Why Do You Need This New Edition?

If you're wondering why you should buy this new edition of *The Prentice Hall Guide for College Writers,* here are a few great reasons!

1. **A completely revised and updated Chapter 12 on doing research** helps you find and evaluate all kinds of sources and shows you how to develop **two new writing projects: the research proposal and annotated bibliography.**
2. **An expanded Chapter 13 on researched writing** provides clear instructions, graphics, and charts to help you organize and draft a source-based essay, and up-to-date, color-coded MLA and APA citation examples to show you how to document your sources properly.
3. **An expanded Chapter 4, Reading Critically, Analyzing Rhetorically,** now provides you with guidelines for a **new writing project: the rhetorical analysis essay** that calls for analyzing and evaluating the rhetorical appeals in a text.
4. **New Shaping Strategies charts** help you identify strategies that can help you achieve your purpose for writing, and **new Shaping Points diagrams** show you how to organize different types of papers.
5. **Increased coverage of issues related to plagiarism**—what it is, how to avoid it, why it is important in academic writing—now appears in several chapters, and a new essay, "Plagiarism in America," helps you learn the best academic practices.
6. **19 new readings** bring you up-to-date perspectives on a wide range of interesting topics—including the value of a college education, the Occupy movement, cyberbullying, social media, and censorship on Facebook—and provide ideas for your own writing.
7. **New media enhancements in the eText** link you to videos, animations, model documents, chapter quizzes, and other resources that will help you master the content in *The Prentice Hall Guide* and improve your writing.

PEARSON

The Prentice Hall Guide for College Writers

Brief Tenth Edition

Brief Tenth Edition

The Prentice Hall Guide for College Writers

STEPHEN REID
Colorado State University

PEARSON

Boston Columbus Indianapolis New York San Francisco Upper Saddle River
Amsterdam Cape Town Dubai London Madrid Milan Munich Paris Montreal Toronto
Delhi Mexico City São Paulo Sydney Hong Kong Seoul Singapore Taipei Tokyo

Senior Acquisitions Editor: Lauren A. Finn
Senior Development Editor: Marion B. Castellucci
Development Editor: Elaine Silverstein
Senior Marketing Manager: Sandra McGuire
Senior Supplements Editor: Donna Campion
Executive Digital Producer: Stefanie Snajder
Digital Editor: Sara Gordus
Production/Project Manager: Eric Jorgensen
Project Coordination, Text Design, and Electronic Page Makeup: Cenveo Publisher Services
Cover Designer: John Callahan
Cover Image: Monarx3d/Shutterstock.com
Senior Manufacturing Buyer: Dennis J. Para
Printer/Binder: RR Donnelley & Sons/Crawfordsville
Cover Printer: Lehigh-Phoenix Color/Hagerstown

This title is restricted to sales and distribution in North America only.

Credits and acknowledgments borrowed from other sources and reproduced, with permission, in this textbook appear on the appropriate page within text [or on page 555].

Library of Congress Cataloging-in-Publication Data

Reid, Stephen
The Prentice Hall Guide for College Writers / Stephen Reid, Colorado State University.—Tenth Brief Edition.
pages cm
ISBN-13: 978-0-205-88305-9
ISBN-10: 0-205-88305-2
1. English language—Rhetoric—Handbooks, manuals, etc. 2. Report writing—Handbooks, manuals, etc.
3. College readers. I. Title. II. Title: Guide for college writers.
PE1408.R424 2013b
808'.042—dc23
2012040643

---

10 9 8 7 6 5 4 3 2—DOC—15 14 13

ISBN-10: 0-205-88305-2
ISBN-13: 978-0-205-88305-9
A la Carte ISBN-10: 0-205-87725-7
A la Carte ISBN-13: 978-0-205-87725-6

http://www.pearsonhighered.com

Contents

Thematic Contents

Thematic Contents

The Prentice Hall Guide for College Writers, tenth edition, contains selections from over 100 writers, artists, poets, and photographers. Thematic clusters of essays, articles, editorials, Web sites, cartoons, poems, short fiction, and images are indicated below. An asterisk (*) indicates a complete essay.

Web 2.0 Literacies

Mini-Casebook on Education

Technology and the Internet

Advertising and the Media

Educational Issues

Literacy and Language

Race and Cultural Diversity

Gender Roles

Social Issues

Cultural Issues

Preface

THE proliferation of texts and voices in today's rapidly expanding, Internet-based world creates a major challenge for writing teachers and their students. On the one hand, we have almost instantaneous access to the widest possible range of texts, genres, and new media; on the other, we have very few signposts to help us critically read and evaluate these sources. Before students can master the academic and workplace genres they need for communication in the contemporary world, they must first master the critical thinking skills that will enable them to judge the credibility and relevance of the texts they encounter. Students' problems with finding credible and relevant sources, their habit of cutting and pasting information into quotation quilts, and their likelihood of plagiarizing stem from this almost effortless access. As teachers, we need to focus more than ever on the indispensable skills of critical thinking and rhetorical analysis.

The current Writing Program Administrator's (WPA) outcomes continue to offer us goals and strategies to help our students understand the importance of key rhetorical skills. Two of these outcomes—building students' *rhetorical knowledge* and improving their *critical thinking, reading, and writing skills*—are crucial to helping our students cope in a world dominated by Google, Facebook, YouTube, and Wikipedia. This new tenth edition of *The Prentice Hall Guide for College Writers* helps teachers implement the WPA goals and helps students master the skills required for evaluating online texts.

WHAT'S NEW IN THE TENTH EDITION?

The most important revisions for the tenth edition of *The Prentice Hall Guide for College Writers* help teachers respond to the digital literacy challenges that students face today. Helping students assess, evaluate, and respond to the wide variety of texts and contexts they will encounter is the focus of many of the new features in this edition.

- **An expanded chapter on working with texts, "Reading Critically, Analyzing Rhetorically,"** provides students with instruction and guidelines for two writing assignments: a critical response paper and a **new rhetorical analysis essay** that calls for analyzing and evaluating the rhetorical appeals in a text. Introducing the appeals of *ethos*, *logos*, and *pathos* early in the text will help develop students' critical and rhetorical reading skills right from the beginning of the course.

- **Expanded coverage of researched writing in two new and revised chapters** that replace a single chapter in the previous edition will help students effectively research and write source-based assignments.
- **Chapter 12, "Researching,"** shows students how to plan their research according to their purpose for writing, and how to find and evaluate a wide range of print and digital sources so that they use only appropriate and credible sources in their college writing.
- Two new writing assignments in Chapter 12, **a research proposal** and an **annotated bibliography**, give students practice in applying their research planning, searching, and evaluating skills.
- **Chapter 13, "Researched Writing,"** shows students how to incorporate sources in their essays without plagiarizing and without letting the sources take over the paper. Clear instructions, graphics, and charts help students draft, organize, and document a source-based essay.
- In both chapters, **a new student writing example** on the Rwandan genocide provides students with models of how to find reliable sources, draft a research proposal, compile an annotated bibliography, shape, draft, and document a source-based essay, and repurpose their research to produce another researched genre such as a Web page.
- **Increased coverage of plagiarism—what it is, how to avoid it, why it is unacceptable in academic writing**—now appears in several chapters. A new essay, "Plagiarism in America," with sample critical reading responses, encourages students to participate in the conversation and learn the best academic practices.
- **A new mini-casebook of readings on education in Chapter 9, "Problem Solving,"** invites students to engage in the national debate on the costs of higher education, the quality of their education, the importance of writing, and the opportunities that await after graduation. Six new essays, by Jane Bodnar, James Surowiecki, Lynn O'Shaughnessy, Gregory Petsko, and others, provide a wide range of viewpoints.
- **Nineteen new professional essays and many new images** will stimulate student discussion of the Internet, social media, cyberbullying, and censorship. Featured professional writers in the tenth edition include Jennifer Holladay, Nicholas Carr, Nathan Brown, Deborah Soloman, Caterina Fake, David Sirota, Manohla Dargis, Jane Bodnar, Richard Arum, Lynn O'Shaughnessy, James Surowiecki, David Leonhardt, and Gregory Petsko.
- **New images and essays related to the Occupy movement and the events at the University of California at Davis** encourage students to analyze and reflect on how contemporary events are portrayed in various texts and in social media.

- **A new and comprehensive Chapter 3, "Observing and Remembering,"** shows students how description and narration work together in the personal narrative essay. Teachers will no longer have to assign sections from two chapters (as in the ninth edition) when their students write experience- and observation-based essays.
- **Two new visual features highlight key content and processes for students.** New Shaping Strategies charts help students identify appropriate rhetorical strategies that can help them achieve their purpose for writing. Shaping Points diagrams show students how to organize different types of papers.
- **New learning objectives** frame each chapter's content so that students know at the start what they will accomplish by working through a chapter.
- **New media enhancements in the eText** link students to videos, animations, model documents, and chapter quizzes to create a rich interactive learning experience. Online resources that extend the instructional content and examples in *The Prentice Hall Guide for College Writers* let students access additional help as needed and provide support for those students who have different learning styles.

CONTINUING KEY FEATURES

Self-Contained Writing Assignment Chapters

Chapters 3 through 13 each focus on a major college writing assignment, providing instruction on critical thinking and rhetorical strategies and techniques as well as guidance on writing the assignment, all gathered together in one convenient place. The first part of each of these purpose-based chapters explains the rhetorical situation and useful strategies and provides professional examples of that type of writing. In the second part of each chapter, students apply what they have learned to writing their own papers, using, specific writing process, research, and peer review guidance and student model papers. With no need to flip back and forth among chapters hunting for information, students will find that working on their assignments goes more smoothly.

Logical Sequence of Purpose-Based Chapters

Within each rhetorical situation, clear aims and purposes guide the writer to select appropriate genres, shaping strategies, appeals to audience, and styles. Early writing assignment chapters in *The Prentice Hall Guide for College Writers* give students practice with invention, focusing on observing and remembering, critical reading and rhetorical analysis, analyzing visuals, and investigating; later chapters emphasize exposition and argumentation (explaining, evaluating, problem solving, arguing, researching, and researched writing).

Emphasis on Student Writing

The tenth edition continues to showcase student writing, featuring the work of more than a dozen student writers from several colleges and universities. This edition contains *sixteen full-length student essays* and ten essays with sample prewriting materials, rough draft peer response sheets, and/or postscripts.

Techniques Boxes

Within each writing assignment chapter, a Techniques Box summarizes for students the techniques for achieving their purpose for writing (such as getting the reader's attention; defining key terms; describing a process, cause, or effect; supporting claims with evidence) and offers tips for developing sections of papers. The boxes preview the more detailed instruction that follows, offering students at-a-glance summaries of key chapter concepts they can reference as they write.

Research Tips

In Chapters 3–13, Research Tips boxes suggest the research strategies most appropriate for writers' different purposes and offer useful advice on formulating interview questions, quoting sources, evaluating sources for bias, and more.

Peer Response Guidelines

Peer Response features within each writing assignment chapter suggest to students the kinds of rhetorical considerations, elements, and features they might consider as they read their peers' drafts (and their own) in order to help them give and receive constructive feedback.

Journal Writing

Throughout the text, write-to-learn and journal activities help writers improve their critical reading skills, warm up for each assignment, and practice the invention and shaping strategies appropriate for understanding their purpose, audience, genre, and social context.

Marginal Quotations

Nearly a hundred short statements by composition teachers, researchers, essayists, novelists, and poets personalize for the inexperienced writer a larger community of writers struggling with the same problems that each student faces.

Thematic Table of Contents

The essays, stories, poems, and images in the tenth edition combine to create thematic clusters of topics throughout the text: Web 2.0 Literacies; Internet and Social Media; Educational Issues; Literacy and Language; Race and Cultural Diversity; Gender Roles; and Social and Cultural Issues.

STRUCTURE OF *THE PRENTICE HALL GUIDE FOR COLLEGE WRITERS*

The text contains thirteen sequenced chapters that gradually build students' rhetorical knowledge and skills.

Chapter 1: Writing Myths and Rituals

Chapter 1 discounts some common myths about college writing courses, introduces the notion of writing rituals, and outlines the varieties of journal writing used throughout the text. Writing process rituals are crucial for all writers, and especially so for novice writers. Illustrating a variety of writing rituals are testimonies from a dozen professional writers on the nature of writing. These quotations continue through the book, reminding students that writing is not a magical process but a madness that has a method to it—a process born of reading, thinking, observing, remembering, discussing, and writing.

Chapter 2: Situations, Purposes, and Processes for Writing

Chapter 2 grounds the writing process in the rhetorical situation. It shows how audience, genre, subject, and context work together with the writer's purpose to achieve a rhetorical end. It demonstrates how meaning evolves from various recursive, multidimensional, and hierarchical activities that we call *the writing process.* Finally, it reassures students that, because individual writing and learning styles differ, they will be encouraged to discover and articulate their own processes from a range of appropriate possibilities.

Chapters 3–10: Purposes for Writing

The text then turns to specific purposes and assignments for writing. Chapters 3–6 ("Observing and Remembering," "Reading Critically, Analyzing Rhetorically," "Analyzing and Designing Visuals," and "Investigating") focus on invention and critical reading strategies. These chapters introduce genres and situations for writing that build students' rhetorical repertoires: observing and remembering people, places, objects, and events; developing critical reading and rhetorical analysis strategies; developing critical reading strategies for visuals and rhetorical principles for designing visuals; and investigating and reporting through genres such as interviews, profiles, and multiple-source articles.

Chapters 7–10 ("Explaining," "Evaluating," "Problem Solving," and "Arguing") emphasize subject- and audience-based purposes and occasions for writing. The sequence in these chapters moves the student smoothly from exposition to argumentation (acknowledging the obvious overlap), building on the strategies and repertoires of the earlier chapters. The teacher may well use Chapters 7–10 as a minicourse in argument, teaching students how to develop and argue claims of fact and definition, claims of cause and effect, claims about values, and claims about solutions or policies.

Chapter 11: Responding to Literature

Chapter 11 guides students through the process of reading and responding to poetry and short fiction, using many of the critical reading strategies, invention techniques, and shaping strategies practiced in earlier chapters.

Chapter 12: Researching

Chapter 12 draws on all the reading, writing, and researching strategies presented in the first eleven chapters. Source-based papers are assigned for specific purposes, audiences, and contexts, but the invention, drafting, and revising processes are more extended. This chapter helps students select and plan their projects, find and critically evaluate library and Internet sources, evaluate print and open-Web documents, write a research proposal, and compile an annotated bibliography.

Chapter 13: Researched Writing

Chapter 13 provides students with clear instructions, graphics, and charts to help them draft, organize, and document a source-based essay. A new student essay on the Rwandan genocide illustrates the entire process, from how to find reliable sources, prepare the topic proposal, and compile an annotated bibliography to how to organize, draft, and document the final version of a source-based essay.

ONLINE RESOURCES FOR INSTRUCTORS AND STUDENTS

Pearson MyLabs

The Pearson English MyLabs empower students to improve their skills in writing, grammar, research, and documentation with market-leading instruction, multimedia tutorials, exercises, and assessment tools. Students can use the MyLab on their own, benefiting from self-paced diagnostics and extra practice in content knowledge and writing skills. Instructors can use MyLabs in ways that best complement their courses and teaching styles. They can work more efficiently and more closely with students by creating their own assignments and using time-saving administrative and assessment tools. The marginal icons found in this book link students to enhanced online resources and assessment through the Pearson eText, which is also available in an iPad version. To learn more, visit www.pearsonhighered.com/englishmylabs or ask your Pearson representative.

Pearson eText

An interactive online version of *The Prentice Hall Guide* is available as an eText in MyWritingLab bringing together the many resources the MyLab with the instructional content of this successful book to create an enhanced learning experience for students. Marginal icons in the Pearson eText link to a wealth of online resources:

- Video tutorials illustrate key concepts, offering tips and guidance on critical reading, evaluating sources, avoiding plagiarism, and many other topics.
- Audio podcasts discuss common questions about grammar, usage, punctuation, and mechanics.
- Sample documents illustrate the range of writing students do in composition classes, their other courses, the workplace, and the community.
- Additional exercises help students assess their understanding of concepts before applying them in their own writing.

Accelerated Composition

Support for acceleration or immersion courses focuses on three fundamental areas: reading, writing, and grammar. Additional questions for professional and student readings help students understand, analyze, and evaluate the strategies writers employ. For each of the text's major writing assignments, additional activities and prompts encourage students to break down the tasks involved in writing a paper into manageable chunks. Grammar support includes diagnostic, practice, instruction, and mastery assessment. Contact your Pearson representative for access through our English MyLab and for ordering information.

Michelle Zollars, Associate Professor and Coordinator of the Accelerated Learning Program at Patrick Henry Community College, authors the reading and writing support for accelerated courses using *The Prentice Hall Guide for College Writers*. She has been teaching the accelerated composition model for over five years; has presented on acceleration at the National Association for Developmental Education conference, the Council on Basic Writing conference, and the Conference on Acceleration; and has served on the Developmental English Curriculum Team of the Virginia Community College System.

CourseSmart eTextbook

Students can subscribe to *The Prentice Hall Guide* at CourseSmart.com. The format of the eText allows students to search the text, bookmark passages, save their own notes, and print reading assignments that incorporate lecture notes.

Android and iPad eTextbooks

Android and iPad versions of the eText provide the complete text and the electronic resources described above.

SUPPLEMENTS

Instructor's Manual: Teaching Composition with *The Prentice Hall Guide for College Writers*

The instructor's manual, written by Stephen Reid, provides classroom activities and ideas, as well as detailed discussion of effective strategies for the teaching of written expression skills. The manual includes chapter commentaries, answers to discussion questions, and sections on composition theory, policy statements, lesson plans, collaborative writing, writing in a computer classroom, teaching ESL writers, small group learning, write-to-learn exercises, reading/writing exercises, journal assignments, suggestions for student conferences, and ideas for responding to and evaluating writing.

PowerPoints to Accompany *The Prentice Hall Guide for College Writers*

Ideal for hybrid or distance learning courses, the PowerPoint presentation deck offers instructors slides to adapt to their own course needs.

Other Supplements

Pearson English offers a wide array of other supplementary items—some at no additional cost, some deeply discounted—that are available for packaging with this text. Please contact your local Pearson representative to find out more.

ACKNOWLEDGMENTS

Because teaching writing is always a situated enterprise, I would like to thank the members of the composition faculty at Colorado State University, whose teaching expertise and enthusiasm have improved every page of the text: Kate Kiefer, Sarah Sloane, Lisa Langstraat, Tobi Jacobi, Carrie Lamanna, Sue Doe, and Anne Reid. Many of the innovative teaching strategies, resources, and syllabi developed by Colorado State University composition faculty members are available at http://writing.colostate.edu.

In addition, I wish to gratefully acknowledge Dominic DelliCarpini, Writing Program Administrator at York College of Pennsylvania, who completely rewrote and redesigned the new chapters on researching and documenting. Many other key suggestions for improvement came from the following teachers, who offered excellent advice about changes and additions for the tenth edition: Patricia Boyd, Arizona State University; Margaret Ehlen, Ivy Tech Community College Southwest; Gloria Koss, Aims Community College; Gayle E. Larson, Dakota County Technical College; Kevin R. Martin, Cochise College; Amanda Mosley, York Technical College; Coretta M. Pittman, Baylor University; Nicholas Schevera, College of Lake County; Sarah Jane Sloane, Colorado State University; Chrishawn Speller, Seminole State College of Florida; Colleen Thorndike, Limestone College; Karol L. Walchak, Alpena Community College; John Wegner, Angelo State University; and Marc Wilson, Ivy Tech Community College.

For the expert crew at Pearson Education, I am especially grateful. Marion Castellucci and Elaine Silverstein did a wonderfully thorough job setting the vision for the tenth edition, developing new ideas, features, and graphics, and assisting expertly with revision and editing. Their timely, creative, and professional advice improved every chapter of this book. Finally, I thank my family for their continued personal and professional support.

—Stephen Reid

The Prentice Hall Guide for College Writers

Brief Edition

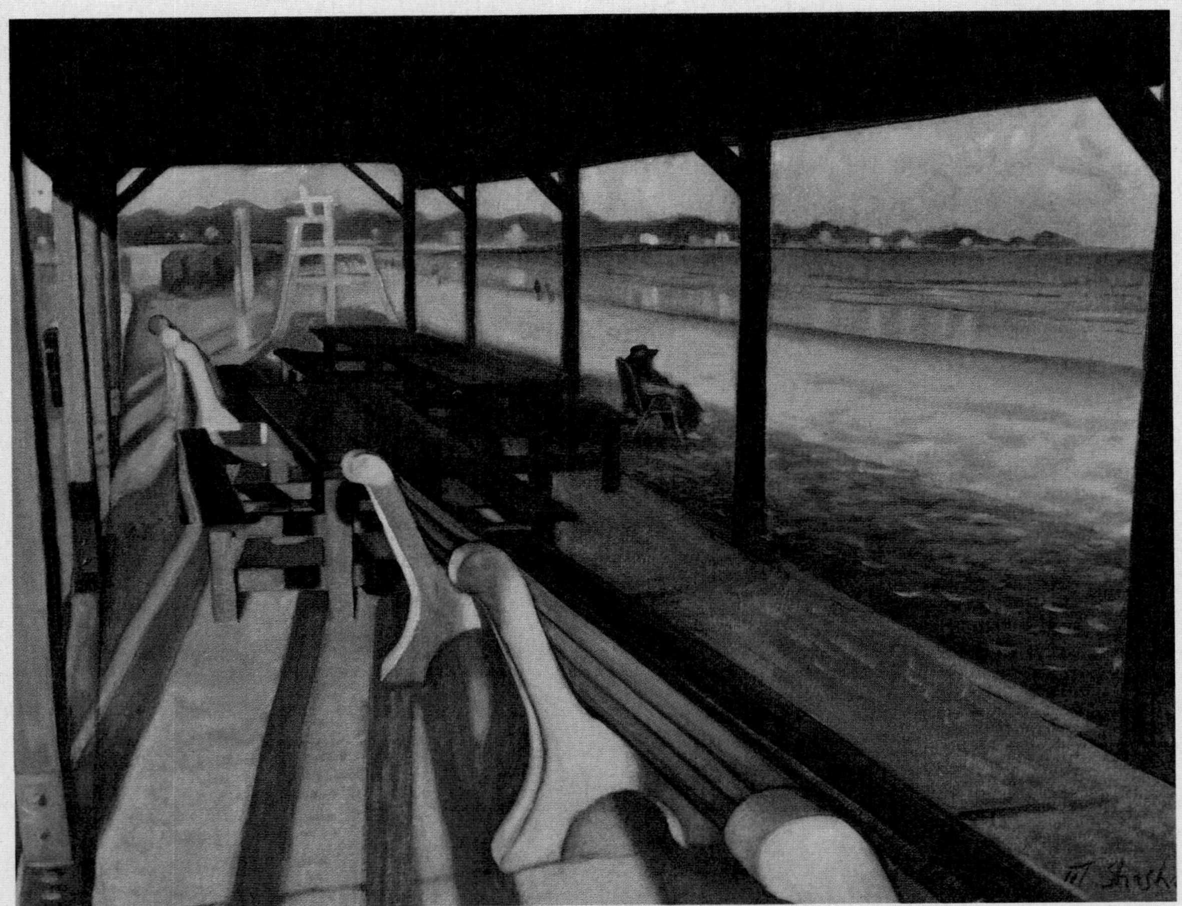

Beach Reader was painted by award-winning artist, actor, and author Mark Shasha. In this chapter, a journal exercise invites you to analyze this painting and relate it to places where you like to read or write.

1

Writing Myths and Rituals

What You Will Learn
In this chapter, you will learn to:

1.1 Establish productive rituals for writing

1.2 Keep a journal to help your reading, writing, and learning

AS YOU begin a college writing course, you need to get rid of some myths about writing that you may have been packing around for some time. Don't allow misconceptions to ruin a good experience. Here are a few common myths about writing, followed by some facts compiled from the experiences of working writers.

> "A writer is someone who writes, that's all."
> —Gore Vidal, Novelist and Social Commentator

> "I always worked until I had something done and I always stopped when I knew what was going to happen next. That way I could be sure of going on the next day."
> —Ernest Hemingway, Journalist and Novelist, Author of *The Old Man and the Sea*

Myth: "Good writers are born, not made. A writing course really won't help my writing."

Fact: *Writers acquire their skills the same way athletes do—through practice and hard work.* There are very few "born" writers. Most writers—even professional writers and journalists—are not continually inspired to write. In fact, they often experience "writer's block," the stressful experience of staring helplessly at a piece of paper, unable to think or to put words down on paper. A writing course will teach you how to cope with your procrastination, anxiety, lack of "inspiration," and false starts by focusing directly on solving the problems that occur during the writing process.

Myth: "Writing courses are just a review of boring grammar and punctuation. When teachers read your writing, the only thing they mark is that stuff, anyway."

Fact: *Learning and communicating—not grammar and punctuation—come first in college writing courses.* Knowledge of grammar, spelling, punctuation, and usage is secondary to discovering ideas, thinking, learning, and communicating. In a writing course, students learn to revise and

> "I work at my writing as an athlete does at . . . training, taking it very seriously. What is important is the truth in it and the way that truth is expressed."
>
> —Edna O'Brien, Novelist and Playwright

improve the content and organization of each other's writing. *Then* they help each other edit for grammar, punctuation, or spelling errors.

Myth: "College writing courses are really 'creative writing,' which is not what my major requires. If I wanted to be another Shakespeare and write poetry, I'd change my major."

Fact: *Writing courses emphasize rhetoric, not poetry.* Rhetoric involves practicing the most effective means or strategies for informing or persuading an audience. All writing—even technical or business writing—is "creative." Deciding what to write, how to write it, how best to get your reader's attention, and how to inform or persuade your reader requires creativity and imagination. Every major requires the skills that writing courses teach: exploring new ideas, learning concepts and processes, communicating with others, and finding fresh or creative solutions to problems.

Myth: "Writing courses are not important in college or the real world. I'll never have to write, anyway."

Fact: *Writing courses do have a significant effect on your success in college, on the job, and in life.* Even if you don't have frequent, formal writing assignments in other courses, writing improves your note-taking, reading comprehension, and thinking skills. When you do have other written tasks or assignments, a writing course teaches you to adapt your writing to a variety of different purposes and audiences—whether you are writing a lab report in biology, a letter to an editor, a complaint to the Better Business Bureau, or a memorandum to your boss. Taking a writing course helps you express yourself more clearly, confidently, and persuasively—a skill that comes in handy whether you're writing a philosophy essay, a job application, or a love letter.

The most important fact about writing is that you are already a writer. You have been writing for years. A writer is someone who writes, not someone who writes a nationally syndicated newspaper column, publishes a bestseller, or wins a Pulitzer Prize. To be an effective writer, you just have to practice writing often enough to get acquainted with its personal benefits for you and its value for others.

Warming Up: Freewriting

Put this text aside—right now—and open your computer or take out pencil or pen and a piece of paper. Use this free exercise (private, unjudged, ungraded) to remind yourself that you are already a writer. Time yourself for five minutes. Write on the first thing that comes to mind—*anything whatsoever.* Write nonstop. Keep writing even if you have to write, "I can't think of anything to say. This feels stupid!" When you get an idea, pursue it.

When five minutes are up, stop writing and read what you have written. Whether you write about a genuinely interesting topic or about the weather, freewriting is an excellent way to warm up, to get into the habit of writing, and to establish a writing ritual.

Watch the **Animation** on Freewriting

WRITING FITNESS: RITUALS AND PRACTICE

1.1
Establish productive rituals for writing

Writing is no more magic or inspiration than any other human activity that you admire: figure skating at the Olympics, rebuilding a car engine, cooking a gourmet meal. Behind every human achievement are many unglamorous hours of practice—working and sweating, falling flat on your face, and picking yourself up again. You can't learn to write just by reading chapters in a textbook or by memorizing other people's advice. You need help and advice, but you also need practice. Consider the following parable about a Chinese painter.

> A rich patron once gave money to the painter Chu Ta, asking him to paint a picture of a fish. Three years later, the patron went to Chu Ta's house to ask why the picture was not done. Chu Ta did not answer but dipped a brush in ink and with a few strokes drew a splendid fish. "If it is so easy," asked the patron, "why didn't you give me the picture three years ago?" Again, Chu Ta did not answer. Instead, he opened the door of a large cabinet. Thousands of pictures of fish tumbled out.

"My idea of a prewriting ritual is getting the kids on the bus and sitting down."

—**Barbara Kingsolver,**
Author of *Prodigal Summer*

"Writing is [like] making a table. With both you are working with reality, a material just as hard as wood. Both are full of tricks and techniques. Basically very little magic and a lot of hard work are involved. . . . What is a privilege, however, is to do a job to your own satisfaction."

—**Gabriel García Márquez,**
Nobel Prize–Winning Author of *One Hundred Years of Solitude*

Most writers develop little rituals that help them practice their writing. A ritual is a *repeated pattern of behavior* that provides structure, security, and a sense of progress to the one who practices it. Creating your own writing rituals and making them part of your routine will help reduce that dreaded initial panic and enable you to call upon your writing process with confidence when you need it.

Place, Time, and Tools

Some writers work best in pen and ink, sprawled on their beds in the afternoon while pets snooze on nearby blankets. Others are most comfortable with their laptops at their desks or in the computer lab. Legal-sized pads help some writers produce, while others feel motivated by spiral notebooks. Only you can determine which place, time, and tools give you the best support as a writer.

The place where you write is also important. If you are writing in a computer lab, you have to adapt to that place, but if you write a draft in long-hand or on your own laptop, you can choose the place yourself. In selecting a place, keep the following tips in mind.

Watch the Video on Todd Pierce's Writing Habits

- **Keep distractions minimal.** Some people simply can't write in the kitchen, where the refrigerator is distractingly close, or in a room that has a TV in it. On the other hand, a public place—a library, an empty classroom, a cafeteria—can be fine as long as the surrounding activity does not disturb them.
- **Control interruptions.** If you can close the door to your room and work without interruptions, fine. But even then, other people often assume that you want to take a break when they do. Choose a place where you can decide when it's time to take a break.
- **Have access to notes, journal, textbooks, sources, and other materials.** Whatever you need—a desk to spread your work out on, access to notes and sources, extra pens, Internet access, or computer supplies—make sure your place has it.

> "Writers are notorious for using any reason to keep from working: overresearching, retyping, going to meetings, waxing the floors—anything."
>
> —Gloria Steinem, Former Editor of *Ms. Magazine*

The time of day you write and the tools you write with can also affect your attitude and efficiency. Some people like to write early in the morning, others like to write in the evening. Whatever time you choose, try to write regularly—at least three days a week—at about the same time. If you're trying to get in shape by jogging, swimming, or doing aerobics, you wouldn't exercise for five straight hours on Monday and then take four days off. Like exercise, writing requires regular practice and conditioning.

Your writing tools—pen, pencil, paper, legal pads, four-by-six-inch notecards, notebooks, computer—should also be comfortable for you. Some writers like to make notes with pencil and paper and write drafts on computers; some like to do all composing on computers. As you try different combinations of tools, be aware of how you feel and whether your tools make you more effective. If you feel comfortable, it will be easier to establish rituals that lead to regular practice.

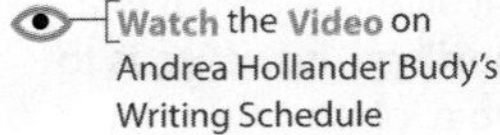

Watch the Video on Andrea Hollander Budy's Writing Schedule

Rituals are important because they help you with the most difficult part of writing: getting started. So use your familiar place, time, and tools to trick yourself into getting some words down on paper. Your mind will devise clever schemes to avoid writing those first ten words—watching TV, texting a friend, drinking more coffee. But if your body has been through the ritual before, it will walk calmly to your favorite place, where all your tools are ready (perhaps bringing the mind kicking and screaming all the way). Then, after you get the first ten words down, the mind will say, "Hey, this isn't so bad—I've got something to say about that!" And off you'll go.

FRANK AND ERNEST ©by Bob Thaves

Each time you perform your writing ritual, the *next* time you write will be that much easier. Soon, your ritual will let you know: "*This is where you write. This is when you write. This is what you write with.*" No fooling around. Just writing.

Energy and Attitude

Once you've tricked yourself into the first ten words, you need to keep your attitude positive and your energy high. When you see an intimidating wall starting to form in front of you, don't ram your head into it; figure out a way to sneak around it. Try these tricks and techniques.

- **Start anywhere, quickly.** No law says that when you sit down to write a draft, you have to "begin at the beginning." If the first sentence is hard to write, begin with the first thoughts that come to mind. Or begin with a good example from your experience. Then come back and rewrite your beginning after you've figured out what you want to say.
- **Write the easiest parts first.** Working on the hardest part first is a sure way to make yourself hate writing. Take the path of least resistance. If you can't get your thesis to come out right, jot down more examples. If you can't think of examples, go back to brainstorming.
- **Keep moving.** Once you've plunged in, write as fast as you can. Maintain your momentum. Reread if you need to, but then plunge ahead.
- **Quit when you know what comes next.** When you quit for the day, stop at a place where you know what comes next. Don't drain the well dry; stop in the middle of something you know how to finish. Make a few notes about what you need to do next. Leave yourself an easy place to get started next time.

"I am by nature lazy, sluggish and of low energy. It constantly amazes me that I do anything at all."

—Margaret Atwood,
Who Has Managed to Produce Numerous Books of Fiction and Poetry

One of the most important strategies for every writer is to *give yourself a break from the past and begin with a fresh image.* Some people are late bloomers. Don't let that C or D you got in English in tenth grade hold you back. Now you are free to start fresh. Your writing rituals should include only positive images about the writer you are today and realistic expectations about what you can accomplish.

- **Visualize yourself writing.** Successful athletes know how to visualize a successful basketball free throw or baseball swing. When you are planning your activities for the day, visualize yourself writing at your favorite place. Seeing yourself writing will enable you to start more quickly and maintain a positive attitude.
- **Discover and emphasize the aspects of writing that are fun for you.** Emphasize whatever is enjoyable for you—discovering an idea, getting

"Since I began writing I have always played games. . . . I have a playful nature; I have never been able to do things because it is my duty to do them. If I can find a way to do my duty by playing a game, then I can manage."

—Maria Irene Fornes,
Obie Award–Winning Playwright

the organization of a paragraph to come out right, clearing the unnecessary words and junk out of your writing. Concentrating on the parts you enjoy will help you make it through the tougher parts.

- **Set modest goals for yourself.** Don't aim for the stars; just work on a sentence. Don't measure yourself against some great writer; be your own yardstick. Compare what you write to what *you* have written before.
- **Congratulate yourself for the writing you do.** Writing is hard work; you're using words to create ideas and meanings. So pat yourself on the back occasionally. Keep in mind the immortal words of comedian and playwright Steve Martin: "I think I did pretty well, considering I started out with nothing but a bunch of blank paper."

"I carry a journal with me almost all the time . . . ."

—Ntozake Shange, Author of the Play *For Colored Girls Who Have Considered Suicide When the Rainbow Is Enuf*

Keeping a Journal

1.2 Keep a journal to help your reading, writing, and learning

Journal writing takes advantage of the special relationship among thinking, writing, and learning: *writing helps you learn what you know* (and don't know) because it shapes your thoughts into language. Because this relationship is so important, many writers keep some kind of notebook in which they record their ideas, thoughts, reactions, and plans.

Journals and blogs can both be places for daily writing. If you choose a private, written journal, you can later select what you want others to read; if you use your blog, your thoughts and ideas are there for others to read and respond to. Whatever medium you choose, use it as part of your daily writing ritual. In it can go notes and ideas, bits and pieces of experience, or responses to essays or books you're reading. Sometimes journals or blogs are assigned as part of your class work. In that case, you may do in-class, write-to-learn entries, plans for your essays, postscripts for an essay, or reflections on a portfolio. Your journal or blog can be a place for formal assignments or just a place to practice, a room where all your "fish paintings" go.

"The most valuable writing tool I have is my daybook. . . . I write in my lap, in the living room or on the porch, in the car or an airplane, in meetings at the university, in bed, or sitting down on a rock wall during a walk. . . . It is always a form of talking to myself, a way of thinking on paper."

—Donald Murray, Journalist, Author of Books and Essays About Writing

As the following list indicates, journal entries fall into three categories: *reading entries, write-to-learn entries,* and *writing entries.*

1. **Reading entries** help you understand and actively respond to student or professional writing.
2. **Write-to-learn entries** help you summarize, react to, or question ideas or essays discussed in class.
3. **Writing entries** help you warm up, test ideas, make writing plans, practice rhetorical strategies, or solve specific writing problems.

All three kinds of journal writing, however, take advantage of the special relationship between thinking, writing, and learning. Simply put, writing helps you learn what you know (and don't know) by shaping your thoughts into language.

Reading Entries

- **Prereading journal entries.** Before you read an essay, read the head-note and write for five minutes on the topic of the essay—what you know about the subject, what related experiences you have had, and what opinions you hold. After you write your entry, the class can discuss the topic before you read the essay. The result? Your reading will be more active, engaged, and responsive.
- **Double-entry logs.** Draw a line vertically down a sheet of paper. On the left-hand side, summarize key ideas as you reread an essay. On the right-hand side, write down your reactions, responses, and questions. Writing while you read helps you understand and respond more thoroughly.
- **Essay annotations.** Writing your comments in the margin as you read is sometimes more efficient than writing separate journal entries. Check out the author on Google and look up any unfamiliar terms or references. Also, in a small group in class, you can share your annotations and collaboratively annotate a copy of the essay.
- **Vocabulary entries.** Looking up unfamiliar words in a dictionary and writing out definitions in your journal will make you a much more accurate reader. Often an essay's thesis, meaning, or tone hinges on the meanings of a few key words.
- **Summary/response entries.** Double-entry logs help you understand while you reread, but a short one-paragraph summary and one-paragraph response after you finish your rereading helps you focus on both the main ideas of a passage and your own key responses.

Write-to-Learn Entries

- **Lecture/discussion entries.** At key points in a class lecture or discussion, your teacher may ask you to write for five minutes by responding to a few questions: What is the main idea of the discussion? What one question would you like to ask? How does the topic of discussion relate to the essay that you are currently writing?

Watch the Video on Tim Schell's Journal

- **Responses to essays.** Before discussing an essay, write for a few minutes to respond to the following questions: What is the main idea of this essay? What do you like best about the essay? What is confusing, misleading, or wrong in this essay? What strategies illustrated in this essay will help you with your own writing?
- **Time-out responses.** During a controversial discussion or argument about an essay, your teacher may stop the class, take time out, and ask you to write for five minutes to respond to several questions: What key issue is the class debating? What are the main points of disagreement? What is your opinion? What evidence, either in the essay or in your experience, supports your opinion?

Writing Entries

- **Warming up.** Writing, like any other kind of activity, improves when you loosen up, stretch, get the kinks out, practice a few lines. Any daybook or journal entry gives you a chance to warm up.
- **Collecting and shaping exercises.** Some journal entries will help you collect information by observing, remembering, or investigating people, places, events, or objects. You can also record quotations or startling statistics for future writing topics. Other journal entries suggested in each chapter of this book will help you practice organizing your information. Strategies of development such as comparison/contrast, definition, classification, and process analysis will help you discover and shape ideas.
- **Writing for a specific audience.** In some journal entries, you need to play a role, imagining that you are in a specific situation and writing for a defined audience. For example, you might write a letter of application for a job or a letter to a friend explaining why you've chosen a certain major.
- **Revision plans and postscripts.** Your journal is also the place to keep a log—a running account of your writing plans, revision plans, problems, and solutions. Include your research notes, peer responses, and postscripts on your writing process in this log.
- **Imitating styles of writers.** Use your journal to copy passages from writers you like. Practice imitating their styles on different topics. Also, try simply transcribing a few paragraphs. Even copying effective writers' words will reveal some of their secrets for successful writing.
- **Writing free journal entries.** Use your journal to record ideas, reactions to people on campus, events in the news, reactions to controversial articles in the campus newspaper, conversations after class or work, or just your private thoughts.

Warming Up: Journal Exercises

Choose three of the exercises below and write for ten minutes on each. Date and number each entry.

1. Make an "authority" list of activities, subjects, ideas, places, people, or events that you know something about. List as many topics as you can. If your reaction is "I'm not really an *authority* on anything," then imagine you've met someone from another school, state, country, or historical period. With that person as your audience, what are you an "authority" on?
2. Choose one activity, sport, or hobby that you do well and that others might admire you for. In the form of a letter to a friend, describe the steps or stages of the process through which you acquired that skill or ability.

3. In a few sentences, complete the following thought: "In my previous classes and from my own writing experience, I've learned that the three most important rules about writing are . . ."
4. Describe your own writing rituals. *When, where,* and *how* do you write best?
5. Look again at the chapter-opening work of art, *Beach Reader*, by Mark Shasha. Mark Shasha is an award-winning artist, author, and actor who travels much of the year to talk to children about the world of reading, writing, and drawing. Describe how Shasha uses color, light, balance, and focus in his painting to create an inviting place for reading, writing, or just relaxing.

Professional Writing

On Keeping a Journal

Roy Hoffman

In a *Newsweek* On Campus essay, Roy Hoffman describes his own experience, recording events and trying out ideas just as an artist doodles on a sketch pad. Your own journal entries about events, images, descriptions of people, and bits of conversation will not only improve your writing but also become your own personal time capsule, to dig up and reread in the year 2040.

Wherever I go I carry a small notebook in my coat or back pocket for thoughts, observations and impressions. As a writer I use this notebook as an artist would a sketch pad, for stories and essays, and as a sporadic journal of my comings and goings. When I first started keeping notebooks, though, I was not yet a professional writer. I was still in college. *1*

I made my first notebook entries . . . just after my freshman year, in what was actually a travel log. A buddy and I were setting out to trek from our Alabama hometown to the distant tundra of Alaska. With unbounded enthusiasm I began: "Wild, crazy ecstasy wants to wrench my head from my body." The log, written in a university composition book, goes on to chronicle our adventures in the land where the sun never sets, the bars never close and the prepipeline employment prospects were so bleak we ended up taking jobs as night janitors. *2*

When I returned to college that fall I had a small revelation: the world around me of libraries, quadrangles, Frisbees and professors was as rich with material for my journals and notebooks as galumphing moose and garrulous fishermen. *3*

These college notebooks, which built to a pitch my senior year, are gold mines to me now. Classrooms, girlfriends, cups of coffee and lines *4* of poetry—from mine to John Keats's—float by like clouds. As I lie beneath these clouds again, they take on familiar and distinctive shapes.

Though I can remember the campus's main quadrangle, I see it more vividly when I read my description of school on a visit during summer break: "the muggy, lassitudinal air . . . the bird noises that cannot be pointed to, the summer emptiness that grows emptier with a few students squeaking by the library on poorly oiled bicycles." An economics professor I fondly remember returns with less fondness in my notebooks, "staring down at the class with his equine face." And a girl I had a crush on senior year, whom I now recall mistily, reappears with far more vitality as "the ample, slightly-gawky, whole-wheat, fractured object of my want gangling down the hall in spring heat today." 5

When, in reading over my notebooks, I am not peering out at quadrangles, midterm exams, professors or girlfriends, I see a portrait of my parents and hometown during holidays and occasional weekend breaks. Like a wheel, home revolves, each turn regarded differently depending on the novel or political essay I'd been most influenced by the previous semester. 6

Mostly, though, in wandering back through my notebooks, I meet someone who could be my younger brother: the younger version of myself. The younger me seems moodier, more inquisitive, more fun-loving and surprisingly eager to stay up all night partying or figuring out electron orbitals for a 9 a.m. exam. The younger me wanders through a hall of mirrors of the self, writes of "seeing two or three of myself on every corner," and pens long meditations on God and society before scribbling in the margin, "what a child I am." The younger me also finds humor in trying to keep track of this hall of mirrors, commenting in ragged verse. 7

I hope that one day
Some grandson or cousin
Will read these books,
And know that I was
Once a youth
Sitting in drugstores with
Anguished looks.
And poring over coffee,
And should have poured
The coffee
Over these lines.

I believe that every college student should attempt to keep some 8
form of notebook, journal or diary. A notebook is a secret garden in which to dance, sing, muse, wander, perform handstands, even cry. In the privacy of this little book, you can make faces, curse, turn somersaults and ask yourself if you're really in love. A notebook or journal is one of the few places you can call just your own. . . .

By keeping notebooks, you improve your writing ability, increasing 9
your capacity to communicate both with yourself and others. By keeping notebooks, you discover patterns in yourself, whether lazy ones that need to be broken or healthy ones that can use some nurturing. By keeping notebooks, you heighten some moments and give substance to others: even a journey to the washateria offers potential for some off-beat journal observations. And by keeping notebooks while still in college, you chart a terrain that, for many, is more dynamically charged with ideas and discussions than the practical, workaday world just beyond. Notebooks, I believe, not only help us remember this dynamic charge, but also help us sustain it.

Not long ago, while traveling with a friend in Yorktown, Va., I 10
passed by a time capsule buried in the ground in 1976, intended to be dug up in 2076. Keeping notebooks and journals is rather like burying time capsules into one's own life. There's no telling what old rock song, love note, philosophical complaint or rosy Saturday morning you'll unearth when you dig up these personal time capsules. You'll be able to piece together a remarkable picture of where you've come from, and may well get some important glimmers about where you're going.

Complete additional exercises and practice in your MyLab

This picture, taken by photographer Layne Kennedy, shows a famous Mona Lisa barn painting on a farm near Cornell, Wisconsin. Mona Lisa's shirt has been repainted to celebrate Wisconsin's victory in the 1994 Rose Bowl. A freewriting assignment in this chapter invites you to describe the purpose, audience, and genre of this image.

Layne Kennedy/Corbis

2

Situations, Purposes, and Processes for Writing

What You Will Learn
In this chapter, you will learn to:

2.1 Identify key elements of the rhetorical situation
2.2 Identify important purposes for writing
2.3 Explain the stages of the writing process

WRITING is valuable for two related reasons. First, writing enables you to learn about something, to help you observe your surroundings, to remember important ideas and events, and to record and analyze what you see and read. Second, writing is an important means to communicate with your readers, to explain or evaluate an idea, to offer a solution, or to argue your point of view. These two reasons for writing are usually related. If you want to persuade others to agree with your point of view, you'll be more effective if you reflect on how your personal observations, memories, experiences, and things you've read and heard might help you convince your readers. Whatever you write, however, you are always writing in a particular situation or context. Understanding how your goals as a writer relate to the writing situation and to your own processes for writing is the focus of this chapter.

“First and foremost I write for myself. Writing has been for a long time my major tool for self-instruction and self-development.”

—Toni Cade Bambara,
Author of *The Salt Eaters*

THE RHETORICAL SITUATION

2.1
Identify key elements of the rhetorical situation

As you begin this writing course, consider how you and your writing fit into a larger context. Anytime you write an e-mail response, a letter to a friend, a posting on your Facebook page, an essay for your English or history class, an application for a job, a letter to the editor, or an entry in your journal, you are in the middle of a rhetorical situation. If rhetoric is the "art of using language effectively or persuasively," then the rhetorical situation is the overall context in which your writing occurs.

Elements of the Rhetorical Situation

"How do I know what I think until I see what I say?"
—E. M. Forster,
Author of *A Passage to India*

The key parts of the rhetorical situation are you, the writer; the immediate occasion that prompts you to write; your intended purpose and audience; your genre or type of writing; and the larger social context in which you are writing. Because these key terms are used repeatedly in this course, you need to know exactly what each term means and how it will help guide your writing.

Watch the Animation on the Rhetorical Situation

The Writer You are the writer. Sometimes you write in response to an assignment, but at other times, you choose to write because of something that happened or something that made you think or react. In college or on the job, you often have writing assignments, but in your life, you are often the one who decides to write when you need to remember something, plan, remind others, express your feelings, or solve a problem.

The Occasion The occasion is the immediate cause or the pressing need to write, whether assigned to you by someone else or just determined by you to be the reason for your desire to write. Often you are motivated by an assignment that a teacher or a boss gives you. Sometimes, however, a particular event or incident makes you want to write. The cause may be a conversation with a friend, an article you read, or something that happened to you.

Purpose Your purpose in writing is the effect you wish to have on your intended audience. Major purposes for writing include **expressing** your feelings; investigating a subject and **reporting** your findings; **explaining** an idea or concept; **evaluating** some object, performance, or image; **proposing a solution** to a problem; and **arguing** for your position and **responding** to alternative or opposing positions.

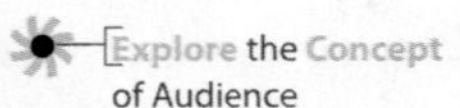
Explore the Concept of Audience

Audience Your knowledge about your intended audience should always guide and shape your writing. If you are writing for yourself, you can just list ideas, express your thoughts, or make informal notes. If you are writing to explain an idea or concept, you should think about who needs or wants to know about your idea. To whom do you want to explain this idea? Are they likely to be novices or experts on the topic? Similarly, if you are arguing a position, you need to consider the thoughts and feelings of readers who may have several different points of view. What do they believe about your topic? Do they agree or disagree with your position, or are they undecided?

Genre The genre you choose is simply the kind, type, or form of writing you select. Everyone is familiar with genres in literature, such as poems, novels, and plays. In nonfiction, typical genres are essays, memoirs, magazine articles, and editorials. In college, you may write in a variety of genres, including e-mail, personal essays, lab reports, summaries, reviews of research, analytical essays, argumentative essays, and even scientific or business reports. Sometimes, you may need to write multi-genre or multimedia reports with graphic images or pictures. For community service learning or on the job, you may write reports, analyses, brochures, or flyers. As a citizen of the community, you may write letters to the editor, responses to an online discussion forum, or letters to your representative.

The genre you choose helps create the intellectual, social, or cultural relationship between you and your reader. It helps you communicate your purpose to your reader or makes possible the social action you wish to achieve. If your purpose is to analyze or critique material you are reading in a class, an essay is a genre suitable to your purpose and your intended audience (your teacher and your peers in class). A lab report is a different genre, requiring your notes, observations, and hypothesis about your experiment, presented for members of a scientific community. Finally, the purpose of a one-page brochure for your community crisis center, for example, may be to advertise its services to a wide audience that includes college students and members of the community. The point is to learn what readers expect of each genre and then choose—or modify—a genre that is appropriate for your purpose and audience.

> **“A rhetorically sound definition of genre must be centered not on the substance or form of discourse but on the action it is used to accomplish.”**
>
> **—Carolyn Miller,**
>
> Teacher and Author of *Genre as Social Action*

Context As both a reader and a writer, you must consider the rhetorical and social context. When you read an essay or other text, think about the **author,** the **place of publication,** the **ongoing conversation** about this topic, and the larger **social or cultural context.** First, consider who wrote an essay and where it appeared. Was the essay a citizen's editorial in the *New York Times,* a journalist's feature article in *Vogue,* a scientist's research report in the *New England Journal of Medicine,* or a blog on the *Huffington Post?* Often, who wrote the article, what his or her potential bias or point of view was, and the place of publication can be just as important as what the article says. Next, consider the ongoing conversation to which this essay contributes. What different viewpoints exist on this topic? Which perspectives does this essay address? Finally, the larger sense of culture, politics, and history in which the article appears may be crucial to your understanding.

Why the Rhetorical Situation is Important

Every decision you make as a writer—how you begin, how much evidence you include, how you organize, whether you use “I” in your writing, what style or tone you should use—depends on the rhetorical situation. The style and organization of a lab report make it different from an essay, which is different from a brochure. If you've ever asked your teacher, “Won't you just tell me what you want?” the answer to that question is always, “Well, it depends.” It depends on what is appropriate for the purpose, audience, genre, and context. To learn the various approaches to writing and how they are most effectively used is the reason that you continually read and practice writing the major genres taught in your composition class.

Freewriting: Inventory of Your Writing

Before you read further in this chapter, make a list of what you have written in the last year or two. Brainstorm a list of all the genres you can think of: shopping lists for a trip, letters to family or friends, applications for jobs, school essays, personal or professional Web sites, science projects, memos for your boss. Then, for one of your longer writing projects, jot down several sentences describing the situation that called for that piece of writing—what was the occasion, purpose, and audience? What form or genre did your writing take? How did that genre help define a relationship between you and your reader? Where did you write it, and what was your writing process?

PURPOSES FOR WRITING

2.2
Identify important purposes for writing

Getting a good grade, sharing experiences with a friend, or contributing to society may be among your motives for writing. However, as a writer, you also have specific rhetorical purposes for writing. These purposes help you make key decisions related to your audience and genre. When your main purpose is to express your feelings, you may write a private entry in your journal. When your main purpose is to explain how your sales promotion increased the number of your company's customers, you may write a formal sales report to your boss. In each case, the intended rhetorical purpose—your desire to create a certain effect on your audience—helps determine what you write and how you say it.

Writer-Based Purposes

“The writer may write to inform, to explain, to entertain, to persuade, but whatever the purpose there should be first of all, the satisfaction of the writer's own learning.”

—**Donald Murray,**
Teacher and Pulitzer Prize–Winning Journalist

Expressing yourself is a fundamental purpose of all writing. Without the satisfaction of expressing your thoughts, feelings, reactions, knowledge, or questions, you might not make the effort to write in the first place.

A closely related purpose is learning: Writing helps you discover what you think or feel, simply by using language to identify and compose your thoughts. Writing not only helps you form ideas but actually promotes observing and remembering. If you write down what you observe about people, places, or things, you can "see" them more clearly. Similarly, if you write down facts, ideas, experiences, or reactions to your readings, you will remember them longer. Writing and rewriting facts, dates, definitions, impressions, or personal experiences will improve your powers of recall on such important occasions as examinations and job interviews.

Subject- and Audience-Based Purposes

Although some writing is intended only for yourself—such as entries in a diary, lists, class notes, reminders—much of your writing will be read by others, by those readers who constitute your "audience."

- You may write to *inform* others about a particular subject—to tell them about the key facts, data, feelings, people, places, or events.
- You may write to *explain* to your readers what something means, how it works, or why it happens.
- You may write to *persuade* others to believe or do something—to convince others to agree with your judgment about a book, record, or restaurant, or to persuade them to take a certain class, vote for a certain candidate, or buy some product you are advertising.
- You may write to *explore* ideas and "truths," to examine how your ideas have changed, to ask questions that have no easy answers, and then to share your thoughts and reflections with others.
- You may write to *entertain*—as a primary purpose in itself or as a purpose combined with informing, explaining, persuading, or exploring. Whatever your purposes may be, good writing both teaches and pleases. Remember, too, that your readers will learn more, remember more, or be more convinced when your writing contains humor, wit, or imaginative language.

"I think writing is really a process of communication. . . . It's the sense of being in contact with people who are part of a particular audience that really makes a difference to me in writing."

—Sherley Anne Williams,
Poet, Critic, and Novelist

Combinations of Purposes

In many cases, you write with more than one purpose in mind. Purposes may appear in combinations, connected in a sequence, or overlapping. Initially, you may take notes about a subject to learn and remember, but later you may want to inform others about what you have discovered. Similarly, you may begin by writing to express your feelings about a movie that you loved; later, you may wish to persuade others to see it.

Purposes can also contain each other, like Chinese boxes, or overlap. An explanation of how an automobile works will contain information about that vehicle. An attempt to persuade someone to buy an automobile may contain an explanation of how it handles and information about its body style or engine. Usually, writing to persuade others will contain explanations and basic information, but the reverse is not necessarily true; you can write simply to give information without trying to persuade anyone to do anything.

"Writing, as a rhetorical act, is carried out within a web of purpose."

—Linda Flower,
Teacher and Researcher in Composition

Subject, Purpose, and Thesis

The *thesis, claim,* or *main idea* in a piece of writing is related to your purpose. As a writer, you usually have a purpose in mind that serves as a guide while you gather information about your subject and think about your audience. However, as you collect and record information, impressions, and ideas you gradually narrow your subject to a specific topic and thus clarify your purpose. You bring your purpose into sharper and sharper focus until you have narrowed your purpose down to a central thesis. That thesis is the dominant idea, explanation, evaluation, or recommendation that you want to impress upon your readers.

The following examples illustrate how a writer moves from a general subject, guided by purpose, to a specific thesis or claim.

Subject	Purpose	Thesis, Claim, or Main Idea
Childhood experiences	To express your feelings and explain how one childhood experience was important	The relentless competition between my sisters and me changed my easygoing personality.
Social networking sites	To inform readers about how to set privacy settings on Facebook	The default settings on Facebook will not always protect your online privacy.
Carbon footprint	To persuade readers to reduce their carbon footprint	Americans should take ten important steps to reduce their carbon footprint when they are at home, when they shop, and when they travel.

PURPOSE AND AUDIENCE

Writing for yourself is relatively easy; after all, you already know your audience and can make spontaneous judgments about what is essential and what is not. However, when your purpose is to communicate to other readers, you need to analyze your audience. Your writing will be more effective if you can anticipate what your readers know and need to know, what they are interested in, and what their beliefs or attitudes are. As you write for different readers, you will select different kinds of information, organize it in different ways, and write in a more formal or less formal style.

Freewriting: Writing for Different Audiences

Before you read further, take a pen or pencil and several sheets of paper and do the following exercise.

1. For your eyes only, write about what you did at a recent party. Write for four minutes.
2. On a second sheet of paper, describe for the members of your writing class what you did at this party; you will read this aloud to the class. Stop after four minutes.
3. On a third sheet of paper, write a letter to a parent or a relative describing what you did at the party. Stop after four minutes.

Audience Analysis

Analyzing your probable audience will help you answer some basic questions.

- What genre—or combination of genres—will best enable me to communicate with my audience?
- How much information or evidence is enough? What should I assume my audience already knows? What do they believe? Will they readily agree with me, or will they be antagonistic?
- How should I organize my writing? How can I get my readers' attention? Should I tell a story, or should I analyze everything in a logical order? Should I put my best examples or arguments first or last?
- Should I write informally, with simple sentences and easy vocabulary, or should I write in a more elaborate or specialized style, with technical vocabulary?

Analyze your audience by considering the following questions. As you learn more about your audience, the possibilities for your own role as a writer will become clearer.

1. **Audience profile.** How narrow or broad is your audience? Is it a defined audience—a single person, such as your Aunt Mary, or a group with clear common interests, such as the readers of *Organic Gardening*? Is it a diverse audience: educated readers who wish to be informed on current events, American voters as a whole, or residents of your state? Do your readers have identifiable roles? Can you determine their age, sex, economic status, ethnic background, or occupational category?
2. **Audience–subject relationship.** Consider what your readers know about your subject. If they know very little about it, you'll need to explain the basics; if they already know quite a bit, you can go straight to more difficult or complex issues. Also estimate their probable attitude toward this subject. Are they likely to be sympathetic or hostile?
3. **Audience–writer relationship.** What is your relationship with your readers? Do you know each other personally? Do you have anything in common? Will your audience be likely to trust what you say, or will they be skeptical about your judgments? Are you the expert on this subject and the readers the novices? Or are you the novice and your readers the experts?
4. **Writer's role.** To communicate effectively with your audience, you should consider your own role or perspective. Of the many roles that you could play (friend, big sister or brother, music fan, employee of a fast-food restaurant, and so on), choose one that will be effective for your purpose and audience. If, for example, you are writing to sixth-graders about nutrition, you could choose the perspective of a concerned older brother or sister. Your writing might be more effective, however, if you assume the role of a person who has worked in fast-food restaurants for three years and knows what goes into hamburgers, french fries, and milkshakes.

Writers may write to real audiences, or they may create audiences. Sometimes the relationship between writer and reader is real (sister writing to brother), so the writer starts with a known audience and writes accordingly. Sometimes, however, writers begin and gradually discover or create an audience in the process of writing. Knowing the audience guides the writing, but the writing may construct an audience as well.

PURPOSE, AUDIENCE, AND GENRE

In addition to considering your purpose and audience, think about the possible forms or genres your writing might take. If you are writing to observe or remember something, you may want to write an informal essay, a letter, a memoir, or even an e-mail. If you are writing to inform your readers or explain some idea, you may write an article, essay, letter, report, or pamphlet. Argumentative writing—writing to evaluate, persuade, or recommend some position or course of action—takes place in many different genres, from e-mails, blogs, and letters, to reviews and editorials, to proposals and researched documents. As you select a topic, consider which genre would most effectively accomplish your purpose for your intended audience.

Below are some of the common genres that you will read or write while in college, on the job, or as a member of your community. Each genre has certain organization and style features that readers expect. Knowing the genre that you are writing or reading helps answer questions about how to write or how to respond to a piece of writing.

Genre	Conventions of Organization and Style
Personal essay	Some narrative and descriptive passages Informal; uses first-person "I" Applies personal experience to larger social question
Research review	Uses concise, accurate summary May be an annotated bibliography or part of a larger thesis Adheres to MLA, APA, or Chicago style
Argumentative essay	Makes a claim about a controversial topic Responds to alternative or opposing positions Carefully considers audience Supports claims with evidence and examples Uses reasonable tone Has formal paragraphing

Laboratory report	May be an informal description of materials, procedures, and results May have formal organization with title, abstract, introduction, method, results, and discussion
Brochure	Mixes graphics, text, and visuals Visually arresting and appealing layout Concise information and language
Letter to the editor	Refers to issue or topic States opinion, point of view, or recommendation Usually concise to fit into editorial page
Posting to an electronic forum	Connects to specific thread in discussion May have informal style Flaming and trolling occur, but are often censured
E-mail, text message, or tweet	Usually short Informal and personal style Often without salutation, caps, or punctuation May use acronyms such as BTW, LOL, FYI, THX

Freewriting: Purpose, Audience, Genre, and Context in an Image

Before you read further, analyze the rhetorical elements in the photograph by Layne Kennedy that appears at the beginning of this chapter. What is the purpose of this barn painting? Who was the intended audience? How would you describe this genre of art? What was the social and cultural context in which this painting appeared? (Search the Web to discover background information.) Overall, how effective is this painting at achieving its rhetorical purpose for its audience and context? Explain.

ANALYZING THE RHETORICAL SITUATION

To review, the rhetorical situation consists of the writer, the occasion, the purpose and audience, the genre and the context. Sometimes several of these are assigned to the writer, but at other times, the writer chooses a purpose, audience, and genre. These elements are interrelated and interconnected. Your overall purpose often depends on your selected audience. Deciding on a particular audience may mean choosing a particular genre. Thinking about the context and conversation surrounding a particular topic may help you be more persuasive for your selected audience. Writing and revising require reconsidering each of these elements to make them work harmoniously to achieve your rhetorical goal.

The following scenarios illustrate how the writer's purpose, the occasion, the audience, genre, and context work together to define rhetorical situation. In the following descriptions, identify each of the key parts of the rhetorical situation.

A student who transferred from a community college to a 4-year school had to give up her well-paying job and move 75 miles. The cost of getting her degree has ballooned to nearly $10,000 per year. She decides to write a letter to her state senator arguing that some 2-year schools in her state should be able to grant bachelor's degrees for high-achieving students. She cites precedents in several states, including California and Florida. Although she acknowledges that such a policy would change the mission of community colleges, she tries to persuade her senator that in these difficult economic times, students need low-cost options for getting a degree.

In response to a request by an editor of a college recruiting pamphlet, a student decides to write an essay explaining the advantages of the social and academic life at his university. According to the editor, the account needs to be realistic but should also promote the university. It shouldn't be too academic and stuffy—the college catalog itself contains all the basic information—but it should give high school seniors a sense of the flavor of college life. The student decides to write a narrative account of his most interesting experiences during his first week at college.

Purpose, Audience, and Context in Two Essays

The two short essays that follow appeared as columns in newspapers. Both relate the writers' own experiences. The essays are similar in genre but have different purposes, they appeal to different readers, and they have different social and cultural contexts. First, read each essay to understand each writer's point of view. Then reread each essay, thinking particularly about each writer's main purpose, his or her intended audience, and the social and cultural context surrounding each topic.

Professional Writing

The Struggle to Be an All-American Girl

Elizabeth Wong

1 It's still there, the Chinese school on Yale Street where my brother and I used to go. Despite the new coat of paint and the high wire fence, the school I knew 10 years ago remains remarkably, stoically the same.

Every day at 5 p.m., instead of playing with our fourth- and fifth-grade friends or sneaking out to the empty lot to hunt ghosts and animal bones, my brother and I had to go to Chinese school. No amount of kicking, screaming, or pleading could dissuade my mother, who was solidly determined to have us learn the language of our heritage. 2

Forcibly, she walked us the seven long, hilly blocks from our home to school, depositing our defiant tearful faces before the stern principal. My only memory of him is that he swayed on his heels like a palm tree, and he always clasped his impatient twitching hands behind his back. I recognized him as a repressed maniacal child killer, and knew that if we ever saw his hands we'd be in big trouble. 3

We all sat in little chairs in an empty auditorium. The room smelled like Chinese medicine, and imported faraway mustiness. Like ancient mothballs or dirty closets. I hated that smell. I favored crisp new scents. Like the soft French perfume that my American teacher wore in public school. 4

Although the emphasis at the school was mainly language—speaking, reading, writing—the lessons always began with an exercise in politeness. With the entrance of the teacher, the best student would tap a bell and everyone would get up, kowtow, and chant, "sing san ho," the phonetic for "How are you, teacher?" 5

Being ten years old, I had better things to learn than ideographs copied painstakingly in lines that ran right to left from the tip of a *moc but,* a real ink pen that had to be held in an awkward way if blotches were to be avoided. After all, I could do the multiplication tables, name the satellites of Mars, and write reports on "Little Women" and "Black Beauty." Nancy Drew, my favorite book heroine, never spoke Chinese. 6

The language was a source of embarrassment. More times than not, I had tried to disassociate myself from the nagging loud voice that followed me wherever I wandered in the nearby American supermarket outside Chinatown. The voice belonged to my grandmother, a fragile woman in her seventies who could outshout the best of the street vendors. Her humor was raunchy, her Chinese rhythmless, patternless. It was quick, it was loud, it was unbeautiful. It was not like the quiet, lilting romance of French or the gentle refinement of the American South. Chinese sounded pedestrian. Public. 7

In Chinatown, the comings and goings of hundreds of Chinese on their daily tasks sounded chaotic and frenzied. I did not want to be thought of as mad, as talking gibberish. When I spoke English, people nodded at me, smiled sweetly, said encouraging words. Even the people in my culture would cluck and say that I'd do well in life. "My, doesn't she move her lips fast," they would say, meaning that I'd be able to keep up with the world outside Chinatown. . . . 8

...continued The Struggle to Be an All-American Girl, **Elizabeth Wong**

After two years of writing with a *moc but* and reciting words with multiples of meanings, I finally was granted a cultural divorce. I was permitted to stop Chinese school. 9

I thought of myself as multicultural. I preferred tacos to egg rolls; I enjoyed Cinco de Mayo more than Chinese New Year. 10

At last, I was one of you; I wasn't one of them. 11

Sadly, I still am. 12

Professional Writing

I'm O.K., but You're Not

Robert Zoellner

The American novelist John Barth, in his early novel *The Floating Opera*, remarks that ordinary, day-to-day life often presents us with embarrassingly obvious, totally unsubtle patterns of symbolism and meaning—life in the midst of death, innocence vindicated, youth versus age, etc. 1

The truth of Barth's insight was brought home to me recently while having breakfast in a lawn-bordered restaurant on College Avenue near the Colorado State University campus. I had asked to be seated in the smoking section of the restaurant—I have happily gone through three or four packs a day for the past 40 years. 2

As it happened, the hostess seated me—I was by myself—at a little two-person table on the dividing line between the smoking and non-smoking sections. Presently, a well-dressed couple of advanced years, his hair a magisterial white and hers an electric blue, were seated in the non-smoking section five feet away from me. 3

It was apparent within a minute that my cigarette smoke was bugging them badly, and soon the husband leaned over and asked me if I would please stop smoking. As a chronic smokestack, I normally comply, out of simple courtesy, with such requests. Even an addict such as myself can quit for as long as 20 minutes. 4

But his manner was so self-righteous and peremptory—he reminded me of Lee Iacocca boasting about Chrysler—that the promptings of original sin, always a problem with me, took over. I quietly pointed out that I was in the smoking section—if only by five feet—and that that fact meant that I had met my social obligation to non-smokers. Besides, the idea of morning coffee without a cigarette was simply inconceivable to me—might as well ask me to vote Republican. 5

The two of them ate their eggs-over-easy in hurried and sullen silence, while I chain-smoked over my coffee. As well as be hung for a sheep as a lamb, I reasoned. Presently they got up, paid their bill, and stalked out in an ambiance of affronted righteousness and affluent propriety. 6

And this is where John Barth comes in. They had parked their car—a diesel Mercedes—where it could be seen from my table. And in the car, waiting impatiently, was a splendidly matched pair of pedigreed poodles, male and female. 7

Both dogs were clearly in extremis, and when the back door of the car was opened, they made for the restaurant lawn in considerable haste. Without ado (no pun intended), the male did a doo-doo that would have done credit to an animal twice his size, and finished off with a leisurely, ruminative wee-wee. The bitch of the pair, as might be expected of any well-brought-up female of Republican proclivities, confined herself to a modest wee-wee, fastidious, diffident, and quickly executed. 8

Having thus polluted the restaurant lawn, the four of them marshalled their collective dignity and drove off in a dense cloud of blue smoke—that lovely white Mercedes was urgently in need of a valve-and-ring job, its emission sticker an obvious exercise in creative writing. . . . 9

. . . The point of this real-life vignette, as John Barth would insist, is obvious. The current controversy over public smoking in Fort Collins is a clear instance of selective virtue at work, coming under the rubric of, what I do is perfectly OK, but what you do is perfectly awful. 10

Questions for Writing and Discussion

1. Choosing only one adjective to describe your main reaction to each essay, answer the following question: "When I finished the _________ [Wong, Zoellner] essay, I was _________ [intrigued, bored, amused, irritated, curious, confused, or _________] because _________." Explain your choice of adjectives in one or two sentences.
2. Referring to specific passages, explain the purpose and state the thesis or main point of each essay.
3. What personality or role does each writer project? Drawing from evidence in the essay, describe what you think both writers would be like if you met them.
4. These two essays are similar in genre—they are both informal essays narrating personal experiences and explaining what each writer discovered or learned. There are differences, however, in structure and style. What differences do you notice in the way each essay begins and concludes, in the order of the paragraphs, and in vocabulary or style of the sentences?

DIMENSIONS OF THE WRITING PROCESS

2.3
Explain the stages of the writing process

Processes for writing vary from one writer to the next and from one writing situation to the next. Most writers, however, can identify four basic stages, or dimensions, of their writing process: collecting, shaping, drafting, and revising. The writing situation may precede these stages—particularly when you are assigned a subject, purpose, audience, and form. Usually, however, you continue to narrow your subject, clarify your purpose, meet the needs of your audience, and modify your form as you work through the dimensions of your writing process.

Collecting

"I don't see writing as communication of something already discovered, as "truths" already known. Rather, I see writing as a job of experiment. It's like any discovery job; you don't know what's going to happen until you try it."

—William Stafford,
Teacher, Poet, and Essayist

Mark Twain, the author of *Adventures of Huckleberry Finn,* once observed that if you attempt to carry a cat around the block by its tail, you'll gain a whole lot of information about cats that you'll never forget. You may collect such firsthand information, or you may rely on the data, experience, or expertise of others. In any case, writers constantly collect facts, impressions, opinions, and ideas that are relevant to their subjects, purposes, and audiences. Collecting involves observing, remembering, imagining, thinking, reading, listening, writing, investigating, talking, taking notes, and experimenting. Collecting also involves thinking about the relationships among the bits of information that you have collected.

Shaping

"We must and do write each our own way."

—Eudora Welty,
Novelist and Essayist

Writers focus and organize the facts, examples, and ideas that they have collected into the recorded, linear form that is written language. When a hurricane hits the Gulf Coast, for example, residents of Texas, Louisiana, Mississippi, Alabama, and Florida are likely to collect an enormous amount of data in just a few hours. Rain, floods, tree limbs snapping, windows shattering, sirens blaring—all occur nearly simultaneously. If you try to write about such devastation, you need to narrow your focus (you can't describe everything that happened) and organize your information (you can't describe all of your experiences at the same time).

The genre of the personal essay, weaving description in a chronological order, is just one of the shapes that a writer may choose to develop and organize experience. Such shaping strategies also help writers collect additional information and ideas. Reconstructing a chronological order, for example, may suggest additional details—perhaps a wet, miserable-looking dog running through the heavy downpour—that you might not otherwise have remembered.

Drafting

Watch the **Video** on Office Hours: Drafting

At some point, writers draft a rough version of what will evolve into the finished piece of writing. Drafting processes vary widely from one writer to the next. Some writers prefer to reread their collecting and shaping notes, find a starting point, and launch themselves—figuring out what they want to say as they write it. Other writers start with a plan—a mental strategy, a short list, or an outline—of how they wish to proceed. Whatever approach you use in your draft, write down as much as possible: You want to see whether the information is clear, whether your overall shape expresses and clarifies your purpose, and whether your content and organization will meet the needs and expectations of your audience.

Revising

When writers revise rough drafts, they "resee" their subjects—and then modify their drafts to fit new visions. Revision is more than just tinkering with a word here and there; revision leads to larger changes—new examples or details, a different organization, or a new perspective. You accomplish these changes by adding, deleting, substituting, or reordering words, sentences, and paragraphs. Although revision begins the moment you get your first idea, most revisions are based on the reactions—or anticipated reactions—of the audience to your draft. You often play the role of audience yourself by putting the draft aside and rereading it later when you have some distance from your writing. Wherever you feel readers might not get your point, you revise to make it clearer. You may also get feedback from readers in a class workshop, suggesting that you collect more or different information, alter the shape of your draft to improve the flow of ideas, or clarify your terminology. As a result of your rereading and your readers' suggestions, you may change your thesis or even write for an entirely different audience.

Watch the **Video** on Office Hours: Revising

Editing—in contrast to revising—focuses on the minor changes that will improve the accuracy and readability of your language. You usually edit your essay to improve word choice, grammar, usage, or punctuation. You also use a computer spell-check program and proofread to catch typos and other surface errors.

Writing Process

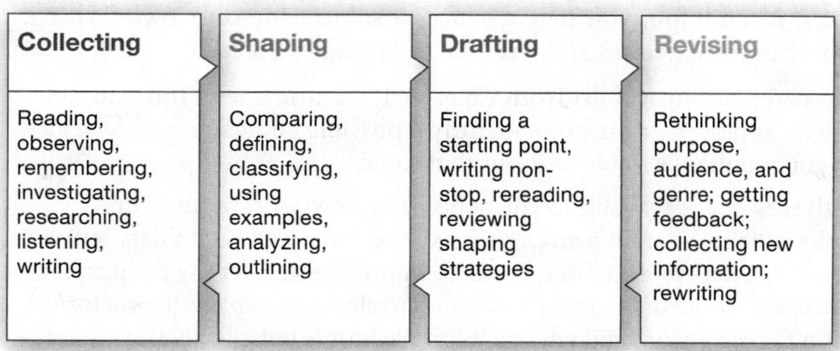

Collecting
Reading, observing, remembering, investigating, researching, listening, writing
Shaping
Comparing, defining, classifying, using examples, analyzing, outlining
Drafting
Finding a starting point, writing non-stop, rereading, reviewing shaping strategies
Revising
Rethinking purpose, audience, and genre; getting feedback; collecting new information; rewriting

The Whole Process

In practice, a writer's process rarely follows the simple consecutive order that these four stages or dimensions suggest. The writing process is recursive: It begins at one point, goes on to another, comes back to the first, jumps to the third, and so forth. While writing a letter to a friend, you may collect, shape, revise, and edit in one quick draft; a research paper may require repeated shaping over a two-week period. As writers draft, they may correct a few mistakes or typos, but they may not proofread until many days later. In the middle of reorganizing an essay, writers often reread drafts, ask more questions, and go back and collect more data. Even while editing, writers may throw out paragraphs, collect additional information, and draft new sections.

Keep in mind that writing often occurs during every stage of the writing process, not just during drafting and revising. During collecting, you will be recording information and jotting down ideas. During shaping, you will be writing out trial versions that you may use later when you draft or revise. Throughout the writing process, you use your writing to modify your subject, purpose, audience, and form.

The most important point to keep in mind is that the writing process is unique to each writer and to each writing situation. What works for one writer may be absolutely wrong for you. Some writers compose nearly everything in their heads. Others write only after discussing the subject with friends or drawing diagrams and pictures.

During the writing process, you need to experiment with various collecting, shaping, and drafting strategies to see what works best for you and for a particular piece of writing. As long as your process works, however, it's legitimate—no matter how many times you backtrack and repeat stages. When you are struggling with a piece of writing, remember that numerous revisions are a normal part of the writing process—even for most professionals.

Warming Up: Journal Exercises

The following exercises will help you review and practice the topics covered in this chapter. In addition, you may discover a subject for your own writing. Choose three of the exercises and write for ten minutes on each.

1. Reread your "authority" list from Chapter 1. Choose one of those topics and then explain your purpose, identify a possible audience, and select a genre you would use to write about that topic.
2. From the resources available to you at home or on your computer, find examples of four different genres, such as advertisements, pamphlets, letters, articles, and letters to the editor. For each sample genre, identify the purpose, audience, and context. Bring these samples to class and explain the rhetorical situation for each genre and why each sample is or is not effective.

3. **Writing Across the Curriculum.** If you have been given a writing assignment in another course, explain the purpose, the intended audience, and the genre for that assignment. Be prepared to explain how you plan to complete that assignment.
4. Read Neil Petrie's essay and postscript that follow. Then find the best paper you've written during the past year or two and write a "postscript" for it. Describe (a) the rhetorical situation, (b) your purpose, and (c) the process you used to write it.

A WRITING PROCESS AT WORK: COLLECTING AND SHAPING

Professional Writing

Athletes and Education

Neil H. Petrie

In the following essay, which appeared in the Chronicle of Higher Education, Neil H. Petrie argues that colleges have a hypocritical attitude toward student athletes. Although most universities claim that their athletes—both male and female—are in college to get a good education, in reality the pressures on athletes compromise their academic careers. In far too many cases, athletes never graduate. These are the students whom, as Petrie says, "the system uses and then discards after the final buzzer."

I have spent all my adult life in academe, first as a student and then as a professor. During that time I have seen many variations in the role of intercollegiate athletics in the university, and I've developed sharply split opinions on the subject. On one hand, I despise the system, clinging as it does to the academic body like a parasite. On the other hand, I feel sympathy and admiration for most of the young athletes struggling to balance the task of getting an education with the need to devote most of their energies to the excessive demands of the gym and the field. 1

My earliest experiences with the intrusion of athletics into the classroom came while I was still a freshman at the University of Colorado. While I was in my English professor's office one day, a colleague of hers came by for a chat. Their talk turned to the football coach's efforts to court the favor of the teachers responsible for his gladiators by treating them to dinner and a solicitous discussion of the academic progress of the players. I vividly recall my professor saying, "He can take me out to dinner if he wants, but if he thinks I'll pass his knuckleheads just because of that, he'd better think again." 2

Later, as a graduate teaching fellow, a lecturer, and then an assistant professor of English, I had ample opportunity to observe a Division 1 3 university's athletics program. I soon discovered that the prevailing stereotypes did not always apply. Athletes turned out to be as diverse as any other group of students in their habits, tastes, and abilities, and they showed a wide range of strategies for coping with the stress of their dual roles.

Some of them were poor students. An extreme example was the All-American football player (later a successful pro) who saw college only as a step to a six-figure contract and openly showed his disdain for the educational process. Others did such marginal work in my courses that I got the feeling they were daring me to give them D's or F's. One woman cross-country star, who almost never attended my composition class, used to push nearly illiterate essays under my office door at odd hours. 4

Yet many athletes were among the brightest students I had. Not so surprising, when you consider that, in addition to physical prowess, success in athletics requires intelligence, competitive drive, and dedication—all qualities that can translate into success in the classroom as well as on the field. The trouble is that the grinding hours of practice and road trips rob student athletes of precious study time and deplete their reserves of mental and physical energy. A few top athletes have earned A's; most are content to settle for B's or C's, even if they are capable of better. 5

The athletes' educational experience can't help being marred by their numerous absences and divided loyalties. In this respect, they are little different from the students who attempt to go to college while caring for a family or working long hours at an outside job. The athletes, however, get extra help in juggling their responsibilities. Although I have never been bribed or threatened and have never received a dinner invitation from a coach, I am expected to provide extra time and consideration for athletes, far beyond what I give other students. 6

Take the midterm grade reports, for example. At my university, the athletic department's academic counselor sends progress questionnaires to every teacher of varsity athletes. While the procedure shows admirable concern for the academic performance of athletes, it also amounts to preferential treatment. It requires teachers to take time from other teaching duties to fill out and return the forms for the athletes. (No other students get such progress reports.) If I were a cynic it would occur to me that the athletic department might actually be more concerned with athletes' eligibility than with their academic work. 7

Special attendance policies for athletes are another example of preferential treatment. Athletes miss a lot of classes. In fact, I think the road trip is one of the main reasons that athletes receive a deficient education. You simply can't learn as much away from the classroom and the library as on the campus. Nevertheless, professors continue to provide make-up tests, 8 alternative assignments, and special tutoring sessions to accommodate athletes. Any other student would have to have been very sick or the victim of a serious accident to get such dispensations.

It is sad to see bright young athletes knowingly compromise their potential and settle for much less education than they deserve. It is infuriating, though, to see the ones less gifted academically exploited by a system that they do not comprehend and robbed of any possible chance to grow intellectually and to explore other opportunities. *9*

One specific incident illustrates for me the worst aspects of college athletics. It wasn't unusual or extraordinary—just the all-too-ordinary case of an athlete not quite good enough to make a living from athletics and blind to the opportunity afforded by the classroom. *10*

I was sitting in my office near the beginning of a term, talking to a parade of new advisees. I glanced up to see my entire doorway filled with the bulk of a large young man, whom I recognized as one of our basketball stars from several seasons ago who had left for the pros and now apparently come back. *11*

Over the next hour I got an intensive course on what it's like to be a college athlete. In high school, John had never been interested in much outside of basketball, and, like many other indifferent students, he went on to junior college on an athletic scholarship. After graduating, he came to the university, where he played for two more years, finishing out hiseligibility. He was picked in a late round of the N.B.A. draft and left college, but in the end he turned out to be a step too slow for the pros. By that time he had a family to support, and when he realized he could never make a career of basketball, he decided to return to college. *12*

We both knew that his previous academic career hadn't been particularly focused, and that because of transferring and taking minimum course loads during the basketball season, he wouldn't be close to a degree. But I don't think either one of us was prepared for what actually emerged from our examination of his transcripts. It was almost as if he had never gone beyond high school. His junior-college transcript was filled with remedial and nonacademic courses. *13*

Credit for those had not transferred to the university. Over the next two years he had taken a hodgepodge of courses, mostly in physical education. He had never received any advice about putting together a coherent program leading to a degree. In short, the academic side of his college experience had been completely neglected by coaches, advisers, and, of course, John himself. *14*

By the time we had evaluated his transcripts and worked out a tentative course of study, John was in shock and I was angry. It was going to take him at least three years of full-time study to complete a degree. He thanked me politely for my time, picked up the planning sheets, and left. I was ashamed to be a part of the university that day. Why hadn't anyone *15*

...continued Athletes and Education, **Neil H. Petrie**

in the athletic department ever told him what it would take to earn a degree? Or at least been honest enough to say, "Listen, we can keep you eligible and give you a chance to play ball, but don't kid yourself into thinking you'll be getting an education, too."

I saw John several more times during the year. He tried for a while. 16
He took classes, worked, supported his family, and then he left again. I lost track of him after that. I can only hope that he found a satisfying job or completed his education at some other institution. I know people say the situation has improved in the last few years, but when I read about the shockingly low percentages of athletes who graduate, I think of John.

Colleges give student athletes preferential treatment. We let them cut 17
classes. We let them slide through. We protect them from harsh realities. We applaud them for entertaining us and wink when they compromise themselves intellectually. We give them special dorms, special meals, special tutors, and a specially reprehensible form of hypocrisy.

I can live with the thought of the athletes who knowingly use the 18
college-athletics system to get their pro contracts or their devalued degrees. But I have trouble living with the thought of the ones whom the system uses and then discards after the final buzzer.

Professional Writing

On Writing "Athletes and Education"

Neil H. Petrie

In the following postscript on his writing process, Neil Petrie describes why he wanted to write the paper, how he collected material to support his argument, and how he shaped and focused his ideas as he wrote. His comments illustrate how his purpose—to expose the hypocrisies of collegiate athletics—guided his writing of the essay.

This essay has its origin, as all persuasive writing should, in a strongly 1
held opinion. I'm always more comfortable if I care deeply about my subject matter. As a teacher, I hold some powerful convictions about the uneasy marriage of big-time athletics and higher education, and so I wanted to write an essay that would expose what I think are the dangers and hypocrisies of that system.

At the beginning of my essay, I wanted to establish some authority to 2
lend credibility to my argument. Rather than gather statistics on drop-out rates of student athletes or collect the opinions of experts, I planned to

rely on my own experiences as both a student and teacher. I hoped to convince my readers that my opinions were based on the authority of firsthand knowledge. In this introduction I was also aware of the need to avoid turning off readers who might dismiss me as a "jock hater." I had to project my negative feelings about the athletic system while maintaining my sympathy with the individual student athletes involved in that system. The thesis, then, would emerge gradually as I accumulated the evidence; it would be more implied than explicitly stated.

Gathering the material was easy. I selected a series of examples from 3
my personal experiences as a college student and instructor, as well as anecdotes I'd heard from other instructors. Most of these stories were ones that I had shared before, either in private discussions with friends or in classrooms with students.

Shaping the material was a little tougher. As I began thinking about 4
my examples and how to order them, I saw that I really wanted to make two main points. The first was that most colleges give preferential treatment to athletes. The second point was that, despite the extra attention, the success of the athlete's academic career is often ignored by all parties involved. Many of my examples, I realized, illustrated the varieties of pressures put upon both athletes and instructors to make sure that the students at least get by in class and remain eligible. These examples seemed to cluster together because they showed the frustrations of teachers and the reactions of athletes trying to juggle sports and academics. This group would make a good introduction to my general exposé of the system. But I had one more example I wanted to use that seemed to go beyond the cynicism of some athletes or the hypocrisy of the educators. This was the case of John, an athlete who illustrated what I thought were the most exploitative aspects of varsity athletics. I originally planned on devoting the bulk of my essay to this story and decided to place it near the end where it would make my second point with maximum emotional effect.

A two-part structure for the essay now emerged. In the first segment 5
following my introductory paragraph, I gave a series of shorter examples, choosing to order them in roughly chronological order (paragraphs 2–4). I then moved from these specific details to a more general discussion of the demands placed upon both students and teachers, such as lengthy practice time, grade reports, road trips, and special attendance policies. This concluded my description of the way the system operates (paragraphs 5–8).

Then it was time to shift gears, to provide a transition to the next 6
part of my essay, to what I thought was my strongest example. I wanted the story of John to show how the system destroyed human potential. To do this, I needed to increase the seriousness of the tone in order to persuade the reader that I was dealing in more than a little bureaucratic

...continued On Writing "Athletes and Education", **Neil H. Petrie**

boondoggling. I tried to set the tone by my word choice: I moved from words such as "sad," "compromise," and "settle" to words with much stronger emotional connotations such as "infuriating," "exploited," and "robbed," all in a single short transitional paragraph (paragraph 9).

I then introduced my final extended example in equally strong language, identifying it as a worst-case illustration (paragraph 10). I elaborated on John's story, letting the details and my reactions to his situation carry the more intense outrage that I was trying to convey in this second part of the essay (paragraphs 10–16). The first version that I tried was a rambling narrative that had an overly long recounting of John's high school and college careers. So I tightened this section by eliminating such items as his progress through the ranks of professional basketball and his dreams of million-dollar contracts. I also cut down on a discussion of the various courses of study he was considering as options. The result was a sharper focus on the central issue of John's dilemma: the lack of adequate degree counseling for athletes. 7

After my extended example, all that was left was the conclusion. As I wrote, I was very conscious of using certain devices, such as the repetition of key words and sentence patterns in paragraph seventeen ("We let them . . . We let them . . . We protect them . . . We applaud them . . . We give them . . .") to maintain the heightened emotional tone. I was also conscious of repeating the two-part structure of the essay in the last two paragraphs. I moved from general preferential treatment (paragraph 17) to the concluding and more disturbing idea of devastating exploitation (paragraph 18). 8

On the whole, I believe that this essay effectively conveys its point through the force of accumulated detail. My personal experience was the primary source of evidence, and that experience led naturally to the order of the paragraphs and to the argument I wished to make: that while some athletes knowingly use the system, others are used and exploited by it. 9

Questions for Writing and Discussion

1. Describe Petrie's audience and purpose for this essay. What sentences reveal his intended audience? What sentences reveal his purpose? What sentences contain his thesis, claim, or main idea? Do you agree with that thesis? Why or why not?
2. Who do you think is most to blame for the situation that Petrie describes: The athletes themselves? The colleges for paying their scholarships and then ignoring them when they drop out? The students and alumni who pay to see their teams win?

3 Petrie does not explicitly suggest a solution to the problem that he describes. Assume, however, that he has been asked by the president of his university to propose a solution. Write the letter that you think Petrie would send to the president.

A WRITING PROCESS AT WORK: DRAFTING AND REVISING

While drafting and revising, writers frequently make crucial changes in ideas and language. The first scribbled sentences, written primarily for ourselves, are often totally different from what we later present to our audience in final, polished versions. Carl Becker's study of the American Declaration of Independence assembles the early drafts of that famous document and compares them with the final version. Shown below is Thomas Jefferson's first draft, with revisions made by Benjamin Franklin, John Adams, and other members of the Committee of Five that was charged with developing the new document.

Professional Writing

Rough Draft of the Opening Sentences of the Declaration of Independence

Thomas Jefferson

one
When in the course of human events it becomes necessary for ~~a~~ people to
dissolve the political bands which have connected them with another, and to
~~advance from that subordination in which they have hitherto remained, & to~~
separate and equal
assume among the powers of the earth the ~~equal & independent~~ station to
which the laws of nature & of nature's god entitle them, a decent respect to
the opinions of mankind requires that they should declare the causes which
the separation.
impel them to ~~the change.~~

self-evident
We hold these truths *to be* ~~sacred & undeniable; that~~ all men are created
they are endowed by their creator with
equal ~~& independent;~~ that ~~from that equal creation they derive in rights~~
rights; that *these*
inherent & inalienable among ~~which~~ are ~~the preservation of~~ life, ~~&~~ liberty, &
the pursuit of happiness. . . .

The Final Draft of the Opening Sentences of the Declaration of Independence, as Approved on July 4, 1776

When in the Course of human events, it becomes necessary for one people to dissolve the political bands which have connected them with another, and to assume among the powers of the earth, the separate and equal station to which the Laws of Nature and of Nature's God entitle them, a decent respect to the opinions of mankind requires that they should declare the causes which impel them to the separation.

We hold these truths to be self-evident, that all men are created equal, that they are endowed by their Creator with certain inalienable Rights, that among these are Life, Liberty and the pursuit of Happiness.

Questions for Writing and Discussion

1. Select one change in a sentence that most improved the final version of the Declaration of Independence. Explain how the revised wording is more effective.
2. Find one change in a word or phrase that constitutes an alteration in meaning rather than a choice of "smoother" or more appropriate language. How does this change affect the meaning?
3. Upon rereading this passage from the Declaration of Independence, one reader wrote, "I was really irritated by that 'all men are created equal' remark. The writers were white, free, well-to-do, Anglo-Saxon, mostly Protestant males discussing their own 'inalienable rights.' They sure weren't discussing the 'inalienable rights' of female Americans or of a million slaves or of nonwhite free Americans!" Revise the passage from the Declaration of Independence using this person as your audience.

4 On the Internet, visit the National Archives at http://www.archives.gov to see a photograph of the original Declaration of Independence and learn how the Dunlap Broadside of the Declaration was read aloud to troops. What does this historical context add to what you know about the Declaration of Independence? Do the revisions help make the document more revolutionary or propagandistic? Do you think the revisions are as important to our history and culture as the Declaration itself? Explain.

Complete additional exercises and practice in your MyLab

Described by Robert F. Kennedy as "one of the heroic figures of our time," César Chávez (1927–1993) spent his lifetime improving the conditions of agricultural workers in America. In 1994, President Clinton posthumously awarded Chávez the Presidential Medal of Freedom, the nation's highest and most prestigious civilian award. In his essay in this chapter, "César Chávez Saved My Life," Daniel Alejandrez remembers Chávez's influence on his life.

Department of Labor

3 Observing and Remembering

What You Will Learn
In this chapter, you will learn to:

3.1 Use techniques for writing about observations

3.2 Use techniques for writing about memories

3.3 Use collecting strategies to develop a personal narrative

3.4 Shape your personal narrative

BOTH observing and remembering are essential to good writing in a variety of genres. Good observing skills come in handy when you are writing up a science experiment, making notes during a field trip, or describing something for a friend. In addition, the strategies that you learn from careful observation and description will help you write about your memories of particular people, places, and events. Observing and remembering are remarkably interrelated skills: observing certain places or events often brings back memories of other experiences; likewise, remembering a person or a place will often bring up specific observed details—the color of someone's hair, the aroma of bacon and eggs for breakfast, or the sounds of the city or country. In this chapter, you will practice key observing techniques and then use them as you write an essay about a personal memory.

Observing is essential to both learning and communicating. Sometimes we want to describe something carefully to help us learn and remember; at other times, we want to share what we have seen. Good writers draw on all their senses: sight, smell, touch, taste, and hearing. In addition, experienced writers notice what is *not* there: a friend who is usually present but is now absent; the absolute quiet in the air that precedes an impending storm. Writers of description also look for *changes* in their subjects—from light to dark or from noise to sudden silence. Good writers of description use their *experiences* to help see and describe a place or event: How is this room or building or neighborhood similar to or different from other places you have been? Finally, writers of effective description are good *researchers*: if you're not sure exactly when it happened or what it means, searching a database or Google can help you—and your readers—identify what something is, where it occurs, or why it is important.

"My task . . . is, by the power of the written word, to make you hear, to make you feel—it is, before all, to make you see."

—Joseph Conrad,
Author of *Heart of Darkness* and Other Novels

"The fact is that there's no understanding the future without the present, and no understanding where we are now without a glance, at least, to where we have been."

—Joyce Maynard,
Columnist and Author of *Looking Backward: A Chronicle of Growing up Old in the Sixties*

" . . . Not that it's raining, but the feel of being rained upon. "

—E. L. Doctorow, Author of *Ragtime* and Other Novels

The key to effective observing is using specific detail *to show* your reader the person, place, object, or image. Good description follows the advice of experienced writers: *Show, don't tell.* Showing through vivid detail allows readers to reach the conclusions that you may be tempted to tell them. Even in writing, experience is the best teacher; you will need to use specific details to communicate the look, the feel, the weight, the sounds, and the smells.

Remembering also has a set of strategies and techniques that effective writers use. The first and most important strategy is to focus on specific scenes set at a particular time and place. Just as good description *shows* rather than tells, an effective narrative picks *key scenes*, sets them in time and place, and then recreates them by using description, dialogue, and important incidents. In addition, effective remembering requires describing key *changes* and *conflicts*. Finally, effective remembering essays emphasize a single key idea. Sometimes that main point shows contrasts between past and present or focuses on what a person learns—or fails to learn.

Techniques for Observing

3.1 Use techniques for writing about observations

" The real voyage of discovery consists not in seeking new landscapes but in having new eyes. "

—Marcel Proust, Author of *Remembrance of Things Past*

This chapter asks you to write a personal narrative about an important event in your life. Your narrative will focus on a few key scenes to support and illustrate your main idea. In addition, you will use descriptive strategies to make your key scenes as vivid and memorable as possible. You may wish to begin your assignment by practicing the following observing techniques in a shorter assignment, journal entry, or forum post. Or you may want to start writing your narrative and then come back to these observing techniques when you have identified the key scenes you want to narrate.

These techniques for observing are illustrated in the following paragraphs by Karen Blixen, who wrote *Out of Africa* under the pen name Isak Dinesen. In this excerpt from her journals, Blixen describes a startling change that occurred when she shot a large iguana. (The annotations in the margin identify all five observing techniques.)

Sensory description

Comparisons, images, and sensory details

In the Reserve I have sometimes come upon the Iguana, the big lizards, as they were sunning themselves upon a flat stone in a riverbed. They are not pretty in shape, but nothing can be imagined more beautiful than their coloring. They shine like a heap of precious stones or like a pane cut out of an old church window. When, as you approach, they swish away, there is a flash of azure, green and purple over the stones, the color seems to be standing behind them in the air, like a comet's luminous tail.

Once I shot an Iguana. I thought that I should be able to make some pretty things from his skin. A strange thing happened then, that I have never afterwards forgotten. As I went up to him, where he was lying dead upon his stone, and actually while I was walking the few steps, he faded and grew pale, all color died out of him as in one long sigh, and by the time that I touched him he was grey and dull like a lump of concrete. It was the live impetuous blood pulsating within the animal, which had radiated out all that glow and splendor. Now that the flame was put out, and the soul had flown, the Iguana was as dead as a sandbag.

Changes in condition

Learning about the subject

What is not there

Dominant idea: Now colorless and dead

Watch the **Video** on Writing Observations

Techniques for Writing About Observations

Technique	Tips on How to Do It
Giving sensory details (sight, sound, smell, touch, taste)	Use *sensory descriptions, comparisons,* and *images.* "Zoom in" on crucial details. Include *actual dialogue* and *names of things* where appropriate.
Describing what is *not* there	Sometimes keen observation requires stepping back and noticing what is *absent*, what is *not* happening, or who is *not* present.
Noting changes in the subject's form or condition	Even when the subject appears static—a landscape, a flower, a building—look for evidence of change: a tree being enveloped by tent worms, a six-inch purple-and-white iris that eight hours earlier was just a green bud, a sandstone exterior of a church being eroded by acid rain.
Learning about your subject	The observant eye requires a critical, inquiring mind. Read about your subject. Google key ideas or terms. Ask other people or experts on the subject. Probe to find what is *unusual*, *surprising*, or *controversial* about your subject.
Focusing on a dominant idea	Focus on those details and images that clarify the main ideas or discoveries. Discovery often depends on the *contrast* between the writer's expectations and the reality.

OBSERVING PEOPLE

Watch the Video on Ron Carlson on Observing

Observing people—their dress, body language, facial features, behavior, eating habits, and conversation—is a pastime that we all share. In a *Rolling Stone* article, Brian Hiatt describes U2 lead singer Bono in his native Dublin. Notice how the descriptive details and images work together to create the dominant impression of Bono as a high-energy rock star, conversationalist, and global philanthropist.

> Bono rounds a corner onto a narrow Dublin street, boots crunching on old cobblestone, sleek, black double-breasted overcoat flapping in the January breeze. . . . He's running late for his next appointment, which is not unusual in what must be one of the most overstuffed lives on the planet: "part-time" rock stardom; global advocacy for Africa's poor that's won him nominations for the Nobel Peace Prize; various multinational business and charitable ventures; an op-ed column for the *New York Times*; and four kids with Ali Hewson, his wife of 26 years. "I find it very hard to leave home," he says, "because my house is full of laughter and songs and kids."
>
> Interviewing Bono is like taking an Alaskan husky for a walk—you can only suggest a general direction, and then hold on for dear life. Over an 80-minute lunch at a favorite Dublin restaurant, Eden, he repeatedly goes off on wild, entertaining tangents, which tend to include names such as Bill Clinton, Microsoft co-founder Paul Allen, genomic researcher Craig Venter and Archbishop Desmond Tutu (Bono calls him "the Arch"). He tosses out one killer sound bite after another, blue eyes moving like tropical fish behind today's pinkish-purple shades.
>
> He eats his chicken breast in big bites, avoiding the potatoes, talking with his mouth full—and when the chicken is gone, he dips a finger into the sauce and licks it off, more than once. "We began this decade well—I think we'll end it better," he says, sitting on a white chair at a white table in a restaurant that's otherwise empty—apparently because management has cleared it out for him. "Wouldn't it be great if, after all these years, U2 has their heyday? That could be true of a painter or a filmmaker at this stage."

OBSERVING PLACES

In the following passage, John Muir describes California and the Yosemite Valley as it looked over 140 years ago. John Muir was the founder of the Sierra Club, whose first mission was to preserve the vision of Yosemite that Muir paints in the following paragraphs. Notice how Muir uses all of the key techniques for observing as he vividly describes the California Sierra.

Arriving by the Panama steamer, I stopped one day in San Francisco and then inquired for the nearest way out of town. "But where do you want to go?" asked the man to whom I had applied for this important information. "To any place that is wild," I said. This reply startled him. He seemed to fear I might be crazy and therefore the sooner I was out of town the better, so he directed me to the Oakland ferry.

So on the first of April, 1868, I set out afoot for Yosemite. It was the bloom-time of the year over the lowlands and coast ranges; the landscapes of the Santa Clara Valley were fairly drenched with sunshine, all the air was quivering with the songs of the meadow-larks, and the hills were so covered with flowers that they seemed to be painted. Slow indeed was my progress through these glorious gardens, the first of the California flora I had seen. Cattle and cultivation were making few scars as yet, and I wandered enchanted in long wavering curves, knowing by my pocket map that Yosemite Valley lay to the east and that I should surely find it.

Looking eastward from the summit of the Pacheco Pass one shining morning, a landscape was displayed that after all my wanderings still appears as the most beautiful I have ever beheld. At my feet lay the Great Central Valley of California, level and flowery, like a lake of pure sunshine, forty or fifty miles wide, five hundred miles long, one rich furred garden of yellow *Compositae*. And from the eastern boundary of this vast golden flower-bed rose the mighty Sierra, miles in height, and so gloriously colored and so radiant, it seemed not clothed with light, but wholly composed of it, like the wall of some celestial city. Along the top and extending a good way down, was a rich pearl-gray belt of snow; below it a belt of blue and dark purple, marking the extension of the forests; and stretching along the base of the range a broad belt of rose-purple; all these colors, from the blue sky to the yellow valley smoothly blending as they do in a rainbow, making a wall of light ineffably fine. Then it seemed to me that the Sierra should be called, not the Nevada or Snowy Range, but the Range of Light.

In general views no mark of man is visible upon it, nor anything to suggest the wonderful depth and grandeur of its sculpture. None of its magnificent forest-crowned ridges seems to rise much above the general level to publish its wealth. No great valley or river is seen, or group of well-marked features of any kind standing out as distinct pictures. Even the summit peaks, marshaled in glorious array so high in the sky, seem comparatively regular in form. Nevertheless the whole range five hundred miles long is furrowed with canyons 2,000 to 5,000 feet deep, in which once flowed majestic glaciers, and in which now flow and sing the bright rejoicing rivers.

Techniques for Writing About Memories

3.2
Use techniques for writing about memories

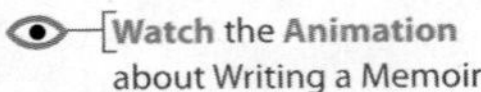
Watch the Animation about Writing a Memoir

Writing vividly about memories includes all the skills of careful observing, but it adds several narrative strategies. Listed below are six techniques that writers use to compose effective remembering essays. As you read the essays that follow, notice how each writer uses these techniques. Then use these techniques when you write your own remembering essay. Remember: Not all writing about memories uses all of these techniques, but one or two of them may transform a lifeless account into an effective narrative.

Techniques for Writing About Memories

Technique	Tips on How to Do It
Using *detailed observation* of people, places, and events	Writing vividly about memories requires many of the skills of careful observation. Use *sensory descriptions*, *comparisons*, and *images*. Include *actual dialogue* where appropriate.
Focusing on *occasion and cultural context*	Think about the personal occasion that motivated you to write about your experience. You may want to set your experiences in a larger cultural context.
Creating *specific scenes* set in time and space	Show your reader the actual events—don't just tell about them. Narrate or recreate specific incidents as they actually happened. Avoid summarizing events or presenting just the conclusions (for instance, "Those experiences really changed my life").
Noting *changes*, *contrasts*, or *conflicts*	Describe changes in people or places. Show contrasts between two memories or between memories of expectations and the subsequent realities. Narrate conflicts between people or ideas. Resolving (or sometimes not resolving) these changes, contrasts, or conflicts can even be the point of your memoir.
Making *connections* between *past* events, people, or places and the *present*	The main idea or focus of your narrative may grow out of the connections you make between the past and the present: what you felt then and how you feel now; what you thought you knew and what you know now.
Discovering and focusing on a *main idea*	Your narrative should not be a random account of your favorite memories. It should have a clear main point—something you learned or discovered or realized—without stating a "moral" to your story.

All of these techniques are important, but you should also keep several other points in mind. Normally, you should write in the *first person,* using *I* or *we.* Although you will usually write in the *past tense,* sometimes you may wish to lend immediacy to the events by retelling them in the *present tense.* Finally, you may choose straightforward *chronological order,* or you may begin near the end and use a *flashback* to tell the beginning of the story.

The key to effective remembering is to go beyond *generalities* and *conclusions* about your experiences ("I had a lot of fun—those days really changed my life"). Your goal is to recall specific incidents set in time and place that *show* how and why those days changed your life. The specific incidents should show your *main point* or *dominant idea.*

The following passage by Andrea Lee began as a journal entry in 1978 when she lived in Moscow and Leningrad following her graduation from college. She later combined these firsthand observations with her memories and published them in a collection called *Russian Journal.* She uses first person and, frequently, present tense as she describes her reactions to the sights of Moscow. In these paragraphs, she weaves observations and memories together to show her main idea: The contrast between American and Soviet Union–style advertising helped her understand both the virtues and the faults of American commercialism. (The annotations in the margin illustrate how Lee uses all five remembering techniques.)

"Time passes and the past becomes the present. . . . These presences of the past are there in the center of your life today. You thought . . . they had died, but they have just been waiting their chance."

—Carlos Fuentes,
Mexican Essayist and Novelist, Author of *The Crystal Frontier*

In Mayakovsky Square, not far from the Tchaikovsky Concert Hall, a big computerized electric sign sends various messages flashing out into the night. An outline of a taxi in green dots is accompanied by the words: "Take Taxis—All Streets Are Near." This is replaced by multicolored human figures and a sentence urging Soviet citizens to save in State banks. The bright patterns and messages come and go, making this one of the most sophisticated examples of advertising in Moscow. Even on chilly nights when I pass through the square, there is often a little group of Russians standing in front of the sign, watching in fascination for five and ten minutes as the colored dots go through their magical changes. The first few times I saw this, I chuckled and recalled an old joke about an American town so boring that people went out on weekends to watch the Esso sign.

Specific scene

Detailed observation

Connections past and present

Advertising, of course, is the glamorous offspring of capitalism and art: Why advertise in a country where there is only one brand, the State brand, of anything, and often not enough even of that? There is nothing here comparable to the glittering overlay of commercialism that Americans, at least, take for granted as part of our cities; nothing like the myriad small seductions of the marketplace, which have led us to expect to be enticed. The Soviet political propaganda posters that fill up a small part of the Moscow landscape with their uniformly cold red color schemes and monumental robot-faced figures are so unappealing that they are dismissable.

Contrast

Detailed observation

Connections past and present

Contrast and change

Main idea

I realize now, looking back, that for at least my first month in Moscow, I was filled with an unconscious and devastating disappointment. Hardly realizing it, as I walked around the city, I was looking for the constant sensory distractions I was accustomed to in America. Like many others my age, I grew up reading billboards and singing advertising jingles; my idea of beauty was shaped—perniciously, I think—by the models with the painted eyes and pounds of shining hair whose beauty was accessible on every television set and street corner.

REMEMBERING PEOPLE

"A writer is a reader moved to emulation."

—Saul Bellow,
Author of *Henderson the Rain King*

In the following passage from his introduction to *The Way to Rainy Mountain*, N. Scott Momaday remembers his grandmother. While details of place and event are also recreated, the primary focus is on the character of his grandmother as revealed in several *specific,* recurring actions. Momaday does not give us generalities about his feelings (for instance, "I miss my grandmother a lot, especially now that she's gone"). Instead, he begins with specific memories of scenes that *show* how he felt.

"There are two ways to live. One is as though nothing is a miracle, the other is as though everything is."

—Albert Einstein,
Author of *What I Believe*

"Some very small incident that takes place today may be the most important event that happens to you this year, but you don't know that when it happens. You don't know it until much later."

—Toni Morrison,
Nobel Prize–Winning Author of *Beloved* And *Song of Solomon*

Now that I can have her only in memory, I see my grandmother in the several postures that were peculiar to her: standing at the wood stove on a winter morning and turning meat in a great iron skillet; sitting at the south window, bent above her beadwork, and afterwards, when her vision failed, looking down for a long time into the fold of her hands; going out upon a cane, very slowly as she did when the weight of age came upon her; praying. I remember her most often at prayer. She made long, rambling prayers out of suffering and hope, having seen many things. I was never sure that I had the right to hear, so exclusive were they of all mere custom and company. The last time I saw her she prayed standing by the side of her bed at night, naked to the waist, the light of a kerosene lamp moving upon her dark skin. Her long, black hair, always drawn and braided in the day, lay upon her shoulders and against her breasts like a shawl. I do not speak Kiowa, and I never understood her prayers, but there was something inherently sad in the sound, some merest hesitation upon the syllables of sorrow. She began in a high and descending pitch, exhausting her breath to silence; then again and again—and always the same intensity of effort, of something that is, and is not, like urgency in the human voice. Transported so in the dancing light among the shadows of her room, she seemed beyond the reach of time. But that was illusion; I think I knew then that I should not see her again.

REMEMBERING PLACES

In the following passage from *Farewell to Manzanar,* Jeanne Wakatsuke Houston remembers the place in California where, as Japanese-Americans, her family was imprisoned during World War II. As you read, look for specific details and bits of description that convey her main idea.

> "Your audience is one single reader. I have found that sometimes it helps to pick out one person—a real person you know, or an imagined person—and write to that one."
>
> —John Steinbeck, Novelist

In Spanish, *Manzanar* means "apple orchard." Great stretches of Owens Valley were once green with orchards and alfalfa fields. It has been a desert ever since its water started flowing south into Los Angeles, sometime during the twenties. But a few rows of untended pear and apple trees were still growing there when the camp opened, where a shallow water table had kept them alive. In the spring of 1943 we moved to block 28, right up next to one of the old pear orchards. That's where we stayed until the end of the war, and those trees stand in my memory for the turning of our life in camp, from the outrageous to the tolerable.

Papa pruned and cared for the nearest trees. Late that summer we picked the fruit green and stored it in a root cellar he had dug under our new barracks. At night the wind through the leaves would sound like the surf had sounded in Ocean Park, and while drifting off to sleep, I could almost imagine we were still living by the beach.

REMEMBERING EVENTS

In his essay "The Boy's Desire," Richard Rodriguez recalls a particular event from his childhood that comes to mind when he remembers Christmas. In this passage, Rodriguez describes both the effort to remember and the memory itself—the one memory that still "holds color and size and shape." Was it all right, he wonders, that a boy should have wanted a doll for Christmas?

The fog comes to mind. It never rained on Christmas. It was never sharp blue and windy. When I remember Christmas in Sacramento, it is in gray: The valley fog would lift by late morning, the sun boiled haze for a few hours, then the tule fog would rise again when it was time to go into the house.

The haze through which memory must wander is thickened by that fog. The rooms of the house on 39th Street are still and dark in late afternoon, and I open the closet to search for old toys. One year there was a secondhand bike. I do not remember a color. Perhaps it had no color even then. Another year there were boxes of games that rattled their parts—dice and pegs and spinning dials. Or perhaps the rattle is of a jigsaw puzzle that compressed into an image. . . of what? of Paris? a litter of kittens? I cannot remember. Only one memory holds color and size and shape: brown hair, blue eyes, the sweet smell of styrene.

That Christmas I announced I wanted a bride doll. I must have been seven or eight—wise enough to know not to tell anyone at school, but young enough to whine out my petition from early November.

My father's reaction was unhampered by psychology. A shrug—"Una muñeca?"—a doll, why not? Because I knew it was my mother who would choose all the presents, it was she I badgered. I wanted a bride doll! "Is there something else you want?" she wondered. No! I'd make clear with my voice that nothing else would appease me. "We'll see," she'd say, and she never wrote it down on her list.

By early December, wrapped boxes started piling up in my parents' bedroom closet, above my father's important papers and the family album. When no one else was home, I'd drag a chair over and climb up to see. . . Looking for the one. About a week before Christmas, it was there. I was so certain it was mine that I punched my thumb through the wrapping paper and the cellophane window on the box and felt inside—lace, two tiny, thin legs. I got other presents that year, but it was the doll I kept by me. I remember my mother saying I'd have "to share her" with my younger sister—but Helen was four years old, oblivious. The doll was mine. My arms would hold her. She would sleep on my pillow.

And the sky did not fall. The order of the universe did not tremble. In fact, it was right for a change. My family accommodated itself to my request. My brother and sisters played round me with their own toys. I paraded my doll by the hands across the floor.

The other day, when I asked my brother and sisters about the doll, no one remembered. My mother remembers. "Yes," she smiled. "One year there was a doll."

The closet door closes. (The house on 39th Street has been razed for a hospital parking lot.) The fog rises. Distance tempts me to mock the boy and his desire. The fact remains: One Christmas in Sacramento I wanted a bride doll, and I got one.

Warming Up: Journal Exercises

To practice writing about your memories, read the following exercises, and then write on three that interest you the most. If another idea occurs to you, write about it.

1. Go through old family photographs and find one of yourself, taken at least five years ago. Describe the person in the photograph—what he or she did, thought, said, or hoped. How is that person like or unlike the person you are now?
2. What are your earliest memories? Choose one particular event. How old were you? What was the place? Who were the people around you? What happened? After you write down your own memories, call members of your family, if possible, and interview them for their memories of this incident. How does what you remember differ from what your family tells you? Revise your first memory to incorporate details provided by your family.
3. At some point in the past, you may have faced a conflict between what was expected of you—by parents, friends, family, coach, or employer—and your own personality or abilities. Describe one occasion when those expectations seemed unrealistic or unfair. Was the experience entirely negative or was it, in the long run, positive?
4. At least at one point in our lives, we have felt like an outsider. Earlier in this chapter, Richard Rodriguez recalls feelings of being different. Write about an incident when you felt alienated from your family, peers, or social group. Focus on a key scene or scenes that show what happened, why it was important, and how it affects you now.
5. Read the following short educational memories written by Junot Diaz, Michelle A. Rhee, and Lisa Randall. Then write a few paragraphs for your classmates, narrating a special memory of a person or an event that had a positive impact on your own education or your life.

In Mrs. Crowell's Library

By Junot Diaz, author

I remember her as a small woman, but what do I know? I was small myself. She's in none of the official photographs I have from my elementary-school days, but in my memory, my first librarian is a gentle white woman who wore glasses and was exceedingly kind to this new immigrant. I do not remember her voice,

...continued In Mrs. Crowell's Library **By Junot Diaz, author**

but I do remember that every time I saw her, she called me to her desk and showed me with an almost conspiratorial glee a book she had picked out for me, a book I always read and often loved.

Every now and then you get lucky in your education and you make a teacher-friend; Mrs. Crowell was my first. By second grade she was allowing me to take out more books than the prescribed limit. By third grade I was granted admission to her librarian's office. My love of books was born of hers. As a newcomer with almost no knowledge of the country in which I'd found myself, I was desperate to understand where the hell I was, who I was. I sought those answers in books. It was in Mrs. Crowell's library that I found my first harbor, my first truly safe place in the United States. I still feel a happy pulse every time I see a library. I'm with Borges in imagining Paradise as "a kind of library." Where instead of angels there will be a corps of excellent librarians.

Calvin in Motion

By Michelle A. Rhee, founder and chief executive, Students First

When I was teaching second grade in Baltimore, there was an adorable but disruptive boy in my class named Calvin. He talked over me, talked over his friends and couldn't participate in an appropriate way. I was constantly urging him to sit still and be quiet, and I even held one of those awfully serious what-do-we-do meetings with his father. Nothing worked. Until the day I put a dustpan in Calvin's hand. It all started when he threw a pile of pencil-sharpener shavings all over the room during story time. I gave Calvin the dustpan and a brush and told him to clean up the mess. Then, I proceeded with the story. As I read, I heard Calvin mumbling while he twirled around with that dustpan. After a few minutes, to my astonishment, I realized Calvin was answering my questions about the story. He sounded like a model student. Never before had I imagined that I would get Calvin on task by telling him to do an activity that was entirely unrelated to my lesson. Because Calvin was a kinesthetic kid, or a physical learner, he could only focus on school if he was up and moving. From that day on, Calvin would play with manipulative toys and sometimes even take a lap around the classroom while I was instructing. He taught me that all kids learn in wildly different ways and that all children are reachable and teachable.

Just Ask. Then Keep Asking.

By Lisa Randall, Professor of Physics, Harvard University, and author of *Knocking on Heaven's Door* and *Warped Passengers*

I was shy the way many geeky girls can be. Professors hardly noticed that they rarely answered girls' questions before some boy who didn't actually know the answer interrupted. But a professor who later became my adviser gave me the best advice I ever received, which was to not be afraid to speak up and ask questions. Suddenly teachers were speaking directly to me, and my questions were usually good enough that I could detect the relief of other students who actually had the same ones, reassuring me I was doing the right thing. Now, as a professor, I know not to see classes as passive experiences. The occasional interruption keeps people engaged and illuminates subtle points, and in research even leads to new research directions. Just participating and questioning makes your mind work better. Don't you agree?

Professional Writing

César Chávez Saved My Life

Daniel "Nene" Alejandrez

Labor leader and civil rights worker César Chávez (1927–1993) founded the National Farm Workers Association and used the nonviolent principles of Mahatma Gandhi and Dr. Martin Luther King, Jr. to gain dignity, fair wages, and humane working conditions for farm workers. The author of this article, Daniel "Nene" Alejandrez, is the founder of *Barrios Unidos* and has spent his life fighting poverty, drugs, and gangs in Latino communities. In this essay, written in 2005 for Sojourners magazine, Alejandrez remembers how the principles and the voice of César Chávez changed his life and inspired him to help others.

I'm the son of migrant farm workers, born out in a cotton field in Merigold, Mississippi. My family's from Texas. A migrant child goes to five or six different schools in one year, and you try to assimilate to whatever's going on at that time. I grew up not having shoes or only having one pair of pants to wear to school all week. I always remembered my experience in Texas, where Mexicans and blacks couldn't go to certain restaurants. That leaves something in you. 1

I saw how my father would react when Immigration would come up to the fields or the boss man talked to him. I would see my father bow his head. I didn't know why my father wasn't standing up to this man. As a child 2 working in the rows behind him, I said to myself, "I'll never do that." A deep anger was developing in me.

But it was also developing in my father; the way that he dealt with it 3 was alcohol. He would become violent when he drank on the weekends. I realized later that the reason he would bow his head to the boss is that he had seven kids to feed. He took that humiliation in order to feed me.

I stabbed the first kid when I was 13 years old. I shot another guy 4 when I was 15. I almost killed a guy when I was 17. On and on and on. Then, in the late 1960s, I found myself as a young man in the Vietnam War. I saw more violence, inflicted more violence, and then tried to deal with the violence.

I came back from the war addicted to heroin, as many, many young 5 men did. I came back to the street war, in the drug culture. Suddenly there were farm workers—who lost jobs because of the bringing of machines into the fields—who turned into drug dealers; it's easier money. 6

But when I was still working in the fields, something happened. I was 17 years old, out in the fields of central California, and suddenly I hear this voice coming out of the radio, talking about how we must better our conditions and better our lives in the migrant camps. It was like this voice was talking just to me.

The voice was César Chávez. He said, "You must organize. You must 7 seek justice. You must ask for better wages."

It's 1967. I'm busting my ass off pitching melons with six guys. 8 Because we're the youngest, they put us on the hardest job, but we're getting paid $1.65 an hour. The guys working the harvesting machines are making $8 an hour. We said to ourselves, "Something's not right."

Having the words of César Chávez, I organized the young men and 9 called a strike. After lunch we just stopped working. We didn't go back on the fields. This was sort of a hard thing because my father was a foreman to this contractor, so I was going against him. He was concerned that we were rocking the boat—but I think he was proud of me. We shut down three of the melon machines, which forced the contractor to come, and then the landowner came. "What's going on?" he said. We said, "We're on strike, because we aren't getting our money." After about two hours, they said, "Okay, we're going to raise it to $1.95."

But it wasn't the $1.95—it was the fact that six young men were being 10 abused, and that this little short Indian guy, César Chávez, had an influence. I kept his words.

When I wound up in Vietnam, I heard about Martin Luther King and 11 his stand against the war. Somebody also told me about Mahatma Gandhi. I didn't know who he was, only that he was a bald-headed dude that had done this kind of stuff.

In Vietnam I realized that there were people that I had never met before, that had never done nothing to me, never called me a dirty Mexican or a greaser or nothing, and all of sudden I had to be an enemy to them. 12

I started looking at the words of César Chávez in terms of nonviolence. I looked at the violence in the community, in the fields, yet Chávez was still calling for peace. 13

It has been an incredible journey since those days. For us this is a spiritual movement. In Barrios Unidos, that's the primary thing—our spirit comes first. How do we take care of ourselves? Whatever people believe in, no matter what faith or religion, how do we communicate to the youngsters who are spiritually bankrupt? Many of us were addicted to drugs or alcohol, and we have to find a spiritual connection. Working with gang members, there's a lot of pain, so you have to find ways for healing. As peacemakers, we are wounded peacemakers. 14 15

This work has taken us into the prisons. Throughout the years, we've been talking about the high rate of incarceration among our people, and the drug laws. Many people are doing huge amounts of time for nonviolent drug convictions; they did not need to be incarcerated—they need treatment. Currently in this country we deal with treatment by incarcerating people, which leads them to more violence and more negative ways of living.

As community-based organizations, we have had to prove to the correctional institutions that we're not in there to create any revolution. We're there to try to help. I'm asking how I can change the men that have been violent. How do I help change their attitude toward society and toward their own relatives? We see them as our relatives—these are our relatives that are incarcerated. How can we support them? 16

We go into the prison as a cultural and spiritual group helping men in prison to understand their own culture and those of different cultures. They come from great warrior societies. But the warrior tradition doesn't just mean going to war, but also fighting for peace. The prisoners who help organize the Cinco de Mayo, Juneteenth, and Native powwow ceremonies within the prison system are a true testament of courage to change the madness of violence that has unnecessarily claimed many lives. By providing those ceremonies, we allow them to see who they really are. They weren't born gang members, or drug addicts, or thieves. 17

My best example of hope in the prisons is when we take the Aztec dancers into the institutions. They do a whole indigenous ceremony. At the end, they invite people to what's called a friendship dance. It's a big figure-eight dance. 18

The first time that we were in prison in Tracy, California, out on the yard, there were 2,000 men out there. The ceremony was led by Laura 19

...continued Teach Diversity—with a Smile, **Barbara Ehrenreich**

Castro, founder of the Xochut Aztec dance group, a very petite woman, very keen to her culture. She says to me, "What do you think, Nane? Do you think that these guys will come out and dance?" I'm looking at those guys—tattoos all over them and swastikas and black dudes that are really big. It's incredible to be in the prison yard. I say to her, "I don't know."

But what ties all those guys together is the drumbeat. Every culture has some ceremonial drum you play. When the drumbeat started in the yard, the men just started coming. They divide themselves by race and then by gang. You got Norteños, Sureños, Hispanos, blacks, whites, Indians, and then "others" (mostly the Asian guys). 20

When the men were invited into the dance, those guys emptied out the bleachers. They came. They held hands. This tiny woman, Laura, led them through the ceremony of the friendship dance. They went round and round. There were black, white, and brown holding hands, which doesn't happen in prison. And they were laughing. For a few seconds, maybe a minute, there was hope. We saw the smiles of men being children, remembering something about their culture. The COs [correctional officers] came out of the tower wondering what the hell was going on with these men dancing in prison, holding hands. It was an incredible sight. That day, the Creator was present. I knew that God's presence was there. Everyone was given a feeling that something had happened that wasn't our doing. 21

Questions for Writing and Discussion

1. One key strategy for writing successful narratives is setting and describing specific scenes. Alejandrez does an excellent job of setting two key scenes—one from his childhood and one from later in life. For each of these scenes, explain how Alejandrez (a) sets up the scene, (b) describes what happens using detailed observations, (c) uses dialogue to make the scene more vivid and dramatic, and (d) makes connections between the past and the present.
2. One key theme or motif in Alejandrez's essay is the idea of a "spiritual connection." Drawing on your description from question 1, explain how the idea of a spiritual connection is important in both of these key scenes. How does this theme connect to the nonviolent movements of Mahatma Gandhi and Martin Luther King, Jr.? How is this theme evoked in the final sentences of Alejandrez's essay? Explain.

3. Using Alejandrez's essay as a guide, write a remembering essay about a person in your life who became a role model or was influential at a key point in your life. Include key scenes showing how, when, and why this person was influential and then tell what you were able to accomplish because of that influence.

4. Go to the official Web sites for César Chávez and Barrios Unidos. What parallels are there between the lives of César Chávez and Daniel Alejandrez? How did both organizations use the nonviolent principles of Gandhi and Martin Luther King, Jr.? How are or were the goals of both organizations different? Explain.

Observing and Remembering: The Writing Process

Assignment for Observing and Remembering

Write an essay about an important person, place, and/or event in your life. Your purpose is to recall and then use specific examples and scenes that *recreate* this memory and *show why* it is important to you. If you don't have a specific audience and genre assigned, use the chart that follows to help you think about your possible audience and genre. You may be considering a personal audience of family and friends, but you may also want to think about a more public audience. Browsing through specialty magazines or Web sites (sports, nature, outdoors, genealogy, cooking, style) may give you an idea of how writers adapt an autobiographical narrative for a particular audience.

Audience	Possible Genres for Writing About Memories
Personal Audience	Autobiographical essay, memoir, journal entry, social networking site entry, blog, photo essay, scrapbook, multigenre document.
Academic Audience	Essay for humanities or social science class, journal entry, forum entry on class site, multigenre document.
Public Audience	Column, memoir, or essay in a magazine, newspaper, or newsletter; memoir or essay in an online site or blog; online memoir in a multigenre document.

"Memory is more indelible than ink."

—Anita Loos,
Author of *Kiss Hollywood Goodbye*

CHOOSING A SUBJECT

Watch the **Video** on Conducting Interviews

If one of the journal exercises suggests a workable subject, try the collecting and shaping strategies described in the following pages. If none of the exercises leads to an interesting subject, consider these ideas:

- Interview (in person or over the phone) a parent, a brother or sister, or a close friend. What events or experiences does your interviewee remember that were important to you?
- Look at a map of your town, city, state, or country and do an inventory of places you have been. Make a list of trips you have taken, with dates and years. Which of those places is the most memorable for you?
- Dig out a school yearbook or look through the pictures and comments on your friends' Facebook profiles. Whom do you remember most clearly? What events do you recall most vividly?
- Go to the library and look through news magazines or newspapers from five to ten years ago. What were the most important events of those years? What do you remember about them? Where were you and what were you doing when these events occurred? Which events had the largest impact on your life?
- Choose an important moment in your life, but write from the *point of view* of another person—a friend, family member, or stranger who was present. Let this person narrate the events that happened to you.

"For me the initial delight is in the surprise of remembering something I didn't know I knew."

—Robert Frost, Poet

Note: Avoid choosing overly emotional topics such as the recent death of a close friend or family member. If you are too close to your subject, responding to your reader's revision suggestions may be difficult. Ask yourself if you can emotionally distance yourself from that subject. If you received a C for that essay, would you feel devastated?

COLLECTING

3.3
Use collecting strategies to develop your personal narrative

Once you have chosen a subject for your essay, try the following collecting strategies.

Brainstorming

Brainstorming is jotting down anything and everything that comes to mind that is remotely connected to your subject: words, phrases, images, or complete thoughts. You can brainstorm by yourself or in groups, with everyone contributing ideas and one person recording them.

Watch the **Animation** on Brainstorming

Clustering

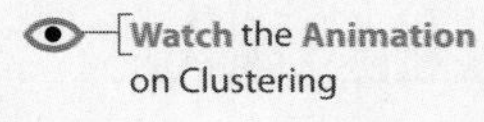

Clustering is a visual scheme for brainstorming and free-associating about your topic. It can be especially effective for remembering because it helps you sketch relationships among your topics and subtopics. As you can see from the sample sketch, the diagram you make should help you see relationships between ideas or get a rough idea about an order or shape you may wish to use.

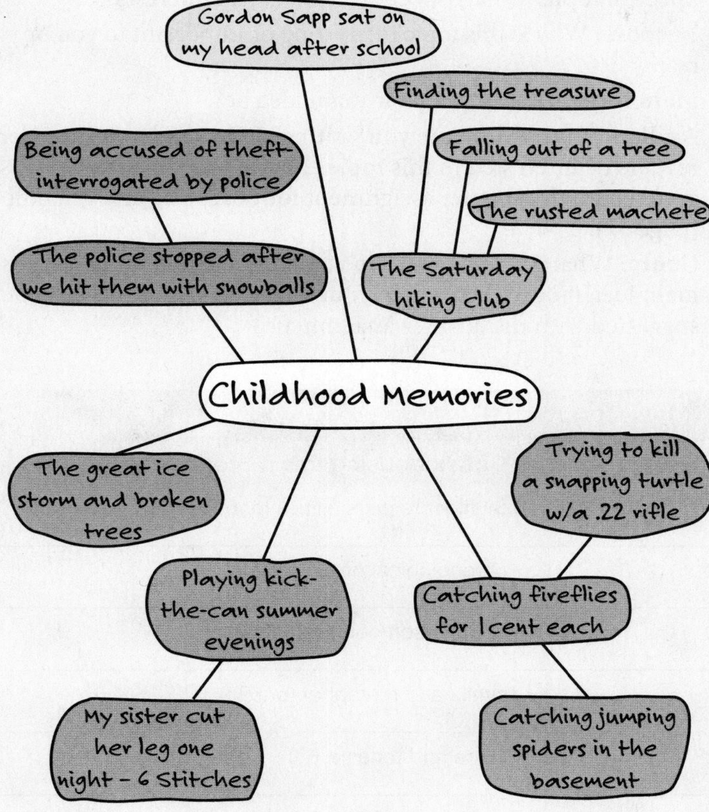

Looping

Looping is a method of controlled freewriting that generates ideas and provides focus and direction. Begin by freewriting about your subject for eight to ten minutes. Then pause, reread what you have written, and *underline* the most interesting or important idea in what you've written so far. Then, using that sentence or idea as your starting point, write for eight to ten minutes more. Repeat this cycle, or "loop," one more time. Each loop should add ideas and details from some new angle or viewpoint, but overall you will be focusing on the most important ideas that you discover.

SHAPING

3.4
Shape your personal narrative

Begin by reconsidering your purpose; perhaps it has become clearer since you recorded it in your journal entry. In your journal, jot down tentative answers to the following questions. If you don't have an answer, go on to the next question.

- **Subject:** What is your general subject?
- **Specific topic:** What aspect of your subject interests you?
- **Purpose:** Why is this topic interesting or important to you or your readers?
- **Main idea:** What might your main idea be?
- **Audience:** For whom are you writing? Why might your reader or readers be interested in this topic? Review possible audiences suggested with the chapter assignment for observing and remembering (page 57).
- **Genre:** What genre might help you communicate your purpose and main idea most effectively to your audience? (Review genre options suggested with the chapter assignment.)

Shaping Strategies

Do you want to . . .	Consider using this rhetorical strategy:
use several images or graphics?	multigenre possibilities (p. 61)
use chronological order or flashback?	chronological order (p. 61)
contrast the present to the past?	comparison/contrast (p. 62)
use figurative language?	simile and metaphor (p. 62)
create a narrator with a distinct voice?	voice and tone (p. 63)
use dialogue between characters?	dialogue (p. 63)
have a catchy title, introduction, or conclusion?	title, introduction, conclusion (p. 65)

As you think about ways to organize and shape your essay, reread your assignment and think about your purpose and possible audience. Review the strategies below for shaping ideas that might work for your topic. After you have written a draft, come back and review these shaping possibilities to see if one will make your essay more dramatic, vivid, or memorable.

Multigenre

As you collect ideas, draft passages, and discuss your assignment with your peers, think about appropriate genre possibilities. Start by reviewing the genre alternatives in the chapter assignment. You may choose to write in a traditional narrative format. Or you may want to use a multigenre or multimedia format with photographs, graphics, drawings, scrapbook materials, video, podcasts, and Web links. Check with your instructor to see if a multigenre approach meets the assignment.

Chronological Order

If you are writing about remembered events, you will probably use some form of chronological order. Try making a chronological list of the major scenes or events. Then go through the list, deciding what you will emphasize by telling about each item in detail and what you will pass over quickly. Normally, you will be using a straightforward chronological order, but you may wish to use a flashback, starting in the middle or near the end and then returning to tell the beginning. In his paragraph about a personal relationship, for example, student writer Gregory Hoffman begins the story at its most dramatic point, returns to tell how the relationship began, and then concludes the story.

Her words hung in the air like iron ghosts. "I'm pregnant," she said as they walked through the park, the snow crackling beneath their feet. Carol was looking down at the ground when she told him, somewhat ashamed, embarrassed, and defiant all at once. Their relationship had only started in September, but both had felt the uneasiness surrounding them for the past months. She could remember the beginning so well and in such favor, now that the future seemed so uncertain. The all-night conversations by the bay window, the rehearsals at the university theater—where he would make her laugh during her only soliloquy, and most of all the Christmas they had spent together in Vermont. No one else had existed for her during those months. Yet now, she felt duped by her affections—as if she had become an absurd representation of a tragic television character. As they approached the lake, he put his arm around her, "Just do what you think is best, babe. I mean, I think you know how I feel." At that moment, she knew it was over. It was no longer "their" decision. His hand touched her cheek in a benedictorial fashion. The rest would only be form now. Exchanging records and clothes with an aside of brief conversation. She would see him again, in the market or at a movie, and they would remember. But like his affection in September, her memory of him would fade until he was too distant to see.

Comparison/Contrast

Although you may be comparing or contrasting people, places, or events from the past, you will probably also be comparing or contrasting the past and the present. You may do that at the beginning, noting how something in the present reminds you of a past person, place, or event. You may do it at the end, as Andrea Lee does in *Russian Journal.* You may do it both at the beginning and at the end, as Richard Rodriguez does in "The Boy's Desire." Comparing or contrasting the past with the present will often clarify your dominant idea.

Simile and Metaphor

Similes and metaphors create vivid word pictures or images by making comparisons. This figurative language may take up only a sentence or two, or it may shape several paragraphs.

- A *simile* is a comparison using *like* or *as*: A is *like* B. In the passage earlier in this chapter from *Out of Africa*, Karen Blixen uses similes to describe the iguanas she comes across:

> [The iguanas] shine *like* a heap of precious stones or *like* a pane cut out of an old church window. When, as you approach, they swish away, there is a flash of azure, green and purple over the stones, the color seems to be standing behind them in the air, *like* a comet's luminous tail. . . . Now that the flame was put out, and the soul had flown, the Iguana was *as* dead *as* a sandbag.

- A *metaphor* is a direct or implied comparison suggesting that A *is* B. In a passage earlier in this chapter, John Muir uses both simile and metaphor when he compares the Great Central Valley of California first to a lake, and then to a garden. He uses simile when he says the valley is *like* a lake, and he uses metaphor when he equates (without using *like* or *as*) the valley to a "vast golden flower-bed":

> At my feet lay the Great Central Valley of California, level and flowery, *like* a lake of pure sunshine, forty or fifty miles wide, five hundred miles long, one rich furred garden of yellow *Compositae.* And from the eastern boundary of this *vast golden flower-bed* rose the mighty Sierra. . . .

Voice and Tone

The term *voice* refers to a writer's personality as revealed through language. Writers may use emotional, colloquial, or conversational language to communicate a sense of personality. Or they may use abstract, impersonal language either to conceal their personalities or to create an air of scientific objectivity.

Tone is a writer's attitude toward the subject. The attitude may be positive or negative. It may be serious, humorous, honest, or ironic; it may be skeptical or accepting; it may be happy, frustrated, or angry. Often voice and tone overlap, and together they help us hear a writer talking to us. In the following passage, we hear student writer Kurt Weekly talking to us directly; we hear a clear, honest voice telling the story. His tone is not defensive or guilty: He openly admits he has a "problem."

> Oh no, not another trash day. Every time I see all those trash containers, plastic garbage bags and junk lined up on the sidewalks, it drives me crazy. It all started when I was sixteen. I had just received my driver's license and the most beautiful Ford pickup. It was Wednesday as I remember and trash day. I don't know what happened. All of a sudden I was racing down the street swerving to the right, smashing into a large green Hefty trash bag filled with grass clippings. The bag exploded, and grass clippings and trash flew everywhere. It was beautiful and I was hooked. There was no stopping me.
>
> At first I would smash one or two cans on the way to school. Then I just couldn't get enough. I would start going out the night before trash day. I would go down the full length of the street and wipe out every garbage container in sight. I was the terror of the neighborhood. This was not a bad habit to be taken lightly. It was an obsession. I was in trouble. There was no way I could kick this on my own. I needed help.
>
> I received that help. One night after an evening of nonstop can smashing, the Arapahoe County Sheriff Department caught up with me. Not just one or a few but the whole department. They were willing to set me on the right path, and if that didn't work, they were going to send me to jail. It was a long, tough road to rehabilitation, but I did it. Not alone. I had the support of my family and the community.

Dialogue

Dialogue, which helps to *re-create* people and events rather than just tell about them, can be a strategy for shaping parts of your narrative. Even though you might not remember the exact words from a conversation, you can write dialogue that re-creates what you remember each person's saying during a scene. In the following excerpt, James Thurber, a master of autobiographical humor, uses dialogue—within his chronological narrative—to shape his account of a frustrating biology class.

> I passed all the other courses that I took at my university, but I could never pass botany. This was because all botany students had to spend several hours a week in a laboratory looking through a microscope at plant cells, and I could never see through a microscope. I never once saw a cell through a microscope. This used to enrage my instructor. He would wander around the laboratory pleased with the progress all the students were making in drawing the involved and, so I am told, interesting structure of flower cells, until he came to me. I would just be standing there. "I can't see anything," I would say. He would begin patiently enough, explaining how anybody can see through a microscope, but he would always end up in a fury claiming that I could too see through a microscope but just pretended that I couldn't. "It takes away from the beauty of flowers anyway," I used to tell him. "We are not concerned with beauty in this course," he would say. "We are concerned solely with the mechanics of flowers." "Well," I'd say, "I can't see anything." "Try it just once again," he'd say, and I would put my eye to the microscope and see nothing at all, except now and again a nebulous milky substance—a phenomenon of maladjustment. You were supposed to see a vivid, restless clockwork of sharply defined plant cells. "I see what looks like a lot of milk," I would tell him. This, he claimed, was the result of my not having adjusted the microscope properly, so he would readjust it for me, or rather, for himself. And I would look again and see milk. I finally took a deferred pass, as they called it, and waited a year and tried again. (You had to pass one of the biological sciences or you couldn't graduate.) The professor had come back from vacation brown as a berry, bright-eyed, and eager to explain cell-structure again to his classes. "Well," he said to me, cheerily, when we met in the first laboratory hour of the semester, "we're going to see cells this time, aren't we?" "Yes, sir," I said. Students to the right of me and to the left of me and in front of me were seeing cells; what's more, they were quietly drawing pictures of them in their notebooks. Of course, I didn't see anything.
>
> "We'll try it," the professor said to me, grimly. "with every adjustment of the microscope known to man. As God is my witness, I'll arrange this glass so that you see cells through it or I'll give up teaching. In twenty-two years of botany, I—" He cut off abruptly for he was beginning to quiver all over, like Lionel Barrymore, and he genuinely wished to hold onto his temper; his scenes with me had taken a great deal out of him.

Title, Introduction, and Conclusion

In your journal, sketch out several titles you might use. You may want a title that is merely an accurate label, such as *Russian Journal* or "The Boy's Desire," or you may prefer something less direct that gets your reader's attention. For example, for his essay about his hat that appears later in this chapter, student writer Todd Petry uses the title "The Wind Catcher."

Introductions or beginning paragraphs take several shapes. Some writers plunge the reader immediately into the action—as Gregory Hoffman does—and later fill in the scene and context. Others are more like Kurt Weekly, announcing his subject—trash cans—and then taking the reader from the present to the past and the beginning of the story. At some point, however, readers do need to know the context—the *who, what, when,* and *where* of your account.

Conclusions are also of several types. Some writers will return to the present and discuss what they have learned, as Andrea Lee does in *Russian Journal.* Some writers conclude with dramatic moments, or an emotional scene, as student writer Juli Bovard does in the essay "The Red Chevy" that appears at the end of this chapter. But many writers will tie the conclusion back to the beginning, as Richard Rodriguez does in "The Boy's Desire": "The closet door closes. . . the fog rises." In your journal, experiment with several possibilities until you find the one that works best for your subject.

"I start at the beginning, go on to the end, then stop."

—Gabriel García Márquez,
Author of *One Hundred Years of Solitude*

"I always know the ending; that's where I start."

—Toni Morrison,
Nobel Prize–Winning Novelist

DRAFTING

When you have experimented with the shaping strategies, reconsider your purpose, audience, and main idea. Have they changed? In your journal, reexamine the notes you made before trying the shaping activities. If necessary, revise your purpose, audience, or main idea based on what you have actually written.

Working from your journal material and from your collecting and shaping activities, draft your essay. It is important *not* to splice parts together or just recopy and connect segments, for they may not fit or flow together. Instead, reread what you have written, and then start afresh. Concentrate on what you want to say and write as quickly as possible.

Avoid interruptions by choosing a quiet place to work. Follow your own writing rituals. Try to write nonstop. If you cannot think of the right word, put a line or a dash, but keep on writing. When necessary, go back and reread what you have written.

"The difference between the right word and the nearly right word is the same as that between lightning and the lightning bug."

—Mark Twain,
Author of *Adventures of Huckleberry Finn*

REVISING

Revising begins when you get your first idea and start collecting and shaping. It continues as you redraft sections of your essay and rework your organization. In many classes, you will give and receive advice from the other writers in your class. Use the guidelines below to give constructive advice about an observing and remembering essay draft.

Guidelines for Revision

- **Reexamine your purpose and audience.** Are you doing what you intended?
- **Reconsider the genre you selected.** Is it working for your purpose and audience? Can you add multigenre elements to make your narrative more effective?
- **Revise to make the main idea of your account clearer.** You don't need a "moral" to the story or a bald statement saying, "This is why this person was important." Your reader, however, should know clearly why you wanted to write about the memory that you chose.
- **Revise to clarify the important relationships in your story.** Consider relationships between past and present, between you and the people in your story, between one place and another place, between one event and another event.
- **Provide close and detailed observation.** *Show,* don't just tell. Can you use any of the collecting and shaping strategies for observing discussed in this chapter?
- **Revise to show crucial changes, contrasts, or conflicts more clearly.** Walker's essay, for instance, illustrates how *conflict and change* are central to an effective observing and remembering essay. See if this strategy will work in your essay.
- **Have you used straight chronological order?** If it works, keep it. If not, should you begin in the middle and do a flashback? Do you want to move back and forth from present to past or stay in the past until the end?
- **Cue your reader by occasionally using transitional words to signal changes.** Transitional words include *then, when, first, next, last, before, after, while, sooner, later, finally, yesterday, today.*
- **Be clear about point of view.** Are you looking back on the past from a viewpoint in the present? Are you using the point of view of yourself as a child or at another point in your life? Are you using the point of view of another person or object in your story?
- **What are the key images in your account?** Should you add or delete an image to show the experience more vividly?
- **What voice are you using?** Does it support your purpose? If you are using a persona, is it an appropriate one for your audience and purpose?

- **Revise sentences to improve clarity, conciseness, emphasis, and variety.**
- **Check your dialogue for proper punctuation and indentation.** See the essay by Alice Walker in this chapter for a model.
- **When you are relatively satisfied with your draft, edit for correct spelling, appropriate word choice, punctuation, and grammar.**

PeerResponse

The instructions below will help you give and receive constructive advice about the rough draft of an observing and remembering essay. You may use these guidelines for an in-class workshop, a take-home review, or a computer e-mail response.

Watch the Video on Office Hours: Peer Review

Writer: Before you exchange drafts with another reader, write out the following information about your own rough draft.

1. State the main idea that you hope your essay conveys.
2. Describe the best *one* or *two* key scenes that your narrative creates.
3. Explain one or two problems that you are having with this draft that you want your reader to focus on.

Reader: Without making any comments, read the *entire* draft from start to finish. Then *reread* the draft and answer the following questions.

1. Locate one or two *key scenes* in the narrative. Are they clearly set at an identified time and place? Does the writer use vivid description of the place or the people? Does the writer use dialogue? Does the writer include his or her reflections? Which of these areas need the most attention during the writer's revision? Explain.
2. Write out a *time line* for the key events in the narrative. What happened first, second, third, and so forth? Are there places in the narrative where the time line could be clearer? Explain.
3. When you finished reading the draft, *what characters or incidents were you still curious about?* Where did you want more information? What characters or incidents did you want to know more about?
4. What *overall idea* does the narrative convey to you? How does your notion of the main idea compare to the writer's answer to

question 1? Explain how the writer might revise the essay to make the main idea clearer.

5. Answer the *writer's questions* in question 3.

After you receive feedback from other readers, you need to distance yourself and objectively reread what you have written. Review the advice from your peer readers. Remember, you will get both good and bad advice, so *you* must decide what you think is important or not important. If you are uncertain about advice you received from one of your peers, ask for a third or fourth opinion. In addition, most writing centers have tutors available who can help you sort through the advice you received and figure out a revision plan. Especially for this observing and remembering essay, make sure your memories are recreated on paper. Don't be satisfied with suggesting incidents that merely trigger your own memories: you must *show* people and events vividly for your reader.

Postscript on the Writing Process

After you finish writing, revising, and editing your essay, you will want to breathe a sigh of relief and turn it in. But before you do, think about the problems that you solved as you wrote this essay. *Remember:* Your major goal is to learn to write and revise more effectively. To do that, you need to discover and adapt your writing processes so you can anticipate and solve the problems you face as a writer. Take a few minutes to answer the following questions. Be sure to hand in this postscript with your essay.

1. Review your writing process. Which collecting, shaping, and revising strategies helped you remember and describe incidents most quickly and clearly? What problems were you unable to solve?
2. Reread your essay. With a small asterisk [*], identify in the margin of your essay sentences where you used sensory details, dialogue, or images to show or re-create the experience for your reader.
3. If you received feedback from your peers, identify one piece of advice that you followed and one bit of advice that you ignored. Explain your decisions.
4. Rereading your essay, what do you like best about it? What parts of your essay need work? What would you change if you had another day to work on this assignment?

Student Writing

The Wind Catcher

Todd Petry

Todd Petry decided to write about his cowboy hat, observing it in the present and thinking about some of the memories that it brought back. His notes, his first short draft paragraphs, and his revised version demonstrate how observing and remembering work together naturally: The details stimulate memories, and memories lead to more specific details.

NOTES AND DETAILS

DETAILS	MORE SPECIFIC DETAILS
Gray	Dirty, dust coated, rain stained cowdung color
Resistol	The name is stained and blurred
Size 7 3/8	
Diamond shape	Used to be diamond shape, now battered, looks abandoned
4" brim	Front tipped down, curled up in back
1" sweat band	blackish
5 yrs. old	still remember the day I bought it
4x beaver	
What it is not:	it is unlike a hat fresh out of the box
What it compares to:	point of crown like the north star like a pancake with wilted edges battered like General Custer's hat
What I remember:	the day I bought the hat a day at Pray Mesa

...continued The Wind Catcher, **Todd Petry**

FIRST DRAFT

The Wind Catcher

The other day while I was relaxing in my favorite chair and listening to Ian Tyson, I happened to notice my work cowboy hat hanging on the wall. Now I look at that old hat no less than a dozen times a day without too much thought, but on that particular day, my eyes remained fixed on it and my mind went to remembering. 1

I still remember I had $100 cash in my pocket the day I went hat shopping. The local tack, feed, and western wear CO-OP was my first and only stop. Finding a hat to meet my general specifications was no big deal. I wanted a gray Resistol, size 7 3/8, with a 4-inch brim and diamond-shaped crown. From there on, though, my wants became very particular. I took 30 minutes to find the one that had the right fit, and five times that long to come to terms with the hat shaper. Boy, but I was one proud young fellow the next day when I went to school sporting my new piece of head gear. I've had that wind catcher five years through rough times, but in a way, it really looks better now, without any shape, dirty, and covered with dust and cowdung. 2

REVISED VERSION

The Wind Catcher

The other day, while I was relaxing in my favorite chair and listening to Ian Tyson, I happened to notice my work cowboy hat hanging on the wall. Now, I look at that old hat no less than a dozen times a day without too much thought, but on that particular day, my eyes remained fixed on it and my mind went to remembering. 1

I was fifteen years old and had $100 cash in my pocket the day I went hat shopping five years ago. The local tack, feed, and western wear CO-OP was my first and only stop. Finding a hat to meet my general specifications was no big deal. I wanted a gray 4X Resistol, size 7 3/8, with a four-inch brim and diamond-shaped crown. I wanted no flashy feathers or gaudy hatbands, which in my mind were only for pilgrims. From there on, though, my wants became very particular. I took thirty minutes to find the one that had the right fit, and five times that long to come to terms with the hat shaper. Boy, but I was one proud young fellow the next day when I went to school sporting my new piece of head gear. 2

About that time, Ian Tyson startled me out of my state of reminiscence by singing "Rose in the Rockies," with that voice of his sounding like ten cow elk cooing to their young in the springtime. As I sat there listening to the music and looking at that old hat, I had to chuckle to myself because that wind catcher had sure seen better days. I mean it looked rode hard and put up wet. The gray, which was once as 3 sharp and crisp as a mountain lake, was now faded and dull where the sun had beat down. Where the crown and brim met, the paleness was suddenly transformed into a gritty black which ran the entire circumference of the hat. This black was unlike any paint or color commercially available, being made up of head sweat, dirt, alfalfa dust, and powdered cow manure. Water blemishes from too much rain and snow mottled the brim, adding to the colors' turbidity. Inside the crown and wherever the slope was less than ninety degrees, dust had collected to hide the natural color even more.

After a while, my attention lost interest in the various colors and 4
began to work its way over the hat's shape, which I was once so critical of. General Custer's hat itself could not have looked worse. All signs of uniformity and definite shape had disappeared. The diamond-shaped crown, which was once round and smooth, now bowed out on the sides and had edges as blunt as an orange crate. The point, which once looked like the North Star indicating the direction, now was twisted off balance from excessive right hand use. Remembering last spring, how I threw that hat in the face of an irate mother cow during calving, I had to chuckle again. Throwing that hat kept my horse and me out of trouble but made the "off-balance look" rather permanent. As I looked at the brim, I was reminded of a three-day-old pancake with all its edges wilted. The back of that brim curled upward like a snake ready to strike, and the front had become so narrow and dipped, it looked like something a dentist would use on your teeth.

For probably half an hour, I sat looking at the wear and tear on 5
that ancient hat. Awhile back, I remember, I decided to try to make my old hat socially presentable by having it cleaned and blocked, removing those curls and dips and other signs of use. However, when a hat shop refused to even attempt the task, I figured I'd just leave well enough alone. As I scanned my eyes over the hat, I noticed several other alterations from its original form, such as the absent hat band, which was torn off in the brush on Pray Mesa, and the black thread that drew together the edges of a hole in the crown. However, try as I might, I could not for the life of me see where any character had been lost in the brush, or any flair had been covered with cowdung.

Questions for Writing and Discussion

1. Close observation often leads to specific memories. In the opening paragraph of his revised version, Todd Petry says that "on that particular day, my eyes remained fixed on it and my mind went to remembering." He then

recalls the time when he was fifteen years old and bought his hat. Identify two other places where observation leads Petry to remember specific scenes from the past.

2. Petry chose "The Wind Catcher" as the title for his essay. Reread the essay and then brainstorm a list of five other titles that might be appropriate for this short essay. Which title do you like best?

3. Where does Petry most clearly express the main idea of his essay? Write out the main idea in your own words.

Student Writing

The Red Chevy

Juli Bovard

In this essay, Juli Bovard recalls several of the most traumatic days of her life. She remembers not just the day she was raped by an unknown assailant, but the days she had to spend in the police station, the day she confronted her attacker in the courtroom, and the days she spent regaining control of her life. In the end, Bovard helps us understand how she overcame being a rape victim and reclaimed her life.

From the moment the man in the Chevy stopped to offer me a ride on that blistering September afternoon, I knew I was in trouble. Before I could say, "No, but thanks anyway," the man in the passenger side of the car jumped at me, twisted my arm and held a shiny piece of steel to my side. I was pushed into the car and driven 30 miles over the county line. During the ride, I did everything every article or specialist on abduction had advised against: I cried, I babbled, and I lost control. In the end it was all futile. Two hours later—after they dumped me off near my home—I was another statistic. I had been raped, and was now a victim of the brutal, demeaning, sad violent crime of sexual assault. *1*

Rape not only has physical repercussions, but has an enormous psychological and emotional impact as well. During my "event" as I like to call it, I remembered an initial feeling of shock and numbness, and soon found myself babbling incoherently. I begged my attackers to let me go. I tried to talk my way out of the car. I even tried to beg or bargain my way out. However, the driver was very much in control of the situation, and my weak efforts failed. Eventually my babbling gave way to cold reason, and I became convinced that not only would I be raped, but that I would also die. My life did not pass before me—as is *2* said to happen to dying people. In fact, I did not think of the past at all, but only the future and all the things I had not yet done. There were too many people I had not told how I really felt, too many people to whom I wanted to say good-bye. I seriously doubted I would ever be given another chance.

I did not die. In fact, other than a few bruises and scratches and several cuts on my neck and cheek—left by the brass knuckle style knife, I was remarkably, physically unhurt. The greatest trauma was to my mind. The psychological and emotional wounds in the ensuing months were far worse than the actual sexual assault. 3

Within a week of my report, the man who raped me was arrested and held without bail (he had previously been convicted of attempted rape), his accomplice was not accused since he agreed to turn state's evidence—which means he made a deal to cover himself and agreed to testify against my assailant. What followed these events, I remember, was a long investigation that involved many tedious hours in the police station, and numbing revisits to the scene of the crime. Through it all I was alone, and I halfheartedly tried to comfort myself for enduring the stress so well. By late October, the month of the preliminary hearing, I had gone back to work, and was back in control of my life—or so I thought. The actual hearing proved me wrong. 4

Though I do not remember much about the actual courtroom or its proceedings, I will always remember the warmth of the day and the overwhelming odor of my perpetrator's cologne (to this day I become nauseous if I smell the cologne Obsession). Seeing my assailant again had an effect on me that I was not prepared for. I felt the same fear that I had experienced the day of my rape, and for the second time in my life I felt terror so deep it paralyzed me. The pressure from the entire incident finally overwhelmed me, and when I returned home that afternoon I climbed into bed and did not leave it for three days. It was weeks before I could focus on everyday tasks, even something as simple as showering. 5

By the middle of November, I had lost close to fifteen pounds. I had constant diarrhea, my menstrual cycle had stopped, and I was constantly bombarded by anxiety attacks. I could no longer get up each day and go to work and act like nothing had happened. Leaving the house left me with cold sweats, and sleeping through the night became impossible. I became paranoid and despondent. I knew I would have to seek professional help. 6

Fortunately, through counseling I learned that my reactions were very common. Through research, I found that all the feelings I was having were very normal. My fear that the rapist would return was natural, and my inability to face unfamiliar situations or people was a classic symptom. I also learned that the guilt that plagued me, which 7 made me think that somehow I had provoked the rape or "wore" the wrong clothes to entice the rapist, was simply untrue. I was feeling a great amount of shame and embarrassment—a stigma I learned society often places on rape victims. My anger, which was the most natural response, was also the most helpful. When you are angry, you tend to want to fight back. My way of fighting back was to get on with living. Still I asked, "Why me?" I had followed all the rules set by society. I did not walk the streets at night, hang out in bars, or talk to strangers. I was an actively employed member of society. So why me? I found it wasn't just me or something I did. It could have been any woman walking the streets that day, and it went far beyond what I wore or how I walked, something noted author Susan Brownmiller eloquently affirms in her statement that, "any female may become a victim of rape. Factors such as youth, advanced age, physical homeliness and virginal lifestyle do not provide a fool-proof deterrent to render a women impervious to sexual assault" (Brownmiller 348).

Through my experience and in talking with other victims I have learned that rape has no typical "face." There is no stereotypical rapist or victim. We can be doctors, lawyers, mothers, or fathers. We are tall, short, fat, and skinny. And, as in most victims' cases, simply in the wrong place at the wrong time. *8*

After the question of "why me?" I asked, "WHY, at all?" Why *does* a man rape a woman? Initially I thought it was obvious—for sex. But I was wrong. The motivations of rape include anger, aggression, dominance, hostility, and power, but generally are not usually associated with just the actual act of sex. Quite simply it is violence. Men who rape do so because they are violent and psychotic. There is no other reason, and no valid excuse. *9*

In the end, before I was to testify, the man who attacked me changed his plea to guilty. I walked out of the district attorney's office and never asked how many years the rapist would serve in prison. It did not matter. He would be behind bars, but more importantly, I would be free to begin living again. Now, instead of dreading the month of September, I celebrate it. I celebrate the month, in which, instead of just existing, I started living. I was a victim of rape, but through years of counseling and support I am not a victim any longer. *10*

Work Cited

Brownmiller, Susan. *Against Our Will.* New York: Simon and Schuster, 1975. Print.

Questions for Writing and Discussion

1. Psychological research has shown that people remember traumatic events more vividly and with more detail than other events. Has that been true in your experience? Recall two experiences—one happy, one traumatic—and consider whether your experiences support or do not support the research.
4. Personal narrative essays should have a purpose—that is, they should focus on having a specific effect on their audience. Why is Juli Bovard writing about this experience? What effect does she want to have on her readers? Is she just giving information, or does she want to convince us about something? Explain.
3. Review the techniques for writing an observing and remembering essay listed at the beginning of this chapter. Which of these techniques does Bovard use? Where does she use them? Which are, in your opinion, most effective? Why?
4. Bovard chose the title "The Red Chevy" for her essay. Brainstorm five other titles she might use for her essay. Compare your ideas with those of your classmates. Did you come up with titles that might be more effective for the purpose of her essay? Explain.

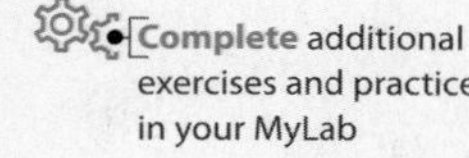
Complete additional exercises and practice in your MyLab

This Tarot card, Rhetorica XXIII, depicts Rhetoric as a woman with a sharp sword that symbolizes the power of words to achieve persuasive goals. The two cherubs blow their horns to announce Rhetorica's presence. A Journal exercise in this chapter asks you to read and think further about rhetoric and Tarot cards.

The Trustees of the British Museum

4

Reading Critically, Analyzing Rhetorically

What You Will Learn
In this chapter, you will learn to:

4.1 Use techniques for critical reading

4.2 Use techniques for summarizing and responding to a text

4.3 Use techniques for rhetorical reading and analysis

4.4 Use collecting strategies to develop a summary and response or rhetorical analysis essay

4.5 Shape your summary and response or rhetorical analysis essay

READING and responding to texts is a crucial part of many college-level writing courses. Because most writing—in any field—exists in a context of ongoing conversation, writing, and debate, college writers need to be effective critical readers. To understand critical and rhetorical reading, we have to define two key terms: *texts* and *reading*. A *text* can be any graphic matter—a textbook, an essay, a blog, a poem, an editorial, a photograph, an advertisement. Some people expand the definition of text to include any phenomenon in the world. In this widest sense, the layout of a restaurant, the behavior of children on a playground, and the clouds in the sky are all "texts" that can be read.

Similarly, the term *reading* has both narrow and broad senses. In the narrow sense, reading is simply understanding the words on a page. But reading has a variety of wider meanings as well. Reading can mean analyzing, as when an architect "reads" the blueprints and knows how to construct a building. Reading can also mean interpreting, as when a sailor "reads" the sky and knows that the day will bring winds and rough seas. And reading can mean examining texts or cultural artifacts and perceiving messages of racism, gender bias, or cultural exploitation. All these "readings" require a close critical and rhetorical attention to the text that involves analyzing, probing, and responding.

In this chapter, you will practice critical and rhetorical reading and responding to written texts. Active, critical reading requires multiple readings, asking

"Reading is not a passive process by which we soak up words and information from the page, but an active process by which we predict, sample, and confirm or correct our hypotheses about the written text."

—Constance Weaver, Author of *Reading Process and Practice*

questions, taking notes, and discussing ideas with other readers. Writing an accurate and objective summary of a text is a key first step to responding to any written text. Once you've written an accurate and objective summary, you are prepared to write a response to the text, analyzing it, agreeing or disagreeing with its ideas, offering your own interpretations of it.

This chapter will also introduce you to a specific kind of critical reading: rhetorical reading. In *rhetorical reading*, you read critically for specific rhetorical strategies that writers use. Your focus is on identifying key rhetorical strategies and then analyzing how and how effectively the writer uses them for his chosen audience. How does the writer get the reader's attention? How, and how effectively, does the writer set forth a thesis, organize key ideas, lead from one point to the next, and conclude an argument? Does the writer use effective appeals to logic, emotion, or character? How do the writer's style, tone, and vocabulary contribute to her or his rhetorical appeals?

Techniques for Reading Critically and Responding to Texts

The critical reading of texts requires several techniques to ensure both comprehension and intelligent response. Although the strategies below are listed in an order typical for most critical reading assignments, remember that the critical reading process is just like any writing process. You may need to circle back and reread, summarize a second time, research key terms, or doublecheck on the author's background or publication context as you work.

Techniques for Reading Critically and Responding to Texts

Technique	Tips on How to Do It
Using active and responsive reading, writing, and discussing strategies.	Preview the author's background and the writing context. Prewrite about your own experiences with the subject. Read initially for information but then reread, make annotations, ask questions, research on the Internet, or do a double-entry log. Discuss the text with other readers in class or online.
Summarizing the main ideas or features of the text.	A summary should accurately and objectively represent the key ideas. Cite the author and title, accurately represent the main ideas, directly quote key phrases or sentences, and describe the main ideas or features of the text.
Responding to or critiquing the ideas in the text.	Responses may *agree or disagree* with the argument in the text; they may *analyze* the argument, organization, or quality of evidence in the text; and/or they may *reflect* on assumptions or implications.

Supporting the response with evidence.	Evidence should cite examples of strengths or weaknesses in the argument, evidence from other texts or outside reading, and/or examples from one's personal experience.
Combining summary and response into a coherent essay.	Usually the summary appears first, followed by the reader's response, but be sure to integrate the two parts. Your response should focus quickly on your main idea. Use a transition between the summary and response or integrate the summary and response throughout.

As you work on these techniques, don't simply read the text, listen to a class discussion, and write out your critique. Instead, annotate the text by circling key ideas and writing your questions and responses in the margin. Continue reading and discussing your ideas after you have written out a draft. Use the interactive powers of reading, writing, and discussing to help you throughout your writing process.

CRITICAL READING STRATEGIES

4.1
Use techniques for critical reading

Critical reading does not mean that you always criticize something or find fault. *Critical reading simply means questioning what you read.* You may end up liking or praising certain features of a text, but you begin by asking questions, by resisting the text, and by demanding that the text be clear, logical, reliable, thoughtful, and honest.

You begin your critical reading by asking questions about every element in the rhetorical situation. Who is the *author,* and what is his or her background or potential bias? What was the *occasion,* and who was the intended *audience?* Is the writer's *purpose* achieved for that occasion and audience? Did the writer understand and fairly represent other writers' positions? Did the writer understand the *genre* and use it to achieve the purpose? How did the *cultural context* affect the author and the text? How did the context affect you as a reader?

You continue your critical reading by asking about the writer's claim or argument, the representation of the background information, the organization, the logical use of evidence, and the effectiveness of the style, tone, and word choice. You start your critical reading by reading and then rereading, by probing key passages, by looking for gaps or ideas not included, by discussing the text with other readers, by assessing your position as a reader, and by continually making notes and asking questions.

Listen to the **Audio** on Critical Reading

Watch the **Animation** on Critical Reading

Double-Entry Log

One of the most effective strategies to promote critical reading is a double-entry log. On the left-hand side, keep a running summary of the main ideas and features that you notice in the text. On the right-hand side, write your questions and reactions.

> **"Reading involves a fair measure of push and shove. You make your mark on a book and it makes its mark on you. Reading is not simply a matter of hanging back and waiting for a piece, or its author, to tell you what the writing has to say."**
>
> —David Bartholomae and Anthony Petrosky,
> Authors of *Ways of Reading*

Double-Entry Reading Log Format

Author and Title: ____________

Summary	**Response**
Main ideas, key features	Your reactions, comments, and questions

Critical Rereading Guide

If your double-entry log does not yield useful ideas, try the ideas and suggestions in this rereading guide. First, read the essay in its entirety. Then, let the following set of questions guide your rereading. The questions on the left-hand side will help you summarize and analyze the text; the questions on the right-hand side will start your critical reading and help focus your response.

Critical Rereading Guide

Summary and Analysis of Text	Critical Response
Purpose	
• Describe the author's overall *purpose* (to inform, explain, explore, evaluate, argue, negotiate, or other purpose). • How does the author/text want to affect or change the reader?	• Is the overall purpose clear or muddled? • Was the actual purpose different from the stated purpose? • How did the text affect you?
Audience/Reader	
• Who is the *intended* audience? • What *assumptions* does the author make about the reader's knowledge or beliefs? • From what *point of view* or *context* is the author writing?	• Are you part of the intended audience? • Does the author misjudge the reader's knowledge or beliefs? • Examine your own personal or cultural bias or point of view. How does that hinder you from being a critical reader of this text?
Occasion, Genre, Context	
• What was the *occasion* for this text? • What *genre* is this text? • What is the *cultural* or *historical context* for this text?	• What conversation was taking place on this topic? • Does the author's chosen genre help achieve the purpose for the audience? • What passages show the cultural forces at work on the author and the text?

Thesis and Main Ideas

- What key *question* or *problem* does the author/text address?
- What is the author's *thesis*?
- What *main ideas* support the thesis?
- What are the key passages or key moments in the text?
- Where is the thesis stated?
- Are the main ideas related to the thesis?
- Where do you agree or disagree?
- Does the essay have contradictions or errors in logic?
- What ideas or arguments does the essay omit or ignore?
- What experience or prior knowledge do you have about the topic?
- What are the implications or consequences of the essay's ideas?

Organization and Evidence

- Where does the author *preview* the essay's organization?
- How does the author *signal* new sections of the essay?
- What kinds of *evidence* does the author use (personal experience, descriptions, statistics, interviews, other authorities, analytical reasoning, or other)?
- At what point could you accurately predict the organization of the essay?
- At what points were you confused about the organization?
- What evidence was most or least effective?
- Where did the author rely on assertions rather than on evidence?
- Which of your own personal experiences did you recall as you read the essay?

Language and Style

- What is the author's *tone* (casual, humorous, ironic, angry, preachy, academic, or other)?
- Are *sentences* and *vocabulary* easy, average, or difficult?
- What key *words* or *images* recur throughout the text?
- Did the tone support or distract from the author's purpose or meaning?
- Did the sentences and vocabulary support or distract from the purpose or meaning?
- Did recurring words or images relate to or support the purpose or meaning?

Remember that not all these questions will be relevant to a given essay or text, but one or two of these questions may suggest a direction or give a *focus* to your overall response. When one of these questions does suggest a focus for your response to the essay, go back to the text, to other texts, and to your experience to gather *evidence* and *examples* to support your response.

SUMMARIZING AND RESPONDING TO AN ESSAY

4.2
Use techniques for summarizing and responding to a text

Before you read the following essay by Barbara Ehrenreich, "Teach Diversity—with a Smile," write for five minutes on the suggested Prereading Journal Entry that precedes the essay. You will be a much more responsive reader if you reflect on your own experiences and articulate your opinions *before* you are influenced by the author and her text. If possible, discuss your experiences and opinions with your classmates after you write your entry but before you read the essay. Next, read the introductory note about Barbara Ehrenreich to understand her background and the context for the essay. Finally, practice active reading techniques as you read. Read first for information and enjoyment. Then, reread and annotate the essay. Either write your comments and questions directly in the text or in a double-entry log.

Prereading Journal Entry

Describe the ethnic groups of people who live in your neighborhood or who attended your previous school. List all the groups you can recall. Then choose one of the following terms and briefly explain what it means: *diversity, multiculturalism,* or *political correctness.* Finally, describe one personal experience that taught you something about diversity or political correctness. What was the experience and how did you react?

Professional Writing

Teach Diversity—with a Smile

Barbara Ehrenreich

Barbara Ehrenreich has been a health policy adviser and a professor of health sciences, but since 1974 she has spent most of her time writing books and articles about socialist and feminist issues. She has received a Ford Foundation Award and a Guggenheim Fellowship for her writings, which include *Nickel and Dimed: On (Not) Getting by in America* (2001), and *This Land Is Their Land: Reports from a Divided Nation* (2008). Her articles and essays have appeared in *Esquire, Mother Jones, Ms., New Republic,* the *New York Times Magazine,* and *Time.* The following essay on cultural diversity appeared in Time magazine.

Something had to replace the threat of communism, and at last a workable substitute is at hand. "Multiculturalism," as the new menace is known, has been denounced in the media recently as the new McCarthyism, the new fundamentalism, even the new totalitarianism—take your choice. According to its critics, who include a flock of tenured 1 conservative scholars, multiculturalism aims to toss out what it sees as the Eurocentric bias in education and replace Plato with Ntozake Shange and traditional math with the Yoruba number system. And that's just the beginning. The Jacobins of the multiculturalist movement, who are described derisively as P.C., or politically correct, are said to have launched a campus reign of terror against those who slip and innocently say "freshman" instead of "freshperson," "Indian" instead of "Native American" or, may the Goddess forgive them, "disabled" instead of "differently abled."

So you can see what is at stake here: freedom of speech, freedom of thought, Western civilization and a great many professorial egos. But before we get carried away by the mounting backlash against multiculturalism, we ought to reflect for a moment on the system that the P.C. people aim to replace. I know all about it; in fact it's just about all I do know, since I—along with so many educated white people of my generation—was a victim of monoculturalism. 2

American history, as it was taught to us, began with Columbus's "discovery" of an apparently unnamed, unpeopled America, and moved on to the Pilgrims serving pumpkin pie to a handful of grateful red-skinned folks. College expanded our horizons with courses called Humanities or sometimes Civ, which introduced us to a line of thought that started with Homer, worked its way through Rabelais and reached a poignant climax in the pensées of Matthew Arnold. Graduate students wrote dissertations on what long-dead men had thought of Chaucer's verse or Shakespeare's dramas; foreign languages meant French or German. If there had been high technology in ancient China, kingdoms in black Africa or women anywhere, at any time, doing anything worth noticing, we did not know it, nor did anyone think to tell us. 3

Our families and neighborhoods reinforced the dogma of monoculturalism. In our heads, most of us '50s teenagers carried around a social map that was about as useful as the chart that guided Columbus to the "Indies." There were "Negroes," "whites" and "Orientals," the latter meaning Chinese and "Japs." Of religions, only three were known—Protestant, Catholic and Jewish—and not much was known about the last two types. The only remaining human categories were husbands and wives, and that was all the diversity the monocultural world could handle. Gays, lesbians, Buddhists, Muslims, Malaysians, Mormons, etc. were simply off the map. 4

So I applaud—with one hand, anyway—the multiculturalist goal of preparing us all for a wider world. The other hand is tapping its fingers impatiently, because the critics are right about one thing: when advocates of multiculturalism adopt the haughty stance of political correctness, they quickly descend to silliness or worse. It's obnoxious, for example, to rely on university administrations to enforce P.C. standards of verbal 5

...continued Teach Diversity—with a Smile, **Barbara Ehrenreich**

inoffensiveness. Racist, sexist and homophobic thoughts cannot, alas, be abolished by fiat but only by the time-honored methods of persuasion, education and exposure to the other guy's—or, excuse me, woman's—point of view.

And it's silly to mistake verbal purification for genuine social reform. 6
Even after all women are "Ms." and all people are "he or she," women will still earn only 65¢ for every dollar earned by men. Minorities by any other name, such as "people of color," will still bear a hugely disproportionate burden of poverty and discrimination. Disabilities are not just "different abilities" when there are not enough ramps for wheelchairs, signers for the deaf or special classes for the "specially" endowed. With all due respect for the new politesse, actions still speak louder than fashionable phrases.

But the worst thing about the P.C. people is that they are such poor 7
advocates for the multicultural cause. No one was ever won over to a broader, more inclusive view of life by being bullied or relentlessly "corrected." Tell a 19-year-old white male that he can't say "girl" when he means "teen-age woman," and he will most likely snicker. This may be the reason why, despite the conservative alarms, P.C.-ness remains a relatively tiny trend. Most campuses have more serious and ancient problems: faculties still top-heavy with white males of the monocultural persuasion; fraternities that harass minorities and women; date rape; alcohol abuse; and tuition that excludes all but the upper fringe of the middle class.

So both sides would be well advised to lighten up. The conservatives 8
ought to realize that criticisms of the great books approach to learning do not amount to totalitarianism. And the advocates of multiculturalism need to regain the sense of humor that enabled their predecessors in the struggle to coin the term P.C. years ago—not in arrogance but in self-mockery.

Beyond that, both sides should realize that the beneficiaries of 9
multiculturalism are not only the "oppressed peoples" on the standard P.C. list (minorities, gays, etc.). The "unenlightened"—the victims of monoculturalism—are oppressed too, or at least deprived. Our educations, whether at Yale or at State U, were narrow and parochial and left us ill-equipped to navigate a society that truly is multicultural and is becoming more so every day. The culture that we studied was, in fact, *one* culture and, from a world perspective, all too limited and ingrown. Diversity is challenging, but those of us who have seen the alternative know it is also richer, livelier and ultimately more fun.

SUMMARIZING

The purpose of a summary is to give a reader a condensed and objective account of the main ideas and features of a text. Usually, a summary has between one and three paragraphs or one hundred to three hundred words, depending on the length and complexity of the original essay and the intended audience and purpose. Typically, a summary will do the following:

- **Cite the author and title of the text.** In some cases, the place of publication or the context for the essay may also be included.
- **Indicate the main ideas of the text.** Accurately representing the main ideas (while omitting the details) is the major goal of a summary.
- **Use direct quotation of key words, phrases, or sentences.** *Quote* the text directly for a few key ideas; *paraphrase* the other important ideas (that is, express the ideas in your own words).
- **Include author tags.** ("According to Ehrenreich" or "as Ehrenreich explains") to remind the reader that you are summarizing the author and the text, not giving your own ideas. ***Note:*** Instead of repeating "Ehrenreich says," choose verbs that more accurately represent the purpose or tone of the original passage: "Ehrenreich argues," "Ehrenreich explains," "Ehrenreich warns," "Ehrenreich advises."
- **Avoid summarizing specific examples or data** unless they help illustrate the thesis or main idea of the text.
- **Report the main ideas as objectively as possible.** Represent the author and text accurately and faithfully. Do not include your reactions; save them for your response.

"Inferences about the writer's intentions appear to be an essential building block—one that readers actively use to construct a meaningful text."

—Linda Flower,
Author of "The Construction of Purpose"

Watch the **Animation** on Summary

Summary of "Teach Diversity—with a Smile"

Following is a summary of Ehrenreich's essay. Do *not* read this summary, however, until you have tried to write your own. After you have made notes and written a draft for your own summary, you will more clearly understand the key features of a summary. ***Note:*** There are many ways to write a good summary. If your summary conveys the main ideas and has the features described above, it may be just as good as the following example. (Key features of a summary are annotated in the margin.)

In "Teach Diversity—with a Smile," journalist Barbara Ehrenreich explains the current conflict between people who would like to replace our Eurocentric bias in education with a multicultural approach and those critics and conservative scholars who are leading the backlash

Title and author

Main idea paraphrase

Context for essay

Author tag

Direct quotations
Main idea paraphrase

Author tag
Main idea paraphrase

against multiculturalism and "political correctness." Writing for readers of *Time* magazine, Ehrenreich uses her own experience growing up in the 1950s to explain that her narrow education left her ill-equipped to cope with America's growing cultural diversity. Ehrenreich applauds multiculturalism's goal of preparing people for a culturally diverse world, but she is impatient at the "haughty stance" of the P.C. people because they mistake "verbal purification for genuine social reform" and they arrogantly bully people and "correct" their language. Ehrenreich argues that the multiculturalists should focus more on genuine social reform—paying equal salaries to men and women, creating access for people with disabilities, and reducing date rape and alcohol abuse. The solution to the problem, according to Ehrenreich, is for both sides to "lighten up." The conservatives should recognize that criticizing the great books of Western civilization is not totalitarian, and the multiculturalists should be less arrogant and regain their sense of humor.

RESPONDING

"Reading the world always precedes reading the word, and reading the word implies continually reading the world."

—Paulo Freire
Author of *Literacy: Reading the Word and the World*

A response requires your reaction and interpretation. Your own perspective—your experiences, beliefs, and attitudes—will guide your response. Your response may be totally different from another reader's response, but that does not make yours better or worse. Good responses say what you think, but then they *show why* you think so. They show the relationships between your opinions and the text, between the text and your experience, and between this text and other texts.

Depending on its purpose and intended audience, a response to a text can take any of several directions. Responses may focus on one or more of the following strategies. Consider your purpose and audience or check your assignment to see which type(s) you should emphasize.

Types of Responses

- **Analyzing the effectiveness of the text.** This response analyzes key features such as the clarity of the main idea, the rhetorical situation, the organization of the argument, the logic of the reasoning, the quality of the supporting evidence, and/or the effectiveness of the author's style, tone, and voice.
- **Agreeing and/or disagreeing with the ideas in the text.** Often responders react to the ideas or the argument of the essay. In this case, the responders show why they agree and/or disagree with what the author/text says.
- **Interpreting and reflecting on the text.** The responder explains key passages or examines the underlying assumptions or the implications of the ideas. Often, the responder reflects on how his or her own experiences, attitudes, and observations relate to the text.

Analyzing, agreeing or disagreeing, and interpreting are somewhat different directions that a response may take. But regardless of the direction, all responses must be supported by evidence, examples, facts, and details. Good responses draw on several kinds of supporting evidence.

Kinds of Evidence

- **Personal experience.** Responders may use *examples* from their personal experiences to show why they interpreted the text as they did, why they agreed or disagreed, or why they reacted as they did.
- **Evidence from the text.** Responders should cite *specific phrases or sentences* from the text to support their explanation of a section, their analysis of the effectiveness of a passage, or their agreement or disagreement with a key point.
- **Evidence from other texts.** Responders may bring in ideas and information from other relevant essays, articles, books, or graphic material.

Not all responses use all three kinds of supporting evidence, but all responses *must* have sufficient examples to support the responder's ideas, reactions, and opinions. Responders should not merely state their opinions. They must give evidence to *show* how and why they read the text as they did.

One final—and crucial—note about responses: A response should make a coherent, overall main point. It should not be just a laundry list of reactions, likes, and dislikes. Sometimes the main point is that the text is not convincing because it lacks evidence. Sometimes the point is that the text makes an original statement even though it is difficult to read. Perhaps the point will be that the author/text stimulates the reader to reflect on his or her experience. Every response should focus on a coherent main idea.

Response to "Teach Diversity—with a Smile"

One possible response to Ehrenreich's essay follows. Before you read this response, however, write out your own reactions. There will be many different but valid responses to any given essay. For this response, marginal annotations indicate the different types of responses and the different kinds of evidence the writer uses.

What I like best about Barbara Ehrenreich's article is her effective use of personal experience to clarify the issues on both sides of the multiculturalism debate. However, her conclusion, that we should "lighten up" and accept diversity because it's "more fun," weakens her argument by ignoring the social inequalities at the heart of the debate. The issue in this debate, I believe, is not just enjoying diversity, which is easy to do, but changing cultural conditions, which is much more difficult.

Analyzing effectiveness of text

Responder's main point

Evidence from text

Evidence from text

Reflecting on the text

Personal experience

Evidence from other texts

Analyzing effectiveness of text

Responder's main point

Ehrenreich effectively uses her own experiences—and her common sense—to let us see both the virtues and the excesses of multiculturalism. When she explains that her monocultural education gave her a social map that was "about as useful as the chart that guided Columbus to the 'Indies,'" she helps us understand how vital multicultural studies are. Interestingly, even her vocabulary reveals—perhaps unconsciously—her Western bias: *Jacobins, pensées, fiat,* and *politesse* are all words that reveal her Eurocentric education. When Ehrenreich shifts to discussing the P.C. movement, her commonsense approach to the silliness of excessive social correctness ("the other guy's—or, excuse me, woman's—point of view") makes us as readers more willing to accept her compromise position.

My own experience with multiculturalism certainly parallels Ehrenreich's impatience with the "haughty stance" of the P.C. people. Of course, we should avoid racist and sexist terms and use our increased sensitivity to language to reduce discrimination. But my own backlash began several years ago when a friend said I shouldn't use the word *girl.* I said, "You mean, not ever? Not even for a ten-year-old female child?" She replied that the word had been so abused by people referring to a "woman" as a "girl" that the word *girl* now carried too many sexist connotations. Although I understood my friend's point, it seems that *girl* should still be a perfectly good word for a female child under the age of twelve. Which reminds me of a book I saw recently, *The Official Politically Correct Dictionary.* It is loaded with examples of political correctness out of control: Don't say *bald,* say *hair disadvantaged.* Don't use the word *pet,* say *nonhuman companion.*

Ehrenreich does recommend keeping a sense of humor about the P.C. movement, but the conclusion to her essay weakens her argument. Instead of focusing on her earlier point that "it's silly to mistake verbal purification for genuine social reform," she advises both sides to lighten up and have fun with the diversity around us. Instead, I wanted her to conclude by reinforcing her point that "actions still speak louder than fashionable phrases." Changing the realities of illiteracy, poverty, alcohol abuse, and sexual harassment should be the focus of the multiculturalists. Of course, changing language is crucial to changing the world, but the language revolution has already happened. Ehrenreich's article would be more effective, I believe, if she concluded with a call for both sides to help change cultural conditions.

RHETORICAL READING AND ANALYSIS

4.3
Use techniques for rhetorical reading and analysis

A rhetorical reading is simply close, critical reading that uses the language and terminology of the study of rhetoric. If *rhetoric* is defined as the "art of persuasion," then rhetorical reading is the analysis of the strategies a speaker or writer employs to persuade her audience or readers. Although rhetoric sometimes has negative connotations—we may refer to a political speech or blog as being "empty rhetoric"—rhetoric typically refers to the study of the most effective ways to communicate a message to a specific audience.

Learning the skills required by a rhetorical analysis is important for improving your ability to read and write a variety of academic and public texts. Understanding how to read text rhetorically and write a rhetorical analysis will help you in three important ways. First, you will become more familiar with the language and the key terms you will use extensively in this writing course. Second, you will acquire the vocabulary and analytical skills to provide helpful and constructive feedback during peer review. Finally—and most important—you will become more proficient at analyzing the strengths and weaknesses of texts you read in your other courses or in your own research. With these skills, you will be able to contribute to any academic or public conversation you encounter.

Watch the **Animation** on Rhetorical Analysis

The Rhetorical Triangle

Below is an example of a contemporary version of the rhetorical triangle (sometimes called a "communication triangle"). This triangle presents the key features of any rhetorical situation: the author or writer, the text, the audience or readers, and the context—the place of publication and the occasion for which the text was written.

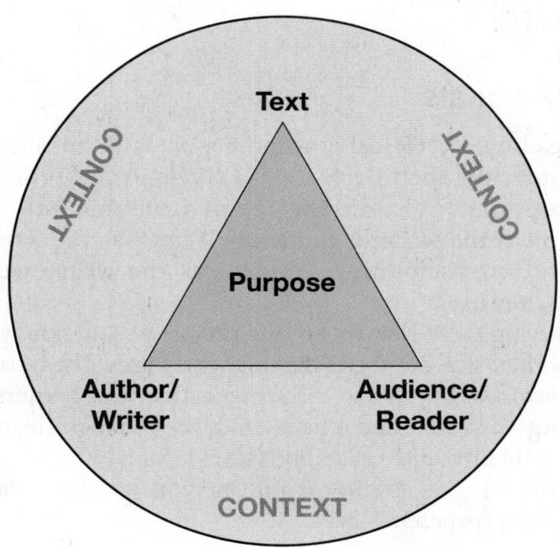

Rhetorical Analysis vs. Critical Reading

Rhetorical analysis relies on the critical reading processes you practiced earlier in this chapter, but here the emphasis is on identifying the key rhetorical

"Wh" Questions

Critical Reading

Who is the writer? *Who* is the intended reader?
When was it written?
Where does it appear?
Why is the writer writing on this topic?
What is the writer saying or arguing?

Rhetorical Analysis

How does the writer construct the essay or text?
What rhetorical strategies does the writer use?
How effective are each of those strategies?

strategies used by a writer and judging whether those strategies are effective, given the writer's purpose, occasion, audience, and genre. The emphasis is less on *what* the writer says—or whether you agree or disagree—and more on *how*, and *how effectively*, the writer constructs the essay or argument.

As the "Wh" Questions chart indicates, critical reading begins with asking *who*, *what*, *when*, *where*, and *why* questions about a text. Rhetorical reading asks—and answers—those questions, but in addition it focuses on the *how* questions: How does the writer construct the essay or text? How effective are the writer's chosen rhetorical strategies in achieving the purpose for the intended audience?

Rhetorical analysis requires knowing and using such key rhetorical terms as the writer's rhetorical occasion and situation; the writer's appeals to logic (logos), emotion (pathos), and character (ethos); and the writer's use of style to connect with readers and support the appeals to logos, pathos, and ethos.

Reminder: In rhetorical analysis, you will *not* explain why you agree or disagree with what the writer says. You will analyze only the rhetorical strategies and explain which strategies are most or least effective for the writer's purpose and audience.

Rhetorical Appeals

[**Watch** the **Video** on the Rhetorical Appeals

Like critical reading, rhetorical reading begins with an understanding of the key elements in the rhetorical situation. Who is the *author*, and what is his or her background? Why did the author write this text—what was the *occasion*? Who was the writer's *audience*? What was the writer's *purpose*? In what cultural or disciplinary *context* was the writer working? What *genre* did the writer use?

After identifying these elements of the rhetorical situation, you're ready to describe the key rhetorical strategies that the writer uses. The most important of them are the *rhetorical appeals to the writer's audience*. Writers appeal to an audience by using reasonable and reliable evidence and logic (logos), by demonstrating their credibility and reliability (ethos), and by appealing effectively to emotions (pathos). For additional information on rhetorical appeals, see Chapter 10, Arguing (pages 337–341).

Appeal to Reason and Logic (Logos) Especially in formal and academic writing, writers convince their readers by being reasonable and logical. Effective writers construct a strong logos appeal by clearly stating their claims and offering sufficient supporting evidence. Evidence can include citations from accepted authorities, statistics or conclusions from scientific or peer-reviewed

Techniques for Rhetorical Analysis and Response

Technique	Tips on How to Do It
Using active reading, writing, and discussing strategies.	Write questions and comments in the text's margins. Find publishing place, date, and context. *Identify* the author's audience, purpose, genre, main arguments and key rhetorical strategies.
Summarizing the author's audience, purpose, and main ideas and then noting the author's main rhetorical strategies.	Indicate the author's purpose, audience, occasion, context, and main arguments and *objectively* describe the key rhetorical strategies, including appeals to logos, pathos, and ethos as well as stylistic strategies.
Responding by analyzing the rhetorical effectiveness (strengths and weaknesses) of the text.	Consider clarity of writer's purpose, use of occasion, connection with audience, effectiveness of rhetorical appeals, clarity of organization, and appropriateness of style. *Focus* on the particular strategies you intend to analyze.
Citing evidence from the text to support your analysis of both the rhetorical strengths and weaknesses of the text.	Support your claims of effectiveness and ineffectiveness with *specific examples* from the text. What rhetorical strategies and appeals were most effective/ineffective for the purpose, audience and context? Note any *gaps* or *missed opportunities* for making the argument *more* effective for its audience and context.
Combining summary and response into a coherent essay containing your thesis about the rhetorical effectiveness of the text.	Begin with the summary, followed by your rhetorical analysis of the text. Present your thesis about the overall effectiveness first, then develop your points and supporting evidence of both effectiveness and ineffectiveness.

studies, and appropriate personal experience. A logos appeal can be strengthened by clear organization, a logical order or sequence to reasons and evidence, and a clear, logical, and grammatically appropriate style.

Problems in logical reasoning—the so-called fallacies of logic—can seriously weaken a writer's logos appeal. Fallacies such as "either-or" reasoning, hasty generalizations, "red herring" arguments, faulty analogies, "post hoc" arguments, "begging the question," circular arguments, "straw man" arguments, and other errors in reasoning will weaken any writer's logos appeal. For a full explanation of these fallacies in logic, see Chapter 10, Arguing (pages 389–391).

Appeal to Character and Credibility (Ethos) Writers are believable and convincing not only when they use good logos appeals but also when they establish their good character, credibility, and trustworthiness. We trust writers who are known experts or authorities, but we also trust writers who present all the relevant information, who give both sides of an argument, who do thorough research and present that research accurately and clearly, and who show fairness and reasonableness in their arguments. Ethos appeals can be undermined, however, by writers who exaggerate, use emotional or loaded language, distort facts and figures, misrepresent alternative arguments, or omit key evidence.

Appeal to Emotion (Pathos) Appeals to emotion can be effective when the emotional content is genuine, appropriate for the subject, and not exaggerated. Often, writers use emotional appeals because they think that if they show they are passionate about the subject, they will win over their readers. However, emotional appeals can backfire because the slightest overuse or exaggeration may negate the writer's logos or ethos appeals.

Combined Appeals Appeals to logos, ethos, and pathos are interconnected and interrelated. An effective logos appeal usually strengthens the author's ethos appeal. A strong ethos appeal makes readers expect a credible and logical argument. An appropriate use of pathos often makes the writer seem more human and credible, which supports the ethos appeal. On the negative side, an excessive use of pathos appeals can undermine a writer's credibility, and a writer's failure to cite logical supporting evidence or authorities will damage the ethos appeal.

In the following excerpt from his classic *Letter from Birmingham Jail,* Martin Luther King, Jr., illustrates how to set up the key elements of a rhetorical situation (occasion, audience, purpose, and genre) and then use logos, ethos, and pathos appeals to persuade his audience. The initial paragraphs (above the text break) show King setting the situation and addressing his audience; below the break, the notes in the margin show how King combines his logos, ethos, and pathos appeals in this famous American document.

April 16, 1963

Rhetorical situation: Audience is fellow clergy; occasion is detainment in jail for disrupting the peace; genre is a letter

My Dear Fellow Clergymen:

While confined here in the Birmingham City Jail, I came across your recent statement calling my present activities "unwise and untimely." Seldom do I pause to answer criticism of my work and ideas. . . . But since I feel that you are men of genuine goodwill and that your criticisms are sincerely set forth, I want to try to answer your statements in what I hope will be patient and reasonable terms.

Ethos appeal: Connects with audience by calling them men of goodwill

I think I should indicate why I am here in Birmingham, since you have been influenced by the view which argues against "outsiders coming in."

I have the honor of serving as president of the Southern Christian Leadership Conference, an organization operating in every Southern state, with headquarters in Atlanta, Georgia. We have some eighty-five affiliated organizations across the South, and one of them is the Alabama Christian Movement for Human Rights.... Several months ago the affiliate here in Birmingham asked us to be on call to engage in a nonviolent direct-action program if such were deemed necessary. We readily consented, and when the hour came we lived up to our promise. So I, along with several members of my staff, am here because I was invited here. I am here because I have organizational ties here.

Ethos appeal: King says he is here not as an outsider, but as an invited member of local organizations

But more basically, I am in Birmingham because injustice is here. Just as the prophets of the eighth century B.C. left their villages and carried their "thus saith the Lord" far beyond the boundaries of their home towns: and just as the Apostle Paul left his village of Tarsus and carried the gospel of Jesus Christ to the far corners of the Greco-Roman world, so am I compelled to carry the gospel of freedom far beyond my own hometown. Like Paul, I must constantly respond to the Macedonian call for aid.

Introduces his purpose: To respond to injustice with direct action

Logos and ethos appeals: Cites comparison with Paul and Jesus

You may well ask: "Why direct action? Why sit-ins, marches and so forth? Isn't negotiation a better path?" You are quite right in calling for negotiation. Indeed, this is the very purpose of direct action. Nonviolent direct action seeks to create such a crisis and foster such a tension that a community which has constantly refused to negotiate is forced to confront the issue. It seeks to so dramatize the issue that it can no longer be ignored. My citing the creation of tension as part of the work of the nonviolent-resister may sound rather shocking. But I must confess that I am not afraid of the word "tension." I have earnestly opposed violent tension, but there is a type of constructive, nonviolent tension which is necessary for growth. Just as Socrates felt that it was necessary to create a tension in the mind so that individuals could rise from the bondage of myths and half-truths to the unfettered realm of creative analysis and objective appraisal, so must we see the need for nonviolent gadflies to create the kind of tension in society that will help men rise from the dark depths of prejudice and racism to the majestic heights of understanding and brotherhood.

Purpose and thesis: To persuade clergy to support direct action now

Pathos appeal: Language and images portray racism as "dark depths" and brotherhood as the "majestic heights"

The purpose of our direct-action program is to create a situation so crisis-packed that it will inevitably open the door to negotiation. I therefore concur with you in your call for negotiation. Too long has our beloved Southland been bogged down in a tragic effort to live in monologue rather than dialogue.

Pathos appeal: King appeals to the clergy's love of their country and region

Logos appeal: Accurately and fairly represents and responds to the clergy's position

One of the basic points in your statement is that the action that I and my associates have taken in Birmingham is untimely. Some have asked: "Why didn't you give the new city administration time to act?" The only answer that I can give to this query is that the new Birmingham administration must be prodded about as much as the outgoing one, before it will act. We are sadly mistaken if we feel that the election of Albert Boutwell as

Logos appeal: King argues reasonably that because Boutwell is a segregationist, he must be pressured mayor will bring the millennium to Birmingham. While Mr. Boutwell is a much more gentle person than Mr. Connor, they are both segregationists, dedicated to maintenance of the status quo. I have hope that Mr. Boutwell will be reasonable enough to see the futility of massive resistance to desegregation. But he will not see this without pressure from devotees of civil rights. My friends, I must say to you that we have not made a single gain in civil rights without determined legal and nonviolent pressure. Lamentably, it is an historical fact that privileged groups seldom give up their privileges voluntarily. Individuals may see the moral light and voluntarily give up their unjust posture; but, as Reinhold Niebuhr has reminded us, groups tend to be more immoral than individuals.

Logos appeal: King cites Reinhold Niebuhr as authority in moral and political issues

We know through painful experience that freedom is never voluntarily given by the oppressor; it must be demanded by the oppressed. Frankly, I have yet to engage in a direct-action campaign that was "well timed" in the view of those who have not suffered unduly from the disease of segregation. For years now I have heard the word "Wait!" It rings in the ear of every Negro with piercing familiarity. This "Wait" has almost always meant "Never." We must come to see, with one of our distinguished jurists, that "justice too long delayed is justice denied."

King restates thesis: We must have direct action now because "justice too long delayed is justice denied."

We have waited for more than 340 years for our constitutional and God-given rights. The nations of Asia and Africa are moving with jetlike speed toward gaining political independence, but we stiff creep at horse-and-buggy pace toward gaining a cup of coffee at a lunch counter. Perhaps it is easy for those who have never felt the stinging darts of segregation to say, "Wait." But when you have seen vicious mobs lynch your mothers and fathers at will and drown your sisters and brothers at whim; when you have seen hate-filled policemen curse, kick and even kill your black brothers and sisters; when you see the vast majority of your twenty million Negro brothers smothering in an airtight cage of poverty in the midst of an affluent society; when you suddenly find your tongue twisted and your speech stammering as you seek to explain to your six-year-old daughter why she can't go to the public amusement park that has just been advertised on television, and see tears welling up in her eyes when she is told that Funtown is closed to colored children, and see ominous clouds of inferiority beginning to form in her little mental sky, and see her beginning to distort her personality by developing an unconscious bitterness toward white people; when you have to concoct an answer for a five-year-old son who is asking: "Daddy, why do white people treat colored people so mean?"; when you take a cross-country drive and find it necessary to sleep night after night in the uncomfortable corners of your automobile because no motel will accept you; when you are humiliated day in and day out by nagging signs reading "white" and "colored"; when your first name becomes "nigger," your middle name becomes "boy" (however old you are) and your last name becomes "John," and your wife and mother are never given the

Pathos appeal: Entire paragraph is an emotional appeal to the injustice of the status quo.

Pathos appeal: Emotional language includes "vicious mobs," "hate-filled policemen," "ominous clouds of inferiority" respected title "Mrs.";... then you will understand why we find it difficult to wait. There comes a time when the cup of endurance runs over, and men are no longer willing to be plunged into the abyss of despair. I hope, sirs, you can understand our legitimate and unavoidable impatience.

Logos appeal: King returns to logos appeal with unemotional language

You express a great deal of anxiety over our willingness to break laws. This is certainly a legitimate concern. Since we so diligently urge people to obey the Supreme Court's decision of 1954 outlawing segregation in the public schools, at first glance it may seem rather paradoxical for us consciously to break laws. One may well ask: "How can you advocate breaking some laws and obeying others?" The answer lies in the fact that there are two types of laws: just and unjust. I would be the first to advocate obeying just laws. One has not only a legal but a moral responsibility to obey just laws. Conversely, one has a moral responsibility to disobey unjust laws. I would agree with St. Augustine that "an unjust law is no law at all."

Logos appeal: Justice of the Supreme Court decision of 1954

Now, what is the difference between the two? How does one determine whether a law is just or unjust? A just law is a man-made code that squares with the moral law or the law of God. An unjust law is a code that is out of harmony with the moral law. To put it in the terms of St. Thomas Aquinas: An unjust law is a human law that is not rooted in eternal law and natural law. Any law that uplifts human personality is just. Any law that degrades human personality is unjust. All segregation statutes are unjust because segregation distorts the soul and damages the personality. It gives the segregator a false sense of superiority and the segregated a false sense of inferiority. Segregation, to use the terminology of the Jewish philosopher Martin Buber, substitutes an "I-it" relationship for an "I-thou" relationship and ends up relegating persons to the status of things. Hence segregation is not only politically, economically and sociologically unsound, it is morally wrong and awful. Paul Tillich has said that sin is separation. Is not segregation an existential expression of man's tragic separation, his awful estrangement, his terrible sinfulness? Thus it is that I can urge men to obey the 1954 decision of the Supreme Court, for it is morally right; and I can urge them to disobey segregation ordinances, for they are morally wrong.

Logos appeal: King cites the religious and philosophical authorities Aquinas, Buber, and Tillich

Rhetorical Analysis Guide

The following questions are intended to help you develop a rhetorical summary and response. As you read a text, you should analyze all the rhetorical features described below. In your response, address primarily the most effective and the least effective rhetorical choices. *Remember:* writers make rhetorical choices throughout an essay or text. Your analytical task is to determine whether they made the most effective choices, given their occasion, purpose, and audience.

Guide to Rhetorical Analysis

Rhetorical Summary of Text	Rhetorical Analysis/Response
Purpose	
• Describe the author's overall purpose (to inform, explain, explore, evaluate, argue, negotiate, or other purpose).	• Is the author's purpose stated or unstated? • Was the actual purpose different from the stated purpose?
Audience/Reader	
• Who is the intended audience? • What assumptions does the author make about the reader's knowledge or beliefs?	• Where does the author effectively address the intended audience? • Is the intended audience the best audience for this purpose and thesis?
Occasion, Genre, Context	
• What was the occasion for this text? • What is the cultural or historical context? • What genre is this text?	• Was the purpose appropriate for the occasion and context? • Considering the author's purpose and audience, did the author choose an appropriate genre for this occasion?
Appeals to Logos, Ethos, and Pathos	
• Where does the writer appeal to logos? • Where does the writer appeal to ethos? • Where does the writer appeal to pathos?	• What strategies make the logos appeals effective or ineffective? • What strategies make the ethos appeals effective or ineffective? • What strategies make the pathos appeals effective or ineffective?
Thesis and Main Ideas (a clear thesis helps support both logos and ethos appeals)	
• What key question or problem does the author address? • What is the author's thesis? • What main ideas or reasons support the thesis?	• Is the writer's focus on a key question or problem effective? • Is the thesis clearly stated? • Are the supporting reasons clearly identifiable and related to the thesis?
Organization (a clear organization helps support both logos and ethos appeals)	
• Where does the author preview the organization of the text? • Where does the author signal new ideas or sections of the text?	• Is the organization clear and effective for the intended audience? Why or why not? • Is the argument easy or difficult to follow? Where is the organization clear or confusing?

Style, Tone, Vocabulary (stylistic elements can support or detract from the appeals)

- Are sentences formal and academic or informal and colloquial?
- What is the author's tone (casual, humorous, ironic, preachy, academic, or other)?
- Is the vocabulary and word choice academic, technical, mainstream, informal, colloquial?
- Which sentences are or are not effective for the purpose and intended audience?
- Where is the author's tone effective or ineffective for the audience?
- Where are the vocabulary and word choices effective or ineffective for the audience?

Rhetorical Summary and Analysis Essays

The following samples of rhetorical summary and analysis discuss Martin Luther King, Jr.'s *Letter from Birmingham Jail.* The annotations in the margin illustrate how the summary essay highlights the key features of the rhetorical situation: the author, the occasion and the historical context, the genre, the thesis, and the main appeals used by King. The rhetorical response essay then analyzes the effectiveness/ineffectiveness of the rhetorical choices, the appeals to logos, ethos, and pathos, and the organization and style of the letter.

A Rhetorical Summary

In April,1963, after he was arrested for staging civil rights demonstrations in Birmingham, Alabama, Martin Luther King, Jr., wrote his famous *Letter from Birmingham Jail.* His intended audience was eight white clergymen who objected to his presence as an outside agitator in Birmingham and called his actions "unwise and untimely." While he was detained, King began drafting sections of the letter, which was published later that year in various magazines, including *The Christian Century* and *The Atlantic Monthly*. In the letter, King explains that he is in Birmingham because he is president of the Southern Christian Leadership Conference and that his affiliates in Birmingham invited him. King then attempts to answer the question posed by the Birmingham clergy: why use direct action instead of negotiation? After explaining his philosophy of "constructive, nonviolent tension," King argues that since "privileged groups seldom give up their privileges voluntarily," direct action must be employed to open the doors to negotiation. King states his thesis when he says that direct action is

Summary points out key elements of the rhetorical situation: writer, occasion, context, genre, and audience

Summary explains King's thesis, citing key phrases

Summary identifies the appeals King uses

Use of ethos appeals

Use of pathos appeals

Use of logos appeals

Description of King's question-and-answer style

necessary because "justice too long delayed is justice denied." To support his thesis, King uses appeals to ethos, logos, and pathos. His ethos appeals start when he addresses the Birmingham clergy as "My Dear Fellow Clergymen" and calls them "men of genuine goodwill." He explains that he is a member of several Christian organizations and he compares himself to the Apostle Paul. In this excerpt, King also employs emotional or pathos appeals to show how his black brothers and sisters have been attacked by "vicious mobs," how his six-year old daughter had tears in her eyes at being denied entrance to an amusement park, and how he has to sleep in his automobile because the motels are closed to him. King uses logos appeals when he explains the difference between a just law and an unjust law and when he cites "authorities" such as St. Thomas Aquinas, Martin Buber, and Paul Tillich to explain why unjust laws, which are not "rooted in eternal law," must be disobeyed. Finally, supporting his logos and ethos appeals, King employs a question-and-answer style that treats the Birmingham clergy as equals by fairly representing their position before advancing his argument.

A Rhetorical Analysis

Rhetorical analysis begins by identifying effective choices King makes about the occasion, title, audience, and genre.

Analysis of audience choice

Analysis of genre choice

King's effective use of ethos appeals

Letter from Birmingham Jail by Martin Luther King, Jr., is a classic and venerated American document, and an analysis of this excerpt reveals its many strengths. First, King uses the rhetorical occasion to his advantage by emphasizing in the title the fact that he has been jailed, unjustly, for leading a demonstration in Birmingham, Alabama. He chooses his audience with care: although he could address the police who arrested him or Birmingham's mayor, Mr. Boutwell, he decides to address the eight white clergymen of Birmingham who objected to his demonstrations. King hopes that this audience will be more open to the religious and moral appeals he wants to make. They are, after all, clergymen who should be sympathetic to his nonviolent demonstrations and to his arguments that segregation laws are unjust and immoral laws that must be changed through negotiation. In deciding to write his arguments in the form of a letter, King chooses a genre that is both personal and public: the letter is addressed to his "fellow clergymen," but King knows that upon publication of this letter, his audience will become anyone who is interested in civil rights. This wider audience, like the Birmingham clergy, needs to know that his civil rights demonstrations are intended not just to disrupt civil life but to lead to negotiations that will change unjust laws.

King uses ethos, logos, and pathos appeals effectively throughout his letter, but he begins by carefully establishing his ethos—his appeal to character and credibility. He is charged with being an outside agitator.

So King spends the first three paragraphs carefully explaining why he is in Birmingham. First, he acknowledges the clergy as "men of genuine goodwill." Because these men had supported the status quo, he could attack them or call them racists. King chooses, however, to address the values they share; they, too, are formally educated clergy who share a Judeo-Christian faith and who recognize injustice when they see it. By comparing himself to the Apostle Paul, King lets the clergymen know that he is on a Christian mission that they should trust: he is carrying "the gospel of freedom" beyond his hometown to the city of Birmingham.

Once King has established his credibility and trustworthiness, he turns to explaining his thesis or argument. His thesis, that direct action is necessary at this moment in order to bring about negotiation and change, is a direct response to the question the clergy have asked: "Why direct action?" In making this argument, King strengthens his ethos appeal by indicating that he shares their goal of negotiation but that he knows that genuine negotiation and change will not happen without "constructive, nonviolent tension." By accurately representing their position before developing his own argument, King effectively uses both logos and ethos appeals to strengthen his argument. King never lets his audience be his adversary. They are always fellow clergymen who deserve a respectful and reasonable style: "My friends, I must say to you that we have not made a single gain in civil rights without determined legal and nonviolent pressure."

King explains his thesis by responding to questions that his audience has.

King's respectful style supports his ethos appeal.

As supporting appeals for his thesis, King first develops the emotional side of the argument. The paragraph that begins "we have waited for more than 340 years for our constitutional and God-given rights" is one extended emotional or pathos appeal. In a controlled but emotional style, he cites the "stinging darts of segration," the "vicious mobs," the "hate-filled policemen," and the tears in the eyes of a six-year-old girl. Although highly emotional, these images are effective because they accurately describe the reality of segregation. Near the end, King turns to biblical language to sum up the emotional devastation: "there comes a time when the cup of endurance runs over," when "men are no longer willing to be plunged into the abyss of despair." And then, at the end of this long paragraph, King seems to sense that perhaps the emotion is too heavy, because he ends with a sentence that restores reason and understates the emotional case: "I hope, sirs, you can understand our legitimate and unavoidable impatience."

King's pathos appeal is controlled and effective.

In the final two paragraphs of this selection, King returns to his argument and to his appeals to logos. He again acknowledges the position of the clergy and admits that they have a "legitimate concern": How can he recommend obeying some laws but breaking others? King's answer is that we must support only those laws that "square with the moral law or the law of God." As support for this argument, King cites religious and philosophical authorities such as St. Thomas Acquinas, Martin Buber, and Paul Tillich. They support his definition that any law that is "not rooted in eternal law" or that "degrades human personality" is an unjust law that should be disobeyed.

King creates logos and ethos appeals by responding to the legitimate concerns of his audience.

King effectively supports his thesis with logos appeals to authorities.

Conclusion summarizes the rhetorical strengths of King's letter.

This excerpt from *Letter from Birmingham Jail* reveals how King makes effective rhetorical choices in deciding to write from jail, choosing an open letter as his genre, and addressing his letter to the eight clergymen in Birmingham. He effectively creates his ethos by treating his audience as men of goodwill and by explaining that he is not an outsider and has legitimate and moral reasons for coming to Birmingham. He helps break down his audience's resistance through extended emotional appeals, and he concludes his argument in this excerpt by citing authorities to support his thesis that unjust laws must be changed now, through direct action, in order to achieve meaningful negotiation and change.

Warming Up: Journal Exercises

The following topics will help you practice reading and responding.

1. **Community Service Learning Project.** Go to your agency or organization and collect texts, images, and brochures that advertise the organization or explain its mission. Choose one or two documents and write a summary and response addressed both to your classmates and to the organization itself. Consider the rhetorical context of these documents (author, purpose, audience, occasion, genre, and cultural context) as you explain why they are or are not effective or appropriate and/or how you interpret the assumptions and implications contained in these texts or images. Your goal is to provide constructive suggestions about ways to revise or improve these texts.

2. Study the print of *Day and Night* by Maurits Escher. How many different ways of perceiving this picture can you see? Describe each perspective. How is "reading" this picture similar to reading a printed text? How is it different?

Day and Night by M. C. Escher.

3 **Writing across the Curriculum.** Because previewing material is an important part of active reading, most recent psychology and social science textbooks use previewing or prereading strategies at the beginning of each new chapter. Find one chapter in a textbook that uses these previewing techniques. How does the author preview the material? Does the preview help you understand the material in the chapter?

4 Reexamine the image of Rhetorica on the opening page of this chapter. What is the connection between the study of rhetoric and this particular Tarot card? As you research, answer these questions: What is rhetoric? Who is Rhetorica? What is the function or power of this Tarot card?

Reading and Writing Processes

Assignment for Reading/Responding/Analyzing

Write an essay that summarizes, analyzes, and then responds to one or more essays, articles, or advertisements. As you review your assignment, make sure you understand what text or texts you should respond to, how long your summary and response should be, who your intended audience should be, and what type(s) of summary and response you should do. You may be doing a critical summary and response, or you may be assigned a rhetorical summary and analysis.

Your purpose is to represent the text(s) accurately and faithfully in your summary and to explain and support your response or analysis for a specific audience. Taken together, your summary and response should be a coherent essay with clear connections between summary and response. Your audience may be other members of the class or specific writers, groups, or organizations.

Your instructor's assignment should indicate which of the audiences and genres suggested below you should use.

Audience	Possible Genres
Personal Audience	Class or laboratory notes, journal entry, blog, scrapbook, multigenre document
Academic Audience	Academic summary, summary and response, rhetorical analysis, synopsis, critique, review, journal entry, forum entry on class site, multigenre document
Public Audience	Column, editorial, letter to the editor, article in a magazine or newspaper, online site, newsletter, or multigenre document

CHOOSING A SUBJECT

"Plagiarism in America," an essay by Dudley Erskine Devlin, will serve as an example to illustrate the various processes, activities, and strategies for reading and writing when summarizing, analyzing, and responding.

Prereading Journal Entry

In your journal, write what you already know about the subject of the essay. The following questions will help you recall your prior experiences and consider your own opinions. The purpose of this entry is to make you aware of your own experiences and opinions before you are influenced by the arguments of the essay.

- Did you or a friend in another writing class ever plagiarize part or all of a paper? What were the circumstances and what was the outcome?
- In your previous writing classes, what were you told about plagiarism? Did you sign an honor code? Did you learn how to paraphrase and use quotations? What were the other penalties for plagiarism?
- Did your other writing teachers use plagiarism detection services such as Turnitin.com? Did knowing that help you avoid plagiarizing?

Professional Writing

Plagiarism in America

Dudley Erskine Devlin

Dudley Erskine Devlin teaches English at Colorado State University and writes editorials and blogs on contemporary issues. The targets for his columns are often controversial issues such as high-stakes testing in schools, texting while driving, and cyberbullying. As you read Devlin's essay, note places where you agree or disagree with his analysis of the problem and his proposed solutions. How would you critically read and respond to Devlin's essay?

Vice President Joe Biden lost his bid for the presidency in 1987 when it was discovered that he had plagiarized a law review article in his first year at law school. Even some well-known authors, such as historians Doris Kearns and Stephen Ambrose, have been found guilty of plagiarism. So perhaps it's not surprising that high school and college students across the nation are also being found guilty of plagiarism. This epidemic of plagiarism, caused largely by students' ease of Internet access to millions of documents, needs to be met head-on with the most direct and effective surveillance and punishment measures possible. 1

Although cheating in schools has always been a problem, today's Wikipedia generation is committing plagiarism in dramatically increased numbers. Recently, a Pew Internet & American Life Project survey showed that cheating and plagiarism have become epidemic—nearly one half of high school students reported that they or their friends cheated, even though the great majority said that cheating was definitely wrong. Researcher Donald McCabe reported in *Education Digest* that in a survey of 22 public high schools, 74% of the surveyed students reported one or more instances of test cheating in the past year and nearly 60% reported an incident involving plagiarism. McCabe also reported in *Liberal Education* that one out of every five or six college papers is plagiarized, and of the 51% of college students who self-reported that they cheated, four out of five indicated that they had bought a paper from the Internet or had cut and pasted material that they found on the Web. According to McCabe, students say, "I got it off the Internet so it's public information." They don't consider it to be a big deal. What's wrong with plagiarism, anyway? The information on the Internet—on Wikipedia, Spark Notes, or Gradesaver—is public, so why not just paste it in your paper? 2

Plagiarism in schools across America has definitely reached an epidemic stage, but students, teachers, and administrators are divided about how to solve the problem. Some say plagiarism has always existed and because of the ease of technological access, we need increased surveillance. Others argue that students need more education in order to understand what plagiarism is and how to avoid it. Although both camps raise good points, rates of plagiarism will keep increasing until teachers and schools introduce zero tolerance rules. Teachers must be more vigilant, and students who plagiarize must be punished swiftly and severely. 3

Some teachers argue that instead of surveillance and punishment, we need to understand *why* students plagiarize, and then address the cause of the problem and educate everyone. When researchers ask students why they plagiarize, they uncover a variety of excuses. Frequently, students rationalize that they cheat because they see other students cheating or buying papers online, because they are in a large lecture class, or because they are taking a boring, required course. Students also blame outside forces—pressure from parents and pressure to get into college and maintain scholarships. Researcher Timothy Dodd of Duke University says that students often feel that they are "scrambling from assignment to assignment just trying to keep their heads above water. Students literally go on a scavenger hunt for information on the Internet, which they throw [into] a word file. Suddenly they think they have a paper." With all this pressure, Dodd says that "we shouldn't be surprised that these students are resorting to plagiarism to 'manage' their time." 4

Those who favor educational solutions point out that honor codes and online tutorials do help explain what plagiarism is, why it is unethical, 5

...continued Plagiarism in America, **Dudley Erskine Devlin**

and how to write a paper that credits all the sources used. Research has shown that educating students about honor codes, especially in very small schools, can have a positive effect. For example, Mountain Lakes High School in New Jersey has an honor code that outlines "pro-active/preventative measures," such as student involvement in creating the honor code and assemblies to explain the code, instead of the punitive approach used in most high schools. Another solution sometimes touted by educators is a tutorial for all students about academic honesty and plagiarism. According to Trip Gabriel, writing in the *New York Times*, students at a selective college who completed a Web tutorial on plagiarism cheated 65% less than students who did not take the tutorial. However, these tutorials did not work as well with the hard core cheaters, students with lower SAT scores, male students, and student athletes.

Honor codes and tutorials for students about plagiarism are not, *6* however, really effective solutions. Students already know what plagiarism is. They know they shouldn't copy someone else's work or buy a paper online. They know that they cannot just cut and paste from the Internet without using quotation marks and citing the author. They know they shouldn't have their parents or roommates write, revise, or edit their papers. So having teachers spend time in class or in tutorials or assemblies talking about plagiarism is not going to lessen this tidal wave of cheating. Teachers and administrators just need to adopt a zero tolerance policy and vigilantly monitor writing and test taking. And students who are caught plagiarizing need to fail the course and be placed on academic probation.

Supervising any test taking or writing situation is really the only solution. *7* Trip Gabriel describes a very effective system used at the University of Central Florida. The testing center does not allow gum chewing (this could disguise a student speaking into a hands-free cell phone to another student outside), the students are not allowed to wear hats (students can hide their eyes or they can write answers on the underside of the brim), and the center has eye-in-the-sky video cameras that record what each student is writing or doing on his computer. In this environment, cheating at UCF dropped significantly, to only 14 suspected students out of 64,000 exams administered. Another effective surveillance system is a plagiarism detection service such as Turnitin.com. This service, which is now used by 9,500 high schools and colleges, checks its ever expanding database for plagiarized essays and undocumented paragraphs, sentences, and phrases. Turnitin needs to be used by every teacher who assigns writing, and students caught plagiarizing should fail the course and be expelled from school, no questions asked.

Although some studies show that teaching students how to do *8* legitimate research, having school honor codes, and practicing citing Internet sources may help to reduce some cases of plagiarism or cheating, basically all students instinctively know what plagiarism is and that it is wrong to steal someone else's ideas, words, or facts. Therefore, high schools and colleges should focus their attention on surveillance and swift punishment. Just like drunk driving, no one quit drinking and driving just because someone else said that it was dangerous. Traffic fatalities began to drop only when increased enforcement and stricter DUI penalties were enforced. Schools and teachers need to increase surveillance, use plagiarism detection services such as Turnitin, and have committees composed of both faculty and students review each case. The minimum punishment should be failure of the paper and failure of the course, and subsequent cases of plagiarism should face academic probation. Maybe, just maybe, students would then learn that plagiarism in school could jeopardize their careers or cost them an election later in life.

COLLECTING

Text Annotation

4.4
Use collecting strategies to develop a summary and response or rhetorical analysis essay

Most experts on reading and writing agree that you will learn and remember more if you write out your comments, questions, and reactions in the margins rather than just highlight sentences. Writing your responses helps you begin a conversation with the text. Reproduced below are one reader's marginal responses to paragraph 6 of Devlin's essay.

Honor codes and tutorials for students about plagiarism are not, however, really effective solutions. Students already know what plagiarism is. They know they shouldn't copy someone else's work or buy a paper online. They know that they cannot just cut and paste from the Internet without using quotation marks and citing the author. They know they shouldn't have their parents or roommates write, revise, or edit their papers. So having teachers spend time in class or in tutorials or assemblies talking about plagiarism is not going to lessen this tidal wave of cheating. Teachers and administrators just need to adopt a zero tolerance policy and vigilantly monitor writing and test taking. And students who are caught plagiarizing need to fail the course and be placed on academic probation.

Clearly, not all students DO know what plagiarism is.

I had to learn how to cite authors to give them credit.

We can get help from students in our class and in the writing center, so why can't roommates help?

Reading Log

A reading log, like text annotations, encourages you to interact with the author and the text and to record your comments and questions as you read. Just open a Word file and write down your thoughts as you read the text. Freewriting in a Word file allows you to develop more of your thoughts than simply writing in the margins of the text. Often, these freewriting responses help you focus on ideas you will want to develop later in your analysis or response.

Here is one reading log response to Devlin's ideas about plagiarism.

> In studies about childhood development, results show that kids follow behaviors they are shown. It is a conditioned response, and if a candidate for President is plagiarizing or an individual's favorite author is plagiarizing, it is logical that kids would do the same thing. From experience, I have had a lot of friends who have copied and pasted entire papers and gotten full credit on them because teachers don't have the proper resources to catch students when they decide to plagiarize. I know a lot of my friends continue to plagiarize because they never got caught so a feeling of invincibility arises and a habit is formed. Plagiarizing is wrong, and I can't say that I have never copied and pasted something because that would be a lie. I know it isn't something anyone should do, but when everyone else is doing it, it is easy to rationalize. Because of the ease of Internet access and the lack of consequences, a lot of students ignore what's wrong and what's right.

SHAPING

4.5
Shape your summary and response or rhetorical analysis essay

As you think about ways to organize and develop your essay, be sure to reread your assignment and consider your purpose and audience. Each of the strategies described below will help you develop and organize specific parts of your summary or response. Even after you have written a first draft, look back and review these strategies to see whether one of them will make your response essay more effective.

Shaping Strategies

Do you want to ...	Consider using this rhetorical strategy:
briefly summarize a text?	paraphrasing and quoting (pp. 107–109)
avoid plagiarizing?	avoiding plagiarism (p. 108)
organize a summary/response/analysis?	sample organizations for summary/response/ analysis essays (pp. 114–115)
understand options for your response?	response-shaping options (pp. 110–113)

Paraphrasing, Quoting, and Avoiding Plagiarism

A summary should convey the main ideas, the essential argument, or the key features of a text. Its purpose should be to represent the text's ideas as concisely and objectively as possible. Paraphrases help you condense key ideas into fewer sentences; direct quotations help you convey the author's ideas as accurately as possible by citing key phrases. You avoid plagiarism by converting the author's ideas into your own language and by using direct quotation marks whenever you use a phrase or sentence written by the author.

Watch the Animation on Avoiding Plagiarism

Paraphrase

The purpose of a paraphrase is to restate concisely the author's ideas in your own language. A good paraphrase retains the original meaning without plagiarizing from the original text.

Original: Those who favor educational solutions point out that honor codes and online tutorials do help explain what plagiarism is, why it is unethical, and how to write a paper that credits all the sources used.

Acceptable Paraphrase: Student honor codes and tutorials do, according to some educators, teach students about plagiarism, how to avoid it, and the ethics of accurately citing resources.

Plagiarism: Some educators argue that tutorials and honor codes actually do help explain what plagiarism is, why it is unethical, and how to credit sources. [This is plagiarism because the writer uses the exact phrases (see highlighting) from the source without using quotation marks. The writer needs to put this information in his or her own language.]

Direct Quotation

Often summaries directly quote key phrases or sentences from the source. *Remember: any words or phrases within the quotation marks must be accurate, word-for-word transcriptions of the original.* Use direct quotations sparingly to convey key ideas in the essay:

Devlin acknowledges that education can help reduce plagiarism through honor codes and tutorials that "help explain what plagiarism is, why it is unethical, and how to write a paper that credits all the sources used."

Use direct quotation of key words or phrases to express the author's thesis or claim:

> In "Plagiarism in America," Devlin argues that our "epidemic of plagiarism" must be "met head-on with the most forceful and effective surveillance and punishment measures possible."

Avoid the direct quotation of long sentences. Instead, use an ellipsis (three spaced points . . .) to indicate words that you have omitted.

> *Original*: Another solution sometimes touted by educators is a tutorial for all students about academic honesty and plagiarism.
>
> *Condensed Quotation*: Devlin explains that "another solution . . . is a tutorial for all students" about avoiding plagiarism.

Avoiding Plagiarism

As you work with your sources, paraphrasing key ideas and quoting key phrases or sentences, keep in mind that in order to avoid plagiarizing, you need to document any ideas, facts, statistics, or actual language you use—both in your text and in a Works Cited or References page. *Plagiarism* is knowingly and deliberately using the language, ideas, or visual materials of another person or source without acknowledging that person or source. Use the following guidelines to avoid plagiarism.

- Do not use language, ideas, or graphics from any essay, text, or visual image that you find online, in the library, or from commercial sources without acknowledging the source.
- Do not use language, ideas, or visual images from any other student's essay without acknowledging the source.

Sometimes students will plagiarize out of carelessness by inadequately citing words, specific language, ideas, or visual images. You can avoid this inadvertent plagiarism by learning how to quote accurately from your sources, how to paraphrase using your own words, and how to cite your sources accurately.

The best way to avoid inadvertent plagiarism is to ask your instructor how to document a source you are using. Your instructor will help you with the conventions of direct quotation, paraphrasing, and in-text reference or citation.

SAMPLE SUMMARIES

Here are two summaries of Devlin's essay on plagiarism, written by different writers. Notice that while both summaries convey the main ideas of the essay by using paraphrase and direct quotation, they are not identical. Check each summary to see how well it meets the guidelines for an effective summary.

Summary 1

Plagiarism. It is the dreaded word that every high school and college student fears. Although every student knows the consequences and fears getting caught, still many students continue to cheat. In "Plagiarism in America," Dudley Erskine Devlin argues that educators need to adopt zero tolerance policies about plagiarism. According to Devlin, plagiarism has reached epidemic proportions because of the Internet's ease of access as well as pressures that students feel to get good grades or earn scholarships. Devlin's main question is simple: How can we put an end to this epidemic? While Devlin notes that some educators believe that plagiarism would be reduced if students were better educated about plagiarism through online tutorials and honor codes, he believes educators should respond with surveillance and harsh punishments. The minimum punishment, Devlin argues, "should be failure of the paper and failure of the course," and repeat offenders should be put on academic probation or even be expelled from school. Devlin cites researchers who show that tutorials and honor codes can lessen the frequency of plagiarism, but he believes that increased surveillance, use of plagiarism detection devices such as Turnitin, and serious punishments are necessary to put an end to this epidemic.

Summary 2

In "Plagiarism in America," Dudley Erskine Devlin argues that plagiarism has become an epidemic in high schools and colleges, largely due to students' increased dependence on the Internet for research. Devlin supports his claim that cheating has become epidemic by citing statistics from researchers who show that approximately 20% of all college papers are plagiarized and that nearly two-thirds of surveyed high school students reported that they or their friends plagiarized an assignment. Devlin argues that although some educators believe this epidemic of plagiarism can be reduced by teaching students what plagiarism is and by encouraging students to sign honor codes, he believes that plagiarism rates will continue to increase until schools and teachers use "the most forceful and effective surveillance and punishment measures possible." Devlin cites statistics that show that educational tutorials and honor codes work for some schools, but he recommends that both cheating on tests and plagiarism be met by careful supervision of test taking environments and by using plagiarism detection devices such as Turnitin.com. According to Devlin, the current epidemic of plagiarism will be reduced only when "the minimum punishment" is failure of both the paper and the course, and when students who are caught more than once should face academic probation or be "immediately expelled from school, no questions asked."

RESPONSE SHAPING

Strategies for organizing a response depend on the purpose of the response. Typically, responses include one or more of four purposes:

- Analyzing the effectiveness of the text
- Agreeing and/or disagreeing with the ideas in the text
- Interpreting and reflecting on the text
- Rhetorically analyzing the effectiveness of the text

As the explanations that follow illustrate, each type of response requires supporting evidence from the text, from other texts, and/or from the writer's own experience.

Analyzing

Analysis requires dividing a whole into its parts in order to better understand the whole. To analyze a text for its effectiveness, start by examining key parts or features of the text, such as the purpose, the intended audience, the thesis and main ideas, the organization and evidence, and the language and style. Notice how the following paragraph analyzes Devlin's illogical argument.

In addition, Devlin's argument in "Plagiarism in America" has clear problems in its logic and the support for his claims. Devlin acknowledges that "students, teachers, and administrators are divided" about how to solve the problem, but after citing two studies that show the statistical importance of educational approaches, he dismisses this evidence by saying "honor codes and tutorials for students" are not effective solutions because "students already know what plagiarism is." His only support for this claim is a series of assertions without any support from surveys or studies. Having dismissed these educational solutions, Devlin seems to commit an either/or fallacy by assuming that we should use either educational solutions or increased surveillance, but not both. And to add to this problem, Devlin cites the example of the surveillance system at the University of Central Florida's testing center. Devlin here confuses monitoring of tests with monitoring for plagiarism. Cheating on tests is not the same as plagiarizing papers or essays, and the two forms of cheating require different solutions. Devlin's problems with logic and lack of support continue into his final paragraph, where he uses the claim that plagiarism is just like drunk driving. He asserts that "traffic fatalities began to drop only when increased enforcement and stricter DUI penalties were enforced." Devlin cites no support for this claim and does not explain how or why the two situations require similar solutions.

Agreeing/Disagreeing

Often a response to a text focuses on agreeing and/or disagreeing with its major ideas. Responses may agree completely, disagree completely, or agree with some points but disagree with others. Responses that agree with some ideas but disagree with others are often the most effective because they show that the responder sees both strengths and weaknesses in an argument. In the following paragraphs, notice how the responder agrees and disagrees and then supports each judgment with evidence.

In "Plagiarism in America," Dudley Erskine Devlin identifies an important problem that definitely needs fixing, but I can't agree with many of his recommended solutions. The statistics he cites from the Pew Internet and American Life project and from the Donald McCabe study appear to be accurate and do fit with my own experiences in high school. My school used Turnitin.com, a plagiarism detection system, in all my writing courses. I was required to turn in my essays to this Web site database, and I discovered the checking system is fairly successful. The majority of my friends who plagiarized essays were caught. However, I don't agree that these detection systems should be the only approach. Students in my class did need to learn about some of the technical aspects of citing sources. Most of us knew that we shouldn't turn in someone else's paper or copy and paste material from the Internet, but we still needed to know how to cite our sources and quote accurately. In addition, Devlin says that we shouldn't accept any help with our papers when he says that students "shouldn't have their parents or roommates write, revise, or edit their papers." In class, we regularly assisted each other with papers in peer review groups. These sessions always helped you see what you missed, what you did wrong, and how to do better. I don't see the difference between getting help from a roommate or the writing center and getting help from peers in your class, as long as no one is writing the paper for you. Finally, Devlin says that if you're caught plagiarizing you should "fail the course and be immediately expelled from school, no questions asked." This "zero tolerance" policy seems much too harsh. Students need a chance to learn from their mistakes, and receiving an F on the paper should be enough to ensure that the student won't do it again.

Interpreting and Reflecting

Many responses contain interpretations of passages that might be read differently depending on one's assumptions or the implications of an idea. An interpretation says, "Here is what the text says, but let me explain what it means, what assumptions the argument carries, or what the implications might be." Here is a paragraph from an interpretive response to Devlin's essay.

In "Plagiarism in America," Devlin spends time talking about surveillance and punishment for plagiarism, but not much time thoughtfully considering his assumptions about what plagiarism is. He says, "Students already know what plagiarism is," and then he gives a few examples of a conventional definition. But the idea of plagiarism is dependent on culture and context. One context he mentions is the Internet. On the Internet, the idea of ownership of language and ideas is regularly challenged. On Wikipedia, for example, it would be extremely difficult to track down the writer of any given sentence or any idea. All of the comments have been posted, taken down, revised, and edited many times. So who is the author who "owns" these words and ideas? To whom should we give credit? Or do we need to give credit at all, since it may be "common knowledge" that we all share, knowledge that does not need documentation. Ideas and language on a wiki site are like a conversation, with many people offering contributions. Similarly, if I have a conversation with a classmate about my topic, and she gives me a suggestion about a different angle or idea, am

I plagiarizing if I incorporate her idea without direct quotation marks and a footnote? What about when I use ideas from another course or even from a paper I wrote several years ago? We really cannot write anything without the ideas and contributions of many people's thoughts and contributions, and it would be impractical and even foolish to try to track down and document the source of every idea that springs to mind.

Analyzing Rhetorically

Rhetorical analysis of a passage uses the same analyzing strategies indicated above, but in addition it uses the language of rhetoric and rhetorical appeals to identify an author's key strategies and to comment on their effectiveness. A rhetorical analysis identifies the author, publication context, intended audience and purpose, and then analyzes the writer's logos, ethos, and pathos appeals. In the next paragraph, the writer focuses on the effectiveness of Devlin's ethos appeals.

Related to his problems with using logos appeals, Devlin's ethos appeal at the beginning of his essay seems strong, but it weakens as the essay proceeds. Although Devlin himself is not a known expert on the topic, he gains early credibility by citing compelling statistics from both the Pew Internet study and Donald McCabe's research. He adds to this credibility and sense of fairness by acknowledging that there are two sides or "camps" to the issue—one that favors increased surveillance and one that favors increased education. At this point, he represents the educational solutions fairly, describing research on both honor codes and tutorial that demonstrate effectiveness. However, his ethos appeal begins to slide when he dismisses the educational solutions out of hand. In paragraph 6, Devlin's ethos continues to deteriorate when he seems to attack students by saying, "they know...," they know..., "they know...," and his language becomes more extreme, recommending "zero tolerance," "vigilantly" monitoring, and "academic probation." He begins paragraph 7 by saying that supervision "is really the only solution," then concludes the paragraph by dramatically increasing the punishment that students caught plagiarizing should receive: "Turnitin needs to be used by every teacher... and students caught plagiarizing should fail the course and be immediately expelled... no questions asked." Suddenly, instead of seeming credible and fair, Devlin's character has become judgmental, intolerant, and unreasonable. Overall, Devlin's ethos appeal is strong at the beginning of his essay, but by the end, the reader has lost confidence in his credibility because of his extreme and judgmental language and recommendations.

ORGANIZING SUMMARY/RESPONSE AND RHETORICAL ANALYSIS ESSAYS

Four common organizations follow. Select or modify one of them to fit your audience, purpose, and kind of response. Typically, a summary/response takes the following form.

Shaping Your Points: Summary/Response with Focus on the Text

Introductory paragraph(s)	Summary	Your response	Concluding paragraph(s)
Introduce the text	Summarize the text	Point 1 Point 2 Point 3 etc.	Wind up your response, emphasizing your main point

A second kind of organization focuses initially on key ideas or issues and then examines the text or texts for their contribution to these key ideas. This form begins with the issues, then summarizes the text(s), and then moves to the reader's responses.

Shaping Your Points: Summary/Response with Focus on the Issues

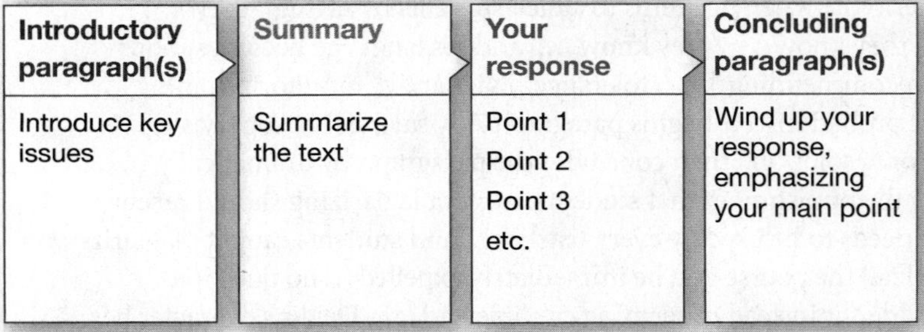

A third organization integrates the summary and the response. It begins by introducing the issue and/or the text, gives a brief overall idea of the text, and then summarizes and responds point by point.

Shaping Your Points: Integrated Summary/Response

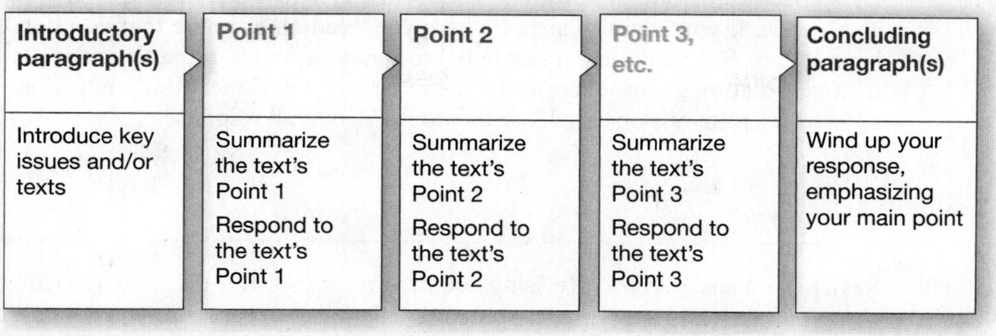

Introductory paragraph(s)	Point 1	Point 2	Point 3, etc.	Concluding paragraph(s)
Introduce key issues and/or texts	Summarize the text's Point 1 Respond to the text's Point 1	Summarize the text's Point 2 Respond to the text's Point 2	Summarize the text's Point 3 Respond to the text's Point 3	Wind up your response, emphasizing your main point

A fourth organization is appropriate especially for rhetorical analyses of a text.

Shaping Your Points: Rhetorical Analysis

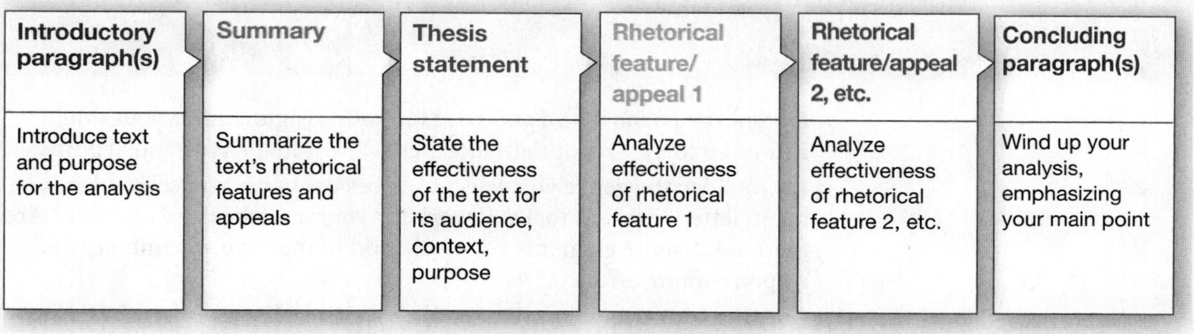

Introductory paragraph(s)	Summary	Thesis statement	Rhetorical feature/appeal 1	Rhetorical feature/appeal 2, etc.	Concluding paragraph(s)
Introduce text and purpose for the analysis	Summarize the text's rhetorical features and appeals	State the effectiveness of the text for its audience, context, purpose	Analyze effectiveness of rhetorical feature 1	Analyze effectiveness of rhetorical feature 2, etc.	Wind up your analysis, emphasizing your main point

DRAFTING

If you have been reading actively, you have been writing throughout the reading/writing/discussing process. At some point, however, you will gather your best ideas, have a rough direction or outline in mind, and begin writing a draft. Some writers like to have their examples and evidence ready when they begin drafting. Many writers have outlines in their heads or on paper. Perhaps you like to put your rough outline on the computer and then expand each section as you write. Finally, most writers like to skim the text and *reread their notes* immediately before they start their drafts.

Once you begin drafting, keep interruptions to a minimum. Because focus and concentration are important to good writing, try to keep writing for as long as possible. If you come to a spot where you need an example that you don't have at your fingertips, just insert in parentheses—(put the example about cosmetics and animal abuse here)—and keep on writing. Concentrate on making all your separate responses add up to a focused, overall response.

REVISING

Revision means *reseeing.* Revising requires rereading the text and rewriting your summary and response as needed. While revision begins as you read and reread the text, it continues until—and sometimes after—you turn in a paper or send it to its intended audience.

A major step in your revision is receiving responses from peer readers and deciding on a revision plan based on the feedback. Use the following guidelines as you read your peers' papers and respond to their advice.

Guidelines for Revision

- **Review the purpose and audience for your assignment.** Is your draft addressed to the appropriate audience? Does it fulfill its intended purpose?
- **Reconsider the genre you selected.** Does the genre you selected (essay, letter, letter to the editor) still work for your audience and purpose? Are there multigenre elements you could add to make your summary and response more effective?
- **Continue to use your active reading/writing/discussing activities as you revise.** If you are uncertain about parts of your summary or response, reread the text, check your notes, or discuss your draft with a classmate.
- **Reread your summary for key features.** Make sure your summary indicates author and title, cites main ideas, uses an occasional direct quotation for key ideas, and includes author tags. Check your summary for accuracy and objectivity. For rhetorical summaries, make sure you identify each of the following key features: author, title, publishing information, context, and genre—as well as the key rhetorical appeals used.
- **Check paraphrases and direct quotations.** When you are paraphrasing you need to put the author's ideas into your own language. If you are quoting directly, make sure the words within the quotation marks are accurate, word-for-word transcriptions.

- **Review the purpose of your response.** Are you analyzing, agreeing/disagreeing, interpreting, doing a rhetorical analysis, or writing some combination of the four? Do your types of responses fit the assignment, meet your purpose, and address your intended audience?
- **Amplify your supporting evidence.** Summary/response drafts often need additional, relevant evidence. Be sure you use sufficient personal experience, evidence from the text, or examples from other texts to support your response.
- **Focus on a clear, overall response.** Your responses should all add up to a focused, overall reaction. Delete or revise any passages that do not maintain your focus.
- **Revise sentences to improve clarity, conciseness, emphasis, and variety.** (See Handbook.)
- **Edit your final version.** Use the spell check on your computer. Have a friend help proofread. Check the Handbook for suspected problems in usage, grammar, and punctuation.

PeerResponse

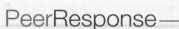

The instructions here will help you give and receive constructive advice about the rough draft of a summary/response or rhetorical analysis essay. You may use these guidelines for an in-class workshop, a take-home review, or a computer e-mail response.

Writer: Before you exchange drafts with another reader, write out the following information about your own rough draft.

1. On your draft, *label* the summary and the response.
2. *Underline* the sentence(s) that signal to the reader that you are shifting from objective summary to personal response or analysis.
3. Indicate your purpose, intended audience, and any special genre features such as graphs or images.
4. Explain *one or two problems* that you are having with this draft that you want your reader to comment on.

Reader: Without making any comments, read the *entire* draft from start to finish. As you *reread* the draft, answer the following questions.

1. Review the guidelines for writing summaries. Has the writer remained *objective* in his or her summary? Does the summary *omit* any key ideas? Does the writer use author tags frequently

and accurately? Can you clearly understand the main ideas of the article? Is the summary written in language appropriate for the intended audience? Do images or graphic material support the writer's purpose?

2. Review the guidelines for writing responses. What type(s) of response is the writer using? In the margin, label the types. What kinds of evidence does the writer use in support of his or her response? In the margin, label the kinds. Is this response addressed appropriately to the audience?
3. In your own words, state the main idea or the focus that organizes the writer's response.
4. Write out your reactions to the writer's response. Where do you disagree with the writer's analysis or interpretation? Explain.
5. Answer the writer's questions in number 4, above.

Postscript on the Writing Process

1. As you finish your essay, what questions do you still have about how to summarize? What questions do you have about writing a good response or rhetorical analysis?
2. Which paragraphs in your response contain your most effective supporting evidence? What kinds of evidence (analysis of the text, evidence from other texts, or personal experience) did you use?
3. What sentences in your response contain your overall reaction to the text?
4. If you had one more day to work on your essay, what would you change? Why?
5. Review the critical reading guide at the beginning of this chapter. Which of its strategies was most successful for you? What did you learn about active, critical reading that you applied to the writing of your response? Cite one passage that illustrates what you learned about critical reading.

Student Writing

Rhetorical Analysis of Gregory Petsko's Open Letter to George M. Philip

Allyson McGrath

Allyson McGrath decided to write a rhetorical analysis essay on the rhetorical strategies and appeals used in "An Open Letter to George M. Philip," by

Gregory Petsko. Before you read her analysis, be sure to read Petsko's letter on pages 299–304 and decide for yourself about the effectiveness of Petsko's rhetorical appeals. McGrath is a student at Colorado State University, majoring in history with an education concentration in social studies. She plans to use her liberal arts education to teach high school history and English.

Gregory Petsko's "An Open Letter to George M. Philip, President of the State University of New York at Albany" expresses his frustration that George M. Philip cut the departments of French, Italian, Classics, Russian, and Theater Arts at SUNY Albany. The cuts were made in October 2010, at a time when many universities were facing a lack of funds. Petsko argues that the elimination of these departments was a bad decision, and that there are more effective ways that the budget problems could have been addressed. He reviews the reasons Philip gave for the cuts, such as a shortage of enrolled students in the programs, budget issues, and a financial drain on the university, as well as the fact that other departments bring in more money through contracts and grants. In addition, Petsko gives examples that explain the importance of these liberal arts departments in order to show why Philip is making a terrible decision. Petsko appeals to ethos by building up himself and criticizing Philip, appeals to logos as he argues the importance of the eliminated departments, and appeals to pathos by using emotional language. *1*

Because Petsko's essay is in the form of an open letter, he is actually addressing two audiences: the current president of SUNY Albany and the public, especially those who may agree with Philip's decision or those who are unaware of why the cuts matter. This means that although the letter begins "Dear President Philip," many parts of the letter appeal not to Philip but to members of the public. If Petsko really wanted to convince Philip that he should reverse his decision and resolve the budget problems in a different manner, his language could have been less inflammatory, and his appeals to emotion could have been more restrained. Petsko's appeals to ethos are effective as he begins his letter, and while his appeals to logos are initially effective, they are eventually undercut by his pathos appeals. Overall, his appeals to ethos, logos, and pathos were more appropriate for the public audience than for Philip. *2*

Initially, Petsko's appeals to ethos are reasonably effective. Petsko mentions that he "started out as classics major." Although he is now a professor of biochemistry and chemistry, his classics courses taught him how "to think, to analyze, and to write clearly," something that none of his science classes taught. This appeal indicates that he has experience with the importance of the departments cut from the university, and the lessons he learned from them have followed him throughout his life. Petsko also builds his credibility by indicating that he has written a monthly column on science and society for ten years. This assures the audience that he knows what he is talking about, that he understands the *3* importance of both science and liberal arts instruction, and that people listen to him. He also assures the audience of his intelligence by his many allusions to books and stories. This reveals him to be a well-rounded individual who has enough knowledge to judge whether or not the departments should have been cut.

However, other ethos appeals are less effective for his audiences. While at first Petsko's recognition of the difficult choices Philip faced helps build his credibility, Petsko undercuts his own ethos by using derisive language toward Philip and the faculty of SUNY Albany. He tries to destroy Philip's authority by stating "from your biography, you don't actually have a PhD or other high degree, and have never really taught or done research at a university," and follows by stating, "I guess I shouldn't be surprised that you have trouble understanding the importance of maintaining programs in unglamorous or even seemingly 'dead' subjects." This was unnecessarily condescending and petty, and it insults the intelligence of his audience. If any audience members don't have a graduate degree, they are also supposedly incapable of understanding. 4

In addition to his ethos appeals, Petsko uses appeals to logos effectively throughout his letter. One effective appeal is the real-life application of knowledge gained by students taking the cut courses. Petsko explains that the courses may seem unimportant now, but they may be vital in the future. Virology was a dying branch of study in the 1970s, Petsko says, but then the growing concern with AIDS made certain universities important because they still supported virology programs. Petsko also brings up the tragedy of 9/11. Programs studying the cultures and languages of the Middle East suddenly became much more valuable. These examples give more logical weight to Petsko's argument. Another effective appeal to logos is the manner in which Petsko structures his letter. With his reiteration of "if only you had [a certain] department, which now, of course, you don't," Petsko uses repetition to hammer home the idea of how important the liberal arts departments are. The departments teach concepts and ideas that go beyond any single discipline and can be applied to everyday life, even in a persuasive letter to a person in power. 5

However, some of Petsko's logos appeals fail to work for his general audience, particularly for the students in that audience. He acknowledges that the courses offered by the eliminated departments had probably experienced lower numbers of enrolled students, so he recommends a mandatory core curriculum that requires students to take courses in French, Italian, Classics, Russian, or Theater Arts because "young people haven't, for the most part, yet attained the wisdom to have that kind of freedom without making poor decisions." While his solution may be convincing to Philip, Petsko's reason for instituting a 6 mandatory curriculum alienates the students in his audience because he implies he does not have much respect for students' decision-making skills. In addition, Petsko tells Philip that he understands that the budget cuts SUNY Albany faced were "very serious." Petsko addresses this situation by noting that his own university handled financial problems without cutting important departments. However, Petsko's logos appeal is somewhat weakened by the fact that he does not describe specifically what should have been done instead of cutting the departments. Petsko only says that it is possible.

Just as Petsko's appeals to ethos and logos have both effective and 7
problematic moments, so are his appeals to pathos effective at some points but strident and condescending at others. The effective appeals to pathos show up in Petsko's unfavorable comparison of Philip to characters in classic tales. In the second comparison, Philip is likened to a traveler in one of Aesop's fables who deserts his friend in a pinch, leaving him to an angry bear. Obviously, the department cuts are not life-threatening, but the emotional comparison makes people feel that Philip abandoned them in a time of financial stress. In another paragraph, he compares Philip to Faust, who made a deal with the devil. While Goethe, the writer of *Faust*, believed that no man should sell his soul even for the world, Philip has apparently sold the soul of his university for a balanced budget. The idea of giving up one's soul for money makes an effective emotional appeal because it has been addressed in so many fashions, from the Bible to plays to television. Petsko also calls on the public to connect with the *idea* of a university and what it stands for. Universities are meant to cover all subjects, to make "the whole." Without its humanities departments, SUNY Albany is not a real university but merely, in Petsko's derogatory term, a "trade school." The public audience may also be influenced by the language Petsko uses. By creating a condescending tone, he makes the president appear unreliable and unintelligent. The audience may join Petsko in his outrage toward the president of SUNY Albany because of the excess of emotion he uses in his writing. Overall, Petsko's pathos appeals were effective, at least for his public audience.

Although Petsko's emotional appeals are effective in persuading his 8
public audience, they would not persuade Philip. The president may be somewhat swayed by the idea that he "sold the soul" of his university, as he probably wants what is best for his university and students, but more often, Petsko's language would have the opposite effect on Philip. By impugning the man with phrases such as "I guess you don't have much clout at your university," and "administrators like you, and your spineless faculty," and ending with the charming "disrespectfully yours," Petsko uses language that one audience may agree with but will only alienate Philip. When an opponent is unwilling or unable to argue politely his or her case without resorting to name-calling, the case appears weaker. Petsko becomes too emotional when writing his letter,

and he crosses the line from sensible to unreasonable. Petsko appears unwilling to listen to Philip, and thus the president may not feel the need to give the letter any real consideration. Instead of adding more appeals to logos or alternative solutions, things that may have been more convincing for Philip, Petsko chooses to argue merely that Philip is incompetent.

Much of the public, and probably the faculty in the dismantled departments, may have been frustrated by President Philip's choices during a time of financial hardship. Petsko voices this irritation in a letter that calls out Philip and attempts to convince him and the public that the cuts were wrong. In his letter, Petsko gives examples of both the effective use of rhetorical appeals and the ineffective use of such appeals. Using ethos appeals, he manages to establish himself as a man of good standing and intelligence, reciting his credentials and including many allusions to literature. Petsko gives logical reasons for not cutting the departments, reasons that undercut the arguments Philip gave for his decision. However, there are also weaknesses in Petsko's letter that make it less than convincing. Petsko's rhetoric seems surprisingly strident and unprofessional because of his language and the way he attacks Philip's perceived incompetence. Petsko also insults Philip (on purpose) as well as members of the public (unintentionally), which weakens his appeals to logos, ethos, and pathos. Petsko tries to tackle two audiences at once, but he fails to take them both into consideration during each part of his letter. Overall, Petsko's letter has strong ethos appeals—because he has a decent reputation—as well as some logos and pathos appeals that are effective for the general public. Unfortunately, many of his other ethos, logos, and pathos appeals are less persuasive, and too frequently Petsko undercuts his previously effective appeals to both Philip and the general public with his highly emotional and unprofessional language. 9

Questions for Writing and Discussion

1. After reading Gregory Petsko's letter on pages 299–304, review the Techniques for Rhetorical Analysis and Response on page 78 of this chapter. Analyze McGrath's essay based on the tips listed there. Which of these guidelines does McGrath follow? Were there analytical strategies that McGrath did not use? Explain.
2. Review the appeals to logos, ethos, and pathos explained in the Rhetorical Reading Strategies on pages 90–92 of this chapter. Does McGrath's essay

explain how effectively (or ineffectively) Petsko uses each of these appeals in his letter? Where, specifically, do you agree or disagree with McGrath about the effectiveness of Petsko's appeals? Explain.

3. As McGrath explains, Petsko's letter addresses two separate audiences: SUNY President Philip and a general audience consisting of students, educators, and others interested in how colleges and universities are responding to budget cuts. After profiling yourself as a member of the general audience, how do you react to Petsko's argument and his appeals? Provide specific examples to support your response.

Student Writing

Two Responses to Deborah Tannen

Jennifer Koester and Sonja H. Browe

The two essays reprinted here were written in response to an essay by Deborah Tannen, "How Male and Female Students Use Language Differently." Jennifer Koester and Sonja H. Browe have opposite responses to Tannen's essay. Jennifer Koester, a political science major at Colorado State University, argues that Tannen's essay uses sufficient evidence and organizes its content clearly. Sonja Browe, an English education major at the University of Wyoming, criticizes Deborah Tannen's focus and supporting evidence. Be sure to read Tannen's essay, which appears on pages 213–218, before you read the following essays.

A Response to Deborah Tannen's Essay

Jennifer Koester

Deborah Tannen's "How Male and Female Students Use Language Differently" addresses how male and female conversational styles influence classroom discussions. Tannen asserts that women speak less than men in class because often the structure of discussion is more "congenial" to men's style of conversing. 1

Tannen looks at three differences between the sexes that shape classroom interaction: classroom setting, debate format, and contrasting attitudes toward classroom discussion. First, Tannen says that during childhood, men "are expected to seize center stage: by exhibiting their skill, displaying their knowledge, and challenging and resisting challenge." Thus, as adults, men are more comfortable than women when speaking in front of a large group of strangers. On the other hand, women are more comfortable in small groups. 2

Second, men are more comfortable with the debate format. Tannen asserts that many classrooms use the format of putting forth ideas followed by "argument and challenge." This too coincides with men's 3

...continued A Response to Deborah Tannen's Essay, **Jennifer Koester**

conversational experiences. However, Tannen asserts that women tend to "resist discussion they perceive as hostile."

Third, men feel it is their duty to think of things to say and to voice them. On the other hand, women often regulate their participation and hold back to avoid dominating discussion. 4

Tannen concludes that educators can no longer use just one format to facilitate classroom discussion. Tannen sees small groups as necessary for any "non-seminar" class along with discussion of differing styles of participation as solutions to the participation gap between the sexes. 5

Three things work together to make Deborah Tannen's essay "How Male and Female Students Use Language Differently" effective: the qualifications of her argument, the evidence used, and the parallel format of comparison/contrast. 6

First, Tannen's efforts to qualify her argument prevent her from committing logical errors. In the first paragraphs of her essay, she states, "This is not to say that all men talk in class, nor that no women do. It is simply that a greater percentage of discussion time is taken by men's voices." By acknowledging exceptions to her claim, Tannen avoids the mistake of oversimplification. 7

Later, Tannen uses another qualification. She says, "No one's conversational style is absolute; everyone's style changes in response to the context and others' styles." Not only does this qualification avoid a logical fallacy, but it also strengthens Tannen's argument that classroom discussion must have several formats. By acknowledging that patterns of participation can change with the setting, Tannen avoids oversimplifying the issue and adds to her argument for classroom variety. 8

Second, Tannen's evidence places a convincing argument before her reader. In the beginning of her essay, Tannen states that a greater percentage of discussion time in class is taken by men and that those women who attend single-sex schools tend to do better later in life. These two pieces of evidence present the reader with Tannen's jumping-off point. These statistics are what Tannen wants to change. 9

In addition, Tannen effectively uses anecdotal evidence. She presents the reader with stories from her colleagues and her own research. Her anecdotal evidence is persuasive because it appeals to the common sense and personal experiences of the audience. While some might question the lack of hard statistics throughout the essay, the anecdotal evidence serves Tannen best because it reminds her audience of educators of their own experiences and she is able makes them see her logic. 10

Third, the parallel format of comparison/contrast between the genders highlights for the reader Tannen's main points. Each time Tannen mentions the reactions of one gender, she follows with the reaction of the other gender. For example, Tannen states, "So one reason men speak in class more than women is that many of them find the 'public' classroom setting more conducive to speaking, whereas most women are more comfortable speaking in private to a small group of people they know well." Here, Tannen places the tendencies of men and of women together, thus preventing the reader from having to constantly refer back to another section of the essay. 11

In an earlier example, Tannen discusses men's comfort with the debate format in class discussion. The majority of that paragraph relates why men feel comfortable with that format. After explaining this idea, Tannen then tells the reader how women feel about the debate structure. Because how men and women feel about the debate format is placed within a paragraph, the readers easily see the difference between the genders. Tannen's use of the parallel format in the above examples and the rest of the essay provides a clear explanation of the differences in men's and women's interactions in the classroom. 12

Tannen writes her essay effectively. She makes the essay convincing by qualifying her claims about gender participation. This strengthens her argument that just as the classroom is diverse, so should the format be diverse. Her supporting evidence is convincing because it comes from Tannen's own experience, reminds the audience of its own experiences, and appeals to the audience's common sense. Finally, her parallel format for discussing the differences between men and women enhances the reader's understanding. 13

Is Deborah Tannen Convincing?

Sonja H. Browe

In her article "How Male and Female Students Use Language Differently," Deborah Tannen explores the issue of gender as it affects the way we use language to communicate. Specifically, she discusses how differences in the way males and females are socialized to use language affect their classroom interactions. She explains that as females are growing up, they learn to use language to talk to friends, and to tell secrets. She states that for females, it is the "telling of secrets, the fact and the way they talk to each other, that makes them best friends." Boys, on the other hand, are "expected to use language to seize center stage: by exhibiting their skill, displaying their knowledge, and challenging and resisting challenge." 1

According to Tannen, these differences make classroom language use more conducive to the way males were taught to use language. 2

Tannen suggests that speaking in front of groups and the debatelike formats used in many classrooms are more easily handled by male students.

Finally, Tannen describes an experiment she conducted in her own classroom which allowed students to evaluate their own conversation transcripts. From this experience, she deduced that small-group interaction is essential in the classroom because it gives students who don't participate in whole-class settings the opportunity for conversation and interaction. 3

Though Tannen's research is a worthwhile consideration and provides information which could be of great interest to educators, this particular article lacks credibility and is unfocused. The points she is trying to make get lost in a world of unsupported assertions, and she strays from her main focus, leaving the reader hanging and confused. 4

Tannen does take some time at the beginning of her article to establish her authority on linguistic analysis, but we may still hold her accountable for supporting her assertions with evidence. However, Tannen makes sweeping declarations throughout the essay, expecting the reader to simply accept them as fact. For example, when discussing the practice of the teacher playing devil's advocate and debating with the students, she states that "many, if not most women would shrink from such a challenge, experiencing it as public humiliation." Following such an assertion, we expect to see some evidence. Whom did Tannen talk to? What did they say? What percentage of women felt this way? This sort of evidence is completely lacking, so that what Tannen states as fact appears more like conjecture. 5

Tannen makes another such unsupported pronouncement when she discusses the debatelike formats used in many classrooms. She explains that this type of classroom interaction is in opposition to the way that females, in contrast to males, approach learning. She states that "it is not that females don't fight, but that they don't fight for fun. They don't ritualize opposition." Again, where is Tannen's evidence to support such a claim? 6

When Tannen does bother to support her assertions, her evidence is trite and unconvincing. For example, she reviews Walter Ong's work on the pursuit of knowledge, in which he suggested that "ritual opposition … is fundamental to the way males approach almost any activity." Tannen supports this claim of Ong's in parentheses, saying, "Consider, for example, the little boy who shows he likes a little girl by pulling her braids and shoving her." This statement may serve as an example but is not enough to convince the reader that ritual opposition is fundamental to the way males approach "almost any activity." 7

Other evidence which Tannen uses to support her declarations comes in the form of conversations she has had with colleagues on 8 these issues. Again, though these may provide examples, they do not represent a broad enough database to support her claims.

Finally, Tannen takes three pages of her article to describe in detail an experiment she conducted in her classroom. Though the information she collected from this experiment was interesting, it strayed from the main point of the essay. Originally, Tannen's article was directed specifically at gender differences in communication. In this classroom activity, she looked at language-use differences in general, including cultural differences. *9*

Finally, at the close of her essay, where we can expect to get the thrust of her argument or at least some sort of summary statement, Tannen states that her experience in her classroom convinced her that "small-group interaction should be a part of any classroom" and that "having students become observers of their own interaction is a crucial part of their education." Again, these are interesting points, but they stray quite a bit from the original intention of the article. *10*

In this article, Tannen discusses important issues. However, her article loses a great deal of its impact because she does not stay focused on her original thesis and fails to support her ideas with convincing evidence. *11*

Questions for Writing and Discussion

1. Do your own double-entry log for Tannen's essay (pages 213–218). On the left-hand side, record Tannen's main points. On the right-hand side, write your own questions and reactions. Compare your notes to Koester's and Browe's responses. Whose response most closely matches your own? Where or how does your response differ from each?

2. Review the critical reading strategies at the beginning of this chapter (pages 79–81). Identify specific places in both Koester's and Browe's essays where they analyze elements of the rhetorical situation—such as purpose, audience, or context. Where do they analyze the effectiveness of the organization, use of evidence, or the style? Based on your analyses of both essays, which writer does a better job of critically reading Tannen's essay? Explain your choice.

3. Koester focuses on three writing strategies that Tannen uses to make her essay more effective. What are they? What weaknesses of Tannen's essay does Koester ignore or downplay?

4. Browe's response focuses on two criticisms of Tannen's essay. What are they? In which paragraphs does Browe develop each criticism? What strengths of Tannen's essay does Browe ignore or downplay?

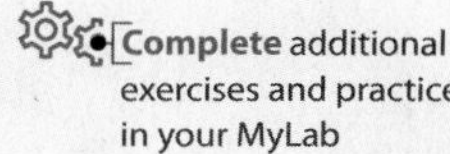

Complete additional exercises and practice in your MyLab

After being pepper sprayed at close range by UC Davis campus police officer John Pike, two protesters were taken to the hospital and 10 people were arrested. Shown here in artist John Trumbell's painting, "Declaration of Independence," Pike is blasting the document with pepper spray.

Jockohomo.com

5

Analyzing and Designing Visuals

What You Will Learn

In this chapter, you will learn to:

5.1 Use techniques for analyzing visuals

5.2 Use techniques for designing visuals

5.3 Use collecting strategies to develop an analysis of a visual

5.4 Shape your visual analysis essay

DURING the Occupy movement protests at UC Davis in November 2011, campus police officer John Pike pepper-sprayed student protesters at close range. Images of Pike's action immediately went viral on the Internet. In the chapter opening image, based on John Trumbell's painting *Declaration of Independence,* Pike is shown pepper-spraying the historical document. Nathan Brown's "Open Letter to Chancellor Linda P. B. Katehi" and a Journal exercise in this chapter deal with the event and the visual.

Communication in the 21st century is, increasingly, multimedia communication. Written texts are interwoven with pictures, photographs, works of art, charts, diagrams, and other graphics. In addition, web sites and electronic communication contain sound and video, with music, podcasts, and video clips often only a mouse click away.

Even though our digital-age technology is new, our means for analyzing and designing visuals remains traditional. In every case, we analyze and design by asking basic rhetorical questions. What is the purpose of this image or bit of media? Who is the intended audience? In what social, political, or cultural context does this visual appear? Who is the author or group of authors? What appeals to logic, emotion, or character does this text make?

The chapter begins by providing the rhetorical questions you need to analyze visuals and hybrid texts. After you understand how to analyze visuals, you can practice composing and designing hybrid texts of your own. This chapter focuses primarily on visuals as one key element of a multimedia text, and the rhetorical principles will help you analyze other kinds of media as well. The diagram on the next page shows the key elements for analyzing visuals, their contexts, and their meanings.

Initially the chapter focuses on you as reader, viewer, or member of the audience. You will examine the visual and its relationship to any accompanying text.

"Graphic design creates visual logic and seeks an optimal balance between visual sensation and graphic information. Without the visual impact of shape, color, and contrast, pages are graphically boring and will not motivate the viewer."

—Patrick Lynch and Sarah Horton, *Web Style Guide*

"Now we make our networks, and our networks make us."

—William Mitchell, *City of Bits*

Then you will consider how the visual and the text interact with the cultural, political, or social context in which the image appears. The context is both immediate (the magazine, newspaper, essay, Web site, or blog in which the image appears) and more general (the cultural context of the image, the written or spoken conversation that is occurring about this image). Finally, throughout the process of analyzing, you will estimate the rhetorical effect: What is the purpose and audience for this image and its text? What appeals to logic and reason, to emotion and feelings, to reliability and character is the writer making? How effective are those appeals?

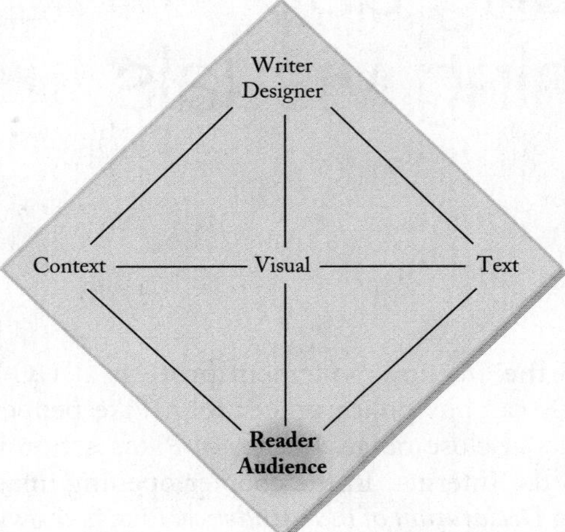

Key elements for analyzing the effects of visuals on audience

After you practice analyzing the rhetorical effect of visuals, you will be better prepared to switch roles from reader or audience to writer or designer of visuals for your own documents. In the second half of this chapter, you will practice several visual or design choices. You will analyze which visuals help support your purpose for your specific audience and how effectively the visuals add to your audience appeals.

Techniques for Analyzing Visuals

5.1
Use techniques for analyzing visuals

Watch the Animation on Reading Visuals Critically

As you analyze images and visuals—as well as any accompanying text or surrounding context—always consider the rhetorical situation, the purpose of the visual, and the intended audience for the visual or hybrid text. The techniques explained here help you **analyze**—that is, look at each part of the visual separately—but the ultimate goal is to **synthesize**, to put the pieces together in an explanation that shows how the parts work together (or do not work together) to achieve a rhetorical purpose for an intended audience. Your conclusion about the visual's significance or meaning becomes your **claim**.

Techniques for Analyzing Visuals

Technique	Tips on How to Do It
Analyzing the composition of the visual itself	Describe the *layout, balance, color, key figures, symbols,* and *cultural references*. Based on your analysis, what is the purpose and who is the audience?
Analyzing the visual with an accompanying text	Does the *accompanying text* or *caption* complement the meaning of the visual? What do the words in the text help you notice in the visual? (What do the words distract you from noticing?) How do the words and the visual work to achieve the same purpose for the intended audience?
Analyzing the visual and the text in context	In what magazine, essay, newspaper, or Web site does the visual appear? What does this publication site tell you about the purpose and audience? How does the larger social, political, or cultural *context* contribute to the overall meaning?
Analyzing the genre of the visual	Visual genres include *advertisements, photographs, art, posters, brochures,* and *charts*. Compare this visual with similar ones. What features do they share? How is your example different? How do these similarities and differences affect the overall meaning and purpose of the visual?
Analyzing the rhetorical appeal of the visual	What *appeals to reason, to emotion,* or *to credibility* does the visual make? Are there multiple appeals? How effective are these appeals in achieving the writer's purpose for the intended audience?
Synthesizing your analyses into an overall claim about the effectiveness of the visual	Your goal is to combine or *synthesize* your analyses of strengths and weaknesses (above) into a claim about the visual's *overall rhetorical effectiveness*. How will the visual's specific strengths affect its intended audience? How will its weaknesses detract from its effectiveness?

ANALYZING STAND-ALONE VISUALS

When we analyze stand-alone visuals and images, we need to pay particular attention to the details of composition, focus, narrative, and genre. We rely primarily on this analysis to reach conclusions about the purpose, intended audience, and effectiveness of the visual. These conclusions will become your claim or thesis for your analysis. Use the following sets of questions to guide your analysis. Depending on the particular image, some questions will be more important than others.

Composition

- Who or what is pictured in the main figure?
- How are key images arranged or organized on the page?
- What is the relationship between the main figure and the background?
- What is excluded from the main figure or background?
- When and where was the image or photograph made?
- What use of color, contrasts of light and shade, or repeated figures are present?
- How do these composition details come together to create a purpose or message for the intended audience?

Focal Point

- What point or image first draws your attention?
- Is this focal point centered or offset?
- Do background figures or diagonal lines draw your attention to or away from the focal point?
- How does the focus (or lack of focus) contribute to the purpose or message of the image?

Narrative

- What story or narrative does the image or visual suggest?
- Do certain objects or figures act as symbols or metaphors?
- How do these story elements support (or not support) the purpose or message for the intended audience?

Themes

- Who has the power in this visual? Who does not? Who is included or excluded?
- What sexist, racist, or body image stereotypes exist? Are these stereotypes promoted and reproduced or are they resisted or challenged? Explain.
- What is this image trying to sell? Does the image make a commodity out of social or cultural values, including holidays (Christmas or Independence Day), ideals (patriotism, charity, or religion), or personal values (integrity or status)?

Now practice applying these questions to two photographs on the following page taken by Dorothea Lange, one of America's most famous documentary photographers of migrant workers and sharecroppers. Lange took these images during the Great Depression of the 1930s, near Berkeley, California.

In the first picture, the composition focuses on several main figures—two women and three children. The makeshift tarp helps to frame these figures, and

the diagonal lines from the chair and the woman on the left bring the viewer's focus to the children standing in the center and then to the mother on the right. The background helps establish the rural, agricultural setting.

In contrast, the second picture has much a much stronger **composition**. The main figure is the woman, with her two children, looking away from the camera, leaving the **focal point** on the mother. The picture is in black and white, which helps focus the viewer's attention on the figures of the mother and the children. Even the angle of the mother's arm, and her chin in her hand, lead the eye to the woman's face. Her expression is determined, but without much hope. All of these compositional features support the purpose and message of the photograph: A migrant mother is caring for her family, as best as she can, in the most primitive of environments.

As viewers, we can construct our own **narrative** based on the information in the picture. This woman is caring for her children in a migrant worker environment. She has no apparent support. This shelter appears to be where she is living. She may have other family members working in the area, but we can only guess at their whereabouts.

Our own conjectural narrative is not very different from the description that Dorothea Lange herself gives of the day when she took these photographs:

> "I saw and approached the hungry and desperate mother, as if drawn by a magnet. I do not remember how I explained my presence or my camera to her, but I do remember she asked me no questions. I made five exposures, working closer and closer from the same direction. I did not ask her name or her history. She told me her age, that she was thirty-two. She said that they had been living on frozen vegetables from the surrounding fields, and birds that the children killed. She had just sold the tires from her car to buy food. There she sat in that lean-to tent with her children huddled around her, and seemed to know that my pictures might help her, and so she helped me. There was a sort of equality about it." (*Popular Photography,* February 1960)

We can put all these analytical pieces together to understand better the purpose and meaning of this photograph. For its **theme**, the photograph brings something hidden (the human story of poverty and exploitation) out into the open and gives it dignity. Lange's purpose was to call attention to the predicament of migrant workers in order to gather support for governmental reform. Her purpose was thus persuasive: she hoped to change public awareness as a first step to improving governmental assistance programs.

ANALYZING VISUALS WITH TEXT

> **"There can be no words without images."**
> —**Aristotle,** Author of *Rhetoric*

Analyzing visuals with accompanying words or text requires that you consider how the composition of the image and the written text function together. Text serves to call attention to and support the message of the visual. Often, words serve as a focusing device, calling our attention to key features, guiding us to "read" the visual in a certain way. (Of course, a text that encourages us to see one meaning in the visual may keep us from seeing other meanings or messages in that visual.) Ideally, image and text should each contribute something unique so that the combined effect is more powerful, appealing, or persuasive than either the text or the image taken separately.

In the recruiting poster for the American Red Cross, the text is spare, simple, and direct: "Join." Notice how the composition of the picture supports this appeal. The foreground figure contrasts clearly with the less distinct background, a representation of a flood-ravaged town. And the figures in the background—a rundown house and a Red Cross nurse who is caring for children—seem to hover in the middle distance, perhaps connected, perhaps not, to the flooded town. The nurse in the foreground extends her hand to the viewer, inviting her or him to join. Thematically, women rather than men are featured in the foreground and background in this stereotypical service role. The patriotic red, white, and blue colors of the nurse's blouse and cape are repeated as a motif in the red of the cross, the blue of the word *join*, and the white of the immediate foreground. The focus on the foreground figure, the color, the center focal point, and the balance of the background figures on the right and left function with the text and the implied narrative (Join the Red Cross and serve your country!) to achieve this visual's persuasive purpose.

In the next image with accompanying text, photographer Jim Goldberg effectively illustrates how visual and text should combine to create a more powerful message than either word or image alone. The photograph, taken in San Francisco in 1982, shows the lady of the house, Mrs. Stone, standing in her modern kitchen with her servant, Vickie Figueroa, standing in the background. The diagonal lines of the white counter and window to the right lead us first to the figure of Mrs. Stone, and then to Ms. Figueroa. This foreground/background juxtaposition sets up a power relationship, confirmed by Mrs. Stone's hands grasping (and owning) the counter while Ms. Figueroa's hands are tucked behind her. The contrast between the pointed and poignant writing and the rather conventional kitchen scene gives the visual a special, combined power. The language in Ms. Figueroa's note supports the power relationship

"My eyes make pictures when they are shut."

—Samuel Taylor Coleridge,
Author of *The Rime of the Ancient Mariner*

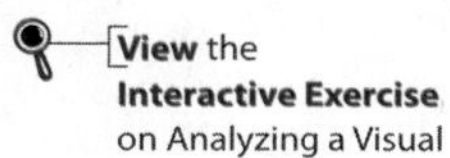
View the **Interactive Exercise** on Analyzing a Visual

My dream Was to became a skool teacher.
Mrs Stone is rich.
I have talents but not opportunity.
I am used to standing behind
mrs Stone.
I have been a servant for 40 years.
Vickie Figueroa.

Jim Goldberg, USA, San Francisco, 1982

of the image: "I am used to standing behind Mrs. Stone." Finally, Goldberg's choice to present the text in what is apparently Ms. Figueroa's own handwriting, complete with crossed out letters, uneven lines, and signature, gives her lost dream of becoming a school teacher remarkable power. If Goldberg had put her note in typeface, much of the authenticity and power of the visual would be lost.

ANALYZING VISUALS IN CONTEXT

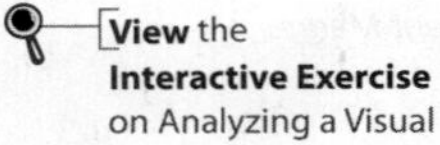
View the
Interactive Exercise
on Analyzing a Visual

A visual often captures a key moment, but the accompanying text and context help viewers understand the wider implications behind the image. The following text and image, which came out of the Occupy movement at the University of California at Davis, illustrate how a visual can graphically illustrate a point in the text, while the text itself complements the image by explaining the wider implications of the moment. In the image, notice how the composition, the color of the pepper spray, the strong diagonal of the officer's arm, the crouching students, and the photographers in the background capture the drama of the moment. The accompanying text is an excerpt from an open letter to the Chancellor of UC Davis written by Nathan Brown, an English department faculty member.

Professional Writing

Open Letter to Chancellor Linda P. B. Katehi

Nathan Brown

I am a junior faculty member at UC Davis. I am an Assistant Professor in the Department of English, and I teach in the Program in Critical Theory and in Science & Technology Studies. I have a strong record of research, teaching, and service. I am currently a Board Member of the Davis Faculty Association. I have also taken an active role in supporting the student movement to defend public education on our camapus and throughout the UC system. In a word: I am the sort of young faculty member, like many of my colleagues, this campus needs. I am an asset to the University of California at Davis.

You are not.

I write to you and to my colleagues for three reasons:

1. to express my outrage at the police brutality which occurred against students engaged in peaceful protest on the UC Davis campus today

2. to hold you accountable for this police brutality
3. to demand your immediate resignation

Today you ordered police onto our campus to clear student protesters from the quad. These were protesters who participated in a rally speaking out against tuition increases and police brutality on UC campuses on Tuesday—a rally that I organized, and which was endorsed by the Davis Faculty Association. These students attended that rally in response to a call for solidarity from students and faculty who were bludgeoned with batons, hospitalized, and arrested at UC Berkeley last week. In the highest tradition of non-violent civil disobedience, those protesters had linked arms and held their ground in defense of tents they set up beside Sproul Hall. In a gesture of solidarity with those students and faculty, and in solidarity with the national Occupy movement, students at UC Davis set up tents on the main quad. When you ordered police outfitted with riot helmets, brandishing batons and teargas guns to remove their tents today, those students sat down on the ground in a circle and linked arms to protect them.

What happened next?

Without any provocation whatsoever, other than the bodies of these students sitting where they were on the ground, with their arms linked, police pepper-sprayed students. Students remained on the ground, now writhing in pain, with their arms linked.

...continued Open Letter to Chancellor Linda..., **Nathan Brown**

What happened next?

Police used batons to try to push the students apart. Those they could separate, they arrested, kneeling on their bodies and pushing their heads into the ground. Those they could not separate, they pepper-sprayed directly in the face, holding these students as they did so. When students covered their eyes with their clothing, police forced open their mouths and pepper-sprayed down their throats. Several of these students were hospitalized. Others are seriously injured. One of them, forty-five minutes after being pepper-sprayed down his throat, was still coughing up blood.

This is what happened. You are responsible for it.

You are responsible for it because this is what happens when UC Chancellors order police onto our campuses to disperse peaceful protesters through the use of force: students get hurt. Faculty get hurt. One of the most inspiring things (inspiring for those of us who care about students who assert their rights to free speech and peaceful assembly) about the demonstration in Berkeley on November 9 is that UC Berkeley faculty stood together with students, their arms linked together. Associate Professor of English Celeste Langan was grabbed by her hair, thrown on the ground, and arrested. Associate Professor Geoffrey O'Brien was injured by baton blows. Professor Robert Hass, former Poet Laureate of the United States, National Book Award and Pulitzer Prize winner, was also struck with a baton. These faculty stood together with students in solidarity, and they too were beaten and arrested by the police. In writing this letter, I stand together with those faculty and with the students they supported.

One week after this happened at UC Berkeley, you ordered police to clear tents from the quad at UC Davis. When students responded in the same way—linking arms and holding their ground—police also responded in the same way: with violent force. The fact is: the administration of UC campuses systematically uses police brutality to terrorize students and faculty, to crush political dissent on our campuses, and to suppress free speech and peaceful assembly. Many people know this. Many more people are learning it very quickly.

You are responsible for the police violence directed against students on the UC Davis quad on November 18, 2011. As I said, I am writing to hold you responsible and to demand your immediate resignation on these grounds.

The next example contains two visuals and their accompanying texts that have been widely circulated on the blogosphere and Facebook. The pictures are of two men, sentenced for crimes of fraud and robbery, with short accompanying texts explaining their similar yet different circumstances. The police mug shots of Roy Brown, a homeless black man, contrast sharply with our mental image of CEO Paul R. Allen in his business attire. The blogger(s)

Ex-Mortgage CEO Sentenced to Prison for $3B Fraud

By THE ASSOCIATED PRESS
Published: June 21, 2011 at 7:04 PM ET

ALEXANDRIA, Va. (AP) — The CEO of what had been one of the nation's largest privately held mortgage lenders was sentenced Tuesday to more than three years in prison for his role in a $3 billion scheme that officials called one of the biggest corporate frauds in U.S. history.

The 40-month sentence for Paul R. Allen, 55, of Oakton, Va., is slightly less than the six-year term sought by federal prosecutors.

Homeless man gets 15 years for stealing $100

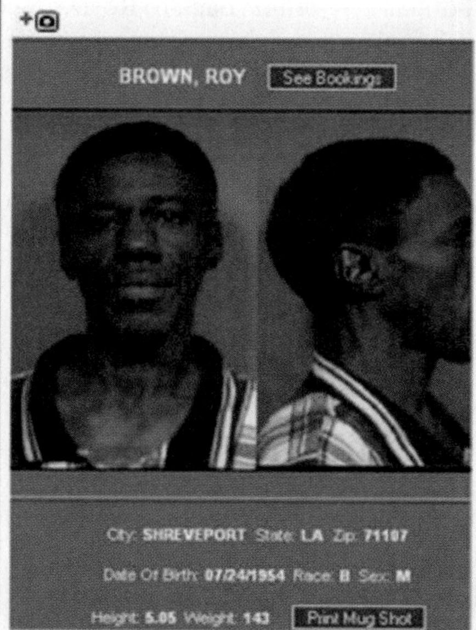

A homeless man robbed a Louisiana bank and took a $100 bill. After feeling remorseful, he surrendered to police the next day. The judge sentenced him to 15 years in prison.

Roy Brown, 54, robbed the Capital One bank in Shreveport, Louisiana in December 2007. He approached the teller with one of his hands under his jacket and told her that it was a robbery.

The teller handed Brown three stacks of bill but he only took a single $100 bill and returned the remaining money back to her. He said that he was homeless and hungry and left the bank.

The next day he surrendered to the police voluntarily and told them that his mother didn't raise him that way.

Brown told the police he needed the money to stay at the detox center and had no other place to stay and was hungry.

In Caddo District Court, he pleaded guilty. The judge sentenced him to 15 years in prison for first degree robbery.

who paired these stories highlighted the significant differences in yellow (another visual strategy) in order to convey a message about injustice in contemporary America. What point is being made about the contrast between these two situations? (Can you find evidence that these stories are accurate representations of actual news stories rather than a creation of politically motivated bloggers?)

ANALYZING THE GENRE OF THE VISUAL

Visuals, like other texts, are of certain kinds or types that we call *genres*. Common visual genres are advertisements, works of art, photographs, charts, and other kinds of graphics. We can learn more about the purpose, audience, and context by understanding how a visual that we are analyzing is similar to (and different from) other visuals belonging to its genre. The two World War II posters shown here, for example, illustrate a visual genre from the 1940s. The purpose of these posters was to recruit men and women to the war effort. The posters were intended to appeal to women to help with war-related tasks.

The first poster is possibly the most famous example of this genre: Rosie the Riveter. The focus is on Rosie's strong right arm, with her sleeves rolled up, ready for work. The strong diagonal of her arm points back to Rosie's face and to the text at the top of the poster. The purpose of this poster was to encourage women to participate in the war effort, both by direct exhortation ("We Can Do It!") and by offering an image of an attractive, capable, and

Rosie the Riveter

"She's a WOW"

courageous woman. The Rosie the Riveter poster helped revolutionize gender images during the war.

The second poster, "She's a WOW," presents a similarly strong image designed to recruit women for ordnance work. Like Rosie, she is capable, attractive, and ready for work, with her hair wrapped in a red and white bandana. Although she is in the foreground against the background image of the soldier, the text keeps her in a supportive role: "The Girl He Left Behind Is Still Behind Him." She is not looking out at the viewer, as Rosie is, but back at the soldier. Still, her color image, accented in red and white, is larger than the soldier's background picture.

The war poster genre continues in contemporary satiric posters questioning our Homeland Security laws. The "Patriotism Means Silence" poster suggests that patriotism requires that one be silent and refrain from speaking out against these laws or other government policies. It uses a popular and patriotic image to imply that the Homeland Security Office is trying to silence freedom of speech. We understand this message partly from the words and partly from the genre of the patriotic wartime poster.

Patriotism Means Silence

RHETORICAL APPEALS TO THE AUDIENCE

All of the features of visuals analyzed earlier—the composition of the visual, the accompanying text, the context, and the genre—contribute to the overall rhetorical purpose and the effect of a visual on its audience or viewer. Visuals, like written texts, make specific rhetorical appeals to reason and logic (logos), to emotion (pathos), and to character and credibility (ethos).

Appeal to Reason

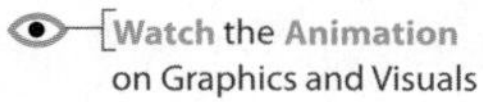

Usually charts, graphs, and diagrams contain appeals to reason, logic, facts, and other kinds of data. The visual diagram on the following page, "Storing the Power of the Wind," which accompanied a newspaper story about alternative sources of energy, illustrates the appeal to reason (*logos*). Using a sequence of logical steps, it explains in text and in image how wind could be used to generate hydrogen to power electric grids as well as automobiles. Its purpose is apparently to inform or explain, but because the information for the graphic is provided by an energy company, its more subtle purpose is to improve public relations by persuading customers that Xcel Energy is doing its part in the search for alternative energies.

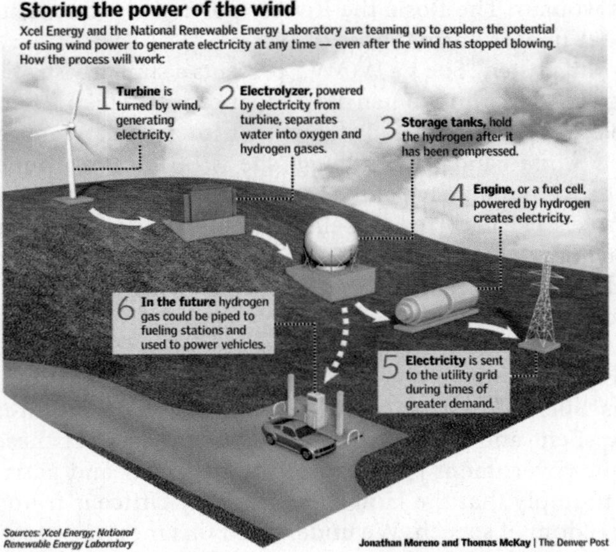

Storing the power of the wind
Xcel Energy and the National Renewable Energy Laboratory are teaming up to explore the potential of using wind power to generate electricity at any time — even after the wind has stopped blowing. How the process will work:
1 Turbine is turned by wind, generating electricity.
2 Electrolyzer, powered by electricity from turbine, separates water into oxygen and hydrogen gases.
3 Storage tanks, hold the hydrogen after it has been compressed.
4 Engine, or a fuel cell, powered by hydrogen creates electricity.
5 Electricity is sent to the utility grid during times of greater demand.
6 In the future hydrogen gas could be piped to fueling stations and used to power vehicles.
Sources: Xcel Energy; National Renewable Energy Laboratory
Jonathan Moreno and Thomas McKay | The Denver Post

Appeal to Emotion

Typically, advertisements use strong appeals to emotion (*pathos*) simply because emotions are so effective in persuading viewers to buy a product. Emotional appeals include positive feelings (beauty, sex, status, image, and sometimes even humor) as well as negative emotions (fear, anxiety, insecurity, and pity). These appeals come from the composition of the image, the text, the context, and even the genre of the visual. Magazines are a good source for advertisements relying primarily on emotional appeals.

Appeal to Character and Credibility

Often visuals use a strong appeal to character and credibility (*ethos*) to convince, move, or persuade viewers. This appeal is not just to the character of any person pictured in the visual, but can also be to the character and credibility of the designer or creator of the image. If viewers sense that the visual conveys a sense of integrity and authenticity, that the maker of the image is sincere and is not relying on cheap emotional appeals, or that the visual communicates a sense of humanity and goodwill, the appeal to character is successful. Look again at Dorothea Lange's images of a migrant mother on page 133. These pictures have an emotional appeal, to be sure, but they are composed with an integrity and credibility that give them a strong character appeal, too. Lange's pictures give the mother and her children dignity at the same time that they call attention to their plight.

Combined Appeals in an Ad

Often visuals and their texts will combine appeals to logic, emotion, and character. Consider the following spoof, posted on Adbusters, of the popular ads for Absolut, a brand of vodka. Emotional appeals emerge from the blood-colored reds and dramatic blacks, the long shadows and spilt liquids, the white chalk outline of the body (the bottle), the police officer taking notes, and the red taillights of the car. The bold caption, "Absolute End" (notice how the spelling has been changed from *Absolut* to *Absolute*), and the statistics cited below the picture appeal to logic, connecting the 100,000 alcohol ads teenagers see with the fact that 50% of automobile fatalities are linked to alcohol. This visual also generates an ethos or character appeal because the creator of the ad is apparently someone we can trust, whose goal is to prevent the needless and tragic fatalities associated with drinking and driving.

As you practice analyzing visuals, remember two important points.

- Although not all analysis strategies will be helpful for every visual or hybrid text, you should experiment with them all until you discover which features are important. Analyze the visual, work through the accompanying text, consider the context and genre, analyze the appeals, and then return to the visual once you know more about the context. Focus on the kinds of analysis that work best for your project.

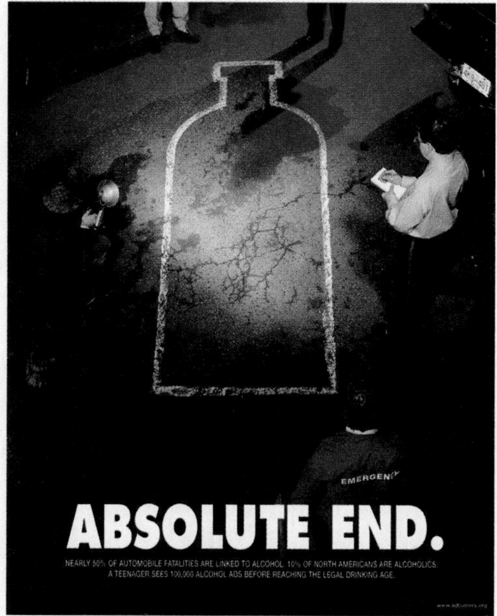

Adbusters

- The ultimate goal of your analysis is a *synthesis*. You examine the parts of a hybrid or multimedia text in order to show how they work together, effectively or ineffectively, to convey a message to an audience. Your explanation of the significance or effectiveness of the visual for its purpose and audience becomes your *claim*.

Techniques for Designing Visuals

5.2
Use techniques for designing visuals

“Effective visual presentation . . . [requires] minimizing the possibility of competition between picture and text and ensuring that the pictures used are relevant to the material presented.”

—**Jennifer Wiley,** “Cognitive and Educational Implications of Visual Rich Media”

When you practiced analyzing visuals, you were the reader or audience in the diagram shown here, judging the visual with its accompanying text, in its context, and considering how the creator of the image worked to achieve a particular purpose for the intended audience.

Now you need to switch roles. Having practiced analyzing a variety of visuals for their overall rhetorical effect, you are better prepared to add or design visuals for your own essay, article, pamphlet, or Web site. As the primary designer or creator, you will also consider the layout of your text as a visual element: typeface, size of font, margins, color, and use of white space all have visual appeal for your readers.

Visuals, illustrations, graphics, photographs, and document design all have a rhetorical effect. Use the following techniques as you consider visuals and text layout possibilities for your document.

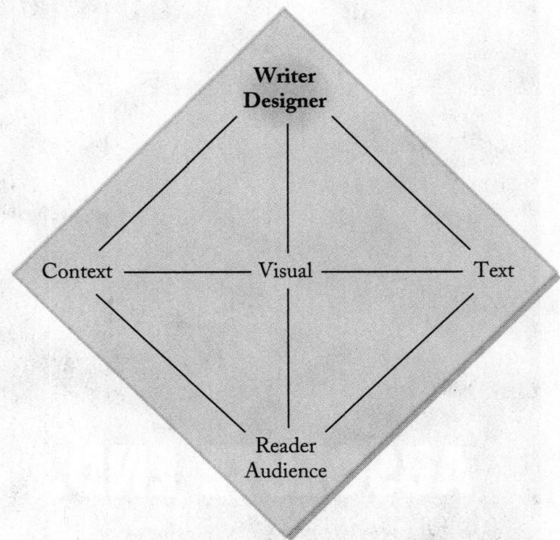

Key elements for understanding visual design

Techniques for Designing Visuals

Technique	Tips on How to Do It	Examples
Designing for your purpose and audience	Your *purpose* and *audience* should guide your selection of an appropriate genre, the most effective visual(s), and a clear document design.	The photograph by Jim Goldberg on page 135 places Vickie Figueroa in the background to support his claim that Vickie's dreams are subordinate to Mrs. Stone's power.
Choosing and understanding your genre	Collect and study *several examples of your genre* (article, brochure, poster, or Web site). Does your genre use many visuals and only a few words? Does it use mostly text with a few visuals? Take notes on the layout typically used, and then choose the best features and creatively modify them for your own purposes.	Examine more posters like "Rosie the Riveter" by searching Google images for World War II posters. Take notes on the common features of the genre.
Selecting or designing visuals for your document	Choose or design visual elements with *strong compositional features*: key figures, strong diagonals, appropriate color, and balance. Make your diagrams, graphs, and charts clear and easy to understand. Choose the most striking illustrations but use them sparingly. Avoid clutter.	In the World War II posters on page 140, notice the strong central figures, bright colors (red, white, blue, yellow), strong diagonals, and large, bold font. Look again at the "Absolute End" visual on page 143 and the American Red Cross image on page 134 for examples of strong compositional features.
Designing your written text to support your purpose	Choose *typeface, font, white space,* and *margins* with an eye to your purpose and audience. Balance chunks of text with visuals on the page. Use bold type and white space to create emphasis.	The World War II posters and the American Red Cross poster are excellent examples of effective use of bold type and white space.

Warming Up: Journal Exercises

The following exercises ask you to analyze and design visuals. Respond to these exercises individually, in groups, or on your class Web site.

1. Examine the photoshopped painting, *Declaration of Independence*, reproduced on the opening page of this chapter. Analyze the visual for composition, focus, narrative, theme, and rhetorical appeals. How does the inserted image of the pepper-spraying officer alter the focus or composition of the painting? Then read Nathan Brown's "Open Letter to Chancellor Linda P. B. Katehi" on pages 136–138. How effectively does the photoshopped image support the main ideas in the letter? Cite sentences from the letter that reinforce the message in this visual.

2. In a visual that contains text or a caption, the image and the words should complement each other, working toward a single meaning. The *New Yorker* regularly sponsors a cartoon caption contest. Drawings are initially published without captions, and readers are invited to contribute their best lines during the following week. Study the cartoon below. By yourself or in a group, suggest possible captions. Once you have a caption or two, explain why your entry complements the drawing. (Beside the cartoon are the three finalist suggestions, printed upside down. Don't read them until you've made your own suggestions.)

3. Study the two famous photographs on the next page. Choose one and write your own analysis. First, analyze the image. Then write a narrative of what you imagine happened before, during, and after the moment recorded in this image. Finally, *research* these two photographs and their

"Well, then, it's unanimous." Anne Whiteside, San Francisco, Calif. (The winning caption.)

"So that settles it. This year, instead of cooking the books, we'll bake them in a light, flaky pastry." Michael Hirson, Washington, D.C.

"Who else found Gary's report a little too angry, white, and male?" Grant Ruple, Morristown, N.J.

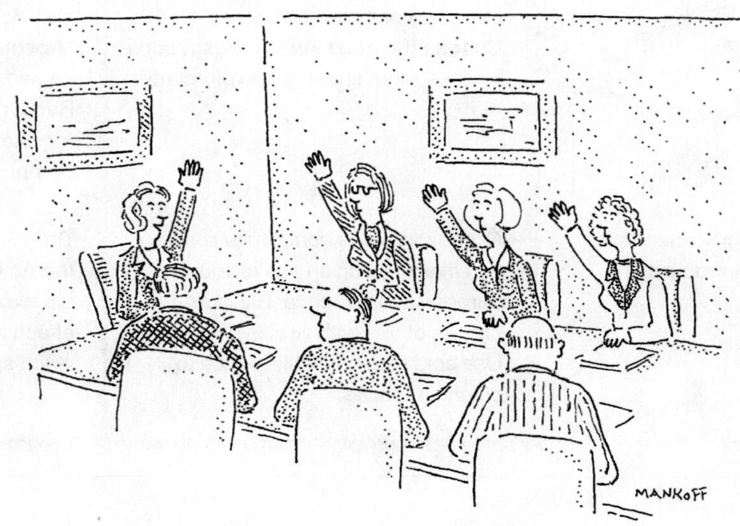

World War II Kiss

Gordon Parks, *American Gothic*

photographers on the Internet and add a final paragraph explaining how the information you discovered confirms or revises your analysis and your narrative.

4. Find three advertisements for the same product (or same kind of product, such as cars, jeans, or perfume) in different magazines directed at different audiences. For example, you might find similar ads in *Time, Wired*, and *Seventeen*. Analyze each ad for its compositional features, and then describe how the ad changes in its composition, focus, narrative, theme, or appeals based on different target audiences. Which of these ads is most effective for its target audience? Why?

5. Choose an essay that you have already written for this course or for a previous writing course. Revise and format it on your computer for a more public audience, choosing the genre of a short newspaper article, brochure, flyer, or poster. Practice using the layout features (sidebars, inserted visuals, double columns, pulled quotations, drop caps, tables, and color) appropriate for that genre. As a postscript for your revision, explain why you made the choices you did during your revision.

6. Choose an advertisement in a magazine and analyze how it works in the context of that particular magazine. First, research the magazine to profile its readers (typical income, class, occupations, or interests). Then examine several advertisements from this magazine to see which ads make the most effective appeals to this group of readers. Choose one particular ad and annotate it for appeals to audience as well as use of key images,

Analysis of Rosetta Stone ad by Sarah Kay Hurst

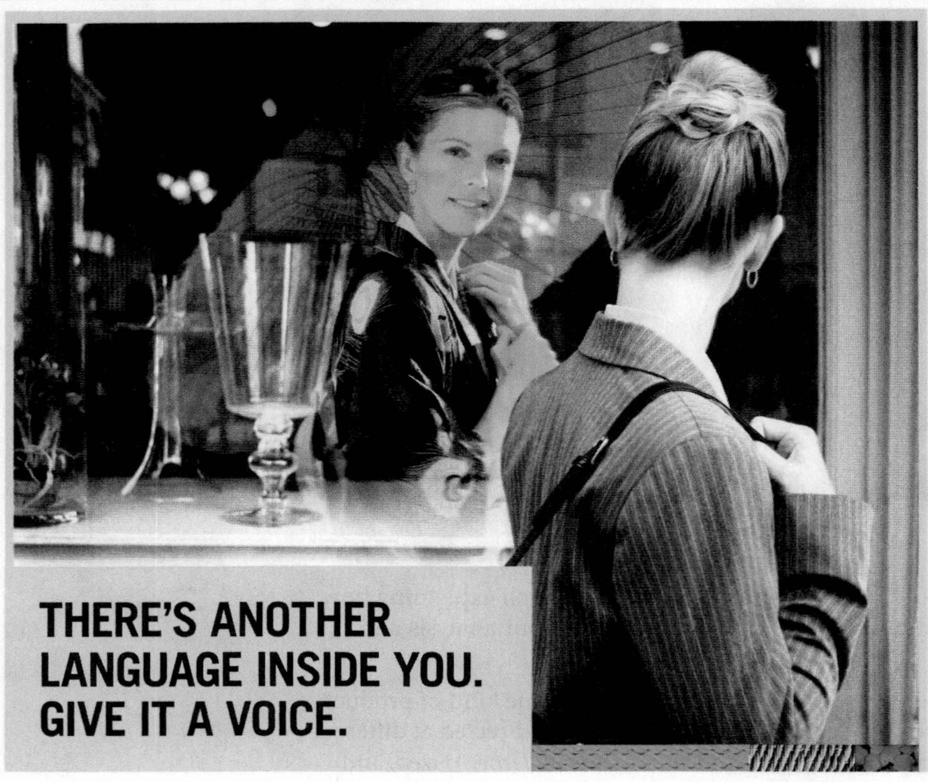
THERE'S ANOTHER
LANGUAGE INSIDE YOU.
GIVE IT A VOICE.

Do you want to communicate a new voice to the world, to express another side of you? With Rosetta Stone® you can. In any language.

- We teach language naturally, pairing words spoken by native speakers with vivid, real-life imagery in context, activating your mind's inherent ability to learn a language.
- Speech recognition coaches you to the right pronunciation, so you'll be speaking quickly and correctly. In no time at all, you'll find that the new language you tried on is a perfect fit.

Rosetta Stone. The fastest way to learn a language. Guaranteed.

Over 30 languages available.

SAVE 10%

Level 1	$233
Level 1&2	$377
Level 1,2&3	$494

100% six-month money-back guarantee.

PICK UP A NEW LANGUAGE TODAY!
(866) 833-8301 RosettaStone.com/sas029a
Use promo code sas029a when ordering. Offer expires June 30, 2009.

RosettaStone®

The woman in this advertisement appears to be a successful and affluent professional based upon her attire. Many of the members of the audience for this publication are likely to be part of this elite class, since 82% of readers have a college degree. There is also an intellectual appeal in the picture: this woman is seeking to broaden her horizons even though she is already successful. Since 51% of readers for *Scientific American Mind* are women, a large number of audience members may be able to identify with her or aspire to her status and success.

The Rosetta Stone program is relatively expensive and must therefore seek to target an affluent audience. *Scientific American Mind* is a good publication to appeal to this audience because the average household income is $119,000, and average household net worth is $827,000.

The bright yellow of the Rosetta Stone logo also frames the picture and serves as a backdrop for the saying "There's another language inside you. Give it a voice." This effectively unifies the elements of the advertisement. The bright yellow is an active appeal to initiative, which is likely to draw the attention of this magazine's audience. *Scientific American Mind's* web site says in its mission statement that it is "aimed at inquisitive adults who are passionate about knowing more about how the mind works." These same individuals who want to know more about the mind are likely to be interested in learning about other cultures and languages.

color, graphics, balance, layout, diagonals, and accompanying text. Use the analysis of a Rosetta Stone advertisement in *Scientific American Mind* by student writer Sarah Kay Hurst on the previous page an example.

Processes for Analyzing and Designing Visuals

Assignment for Analyzing Visuals

Choose an audience and genre and analyze the effectiveness of a visual by itself or a visual with accompanying text and/or social context. For example, you might analyze an advertising campaign, a political document with photographs, a prize-winning or historical photograph, fine art, an Internet visual, or another text that uses images and visuals.

Your purpose for this assignment is to analyze the visual for its composition, focus, narrative, themes, and/or rhetorical appeals in order to show how—and how effectively—it works with any accompanying text in its social context for the intended purpose and audience.

Audience	Possible Genres for Analyzing Visuals
Personal Audience	Class notes, journal entry, blog, scrapbook, social networking page.
Academic Audience	Academic analysis, media critique, review, journal entry, forum entry on class site, multigenre document.
Public Audience	Column, editorial, article, or critique in a magazine, newspaper, online site, newsletter, or multigenre document.

Assignment for Designing Visuals

Choose a piece of writing that you are currently working on or have already written for this class or another class. Your assignment is to add visual elements (pictures, art, charts, graphic material) to your writing that will support the message for your particular audience. Start by explaining the audience, purpose, genre, and context for this particular piece of writing. Then look for opportunities to provide visual elements that will help achieve your purpose for your audience. Select or design the visuals you will be using and insert them into your document. When you finish this assignment, write a postscript explaining the process you went through of selecting, designing, and integrating the material into your piece of writing. Illustrate your choices by referring to graphs or visuals that you decided **not** to use because they were not effective or appropriate for your audience or purpose.

Audience	Possible Visual Genres
Personal Audience	Photographs, art, digitized scrapbook images, collage, video, comics.
Academic Audience	Graphs, charts, diagrams, flow charts, organizational diagrams, photographs, digital images, art, video.
Public Audience	Graphs, charts, diagrams, flow charts, organizational diagrams, photographs, digital images, art, comics, graphic novel, video.

CHOOSING A SUBJECT

Unless you have a particular assignment, choose a contemporary image that you find incorporated in your reading for your other classes, reading and research that you do for your job, news items, Internet sites, billboards, or any other place where visuals appear in a clear rhetorical context. Video clips from the Internet can work if they are short and if you are submitting your document online or in a digital environment. You may wish to choose a visual and compare it to other examples from that genre. You may wish to consider several similar images used for different gender, racial, or cultural contexts. Your assignment may even be to analyze a variety of possible visuals you could choose for an essay you are writing and to show why the ones you select are best suited to your purpose, audience, and genre. *Remember that when you download images from the Internet, you must give credit to the photographer, artist, or designer of the visual.*

COLLECTING

5.3
Use collecting strategies to develop an analysis of a visual

Many images are available on the Internet through Google or Yahoo! searches, or on popular image sites such as Corbis. Once you locate several appropriate visuals, begin by analyzing and taking notes on them, looking for key parts of the composition, focus, narrative, themes, and rhetorical appeals. You should also collect and analyze any accompanying text or evidence that illustrates the social or historical context. Collecting visuals belonging to the same genre (historical photographs, advertising campaigns, political photographs, or Internet images) will also provide evidence helpful for your analysis. Researching the background, context, origin, or maker/designer of the image can be important, as is finding other commentaries and analyses of your particular type or genre of visuals. Use your *critical reading skills* to understand key points in these commentaries. Be sure to use your *observing* skills to help your analysis. Try closing your eyes and drawing the visual for yourself—what details did you remember and reproduce and what details did you forget? If you have any particular *memories* of this image or of the first time you saw this visual, you may want to add them to your account.

SHAPING

How you organize your analysis depends on the assignment, purpose, audience, and genre for your analysis. Two effective strategies for organizing are explained and illustrated here.

5.4
Shape your visual analysis essay

Analysis Focused on the Visual

Often the details of the visual are the primary focus of the analysis. This may be the case with complex images whose meaning or significance may not be immediately obvious. The analysis focuses on composition, arrangement, foreground and background images, images in the center and on the margin, symbols, cultural references, and key features of the genre. Only after analyzing these details will the commentary explain how these details are related to the cultural or historical context and thus contribute to the overall meaning.

The following analysis, by Charles Rosen and Henri Zerner, is of a painting by Norman Rockwell. The authors devote over half of their essay to an analysis of the picture before they interpret the significance of Rockwell's self-portrait. Before you read Rosen's and Zerner's analysis, however, study the painting. What are the important details in the picture? What is its overall meaning or significance, based on your analysis?

Professional Writing

Triple Self-Portrait

Charles Rosen and Henri Zerner

Triple Self-Portrait of 1960 is clever and witty. It is not simply a portrait of the artist by himself but represents the process of painting a self-portrait, and in the bargain Rockwell takes the opportunity to comment on his brand of "realism" and his relation to the history of art. A sheet of preparatory drawings in different poses is tacked onto the left of the canvas. The artist represents himself from the back; the canvas he works on already has a fully worked-out black-and-white drawing of his face with the pipe in his mouth, based on the central drawing of the sketch sheet. The artist gazes at his own reflection in a mirror propped up on a chair. The reflection we see in the mirror is similar to, but not identical with, the portrait sketched on the canvas. The artist wears glasses, and the glare of the lenses completely obliterates his gaze, while the portrait he works on is without glasses and a little younger-looking, certainly less tense than the reflection. Rockwell seems to confess that the reality of his depicted world, compelling as it may be, is in fact a make-believe. 1

Claim: The portrait is a clever and witty comment on the artist's own art.

Layout and composition of portrait

Description of details

...continued Triple Self-Portrait, **Charles Rosen and Henri Zerner**

More description of details

Tacked on the upper right corner of the canvas is a series of reproductions of historical self-portraits: Dürer, Rembrandt, Van Gogh, and Picasso—grand company to measure oneself against, although the humorous tone of the image preserves it from megalomania. But there is a problem: "If Rockwell nodded humbly in Picasso's direction," as Robert Rosenblum suggests, how humbly was it? It is "most surprising," Rosenblum observes, that Rockwell chose "a particularly difficult Picasso that mixes in idealized self-portrait in profile with an id-like female monster attacking from within" rather than something easily recognizable. This was a cover for *The Saturday Evening Post*. The strength of Rockwell is that he knew his public, and knew that such subtleties would be entirely lost on its readers, that most of them would not recognize the Picasso as a self-portrait at all but would consider it as pretentious humbug compared to Rockwell's honest picture and those of the illustrious predecessors he claims. Nor does he seem to have been particularly anxious to change their minds, whatever he himself may have thought. 2

Interpreting the meaning and significance of the painting

Analysis Focused on the Social or Historical Context

In this organizational pattern, the photograph or other visual receives some analysis and commentary, but most of the analysis examines the history of the photograph and the personal story of the key figures in the visual. The following example,

"Coming Home," by Carolyn Kleiner Butler, was published in *Smithsonian* in 2003, at a time when many families in the United States had loved ones serving in Iraq or Afghanistan. Butler chooses to analyze a famous Vietnam-era photograph by Sal Veder, *Burst of Joy*. Butler emphasizes how the reality behind the photograph contrasts sharply with the reality in the photograph. In other words, Butler contrasts the happy story the image reveals with the reality that it conceals.

Professional Writing

Coming Home

Carolyn Kleiner Butler

To a war-weary nation, a U.S. POW's return from captivity in Vietnam in 1973 looked like the happiest of reunions.

Sitting in the back seat of a station wagon on the tarmac at Travis Air Force Base, in California, clad in her favorite fuchsia miniskirt, 15-year-old Lorrie Stirm felt that she was in a dream. It was March 17, 1973, and it had been six long years since she had last seen her father, Lt. Col. Robert L. Stirm, an Air Force fighter pilot who was shot down over Hanoi in 1967 and had been missing or imprisoned ever since. She simply couldn't believe they were about to be reunited. The teenager waited while her father stood in front of a jubilant crowd and made a brief speech on behalf of himself and other POW's who had arrived from Vietnam as part of "Operation Homecoming." 1

The context just before the photograph was taken

The minutes crept by like hours, she recalls, and then, all at once, the car door opened. "I just wanted to get to Dad as fast as I could," Lorrie says. She tore down the runway toward him with open arms, her spirits—and feet—flying. Her mother, Loretta, and three younger siblings—Robert Jr., Roger and Cindy—were only steps behind. "We didn't know if he would ever come home," Lorrie says. "That moment was all our prayers answered, all our wishes come true." 2

Lorrie's memories of her feelings when her dad returned

Associated Press photographer Slava "Sal" Veder, who'd been standing in a crowded bullpen with dozens of other journalists, noticed the sprinting family and started taking pictures. "You could feel the energy and the raw emotion in the air," says Veder, then 46, who had spent much of the Vietnam era covering antiwar demonstrations in San Francisco and Berkeley. The day was overcast, meaning no shadows and near-perfect light. He rushed to a makeshift darkroom in a ladies' bathroom on the base (United Press International had commandeered the men's). In less than half an hour, Veder and his AP colleague Walt Zeboski had developed six remarkable images of that singular moment. Veder's pick, which he instantly titled *Burst of Joy*, was sent out over the 3

Shift to the photographer's history

The photographer's recollection of the emotions of that day

...continued Coming Home, **Carolyn Kleiner Butler**

A hero's welcome: Lorrie, Robert Jr., Cindy, Loretta and Roger Stirm greet Lt. Col. Robert Stirm after his six years as a prisoner of war.

news-service wires, published in newspapers around the nation and went on to win a Pulitzer Prize in 1974.

The story from the soldier's or father's point of view

It remains the quintessential homecoming photograph of the time. Stirm, 39, who had endured gunshot wounds, torture, illness, starvation and despair in North Vietnamese prison camps, including the infamous Hanoi Hilton, is pictured in a crisp new uniform. Because his back is to the camera, as Veder points out, the officer seems anonymous, an everyman who represented not only the hundreds of POW's released that spring but all the troops in Vietnam who would return home to the mothers, fathers, wives, daughters and sons they'd left behind. "It's a hero's welcome for guys who weren't always seen or treated as heroes," says Donald Goldstein, a retired Air Force lieutenant colonel and a coauthor of *The Vietnam War: The Stories and The Photographs*, of the Stirm family reunion picture. "After years of fighting a war we couldn't win, a war that tore us apart, it was finally over, and the country could start healing." 4

Events behind the moment of this photograph

But there was more to the story than was captured on film. Three days before Stirm landed at Travis, a chaplain had handed him a Dear John letter from his wife. "I can't help but feel ambivalent about it," 5

Stirm says today of the photograph. "I was very pleased to see my children—I loved them all and still do, and I know they had a difficult time—but there was a lot to deal with." Lorrie says, "So much had happened—there was so much that my dad missed out on—and it took a while to let him back into our lives and accept his authority." Her parents were divorced within a year of his return. Her mother remarried in 1974 and lives in Texas with her husband. Robert retired from the Air Force as a colonel in 1977 and worked as a corporate pilot and businessman. He married and was divorced again. Now 72 and retired, he lives in Foster City, California.

As for the rest of the family, Robert Jr. is a dentist in Walnut Creek, California; he and his wife have four children, the oldest of whom is a marine. Roger, a major in the Air Force, lives outside Seattle. Cindy Pierson, a waitress, resides in Walnut Creek with her husband and has a daughter in college. And Lorrie Stirm Kitching, now 47, is an executive administrator and mother of two sons. She lives in Mountain View, California, with her husband. All four of Robert Stirm Sr.'s children have a copy of *Burst of Joy* hanging in a place of honor on their walls. But he says he can't bring himself to display the picture. 6

How the lives of all the family members have changed

Three decades after the Stirm reunion, the scene, having appeared in countless books, anthologies and exhibitions, remains part of the nation's collective consciousness, often serving as an uplifting postscript to Vietnam. That the moment was considerably more fraught than we first assumed makes it all the more poignant and reminds us that not all war casualties occur on the battlefield. 7

Concluding comments leading up to Butler's thesis: Pictures do not always tell the complete story, and not all casualties occur on the battlefield.

"We have this very nice picture of a very happy moment," Lorrie says, "but every time I look at it, I remember the families that weren't reunited, and the ones that aren't being reunited today—many, many families—and I think, I'm one of the lucky ones." 8

DRAFTING

Before you begin drafting, collect all your notes, your visuals, and your research. Based on your materials, determine what you want the *focus* of your analysis to be—the visual itself, its relationship to an accompanying text or context, its relation to other images in its genre, or the rhetorical appeals that the visual makes. Depending on the assignment, your visuals, and your own purpose, narrow the strategies to the few that are most helpful in understanding the rhetoric of the visual.

If you are designing your own document, write out your accompanying text in a draft, and then experiment with the overall placement of text, images, and graphs. Arrange/rearrange the chunks of your text and visuals on a blank page until you find a combination of text, image, and use of white space that has the best effect for your purpose and audience.

Finally, obtain feedback or peer response to help you as you move from drafting to revising.

REVISING

As you revise your visual analysis or visual design project, consider your peer-response feedback. Some of it will be helpful, but some may not help you achieve your purpose. You must decide which changes to make.

Guidelines for Revision

- **Review the purpose and audience for your assignment.** Does your draft analyze the key parts of the visual? If you are designing a document, give a draft to someone who is your intended audience or who might understand the needs of your intended audience. What suggestions does that person have?
- **Reexamine the visual.** What else do you notice about its composition, focus, narrative, or themes?
- **Reconsider relationships between the image and its text and context.** Much of the meaning and impact of the visual depends on the accompanying text and on the social, political, and cultural context. Look again at these possible relationships.
- **Reconsider the genre of your visual or your document.** If you are analyzing a visual, have you collected other examples of visuals in that genre? How are these examples similar to or different from your visual? If you are designing a document, have you checked other documents belonging to this genre? How does yours compare to them? How could you use their ideas to improve your document?
- **Check your visual or your document for its rhetorical appeals.** Make sure your draft comments on or makes use of appropriate rhetorical appeals to logic, to character, and to emotion. Are these appeals effective for the purpose and audience of the visual or the document?
- **Organize your analysis.** Check your draft to make sure the parts of your analysis add up to your overall thesis or claim.
- **Revise and edit sentences to improve clarity, conciseness, and emphasis.** Check your handbook for suspected problems with usage, grammar, and punctuation. Spell check your final version.

PeerResponse

The instructions that follow will help you give and receive constructive advice about the rough draft of your visual analysis or design document. Use these guidelines for an in-class workshop, a take-home review, or an electronic class forum response.

Writer: Before you exchange drafts, write out your responses to the following questions.

1. **Purpose** Briefly describe the purpose and intended audience of your essay or document. What is the main point you are trying to communicate?
2. **Revision Plans** Point out one part of your essay that is successful at achieving your purpose. Describe the parts of your essay that do not seem to be working or are not yet completed.
3. **Questions** Write out one or two specific questions that you still have about your visual analysis or your design. Where exactly would you like help on this project?

Reader: First, read the entire draft or document from start to finish without making any comments. Then reread the draft, and answer the following questions.

1. **Techniques for analyzing visuals** Where in the draft do you see the writer using the techniques for analyzing visuals discussed in this chapter? Which techniques should be more developed to help achieve the writer's purpose? Explain.
2. **Context** Where do you see the writer analyzing or using the social, political, or cultural context of the visuals? What other aspects of context might the writer consider?
3. **Responses to visuals** Write out your response to these visuals. What key elements of these visuals do you see that the writer does not comment on? Where would you disagree with the writer's analysis? Explain.
4. **Response to design** Analyze the writer's document design. Is it too busy, cluttered, or crowded? Does the document need more text and fewer visuals? Does it need to cut text and increase white space? What might the audience for this document say about its attractiveness, simplicity of message, or overall effectiveness?
5. **Response to the assignment** The visual analysis or document design needs to respond to the assignment. Where does this draft

respond to the assignment? Where doesn't it respond to the assignment? Explain.

6. **Answer the writer's questions** Briefly respond to the writer's questions listed above.

Postscript on the Writing Process

1. Describe the process you used to analyze your visual in its context or to design your own document. What did you do first? How did your research help? What advice did you get from your peers? What major change(s) did you make for your final version?
2. Write out the sentence or sentences that contain your thesis or the main claim of your visual analysis. If you are designing a document, explain where you put the focus and how you related both your text and your images to that focus or main idea.
3. Explain the two or three most important things you learned about visual analysis or document design as you wrote your analysis or worked through your project.
4. What parts of your analysis or document still need revision? If you had one more day to work on the project, what changes would you make? Explain.

Student Writing

Some Don't Like Their Blues at All

Karyn M. Lewis

Karyn Lewis wrote an analysis of a magazine advertisement for Fila jeans. She chose this particular advertisement because it created an image for the product that was based on stereotyped portrayals of gender roles. Instead of using its power to break down gender stereotypes, Fila deliberately used common stereotypes (men are strong and hard; women are weak and soft) to help sell their clothing. Lewis's analysis explains how Fila's images perpetuate gender stereotypes, leaving viewers of the advertisement without positive gender role models.

He strides toward us in navy and white, his body muscled and heavy-set, one arm holding his casually flung jeans jacket over his shoulder. A man in his prime, with just the right combination of macho and sartorial flair. 1

He is also black. 2

She is curled and giggling upon a chair, her hair loose and flowing around her shoulders, leaning forward innocently—the very picture of a blossoming, navy flower. 3

She is white. 4

They are each pictured on a magazine page of their own, situated opposite each other in a complementary two-page spread. They are stationed in front of a muted photograph which serves as a background for each one. They both merit their own captions: bold indigo letters presiding over them in the outer corners of each page. 5

His says: SOME LIKE THEIR BLUES HARD. 6

Hers says: SOME LIKE THEIR BLUES SOFT. 7

His background depicts a thrusting struggle between a quarterback and a leaping defender, a scene of arrested violence and high tension. 8

Her background is a lounging, bikini-clad goddess, who looks at the camera with intriguing, calm passion. She raises her hand to rest behind her head in a languid gesture as she tries to incite passion within the viewer. 9

At the bottom of the page blazes the proud emblem of the company that came up with this ad: FILA JEANS. 10

This advertisement blatantly uses stereotypes of men and women to sell its product. It caters to our need to fit into the roles that society has deemed right for the individual sexes ever since patriarchal rule rose up and replaced the primitive worship of a mother goddess and the reverence for women. These stereotypes handed down to us throughout the centuries spell out to us that men are violence and power incarnate, and that the manly attitude has no room for weakness or softness of nature. And we find our role model of women in the compliant and eager female who obeys her man in all things, who must not say no to a male, and who is not very bright—someone who flutters her eyelashes, giggles a lot, and uses tears to get her way. 11

This ad tells us, by offering the image of a hard, masculine male, who is deified in violence, that he is the role model men should aspire to, and that for women, their ideal is weak but sexual, innocent and at the same time old enough to have sex. In viewing this ad, we see our aspirations clothed in Fila jeans, and to be like them, we must buy the clothes pictured here. This ad also suggests that a man can become hard and powerful (or at least look it) dressed in these jeans; a woman can become sexually intense and desirable dressed in Fila's clothing. 12

The words of the captions tantalize with their sexual innuendo. The phrase "Some like their blues hard" hints at male sexual prowess. Most men and women in this country are obsessed with males' need to prove their virility, and Fila plays on this obsession. Females too have their own stereotype of what constitutes their sexuality. "Some like their blues soft" exemplifies this ideal: A woman should be soft and yielding. Her soft, sensuous body parts, which so excite her 13

...continued Some Don't Like Their Blues at All, **Karyn M. Lewis**

partners, have been transformed into her personal qualities. By using the term *soft,* Fila immediately links the girl with her sexuality and sexual organs.

14 We are shown by the models' postures that men and women are (according to Fila) fundamentally different and total antonyms of one another. He is standing and walking with purpose; she sits, laughing trivially at the camera. Even the background hints at separation of the sexes.

15 The football players on the man's page are arranged in a diagonal line which starts at the upper left-hand corner and runs to the opposite corner, which is the center of the ad. On her page, the enchanting nymph in the bathing suit runs on a diagonal; beginning where his ends, and traveling up to the upper right-hand corner of her page. These two photos in effect create a *V*, which both links the two models and suggests movement away from one another. Another good example of their autonomy from one another is their skin color. He is a black man, she's white. Black is the opposite color of white on an artist's color wheel and palette and symbolizes dynamically opposed forces: good and evil, night and day, man and woman. This ad hits us with the idea that men and women are not parallel in nature to one another but are fundamentally different in all things. It alienates the sexes from each other. Opposites may attract, but there is no room for understanding a nature completely alien to your own.

16 So in viewing this ad, and reading its captions, the consumer is left with the view that a woman must be "soft" and sensual, a male's sexual dream. She must be weak, the opposite of the violence which contrasts with her on the opposite page. The men looking at this ad read the message that they are supposed to be well-dressed and powerful and possess a strength that borders on violence. As we are told by the caption, men should be "hard." Furthermore, men and women are opposite creatures, as different as two sides of a coin.

17 This ad is supposed to cause us to want to meet these requirements, but it fills me with a deep-rooted disgust that we perpetuate the myth that men are unyielding creatures of iron and women are silly bits of fluff. The ad generates no good role models to aspire to, where men and women are equal beings, and both can show compassion and still be strong. Fila may like their blues hard and soft, but I don't like their blues at all.

Questions for Writing and Discussion

1. Fila did not grant permission to reproduce their advertisement for this text. However, Lewis does an excellent job of describing the layout, balance, color, key figures, diagonals, and background. In the margin of this essay, indicate those sentences where Lewis describes the advertisement, enabling us to visualize it clearly.
2. Parts of Lewis's essay describe and analyze the text that accompanies the advertisement, but she spends most of her time discussing the social, cultural, and gendered contexts of the advertisement. In the margin of the essay, indicate places where she analyzes the accompanying *text* and where she analyzes the *context* of the advertisement. Where in her analysis do you see her showing how text and context relate to each other? Explain.
3. Examine how Lewis *organizes* her analysis of the Fila advertisement. How does her organization reflect her thesis that the two figures, hers and his, are opposites? In other words, where and how does she use sentences and paragraphs to show that these two figures are "fundamentally different and total antonyms of each other"?
4. The genre of the Fila promotion is the clothing or fashion advertisement. Find at least three other advertisements for clothing or fashion. Use Lewis's strategy and analyze how the images, text, and context function together. How are the overall messages in these advertisements similar to or different from the messages that Lewis finds? Explain.

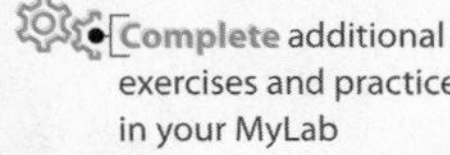
Complete additional exercises and practice in your MyLab

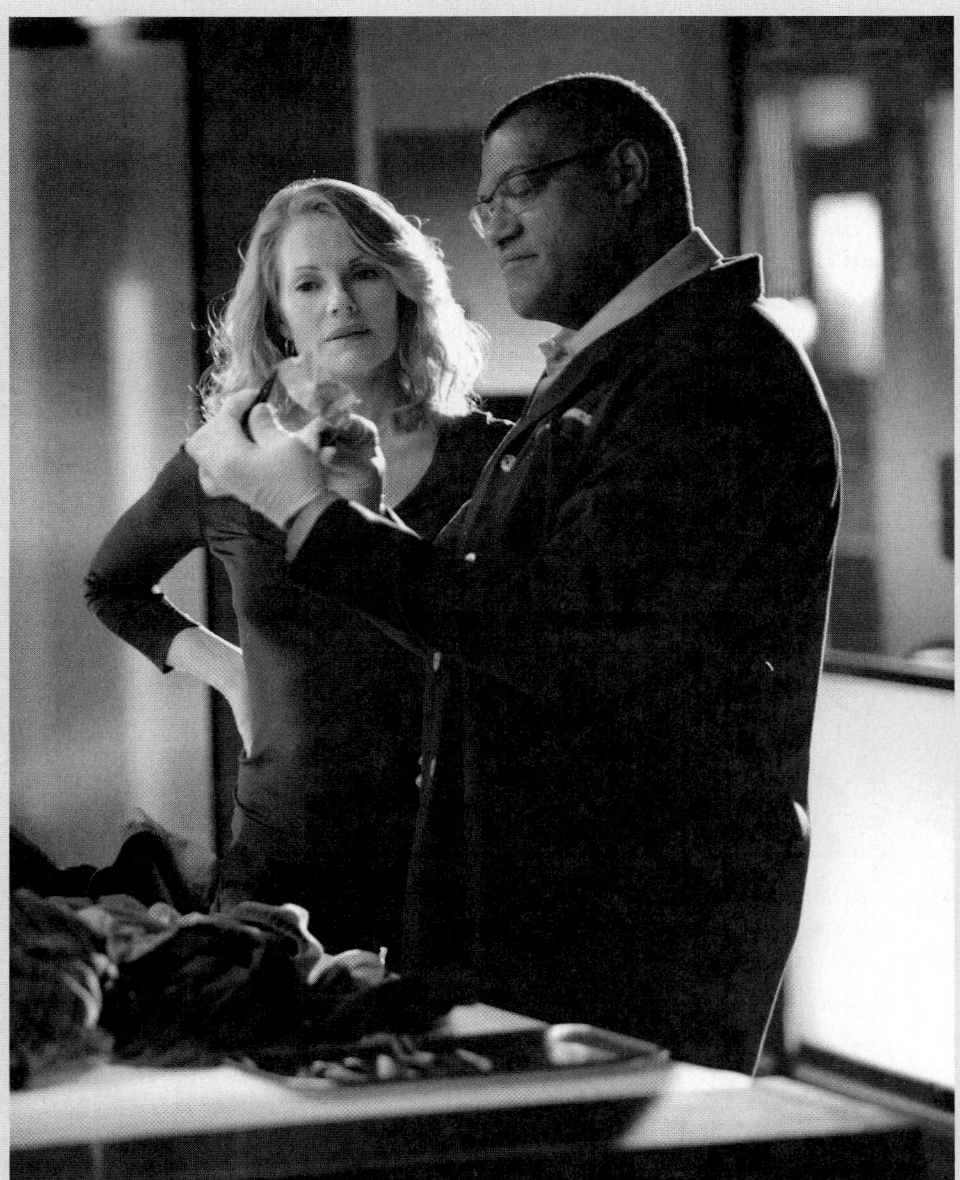

Investigating can be a fruitful technique for writers, even though writers may not get results as dramatic as the police officers do on *CSI: Crime Scene Investigation*. After examining this photo from the television program, do Journal exercise 5 on page 173.

Photofest

6 Investigating

What You Will Learn

In this chapter, you will learn to:

6.1 Use techniques for investigative writing

6.2 Use collecting strategies to develop an investigative essay

6.3 Shape your investigative essay

INVESTIGATING begins with questions. What causes the greenhouse effect? When will the world begin to run out of oil? How does illiteracy affect a person's life? How was the World Wide Web created? Is talking on a cell phone while driving as dangerous as driving drunk? How do colleges recruit applicants? What can you find out about a famous person's personality, background, and achievements? What is Bono really like?

Investigating also carries an assumption that probing for answers to such questions—by observing and remembering, researching sources, interviewing key people, or conducting surveys—will uncover truths not generally known or accepted. As you dig for information, you learn *who, what, where,* and *when.* You may even learn *how* and *why.*

The purpose of investigating is to uncover or discover facts, opinions, information, and reactions and then to report that information to people who want to know. Although no writing is ever free from cultural or personal bias, investigative writing strives to be as neutral and objective as possible. It may summarize other people's judgments, but it does not consciously editorialize. It may represent opposing viewpoints or arguments, but it does not argue for one side or the other. Investigative writing attempts to be a window on the world, allowing readers to see the information for themselves.

> **"When you stop learning, stop listening, stop looking and asking questions, always new questions, then it is time to die."**
>
> —**Lillian Smith,**
> Civil Rights Activist, Journalist, Author of *Killers of the Dream*

> **"As the free press develops, the paramount point is whether the journalist, like the scientist or scholar, puts truth in the first place or in the second."**
>
> —**Walter Lippmann,**
> Journalist and Author

Techniques for Investigative Writing

6.1
Use techniques for investigative writing

Investigative writing builds on the writing processes you have already practiced, but it emphasizes these skills:

- Asking questions and conducting research that will lead you to key sources of information and knowledgeable people.
- Summarizing, quoting, and paraphrasing information accurately and objectively from reliable sources.
- Conducting field research by interviewing experts on a topic, designing questionnaires or surveys, and personally observing events.
- Writing a report whose primary purpose is to inform rather than to argue or persuade.

Watch the Animation on Informative Essays and Reports

The techniques for investigative writing described below illustrate specifically how to use these skills as you write a report. The sample investigative reports that follow illustrate a variety of journalistic genres, styles, and audiences.

Techniques for Investigative Writing

Technique	Tips on How to Do It
Beginning with an interesting title and a catchy lead-in	Titles should announce the topic in a *concise but original* way. Lead-in sentences should arouse your *readers' interest* and focus their attention on the subject.
Giving background information by answering relevant *who, what, when, where, how,* and *why* questions	Answering the reporter's questions *early in your report or article* ensures that readers have sufficient information to understand your report.
Stating the main idea, question, or focus of the investigation	The purpose of a report is to convey information as *clearly as possible*. Readers shouldn't have to guess the main idea.
Summarizing or quoting information from written or oral sources	Reports quote *accurately* any statistics, data, or sentences from the sources; they cite authors and titles in the text of the report.
Following appropriate genre conventions	A news report, a profile, an interview, and an investigative report follow different style and format conventions. Learn the key features of the particular *genre* with which you are working.
Writing in a readable and interesting style for the intended audienc	*Clear, direct, and readable language* is essential in a report. Be as *accurate* and *factual* as possible. Use visuals, photos, graphs, and charts as appropriate.

The intended audience for each report is often determined by the publication in which the report appears: *Psychology Today* assumes that its readers are interested in personality and behavior; *Discover* magazine is for readers interested in popular science; readers of *Ms.* magazine expect coverage of contemporary issues concerning women.

REPORT ON A RESEARCH STUDY

The following report, prepared by the University of Utah News Center, describes a research study on the effects of driving while using cell phones. Notice that the report cites the authors of the study, gives the research methodology, and summarizes the detailed findings of the study.

Professional Writing

Drivers on Cell Phones Are as Bad as Drunks

Attention-getting title

June 29, 2006—Three years after the preliminary results first were 1
presented at a scientific meeting and drew wide attention, University of Utah psychologists have published a study showing that motorists who talk on handheld or hands-free cellular phones are as impaired as drunken drivers.

Background information on study

"We found that people are as impaired when they drive and talk on 2
a cell phone as they are when they drive intoxicated at the legal blood-alcohol limit" of 0.08 percent, which is the minimum level that defines illegal drunken driving in most U.S. states, says study co-author Frank Drews, an assistant professor of psychology. "If legislators really want to address driver distraction, then they should consider outlawing cell phone use while driving."

Most important findings of study

Psychology Professor David Strayer, the study's lead author, adds: 3
"Just like you put yourself and other people at risk when you drive drunk, you put yourself and others at risk when you use a cell phone and drive. The level of impairment is very similar."

"Who" information: the authors of the study

"Clearly the safest course of action is to not use a cell phone while 4
driving," concludes the study by Strayer, Drews and Dennis Crouch, a research associate professor of pharmacology and toxicology. The study was set for publication June 29 in the summer 2006 issue of *Human Factors: The Journal of the Human Factors and Ergonomics Society*.

"When" and "Where" information: When and Where the study was published.

The study reinforced earlier research by Strayer and Drews showing 5
that hands-free cell phones are just as distracting as handheld cell phones because the conversation itself—not just manipulation of a handheld phone—distracts drivers from road conditions.

...continued Drivers on Cell Phones Are as Bad as Drunks

Human Factors Editor Nancy J. Cooke praised the study: "Although we all have our suspicions about the dangers of cell phone use while driving, human factors research on driver safety helps us move beyond mere suspicions to scientific observations of driver behavior." 6

Key Findings: Different Driving Styles, Similar Impairment

"How" information: The methodology of the study

Each of the study's 40 participants "drove" a PatrolSim driving simulator four times: once each while undistracted, using a handheld cell phone, using a hands-free cell phone and while intoxicated to the 0.08 percent blood-alcohol level after drinking vodka and orange juice. Participants followed a simulated pace car that braked intermittently. 7

Both handheld and hands-free cell phones impaired driving, with no significant difference in the degree of impairment. That "calls into question driving regulations that prohibited handheld cell phones and permit hands-free cell phones," the researchers write. 8

The study found that compared with undistracted drivers:

Results of the study

- Motorists who talked on either handheld or hands-free cell phones drove slightly slower, were 9 percent slower to hit the brakes, displayed 24 percent more variation in following distance as their attention switched between driving and conversing, were 19 percent slower to resume normal speed after braking and were more likely to crash. Three study participants rear-ended the pace car. All were talking on cell phones. None were drunk.

Results of the study

- Drivers drunk at the 0.08 percent blood-alcohol level drove a bit more slowly than both undistracted drivers and drivers using cell phones, yet more aggressively. They followed the pace car more closely, were twice as likely to brake only four seconds before a collision would have occurred, and hit their brakes with 23 percent more force. "Neither accident rates, nor reaction times to vehicles braking in front of the participant, nor recovery of lost speed following braking differed significantly" from undistracted drivers, the researchers write.

"Impairments associated with using a cell phone while driving can be as profound as those associated with driving while drunk," they conclude. 9

Are Drunken Drivers Really Less Accident-Prone than Cell Phone Users?

Analysis and discussion of results

Drews says the lack of accidents among the study's drunken drivers was surprising. He and Strayer speculate that because simulated drives were conducted during mornings, participants who got drunk were well-rested and in the "up" phase of intoxication. In reality, 80 percent of all fatal alcohol-related accidents occur between 6 P.M. and 6 A.M. when drunken 10 drivers tend to be fatigued. Average blood-alcohol levels in those accidents are twice 0.08 percent. Forty percent of the roughly 42,000 annual U.S. traffic fatalities involve alcohol.

While none of the study's intoxicated drivers crashed, their hard, late braking is "predictive of increased accident rates over the long run," the researchers wrote. 11

One statistical analysis of the new and previous Utah studies showed cell phone users were 5.36 times more likely to get in an accident than undistracted drivers. Other studies have shown the risk is about the same as for drivers with a 0.08 blood-alcohol level. 12

Analysis and discussion of results

Strayer says he expects criticism "suggesting that we are trivializing drunken-driving impairment, but it is anything but the case. We don't think people should drive while drunk, nor should they talk on their cell phone while driving." 13

Drews says he and Strayer compared the impairment of motorists using cell phones to drivers with a 0.08 percent blood-alcohol level because they wanted to determine if the risk of driving while phoning was comparable to the drunken driving risk considered unacceptable. 14

"This study does not mean people should start driving drunk," says Drews. "It means that driving while talking on a cell phone is as bad as or maybe worse than driving drunk, which is completely unacceptable and cannot be tolerated by society." 15

BRIEF REPORT WITH GRAPHICS

The following passage illustrates the genre of the brief report with graphics that was popularized by *USA Today.* Abigail Sullivan Moore's report, which appeared in the Education Life section of the *New York Times,* illustrates how a simple graphic can enhance the impact of a report.

Professional Writing

Gimme an A (I Insist!)

Abigail Sullivan Moore

Grade inflation seems to be reaching record levels at the nation's high schools, according to a new survey of incoming freshmen at more than 400 colleges and universities. Almost half reported an A average in high school, up from 18 percent in 1968. "Something is amiss," says Linda J. Sax, who directed the survey of 276,000 students for the 1

...continued Gimme an A (I Insist!), **Abigail Sullivan Moore**

Higher Education Research Institute at the University of California at Los Angeles. At the same time, she says, "students are studying, but not as often as they were."

Based on conversations with educators, Dr. Sax believes that parents and pupils are pushing teachers for higher grades amid the intense competition for desirable colleges. Also, she says: "What I'm hearing is that teachers feel a pressure to not shatter students' self-esteem. Teachers are caught up in this web of pressure." 2

A study by the College Board released in January confirms the findings: high school seniors' grades have climbed but SAT scores remain nearly unchanged. Wayne J. Camara, the board's vice president for research and development, says the trend started to accelerate in the early 90's, when "more and more middle-income families had much more awareness of college, and at the same time there was more discretionary income" to pay for the expensive, hard-to-get-into institutions. He predicts a correction is due. "Everyone can't get A's," he says. 3

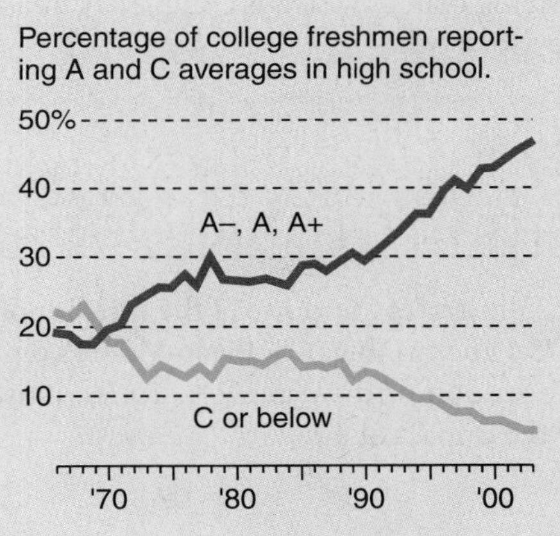

PROFILE OF A PERSON

Watch the Animation on Writing Profiles

The following article is a profile—a biographical sketch intended to give a sense of a person's appearance, character, and accomplishments. In "How Many Stephen Colberts Are There?" Charles McGrath, writing in the *New York Times*, reveals the many facets of comedian Stephen Colbert.

Professional Writing

How Many Stephen Colberts Are There?

Charles McGrath

There used to be just two Stephen Colberts, and they were hard enough to distinguish. The main difference was that one thought the other was an idiot. The idiot Colbert was the one who made a nice paycheck by appearing four times a week on *The Colbert Report* (pronounced in the French fashion, with both t's silent), the extremely popular fake news show on Comedy Central. The other Colbert, the non-idiot, was the 47-year-old South Carolinian, a practicing Catholic, who lives with his wife and three children in suburban Montclair, N.J., where, according to one of his neighbors, he is "extremely normal." One of the pleasures of attending a live taping of *The Colbert Report* is watching this Colbert transform himself into a Republican superhero. 1

Suburban Colbert comes out dressed in the other Colbert's guise—dark two-button suit, tasteful Brooks Brothersy tie, rimless Rumsfeldian glasses—and answers questions from the audience for a few minutes. (The questions are usually about things like Colbert's favorite sport or favorite character from *The Lord of the Rings* but on one memorable occasion a young black boy asked him, "Are you my father?" Colbert hesitated a moment and then said, "Kareem?") Then he steps onstage, gets a last dab of makeup while someone sprays his hair into an unmussable Romney-like helmet, and turns himself into his alter ego. His body straightens, as if jolted by a shock. A self-satisfied smile creeps across his mouth, and a maniacally fatuous gleam steals into his eyes. 2

Lately, though, there has emerged a third Colbert. This one is a version of the TV-show Colbert, except he doesn't exist just on screen anymore. He exists in the real world and has begun to meddle in it. In 2008, the old Colbert briefly ran for president, entering the Democratic primary in his native state of South Carolina. (He hadn't really switched parties, but the filing fee for the Republican primary was too expensive.) In 2010, invited by Representative Zoe Lofgren, he testified before Congress about the problem of illegal-immigrant farmworkers and remarked that "the obvious answer is for all of us to stop eating fruits and vegetables." 3

But those forays into public life were spoofs, more or less. The new Colbert has crossed the line that separates a TV stunt from reality and 4

...continued How Many Stephen Colberts Are There?, **Charles McGrath**

a parody from what is being parodied. In June, after petitioning the Federal Election Commission, he started his own super PAC—a real one, with real money. He has run TV ads, endorsed (sort of) the presidential candidacy of Buddy Roemer, the former governor of Louisiana, and almost succeeded in hijacking and renaming the Republican primary in South Carolina. "Basically, the F.E.C. gave me the license to create a killer robot," Colbert said to me in October, and there are times now when the robot seems to be running the television show instead of the other way around.

INTERVIEW

Typically interviews are conducted by one person, the interviewer, who asks questions over the phone, in writing, or in person. Whoever is being interviewed answers the questions, and then the interviewer often edits the interview to focus on the most relevant questions and answers. The following interview is of Regina Benjamin, the United States surgeon general, and the interviewer is Deborah Solomon. The interview appeared in the *New York Times*.

Professional Writing

Doctor's Orders

As the United States surgeon general, you just released a report on tobacco smoke that claims, not completely convincingly, that one puff of one cigarette can trigger inflammation and a fatal heart attack. Is that intended as a slogan?

Well, it's more than a slogan. The scientific basis is that tobacco smoke is a toxic mix of more than 7,000 chemicals and chemical compounds. When you inhale the smoke, the chemicals can reach your lungs very quickly and enter the bloodstream. Whether it's second-hand smoke or if it's from a cigarette, it damages the lining of the blood vessels; it makes your blood more likely to clot.

As the nation's chief health educator, have you ordered President Obama to quit smoking?

I cannot order the president. However, because he's been trying really hard, I encourage him to keep it up. I want to encourage him and other people to quit because we tend to villainize them, and it's not always their fault.

It's amazing how many people have quit smoking in the past generation.

Since 1964, our rate of smoking in the U.S. has been cut in half.

Have you ever used marijuana?

No, I've never used it. I was a good Catholic girl growing up.

What do you think of its medical use?

There's evidence that shows that it's useful for medicine, but we need to investigate how to avoid the adverse effects of smoking marijuana.

In the summer of 1990, you founded a now-famous clinic in Bayou La Batre, a shrimping village in your native Alabama where you ministered to the health needs of impoverished residents.

I learned that people worked for a living and didn't have health insurance. But they would pay what they could.

Your clinic was destroyed by Hurricane Katrina and rebuilt in short order. In 2008, you won a MacArthur award. I assume you are still receiving installments of your $500,000 grant?

Actually, no. When I accepted this government position—they can't give money to a government employee, so I had to stop.

While running the clinic, you watched your older brother and only sibling die of AIDS. How did he contract it?

My brother was gay, and he was part of the gay community, and many of his friends contracted the disease. It was hard, because he and his friends were so vibrant, such bright energetic people who were contributing to the world.

How old was your brother when he died?

He was 44. It was diagnosed; he lived eight months, and he died about a year before my mother died. She was actually diagnosed with her lung cancer six weeks after his death. I think she died of a broken heart.

You were raised by your mom, after your parents separated. Did your mother work?

She was a housewife, but she also did hair. She was a cosmetologist.

...continued Doctor's Orders

Were you the first person in your family to go to medical school?

Yes. I had never seen a black doctor before I went to college.

When you were nominated for surgeon general, your critics tried to disqualify you on the basis of your weight, saying you were perpetuating obesity rather than battling it.

My thought is that people should be healthy and be fit at whatever size they are.

What sort of exercise do you recommend for people who don't love it?

I want exercise to be fun; don't want it to be work. I don't want it to be so routine that you're bored with it. We used to jump rope a lot and double Dutch and went to a disco to have fun and enjoy ourselves. We didn't go to the disco because somebody said, Go dance for 30 minutes.

When was this? When did you go to a disco?

When I was younger. I want us to get back to doing things because they're fun.

Maybe we need to dance more as a nation.

Yes, I love to dance, and whenever I'm at events and places with music, I will dance. That exercise is medicine. It's better than most pills.

Warming Up: Journal Exercises

The following exercises will help you practice investigative writing. Read all of the exercises and then, in your journal, write about the three that interest you most. One of these exercises may suggest an idea for your investigative essay.

1. Write an "authority" list of topics about which you have some information or experience. Consider your hobbies, academic interests, job skills, community experiences, or other experience with art, music, sports, travel, films, and so forth. Jot down a few sentences about three or four possible topics. Then go to the Internet and use your favorite search engine to continue investigating these topics. When you are finished browsing, write out the key questions you could answer about each of these topics.
2. **Writing Across the Curriculum.** Look through the assignments and texts from another course you are taking or have taken recently. Find an article or research report from that class that was recommended or assigned reading.

Following the model of the report on cell phone research earlier in this chapter, write a summary of the research that answers the *who*, *what*, *when*, and *where* questions about the study and then summarizes the findings of the study. Write this summary so that other members of your writing class can understand the research findings.

3. Watch an investigative news show such as *60 Minutes*, taking notes on the interviewer's techniques. Is there a sequence to the questions—say, from gentle and polite to critical or controversial? What information does the interviewer have *before* the interview? Can you tell which questions are planned or scripted and which are spontaneous? After taking notes on a show, explain what you think are the three most important tips for successful interviewing.
4. Interview a classmate for a 200-to 250-word personal profile. Your object is to describe this person and one of his or her major interests. First, in your daybook, prepare questions you need to ask for biographical information. Then, in an eight- to ten-minute interview, ask questions about the person and about several topics from that person's "authority" list. After the interview, take two or three minutes to review your notes. At home, write up the results of your interview, which will appear in your local or campus newspaper.
5. If you have watched the television program, *CSI: Crime Scene Investigation,* explain the kinds of investigations that the CSI team uses during a typical case. How does the team use crime scene observations, interviews, online or file research, or other investigative strategies in order to solve their crimes? Support your explanation with specific references to a program you have seen recently or that you watch specifically for this assignment.
6. Read the following article by Elizabeth Larson, "Surfin' the Louvre." Use her model to write your own investigative essay comparing online learning to a traditional textbook-based course. Choose a course you are taking or have recently taken, and then find and report on key Web sites that enable you to learn about your subject without going to a single class, reading a textbook, or taking an exam.

Professional Writing

Surfin' the Louvre

Elizabeth Larsen

I first studied art history the old-fashioned way: scribbling notes in a dark auditorium as a parade of yellowing slides whizzed past in an overwhelming progression from ancient Greece to Andy Warhol. Four years and tens of thousands of dollars later, I had traveled from the ruins of Tikal in Guatemala *1*

...continued Surfin' the Louvre, **Elizabeth Larsen**

to a tiny Giotto-decorated chapel in Padua to Rodin's Paris atelier without ever leaving my college's urban campus.

Today it's possible to get a similar education—minus the sometimes inspired (and sometimes not-so-inspired) comments of a professor—on the Internet. In the past few years, virtually every museum of note has established a presence on the World Wide Web. While some sites still stick to the basics (cost of admission, hours, information about the permanent collection and current exhibits), more and more institutions are following the lead of the Fine Arts Museums of San Francisco (www.famsf.org) which is using the Web to promote its new commitment to "behave more like a resource and less like a repository." Currently the site houses over 65,000 images—from Mary Cassatt's *Woman Bathing* to more than 3,000 examples of Japanese ukiyo-e printmaking—with plans to double that number as the museum digitizes its entire collection. 2

That's a heck of a lot more reproductions than you'll find in that chiropractically unfriendly art history text, H. W. Janson's *History of Art.* Inspired by the sheer volume of images available on FAMSF's "Imagebase," I decided to try my hand at digitally designing my own art education. 3

My self-directed syllabus started in Spain at the new Guggenheim Museum in Bilbao (www.guggenheim.org/bilbao), the recently opened critic's darling designed by maverick California architect Frank Gehry. As befits a museum where the architecture is as much a piece of art history as the works it houses, much of the site is devoted to Gehry's oddly gorgeous design, which looks like a cross between a medieval fortress and a bouquet of flowers sculpted in titanium. But there's a lot of other great stuff as well, including reproductions of the museum's most famous acquisitions—like Richard Serra's *Snake,* an appropriately jarring-yet-graceful panel of curving steel set smack dab in the middle of a gallery. 4

Eager to see more, I moved on to the Museums page of the World Wide Web Virtual Library (museumca.org). A clearinghouse of links to museums, the site is most helpful for those who want to search according to the countries the museums are in. I started in Italy, which I soon discovered doesn't include that country-within-a-country, the Vatican (mv.vatican.va). At the Uffizi Gallery in Florence (www.uffizi.com), I checked out a number of Renaissance heavy hitters, including Botticelli's *The Birth of Venus* and Paolo Ucello's *Battle of San Romano*. To get more of a feeling for Florentine art as it exists on the streets and in the churches of Florence, I used the Florence Art Guide to take me all over the city, from the Ponte Vecchio to the Piazzale Michelangelo. 5

My next stop was Paris, where my first visit was to—where else?—the Louvre (www.louvre.fr), where I lingered over a Watteau and a Poussin 6 before getting absorbed in the history of the building. From there it was an easy trek to the countryside and the Giverny home page (giverny.org) to check out the gardens that inspired Monet.

From Giverny I hopped over to Greece and the Hellenic Ministry of Culture's Guide to Athens (odysseus.culture.gr/index_en.html) where I gazed out over the Acropolis. Then I spent the rest of the afternoon in Japan at the Kyoto National Museum (www.kyohaku.go.jp/eng/index_top.html), where I studied up on the intricacies of Chinese and Japanese lacquerware. 7

I know I'm starting to sound pretty starry-eyed about my cyber-education, so I'll temper my enthusiasm with a few caveats. From the vantage point of my office chair, I obviously wasn't able to glean insights from the people standing next to me as I contemplated de Kooning's *Woman I*. But I don't require that every symphony I listen to be live, and I'm equally comfortable with the trade-offs inherent in a digital visual experience. Especially since I won't need to worry about those threatening form letters from the bursar's office. 8

Investigating: The Writing Process

Assignment for Investigating

Choose a subject to investigate: one aspect of a current social or political policy, a scientific discovery or principle, a historical event, a profile of a controversial public figure, or perhaps just an ordinary event, person, process, or place that you find interesting. Your initial purpose should be to discover or learn about your subject. Then, with a specific audience in mind, report your findings. A report presents the information that you find; it should not argue for or against any idea or plan. With the final copy of your investigative report, turn in photocopies of any sources you have summarized or cited, notes from your interview(s), and/or copies of questionnaires that you used.

Selecting your audience and genre is especially important for your investigative report. If an audience is not specified in your assignment, use the chart below to brainstorm possible audiences and genres. Where possible, think globally but focus locally—what global or national topic has local implications that you can investigate, and what local publication might be interested in your report?

Audience	Possible Genres for Investigating Assignments
Personal Audience	Personal or family interview or profile, journal entry, social networking site profile, photo essay, multigenre document.
Academic Audience	Reports for academic classes, summary of article or research study, forum entry on class site, multigenredocument.
Public Audience	Survey, interview, profile, investigation, or report of research for a newspaper, magazine, blog, newsletter, community service organization, online site, or multigenre document.

CHOOSING A SUBJECT

If one of your journal topics does not suggest a subject for your investigation, consider the following ideas. If you have a subject, go on to the collecting and shaping strategies.

- Choose some idea, principle, process, or theory discussed in a class that you are currently taking. In biology, you might focus on the Krebs cycle; in art, investigate the Dutch school of painters; or in education, investigate community literacy programs. In physics, research low-temperature conductivity or hydrogen fuels, or in astronomy, investigate competing theories about the formation of the universe. Begin by interviewing a professor, graduate students, or classmates about how to research the history, development, or personalities behind this idea. With information from the interview, continue your investigation in the library and online. As you read, focus your question on one narrow or specific area.
- Investigate and report on a campus or community service organization. Choose any academic, minority, cultural, or community organization. Visit the office. Interview an official. Read the organization's literature. Talk to students or community members who have used the service. Check the library for background information. Find people who are dissatisfied with or critical of the organization. Select an audience who might use this service or who might be interested in volunteering for the organization, and report the relevant *who, what, when, where, why,* and/or *how* information.
- For practice, investigate one of the following questions on the Internet and/or in the library (and be prepared to explain your answers to your class members): How can you minimize jet lag? Can aspirin prevent heart attacks? How expensive is television advertising? How do

Facebook's privacy controls work? Why is the Antarctic ice shelf melting? How do endorphins work? What is a melanoma? What causes seasonal affective disorder? How does a "Zamboni" work? What effects does Megan's law have? Do Americans spend more money on cosmetics than on education? What are the newest ways to repair torn ACLs (anterior cruciate ligaments) in your knee? What is computer morphing, and how does it work?

- Investigate an academic major, a career, or a job in which you are interested. List some of the *who, what, when, where,* and *why* questions you want to answer. Who is interested in this major? What background or courses are required? What is the pay scale and what are the opportunities for advancement? What appeals to you about this major or job? What are the disadvantages of this major or career? Research your major or career on the Internet and in the library. Plan to interview an adviser, a friend who majors in the field, or a person who works at that job. Be prepared to report your findings to your classmates.

COMMUNITY SERVICE LEARNING

If you have a service-learning project connected with your writing course, here is background information to help you understand your project.

Definition Community service learning is simply a mutually beneficial partnership with a community agency.

Goals Teachers, students, and the partnering agency work together to set mutual goals promoting both civic action and academic learning. The agency receives your assistance with projects involving planning, writing, and communicating. You receive valuable experience related to your writing class goals: working and writing collaboratively, assessing and addressing agency needs, and getting practice with real-world writing situations, tasks, and genres.

Requirements Most service-learning projects require both a certain number of hours of service and a portfolio of pieces of writing *about* the agency, *for* the agency, and *with* the agency. A major requirement of service-learning projects is a reflective account about your participation, about the agency and its mission, and about what you have learned.

Writing Situations and Genres Depending on the goals and mission of the agency, you may write any combination of the following genres or kinds of writing: journal writing, online discussion forums, observation of the agency, profile of the agency, research, needs assessment, audience analysis, interviews, pamphlets, Web site design, public service announcements, feature articles, and impact assessment.

Benefits The agency benefits from your help with its ongoing projects (but remember that it also gives its time to help you learn). You benefit from getting to write in real-world situations—not just for your teacher and classmates. You also gain civic and crosscultural awareness, experience in working and writing collaboratively, increased problem-solving skills, contacts for possible job or career choices, and personal satisfaction for helping with a worthy civic cause.

COLLECTING

6.2
Use collecting strategies to develop an investigative essay

The collecting strategies discussed in Chapters 3 and 4 (brainstorming, clustering, looping, mapping, sketching, reading, summarizing, taking double-entry notes) may be useful as you collect ideas. Other strategies particularly useful for investigating are suggested here.

Asking Questions Asking the *right questions* is crucial to investigative writing. Sets of questions (often called *heuristics*) will help you narrow and focus your subject and tailor your approach to the expectations or needs of your audience. You don't know what information you will need to collect until you know what questions your investigation needs to answer.

> "Had I known the answer to any of these questions, I would never have needed to write."
>
> —Joan Didion, Essayist and Novelist

1. The reporter's questions are one basic heuristic: *who? what? when? where? why?* Asking these questions of a topic ensures that you're not leaving out any crucial information. If, for example, you are investigating recreational opportunities in your city or on campus, you might ask the following questions to focus your investigation (but remember to ask the negative version of each question, too).
   - *Whom* is the recreation for?
   - *Who* runs the programs?
   - *Who* is excluded from the programs?
   - *Who* pays for the programs?
   - *What* is the program?
   - *What* sports are included in the program?
   - *What* sports are not included?
   - *What* is the budget for these programs?
   - *When* are these opportunities available or not available?
   - *Where* do the activities take place?
   - *Where* are they restricted?
   - *Why* are these programs offered?
   - *Why* are certain activities not offered?
   - *Why* have activities been changed?

   These questions might lead you to focus your investigation on the scheduling, on why soccer has been excluded, or on why participants are charged a fee for one class or program but not for another.

Watch the Animation on Questioning

2. The classical "topics" provide a second set of questions for an investigation.

Definition:	What is it?
Comparison:	What is it like or unlike?
Relationship:	What caused it? What are its consequences?
Testimony:	What has been said or written about it?

These questions can be used in conjunction with the reporter's questions to focus an investigation. Applied to the topic on recreational opportunities, the questions might be as follows.

Definition:	What activities exist?
	How can the activities be described, classified, or analyzed?
Comparison:	What are similarities to or differences from other programs?
Relationship:	What caused these programs to be offered?
	What causes people to use or avoid these activities?
	What are the consequences of these programs?
Testimony:	What do students think about these activities?
	What do administrators think?
	What have other schools done?
	What does research show?
	What proverbs or common sayings apply here?

Research Tips

As you work on your investigating essay, use the following research strategies. For additional information, see Chapter 12.

Library Orientation Every library is different, so be sure to take your library's tour and find out how the online catalog searches and databases work. Knowing which databases to use and how to use their search strategies makes your research quicker and more effective.

Internet Searches Use Internet search engines such as Google primarily for introductory or background information. Remember that the sites you find online may not be as reliable as information you find through your library's academic databases.

Evaluate Your Sources For all your Internet and library database sources, carefully evaluate the reliability, accuracy, and bias of your sources. Is the author of the text or Web site an authority on the subject? What is the author's connection to the subject, point of view, or bias? Has the text been published by a reputable magazine, or is it a self-published Web site?

Talk to Your Reference Librarian An informal interview with a reference librarian may be the most important ten minutes you spend doing research. Start by telling the librarian about your assignment—the topic and issue you're investigating—and then ask which databases, sources, or reference guides might be most helpful.

Do Field Research Field research, including personal observations, interviews, and questionnaires, can be effective in almost every research project. An interview with a campus or community expert on your topic may be a great place to start. A questionnaire for other students or potential readers may give you a better sense of what your audience knows about your topic and what points of view they have on the issue.

The two sets of questions above will expand your information, helping you collect facts, data, examples, and ideas—probably more than you can use in a short essay. Once you have all of this information, you can then *narrow* your topic.

Summarizing

As explained in Chapter 4, a *summary* is a concise version of the main and supporting ideas in a passage, report, essay, book, or speech. It is usually written in the present tense. It identifies the author and title of the source; it may refer to the context or the place where the study was made; it contains the passage's main ideas; and it may quote directly a few forceful or concise sentences or phrases. It will not usually cite the author's examples. A *paraphrase* usually expresses all the information in the passage—including examples—in your own words. Summary, paraphrase, and direct quotation often occur together as you use sources. (See Chapter 4 for more details.)

Citing Sources in Your Text

Typically, journalistic reports name their sources in the text, without using footnotes or a works-cited page. In the University of Utah report, early in this chapter, quotations are attributed, the authors are identified, and the journal is cited directly in the text:

> "Clearly the safest course of action is not to use a cell phone while driving," concludes the study by Strayer, Drews and Dennis Crouch,

> a research associate professor of pharmacology and toxicology. The study was set for publication June 29 in the summer 2006 issue of *Human Factors: The Journal of the Human Factors and Ergonomics Society.*

The policy of not citing sources is common in magazines and newspapers where articles and news reports typically go through a fact-checking process to ensure accuracy. If you are writing an academic report, however, your professor may require you to use in-text citation, footnotes, or a works-cited page. Be sure to check with your teacher to see how to refer to or document your sources for your investigating report. For information on citing sources using the Modern Language Association (MLA) style or the American Psychological Association (APA) style, see Chapter 13.

DOING FIELD RESEARCH

Field research is essential for many kinds of investigative reports. Typically, field research—as opposed to library research—involves firsthand observations, interviews, and questionnaires. For observing strategies, see Chapter 3, "Observing and Remembering." Using interviews and writing questionnaires are discussed below.

Interviewing

After you have done some initial research, interviews are a logical next step. Remember that the more you know about the subject (and the person you're interviewing), the more productive the interview will be. In planning an interview, keep the following steps in mind.

1. Make an *appointment* with the person you wish to interview. Although you may feel hesitant or shy about calling or e-mailing someone for an interview, remember that most people are flattered that someone else wants to hear their opinions or learn about their areas of expertise.
2. Make a *list of questions,* in an appropriate *sequence,* that you can ask during the interview. The interview itself will generate additional topics, but your list will jog your memory if the interview gets off track. Begin with relatively objective or factual questions and work your way, gradually, to more subjective questions or controversial issues. Try to phrase your questions so that they require more than a yes or no answer.
3. Begin the interview by *introducing yourself* and describing your investigation. Keep your biases or opinions out of the questions. Be sure to *listen* carefully and ask follow-up questions: "What information do you have on that? What do the statistical studies suggest? In your opinion, do these data show any trends? What memorable experiences have you had

relating to this topic?" Like a dog with a good bone, a reporter doesn't drop a topic until the meat's all gone.

4. During the interview, *take notes* and, if appropriate, use a tape recorder to ensure accuracy. Don't hesitate to ask your interviewee to repeat or clarify a statement. Remember: People want you to get the facts right and quote them accurately. Especially if you're doing a personality profile, describe notable features of your interviewee: hair color, facial features, stature, dress, gestures, and nervous habits, as well as details about the room or surroundings. Finally, don't forget to ask your interviewee for additional leads or sources. At the conclusion of the interview, *express your thanks* and ask if you can check with him or her later, perhaps by e-mail, for additional details or facts.
5. Immediately after the interview, *go over your notes*. If you recorded the interview, listen to the tape and transcribe important responses. List other questions you may still have.

Writing Questionnaires

Watch the **Animation** on Writing Surveys

Questionnaires are useful when you need to know the attitudes, preferences, or opinions of a large group of people. If you are surveying customers in your business, you may discover that 39 percent of those surveyed would prefer that your business stay open an additional hour, from 5 P.M. to 6 P.M. If you are surveying students to determine their knowledge of geography, you might discover that only 8 percent can correctly locate Beirut on a map of the Middle East. The accuracy and usefulness of a survey depend on the kinds of questions you ask, on the number of people you survey, and on the sample of people you select to respond to your questionnaire.

Open questions are easy to ask, but the answers can be difficult to interpret. For example, if you want to survey customers at a department store where you work, you might ask questions requiring a short written response:

- What is your opinion of the service provided by the clerks at Macy's?
- What would make your shopping experience at Macy's more enjoyable?

While these questions may give you interesting—and often reliable—responses, the results may be difficult to tabulate. Open questions are often valuable in initial surveys because they can help you to determine specific areas or topics for further investigation.

Closed questions are more typical than open questions in surveys. They limit responses so that you can focus on a particular topic and accurately tabulate the responses. Here are four types of closed questions:

- *Yes/no questions:* Have you shopped at Macy's in the last three months?
  ______ Yes
  ______ No

- *Multiple choice:* How far did you travel to come to Macy's?

  ______ 0–5 miles ______ 10–15 miles
  ______ 5–10 miles ______ Over 15 miles

- *Checklists:* Which departments at Macy's do you usually visit?

  ______ Women's Wear ______ Kitchen Products
  ______ Sporting Goods ______ Men's Wear
  ______ Children's Wear ______ Household Goods

- *Ranking lists:* Rank the times you prefer to shop (1 indicates most convenient time, 2 indicates slightly less convenient, and so on).

  ______ 9 A.M.–11 A.M. ______ 1 P.M.–4 P.M.
  ______ 11 A.M.–1 P.M. ______ 4 P.M.–8 P.M.

As you design, administer, and use your questionnaire, keep the following tips in mind.

- Focus and limit your questions so that respondents can fill out the questionnaire quickly.
- Avoid loaded or biased questions. For example, don't ask, "How do you like the high-quality merchandise in Macy's sports department?"
- At the top of your questionnaire, write one or two sentences describing your study and thanking participants.
- Pretest your questionnaire by giving it to a few people. Based on their oral and written responses, focus and clarify your questions.
- Use a large sample group. Thirty responses will give you more accurate information about consumer attitudes than will three responses.
- Make your sample as *random* or as evenly representative as possible. Don't survey customers on only one floor, in only one department, or at only one time of day.
- Be sure to include a copy of your questionnaire with your article or essay.

Note: If you intend to do a formal study using questionnaires, check your library for additional sources to help you design and administer statistically reliable surveys.

SHAPING

6.3
Shape your investigative essay

As you think about ways to organize and develop your essay, be sure to reread your assignment and consider your purpose and audience. Limit your subject to create a narrowed and focused topic. Don't try to cover everything—focus on the most interesting questions and information. Take the time to write out a statement of your topic, key questions, purpose, and audience. Then try the following strategies.

Shaping Strategies

Do you want to . . .	Consider using this rhetorical strategy:
put the most important information first to seize your reader's interest?	inverted pyramid structure (p. 184)
present your investigative report as a story?	chronological order (p. 185)
enliven your report with a vivid or personal style?	create a persona (p. 186)
engage your reader's interest and curiosity?	appeal to your reader with a catchy title, introduction, and conclusion (p. 186)

"But for whom have I tried so steadfastly to communicate? Who have I worried over in this writing? Who is my audience?"

—Cherrie Moraga,
Social Critic and Poet

Inverted Pyramid

A common form for reports, especially in journalism, is the *inverted pyramid.* The writer begins with a succinct but arresting title, opens the story with a sentence or short paragraph that answers the reporter's questions, and then fills in the background information and details in order of importance, from the *most important* to the *least important.*

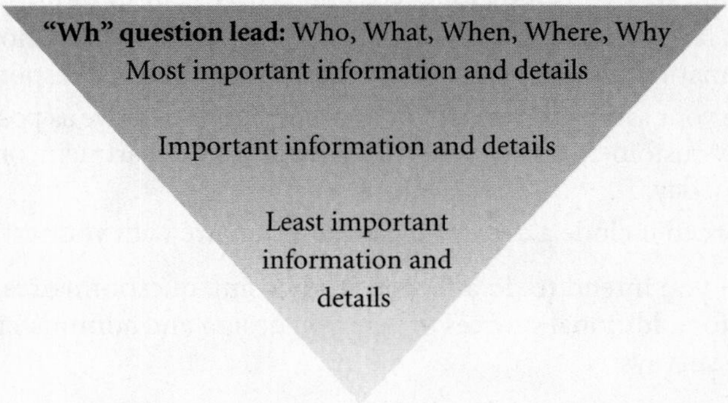

"Wh" question lead: Who, What, When, Where, Why
Most important information and details

Important information and details

Least important information and details

Writers use the inverted pyramid when concrete information and the convenience of the reader are most important. The advantage of the inverted pyramid is that a hurried reader can quickly gather the most important information and determine whether the rest of the story is worth reading. The disadvantage is that some details or information may be scattered or presented out of clear sequence. In investigative writing, therefore, writers often supplement the inverted pyramid with other forms of development: chronological order, definition, classification, and comparison/contrast.

Chronological Order

Often, writers present their information in the order in which they discovered it, enabling the reader to follow the research process as if it were a narrative or a story. In this format, the writer presents the steps of the investigation, from the earliest incidents to the discoveries along the way and to the final pieces of information.

Elizabeth Larsen, for example, uses chronological order to make a story out of her report on Web sites in art history. The following sentences—most of them appear at the beginning of a paragraph—illustrate how she uses time signals ("first," "today," "started," "my next stop," and "then") to create an interesting story about surfing the Web.

> I first studied art history the old-fashioned way: scribbling notes in a dark auditorium …
> Inspired by the sheer volume of images available … I decided to try my hand at digitally designing my own art education.
> My self-directed syllabus started in Spain …
> I started in Italy, which I soon discovered doesn't include … the Vatican.
> My next stop was Paris, where my first visit was to … the Louvre.
> From Giverny I hopped over to Greece …

As these sentences illustrate, chronological order can transform a potentially boring list of Web sites into an interesting narrative journey.

Comparison and Contrast

Comparison and contrast are as essential to investigating and reporting as they are to observing and remembering. In "Surfin' the Louvre," Elizabeth Larsen organizes her essay around a comparison between her traditional campus art course and her online education. Similarly, Charles McGrath, in his article on Stephen Colbert, uses comparison to organize sections of his profile: "There used to be just two Stephen Colberts, and they were hard enough to distinguish. The main difference was that one thought the other was an idiot. . . . The other Colbert, the non-idiot, was the 47-year-old Souh Carolinian. . . ."

Additional Shaping Strategies

Other shaping strategies, discussed in previous chapters, may be useful for your investigation, too. *Simile, metaphor,* or *analogy* may develop and shape parts of your article. Even in investigative reporting, writers may create an identifiable *persona* or adopt a humorous tone. Elizabeth Larsen, in "Surfin' the Louvre," establishes a friendly and humorous tone: "That's a heck of a lot more reproductions than you'll find in that chiropractically unfriendly art history text, H. W. Janson's *History of Art*." Larsen demonstrates that even journalistic writing can have a sense of fun.

Title, Introduction, and Conclusion

Especially in an investigative report, a catchy title is important to help get your readers' interest and attention. Jot down several ideas for titles now and add to that list *after* you've drafted your essay.

In your introductory paragraph(s), answering the reporter's questions will help focus your investigation. Or you may wish to use a short *narrative,* as Larsen does in "Surfin' the Louvre." Other types of lead-ins, such as a short *description,* a *question,* a *statement of a problem,* a *startling fact* or *statistic,* or an arresting *quotation,* may get the reader's interest and focus on the main idea you wish to investigate. (See Chapter 7 for additional examples of lead-ins.)

The conclusion should resolve the question or questions posed in the investigation, summarize the most important information (useful primarily for long or complicated reports), and give the reader a sense of completion, often by picking up an idea, fact, quotation, or bit of description from the introduction.

Some writers like to have a title and know how they're going to start a piece of writing before they begin drafting. However, if you can't think of the perfect title or introduction, begin drafting and work on the title, the introduction, and the conclusion later.

DRAFTING

"All good writing is swimming under water and holding your breath."

—F. Scott Fitzgerald,
Author of *The Great Gatsby*

Before you begin a first draft, reconsider your purpose in writing and further focus your questions, sense of audience, and shaping strategies.

The drafting of an investigative essay requires that you have all your facts, statistics, quotations, summaries, notes from interviews, or results of surveys ready to use. Organize your notes, decide on an overall shaping strategy, or write a sketch outline. In investigative writing, one danger is postponing writing too long in the mistaken belief that if you read just one more article or interview just one more person, you'll get the information you need. At some point, usually *before* you feel ready, you must begin writing. (Professional writers rarely feel they know enough about their subject, but deadlines require them to begin.) Your main problem will be having too much to say rather than not enough. When you have too much, go back to your focusing questions to see whether you can narrow your topic further.

REVISING

After you have drafted your essay, you may wish to get feedback from your peers about your work. The peer response guidelines below will help you to review your goals for this assignment and to construct a revision plan. When you read other students' drafts or ideas, be as constructively critical as possible. Think carefully about the assignment. Be honest about your own reactions as a reader. What would make the draft better?

Guidelines for Revision

As you add, delete, substitute, or rearrange materials, keep the following tips in mind.

- **Reexamine your purpose and audience.** Are you doing what you intended? You should be *reporting* your findings; you should *not* be arguing for or against any idea.
- **Is the genre of your report responsive to audience needs and expectations?** Use samples of other writing for your audience (from newspapers, magazines, or journals) as models. Would visuals be effective in your essay?
- **Can you add your own observations or experiences to the investigation?** Remember that your own perceptions and experiences as a reporter are also relevant data.
- **Review the reporter's questions.** Are you providing your readers with relevant information *early* in the report and also catching their interest with a key statistic, fact, quotation, example, question, description, or short narrative?
- **Recheck your summaries, paraphrases, or direct quotations.** Are they accurate, and have you cited these sources in your text?
- **Use signals, cues, and transitions to indicate your shaping strategies.** *Chronological order:* before, then, afterward, next, soon, later, finally, at last *Comparison/contrast:* likewise, similarly, however, yet, even so, in contrast *Analysis:* first, next, third, fourth, finally
- **Revise sentences for directness, clarity, and conciseness.** Avoid unnecessary use of the passive voice.
- **Edit your report for appropriate word choice, usage, and grammar.** Check your writing for problems in spelling and punctuation.

PeerResponse

The instructions that follow will help you give and receive constructive advice about the rough draft of your investigative essay. You may use these guidelines for an in-class workshop, a take-home review, or an e-mail response.

Writer: Before you exchange drafts with another reader, write out the following on your essay draft or in an e-mail message.

1. **Purpose** Briefly describe your purpose and intended audience. For your audience, write out the title of a newspaper or magazine that might print your investigative report.
2. **Revision plans** Obviously, your draft is just a draft. What still needs work as you continue revising? Explain. (You don't want your reader to critique problems you intend to fix.)
3. **Questions** Write out one or two questions that you still have about your draft. What questions would you like your reader to answer?

Reader: First, read the entire draft from start to finish. As you reread the draft, answer the following questions.

1. **Purpose** Remember that the purpose of this essay is to report information accurately and objectively, not to argue or editorialize. Does this writer go beyond reporting to editorializing or arguing? If so, point out specific sentences that need revision.
2. **Evidence** List the kinds of evidence the writer uses. What additional kinds of sources might the writer use: An interview? A source on the Web? Personal observation? Other print sources? A survey?
3. **Key investigative question** When you read the essay, the key question should become apparent. Write it out. If there are places in the essay that don't relate to that key question, should they be omitted? Explain. Are there other aspects of the key question that the writer should address? Explain.
4. **Reader's response** An investigative essay should satisfy your curiosity about the topic. What did you want to learn about the topic that the essay does not answer? Write out any questions that you would like the writer to answer as he or she revises the essay.
5. **Answer the writer's questions in number 3.**

Postscript on the Writing Process

While the process of writing an investigative essay is still fresh in your mind, answer the following questions in your journal.

1. What sources of information (articles, books, interviews, surveys) were most helpful in your investigation? Explain.
2. Most researchers discover that the more they learn, the more they still need to know about their subjects. If you had more time to work on this essay, which sources would you investigate further?
3. What was the most difficult problem you had to solve during your collecting, shaping, drafting, and revising? What helped you most as you tried to solve this problem (further reading, additional writing, advice from peers)? Explain.
4. What was the single most important thing you learned about investigating as you wrote this paper?
5. What do you like best about the final version of your report?

“We are all apprentices at a craft where no one ever becomes a master.”

—Ernest Hemingway, Novelist

Read a model report

Student Writing

Permanent Tracings

Jennifer Macke

Jennifer Macke, a student in Professor Rachel Henne-Wu’s class at Owens Community College in Findlay, Ohio, decided to write her *investigative* essay about a tattoo parlor. She visited the Living Color Tattoo Parlor and took notes on the office, the clientele, the conversations, the artwork of the tattoos, and the owner of the establishment. Here are some of her original notes, questions and answers, an outline, and the final version of her essay.

NOTES ON A VISIT

- A couple with a young school-aged daughter looks at the artwork on the walls for about 15 minutes before saying anything to the owner. They are looking for a design for the wife for her birthday. They appear to be a typical young couple with a limited amount of money. They ask how much a particular design will be and say they will have to save for it. “How much for this ankle bracelet?” he says. “It’ll run you between $45 and $60, depending on how thick you want the rose vine,” Gasket says.

...continued Permanent Tracings, **Jennifer Macke**

- Two Latino men enter the waiting room. One peeks his head into the office and says, "I'm here early for my appointment because I'm not sure exactly what I want. Do you have any books or more pictures I can look through?" Gasket gives him six photo albums full of ideas (designs).
- Five young adult black men enter. They begin browsing through the photos on the wall. There are designs with prices below them so you know what it costs without asking. They too look through the photo albums the Latinos left on the floor. One of the black guys announces, "I'll go first 'cause I want to get it over with." One says, "I'm not going to do this. I can't stand the sound of that needle!" Gasket looks at me and says, "It's amazing how many people just think all you have to do is walk through the door like a walk-in barber shop. They don't know I'm booked for at least a week. During the summer, it's three weeks."
- The next girl is going to have lips tattooed on her right hip. She is a petite nurse whom you would never guess would even consider such a thing. Her husband put lipstick on and kissed a napkin which she brought to use for the pattern. Gasket took a photocopy of this and made a transfer from it to use as the template. She dropped her shorts to expose where the art would be placed. She lay down on the table which Gasket explained he had gotten in trade for a tattoo. He also said the stirrups were still in the drawer. The girl smiled and talked the whole time he worked. At one point, he asked her, "Does it hurt?" She said, "No." He said, "I can go deeper!" She said, "Are you supposed to?" He said, laughing, "It's just a joke. If I see someone who's comfortable, I'll ask them this." It only took about 30 minutes to complete this one. You would swear someone just kissed her with bright red lipstick. It's amazing how realistic his work looks.

QUESTIONS AND ANSWERS

"Why do people get tattoos?"

"A tattoo is a very personal thing. It's an expression of one's self."

"Does it hurt to get a tattoo?"

"It all depends on the placement and the person. Guys tend to be bigger wimps. I'd rather do women any day. The most painful areas are the ankle and higher up on the belly. I've had the pain described as something annoying but not necessarily painful to such a point that they cannot stand it. I've never had anyone pass out, though."

"What kind of person gets a tattoo?"

"There's not one particular type of person who gets a tattoo. I once had a call from some lawyers from Findlay. They wanted to know if they had five or so people who wanted a tattoo, would I come over? I said, yes, and I tattooed six lawyers at a party."

"What is the process of getting a tattoo?"

"Depending if it will be freehand or something the people bring in, it starts with drawing the art. It is drawn either on the person or on carbon paper backwards. The carbon design is transferred to the skin with Speed Stick deodorant. The outline is applied first. As the single needle picks up and sews into the skin, excess ink covers the work area."

As Gasket works, it's hard to see the actual area he's working on because of the excess ink. When asked how he can work with the excess ink obstructing the guidelines, he says he just knows where the line goes. (I wouldn't.) Once the outline is complete he changes to use a 3 or 4 needle set, depending on the coverage necessary. He colorizes the art, which brings it to life. After it's complete, he puts a thick coat of Bacitracin on and covers it with a gauze bandage. The gauze must remain on for one and a half to two hours.

"What is the most common place for a tattoo?"

"Placement runs in cycles, sometimes the upper arm, sometimes the ankle." While we were talking, a man came in with one on the back of his neck.

"How expensive are tattoos?"

The minimum is $30. Depending on how detailed and how big. Gasket has bartered for the tattoos, too.

"Do most people get more than one tattoo?"

"I've seen people go through life with only one or maybe two, but it's said when you get your third, you're hooked. You'll be back for more."

"Are there health department requirements?"

"At the beginning, the requirements (laws) weren't very strict. I knew I wanted to be supersterile, so I put my needles and equipment through a much stricter procedure. Since then, the health department has taken on my policy and requires everyone to process their stuff like me. They drop in to make sure the laws are being followed."

...continued Permanent Tracings, **Jennifer Macke**

"How many times do you use your needles?"

"They are single-application needles, but they still need to be sterilized. People ask me if they can watch their needles being sterilized so they can make sure. I say fine, but it will be two and a half hours until I can work on you."

Outline

Working Thesis: "Gasket's creative artistic ability and perfectionist work ethic make his designs worth sewing into your body for a lifetime."

I. Describe the Tattoo Parlor
- A. Outer area (waiting room)
- B. Inner office

II. Describe the owner
- A. The way he looks
- B. The way he feels about his work

III. Describe the people
- A. People getting a tattoo
- B. People not getting a tattoo

FINAL VERSION

Permanent Tracings

At first glance, the Living Color Tattoo Parlor appears to be just another typical tattoo establishment. You enter through a glass door only to find a waiting room with the decor reminiscent of the 1970s. The dark paneled walls display numerous types of artwork that range from pencil sketching to color Polaroid snapshots of newly completed tattoos. The gold and green davenport looks as if it came from a Saturday morning garage sale. The inner office is celery green with a dental chair and an obstetrics table that the owner bartered for a tattoo (the stirrups are still in the drawer). A filing cabinet, desk, and copy machine make you feel as if you're in a professional office. The sterilizer is in plain sight and is in operation. Bottle after bottle of brightly colored inks are neatly arranged on a tiered wooden stand. The sound of the oscillating fan that cools the client interrupts the buzz of the needle sewing the paint into the client's skin. A freeze-dried turtle is displayed on a table in the office. 1

I still wondered, though. Could tattoos actually be a form of art? 2

As soon as I could, I asked the owner, a man called Gasket, about his occupation. "I was a suit for fifteen years and now I can work as much as 3

I want. There's always somebody wanting a tattoo or something pierced," Gasket said. He's often asked if he'll scratch out the name of a previous girlfriend, and he always replies that he would never even consider it. "That would be defacement," he said. "When I'm done, the design should look better than when I started." Gasket is not his given name but one he acquired because of his expert repair work on Harley Davidson motorcycles. Gasket is the owner of this establishment, and to look at him, you would never guess he is a college-educated engineer. His long curly, graying hair flows from under his Harley hat, and examples of his handiwork are visible under the rolled up sleeves of his black Harley T-shirt. The harshness of his heavily bearded face is softened by his slate-blue eyes, which mirror his gentle demeanor. If you look past his casual exterior, you will find a code of steel. "At the beginning, the laws weren't very strict. I knew I wanted to be supersterile, so I put my single-use needles and equipment through a much stricter procedure. Since then, the health department has taken on my policy and requires everyone to process their stuff like me," he said.

The appearance of the Living Color Tattoo Parlor may be typical, but two things are distinctly different: the quality and the creativity of the tattoo designs. A young college couple from Toledo was asked why they would drive to Fremont for an appointment. They answered, "Gasket's the best! We wouldn't trust something that's going to be on our body for the rest of our lives to someone other than him." *4*

"I already have two tattoos from you, and I love your work," a middle-aged woman said. Displaying two greeting cards, she asked, "Is it possible to get a combination of these two designs?" *5*

"I can create anything you want," Gasket said. *6*

"I'll have to wait a couple of weeks because I'm not working much and my other bills come first," she said. *7*

"Yes, you have to get your priorities straight. When you're ready, I'm here," he said. *8*

Gasket is performing his tattoo magic on a young college female. He's creating a rose with a heart stem wrapping around her belly button, which is pierced. The girl is nervously seated in the green dental chair, which is tilted back to flatten the skin surface. First, Gasket draws the sketch on her belly. He covers his hands with a thin layer of latex once the exact position and specific details are decided upon. A small device resembling a fountain pen with a brightly colored motor and a single needle moving at 1,000 rpm is used to apply the black outline first. As the needle moves up and down, it picks up a small amount of ink and deposits it just under the surface of the skin. When asked how he can work with the excess ink obstructing the guidelines, he simply said he just knows where the line goes. This is a difficult task because unlike a paint-by-number design, the image not only has to be in his mind but he also has to have the artistic ability to convert the image to the skin. The girl asks a pain-filled question, "How much longer?" *9*

...continued Permanent Tracings, **Jennifer Macke**

10 "I can stop and let you take a break at any time," Gasket says. His soft tone and slow-paced voice help soothe the girl. "The higher up on the belly, the more painful," he says. The process of colorizing the tattoo begins once the outline is complete. This is accomplished with a three- or four-needle set, depending on the amount of coverage desired. It takes about forty-five minutes to complete the multicolored masterpiece, which is literally sewn into her skin. Some of Gasket's designs can be compared to Picasso's brilliantly colored, dreamlike images. Upon completion, the girl is directed to a full-length mirror to inspect her permanently altered abs.

11 "It looks fantastic!" she exclaims. "I was a little vague on how I pictured it would look, but it looks even better than I had imagined. I'm thrilled."

12 Once thought of as green-toned disfigurements that only drunken sailors and lowlife people would don, tattoos are now high fashion. Now it is possible to see skin art on TV stars, sports superstars, and a multitude of individuals you might not suspect. The future of this trendy fashion has its roots firmly planted in today's society. Young people seem to be one of its biggest supporters.

13 "I'll go first 'cause I want to get it over with," one young black man states to his four companions.

14 "I'm not going to do this. I can't stand the sound of that needle!" another man proclaims.

15 "It's amazing how many people think all you have to do is just walk through the door like a walk-in barber shop. They don't know I'm booked for at least a week. During the summer, it's three weeks," Gasket claims. He explains this to the young men, who make appointments. They leave, disappointed.

16 Gasket's tattoo designs can be compared to the famous fashion designs by Bob Mackie. Like Mackie's one-of-a-kind designs, they are not mass-produced, but are hand-sewn for a specific individual. As I left, my first impression of the Living Color Tattoo Parlor was changed by the incredibly beautiful skin art and the comments of the satisfied clients. For many, Gasket's artistic ability and perfectionism make his designs worth sewing into your body for a lifetime.

Questions for Writing and Discussion

1. Review the techniques for writing an investigative paper at the beginning of the chapter. Did Macke ask good questions to get information? Did she conduct field research? Did she include a short profile of Gasket? What other investigating strategies did she use?

2. Reread Macke's notes of her visit, including her questions and answers. What interesting ideas and descriptions in her notes might be included in her final draft? Why might Macke have left these details out? Assume that you are a peer reader for Macke's essay. Fill out the peer response questions printed earlier in this chapter so you can help her with a revision of her essay.
3. List the three things that you like best about Macke's essay. Which of her strategies might work for a revision of your own essay? Make a revision plan for your own essay, based on what you learned from reading "Permanent Tracings."

Complete additional exercises and practice in your MyLab

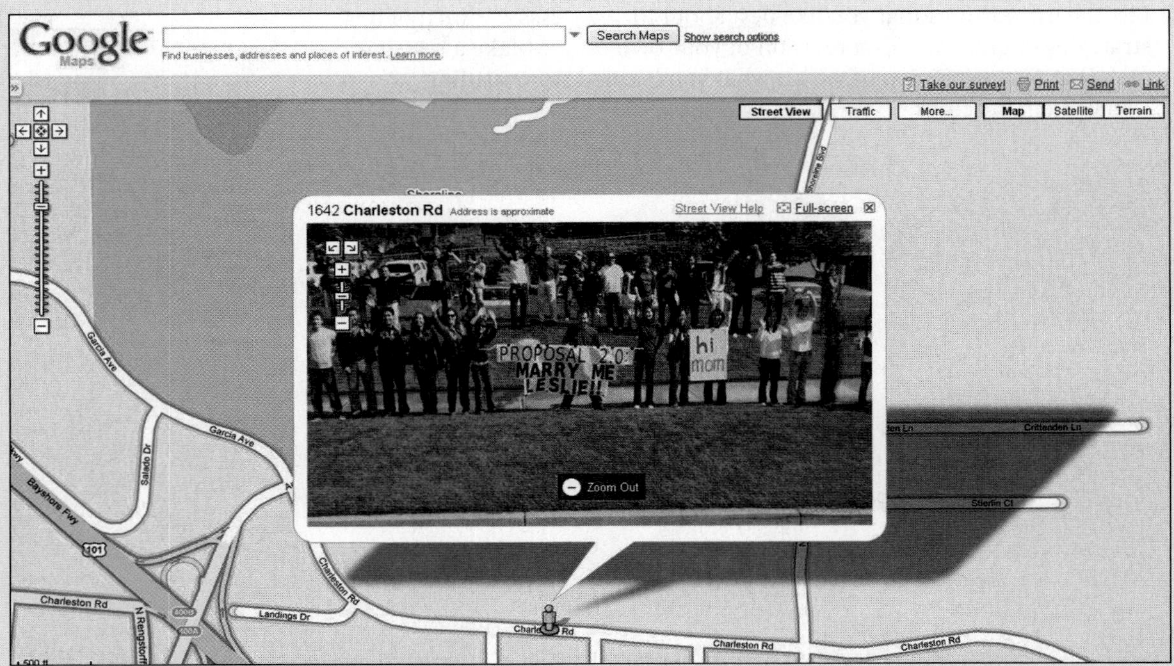

The image above was captured from Google Street Views. Although many Google street views show people unaware that the Google camera car is passing, these people knew the camera car was coming and prepared to have their picture taken. A Journal exercise in this chapter considers the ethics of publishing such a photo.

7 Explaining

What You Will Learn
In this chapter, you will learn to:

- **7.1** Use techniques for explaining what (definition)
- **7.2** Use techniques for explaining how (process analysis)
- **7.3** Use techniques for explaining why (causal analysis)
- **7.4** Use collecting strategies for developing your explanatory essay
- **7.5** Shape your explanatory essay

EXPLAINING and demonstrating relationships is a frequent purpose for writing. Explaining goes beyond investigating the facts and reporting information; it analyzes the component parts of a subject and then shows how the parts fit in relation to one another. Its goal is to clarify for a particular group of readers *what* something is, *how* it happened or should happen, and/or *why* it happens.

Explaining begins with assessing the rhetorical situation: the writer, the occasion, the intended purpose and audience, the genre, and the cultural context. As you begin thinking about a topic, keep in mind your own interests, the expectations of your audience, the possible genre you might choose (essay, article, pamphlet, multigenre essay, Web site), and the cultural or social context in which you are writing or in which your writing might be read.

Explaining any idea, concept, process, or effect requires analysis. Analysis starts with dividing a thing or phenomenon into its parts. Then, once you explain the various parts, you put them back together (synthesis) to explain their relationship or how they work together.

> **"Become aware of the two-sided nature of your mental make-up: one thinks in terms of the connectedness of things, the other thinks in terms of parts and sequences."**
>
> —Gabriele Lusser Rico, Author of *Writing the Natural Way*

"What [a writer] knows is almost always a matter of the relationships he establishes, between example and generalization, between one part of a narrative and the next, between the idea and the counter idea that the writer sees is also relevant."

—Roger Sale,
Author of *On Writing*

Explaining how to play the piano, for example, begins with an analysis of the parts of the learning process: playing scales, learning chords, getting instruction from a teacher, sight reading, and practicing. Explaining why two automobiles collided at an intersection begins with an analysis of the contributing factors: the nature of the intersection, the number of cars involved, the condition of the drivers, and the condition of each vehicle. Then you bring the parts together and show their *relationships:* you show how practicing scales on the piano fits into the process of learning to play the piano; you demonstrate why one small factor—such as a faulty turn signal—combined with other factors to cause an automobile accident.

The emphasis you give to the *analysis* of the object or phenomenon and the time you spend explaining *relationships* of the parts depends on your purpose and audience. If you want to explain how a flower reproduces, for example, you may begin by identifying the important parts, such as the pistil and stamen, that most readers need to know about before they can understand the reproductive process. However, if you are explaining the process to a botany major who already knows the parts of a flower, you might spend more time discussing the key operations in pollination or the reasons why some flowers cross-pollinate. In any effective explanation, analyzing parts and showing relationships must work together for that group of readers.

Because its purpose is to teach the reader, *expository writing,* or writing to explain, should be as clear as possible. Explanations, however, are more than organized pieces of information. Expository writing contains information that is focused by your point of view, by your experience, and by your reasoning powers. Thus, your explanation of a thing or phenomenon makes a point or has a thesis: This is the *right* way to define *happiness.* This is how one *should* bake lasagne or do a calculus problem. To make your explanation clear, you use specific support: facts, data, examples, illustrations, statistics, comparisons, analogies, and images. Your thesis is a *general* assertion about the relationships of the *specific* parts. The support helps your reader identify the parts and see the relationships. Expository writing teaches the reader by alternating between generalizations and specific examples.

Techniques for Explaining

"The main thing I try to do is write as clearly as I can."

—E. B. White,
Journalist and Coauthor of *Elements of Style*

Explaining requires first that you assess your rhetorical situation. Your purpose must work for a particular audience, genre, and context. You may revise some of these aspects of the rhetorical situation as you draw on your own observations and memories about your topic. On the next page are techniques for writing clear explanations.

Techniques for Explaining

Technique	Tips on How to Do It
Considering (and reconsidering) your purpose, audience, genre, and social context	As you change your *audience* or your *genre,* you must change how you explain something as well as how much and what kind of evidence you use.
Getting the reader's attention and stating the thesis	Devise an accurate but interesting *title*. Use an attention-getting *lead-in*. State the *thesis* clearly.
Defining key terms and describing *what* something is	Analyze and define by *describing, comparing, classifying* and/or *giving examples*.
Identifying the steps in a process and showing *how* each step relates to the overall process	Describe *how* something should be done or *how* something typically happens.
Describing causes and effects and showing *why* certain causes lead to specific effects	Analyze how several causes lead to a *single effect,* or show how a single cause leads to *multiple effects*.
Supporting explanations with specific evidence	Use descriptions, examples, comparisons, analogies, images, facts, data, or statistics to *show* what, how, or why.

In *Spirit of the Valley: Androgyny and Chinese Thought,* psychologist Sukie Colgrave illustrates many of these techniques as she explains an important concept from psychology: the phenomenon of *projection.* Colgrave explains how we "project" attributes missing in our own personality onto another person—especially someone we love.

A one-sided development of either the masculine or feminine principles has [an] unfortunate consequence for our psychological and intellectual health: it encourages the phenomenon termed "projection." This is the process by which we project onto other people, things, or ideologies, those aspects of ourselves which we have not, for whatever reason, acknowledged or developed. The most familiar example of this is the obsession which usually accompanies being "in love." A person whose feminine side is unrealised will often "fall in love" with the feminine which she or he "sees" in another person, and similarly with the masculine. The experience of being "in love" is one of powerful dependency. As long as the projection appears to fit its object nothing

Explaining what: Definition example

Explaining why: Effects of projection

awakens the person to the reality of the projection. But sooner or later the lover usually becomes aware of certain discrepancies between her or his desires and the person chosen to satisfy them. Resentment, disappointment, anger and rejection rapidly follow, and often the relationship disintegrates. . . . But if we can explore our own psyches we may discover what it is we were demanding from our lover and start to develop it in ourselves. The moment this happens we begin to see other people a little more clearly. We are freed from some of our needs to make others what we want them to be, and can begin to love them more for what they are.

Explaining how: The process of freeing ourselves from dependency

EXPLAINING *WHAT:* DEFINITION

7.1
Use techniques for explaining what (definition)

Explaining *what* something is or means requires showing the relationship between it and the *class* of beings, objects, or concepts to which it belongs. *Formal definition,* which is often essential in explaining, has three parts: the thing or term to be defined, the class, and the distinguishing characteristics of the thing or term. The thing being defined can be concrete, such as a turkey, or abstract, such as democracy.

Thing or Term	Class	Distinguishing Characteristics
A turkey is a	bird	that has brownish plumage and a bare, wattled head and neck; it is widely domesticated for food.
Democracy is	government	by the people, exercised directly or through elected representatives.

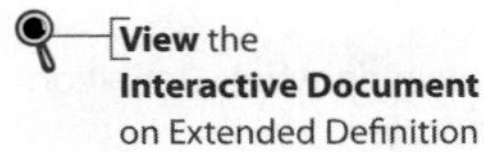
View the **Interactive Document** on Extended Definition

Frequently, writers use *extended definitions* when they need to give more than a mere formal definition. An extended definition may explain a word's etymology or historical roots, describe sensory characteristics (how an object looks, feels, sounds, tastes, smells), identify its parts, indicate how something is used, explain what it is not, provide an example, and/or note similarities or differences between this term and other words or things.

The following extended definition of democracy, written for an audience of college students and appearing in a textbook, begins with the etymology of the word and then explains—using analysis, comparison, example, and description—what democracy is and what it is not.

Since democracy is government of the people, by the people, and for the people, a democratic form of government is not fixed or static. Democracy is dynamic; it adapts to the wishes and needs of the people. The term *democracy* derives from the Greek word *demos,* meaning "the common people," and *-kratia,* meaning "strength or power" used to govern or rule. Democracy is based on the notion that a majority of people creates laws and then everyone agrees to abide by those laws in the interest of the common good. In a democracy, people are not ruled by a king, a dictator, or a small group of powerful individuals. Instead, people elect officials who use the power temporarily granted to them to govern the society. For example, the people may agree that their government should raise money for defense, so the officials levy taxes to support an army. If enough people decide, however, that taxes for defense are too high, then they request that their elected officials change the laws or they elect new officials. The essence of democracy lies in its responsiveness: Democracy is a form of government in which laws and lawmakers change as the will of the majority changes.

Formal definition

Description: What democracy is

Etymology: Analysis of the word's roots

Comparison: What democracy is not

Example

Formal definition

More typically, extended definitions are informal and are followed by examples that illustrate and explain the concept. In the following definition, Caterina Fake, the founder of *Flickr* and *Hunch,* defines on her blog the social phenomenon of FOMO.

FOMO and Social Media

I've been watching Twitter and Ditto feeds of people at SxSW [South by Southwest], and, from a distance, I get a distinct sense of the social anxiety and FOMO that's going on there. "FOMO" stands for "Fear of Missing Out" and it's what happens everywhere on a typical Saturday night, when you're trying to decide if you should stay in, or muster the energy to go to the party. At SxSW I see people wondering if they're at the wrong party—the party where they are is lame, feels uncool, has too much brand advertising or doesn't have anyone there they'd want to hook up with—and so they move on to the next party where they have to wait in line too

Caterina Fake, cofounder of *Hunch* and *Flickr.*

long, can't get a beer, or don't find their friends, and so move on to the next venue where ... and so on.

FOMO is a great motivator of human behavior, and I think a crucial key to understanding social software, and why it works the way it does. Many people have studied the game mechanics that keep people collecting things (points, trophies, check-ins, mayorships, kudos). Others have studied how the neurochemistry that keeps us checking Facebook every five minutes is similar to the neurochemistry fueling addiction. Social media has made us even more aware of the things we are missing out on. You're home alone, but watching your friends status updates tell of a great party happening somewhere. You are aware of more parties than ever before. And, like gym memberships, adding Bergman movies to your Netflix queue and piling up unread copies of the New Yorker, watching these feeds gives you a sense that you're participating, not missing out, even when you are.

EXPLAINING *HOW:* PROCESS ANALYSIS

7.2
Use techniques for explaining how (process analysis)

Explaining how something should be done or how something happens is called process analysis. There are two kinds of process analysis: *prescriptive* and *descriptive*.

- *Prescriptive* analyses: Typically, prescriptive processes involve a "how to" explanation—how to cook a turkey, how to tune an engine, how to get a job. The analysis is "prescriptive" because it explains the right way to do something to get the best results.
- *Descriptive* analyses: Usually, descriptive process analyses simply explain how something typically happens without suggesting that this is the right way or best way to do something.

In both prescriptive and descriptive process analyses, you analyze a process—dividing the sequence into steps or parts—and then show how the parts contribute to and explain the whole process.

Cookbooks, automobile-repair manuals, instructions for assembling toys or appliances, and self-improvement books are all examples of *prescriptive* process analysis. Writers of recipes, for example, begin with analyses of the ingredients and the steps in preparing the food. Then they carefully explain how the steps are related, how to avoid problems, and how to serve mouth-watering concoctions. Farley Mowat, naturalist and author of *Never Cry Wolf,* gives his readers the following detailed recipe for creamed mouse. Mowat became interested in this recipe when he decided to test the nutritional content of the wolf's diet. "In the event that any of my readers may be interested in personally exploiting this hitherto overlooked source of excellent animal protein," Mowat writes, "I give the recipe in full."

Souris à la Crème

Ingredients:

One dozen fat mice	Salt and pepper	One cup white flour
Cloves	One piece sowbelly	Ethyl alcohol

Skin and gut the mice, but do not remove the heads; wash, then place in a pot with enough alcohol to cover the carcasses. Allow to marinate for about two hours. Cut sowbelly into small cubes and fry slowly until most of the fat has been rendered. Now remove the carcasses from the alcohol and roll them in a mixture of salt, pepper and flour; then place in frying pan and sauté for about five minutes (being careful not to allow the pan to get too hot, or the delicate meat will dry out and become tough and stringy). Now add a cup of alcohol and six or eight cloves. Cover the pan and allow to simmer slowly for fifteen minutes. The cream sauce can be made according to any standard recipe. When the sauce is ready, drench the carcasses with it, cover and allow to rest in a warm place for ten minutes before serving.

Explaining *how* something happens or is typically done involves a *descriptive* process analysis. It requires showing the chronological relationship between one idea, event, or phenomenon and the next—and it depends on close observation. In *The Lives of a Cell,* biologist and physician Lewis Thomas explains that ants are like humans: while they are individuals, they can also act together to create a social organism. Although exactly how ants communicate remains a mystery, Thomas explains how they combine to form a thinking, working organism.

[Ants] seem to live two kinds of lives: they are individuals, going about the day's business without much evidence of thought for tomorrow, and they are at the same time component parts, cellular elements, in the huge, writhing, ruminating organism of the Hill, the nest, the hive. . . .

A solitary ant, afield, cannot be considered to have much of anything on his mind; indeed, with only a few neurons strung together by fibers, he can't be imagined to have a mind at all, much less a thought. He is more like a ganglion on legs. Four ants together, or ten, encircling a dead moth on a path, begin to look more like an idea. They fumble and shove, gradually moving the food toward the Hill, but as though by blind chance. It is only when you watch the dense mass of thousands of ants, crowded together around the Hill, blackening the ground, that you begin to see the whole beast, and now you observe it thinking, planning, calculating. It is an intelligence, a kind of live computer, with crawling bits for its wits.

At a stage in the construction, twigs of a certain size are needed, and all the members forage obsessively for twigs of just this size. Later, when outer walls are to be finished, thatched, the size must change, and as though given new orders by telephone, all the workers shift the search to the new twigs. If you disturb the arrangement of a part of the Hill, hundreds of ants will set it vibrating, shifting, until it is put right again.

EXPLAINING *WHY:* CAUSAL ANALYSIS

7.3
Use techniques for explaining why (causal analysis)

"Why?" may be the question most commonly asked by human beings. We are fascinated by the reasons for everything that we experience in life. We ask questions about natural phenomena: Why is the sky blue? Why does a teakettle whistle? Why do some materials act as superconductors? We also find human attitudes and behavior intriguing: Why is chocolate so popular? Why did the United States go to war in Iraq?

Explaining *why* something occurs can be the most fascinating—and difficult—kind of expository writing. Answering the question "why" usually requires analyzing *cause-and-effect relationships.* The causes, however, may be too complex or intangible to identify precisely. We are on comparatively secure ground when we ask *why* about physical phenomena that can be weighed, measured, and replicated under laboratory conditions. Under those conditions, we can determine cause and effect with precision.

Fire, for example, has three *necessary* and *sufficient* causes: combustible material, oxygen, and ignition temperature. Without each of these causes, fire will not occur (each cause is "necessary"); taken together, these three causes are enough to cause fire (all three together are "sufficient"). In this case, the cause-and-effect relationship can be illustrated by an equation:

Cause 1 +	Cause 2 +	Cause 3 =	Effect
(combustible material)	(oxygen)	(ignition temperature)	(fire)

Analyzing both necessary and sufficient causes is essential to explaining an effect. You may say, for example, that wind shear (an abrupt downdraft in a storm) "caused" an airplane crash. In fact, wind shear may have *contributed* (been necessary) to the crash but was not by itself the total (sufficient) cause of the crash: an airplane with enough power may be able to overcome wind shear forces in certain circumstances. An explanation of the crash is not complete until you analyze the full range of necessary *and* sufficient causes, which may include wind shear, lack of power, mechanical failure, and even pilot error.

Cause-and-effect relationships are particularly tricky to prove. What kind of evidence do we need to prove that A causes B? The following short editorial shows how racial prejudice in major league baseball affects umpires' judgment in calling balls and strikes. In support of his claim of cause and effect, David Sirota cites extensive statistical evidence from 3.5 million pitches over a period of four years to demonstrate that racial prejudice still exists and that it impairs the judgment of umpires. Sirota is the author of *Back to Our Future: How the 1980s Explain the World We Live in Now.*

Professional Writing

How Baseball Explains Modern Racism

David Sirota

Despite recent odes to "post-racial" sensibilities, persistent racial wage and unemployment gaps show that prejudice is alive and well in America. Nonetheless, that truism is often angrily denied or willfully ignored in our society, in part because prejudice is so much more difficult to recognize on a day-to-day basis. As opposed to the Jim Crow era of white hoods and lynch mobs, 21st century American bigotry is now more often an unseen crime of the subtle and the reflexive—and the crime scene tends to be the shadowy nuances of hiring decisions, performance evaluations, and plausible deniability. *1*

Thankfully, though, we now have baseball to help shine a light on the problem so that everyone can see it for what it really is. *2*

Today, Major League Baseball games using the QuesTec computerized pitch-monitoring system are the most statistically quantifiable workplaces in America. Match up QuesTec's accumulated data with demographic information about who is pitching and who is calling balls and strikes, and you get the indisputable proof of how ethnicity does indeed play a part in discretionary decisions of those in power positions. *3*

This is exactly what Southern Methodist University's researchers did when they examined more than 3.5 million pitches from 2004 to 2008. Their findings say as much about the enduring relationship between sports and bigotry as they do about the synaptic nature of racism in all of American society. *4*

First and foremost, SMU found that home-plate umpires call disproportionately more strikes for pitchers in their same ethnic group. Because most home-plate umpires are white, this has been a big form of racial privilege for white pitchers, who researchers show are, on average, getting disproportionately more of the benefit of the doubt on close calls. *5*

...continued How Baseball Explains Modern Racism, **David Sirota**

Second, SMU researchers found that "minority pitchers reacted to umpire bias by playing it safe with the pitches they threw in a way that actually harmed their performance and statistics." Basically, these hurlers adjusted to the white umpires' artificially narrower strike zone by throwing pitches down the heart of the plate, where they were easier for batters to hit. *6*

Finally, and perhaps most importantly, the data suggest that racial bias is probably operating at a subconscious level, where the umpire doesn't even recognize it. *7*

To document this, SMU compared the percentage of strikes called in QuesTec-equipped ballparks versus non-QuesTec parks. *8*

Researchers found that umpires' racial biases diminished when they knew they were being monitored by the computer. Same thing for high-profile moments. During those important points in games when umpires knew fans were more carefully watching the calls, the racial bias all but vanished. Likewise, the same-race preference was less pronounced at high-attendance games, where umps knew there would be more crowd scrutiny. *9*

Though gleaned from baseball, these findings transcend athletics by providing a larger lesson about conditioned behavior in an institutionally racist society. *10*

Whether the workplace is a baseball diamond, a factory floor or an office, when authority figures realize they are being scrutinized, they are more cognizant of their own biases—and more likely to try to stop them before they unduly influence their behavior. But in lower-profile interludes, when the workplace isn't scrutinized and decisions are happening on psychological autopilot, pre-programmed biases can take over. *11*

Thus, the inherent problem of today's pervasive "post-racial" fallacy. By perpetuating the lie that racism doesn't exist, pretending that bigotry is not a workplace problem anymore, and resisting governmental efforts to halt such prejudice, we create the environment for our ugly subconscious to rule. In doing so, we consequently reduce the potential for much-needed self-correction. *12*

Warming Up: Journal Exercises

The following exercises ask you to write explanations. Read all the exercises and then write on the three that interest you most. If another idea occurs to you, write about it.

1. **Writing Across the Curriculum.** Write a one-paragraph explanation of an idea, term, or concept that you have discussed in a class that you are currently taking. From biology, for example, you might define *photosynthesis* or *gene splicing*. From psychology, you might define *psychosis* or *projection*. From computer studies, you might define *cyberspace* or *morphing*. First, identify someone who might need to know about this subject. Then give a definition and an illustration. Finally, describe how the term was discovered or invented, what its effects or applications are, and/or how it works.

2. Review the Calvin and Hobbes cartoon above. Working by yourself or in a group, determine what idea or concept the cartoon is explaining. Then study each panel. What aspect of the overall idea or concept does each picture and dialogue explain? Finally, determine whether the cartoon clearly—and accurately—explains the concept. Be prepared to post your analysis on a forum or present your analysis in class.

3. Novelist Ernest Hemingway once defined *courage* as "grace under pressure." Using this definition, explain how you or someone you know showed this kind of courage in a difficult situation.

4. Choose a skill that you've acquired (for example, operating a machine, playing a sport, drawing, counseling others, dieting) and explain to a novice how he or she can acquire that skill. Reread what you've written. Then write another version addressed to an expert. What parts can you leave out? What must you add?

5 Examine the illustration of Google Street Views shown on the opening page of this chapter. Do some research online about what Google Street Views are, how these images are captured, and how to access them online. Then consider their possible effects. Although Google says that they blur the faces of people so that they are not identifiable, is this always true? Are there images that are clear invasions of privacy? Google has already captured images of apparent crimes—does that mean that these images could protect public safety or help send alleged criminals to jail? For a private, public, or academic audience, write your own blog or essay explaining the real or potential good or bad effects of Google Street Views.

6 Sometimes writers use standard definitions to explain a key term, but sometimes they need to resist conventional definition in order to make a point. LaMer Steptoe, an eleventh-grader in West Philadelphia, was faced with a form requiring her to check her racial identity. Like many Americans of multicultural heritage, she decided not to check one box. In the following paragraphs, reprinted from National Public Radio's *All Things Considered,* Ms. Steptoe explains how she decided to (re)define herself. As you read her response, consider how you might need to resist a conventional definition in your own explaining essay.

Professional Writing

Multiracialness

Caucasian, African-American, Latin American, Asian-American. Check one. I look black, so I'll pick that one. But, no, wait, if I pick that, I'll be denying the other sides of my family. So I'll pick white. But I'm not white or black, I'm both, and part Native American, too. It's confusing when you have to pick which race to identify with, especially when you have family who, on one side, ask, "Why do you talk like a white girl?" when, in the eyes of the other side of your family, your behind is black. *1*

I never met my dad's mom, my grandmother, Maybelle Dawson Boyd Steptoe, and my father never knew his father. But my aunts or uncles or cousins all think of me as black or white. I mean, I'm not the lightest-skinned person, but my cousins down South swear I'm white. It bothers them, and that bothers me, how people could care so much about your skin color. *2*

My mother's mother, Sylvia Gabriel, lives in Connecticut, near where my aunt, uncle and cousins on that side of the family live. Now, they're white, and where my grandma lives, there are very few black people or people of color. And when we visit, people look at us a lot, staring like, "What is that woman doing with those people?" It shocks the heck out of them when my brother and I call her Grandma. *3*

My mother's side is Italian. I really didn't get any Italian culture except for the food. My father was raised much differently from my mother. My father is superstitious; he believes that a child should know his or her place and not speak unless spoken to. My father is very much into both his African-American and Native American heritage. 4

Multiracialness is a very tricky subject for my father. He'll tell people that I'm Native, African-American and Caucasian American, but at the same time he'll say things like, "Listen to jazz, listen to your cultural music." He says, "LaMer, look in the mirror. You're black. Ask any white person: they'll say you're black." He doesn't get it. I really would rather be colorless than to pick a race. I like other music, not just black music. 5

The term African-American bugs me. I'm not African. I'm American as a hot dog. We should have friends who are yellow, red, blue, black, purple, gay, religious, bisexual, trilingual, whatever, so you don't have a stereotypical view. I've met mean people and nice people of all different backgrounds. At my school, I grew up with all these kids, and I didn't look at them as white or Jewish or heterosexual; I looked at them as, "Oh, she's funny, he's sweet." 6

I know what box I'm going to choose. I pick D for none of the above, because my race is human. 7

Professional Writing

How to Take Control of Your Credit Cards

Suze Orman

The author of several best-selling books, including The Money Book for the Young, Fabulous & Broke *(2005) and* Women and Money: Owning the Power to Control Your Destiny *(2007), Suze Orman was born in 1951 in Chicago, earned a degree in social work from the University of Illinois, and started her career not as a financial expert but as a waitress. After working at a restaurant for seven years, she talked her way into a job as a financial advisor with Merrill Lynch. Six of her most recent books have been* New York Times *best sellers. Now that she is young(ish), fabulous, and very wealthy, Suze Orman has her own CNBC TV show. "How to Take Control of Your Credit Cards" appeared originally as one of her regular columns for* Money Matters *on Yahoo! Finance.*

I'm all for taking credit where credit is due, but when it comes to credit cards, way too many of you are overdoing it. For Americans who don't pay their entire credit card bill each month, the average balance is close to $4,000. And when we zoom in on higher-income folks—those with annual incomes between $75,000 and $100,000—the average balance clocks in at nearly $8,000. If you're paying, say, 18 percent 1 interest on an $8,000 balance, and you make only the 2 percent minimum payment due each month, you are going to end up paying more than $22,000 in interest over the course of the 54 years it will take to get the balance down to zero.

That's absolute insanity. 2

And absolutely unnecessary. 3

If you have the desire to take control of your credit card mess, you can. 4
It's just a matter of choice. I am not saying it will be easy, but there are plenty of strategies that can put you on a path out of credit card hell. And as I explain later, even those of you who can't seem to turn the corner and become credit responsible on your own, can get plenty of help from qualified credit counseling services.

How to Be a Credit Card Shark

If you overspend just because you like to buy buy buy on credit, then 5
you are what I call Broke by Choice. You are willfully making your own mess. I am not going to lecture you about how damaging this is; I'm hoping the fact that you're reading this article means you are ready to make a change.

But I also realize that some of you are Broke by Circumstance. I 6
actually tell young adults in the dues-paying stage of their careers to lean on their credit cards if they don't yet make enough to always keep up with their bills. But the key is that if you rely on your credit cards to make ends meet, you must limit the plastic spending to true necessities, not indulgences. Buying groceries is a necessity. Buying dinner for you and your pals at a swank restaurant is an indulgence you can't afford if it will become part of your unpaid credit card balance.

But whether you are broke by choice or by circumstance, the strategy 7
for getting out of credit card debt is the same: to outmaneuver the card companies with a strategy that assures you pay the lowest possible interest rate, for the shortest possible time, while avoiding all of the many snares and traps the card companies lay out for you.

Here's how to be a Credit Card Shark. 8

Take an Interest in Your Rate

The average interest rate charged on credit cards is 15 percent, with 9
plenty of folks paying 18 percent, 20 percent, or even more. If you carry a balance on any credit cards, your primary focus should be to get that rate down as low as possible.

Now then. If you have a FICO score of at least 720, and you make at 10
least the minimum payment due each month, on time, you should be able to negotiate with your current credit card issuer to lower your rate.

Call'em up and let them know you plan to transfer your entire balance to another card with a lower rate—more on this in a sec—if they don't get your rate down.

If your card issuer doesn't step up to the plate and give you a better deal, then do indeed start shopping around for a new card with a sweet intro offer. For those of you with strong FICO scores, a zero-rate deal ought to be possible. You can search for top card deals at the Yahoo! Finance Credit Card Center. *11*

Don't forget, though, that the key with balance transfer offers is to find out what your rate will be when the intro period expires in six months to a year. If your zero rate will skyrocket to 20 percent, that's a crappy deal, unless you are absolutely 100 percent sure you will get the balance paid off before the rate changes. (And if you got yourself into card hell in the first place, I wouldn't be betting on you having the ability to wipe out your problem in just six months. . . .) *12*

Once you are approved for the new low- or zero-rate card, move as much of your high-rate balances onto this new card. But don't—I repeat, do NOT—use the new card for new purchases. Hidden in the fine print on these deals are provisions stating, first, that any new purchases you make on the card will come with a high interest rate, and second, that you'll be paying that high interest on the entirety of your new purchase charges until you pay off every last cent of the balance transfer amount. This, to put it mildly, could really screw up your zero-rate deal. So please, use the new card only to park your old high-rate debt, and not to shop with. *13*

Another careless mistake you can make is to cancel your old cards. Don't do that either. Those cards hold some valuable "history" that's used to compute your FICO credit score. If you cancel the cards, you cancel your history, and your FICO score can take a hit. If you are worried about the temptation of using the cards, just get out your scissors and give them a good trim. That way you can't use 'em, but your history stays on your record. *14*

Coddle Your New Card

When you do a balance transfer, you need to protect your low rate as if it were an endangered species—because if the credit card issuer has anything to say about it, it will be. Look, you don't really think the card company is excited about charging you no interest, do you? How the heck do they make money off of that? They only offer up the great deal to lure you over to their card. Then they start working overtime trying to get you to screw up so they have an excuse to change your zero interest rate, often to as much as 20 percent or more. *15*

And the big screw-up they are hoping you don't know about is buried down in the fine print of your card agreement: make one late payment and you can kiss your zero deal good-bye. Even worse is that card companies are *16*

...continued How to Take Control of Your Credit Cards, **Suze Orman**

now scouring all your credit cards—remember, they can check your credit reports—to see if you have been late on any card, not just their card. So even if you always pay the zero-rate card on time, if you are late on any other card, your zero deal can be in jeopardy.

That's why I want you to make sure every credit card bill is paid 17
ahead of schedule. Don't mail it in on the day it is due; that's late. Mail it in at least five days early. Better yet, convert your card to online bill pay so you can zap your payments over in time every month. And remember, it's only the minimum monthly payment that needs to be paid. That's not asking a lot.

Dealing with High-Rate Debt

Okay, I realize not everyone is going to qualify for these low-rate 18
balance transfer deals, so let's run through how to take control of your cards if you are stuck with higher rates.

I want you to line up all your cards in descending order of their 19
interest rates. Notice I said the card with the highest interest rate comes first. Not the one with the biggest balance.

Your strategy is to make the minimum monthly payment on every 20
card, on time, every month. But your card with the highest interest rate gets some special treatment. I want you to pay more than the minimum amount due on this card. The more you can pay, the better; but everyone should put in, at the minimum, an extra $20 each month. Push yourself hard to make that extra payment as large as possible. It can save you thousands of dollars in interest charges over time.

Keep this up every month until your card with the highest rate is 21
paid off. Then turn your attention to the card with the next highest rate. In addition to the usual monthly minimum payment due on that second card, I want you to add in the entire amount you were previously paying on the first card (the one that's now paid off). So let's say you were paying a total of $200 a month on your original highest-rate card, and making a $75 monthly minimum on the second card. Well, now you are going to fork over $275 a month to the second card. And, of course, you'll continue to make the minimum monthly payment due on any other cards. Once your second card is paid off, move on to the third. If your monthly payment on that second card was $275, then that's what you should add to the minimum payment due on your third card. Get the idea? Rinse and repeat as often as needed, until you have all your debt paid off. For some of you this may take a year, for others it may take many years. That's okay. Just get yourself moving in the right direction and you'll be amazed how gratifying it is to find yourself taking control of your money rather than letting it control you.

And be sure to keep an eye on your FICO credit score. As you pay down your card balances—and build a record of paying on time—your score is indeed going to rise. Eventually your score may be high enough to finally qualify for a low-rate balance transfer offer. 22

Questions for Writing and Discussion

1. Writers of effective explaining essays focus their thesis for a specific audience. Describe the audience Suze Orman addresses in her essay. Which sentences help you identify this audience? Which sentences in Orman's essay most clearly express her thesis?
2. Explaining essays typically use definition of terms, explanation of processes, and analyses of causes and effects. Identify at least one example of each of these strategies in Orman's essay. In each case, decide whether the information Orman gives is clear to you. Where do you need additional information or clarification?
3. Two strategies that Orman uses to connect with her readers are addressing them in the second person, "you," and using informal language such as "you and your pals," "call 'em up," "more on this in a sec," and "sweet intro offer." Find other examples of informal language in her essay. Does this language work for her audience? Does it make the essay more lively and readable for you? Is this language appropriate in an essay about finances? Explain.
4. Find an offer for credit cards that you, a friend, or a family member has recently received. Study the fine print. Then, in your own words, explain what the fine print means in language that another member of your class can understand. Is Orman right about the "many snares and traps" that the card companies set for their customers?

Professional Writing

How Male and Female Students Use Language Differently

Deborah Tannen

Everyone knows that men and women communicate differently, but Deborah Tannen, a linguist at Georgetown University, has spent her career studying how and why their conversational styles are different. Tannen's books include her best-selling You Just Don't Understand: Women and Men in Conversation *(1990) and* I Only Say This Because I Love You *(2001). In the following article from the* Chronicle of Higher Education, *Tannen applies her knowledge of conversational styles to the classroom. As you read her essay, think about your own classes. Do men class talk more than women? Do men like to argue in large groups, while women prefer conversations in small groups? How clearly—and convincingly—does Tannen explain discussion preferences and their effects in the classroom?*

When I researched and wrote my latest book, *You Just Don't Understand: Women and Men in Conversation,* the furthest thing from my mind was reevaluating my teaching strategies. But that has been one of the direct benefits of having written the book. 1

The primary focus of my linguistic research always has been the language of everyday conversation. One facet of this is conversational style: how different regional, ethnic, and class backgrounds, as well as age and gender, result in different ways of using language to communicate. *You Just Don't Understand* is about the conversational styles of women and men. As I gained more insight into typically male and female ways of using language, I began to suspect some of the causes of the troubling facts that women who go to single-sex schools do better in later life, and that when young women sit next to young men in classrooms, the males talk more. This is not to say that all men talk in class, nor that no women do. It is simply that a greater percentage of discussion time is taken by men's voices. 2

The research of sociologists and anthropologists such as Janet Lever, Marjorie Harness Goodwin, and Donna Eder has shown that girls and boys learn to use language differently in their sex-separate peer groups. Typically, a girl has a best friend with whom she sits and talks, frequently telling secrets. It's the telling of secrets, the fact and the way that they talk to each other, that makes them best friends. For boys, activities are central: their best friends are the ones they do things with. Boys also tend to play in larger groups that are hierarchical. High-status boys give orders and push low-status boys around. So boys are expected to use language to seize center stage: by exhibiting their skill, displaying their knowledge, and challenging and resisting challenges. 3

These patterns have stunning implications for classroom interaction. Most faculty members assume that participating in class discussion is a necessary part of successful performance. Yet speaking in a classroom is more congenial to boys' language experience than to girls', since it entails putting oneself forward in front of a large group of people, many of whom are strangers and at least one of whom is sure to judge speakers' knowledge and intelligence by their verbal display. 4

Another aspect of many classrooms that makes them more hospitable to most men than to most women is the use of debate-like formats as a learning tool. Our educational system, as Walter Ong argues persuasively in 5 his book *Fighting for Life* (Cornell University Press, 1981), is fundamentally male in that the pursuit of knowledge is believed to be achieved by ritual opposition: public display followed by argument and challenge. Father Ong demonstrates that ritual opposition—what he calls "adversativeness" or "agonism"—is fundamental to the way most males approach almost any activity. (Consider, for example, the little boy who shows he likes a little girl by pulling her braids and shoving her.) But ritual opposition is antithetical to the way most females learn and like to interact. It is not that females don't fight, but that they don't fight for fun. They don't *ritualize* opposition.

Anthropologists working in widely disparate parts of the world have found contrasting verbal rituals for women and men. Women in completely unrelated cultures (for example, Greece and Bali) engage in ritual laments: spontaneously produced rhyming couplets that express their pain, for example, over the loss of loved ones. Men do not take part in laments. They have their own, very different verbal ritual: a contest, a war of words in which they vie with each other to devise clever insults. *6*

When discussing these phenomena with a colleague, I commented that I see these two styles in American conversation: many women bond by talking about troubles, and many men bond by exchanging playful insults and put-downs, and other sorts of verbal sparring. He exclaimed: "I never thought of this, but that's the way I teach: I have students read an article, and then I invite them to tear it apart. After we've torn it to shreds, we talk about how to build a better model." *7*

This contrasts sharply with the way I teach: I open the discussion of readings by asking, "What did you find useful in this? What can we use in our own theory building and our own methods?" I note what I see as weaknesses in the author's approach, but I also point out that the writer's discipline and purposes might be different from ours. Finally, I offer personal anecdotes illustrating the phenomena under discussion and praise students' anecdotes as well as their critical acumen. *8*

These different teaching styles must make our classrooms wildly different places and hospitable to different students. Male students are more likely to be comfortable attacking the readings and might find the inclusion of personal anecdotes irrelevant and "soft." Women are more likely to resist discussion they perceive as hostile, and, indeed, it is women in my classes who are most likely to offer personal anecdotes. *9*

A colleague who read my book commented that he had always taken for granted that the best way to deal with students' comments is to challenge them; this, he felt it was self-evident, sharpens their minds and helps them develop debating skills. But he had noticed that women were relatively silent in his classes, so he decided to try beginning discussion with relatively open-ended questions and letting comments go unchallenged. He found, to his amazement and satisfaction, that more women began to speak up. *10*

Though some of the women in his class clearly liked this better, perhaps some of the men liked it less. One young man in my class wrote in a questionnaire about a history professor who gave students questions to think about and called on people to answer them: "He would then play devil's advocate . . . *i.e.,* he debated us. . . . That class *really* sharpened me intellectually. . . . We as students do need to know how to defend ourselves." This young man valued the experience of being attacked and challenged publicly. Many, if not most, women would shrink from such "challenge," experiencing it as public humiliation. 11

A professor at Hamilton College told me of a young man who was upset because he felt his class presentation had been a failure. The professor was puzzled because he had observed that class members had listened attentively and agreed with the student's observations. It turned out that it was this very agreement that the student interpreted as failure: since no one had engaged his ideas by arguing with him, he felt they had found them unworthy of attention. 12

So one reason men speak in class more than women is that many of them find the "public" classroom setting more conducive to speaking, whereas most women are more comfortable speaking in private to a small group of people they know well. A second reason is that men are more likely to be comfortable with the debate-like form that discussion may take. Yet another reason is the different attitudes toward speaking in class that typify women and men. 13

Students who speak frequently in class, many of whom are men, assume that it is their job to think of contributions and try to get the floor to express them. But many women monitor their participation not only to get the floor but to avoid getting it. Women students in my class tell me that if they have spoken up once or twice, they hold back for the rest of the class because they don't want to dominate. If they have spoken a lot one week, they will remain silent the next. These different ethics of participation are, of course, unstated, so those who speak freely assume that those who remain silent have nothing to say, and those who are reining themselves in assume that the big talkers are selfish and hoggish. 14

When I looked around my classes, I could see these differing ethics and habits at work. For example, my graduate class in analyzing conversation had twenty students, eleven women and nine men. Of the men, four were foreign students: two Japanese, one Chinese, and one Syrian. With the exception of the three Asian men, all the men spoke in class at least occasionally. The biggest talker in the class was a woman, but there were also five women who never spoke at all, only one of whom was Japanese. I decided to try something different. 15

I broke the class into small groups to discuss the issues raised in the readings and to analyze their own conversational transcripts. I devised three ways of dividing the students into groups: one by the degree program they were in, one by gender, and one by conversational style, as closely as I could guess it. This meant that when the class was grouped according to conversational style, I put Asian students together, fast talkers together, and quiet students together. The class split into groups six times during the semester, so they met in each grouping twice. I told students to regard the groups as examples of interactional data and to note the different ways they participated in the different groups. Toward the end of the term, I gave them a questionnaire asking about their class and group participation. 16

I could see plainly from my observation of the groups at work that women who never opened their mouths in class were talking away in the small groups. In fact, the Japanese woman commented that she found it particularly hard to contribute to the all-woman group she was in because "I was overwhelmed by how talkative the female students were in the female-only group." This is particularly revealing because it highlights that the same person who can be "oppressed" into silence in one context can become the talkative "oppressor" in another. No one's conversational style is absolute; everyone's style changes in response to the context and others' styles. 17

Some of the students (seven) said they preferred the same-gender groups; others preferred the same-style groups. In answer to the question "Would you have liked to speak in class more than you did?" six of the seven who said yes were women; the one man was Japanese. Most startlingly, this response did not come only from quiet women; it came from women who had indicated they had spoken in class never, rarely, sometimes, and often. Of the eleven students who said the amount they had spoken was fine, seven were men. Of the four women who checked "fine," two added qualifications indicating it wasn't completely fine: One wrote in "maybe more," and one wrote, "I have an urge to participate but often feel I should have something more interesting/relevant/wonderful/intelligent to say!!" 18

I counted my experiment a success. Everyone in the class found the small groups interesting, and no one indicated he or she would have preferred that the class not break into groups. Perhaps most instructive, however, was the fact that the experience of breaking into groups, and of talking about participation in class, raised everyone's awareness about classroom participation. After we had talked about it, some of the quietest women in the class made a few voluntary contributions, though sometimes I had to ensure their participation by interrupting the students who were exuberantly speaking out. 19

...continued How Male and Female Students Use Language..., **Deborah Tannen**

Americans are often proud that they discount the significance of 20
cultural differences: "We are all individuals," many people boast. Ignoring such issues as gender and ethnicity becomes a source of pride: "I treat everyone the same." But treating people the same is not equal treatment if they are not the same. . . .

In a class where some students speak out without raising hands, those 21
who feel they must raise their hands and wait to be recognized do not have equal opportunity to speak. Telling them to feel free to jump in will not make them feel free; one's sense of timing, of one's rights and obligations in a classroom, are automatic, learned over years of interaction. They may be changed over time, with motivation and effort, but they cannot be changed on the spot. And everyone assumes his or her own way is best. When I asked my students how the class could be changed to make it easier for them to speak more, the most talkative woman said she would prefer it if no one had to raise hands, and a foreign student said he wished people would raise their hands and wait to be recognized.

My experience in this class has convinced me that small-group 22
interaction should be part of any class that is not a small seminar. I also am convinced that having the students become observers of their own interaction is a crucial part of their education. Talking about ways of talking in class makes students aware that their ways of talking affect other students, that the motivations they impute to others may not truly reflect others' motives, and that the behaviors they assume to be self-evidently right are not universal norms.

The goal of complete equal opportunity in class may not be attainable, 23
but realizing that one monolithic classroom-participation structure is not equal opportunity is itself a powerful motivation to find more-diverse methods to serve diverse students—and every classroom is diverse.

Questions for Writing and Discussion

1. In her essay, Deborah Tannen states and then continues to restate her thesis. Reread her essay, underlining all the sentences that seem to state or rephrase her main idea. Do her restatements of the main idea make her essay clearer? Explain.

2. Explaining essays may explain *what* (describe and define), explain *how* (process analysis), and/or explain *why* (causal analysis). Find one example of each of these strategies in Tannen's essay. Which of these three is the

dominant shaping strategy? Support your answer with references to specific sentences or paragraphs.

3. Effective explaining essays must have supporting evidence—specific examples, facts, quotations, testimony from experts, statistics, and so on. Choose four consecutive paragraphs from Tannen's essay and list the kinds of supporting evidence she uses. Based on your inventory, rate her supporting evidence as weak, average, or strong. Explain your choice.

4. Does the style of Tannen's essay support her thesis that men and women have different ways of communicating? Does Tannen, in fact, use a "woman's style" of writing that is similar to women's conversational style? Examine Tannen's tone (her attitude toward her subject and audience), her voice (the projection of her personality in her language), and her supporting evidence (her use of facts and statistics or anecdotal, contextual evidence). Cite specific passages to support your analysis.

Explaining: The Writing Process

Assignment for Explaining

After assessing your rhetorical situation, *explain* what something means or is, *how* it should be done or *how* it occurs, and/or *why* something occurs. Your purpose is to explain something as clearly as possible for your audience by analyzing, showing relationships, and demonstrating with examples, facts, illustrations, data, or other information.

With a topic in mind, use the grid below to think about a possible audience and genre that would meet your assignment. Once you've chosen an audience, think about how much they already know about the subject. Are they experts, novices, or somewhere in between? What do they already know? What information are they least likely to know?

Audience	Possible Genres for Explaining
Personal Audience	Class notes, annotations in a textbook, journal entry, blog, scrapbook, social networking page
Academic Audience	Expository essay, academic analysis and synthesis, journal entry, forum entry on class site, multigenre document
Public Audience	Column, editorial, letter, or article in a magazine, newspaper, online site, newsletter, or multigenre document

CHOOSING A SUBJECT

> "You can write about anything, and if you write well enough, even the reader with no intrinsic interest in the subject will become involved."
>
> —Tracy Kidder, Novelist

If one of your journal entries suggested a possible subject, go on to the collecting and shaping strategies. If you still need an interesting subject, consider the following suggestions.

- Reread your authority list or your most interesting journal entries from previous chapters. Do they contain ideas that you might define or explain, processes suitable for how-to explanations, or causes or effects that you could analyze and explain for a certain audience?
- **Writing Across the Curriculum.** Reread your notes from another class in which you have an upcoming examination. Select some topic, idea, principle, process, famous person, or event from the text or your notes. Investigate other texts, popular magazines, or journals for information on that topic. If appropriate, interview someone or conduct a survey. Explain this principle or process to a member of your writing class.
- **Community Service Learning.** If you are doing a community-service-learning project, consider a writing project explaining the agency's mission to the public or to a potential donor. You might also write an article for a local or campus newspaper explaining a recent contribution the agency has made to the community.
- Write an artistic, cultural, historical, or social explanation of a visual image or a set of visual images. One excellent Web site for famous photographs is the Pulitzer site at http://www.gallerym.com/pulitzer photos.htm. Decide on a particular audience, genre, and context appropriate for the photograph.
- Choose a current controversy and, instead of arguing for one side or the other, explain the different points of view. Who are the leading figures or groups representing each position? Choose a particular audience, genre, and context, and explain what each of these people or groups has to gain or lose and how their personal investments in the topic determine their position.

COLLECTING

7.4
Use collecting strategies for developing your explanatory essay

Questions

Once you have a tentative subject and audience, consider which of the following will be your primary focus (all three may be relevant).

- *What* something means or is
- *How* something occurs or is done (or should be done)
- *Why* something occurs or what its effects are

Focus on Definition To explain *what* something is, jot down answers to each of the following questions. The more you can write on each question, the more details you'll have for your topic.

- What are its class and distinguishing characteristics?
- What is its etymology?
- How can you describe it?
- What examples can you give?
- What are its parts or its functions?
- What is it similar to? What is it *not?*
- What figurative comparisons apply?
- How can it be classified?
- Which of the above is most useful to your audience?

Focus on Process Analysis To explain *how* something occurs or is done, answer the following questions.

- What are the component parts or steps in the whole process?
- What is the exact sequence of steps or events?
- Are several of the steps or events related?
- If steps or events were omitted, would the outcome change?
- Which steps or events are most crucial?
- Which steps or events does your audience most need to know?

Focus on Causal Analysis To explain *why* something occurs or what its effects are, consider the following questions.

- Which are the necessary or sufficient causes?
- Which causes are remote in time, and which are immediate?
- What is the order or sequence of the causes? Do the causes occur simultaneously?
- What are the effects? Do they occur in a sequence or simultaneously?
- Do the causes and effects occur in a "chain reaction"?
- Is there an action or situation that would have prevented the effect?
- Are there comparable things or events that have similar causes or effects?
- Which causes or effects will need special clarification for your audience?

Branching

Often, *branching* can help you analyze your subject visually. Start with your topic and then subdivide each idea into its component parts. The resulting analysis will not only help generate ideas but may also suggest ways to shape an essay.

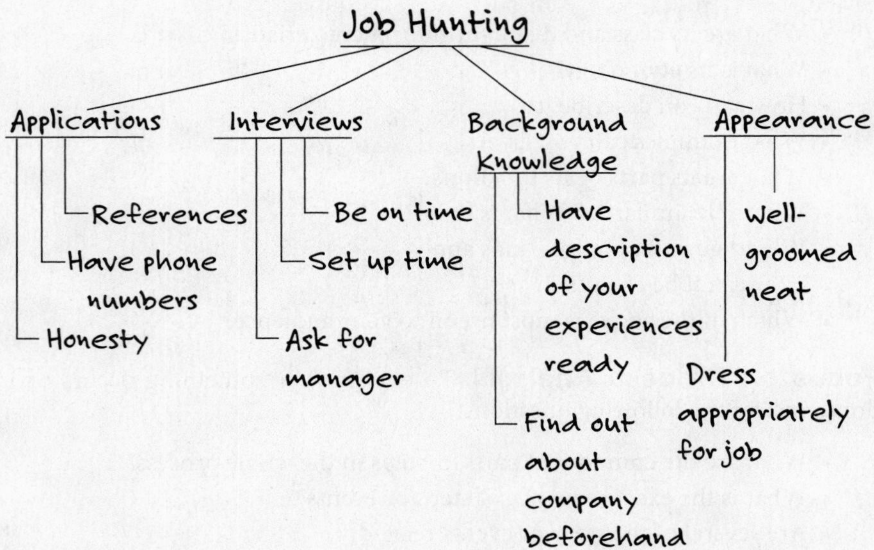

Observing

If you can observe your subject, try drawing it, describing it, or taking careful notes. Which senses can you use to describe it—sight, sound, touch, smell, taste? If it is a scientific experiment that you can reproduce or a social situation you can reconstruct, go through it again and observe carefully. As you observe it, put yourself in your readers' shoes: What do you need to explain to them?

Remembering

Your own experience and memory are essential for explaining. *Freewriting, looping,* and *clustering* may all generate detailed information, good examples, and interesting perspectives that will make your explanation clearer and more vivid. (See Chapter 3 for an explanation of looping and clustering.)

> "Readers may be strangers who have no immediate reason to care about your writing. They want order, clarity, and stimulation."
>
> —Elizabeth Cowan Neeld, Teacher and Author

Reading

When you find written texts about your subject, be sure to use your active reading strategies. You may need only a few sources if you reread them carefully. Write out a short summary for each source. Respond to each source by analyzing its effectiveness, agreeing or disagreeing with its ideas, or interpreting the text. The quality of your understanding is more important than the sheer number of sources you cite.

Investigating

Use sources available in the library, textbooks containing relevant information, or interviews with teachers, participants, or experts. Interview your classmates about their own subjects for this assignment: Someone else's subject may trigger an idea that you can write about or may suggest a fresh approach to the subject that you have already chosen.

SHAPING

7.5
Shape your explanatory essay

As you think about ways to organize and develop your essay, be sure to reread your assignment and reconsider your purpose and audience. Limit your subject to create a *narrowed* and *focused* topic. You will not be able to cover everything you've read, thought, or experienced about your topic, so choose the most interesting ideas—for you and for your audience—and then try the following strategies.

Shaping Strategies

Do you want to...	Consider using these rhetorical modes or strategies:
define key terms or concepts?	definition, classification, example (p. 224)
describe how a process works?	chronological order (p. 226)
explain relationships between causes and effects?	causal analysis, example (pp. 226–227)
structure your essay so your reader understands your thesis and can follow your explanation?	an introduction, thesis, essay map, and paragraph transitions (pp. 229–231)

Audience and Genre

An essay directed at a general audience composed of peers like your classmates is just one possibility. A letter to the editor, a pamphlet for a community agency, a job analysis for your employer, an article for a local or school newspaper, a posting or response to a listserve, or an essay for students in your major are other possibilities. Once you have a tentative audience and genre, you'll have a better idea about how to organize your explanation. Reread your assignment for specific suggestions and guidelines about audience and genre.

Definition and Classification

An essay explaining *what* something means or is can be shaped by using a variety of definition strategies or by classifying the subject.

Definition itself is not a single organizing strategy; it supports a variety of strategies that may be useful in shaping your essay: description, analysis of parts or function, comparison/contrast, development by examples, or figures of speech such as simile, metaphor, and analogy.

ResearchTips

Review your audience, purpose, and possible focus. Which of the following four research strategies would help you gather information on your topic?

1. Direct *observation* (see Chapter 3)
2. Use of *memories* and personal experience (see Chapter 3)
3. *Field research* including interviews and surveys (see Chapter 6)
4. *Library/Internet* research (see Chapter 12)

As you do your research, keep the following in mind:

- Save all your *links* or *Word files* or make *photocopies* or *printouts* of all the sources that you plan to cite in your essay.
- Be sure to *write all relevant bibliographic information*, such as author, date, publisher, place of publication, journal title, and volume and issue numbers. in your Word files or on the photocopies or printouts. Note the Web site sponsor and your access date for Web sources.
- When you cite sources in your text, be sure to *introduce* the sources. Make sure your direct quotations are *accurate* word-for-word transcriptions.

For more details on these suggestions, see Chapter 12.

Classification, on the other hand, is a single strategy that can organize a paragraph or even a whole essay quickly. Observers of human behavior, for example, love to use classification. Grocery shoppers might be classified by types: racers (the ones who seem to have just won forty-five seconds of free shopping and run down the aisles filling their carts as fast as possible), talkers (the ones who stand in the aisles gossiping forever), penny-pinchers (who always have their calculators out and read the unit price labels for everything), and dawdlers (who leave their carts crosswise in the aisles while they read twenty-nine different soup can labels). You can write a sentence or two about each type or devote a whole paragraph to explaining a single type.

Example

Development by example can illustrate effectively what something is or means, and it can also help explain how or why something happens. Usually, an example describes a specific incident that *shows* or *demonstrates* the main idea. In the following paragraph from *Mediaspeak*, Donna Woolfolk Cross explains what effects soap operas can have on addicted viewers. This paragraph is developed by several examples—some described in detail, others referred to briefly.

> Dedicated watchers of soap operas often confuse fact with fiction.... Stars of soap operas tell hair-raising stories of their encounters with fans suffering from this affliction. Susan Lucci, who plays the promiscuous Erica Kane on "All My Children," tells of a time she was riding in a parade: "We were in a crowd of about 250,000 traveling in an antique open car moving ver-r-ry slowly. At that time in the series I was involved with a character named Nick. Some man broke through, came right up to the car and said to me, 'Why don't you give me a little bit of what you've been giving Nick?'" The man hung onto the car, menacingly, until she was rescued by the police. Another time, when she was in church, the reverent silence was broken by a woman's astonished remark, "Oh, my god, Erica prays!"

Voice and Tone

Writers use voice and tone to shape and control whole passages, often in combination with other shaping strategies. In the following paragraph, Toni Bambara, author of *The Salt Eaters* and numerous short stories, explains *what* being a writer is all about. This paragraph is shaped both by a single extended example and by Bambara's voice speaking directly to the reader.

> When I replay the tapes on file in my head, tapes of speeches I've given at writing conferences over the years, I invariably hear myself saying—"A writer, like any other cultural worker, like any other member of the community, ought to try to put her/his skills in the service of the community." Some years ago when I returned south, my picture in the paper

> prompted several neighbors to come visit. "You a writer? What all you write?" Before I could begin the catalogue, one old gent interrupted with—"Ya know Miz Mary down the block? She need a writer to help her send off a letter to her grandson overseas." So I began a career as the neighborhood scribe—letters to relatives, snarling letters to the traffic chief about the promised stop sign, nasty letters to the utilities, angry letters to the principal about that confederate flag hanging in front of the school, contracts to transfer a truck from seller to buyer, etc. While my efforts have been graciously appreciated in the form of sweet potato dumplings, herb teas, hair braiding, and the like, there is still much room for improvement—"For a writer, honey, you've got a mighty bad hand. Didn't they teach penmanship at that college?" Another example, I guess, of words setting things in motion. What goes around, comes around, as the elders say.

Chronological Order and Process Analysis

Writers use chronological order in expository writing to help explain how something is typically done. In her essay "Anorexia Nervosa," student writer Nancie Brosseau uses transitional words to signal the successive stages of anorexia. In the following sentences, the *italicized* words mark the chronological stages of her anorexia.

> Several serious health problems bombarded me, and it's a wonder I'm still alive. . . . *As my weight plummeted,* my circulation grew *increasingly worse.* . . . My hair *started* to fall out, and my whole body took on a very skeletal appearance. . . . I would force myself to vomit *as soon as possible* if I was forced to eat. The enamel on my teeth *started to be eaten away* by the acid in the vomit, and my lips cracked and bled regularly. I *stopped* menstruating completely because I was not producing enough estrogen. . . . *One time,* while executing a chain of back handsprings, I broke all five fingers on one hand and three on the other because my bones had become so brittle. . . . I chose to see a psychologist, and she helped me sort out the emotional aspects of anorexia, *which in turn* solved the physical problems.

Causal Analysis

In order to explain *why* something happens or what the effects of something are, writers often use one of three patterns of cause and effect to shape their material.

Shaping Your Points: Several Causes, One Effect

In the case of fire, for example, we know that three causes lead to a single effect. These causes do not occur in any special sequence; they must all be present at the same time. For historical events, however, we usually list causes in chronological order.

Sometimes one cause has several effects. In that case, we reverse the pattern:

Shaping Your Points: One Cause, Several Effects

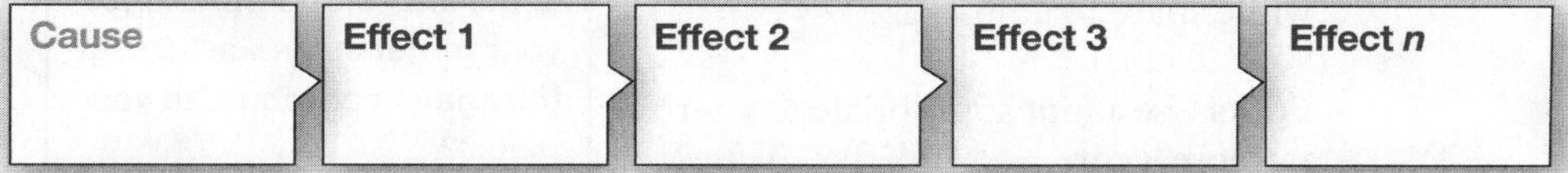

Tips for Integrating Images

For your explaining essay, you may wish to integrate images (photographs, graphics, or charts), and you may wish to work with your document design. To integrate images with your text, first consider your rhetorical situation.

- **What is your purpose?** Does the visual contribute to your thesis or main idea, or would it be just a distraction?
- **Who is your audience?** Is the image appropriate for your target audience? Would it make your document more appealing or attractive? Would it offend? Would it amuse? Would it make your point in a way that words could not?
- **What is your intended genre?** Look at other examples of your genre (essay, pamphlet, Web page, article, advertisement, brochure, laboratory report, letter, or flyer). How do they use images or graphics?
- **What is the social/cultural context of your text?** Consider whether the subject, topic, or issue you are discussing could or should be illustrated with an image or a certain document design.

Use search engines and library sources to find images relevant to your topic. Start with an image search on Google or Yahoo!, but don't forget that your library has a wealth of online image databases. If you're looking for paintings or fine art, check Web sites for museums around the world. Having several potential images enables you to choose the one most effective for your rhetorical situation.

Finally, don't forget about your document design. Start with your purpose, audience, and genre. Consider how the genre you have selected uses the following document features.

Is the image appropriate for your target audience? Does the image contribute to your thesis?

- **Columns** Would a text with two columns work for your purpose?
- **Margins and white space** Avoid overcrowding words, images, and graphics on a page. Use margins and white space to emphasize key parts of your text.
- **Fonts** Use a font appropriate to your purpose, genre, and audience. Times New Roman and Palatino Linotype are widely accepted, but do you need **Franklin Gothic Demi** for particular parts of your text? For special situations, perhaps consider a script face such as Felt Tip or a bolder face such as TRADE GOTHIC.
- **Sidebars** If appropriate for your text, use a sidebar for emphasis or to add related information.

For example, an explanation of the collapse of the economy following the stock market crash of 1929 might follow this pattern. The crash (itself a symptom of other causes) led to a depreciated economy, widespread unemployment, bankruptcy for thousands of businesses, and foreclosures on farms. An essay on the effects of the crash might devote one or two paragraphs to each effect.

In the third pattern, causes and effects form a pattern of chain reactions. One cause leads to an effect that then becomes the cause of another effect, and so on:

Shaping Your Points: Causal Chain

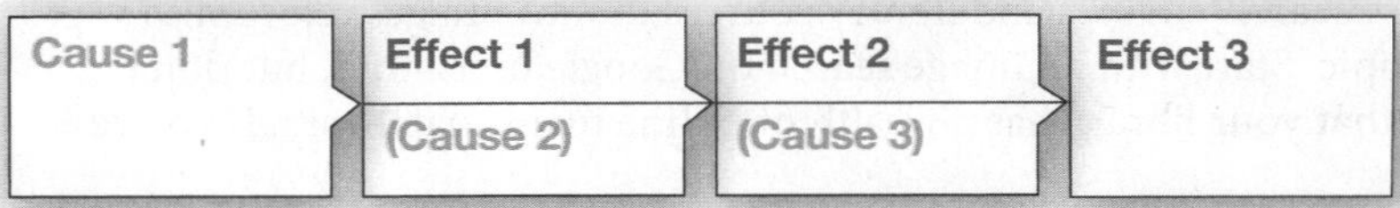

We could analyze events in the Middle East during and after the Iraq War as a series of actions and reactions in which each effect becomes the cause of the next effect in the chain of car bombings, air raids, terrorist hijackings, and kidnappings. An essay on the chain reaction of events in the Middle East might have a paragraph or two on each of the links in this chain.

Introduction and Lead-in

Often, the first sentences of the introductory paragraph of an essay are the hardest to write. You want to get your reader's attention and focus on the main idea of your essay, but you don't want to begin, boringly, with your thesis statement. Several kinds of opening sentences are designed to grab your reader's interest. Consider your topic—see if one of these strategies will work for you.

A Personal Example

I knew my dieting had gotten out of hand, but when I could actually see the movement of my heart beating beneath my clothes, I knew I was in trouble.

—Nancie Brosseau, "Anorexia Nervosa"

A Description of a Person or Place

It's still there, the Chinese school on Yale Street where my brother and I used to go. Despite the new coat of paint and the high wire fence, the school I knew ten years ago remains remarkably, stoically the same.

—Elizabeth Wong, "The Struggle to Be an All-American Girl"

A Statement from a Book

The American novelist John Barth, in his early novel *The Floating Opera,* remarks that ordinary, day-to-day life often presents us with embarrassingly obvious, totally unsubtle patterns of symbolism and meaning—life in the midst of death, innocence vindicated, youth versus age, etc.

—Robert Zoellner, "I'm O.K., but You're Not"

A Striking Question or Questions

Do non-human animals have rights? Should we humans feel morally bound to exercise consideration for the lives and well-being of individual members of other animal species? If so, how much consideration, and by what logic?

—David Quammen, "Animal Rights and Beyond"

A Common Error or Mistaken Judgment

There was a time when, in my search for essences, I concluded that the canyonland country has no heart. I was wrong. The canyonlands did have a heart, a living heart, and that heart was Glen Canyon and the golden, flowing Colorado River.

—Edward Abbey, "The Damnation of a Canyon"

Lead-in, Thesis, and Essay Map

The introduction to an explaining essay usually contains the following features.

- **Lead-in:** Some example, description, startling statement, statistic, short narrative, allusion, or quotation to get the reader's interest *and* focus on the topic the writer will explain.
- **Thesis:** Statement of the main idea; a "promise" to the reader that the essay will fulfill.
- **Essay map:** A sentence, or part of a sentence, that *lists* (in the order in which the essay will discuss them) the subtopics for the essay.

In her essay on anorexia nervosa, Nancie Brosseau's introductory paragraph has all three features.

Lead-in: Startling statement

Description

Statistics

Thesis and essay map

I knew my dieting had gotten out of hand, but when I could actually see the movement of my heart beating beneath my clothes, I knew I was in trouble. At first, the family doctor reassured my parents that my rapid weight loss was a "temporary phase among teenage girls." However, when I, at fourteen years old and five feet tall, weighed in at sixty-three pounds, my doctor changed his diagnosis from "temporary phase" to "anorexia nervosa." Anorexia nervosa is the process of self-starvation that affects over 100,000 young girls each year. Almost 6,000 of these girls die every year. Anorexia nervosa is a self-mutilating disease that affects its victim both physically and emotionally.

The essay map is contained in the phrase "both physically and emotionally": The first half of the essay discusses the physical effects of anorexia nervosa; the second half explains the emotional effects. Like a road map, the essay map helps the reader anticipate what topics the writer will explain.

Paragraph Transitions and Hooks

Listen to the **Podcast** Transitional Expressions

Transition words and paragraph hooks are audience cues that help the reader shift from one paragraph to the next. These connections between paragraphs enable the reader to see the relationships of the various parts. Transition words—*first, second, next, another, last, finally,* and so forth—signal your reader that a new idea or a new part of the idea is coming up. In addition to transition words, writers often tie paragraphs together by using a key word or idea from one paragraph in the first sentence of the next paragraph to "hook" the paragraphs together.

The following paragraphs from Deborah Tannen's essay illustrate how transition words and paragraph hooks work together to create smooth connections between paragraphs.

> The research of sociologists and anthropologists . . . has shown that girls and boys learn to use language differently in their sex-separate peer groups. Typically, a girl has a best friend with whom she sits and talks, frequently telling secrets. It's the telling of secrets, the fact and the way that they talk to each other, that makes them best friends. For boys, activities are central: their best friends are the ones they do things with. Boys also tend to play in larger groups that are hierarchical. High-status boys give orders and push low-status boys around. So boys are expected to use language to seize center stage: by exhibiting their skill, displaying their knowledge, and challenging and resisting challenges.
>
> These patterns have stunning implications for classroom interaction. Most faculty members assume that participating in class discussion is a necessary part of successful performance. Yet speaking in a classroom is more congenial to boys' language experience than to girls', since it entails putting oneself forward in front of a large group of people, many of whom are strangers and at least one of whom is sure to judge speakers' knowledge and intelligence by their verbal display.
>
> Another aspect of many classrooms that makes them more hospitable to most men than to most women is the use of debate-like formats as a learning tool. . . .

Idea hook: "These patterns" refers back to the language patterns of boys and girls in the previous paragraph.

Transition word: "Another" helps readers move from the previous example about verbal display in a classroom to the debate-like structure.

Body Paragraphs

Body paragraphs in expository writing are the main paragraphs in an essay, excluding any introductory, concluding, or transition paragraphs. They often contain the following features.

- **Topic sentence:** To promote clarity and precision, writers often use topic sentences to announce the main ideas of paragraphs. The main idea should be clearly related to the writer's thesis. A topic sentence usually occurs early in the paragraph (first or second sentence) or at the end of the paragraph.

Watch the Animation on Unity

- **Unity:** To avoid confusing readers, writers focus on a single idea for each paragraph. Writing unified paragraphs helps writers—and their readers—concentrate on one point at a time.

Watch the Animation on Coherence

- **Coherence:** To make their writing flow smoothly from one sentence to the next, writers supplement their shaping strategies with coherence devices: repeated key words, pronouns referring to key nouns, and transition words.

One body paragraph from Deborah Tannen's essay illustrates these features. The first sentence is the *topic sentence*, which focuses our attention on the key idea to be discussed in the paragraph: "girls and boys learn to use language differently." The paragraph has *unity* because it follows this topic sentence by first describing how girls use language and then discussing how boys use language. Paragraph *coherence* is achieved by focusing on the one idea of different language use, and by discussing first the girls' use of language and then the boys' use of language—as forecast, or promised, in the topic sentence.

Topic sentence is the first sentence

Paragraph *unity* is achieved by focusing on how boys and girls use language differently

Paragraph *coherence* is achieved by discussing girls' use of language and then boys' use of language—and by the repeated key words

> The research of sociologists and anthropologists . . . has shown that girls and boys learn to use language differently in their sex-separate peer groups. Typically, a girl has a best friend with whom she sits and talks, frequently telling secrets. It's the telling of secrets, the fact and the way that they talk to each other, that makes them best friends. For boys, activities are central: their best friends are the ones they do things with. Boys also tend to play in larger groups that are hierarchical. High-status boys give orders and push low-status boys around. So boys are expected to use language to seize center stage: by exhibiting their skill, displaying their knowledge, and challenging and resisting challenges.

PeerResponse

These instructions will help you give and receive constructive advice about the rough draft of your explaining essay. You may use these guidelines for an in-class workshop, a take-home review, or a computer e-mail response.

Writer: Before you exchange drafts with another reader, write out the following on your essay draft.

1. **Purpose** Briefly describe your purpose, genre, and intended audience.
2. **Revision plans** What do you still intend to work on as you revise your draft?
3. **Questions** Write out one or two questions that you still have about your draft. What questions would you like your reader to answer?

Reader: First, read the entire draft from start to finish. As you reread the draft, answer the following questions.

1. **Clarity** What passages were clearest? Where were you most confused? Refer to specific sentences or passages to support your response. How and where could the writer make the draft clearer?
2. **Evidence** Where does the writer have good supporting evidence (examples, facts, visuals, statistics, interview results, or citations from sources)? Where does the writer need additional evidence? Refer to specific sentences or passages to support your response.
3. **Organization** Summarize or briefly outline the main ideas of the essay. Where was the organization most clear? Where were you confused? Refer to specific passages as you suggest ways to improve the draft.
4. **Purpose** Underline sentences that express the purpose or contain the thesis of the essay. Does your understanding of the essay's purpose match the writer's statement about purpose? Explain. How might the writer clarify the thesis for the intended audience?
5. **Reader's response** Overall, describe what you liked best about the draft. Then identify one major area that the writer should focus on during the revision. Does your suggestion match the writer's revision plans? Explain. Answer the writer's own question or questions about the draft.

DRAFTING

Before you begin drafting, reconsider your purpose and audience. What you will explain depends on what your audience needs to know or what would demonstrate your point most effectively.

As you work from an outline or from an organizing strategy, remember that all three questions—*what, how,* and *why*—are interrelated. When you are writing about causes, for example, an explanation of *what* the topic is and *how* the causes function may be necessary to explain your subject clearly. As you write, balance your sense of plan and organization with a willingness to pursue ideas that you discover as you write. You should be ready to change course if you discover a more interesting idea or angle.

REVISING

As you revise your explaining essay, concentrate on making yourself clear, on illustrating with examples where your reader might be confused, and on signaling the relationship of the parts of your essay to your reader.

Guidelines for Revision

"I wish he would explain his explanation."
—Lord Byron, Poet

- **Review your purpose, audience, and genre.** Will your purpose be clear to your target audience? Should you modify your chosen genre to appeal to your audience?
- **Review possibilities for visuals or graphics.** What additions or changes to images might be appropriate for your purpose, genre, or audience?
- **Compare your thesis sentence with what you say in your conclusion.** You may have formed a clearer statement of your thesis near the end of your paper. Revise your original thesis sentence to make it clearer, more focused, or more in line with what your essay actually says.
- **Explaining means *showing* and *demonstrating* relationships.** Be sure to follow general statements with *specific examples, details, facts, statistics, memories, dialogues,* or other *illustrations.*
- **In a formal definition, be sure to state the class of objects or concepts to which the term belongs.** Avoid ungrammatical writing, such as "Photosynthesis is *when* plants absorb oxygen" or "The lymphatic system is *where* the body removes bacteria and transports fatty cells."
- **Avoid introducing definitions with "Webster says. . . ."** Instead, read definitions from several dictionaries and give the best or most appropriate definition.

- **Remember that you can modify the dictionary definition of a term or concept to fit your particular context.** For example, to you, *heroism* may mean having the courage to *say* what you believe, not just to endanger your life through selfless actions.
- **Don't mix categories when you are classifying objects or ideas.** If you are classifying houses *by floor design* (ranch, bilevel, split-level, two-story), don't bring in other categories, such as passive-solar, which could be incorporated into any of those designs.
- **In explaining *how* something occurs or should be done, be sure to indicate to your audience which steps are *most important*.**
- **In cause-and-effect explanations, avoid post hoc fallacies.** This term comes from the Latin phrase *post hoc, ergo propter hoc:* "After this, therefore because of this." For example, just because Event B occurred after Event A, it does not follow, necessarily, that A caused B. If, for example, statistics show that traffic fatalities in your state declined after the speed limit on interstate highways was increased, you should not conclude that higher speeds caused the reduction in fatalities. Other causes—increased radar patrols, stiffer drunk-driving penalties, or more rigorous vehicle-maintenance laws—may have been responsible.
- **As you revise to sharpen your meaning or make your organization clearer, use appropriate transitional words and phrases to signal the *relationships among the parts of your subject.***

  —*To signal relation in time:* before, meanwhile, later, soon, at last, earlier, thereafter, afterward, by that time, from then on, first, next, now, presently, shortly, immediately, finally

  —*To signal similarity:* likewise, similarly, once again, once more

  —*To signal difference:* but, yet, however, although, whereas, though, even so, nonetheless, still, on the other hand, on the contrary

  —*To signal consequences:* as a result, consequently, therefore, hence, for this reason

Postscript on the Writing Process

Before you hand in your essay, reflect on your writing and learning process. In your journal, spend a few minutes answering the following questions.

1. Describe the purpose and intended audience for your essay.
2. What was the best workshop advice that you received? What did you revise in your draft because of that advice? What piece of advice did you ignore? Why?

3. What caused you the most difficulty with this essay? How did you solve the problem—or attempt to solve it? With what parts are you still least satisfied?
4. What are the best parts of your paper? Refer to specific paragraphs—what do you like most about them?
5. If you added images or special document-design features to your essay, explain how they supported your purpose or rhetorical goals.
6. What was the most important thing you learned about writing or your writing process as you wrote this paper?

Student Writing

White Lies: White-Collar Crime in America

Chris Blakely

Chris Blakely decided to write his essay on white-collar crime after the collapse of financial institutions such as AIG and the revelation of pyramid schemes such as the one perpetrated by Bernie Madoff that cost investors $65 billion. After gathering information about the nature of white-collar crime and its effects, Blakely decided to focus on two examples: the Enron collapse and the Adelphia Communications scandal. His purpose was to explain what white-collar crime is and how its effects can be more devastating than those of street crime. As his essay overview explains, he also wrote a graphic novel to help make his point more visually and memorably for his audience. Sample pages from his graphic novel appear on the next page.

ESSAY OVERVIEW

In this paper, I planned to analyze the state of white collar crime and how it is perceived by the general public and the justice system. I found in my early research that white-collar criminals are perceived as less of a threat than street criminals (Holtfreter). This helped me to realize that public perception needs to change—and helping to change that perception was the main goal of my paper. I first needed to define white-collar crime, which I limited to cases where an employee of a public company engaged in illegal activity that seems to benefit that person and the company, but in the end harms the company, its employees, and its stockholders. I found examples of crime on a large scale, such as the Enron, Tyco, and WorldCom scandals, to show how damaging white-collar crime can be at its highest levels. 1

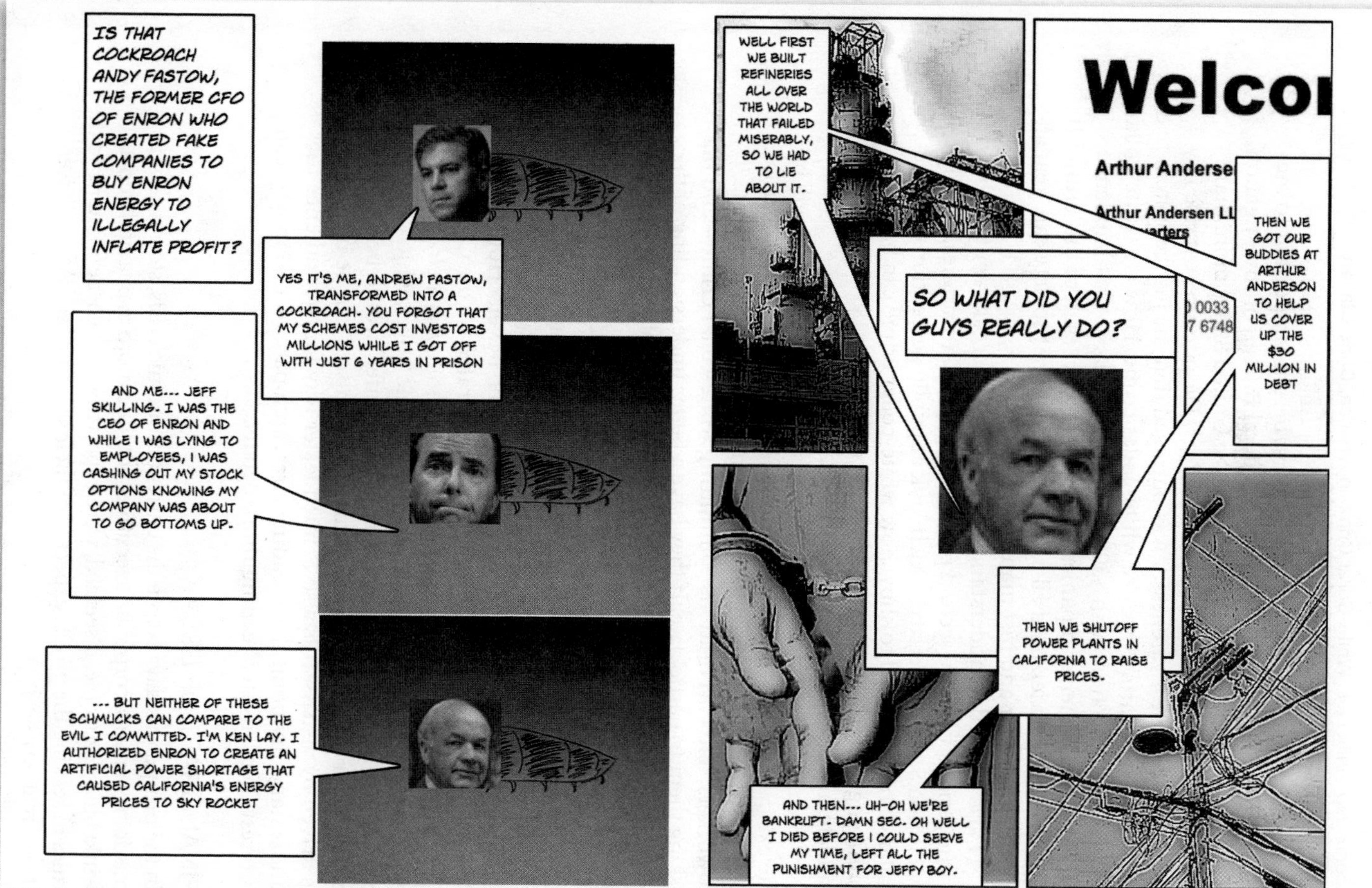
IS THAT COCKROACH ANDY FASTOW, THE FORMER CFO OF ENRON WHO CREATED FAKE COMPANIES TO BUY ENRON ENERGY TO ILLEGALLY INFLATE PROFIT?
YES IT'S ME, ANDREW FASTOW, TRANSFORMED INTO A COCKROACH. YOU FORGOT THAT MY SCHEMES COST INVESTORS MILLIONS WHILE I GOT OFF WITH JUST 6 YEARS IN PRISON
AND ME... JEFF SKILLING. I WAS THE CEO OF ENRON AND WHILE I WAS LYING TO EMPLOYEES, I WAS CASHING OUT MY STOCK OPTIONS KNOWING MY COMPANY WAS ABOUT TO GO BOTTOMS UP.
... BUT NEITHER OF THESE SCHMUCKS CAN COMPARE TO THE EVIL I COMMITTED. I'M KEN LAY. I AUTHORIZED ENRON TO CREATE AN ARTIFICIAL POWER SHORTAGE THAT CAUSED CALIFORNIA'S ENERGY PRICES TO SKY ROCKET
SO WHAT DID YOU GUYS REALLY DO?
WELL FIRST WE BUILT REFINERIES ALL OVER THE WORLD THAT FAILED MISERABLY, SO WE HAD TO LIE ABOUT IT.
THEN WE GOT OUR BUDDIES AT ARTHUR ANDERSON TO HELP US COVER UP THE $30 MILLION IN DEBT
THEN WE SHUTOFF POWER PLANTS IN CALIFORNIA TO RAISE PRICES.
AND THEN... UH-OH WE'RE BANKRUPT. DAMN SEC. OH WELL I DIED BEFORE I COULD SERVE MY TIME, LEFT ALL THE PUNISHMENT FOR JEFFY BOY.

...continued White Lies: White-Collar Crime in America, **Chris Blakely**

Understanding this type of crime first became important to me when I found that, "according to the Federal Bureau of Investigation, white-collar crime is estimated to cost the United States more than $300 billion annually" (Cornell Law Index). Despite a recent rise in white-collar crime awareness, I was outraged that the justice system had not shifted its efforts to reduce white-collar crime. How are white-collar criminals getting away with $300 billion every year? What happens to the employees when companies go bankrupt as a result of this crime? It is necessary to understand all types of crime so that society can treat all criminals in a fair and just manner. 2

I also wanted to understand why people didn't take white-collar crime seriously, so the second part of my paper used studies, mainly one by Florida State University, which look at public perception of white-collar crime. I wanted to show how white-collar crime can be just as damaging to the general public as street crime. This part helped to validate my thesis and show that this paper is exigent. 3

One major audience for this paper is business students. It will be their decisions that shape the business world, and the ethical decisions they make could reduce white-collar crime. It will be their bosses, coworkers, and corporations committing white-collar crime—and maybe asking them to participate. If they have a better understanding of the term, as well as a sense of how damaging it can be, businesses may act more ethically. 4

Considering the audience of students, I then created a short graphic novel about a CEO who is tempted to commit white-collar crime, but is dissuaded after meeting characters like Jeff Skilling, Dennis Kozlowski, and Karl Marx. My graphic novel, "Hope for America," looks at the illegal activity orchestrated by the CEOs of Enron. I wanted readers to be intrigued but not overwhelmed by the magnitude of the crimes. I felt that the graphic novel, which I created by learning and using the program "Comic Life," would be a great medium for presenting the information because it can be informal and is driven by visuals. It is also a much faster way for the audience to understand my point than reading a research paper—and maybe can interest them in later reading more details. 5

FINAL DRAFT OF ESSAY

In the prosperous days before the current economic crisis, stories about misdoings among corporate executives got little more than a nod and a wink; businesspeople, it seemed, were expected to cut corners and bend the rules in seeking the profits expected of their shareholders. After all, were these "real" crimes? 1

2 But times have changed. In the face of growing unemployment, numerous bankruptcies, and shrinking retirement funds, suddenly the public (and the justice system) have turned their attention—and sometimes their rage—toward the white-collar criminal. Joe Nacchio, CEO of Qwest Communication, has been sentenced to six years in federal prison; Bernie Madoff, who pled guilty to defrauding clients out of some $65 billion, has faced not only criminal penalties but also death threats; and bonuses paid to executives at the American International Group (AIG) have caused public outrage by citizens and legislators. But while these and countless other abuses have finally caught the public and governmental eye, white-collar crime is no new phenomenon. A look back at the all-but-forgotten Aldephia Communications scandal and the Enron debacle before that demonstrates how, despite the spectacular headlines, we largely ignored this building storm until it was too late.

3 On March 27, 2002, John Rigas and his executive board at Adelphia prepared for a routine financial check by the Securities and Exchange Commission. The investigation disclosed that the Rigas family had illegally co-borrowed $2.3 billion from the company. To cover the loans, it was estimated that Adelphia would have to borrow $1 billion. In response, investors pushed Adelphia's stock down 30% the very next day. Adelphia's shares were temporarily taken off the market and by summer the company filed for bankruptcy. On July 24, 2002, Rigas and his sons were arrested in New York City. Rigas's son Tim was sentenced to twenty years, while his father was given fifteen years for securities fraud (Cauley). After his trial, John Rigas maintained that, "It was a case of being in the wrong place at the wrong time. If this happened a year before, there would have been no headlines" (Cauley). In other words, Rigas felt that few would have noticed his actions if he had been caught before Enron and other corporate scandals of 2001 were exposed. And perhaps he was right.

4 The Adelphia story would be a tragedy in its own right, but when it is looked at in conjunction with companies like Enron, WorldCom, Tyco, Global Crossing, Qçwest, Xerox, and several other Fortune 500 companies that went bankrupt after white-collar crime was exposed, a pattern of corruption that has existed for many years emerges. In the film *Enron: The Smartest Guys in the Room,* Bethany Mclean, a co-author of the book of the same title, shows a significant problem with how white-collar crime is perceived: "The Enron story is so fascinating because people perceive it as a story that's about numbers, that it's somehow about all these complicated transactions. In reality it's a story about people, and it's really a human tragedy" (Gibney).

5 By explaining the human costs behind these white collar crimes, I hope to show why the public must pay attention to this public scourge.

First, I want to show how the sentencing of these criminals, as compared to the sentencing of street criminals, sends the wrong message about the serious nature of white-collar crime. Second, I hope to demonstrate that public perception of white-collar crime is flawed and out of sync with the personal tragedies that crime causes.

The term *white-collar crime* was originally coined by Edward Sutherland in 1939. Suthe°rland defined white-collar crime as "crime committed by a person of respectability and high social status in the course of their occupation" (Strader 1). Recently, sociologists and criminologists have debated what crimes are considered white-collar. Often, the term refers to a crime committed in the course of a person's occupation—no matter the social class. But, as Sutherland suggests, true white-collar crime is that which has a great impact upon society. 6

White-collar crime is often very difficult to detect. The crimes take place in private offices where there are rarely eye-witnesses. The government has to base their prosecution on complex paper trails instead of concrete evidence (Strader 1-4). Also, white-collar criminals of high social status are able to hire better-trained, more experienced lawyers. This makes convicting white-collar criminals much more difficult than convicting street criminals. 7

Because white-collar crimes are often not given due attention, it is difficult for the majority of Americans to understand their financial complexity. Understanding the methods used to commit the crimes, however, is not nearly as important as recognizing the damage that is done to countless employees who lose everything that they worked years to accomplish. Americans need to realize that their ignorance of the effects of white collar crime has allowed the American justice system to be unfairly lax in the way it treats white-collar criminals. 8

If we compare white collar crime to a typical armed robbery, we can see the inequality of the current justice system. For example, compare the sentencing of John Rigas to that of three Kentuckians who robbed a small grocery store. In November 2007, Morgan Wallace, 30, entered the grocery store with a handgun and demanded money. Geneva S. Goodin and Megan Johnston assisted in the escape before the three were apprehended on a highway near the scene of the crime. All three were held in a detention center after the robbery. On April 11, 2008, Wallace and Goodin were sentenced to ten years in prison while Johnston was sentenced to five years ("Three Plead"). Unlike Rigas, Wallace, Goodin, and Johnston were not able to obtain bail money so that they could go to their homes before their trial. The three robbers were arrested, tried, and convicted within five to six months. That period is a stark contrast to the five years of freedom that Rigas was allowed before a judge requested he begin his jail time (Cauley). There is also a clear disparity in the punishment that was handed 9 out in relation to the damage of the crimes to society. The amount that the Kentuckians made off with was not disclosed, but it is certainly a miniscule amount compared with the $2.3 billion that Rigas gained, followed by the millions of dollars that were lost to shareholders. However, Wallace's term is only five years shorter than that of John Rigas, and there was no stipulation that the sentence could be as short as two years (as with Rigas's case), if Wallace's health declined.

The Rigas case is important in its own right, but it is impossible to 10
explain the devastation caused by white-collar crime without also examining the Enron scandal. In January 2001, Enron was the seventh largest corporation in America. Enron had built oil-extracting stations all over the world, but most of them were performing terribly. However, instead of accurately releasing the correct financial statistics, Enron's executives included prospective profits in its bottom line. Enron and its accounting firm, Arthur Anderson, were able to hide the fact that Enron was $30 million in debt. Enron's CFO, Andy Fastow, created fake partnerships that would buy energy from Enron, in order to increase Enron's value. However, Fastow was merely working under Kenneth Lay, the founder of the company, and Jeffrey Skilling, the CEO. When investors started to question Enron's finances, Enron was not able to provide legitimate documentation for their profits. The final straw was when Enron began shutting down power plants in California in order to create artificial power shortages to increase the price of energy. Then the SEC began to inquire into Enron. In response, Enron began to release massive restatements, and Arthur Anderson began to shred documents concerning Enron. Six weeks after the investigations began, Enron filed for bankruptcy (Gibney). Ken Lay passed away before he could be sentenced. Jeff Skilling was sentenced to twenty-four years and $60 million in fines; however, he was allowed to keep his $5 million mansion and $50 million in stocks and bonds. Andy Fastow was sentenced to just six years in prison.

The difference between Enron and other corporate scandals is that 11
no other company has ever been so high and fallen with such damaging consequences. While Adelphia was partially bought up by Time Warner (Cauley), Enron completely collapsed. The stock value went from $90.75 at its peak to just $.08 after the company filed for bankruptcy. Five thousand employees lost their jobs, along with $800 million in pension funds. It is also important to remember that not all of the damage was financial. Enron employees and investors were personally affected. After losing their jobs, former employees were forced to deal with the stress that surrounds finding a new job and making ends meet while providing for a family. The employees went from having a secure future in a successful company to being unemployed with most of their stock and their retirement funds erased. Enron was white-collar crime at its worst.

These personal tragedies are often lost in the extravagant numbers 12
and complex business practices. As a result of the fraud committed by a

small group of men, thousands of people lost their livelihood. This problem cannot be considered an isolated incident. Doing that would ignore the damage that white-collar crime has already done and foster ignorance of future corporate fraud. As Ben Lerach, the chief attorney for Enron employees stated, "It's the same old adage; if it looks to good to be true, then it is. Enron was making millions of dollars out of nowhere, and no one inside the company was there to stand up and question where this money was coming from" (Gibney). But is the public aware?

Following these high-profile white-collar crimes, researchers took specific interest in how white-collar crime is perceived by the general public. Researchers at the College of Criminology at Florida State University published a study in February 2008 that addressed this topic. In preliminary research it was found that white-collar crime costs the United States about $250 billion per year, whereas personal, or "street crimes," and household crimes account for only $17.6 billion lost. Despite this large disparity, the focus of criminal justice authorities and criminologists has been on explaining and preventing personal crime. *13*

A study by researchers at Cal State and the University of Florida published in February 2007 provides more data on the topic. Researchers used data from a national phone poll of 1,106 participants and found that three-quarters of the sample believed that street criminals were more likely to be caught and more likely to receive a harsher punishment. The sample was split on who *should* receive a harsher punishment. This study suggests that while the public may believe all criminals should receive the same punishment, it is clear that Americans believe white-collar criminals will receive less of a punishment (Schoepfer). *14*

Interesting conclusions can be drawn from both of these studies. From the Florida State study, participants believed that in a case where a white-collar and a street criminal commit crimes of equal financial damage, the street criminal should receive a harsher punishment. This may be because street crime is usually a crime where the victim is personally involved in a confrontation, whereas white-collar crime is a more indirect form of victimization. However, it is obvious, due to the large gap in total damages, that white-collar criminals are acting more frequently and doing more financial damage than street criminals. The second study shows that the public acknowledges a disparity in the sentencing of white-collar and street criminals, yet no major reforms have attempted to change this pattern. These studies show that public perception is inaccurate as based on the threat that each type of crime poses financially. *15*

The American business model is an institution that has shown sustainability and reliability for the past two hundred years. However, it is through this institution that Americans are stealing *16* nearly fifteen times more money than through conventional street crimes. The devastating effects of white-collar crime need to be discussed by all Americans and addressed in a systematic way. The current outrage is not sufficient for a long-term fix. People lock their doors when they leave their house, but they see no problem in putting ninety percent of their 401k stock options into one company. White-collar crime has produced real damage, and without change in public opinion, there are no signs that it will decline. Understanding white-collar crime now can prevent or reduce the damage that white-collar crime inflicts on America.

Works Cited

Cauley, Leslie. "John Rigas Tells His Side of the Adelphia Story." *USA Today*. Gannett, 10 Apr. 2008. Web. 12 Apr. 2009.

"Former Enron CEO Skilling Gets 24 Years." *Associated Press*. Associated Press, 23 Oct. 2006. Web. 11 Apr. 2009.

Gibney, Alex, dir. *Enron: The Smartest Guys in the Room*. Perf. Peter Coyote. Jigsaw, 2005. Film.

Holtfreter, Kristy, et al. "Public Perception of White-Collar Crime." *Journal of Criminal Justice* 36:1 (2008): 50-60. Print.

Meier, Barry. "Founder of Adelphia Is Found Guilty of Conspiracy." *New York Times*. New York Times, 8 July 2004. Web. 13 Apr. 2009.

Schoepfer, Andrea, et al. "Do Perceptions of Punishment Vary between White Collar and Street Crimes?" *Journal of Criminal Justice* 35:2 (2007): 151-63. Print.

Strader, Kelly. "Understanding White Collar Crime." *Understanding White Collar Crime*. New York: Mathew Bender, 2002. 1-13. Print.

"Three Plead Guilty in Store Robbery." *McCreary County Voice*. McCreary County Voice, 11 Apr. 2008. Web. 13 Apr. 2009.

Questions for Writing and Discussion

1. In his essay overview, Chris Blakely says his purpose is to change public perception about the effects of white-collar crime. Cite at least two specific sentences from his essay where Blakely states this purpose.
2. Explaining essays typically use definition, process analysis, and cause-and-effect reasoning to demonstrate the main points. Reread

Blakely's essay. Then cite examples of all of these strategies from his paper. Which of the strategies is most closely related to his purpose or thesis? Explain.

3. In an explaining essay, transitions from paragraph to paragraph help to clarify the subject for the audience. Review the section on "Paragraph Transitions and Hooks" in this chapter (page 214). Then find two places where Blakely makes clear and smooth transitions from one paragraph to the next. Identify the transition words and hooks he uses to connect these paragraphs.

4. Review the selections from Blakely's graphic novel. How do the scenes he depicts relate to the subject and purpose of his essay? Do the cartoon-like pictures and captions make white-collar crime seem humorous? How do Blakely's images and captions convey the seriousness of these crimes? Explain, citing specific images and dialogue.

Student Writing

Anorexia Nervosa

Nancie Brosseau

In her essay on anorexia nervosa, Nancie Brosseau writes from her own experience, explaining what anorexia nervosa is and what its effects are. Her essay succeeds not only because it is organized clearly, but also because it is so vivid and memorable. Relying on specific details, her explanation shows the effects of anorexia on her life.

I knew my dieting had gotten out of hand, but when I could actually see the movement of my heart beating beneath my clothes, I knew I was in trouble. At first, the family doctor reassured my parents that my rapid weight loss was a "temporary phase among teenage girls." However, when I, at fourteen years old and five feet tall, weighed in at sixty-three pounds, my doctor changed his diagnosis from "temporary phase" to "anorexia nervosa." Anorexia nervosa is the process of self-starvation that affects over 100,000 young girls each year. Almost 6,000 of these girls die every year. Anorexia nervosa is a self-mutilating disease that affects its victim both physically and emotionally. 1

As both a gymnast and a dancer, I was constantly surrounded by lithe, muscular people, all of them extremely conscious about their weight. Although I wasn't overweight to begin with, I thought that if I lost five to ten pounds I would look, feel, dance, and tumble better. 2

I figured the quickest way to accomplish this was by drastically limiting my intake of food. By doing this, I lost ten pounds in one week and gained the approval of my peers. Soon, I could no longer control myself, and ten pounds turned into twenty, twenty into forty, and so on, until I finally ended up weighing fifty-eight pounds.

Several serious health problems bombarded me, and it's a wonder I'm still alive. Because my body was receiving no nourishment at all, my muscles and essential organs, including my heart, liver, kidneys, and intestines, started to compensate by slowly disintegrating. My body was feeding on itself! As my weight plummeted, my circulation grew increasingly worse. My hands, feet, lips, and ears took on a bluish-purple tint, and I was constantly freezing cold. My hair started to fall out and my whole body took on a very skeletal appearance. My eyes appeared to have sunken into my face, and my forehead, cheekbones, and chin protruded sharply. My wrists were the largest part of my entire arm, as were my knees the widest part of my legs. My pants rubbed my hips raw because I had to wear my belts at their tightest notch to keep them up. I would force myself to vomit as soon as possible if I was forced to eat. The enamel on my teeth started to be eaten away by the acid in the vomit, and my lips cracked and bled regularly. I stopped menstruating completely because I was not producing enough estrogen. Instead of improving my skills as a dancer and a gymnast, I drastically reduced them because I was so weak. One time, while executing a chain of back handsprings, I broke all five fingers on one hand and three on the other because my bones had become so brittle. My doctor realized the serious danger I was in and told me I either had to see a psychologist or be put in the hospital. I chose to see a psychologist, and she helped me sort out the emotional aspects of anorexia, which in turn solved the physical problems. 3

The emotional problems associated with anorexia nervosa are equally disastrous to the victim's health. Self-deception, lying, and depression are three examples of the emotions and actions an anorexic often experiences. During my entire bout with anorexia, I deceived myself into thinking I had complete control over my body. Hunger pains became a pleasant feeling, and sore muscles from overexercising just proved to me that I still needed to lose more weight. When my psychologist showed me pictures of girls that were of normal weight for my age group, they honestly looked obese to me. I truly believed that even the smallest amount of food would make me extremely fat. 4

Another problem, lying, occurred most often when my parents tried to force me to eat. Because I was at the gym until around eight o'clock 5 every night, I told my mother not to save me dinner. I would come home and make a sandwich and feed it to my dog. I lied to my parents every day about eating lunch at school. For example, I would bring a sack lunch and sell it to someone and use the money to buy diet pills. I always told my parents that I ate my own lunch. I lied to my doctor when he asked if I was taking an appetite suppressant. I had to cover one lie with another to keep from being found out, although it was obvious that I was not eating by looking at me.

Still another emotion I felt, as a result of my anorexia, was severe 6
depression. It seemed that, no matter how hard I tried, I kept growing fatter. Of course, I was getting thinner all the time, but I couldn't see that. One time, I licked a postage stamp to put on a letter and immediately remembered that there was 1/4 of a calorie in the glue on the stamp. I punished myself by doing 100 extra situps every night for one week. I pinched my skin until it bruised as I lay awake at night because I was so ashamed of the way I thought I looked. I doomed myself to a life of obesity. I would often slip into a mood my psychologist described as a "blue funk." That is, I would become so depressed, I seriously considered committing suicide. The emotional instabilities associated with anorexia nervosa can be fatal.

Through psychological and physical treatment, I was able to 7
overcome anorexia nervosa. I still have a few complications today due to anorexia, such as dysmenorrhea (severe menstrual cramps) and the tendency to fast. However, these problems are minute compared to the problems I would have had if I hadn't received immediate help. Separately, the physical and emotional problems that anorexia nervosa creates can greatly harm its victim. However, when the two are teamed together, the results are deadly.

Questions for Writing and Discussion

1. Without looking back at this essay, jot down the specific examples that you found most memorable. How would you describe these examples: tedious and commonplace, eye-opening, shocking, upsetting, persuasive? Explain.
2. Identify the thesis statement and essay map. Referring to paragraph numbers, show how the essay map sets up the organization of the essay.

3. Reread the opening sentences of each body paragraph. Identify one opening sentence that creates a smooth transition from the previous paragraph. Identify one opening sentence in which the transition could be smoother. Revise this sentence to improve the transition with a paragraph hook.
4. In this essay, Brosseau defines anorexia nervosa, explains its physical and emotional effects (and hints at its causes), and analyzes the process of the disorder, from its inception to its cure. Identify passages that illustrate each of these strategies: definition, cause-and-effect analysis, and process analysis.

Complete additional exercises and practice in your MyLab

The car spindle was created by Dustin Shuler and erected in a shopping center in Berwyn, Illinois, in 1989. The spindle had attained the status of a pop art icon by the time it was torn down in 2007. After reading in this chapter about evaluating works of art, write your own evaluation of this sculpture.

Adolph F. Rohrer/ Superstock

8 Evaluating

What You Will Learn
In this chapter, you will learn to:

8.1 Use techniques for evaluating

8.2 Use collecting strategies to develop your evaluation

8.3 Shape your evaluation essay

HARDLY a day passes that we do not express our likes or dislikes. We constantly pass judgment on people, places, objects, events, ideas, and policies. "Sue is a wonderful person." "The food in this cafeteria is horrible." "That movie ought to get an Oscar nomination for best picture." "That candidate should be re-elected." In addition to our own reactions, we are constantly exposed to the opinions of our friends, family members, teachers, and business associates. The media also barrage us with claims about products, famous personalities, and candidates for political office.

A claim or opinion, however, is not an *evaluation.* Your reaction to a person, a sports event, a meal, a movie, or a public policy becomes an evaluation *only* when you support your value judgment with clear standards and specific evidence. Your goal in evaluating something is not only to express your viewpoint, but also to *persuade* others to accept your judgment. You convince your readers by indicating the standards for your judgment and then supporting it with evidence: "The food in this cafeteria is horrible [your claim]. I know that not all cafeteria food tastes great, but it should at least be sanitary [one standard of judgment]. Yesterday, I had to dig a piece of green mold out of the meat loaf, and just as I stuck my fork into the green salad, a large black roach ran out [evidence]."

Most people interested in a subject will agree that certain standards are important; for example, that a cafeteria be clean and pest-free. The standards that you share with your audience are the *criteria* for your evaluation. You convince your readers that something is good or bad, ugly or beautiful, tasty or nauseating, by analyzing your subject in terms of your criteria. For each criterion, you support your judgment with specific *evidence:* descriptions, statistics, testimony, or examples from your personal experience. If your readers agree that your standards or criteria are appropriate, and if you supply sufficient evidence, your readers should be convinced. They will take your evaluation seriously—and think twice about eating at that roach-infested cafeteria.

"When we evaluate, we have in mind . . . an ideal of what a good thing—pianist, painting, or professor—should be and do, and we apply that ideal to the individual instance before us."

—Jeanne Fahnestock and Marie Secor,
Authors of *A Rhetoric of Argument*

"Purpose and craftsmanship—ends and means—these are the keys to your judgment."

—Marya Mannes,
Journalist and Social Commentator

Techniques for Writing Evaluations

8.1
Use techniques for evaluating

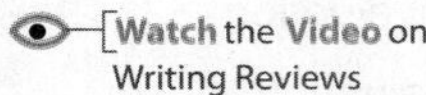
Watch the Video on Writing Reviews

The most common genre for an evaluation is the review. Most frequently, we read reviews of films, books, restaurants, commercial products, public performances, and works of art. Reviews vary widely in style depending on the topic, the place of publication, and the social context. Some reviews seem to be little more than thinly disguised promotions, while other reviews are thorough, complex, and highly critical. For any substantive evaluation, the review must set standards of judgment, rely on fair criteria, balance the positive and the negative, and provide sufficient evidence to persuade its readers. Use the following techniques as you write your evaluation.

Techniques for Evaluating

Technique	Tips on How to Do It
Assessing *the* rhetorical situation	What is the occasion and context for your review? Find examples of the genre you propose to write—where are these reviews or critiques typically published? Who is the audience, and what do they already believe or know about the topic?
Stating an *overall claim* about your subject	The overall claim is your *thesis* for your evaluation. It sums up the positive and negative judgments you make for each criterion.
Clarifying the *criteria* for your evaluation	A criterion is a standard of judgment that most people who are knowledgeable about your subject agree is important. A criterion serves as a yardstick against which you measure your subject.
Stating a *judgment* for each criterion	The overall claim is based on your *judgment* of each criterion. Avoid being too critical or too enthusiastic by including both positive and negative judgments.
Supporting each judgment with *evidence*	Support should include *detailed observations, facts, examples, testimonials, quotations from experts,* or *statistics*.
Balancing your evaluation with both *positive* and *negative* judgments about your subject	Evaluations that are all positive are merely advertisements; evaluations that are entirely negative may seem too harsh or mean-spirited.

In the following evaluation of a Chinese restaurant in Washington, D.C., journalist and critic Phyllis C. Richman illustrates the main features of a restaurant review.

Professional Writing

Hunan Dynasty

215 Pennsylvania Ave. SE, 546-6161
Open daily 11 A.M. to 3 P.M. for lunch, 3 P.M. to 10 P.M.
for dinner, until 11 P.M. on Friday and Saturday.
Reservations suggested for large parties.

Information and description

1 Chinese restaurants in America were once places one went just to eat. Now one goes to dine. There are now waiters in black tie, cloths on the tables and space between those tables, art on the walls and decoratively carved vegetables on the plate—elegance has become routine in Chinese restaurants. What's more, in Chinese restaurants the ingredients are fresh (have you ever found frozen broccoli in a Chinese kitchen?), and the cooking almost never sinks below decent. . . . And it is usually moderately priced. In other words, if you're among unfamiliar restaurants and looking for good value, Chinese restaurants now are routinely better than ever.

Description

Overall claim

2 The Hunan Dynasty is an example of what makes Chinese restaurants such reliable choices. A great restaurant? It is not. A good value? Definitely. A restaurant to fit nearly any diner's need? Probably.

3 First, it is attractive. There are no silk tassels, blaring red lacquer or Formica tables; instead there are white tablecloths and subtle glass etchings. It is a dining room—or dining rooms, for the vastness has been carved into smaller spaces—of gracefulness and lavish space.

Criterion #1: Nice setting

Judgment: Attractive

Evidence

4 Second, service is a strong priority. The waiters look and act polished, and serve with flourishes from the carving of a Peking duck to the portioning of dishes among the diners. I have found some glitches—a forgotten appetizer, a recommendation of two dishes that turned out nearly identical—but most often the service has been expert. . . .

Criterion #2: Good service

Judgment: Often expert

Evidence

5 As for the main dishes, don't take the "hot and spicy" asterisks too seriously, for this kitchen is not out to offer you a test of fire. The peppers are there, but not in great number. And, like the appetizers, the main dishes are generally good but not often memorable. Fried dishes—and an inordinate number of them seem to be fried—are crunchy and not greasy. Vegetables are bright and crisp. Eggplant with hot garlic sauce is properly unctuous; Peking duck is as fat-free and crackly-skinned as you could hope (though pancakes were rubbery). . . .

Criterion #3: Good main dishes

Judgment: Good but not memorable

Evidence

6 I have found only one dismal main dish in a fairly broad sampling: lemon chicken had no redeeming feature in its doughy, greasy, overcooked and underseasoned presentation. Otherwise, not much goes wrong. Crispy shrimp with walnuts might be preferable stir-fried rather than batter-fried, but the tomato-red sauce and crunchy walnuts made a good dish. Orange beef could use more seasoning but the coating was nicely crusty and the meat tender. . . .

Criterion #3 cont.

Judgment: Sometimes bad

Evidence

Overall claim restated

...continued Hunan Dynasty

So with the opening of the Hunan Dynasty, Washington did not add a stellar Chinese restaurant to its repertoire, but that is not necessarily what the city needed anyway. Hunan Dynasty is a top-flight neighborhood restaurant—with good food, caring service and very fair prices—that is attractive enough to set a mood for celebration and easygoing enough for an uncomplicated dinner with the family after work. 7

EVALUATING COMMERCIAL PRODUCTS OR SERVICES

“It is as hard to find a neutral critic as it is a neutral country in a time of war.”

—Katherine Anne Porter, Novelist and Short Story Writer

Writers frequently evaluate commercial products or services. Consumer magazines test and rate every imaginable product or service—from cars and dishwashers to peanut butter and brokerage houses. Guidebooks evaluate tourist spots, restaurants, colleges, and hunting lodges. Specialty magazines such as *Modern Photography, Road and Track, Skiing,* and *Wired* often rate products and services. To qualify as evaluation—and not just advertising—the authors and the publishers must maintain an independent status, uninfluenced by the manufacturers of the products or services they are judging.

Consider the “evaluation” of a wine found on a bottle of Cabernet Sauvignon:

> This Cabernet Sauvignon is a dry, robust, and complex wine whose hearty character is balanced by an unusual softness.

This “evaluative” language is so vague and esoteric that it may mean very little to the average consumer who just wants some wine with dinner. *Dry:* How can a liquid be dry? *Robust:* Does this refer to physique? *Soft:* Wine is not a pillow, though it might put you to sleep. *Complex:* Are they describing a wine or conducting a psychological analysis? While an independent evaluator may legitimately use these terms for knowledgeable wine drinkers, this particular description suggests that the wine is everything the buyer would like it to be—dry yet robust, hearty but at the same time soft. Apparently, the writer's purpose here is not to evaluate a product but to flatter customers who imagine themselves connoisseurs of wine.

Now consider an evaluation of two popular lines of cell phone, Android phones versus iPhones. In this comparative evalution, the editors at *Consumer Reports* judge these cell phones in terms of display, navigation, Web browsing, 4G compatibility, shopping, apps, cloud computing, and voice assistance. Notice that the editors comment on both the strengths and the weaknesses of each phone.

Professional Writing

Android vs. iPhone

The most important determinant of what a smart phone can do, and how well it can do it, is its operating system. While Windows Phone and, even more so, BlackBerry have a significant presence, two rivals dominate the OS market: Apple, with its three models of iPhone (the new 4s along with the 4 and 3G S), and Google's Android, with dozens of phones from a host of manufacturers. Here's how those two titans compare on key attributes: 1

Advantage: Android

Large displays. Back in 2007, iPhone's 3.5-inch display was one of the largest, brightest, and sharpest you could get, and its recent color and resolution upgrades have been impressive. But the larger (4.3 inches and up) and equally dazzling screens on Android phones from HTC, Motorola, Samsung, and other makers seem better suited to the Web pages, games, and videos that users are increasingly accessing from their phones. 2

Navigation. Android phones offer free, spoken, turn-by-turn directions and traffic updates out of the box via Google Maps Navigation software. To get comparable performance and convenience, iPhone users have to shell out $40 to $50 for a navigation app from TomTom, Navigon, and others. But those aftermarket iPhone apps have an advantage: Their maps are stored on the phone, so you can navigate even when you lack good cellular reception. (Next month's issue will include Ratings of the newest versions of those apps.) 3

Web browsing. Apple has its pluses here, including a "reader" mode built into the Safari browser of the new iOS 5 operating system. You can tap it to read articles without the clutter of ads and other graphics and to save articles to read later. 4

Customization of the interface. Apple's interface is fairly fixed, albeit in a highly intuitive manner, but the Android platform can be customized. Phone makers can tweak the interface, carriers can install apps, and users can customize a phone's look and feel using widgets and other tools. For example, some blend updates from friends on Facebook, Twitter, and other social networks, and others manage all of your phone's wireless connections. 5

4G compatibility. More than a dozen Android smart phones support this technology, far more than any other platform. Technically, only the AT&T version of the iPhone 4S supports 4G; it runs on the carrier's HSPA+ network. 6

...continued Android vs. iPhone

Shopping by phone. Android and Apple have apps that allow you to check the prices of products and other details by scanning bar codes or QR codes (those square blotches you might have seen in ads) using the phone's camera and a connection to the Web. 7

However, only Android has the Google Wallet app, which allows you to make a purchase using your smart phone as though it were a digital credit card. Use of that app is limited to a handful of phones with near-field communications (NFC) capability. Phones in our Ratings with that feature include the Sprint version of the Samsung Nexus S 4G, the HTCAmaze 4G, and the T-Mobile Samsung Galaxy S II. The carrier must offer the service (now only Sprint does), and merchants must be in the MasterCard PayPass network, which operates in 150,000 U.S. locations. 8

Advantage: iPhone

Selection of apps and entertainment. No contest. Not only does Apple have the most apps, games, songs, movies, and other forms of entertainment for download but its platform also makes it very easy to pay for them—via your iTunes account. On Android phones, payment arrangements are often between you and the individual app seller, which means you're giving your credit-card number to multiple sources instead of to just one. 9

Cloud computing. Android is the true pioneer when it comes to syncing contacts, calendars, apps, and other phone-based elements via the Web and intelligently linking them with Web-based data such as maps, social networks such as Facebook and Twitter, photos, search-engine results, and more. Apple's iCloud feature takes the game to a whole new level, giving users 5 gigabytes of free storage on its servers, to which they can upload photos, music, documents created with apps from Apple or third parties that support iCloud, and more that can be accessed by up to 10 devices on one iTunes account. Ditto for most apps and content, including videos and books bought from Apple, which don't count against your limit. To get more storage for non-Apple files, you'll have to pay up to $100 a year for 50GB. Both Google and Apple have new services that use the cloud to stream music, but it's premature to compare them, because Google's app is still in beta. 10

Consistent and intuitive interface and "ecosystem." Apple sustains a familiar, highly intuitive interface across its various devices and programs. That aids in the sharing and integration of tasks across your digital life, especially if you own various Apple devices. 11

Voice assistance. While Android efficiently allows users to perform universal searches, launch apps, and even dictate and send messages through voice commands, Apple now offers all that and more with its 12 built-in Siri voice-activated assistant. Currently available only on the iPhone 4S, Siri not only understands and executes requests but speaks back to you, in a female voice. Tell Siri to remind you about an appointment, and she'll set it up in the calendar after confirming with you that she got it right.

Siri sometimes demurs from speaking when you ask her questions involving calculations, such as, "Convert 42 pounds into ounces." But she's smart enough to show you the correct answer—in this case, 672 ounces—on her display. 13

While the cell phone evaluation considers several criteria (shown in boldface) the following review of light beers focuses on aspects of just one criterion. As you read this short piece by Eric Asimov, wine critic for the *New York Times*, see if you can determine his main criterion, his judgment for that criterion, and his supporting evidence. Is his evidence sufficient to persuade you of his overall claim?

Professional Writing

Bud Light, Coors Light, Miller Lite: Is There Any Difference?

Eric Asimov

It's true that the craft-beer movement of the last 30 years has exposed a lot of Americans to the idea that good beer is complex, flavorful and distinctive.

It's also true that Americans buy an enormous amount of terrible beer. Six of the 10 best-selling beers in the United States are light beers, including Bud Light at No. 1 (it outsells No. 2 Budweiser by more than 2 to 1), Coors Light at No. 3 and Miller Lite at No. 4. Because huge budgets are devoted to television advertising, industry analysts say that light-beer sales are "marketing driven." Basically, what the beers taste like is less important than the effectiveness of their ads—Bud Light's "Real Men of Genius" or Miller Lite's "Be a Man" campaign or Coors Light's labels that turn blue when properly cold. And apparently there is a need for the latter—sales of Bud Light and Miller Lite have declined for three straight years as Coors Light has shown modest growth.

I recently sampled the best-selling light beers to see if there was any palatable difference between them. The results: Coors Light offered no smell and no taste, but as the label indicated, it was indeed cold. Bud Light, which promises "superior drinkability," had only the faintest hint of bitterness but was otherwise devoid of flavor. Miller Lite was the clear winner. It seemed almost robust by comparison, but still hardly bitter.

...continued Bud Light, Coors Light, Miller Lite..., **Eric Asimov**

For added thrills, I drank a Michelob Ultra, the 12th-best-selling brand. Now here was a beer that truly tasted like nothing—no smell, no taste, not even the cold sensation of the Coors Light. If you want to drink basically nothing, Michelob Ultra is for you.

EVALUATING WORKS OF ART

Evaluations of commercial products and services tend to emphasize usefulness, practicality, convenience, and cost. Evaluations of works of art, on the other hand, focus on form, color, texture, design, balance, image, or theme. Through evaluation, writers teach us to appreciate all kinds of art: paintings, sculpture, photographs, buildings, antique cars and furniture, novels, short stories, essays, poems, tapestries. A Dior fashion, a quilt, a silverware pattern, even an old pair of jeans might be evaluated primarily on aesthetic rather than on practical grounds.

In the following selection, Paul Richard, art critic for the *Washington Post,* evaluates the painting *American Gothic* by Grant Wood. (Grant Wood's painting, *American Gothic,* can be accessed quickly through Google images.) Although the painting was completed in 1930, the occasion for Richard's review was a 2006 Grant Wood exhibition at the Renwick Gallery of the Smithsonian American Art Museum. Richard's overall claim is that *American Gothic* is a famous and even iconic example of American art—as well known as Andy Warhol's Campbell, soup can or Norman Rockwell's Thanksgiving turkey. The fact that *American Gothic* has so often been the subject of parody (search Google images, "American Gothic Parodies") is further evidence of the painting's iconic status.

Professional Writing

"American Gothic," Pitchfork Perfect

Paul Richard

Is "American Gothic" America's best-known painting? Certainly it's one of them. Grant Wood's dual portrait—with its churchy evocations, its stiffness and its pitchfork—pierced us long ago, and got stuck into our minds. Now, finally, it's here. 1

"American Gothic," which hasn't been in Washington in 40 years, goes on view today at the Renwick Gallery of the Smithsonian American Art Museum. By all means, take it in—although, of course, you have already. 2

It should have gone all fuzzy—it's been parodied so often, and parsed so many ways—but the 1930 canvas at the Renwick is as sharp as ever. Its details are finer than its travesties suggest, its image more absorbing. It's also smaller than one might have imagined, at only two feet wide. Wood painted it in his home town of Cedar Rapids, Iowa, showed it only once and then sold it, with relief, to the Art Institute of Chicago—for $300. 3

The picture with a pitchfork is an American unforgettable. Few paintings, very few, have its recognizability. Maybe Whistler's mother. Maybe Warhol's soup can. Maybe Rockwell's Thanksgiving turkey. They're national emblems, all of them, visual manifestations of the American dream. 4

Whistler's figure, stiff and dark, looks half-enthroned and half-embalmed; what she evokes is Mom. Family and food are the twin themes of the Rockwell. And with his Campbell's can, fluorescent-lit, Warhol nails shopping. 5

"American Gothic," too, hits the psychic bull's-eye. Wood's sly painting gives us the bedrock Christian values, the sober rural rectitude and the gnawing fear of sex that have made this country great. 6

The dangers of the dirty deed might not be depicted, but they're present nonetheless. The sinful is suggested by the serpent made of hair that slithers up the woman's neck to whisper in her ear, by the lightning rod atop the house and, of course, by the Devil's pitchfork. Wood's painting has a wink in it. No wonder it has been so frequently cartooned. 7

"The couple in front of the house have become preppies, yuppies, hippies," writes critic Robert Hughes, "Weathermen, pot growers, Ku Kluxers, jocks, operagoers, the Johnsons, the Reagans, the Carters, the Fords, the Nixons, the Clintons, and George Wallace with an elderly black lady." 8

But cartoons tend toward the slapdash, and Wood's calculated image is not at all haphazard. Nothing's out of place. The bright tines of the fork have been echoed one, two, three, by, at the left, the distant steeple, the window's pointed arch and the sharp roof at the right. The pitchfork rhymes as well with the seams of the man's overalls. When Wood painted "American Gothic," he fit its symmetries together as if he were making a watch. . . . 9

The picture takes its title from an architectural fashion. In its higher manifestations, American Gothic gave us the Washington Cathedral and the colleges at Yale. Far out in the sticks (in, for instance, rural Iowa), the style left its mark on the factory-made windows, porch columns and pattern books that in the 19th century were shipped in by train. 10

"American Gothic's" farmhouse, with its pointed gable window, is another local artifact. Wood discovered that wooden building in nearby Eldon, Iowa. It's still there. His figures were local, too. The bald man is his dentist, B. H. McKeeby. The woman is Wood's sister, Nan. (She was 30 at the time, McKeeby, 62.) Their eyes are cold, their mouths are prim. They wear period clothes. He stares the viewer down, she averts her gaze. They understand their roles. 11

...continued American Gothic," Pitchfork Perfect, **Paul Richard**

Modern art, this isn't. Wood's painting is behind its times, rather than ahead of them. What gives the work its punch is its slippery ambiguities. These haven't aged at all. 12

Try asking it a question. Is the woman the farmer's wife, or might she be (nudge, nudge) the famous farmer's daughter of countless naughty jokes? 13

What does this painting mean to do, celebrate or satirize? Do its figures dwell in paradise, where the pioneering Protestant verities still hold, or is their rural neighborhood not so far from Hell? ... 14

I don't know whether Wood expected "American Gothic" to become an American icon, but he wouldn't have been surprised. In the early 1930s, mythic American icons were very much on his mind. 15

Had you asked him to identify America's best-known paintings, you can bet he would have named two pictures of George Washington: Gilbert Stuart's likeness, the so-called Atheneum Portrait of 1796, the one that's on the dollar; and "Washington Crossing the Delaware" (1851), Emanuel Leutze's famous river scene with ice floes. In fact, both of these chestnuts can be found in Wood's own art. . . . 16

What is remarkable about "American Gothic" is its famousness. What is equally remarkable is that the picture's fame was not achieved by accident. The Renwick's show suggests that's what Grant Wood had in mind. 17

EVALUATING PERFORMANCES

Evaluating live, recorded, or filmed performances of people in sports, dance, drama, debate, public meetings or lectures, and music may involve practical criteria such as the prices of tickets to sports events or rock concerts. However, aesthetic criteria also apply. In film evaluations, for example, the usual criteria are good acting and directing, an entertaining or believable story or plot, memorable characters, dramatic special effects, and so forth.

In her review of *The Help*, Manohla Dargis, writing in the *New York Times*, evaluates key elements of director Tate Taylor's adaption of Kathryn Stockett's best-selling novel. As is typical of the film review genre, Dargis is writing for readers who have seen the film but also for those still deciding whether to watch it. To appeal to both sets of readers, Dargis weaves her evaluation into a summary of the film that gives a sense of the story from the novel and its historical and cultural context without revealing all the turns of the plot. As you read this review, look for her judgments about specific criteria (acting, directing, the effectiveness of specific scenes, the use of dialect) and her overall claim about the film.

Professional Writing

"The Maids" Now Have Their Say

Manohla Dargis

There's a scene in "The Help," the new movie based on Kathryn Stockett's novel, that cracks open the early-'60s world of strained smiles and gentility that rarely leaps out of this big, ole slab of honey-glazed hokum. It's after hours, and Aibileen, a maid played with determined grace by Viola Davis, is going home. Suddenly the bus stops, and a white man orders the black passengers off, explaining that a black man has been shot—except that he doesn't say black, Negro or colored. In a pool of dreadful night, Aibileen and a young man trade goodbyes and rush off. And then this sturdy, frightened woman starts running as if her life were in danger, because it's Mississippi, and it is. 1

When she gets to safety, Aibileen learns that the man who has been shot is Medgar Evers, the civil rights activist who was gunned down in Jackson, Miss., on June 12, 1963, in front of his home. His wife and three young children, who were trained to lie on the floor in case of gunfire, found him, and Evers died shortly afterward. Hours before, President John F. Kennedy, spurred on by different national events, including the demonstrations in Birmingham led by the Rev. Dr. Martin Luther King Jr., 2

Emma Stone, Octavia Spencer, and Viola Davis in *The Help*.

had delivered his landmark speech about civil rights. He said we were facing a "moral crisis as a country and a people" and soon introduced legislation that would become the Civil Rights Act of 1964, the same year "The Help" rises to its teary, insistently uplifting end.

If the movie's director, Tate Taylor, had his way, your tear ducts would be sucked dry by that big finish, emptied out by a pileup of calamities that include a painful romantic breakup, the devastations of cancer and the mighty wailing of an emotionally abandoned toddler. And that's just what's ailing the white folks. The black characters have it tough too, no question, and Mr. Taylor includes enough scenes of Aibileen and her best friend, Minny (Octavia Spencer), cleaning white houses and polishing the silver—and cooking meals and tending children and smiling, always smiling, even as they pretend not to hear the insults—to remind you that this is at least partly about backbreaking, soul-killing black labor. *3*

Aibileen works hard for one family in Jackson, minding a pale dumpling named Mae Mobley, whose own mother, Elizabeth (Ahna O'Reilly), called Miss Leefolt by Aibileen, scarcely touches the child. Aibileen loves the white babies she helps raise, though that affection comes with so many choking complexities that they can leave her near-speechless, as the promising first scene shows. Did you always think you would be a maid? an off-screen woman asks. Aibileen answers quietly but with matter-of-fact directness, yes: Her mother was a maid, and her grandmother had been a house slave. Did you have dreams of being something else? the unseen woman asks, her voice so guileless and so maddeningly oblivious that it's a wonder that Ms. Davis, who has been looking directly into the camera, nearly burning right through it, doesn't sneer. *4*

But Ms. Davis keeps her cool even as she warms your heart and does her job, often beautifully. She doesn't just turn Aibileen, something of a blur in the novel, into a fully dimensional character, she also helps lift up several weaker performances and invests this cautious, at times bizarrely buoyant, movie with the gravity it frequently seems to want to shrug off. She keeps your attention focused on her and Minny even when the story drifts over to Elizabeth and her white friends, who include a segregationist housewife, Hilly (Bryce Dallas Howard, energetic in a thankless role), and the far more liberal Skeeter (Emma Stone, uncharacteristically wan). A would-be writer, Skeeter is the one asking Aibileen all those questions. *5*

The story, which Mr. Taylor adapted for the screen, involves Skeeter's attempts to interview Aibileen, Minny and others about their experiences as maids. Skeeter, recently graduated from the University of Mississippi, *6* has returned home to find that Constantine (a frail-looking Cicely Tyson), her family's longtime maid and the woman who raised her, has disappeared. As Skeeter tries to find out what happened to Constantine—Skeeter's ill mother, Charlotte (Allison Janney), isn't saying—she begins a process of discovery. She lands a newspaper job, meets a boy (Chris Lowell) and slowly starts to see her friends for the bigots they are. Alas, she doesn't cozy up to the only interesting white woman in town, Celia (a winning Jessica Chastain), a bottle blonde shunned by almost everyone but her own maid, Minny.

Mr. Taylor handles these story threads ably as he moves from one household to another, from the bright, open plantation where Skeeter lives to the shotgun shacks that Aibileen and Minny call home. Everything looks good, polished to a high industrial gleam. Save for Ms. Davis's, however, the performances are almost all overly broad, sometimes excruciatingly so, characterized by loud laughs, bugging eyes and pumping limbs. Ms. Chastain and Ms. Spencer make quite the raucous comedy team, and while there's pleasure in their routine, all that comedy can feel misplaced. They have some genuinely touching moments together when you see two women, each struggling with the burdens of race and class. But just when you think it might get too heavy, Minny starts vacuuming a stuffed bear for some laughs. 7

Born in Mississippi in 1969, Ms. Stockett, a white woman, has suggested that she was somewhat inspired by Demetrie McLorn, a black woman who worked as a maid for her family, who died when Ms. Stockett was 16 and spoke, to judge from the book's afterword, in dialect. Some readers have objected to Ms. Stockett's decision to use black dialect that, in the case of Aibileen, is so thick and old-timey ("sho nuff") that it's as if Ms. Stockett were trying to channel Mark Twain. Her white characters, by contrast, are mostly written in "correct" English, even Celia, who in less genteel quarters would be called poor white trash. The dialect doesn't register as weighty in the movie, largely because Ms. Davis's performance speaks louder than her accent. 8

What does remain, though, is the novel's conceit that the white characters, with their troubled relationships and unloved children, carry burdens equal to those of the black characters. Like the novel, the movie is about ironing out differences and letting go of the past and anger. It's also about a vision of a divided America that while consistently insulting and sometimes even terrifying, is rarely grotesque, despite Hilly's best (worst) segregationist efforts. Inside all these different homes, black and white women tend to the urgent matters of everyday life, like the care and feeding of children. And while every so often the roar of the outside world steals in like thunder, Mr. Taylor makes sure it doesn't rattle the china or your soul. 9

Warming Up: Journal Exercises

The following exercises ask you to write evaluations. Read all of the exercises and then write on the three that interest you most. If another idea occurs to you, write about it.

1. **Writing Across the Curriculum.** Choose the best of the courses that you are currently taking. To persuade a friend to take it, evaluate the course, the teacher, or both. What criteria and evidence would you select to persuade your friend?
2. To gather information for yourself about a possible job or career, interview a person in your prospective field about his or her job or profession. Focus your questions on the person's opinions and judgments about this career. What criteria does this person use to judge it? What other jobs would serve as a good basis for comparison? What details from this person's daily routine support his or her judgments?
3. At your place of work, evaluate one of your products or services. Write down the criteria and evidence that your business might use to determine whether it is a "good" product or service. Then list the criteria and evidence that your customers or patrons probably use. Are these two sets of criteria and evidence identical? Explain.
4. Choose a work of modern art (painting, drawing, poster, sculpture, ceramic, and so forth). Describe and evaluate it for an audience that is indifferent or possibly even hostile to contemporary art. Explain why your readers should appreciate this particular art object.

While evaluations of restaurants typically focus on objective details such as the menu, the price of entreés, or a description of the restaurant itself, David Sedaris in the following piece of creative non-fiction uses a partly fictitious humorous narrative to evaluate not a single restaurant but a group of New York restaurants he calls "precious little bistros," As you read his narrative, consider how Sedaris alters the genre of the "restaurant review" in order to entertain his readers by satirizing the pretentions of these restaurants. The author of several best-selling books, including *Squirrel Seeks Chipmunk: A Modest Bestiary,* Sedaris provides an excellent model of how bend typical genre features to achieve his own purposes.

Professional Writing

Today's Special

David Sedaris

It is his birthday, and Hugh and I are seated in a New York restaurant, awaiting the arrival of our fifteen-word entreés. He looks very nice, 1 dressed in the suit and sweater that have always belonged to him. As for me, I own only my shoes, pants, shirt, and tie. My jacket belongs to the restaurant and was offered as a loan by the maître d', who apparently thought I would feel more comfortable dressed to lead a high-school marching band.

I'm worrying the thick gold braids decorating my sleeve when the waiter presents us with what he calls "a little something to amuse the palette." Roughly the size and color of a Band-Aid, the amusement floats on a shallow, muddy puddle of sauce and is topped with a sprig of greenery. 2

"And this would be . . . what, exactly?" Hugh asks. 3

"This," the waiter announces, "is our raw Atlantic sword-fish served in a dark chocolate gravy and garnished with fresh mint." 4

"Not again," I say. "Can't you guys come up with something a little less conventional?" 5

"Love your jacket," the waiter whispers. 6

As a rule, I'm no great fan of eating out in New York restaurants. It's hard to love a place that's outlawed smoking but finds it perfectly acceptable to serve raw fish in a bath of chocolate. There are no normal restaurants left, at least in our neighborhood. The diners have all been taken over by precious little bistros boasting a menu of indigenous American cuisine. They call these meals "traditional," yet they're rarely the American dishes I remember. The patty melt has been pushed aside in favor of the herb-encrusted medallions of baby artichoke hearts, which never leave me thinking, Oh, right, those! I wonder if they're as good as the ones my mom used to make. 7

Part of the problem is that we live in the wrong part of town. SoHo is not a macaroni salad kind of place. This is where the world's brightest young talents come to braise carmelized racks of corn-fed songbirds or offer up their famous knuckle of flash-seared crappie served with a collar of chided ginger and cornered by a tribe of kiln-roasted Chilean toad-stools, teased with a warm spray of clarified musk oil. Even when they promise something simple, they've got to tart it up—the meatloaf has been poached in sea water, or there are figs in the tuna salad. If cooking is an art, I think we're in our Dada phase. 8

I've never thought of myself as a particularly finicky eater, but it's hard to be a good sport when each dish seems to include no fewer than a dozen ingredients, one of which I'm bound to dislike. I'd order the skirt steak with a medley of suffocated peaches, but I'm put off by the aspirin sauce. The sea scallops look good until I'm told they're served in a broth of malt liquor and mummified litchi nuts. What I really want is a cigarette, and I'm always searching the menu in the hope that some courageous young chef has finally recognized tobacco as a vegetable. Bake it, steam it, grill it, or stuff it into littleneck clams, I just need something familiar that I can hold on to. 9

When the waiter brings our entrées, I have no idea which plate might be mine. In yesterday's restaurants it was possible both to visualize and to recognize your meal. There were always subtle differences, but for the most part, a lamb chop tended to maintain its basic shape. That is to say that it looked choplike. It had a handle made of bone and a teardrop of meat hugged by a thin rind of fat. Apparently, though, that was too predictable. Order the modern lamb chop, and it's likely to look no different than your companion's order of shackled pompano. The current food is always arranged into a senseless, vertical tower. No longer content to recline, it now reaches for the sky, much like the high-rise buildings lining our city streets. It's as if the plates were valuable parcels of land and the chef had purchased one small lot and unlimited air rights. Hugh's saffron linguini resembles a miniature turban, topped with architectural spires of shrimp. It stands there in the center while the rest of the vast, empty plate looks as though it's been leased out as a possible parking lot. I had ordered the steak, which, bowing to the same minimalist fashion, is served without the bone, the thin slices of beef stacked to resemble a funeral pyre. The potatoes I'd been expecting have apparently either been clarified to an essence or were used to stoke the grill. *10*

"Maybe," Hugh says, "they're inside your tower of meat." *11*

This is what we have been reduced to. Hugh blows the yucca pollen off his blackened shrimp while I push back the sleeves of my borrowed sport coat and search the meat tower for my promised potatoes. *12*

"There they are, right there." Hugh uses his fork to point out what could easily be mistaken for five cavity-riddled molars. The dark spots must be my vegetable. *13*

Because I am both a glutton and a masochist, my standard complaint, "That was so bad," is always followed by "And there was so little of it!" *14*

Our plates are cleared, and we are presented with dessert menus. I learn that spiced ham is no longer considered just a luncheon meat and that even back issues of *Smithsonian* can be turned into sorbets. *15*

"I just couldn't," I say to the waiter when he recommends the white chocolate and wild loganberry couscous. *16*

"If we're counting calories, I could have the chef serve it without the crème fraîche." *17*

"No," I say. "Really, I just couldn't." *18*

We ask for the check, explaining that we have a movie to catch. It's only a ten-minute walk to the theater, but I'm antsy because I'd like to get something to eat before the show. They'll have loads of food at the concession stand, but I don't believe in mixing meat with my movies. Luckily there's a hot dog cart not too far out of our way. *19*

Friends always say, "How can you eat those? I read in the paper that 20
they're made from hog's lips."

"And . . . ?" 21

"And hearts and eyelids." 22

That, to my mind, is only three ingredients and constitutes a refresh- 23
ing change of pace. I order mine with nothing but mustard, and am thrilled to watch the vendor present my hot dog in a horizontal position. So simple and timeless that I can recognize it, immediately, as food.

Questions for Writing and Discussion

1. In his essay, David Sedaris claims to enjoy simple food like potatoes and hot dogs, yet he knows and uses the vocabulary of a sophisticated gourmand. List the words and phrases Sedaris uses to describe the cuisine of this restaurant. Does he use this vocabulary to praise the cooking or to ridicule it? Explain.

2. As a humorist, Sedaris looks for the amusing and absurd in people, places, and events. As a restaurant critic, however, Sedaris uses evaluation to make a serious point. He doesn't explicitly state his overall claim about this restaurant, but his opinion is evident throughout. What exactly does Sedaris like and dislike? Write your own three-column log for this essay. List the *criteria* (such as ambiance, service, presentation, etc.) that Sedaris uses in this review, the *evidence* he gives, and his *judgment* for each criterion. State in your own words Sedaris's overall judgment or claim.

3. In his essay, Sedaris uses several descriptive and narrative strategies to convey the scene and describe the action. Review the techniques for observing and remembering in Chapter 3. Where in his essay does Sedaris give vivid and detailed descriptions or use images, similes, and metaphors? Where does Sedaris use narrative techniques such as scene setting, dialogue, and characterization? Support your response by citing specific sentences, phrases, or images.

4. Visit a local restaurant—preferably one you are already familiar with—for the purpose of writing a review. Take notes during the meal so you won't miss any details. Then write two versions of your review. For the first one, follow the informative model of the Hunan Dynasty review at the beginning of this chapter. Organize your comments clearly by the criteria you choose. For your second version, write in a narrative fashion as Sedaris does, including scene description, key events, characters, and dialogue. When you finish, evaluate your reviews. Which do you like best? What magazine, newspaper, or Web site would be the best choice for each of your versions?

Evaluating: The Writing Process

> “I love criticism so long as it’s unqualified praise.”
>
> —Noel Coward, Playwright, Songwriter, Novelist, Director, and Performer

Assignment for Evaluating

With a specific audience and genre in mind, evaluate a product or service, a work of art, or a performance. Choose a subject that you can revisit or review as you write your essay. Select criteria appropriate for your subject, genre, and audience. Collect evidence to support your judgment for each criterion. *Remember: In order to remain objective and credible, your review or critique should contain both positive and negative judgments.*

As the grid below indicates, the review is the most common genre for evaluating, but “reviews” cover a wide range of documents. Some film reviews, for example, are academic and critical whereas others merely indicate the major plot line without much critical evaluation. As you choose your topic, be sure to reread your assignment and consider the requirements or expectations of your audience. Are they expecting merely to be informed or entertained, or do they want the thorough and critical evaluation described in this chapter?

Audience	Possible Genres for Evaluating
Personal Audience	Class notes, journal entry, blog, scrapbook, or social networking page
Academic Audience	Academic critique, media critique, review, journal entry, forum entry on class site, multigenre document
Public Audience	Column, editorial, article, or critique in a magazine, news-paper, newsletter, online site, or multigenre document

CHOOSING A SUBJECT

If you have already settled on a possible subject, go on to the collecting and shaping strategies. If you have not found a subject, consider these ideas.

- Comparing and contrasting lead naturally to evaluation. For example, compare two places you’ve lived, two friends, or two jobs. Compare two famous people from the same profession. Compare your expectations about a person, place, or event with the reality. The purpose of your comparison is to determine, for a specific audience, which is "better," based on the criteria you select and the evidence you find.

- Evaluating a possible career choice can help you choose courses, think about summer jobs, and prepare for job interviews. Begin by describing several jobs that fit your career goals. Then go to the following Web sites and gather information.

  http://www.monster.com
  http://www.careers.com
  http://careers.yahoo.com
  http://www.bestjobsusa.com
  money.cnn.com/services/careerbuilder
  http://www.getthatgig.com

  Choose the career criteria that are most important for you, such as job satisfaction, location, benefits, salary, or education requirements. Is job satisfaction more important than pay or location? Rank your criteria in order of importance. Then write an evaluation of one or two jobs that you find described on the Internet or in your local newspaper.
- **Community Service Learning.** Community service-learning projects often require an assessment at the end of the period of service. These reflective evaluations start with the goals of the agency, the goals of your class project, and your goals as a learner as the major criteria. Then you gather evidence to see how well the actual experiences and projects met the overall project goals. Sometimes participants use short evaluation questionnaires to get feedback at the midpoint and then again at the end of the project. If you are participating in a community service-learning project, check with your teacher or coordinator about how to write this assessment.

COLLECTING

8.2
Use collecting strategies to develop your evaluation

Once you have a tentative subject and audience in mind, ask the following questions to focus your collecting activities.

- Can you *narrow*, *restrict*, or *define* your subject to focus your paper?
- What *criteria* will you use to evaluate your subject?
- What *evidence* might you gather? As you collect evidence, focus on three questions:

  What *comparisons* can you make between your subject and similar subjects?
  What are the *uses* or *consequences* of this subject?
  What *experiments* or *authorities* might you cite for support?
- What initial *judgments* are you going to make?

Observing

Observation and description of your subject are crucial to a clear evaluation. In most cases, your audience will need to know *what* your subject is before they can understand your evaluation.

- Examine a place or object repeatedly, looking at it from different points of view. Take notes. Describe it. Draw it, if appropriate. Analyze its component parts. List its uses. To which senses does it appeal—sight, sound, touch, smell, taste? If you are comparing your subject to similar subjects, observe them carefully. Remember: Each time you observe your subject, you will see more key details.
- If you are evaluating a person, collect information about this person's life, interests, abilities, accomplishments, and plans for the future. If you are able to observe the person directly, describe his or her physical features, write down what he or she says, and describe the person's environment.
- If you are evaluating a performance or an event, a recording or video can be extremely useful. If possible, choose a concert, film, or play on tape that you can stop and review as necessary. If a recording or video is not available, attend the performance or event twice.

Making notes in a *three-column log* is an excellent collecting strategy for evaluations. Using the following example from Phyllis Richman's evaluation of the Hunan Dynasty restaurant, list the criteria, evidence, and judgments for your subject.

Subject: Hunan Dynasty Restaurant

Criteria	Evidence	Judgment
Attractive setting	No blaring red-lacquer tables	Graceful
	White tablecloths	
	Subtle glass etchings	
Good service	Waiters serve with flourishes	Often expert
	Some glitches, such as forgotten appetizer	

Remembering

You are already an authority on many subjects, and your personal experiences may help you evaluate your subject. Try *freewriting, looping, branching,* or *clustering* your subject to help you remember relevant events, impressions, and information. In evaluating appliances for consumer magazines, for example, reporters often use products over a period of months, recording data, impressions, and experiences. Those experiences and memories are then used to support criteria and judgments. Evaluating a film often requires remembering similar films that you have liked or disliked. A vivid narrative of those memories can help convince an audience that a performance is good or bad.

Reading

Some of the ideas and evidence for your evaluation may come from reading descriptions of your subject, other evaluations of your subject, or the testimony of experts. Be sure you read these texts critically: Who is the intended audience for the text? What evidence does the text give? What is the author's bias? What are other points of view? Read your potential sources critically.

Investigating

All evaluations involve some degree of formal or informal investigation as you probe the characteristics of your subject and seek evidence to support your judgments.

Use the Library or the Internet Check the library and Internet resources for information on your subject, for ideas about how to design and conduct an evaluation of that subject, for possible criteria, for data in evaluations already performed, and for a sense of different audiences. In its evaluation of chocolate chip cookies, for example, *Consumer Reports* suggests criteria and outlines procedures. The magazine rated some two dozen popular store-bought brands, as well as four "boutique" or freshly baked varieties, on "strength of chocolate flavor and aroma, cookie and chip texture, and freedom from sensory defects."

Gather Field Data You may want to supplement your personal evaluation with a sample of other people's opinions by using *questionnaires* or *interviews*. (See Chapter 6.) If you are rating a film, for example, you might give people leaving the theater a very brief *questionnaire*, asking for their responses on key criteria relating to the movie they just saw. If you are rating a class, you might want to *interview* several students to support your claim that the class was either effective or ineffective. The interviews might also give you specific examples that you can then use as evidence to support your own judgments.

SHAPING

8.3
Shape your evaluation essay

As you think about ways to organize and develop your essay, be sure to reread your assignment and reconsider your purpose and audience. For your evaluating essay, you can use shaping strategies from your previous essays, but be sure to consider the following strategies designed for evaluative essays.

Shaping Strategies

Do you want to. . .	Consider using these rhetorical modes or strategies:
write for a particular audience or publication?	possible audiences and genres (p. 270)
organize your evaluation by specific criteria?	analysis by criteria (pp. 270–271)
compare two subjects for your evaluative essay?	comparison and contrast (pp. 271–272)
evaluate the effect of the subject on your audience?	causal analysis (p. 273)
get your reader's attention and make your overall claim clear?	title, introduction, and conclusion (p. 273)

Audience and Genre

As you consider ways to organize and shape your explaining essay, think about your probable audience and genre. Reviews vary greatly in length, critical depth, complexity, and reader appeal Think about your own purpose and goal; find several magazines, newspapers, or Web sites that publish the kind of review you would like to write, and use the best ones as genre models—not as blueprints—to guide your own writing.

Analysis by Criteria

Watch the Animation on Evaluation Essays

Often, evaluations are organized by criteria. You decide which criteria are appropriate for the subject and audience, and then you use those criteria to outline the essay. Your first few paragraphs of introduction establish your thesis or overall claim and then give background information: what the subject is, why you are evaluating it, what the competition is, and how you gathered your data. Then you order the criteria according to some plan: chronological order, spatial order, order of importance, or another logical sequence. Phyllis Richman's evaluation of the Hunan Dynasty restaurant follows the criteria pattern:

Shaping Your Points: Analysis by Division or Criteria

Introductory paragraphs	Criterion 1: Setting and atmosphere	Criterion 2: Service	Criterion 3: Quality of food	Concluding paragraphs
Information about the Hunan Dynasty, etc.	**Judgment:** Hunan Dynasty is attractive	**Judgment:** Hunan Dynasty has expert service despite an occasional glitch	**Judgment:** Main dishes are good but not memorable	Hunan Dynasty is a top-flight neighborhood restaurant

Comparison and Contrast

Many evaluations compare two subjects in order to demonstrate why one is preferable to the other. Books, films, restaurants, courses, music, writers, scientists, historical events, sports—all can be evaluated by means of comparison and contrast. In evaluating two Asian restaurants, for example, student writer Chris Cameron uses a comparison-and-contrast structure to shape her essay. In the following body paragraph from her essay, Cameron compares two restaurants, the Unicorn and the Yakitori, on the basis of her first criterion—an atmosphere that seems authentically Asian.

Watch the **Animation** on Comparison and Contrast

Of the two restaurants, we preferred the authentic atmosphere of the Unicorn to the cultural confusion at the Yakitori. On first impression, the Yakitori looked like a converted truck stop, sparsely decorated with a few bamboo slats and Japanese print fabric hanging in slices as Bruce Springsteen wailed loudly in the ears of the customers. The feeling at the Unicorn was quite the opposite as we entered a room that seemed transported from Chinatown. The whole room had a red tint from the light shining through the flowered curtains, and the place looked truly authentic, from the Chinese patterned rug on the wall to the elaborate dragon on the ceiling. Soft oriental music played as the customers sipped tea from small porcelain cups and ate fortune cookies.

Cameron used the following *alternating* comparison-and-contrast shape for her whole essay.

Shaping Your Points: Alternating Comparison and Contrast of Two Subjects

Introductory paragraph(s) with thesis	Criterion 1: Setting and atmosphere	Criterion 2: Service	Criterion 3: Quality of food	Concluding paragraphs
Although friends recommended the Yakitori, we preferred the Unicorn for its authentic atmosphere, courteous service, and well-prepared food.	Yakitori versus Unicorn	Yakitori versus Unicorn	Yakitori versus Unicorn	Expresses preference for the Unicorn

On the other hand, Cameron might have used a *block* comparison-and-contrast structure an organizational pattern that would take this shape.

Shaping Your Points: Block Comparison/Contrast of Two Subjects

Introductory paragraph(s) with thesis	Yakitori Restaurant	Unicorn Restaurant	Concluding paragraphs
Although friends recommended the Yakitori, we preferred the Unicorn for its authentic atmosphere, courteous service, and well-prepared food.	Atmosphere, service, and food	Atmosphere, service, and food as compared to the Yakitori's	Expresses preference for the Unicorn

Chronological Order

Writers often use chronological order, especially in reviewing a book or a film, to shape parts of their evaluations. Film reviewers rely on chronological order to sketch the main outline of the plot as they comment on the quality of the acting, directing, or cinematography.

Causal Analysis

Evaluations of works of art, performances, or visuals often measure the *effect* on the audience. Robin Williams and John Tollett, in "Evaluating a Web Site," use several criteria, including a clear organization and the avoidance of irritating "chain-yanks." Their evidence illustrates that Web sites should have a positive effect on the user.

- **Criteria:** The organization of a Web site must make information easily accessible for the user.
- **Evidence:** "Recently I needed to buy a new carafe for my coffee pot. I went to the Web site our local store recommended, and in THREE SECONDS I found exactly the carafe I needed. . . . This site was so well organized that I could scan and find the first topic I needed in about one second. . . . Amazing."
- **Judgment:** The site was very well organized for the user.
- **Criteria:** Web sites should not create false expectations or "chain-yanks" for the user.
- **Evidence:** "For example, you click next to a graphic that says 'Click here for a larger image.' You click, expecting a larger image and perhaps some additional information, but you get a page with the same image. . . . This makes you feel stupid. Or worse, it makes you think the Web site is stupid."
- **Judgment:** The Web site frustrated the user.

Title, Introduction, and Conclusion

Titles of evaluative writing tend to be short and succinct, stating what product, service, work of art, or performance you are evaluating ("The Help" or "'American Gothic,' Pitchfork Perfect").

Introductory paragraphs provide background information and description and usually give an overall claim or thesis. In some cases, however, the overall claim comes last, in a "Recommendations" section or in a summary paragraph. If the overall claim appears in the opening paragraphs, the concluding paragraph may simply review the strengths or weaknesses or advise the reader: This *is* or *is not* worth seeing, reading, watching, doing, or buying.

"I have to stop being afraid of being wrong; I can't wait until everything is perfect before the work comes out. I don't have that kind of time."

—Sherley Anne Williams,
Novelist and Critic

ResearchTips

Before you draft your evaluating essay, stop for a moment and *evaluate your sources* of information and opinion. If you are citing ideas or information from library articles—or especially from the Internet—be skeptical. How reliable is your source? What do you know about your source's reliability or editorial slant? Does the author have a particular bias? Be sure to *qualify* any biased or absolute statements you use from your sources. (See Chapter 12 for additional ideas on evaluating written sources.)

If you cite observations or field sources (interviews, surveys), evaluate the information you collected. Does it reflect only one point of view? How is it biased? Are your responses limited in number or point of view? Remember: You may use sources that reflect a limited perspective, but *be sure to alert your readers to those limitations.* For example, you might say, "Of course, the administrator wanted to defend this student program when he said. . . ."

PeerResponse

These instructions will help you give and receive constructive advice about the rough draft of your evaluating essay. You may use these guidelines for an in-class workshop, a take-home review, or an e-mail response.

Writer: Before you exchange drafts, write out the following information about your essay draft.

1. **Purpose, audience, and genre.** Briefly, describe your overall purpose, your genre, and your intended audience. Do you plan to incorporate visuals? If so, where?
2. **Revision plans.** What do you know you still need to work on as you revise your draft?
3. **Questions.** Write one or two questions about your draft that you would like your reader to answer.

Reader: Before you answer the following questions, read the entire draft from start to finish. As you *reread* the draft, do the following.

1. Underline the sentence(s) that state the writer's *overall claim* about the subject.
2. In the margin, put large brackets [ ] around paragraphs that *describe* what the writer is evaluating.
3. On a separate piece of paper or at the end of the writer's essay, make a *three-column log* indicating the writer's criteria, evidence, and judgments. (Does the log include both positive and negative judgments?)
4. Identify with an asterisk (*) any passages in which the writer needs more *evidence* to support the judgments.
5. Write out one *criterion* that is missing or that is not appropriate for the given subject.
6. Assess how well the writer explains the purpose and addresses the intended audience. Do you agree with the writer about his or her revision plans? Finally, answer the writer's questions.

Writer: As you read your peer reviewer's notes and comments, do the following.

1. Consider your peer reviewer's comments and notes. Has your reviewer correctly identified your overall claim? Do you need to add more description of your subject? Does the reviewer's three-column log look like yours? Do you need to revise your criteria or add additional evidence? Do you balance positive and negative judgments?
2. Based on your review, draw up a *revision plan.* Write out the three most important things you need to do as you revise your essay.

DRAFTING

With your criteria in front of you, your data or evidence at hand, and a general plan or sketch outline in mind, begin writing your draft. As you write, focus on your audience. If your evaluation needs to be short, you may have to use only those criteria that will appeal most effectively to your audience. As you write, check occasionally to be sure that you are including your key criteria. While some parts of the essay may seem forced or awkward as you write, other parts will grow and expand as you get your thoughts on paper. As in other papers, don't stop to check spelling or worry about an occasional awkward sentence. If you stop and can't get going, reread what you have written, look over your notes or sketch outline, and pick up the thread again.

"I have rewritten—often several times—every word I have ever published. My pencils outlast their erasers."

—Vladimir Nabokov,
Novelist

REVISING

Remember that revision is not just changing a word here and there or correcting occasional spelling errors. Make your evaluation more effective for your reader by including more specific evidence, changing the order of your paragraphs to make them clearer, cutting out an unimportant point, or adding a point that one of your readers suggests.

Guidelines for Revision

- **Review your purpose, audience, and genre.** Is your purpose clear to your target audience? Should you modify your chosen genre to appeal to your audience?
- **Review possibilities for visuals or graphics.** What additions or changes to images might be appropriate for your purpose, genre, or audience?
- **Criteria are *standards of value.*** They contain categories and judgments, as in "good fuel economy," "good reliability," or "powerful use of light and shade in a painting." Some categories, such as "price," have clearly implied judgments ("low price"), but make sure that your criteria refer implicitly or explicitly to a standard of value.
- **Examine your criteria from your audience's point of view.** Which criteria are most important in evaluating your subject? Will your readers agree that the criteria you select are indeed the most important ones? Will changing the order in which you present your criteria make your evaluation more convincing?
- **Include both positive and negative evaluations of your subject.** If all of your judgments are positive, your evaluation will sound like an advertisement. If all of your judgments are negative, your readers may think you are too critical.
- **Be sure to include supporting evidence for each criterion.** Without any data or support, your evaluation will be just an opinion that will not persuade your reader.
- **Avoid overgeneralizing in your claim.** If you are evaluating only three cell phones, for example, you cannot claim that one of those phones is the best cell phone available. You can only say it is the best of the three you evaluated.
- **Unless your goal is humor or irony, compare subjects that belong in the same class.** Comparing a Ford Focus to a BMW is absurd because they are not similar in terms of cost, design, or purpose.

- **If you need additional evidence to persuade your readers, review the questions at the beginning of the "Collecting" section of this chapter.** Have you addressed all the key questions listed there?
- **If you are citing other people's data or quoting sources, check to make sure your summaries and data are accurate.**
- ***Signal* the major divisions in your evaluation to your reader using clear transitions, key words, and paragraph hooks.** At the beginning of new paragraphs or sections in your essay, let your reader know where you are going.
- **Revise sentences for directness and clarity.**
- **Edit your evaluation for correct spelling, appropriate word choice, punctuation, usage, and grammar.**

Postscript on the Writing Process

When you finish writing your essay, answer the following questions.

1. Who is the intended audience for your evaluation? Write out one sentence from your essay in which you appeal to or address this audience.
2. Describe the main problem that you had writing this essay, such as finding a topic, collecting evidence, or writing or revising the draft.
3. What parts or paragraphs of your essay do you like best? Indicate the words, phrases, or sentences that make it effective. What do you like about them?
4. Explain what helped you most with your revision: advice from your peers, conference with the teacher, advice from a writing center tutor, rereading your draft several times, or some other source.
5. Write out one question that you still have about the assignment or about your writing and revising process.

Student Writing

Vulgar Propriety

Courtney Klockeman

For her evaluative essay, Courtney Klockeman wrote a critical review of the 2001 Academy Award–winning musical, *Moulin Rouge*. The original story is of a young English writer who arrives in Paris in 1899 and falls in love with the nightclub's leading performer and courtesan, Satine. The director's challenge, as Klockeman explains, was to convey the exciting and sensual scene of Montmartre in 1899 for a twenty-first century audience. As you read her essay, see if Klockeman evaluates the film based on clear criteria and evidence that support her thesis that the film "is over the top, but intentionally and meticulously so."

Baz Luhrmann's rock opera *Moulin Rouge* has been called everything 1
from vulgar and over the top to innovative and spectacular. Love it or hate it, Luhrmann knows how to draw attention. Luhrmann seems to have emulated the things that entertain us: music videos, rock concerts, and "high octane thrill ride" movies. He managed to create a musical romance with the thrills and explosive appeal of all of the above, successfully captivating the A.D.D. MTV generation. The pure opulence of the film, especially the club, might over-stimulate some, but it accurately conveys the exciting lure that the Moulin Rouge has represented since its opening. The film *is* over the top, but intentionally and meticulously so. Each artistic decision reflects careful consideration for historical context and authenticity of costumes and sets while still keeping modern audiences enthralled.

Luhrmann faced a tremendous challenge in trying to shock a 2
desensitized generation. He had to convey to a 21st century audience the temptations of the Moulin Rouge to its 19th century audience while still being fairly faithful to the period. In today's world girls walk around in low cut crop tops and high cut shorts on a regular basis, and shows on HBO would have been deemed pornography 30 years ago. The only way to shock us anymore is with excess—vibrant color, ornate detail and flamboyant movement so that we are repulsed yet strangely attracted to the frenzied energy of it all. It is a delicate and complex balance, for which Luhrmann turned to his wife and artistic director Catherine Martin. He had a vision and she made it a reality.

With an ambition for authenticity Martin and her co-costume designer 3
Angus Strathie thoroughly researched 19th century France and the Moulin Rouge before beginning production. Their research spanned over several years and included much time in Montmartre and Paris Libraries (Litson). The trouble was to reconcile their vision of the film's impact with their research. To remain historically accurate while still connecting to their modern audience, they agreed to follow one main rule: if it existed in the 19th century, even if it wasn't used in every day life, they could use it. For instance, there is a bohemian musician wearing sunglasses when Christian first arrives in Montmartre. Martin explains that "sunglasses did exist in the 19th century, but they were a specific purpose item. Like if you were climbing Mount Everest and there was a glare from the snow" (Kaye). The sunglasses are a tiny stretch, but they make the musician easier for us to relate to, like one we might see on Pearl Street in Boulder.

Through their research, Martin and Strathie also learned that part of the appeal at the actual Moulin Rouge was that the dancers wore knickers that were split down the middle. If some of us were wondering what was so naughty about the cancan . . . mystery solved. Leaving that dirty little detail out was not an option if they were going to stay true to the times and share the shock with us. At the same time an uncensored split knicker cancan would have earned them an R or possibly NC-17 rating, effectively eliminating a large portion of the movie-going public. Martin solved the problem by "conceal[ing] the areas that can be seen [so the girls had] a pink, smooth, Barbie-like area!" (Litson). Corsets, of course, were also essential to the costuming. Women used to cinch themselves up so tightly that they would fracture ribs and sometimes damage their internal organs. Naturally, clothing so tight restricts movement and makes dancing extremely difficult. Martin designed smaller corsets to mitigate the issue while keeping the extreme hourglass figures, but Nicole Kidman still cracked a rib during a scene (Litson). *4*

Compared to the costumes, the set was fairly straightforward. The original Moulin Rouge was excessive enough that Martin and Strathie needed only to create a replica of it. Even Satine's Hindi elephant was a part of the original (Litson). The inside of the dance hall was and still is very much like a circus, as it is portrayed in the film (Mac Devitt). There were some minor changes to the design for the sake of convenience or emphasis. The garden was placed in front instead of to the side of the dance hall to allow for smooth filming in and out of the club. Martin also added the gothic "brothel room." There were such rooms near the notorious dance hall and the dancers were, in fact, prostitutes, but there wasn't one in the hall itself (Litson). Martin's addition makes these particulars more assertive by visually and spatially combining the dance hall with its shady brothel aspect. *5*

For some sets Martin sacrificed authenticity for effect. The city of Paris from afar looks more like a picture book than a movie set. Some question the choice to use such post-card like scenery, but the dreamy image with the Eiffel Tower surrounded by quaint little buildings is just a flimsy romanticized façade for the gritty truth. Why not portray it for what it is? Montmartre was, and nightly still is, a seedy district. It is home to pimps and prostitutes, where beatnik artists earn wages on the streets. In the film, Christian seeks the romantic, iconic version and discovers instead the disturbing truth. The styles of the sets represent their distance from or closeness to the truth. During "Your Song" the set becomes surreal with a miniature Eiffel Tower and a singing moon while Satine and Christian dance on the clouds. In that scene, Satine is under the false impression that Christian is the Duke and Christian seems to be naïve of Satine's work as a prostitute. Essentially, they fall in love under false pretenses and the scenery reflects that falseness. Alternately, in the scene where they declare their love with full awareness of each others' identities *6*

...continued Courtney Klockeman, **Vulgar Propriety**

("Elephant Love Medley"), realism returns because there is no deception or misunderstanding. The scenes with Christian, Satine, and the Duke once again enter the realm of surreal due to his blissful ignorance of their love affair.

To keep us spellbound, Strathie and Martin replaced a line of girls in matching outfits with a fascinating diversity in color and style to "make [it as] extraordinary for now" as it was in 1899 (Litson). They turned an already challenging task into a Herculean feat by designing each individual dancer's costume with a theme in mind. There is a Hindi girl, a baby doll, a Greek goddess, a very heavily tattooed dominatrix, and more than 50 others. They started with sexual fetishes and moved on to nationalities when they ran out (Litson). Even in the "Tango de Roxanne," each dancer sports a unique undergarment. By the end of filming, the creative duo had meticulously clothed 15 primary actors, 60 dancers, and more than 600 extras in various scenes. Nicole Kidman alone wears more than 20 costumes throughout (Kaye). 7

The Moulin Rouge seems all the more opulent because of its stark contrast from the outside world. The costumes and sets are more overwhelming in and around the Moulin Rouge than anywhere else. The color scheme is all red, black and gold and everything is heavily ornamented. Away from its influence, Christian's "humble abode" is comparatively minimalistic. It is dominated by whites and light neutrals and has only the bare essentials in furniture. Satine's costumes tend to match the surroundings. In and around the Moulin Rouge she is always corseted and fully accessorized. Like all of the dancers, she is trapped where "the show must go on." At Christian's flat, she is usually wearing only a white sheet or robe, free to be herself—not the temptress of the stage. The view from Christian's flat is the Moulin Rouge, seemingly innocent by day but lit up and dangerously alluring by night. The story's conflict arises in trying to reconcile these apparently incompatible worlds or else leave one behind. 8

Moulin Rouge may be an "audacious, rapid-fire assault on the senses," but even Guthmann concedes that "it works." The gaudy display is not without a purpose, exposing us to the lurid temptations of the "tantric cancan" in a way we understand while revealing their destructive consequences. David Ansen and Dan Ephron eloquently conclude that "by reveling in all things artificial, [Moulin Rouge] arrives, giddily, at the genuine." Luhrmann and Martin set out to shock us, thrill us, entertain us, and give us a musical like never before. Even their most "over-stimulated" and conservative critics can't deny that they achieved just that. 9

Works Consulted

Ansen, David, and Dan Ephron. "Yes, 'Rouge' Can Can Can." *Newsweek* 137.22 (2001): 61. *LexisNexis Academic*. Web. 5 Mar. 2009.

Guthmann, Edward. "Red Hot." *San Francisco Chronicle* 1 June 2001, final ed.: C1. *LexisNexis Academic*. Web. 5 Mar. 2009.

Kaye, Lori. "Clothes That Cancan." *Advocate* 839 (2001): 58. *Academic Search Premiere*. Web. 5 Mar. 2009.

Litson, Jo. "Rouging It." *Entertainment Design* 35.5 (2001): 22. *LexisNexis Academic*. Web. 5 Mar. 2009.

Mac Devitt, Aedin. "Le Moulin Rouge Cabaret." *About.com*. New York Times, 2008. Web. 5 Mar. 2009.

Moulin Rouge. Dir. Baz Luhrmann. Perf. Nicole Kidman, Ewan McGregor. 2001. 20th Century Fox, 2003. DVD.

Questions for Writing and Discussion

1. In her review, Courtney Klockeman explains that the director's main task was to maintain historical accuracy while updating the context, costumes, and sets for a modern audience. If you have seen the film, would you agree that these adjustments do make the film historically real and yet contemporary and exciting for a twenty-first century audience? Explain your response by commenting on scenes that you remember from the film.
2. Reread Klockeman's essay and then write out a three-column log (criteria, evidence, judgments) that she might have used to organize her evaluation. List the evidence for each of her criteria. Does she have sufficient evidence from the film to support her judgment of each criterion? Explain.
3. In her title, Klockeman tries to capture the edginess of the film by using the phrase, "vulgar propriety." Is this title effective for the essay? What other oxymorons or phrases such as "tasteful pornography" would work for her title? Explain your choices.
4. Go online and read other reviews of *Moulin Rouge*. After reading those reviews, do you agree with Klockeman's evaluation? Do those reviews consider other criteria such as acting ability, plot, or dialogue that you believe are important for evaluating the film? What criteria would you choose for your evaluation of this film?

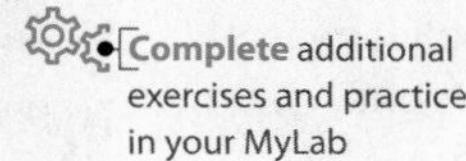
Complete additional exercises and practice in your MyLab

I am a College Student. I will graduate ONly $30,000 in debt.
I AM LUCKY.
I work hard. I got a loan and bought My OWN car which I have since paid off. I've written a Novel. I work 30+ hours a week at MINIMUM wage.
BUT I AM HEALTHY. If I were to get sick, or injured, I would have to stop working and could Not afford school.
If this private school had Not accepted me, my second option (Public school) would have left me over $60,000 in debt.
I am LUCKY but I realize MaNY are Not. This system is about luck, Not hard work. EveryONE Should be giVEN a chance to succeed. I AM THE 99%

One goal of the Occupy movement has been to dramatize the growing disparity between the very rich (the 1%) and the rest of us (the 99%). A discussion question in this chapter asks you to analyze this visual statement and compare it to another student's similar declaration, considering the credibility and effectiveness of each one.

We Are the 99 Percent

9 Problem Solving

What You Will Learn

In this chapter, you will learn to:

- **9.1** Use techniques for problem solving
- **9.2** Use collecting strategies to define a problem and develop solutions
- **9.3** Shape your proposal

WE don't have to look hard to locate problems in our lives. They have a habit of seeking us out. It seems that if something can go wrong, it will. Countries fight, greenhouse gases cause climate change, prejudice is rampant, television shows are too violent, sports are corrupted by drugs and money, education is impersonal, and people text while driving. Everywhere we look, someone creates problems for us—from minor bureaucratic hassles to serious, life-threatening situations. (On occasions we're part of the problem ourselves.)

> **"This country has more problems than it should tolerate and more solutions than it uses."**
>
> —Ralph Nader, Consumer Rights Advocate and Presidential Candidate

Once we identify a problem, we must critically question and investigate the issue. Just because we think something is a problem does not mean that other people will agree that it is a problem. For example, let's critically analyze what appears to be a straightforward issue: grade inflation. First, notice the language we use to describe the issue. The word *inflation* suggests a negative bias; we are predisposed to think that inflation is bad. Next, we need to know who is involved in this issue and who has the most to gain or lose from it. What positions are students, teachers, parents, school administrators, admissions officers at colleges, and companies who hire likely to take? Some of these groups may see grade inflation as a serious problem; others may not agree that a problem exists. Finally, we must gather the "facts" about grade inflation and the various definitions commonly used to describe it. There are a variety of definitions for grade inflation and statistics both proving and disproving that it exists.

> **"Whenever life doesn't seem to give an answer, we create one."**
>
> —Lorraine Hansberry, Author of *a Raisin in the Sun*

Once you can identify something that is a real problem for a specific group of people, the difficult task is to propose a solution and then persuade others that your solution will solve the problem—without creating new problems or costing too much. Because your proposal may ask readers to take some action, you must make sure that your readers vividly perceive the problem and agree that your plan outlines the most logical and feasible solution.

Techniques for Problem Solving

9.1
Use techniques for problem solving

Problem solving requires all your skills as a writer. You need to *observe* carefully to see what problem exists. You may need to *remember* experiences that illustrate the seriousness of the problem. You need to *read* and *investigate* to learn which solutions have worked or not worked. You will have to *explain* what the problem is and why or how your proposal would remedy the situation. You may need to *evaluate* both the problem and alternative solutions. To help you identify the problem and convince your readers of the soundness of your proposal, keep the following techniques in mind.

Techniques for Problem Solving

Technique	Tips on How to Do It
Analyzing the political, social, and cultural *contexts* of the problem	Determine *when, where,* and *why* some people perceive this problem. *What* groups are affected, and what do they have to gain or lose? *Who* would be most affected by a particular solution?
Identifying and understanding your *audience*	When you want something changed, fixed, improved, subsidized, banned, reorganized, or made legal or illegal, write to an audience that has the *power to help make this change*.
Demonstrating that a *problem exists*	Some problems are so obvious that your readers will readily acknowledge them: conflicts in the Middle East, air pollution and greenhouse gases, childhood obesity, unemployment, and outsized CEO bonuses. Often, however, you must first convince your audience that a problem exists: Are genetically engineered crops a problem or would eliminating them cause even more problems?
Proposing a *solution* that will solve the problem	After convincing your readers of the seriousness of the problem, offer a *remedy, plan,* or *course of action* that will reduce or eliminate the problem.
Persuading your readers that your proposal *will work*	Show that your solution is *feasible* and better than *alternative solutions* by supporting your proposal with *reasons* and *evidence*.

As you start to plan your problem-solving paper, concentrate on ways to *narrow and focus* your topic. When you think about possible topics, follow the advice of environmentalists: "Think Globally, Act Locally." Rather than write about drugs or crime or pollution on a national scale, find out how your community or campus is dealing with the problem. A local focus will help narrow your topic—and provide opportunities for firsthand observations, personal experience, and interviews.

DEMONSTRATING THAT A PROBLEM EXISTS

A proposal begins with the description of a problem. Demonstrating that the problem exists (and is serious) will make your readers more receptive to your plan for a solution. The following selection from Frank Trippett's *Time* magazine essay "A Red Light for Scofflaws" identifies a problem and provides sufficient examples to demonstrate that scofflawry is pervasive and serious. Even if we haven't been personally attacked while driving the Houston or Miami or Los Angeles freeways, Trippett convinces us that *scofflawry*—deliberately disobeying ("scoffing at") laws—is serious. His vivid description makes us aware of the problem.

"You see things; and you say, Why? But I dream things that never were; and I say, Why not?"

—George Bernard Shaw, Dramatist

Watch the Animation on Proposals

Law and order is the longest-running and probably the best-loved political issue in U.S. history. Yet it is painfully apparent that millions of Americans who would never think of themselves as lawbreakers, let alone criminals, are taking increasing liberties with the legal codes that are designed to protect and nourish their society. Indeed, there are moments today—amid outlaw litter, tax cheating, illicit noise, and motorized anarchy—when it seems as though the scofflaw represents the wave of the future. Harvard sociologist David Riesman suspects that a majority of Americans have blithely taken to committing supposedly minor derelictions as a matter of course. Already, Riesman says, the ethic of U.S. society is in danger of becoming this: "You're a fool if you obey the rules."

Demonstrating that a problem exists

Evidence: Authority

The dangers of scofflawry vary wildly. The person who illegally spits on the sidewalk remains disgusting, but clearly poses less risk to others than the company that illegally buries hazardous chemical waste in an unauthorized location. The fare beater on the subway presents less threat to life than the landlord who ignores fire safety statutes. The most immediately and measurably dangerous scofflawry, however, also happens to be the most visible. The culprit is the American driver, whose lawless activities today add up to a colossal public nuisance. The hazards range from routine double parking that jams city streets to the drunk driving that kills some 25,000 people and injures at least 650,000 others yearly.

Evidence: Examples

Evidence: Statistics

The most flagrant scofflaw of them all is the red-light runner. The flouting of stop signals has got so bad in Boston that residents tell an anecdote about a cabby who insists that red lights are "just for decoration." The power of the stoplight to control traffic seems to be waning everywhere. In Los Angeles, red-light running has become perhaps the city's most common traffic violation. In New York City, going through an intersection is like Russian roulette. Admits Police Commissioner Robert J. McGuire: "Today it's a 50–50 toss-up as to whether people will stop for a red light." Meanwhile, his own police largely ignore the lawbreaking.

Evidence: Authority

The prospect of the collapse of public manners is not merely a matter of etiquette. Society's first concern will remain major crime, but a foretaste of the seriousness of incivility is suggested by what has been happening in Houston. Drivers on Houston freeways have been showing an increasing tendency to replace the rules of the road with violent outbreaks. Items from the Houston police department's new statistical category—freeway traffic violence: (1) Driver flashes high-beam lights at car that cut in front of him, whose occupants then hurl a beer can at his windshield, kick out his tail lights, slug him eight stitches worth. (2) Dump-truck driver annoyed by delay batters trunk of stalled car ahead and its driver with steel bolt. (3) Hurrying driver of 18-wheel truck deliberately rear-ends car whose driver was trying to stay within 55 m.p.h. limit.

Evidence: Examples

PROPOSING A SOLUTION AND CONVINCING YOUR READERS

Once you have described the problem, you are ready to propose a solution and persuade your readers. In the following article, Janet Bodnar, an award-winning journalist and editor of *Kiplinger's Personal Finance*, gives advice to parents about college financing. After stating the obvious problem—that a college education is expensive—she devotes most of her article to outlining practical steps that parents can take to avoid the student-debt trap. Notice how she gives a variety of courses of action and then supports her proposals with specific financial examples.

Professional Writing

The College Debt Trap

Janet Bodnar

Briefly describes the problem

Is it worth it to pay $200,000 for a liberal arts education, especially if it means taking out loans? One of my 20-something Kiplinger colleagues answers bluntly: "If I had realized how much debt I was getting into, I would have gone to my state school instead of an expensive private college." 1

As important as education is in today's world, families need to find more affordable ways to pay for it. Mark Kantrowitz, publisher of FinAid.org and FastWeb.com, has calculated that total student-loan debt exceeds revolving credit (mostly credit-card debt). 2

Here's my guide for parents about avoiding the student-debt trap: 3

Sets up guide for the solution

Save as much as you can. It's never too late to start, especially if you 4
live in a state that gives you an income-tax break for contributions to state-sponsored 529 plans. Plus, money withdrawn from 529 accounts and used to pay for qualified college expenses is tax-free.

Recommendation and supporting specifics

Don't let the total cost of college discourage you. If it seems intimidat- 5
ing, aim for a more manageable goal—such as saving enough to pay first-year expenses or one-third of the total cost (the rest could be covered by a combination of current income, both yours and your child's, and financial aid). Remember, every dollar you save is a dollar you won't have to borrow.

Recommendation

Be straight with your kids about what you can afford. Have the 6
"college talk" with your teenagers before they start their search so that they know what fits into your budget and how much they'll have to contribute. At a minimum, kids should be expected to earn their own spending money.

Recommendation

Choose schools strategically. You're looking for colleges that deliver 7
good value—a high-quality education at an affordable price. That might mean a state institution, or it could mean a pricey private school that offers a generous financial-aid package. To better their chances for a scholarship, students should focus on schools at which their GPA or other achievements would make them a standout.

Recommendation

Think outside the box. Students can follow the example of one of our 8
top Kiplinger editors, who started at a lower-cost community college and then transferred to a four-year school. And more colleges are offering online classes to keep costs under control. Taking Advanced Placement classes in high school can slice a year off your child's education and cut your expenses by 25 percent. Uncle Sam will help pay the bill if your child joins the military. You could also take advantage of the growing number of colleges offering accelerated, three-year degree programs.

Recommendation with alternatives

Or, here's a radical thought: Your child may be better off passing up 9
college, at least for a year. Not everyone is ready for college at 18. It might literally pay if your child takes a year off to mature, earn some money and figure out what he really wants to study. Education and training are critical in today's economy, but rather than spend time and money on a degree from a four-year institution, it might be more appropriate for some kids to consider a one- or two-year certificate program from a community college in a field such as health care or engineering.

Recommendation with alternatives

Borrow smart. If your family must borrow to pay the bills, stick with 10
government-sponsored Stafford loans for students and PLUS loans for parents (or a home-equity line of credit, if you qualify). Current interest rates on government loans are 6.8 percent for students (lower if you're eligible for financial subsidies) and 7.9 percent for new PLUS loans (for more information on student loans, go to StudentLoans.gov). With that combination, you shouldn't have to resort to more-expensive private loans.

Recommendation with evidence

...continued The College Debt Trap, **Janet Bodnar**

Recommendation with specific examples

Run the numbers. Perhaps the most important mathematical exercise your child will ever have to do—and the most widely neglected—is figure out how much it will cost to pay back her student loans. At FinAid.org, you can use the Student Loan Advisor calculator to determine the monthly payment amount based on a future salary. 11

Let's say your daughter plans to major in accounting, with a projected starting salary of $47,200. If she wanted to hold the loan payments to 10 percent of her monthly income and repay the loans over 10 years, her monthly payment would be $393, assuming a student-loan interest rate of 6.8 percent, and her maximum manageable debt would be $34,200. 12

Recommendation with specific examples

Pick a marketable major. Majors that are most likely to yield an immediate job offer after college are accounting, business administration, computer science, engineering and math, according to the National Association of Colleges and Employers. But students can still major in liberal arts and make themselves attractive to potential employers by choosing subjects that are marketable. 13

Personal experience

As an editor, I always counsel budding journalists who are majoring in something as general as "mass communications" to add a minor or a concentration in another subject—business, health or computer skills, for instance. As the editor of a personal-finance magazine, I can attest that our most attractive job candidates are those who combine writing ability with knowledge of the subjects we cover. 14

That applies to other fields as well. If your daughter is majoring in economics, she should take accounting. If she's studying history or government, she could learn a foreign language. An English major could take classes in technical writing. Then she'd have a better shot at landing a well-paying job to help pay back those college loans. 15

Warming Up: Journal Exercises

The following exercises ask you to practice problem solving. Read all of the exercises and then write on one or two that interest you. If another idea occurs to you, write about it.

1. Wishful-thinking department: Assume that you are a member of the student government, and your organization has $10,000 to spend on a campus improvement project. Think of some campus problem that needs solving. Describe why it is a problem. Then outline your plan for a solution, indicating how you would spend the money to help solve the problem.

2 Eldridge Cleaver once said, "You're either part of the solution or part of the problem." Examine one of your activities or pastimes—sports, shopping, cruising, eating, drinking, or even studying. How might what you do create a problem from someone else's point of view? Explain.

3 The following visual, with an accompanying paragraph, appears on the United Nations Children's Fund (UNICEF) Web site at http://www.unicef.org. Analyze the effectiveness of the image and text in demonstrating the problem of child labor. What details in the picture support the argument that child labor is a problem we must solve?

> "A good solution solves more than one problem, and it does not make new problems. I am talking about health as opposed to almost any cure, coherence of pattern as opposed to almost any solution produced piecemeal or in isolation."
>
> —Wendell Berry, Author of *the Gift of the Good Land*

A small boy sleeps at the table where he was making softballs in the village of Cholomo, Honduras.

Some people say that boycotts—that is, refusing to buy goods made by children—will help put an end to child labour. But boycotts can also hurt working children and their families, as the children lose their jobs, and then their families have even less money to live on. If employers provided parents with jobs at a living wage, fewer children would be forced to go to work. (UNICEF/89-0052/Vauclair)

> "God, give us grace to accept with serenity the things that cannot be changed, courage to change the things which should be changed, and the wisdom to distinguish the one from the other."
>
> —Reinhold Niebuhr, Author and Theologian

4 Changing the rules of some sports might make them more enjoyable, less violent, or fairer: moving the three-point line farther out, introducing the 30-second clock in NCAA basketball, using TV instant replays in college football and basketball, imposing stiffer fines for brawls in hockey games, giving equal pay and media coverage to women's sports. Choose a sport you enjoy as a participant or observer, identify and explain the problem you want to solve, and justify your solution in a letter to the editors of *Sports Illustrated*.

MINI-CASEBOOK ON EDUCATION

Higher education today is struggling with many problems, but the most frequently discussed are the high costs and increasing student debt, the decline of students' critical thinking skills, and the lack of jobs for graduates. These problems are all interrelated. In a weak economy, many students lack the money to go to college. The high costs of college cause students to take on debt that they cannot easily repay, especially when the jobs they find after graduation may pay little more than minimum wage. And if students are not getting the critical thinking skills they need in college, they won't be able to get the jobs they want.

How to identify and solve these problems is the subject of the articles in this mini-casebook. Richard Arum and Josipa Roksa, authors of "Your So-Called Education," have written a highly publicized study of current problems in education, *Academically Adrift: Limited Learning on College Campuses*, which finds that many students are not making sufficient progress in tests of critical thinking and complex reasoning. Lynn O'Shaughnessy, author of *The College Solution: A Guide for Everyone Looking for the Right School at the Right Price*, recommends in "But Can They Write?" that students major in science or liberal arts rather than business if they want to get a good jobs. In "Debt by Degrees," James Surowiecki, financial page editor of the *New Yorker*, explains that because college costs have increased three times faster than inflation, many students end up in debt without getting a degree. The anonymous author of the image "College Senior" claims that he or she will complete college debt free by having two scholarships, working part time, and living frugally. In "Even for Cashiers, College Pays Off," David Leonhardt, business columnist for the *New York Times*, argues that college graduates still have a significant financial advantage over nongraduates. Shifting the focus from student debt to the higher education funding crisis, Brandeis University professor Gregory Petsko, in "An Open Letter to George M. Philip," attacks the president of SUNY Albany for his plan to eliminate the departments of French, Italian, Classics, Russian, and Theater Arts.

As you read these articles, look for the common problems of higher education that these writers describe, the evidence they give to support their claims, and the solutions they recommend.

Professional Writing

Your So-Called Education

Richard Arum and Josipa Roksa

Commencement is a special time on college campuses: an occasion for students, families, faculty and administrators to come together to celebrate a job well done. And perhaps there is reason to be pleased. In recent surveys of college seniors, more than 90 percent report gaining subject-specific knowledge and developing the ability to think critically and analytically. Almost 9 out of 10 report that overall, they were satisfied with their collegiate experiences. 1

We would be happy to join in the celebrations if it weren't for our recent research, which raises doubts about the quality of undergraduate learning in the United States. Over four years, we followed the progress of several thousand students in more than two dozen diverse four-year colleges and universities. We found that large numbers of the students were making their way through college with minimal exposure to rigorous coursework, only a modest investment of effort and little or no meaningful improvement in skills like writing and reasoning. 2

In a typical semester, for instance, 32 percent of the students did not take a single course with more than 40 pages of reading per week, and 50 percent did not take any course requiring more than 20 pages of writing over the semester. The average student spent only about 12 to 13 hours per week studying—about half the time a full-time college student in 1960 spent studying, according to the labor economists Philip S. Babcock and Mindy S. Marks. 3

Not surprisingly, a large number of the students showed no significant progress on tests of critical thinking, complex reasoning and writing that were administered when they began college and then again at the ends of their sophomore and senior years. If the test that we used, the Collegiate Learning Assessment, were scaled on a traditional 0-to-100 point range, 45 percent of the students would not have demonstrated gains of even one point over the first two years of college, and 36 percent would not have shown such gains over four years of college. 4

Why is the overall quality of undergraduate learning so poor? 5

While some colleges are starved for resources, for many others it's not for lack of money. Even at those colleges where for the past several decades tuition has far outpaced the rate of inflation, students are taught by fewer full-time tenured faculty members while being looked after by a greatly expanded number of counselors who serve 6

...continued Your So-Called Education, **Richard Arum and Josipa Roksa**

an array of social and personal needs. At the same time, many schools are investing in deluxe dormitory rooms, elaborate student centers and expensive gyms. Simply put: academic investments are a lower priority.

The situation reflects a larger cultural change in the relationship between students and colleges. The authority of educators has diminished, and students are increasingly thought of, by themselves and their colleges, as "clients" or "consumers." When 18-year-olds are emboldened to see themselves in this manner, many look for ways to attain an educational credential effortlessly and comfortably. And they are catered to accordingly. The customer is always right. 7

Federal legislation has facilitated this shift. The funds from Pell Grants and subsidized loans, by being assigned to students to spend on academic institutions they have chosen rather than being packaged as institutional grants for colleges to dispense, have empowered students—for good but also for ill. And expanded privacy protections have created obstacles for colleges in providing information on student performance to parents, undercutting a traditional check on student lassitude. 8

Fortunately, there are some relatively simple, practical steps that colleges and universities could take to address the problem. Too many institutions, for instance, rely primarily on student course evaluations to assess teaching. This creates perverse incentives for professors to demand little and give out good grades. (Indeed, the 36 percent of students in our study who reported spending five or fewer hours per week studying alone still had an average G.P.A. of 3.16.) On those commendable occasions when professors and academic departments do maintain rigor, they risk declines in student enrollments. And since resources are typically distributed based on enrollments, rigorous classes are likely to be canceled and rigorous programs shrunk. Distributing resources and rewards based on student learning instead of student satisfaction would help stop this race to the bottom. 9

Others involved in education can help, too. College trustees, instead of worrying primarily about institutional rankings and fiscal concerns, could hold administrators accountable for assessing and improving learning. Alumni as well as parents and students on college tours could ignore institutional facades and focus on educational substance. And the Department of Education could make available nationally representative longitudinal data on undergraduate learning outcomes for research purposes, as it has been doing for decades for primary and secondary education. 10

Most of all, we hope that during this commencement season, our faculty colleagues will pause to consider the state of undergraduate learning and our collective responsibility to increase academic rigor on our campuses. 11

Professional Writing

But Can They Write?

Lynn O'Shaughnessy

Several years ago my daughter Caitlin told me that she wanted to major in business. I would have been depressed by her decision to pursue what I consider to be a slacker major, but she added that she also planned to major in Spanish. 1

Caitlin is graduating from a liberal arts college in Pennsylvania next month, and I emailed her today to ask which was harder during the past four years—her business classes or her Spanish courses. Her reply was "Spanish hands down." 2

For four years she had to think, talk, write and read in a foreign language. In contrast to business (with the exception of accounting and finance), it's far more difficult to coast if you major in the liberal arts or sciences. My son, who is studying math and physics at a college in Wisconsin, told me recently that he spent seven hours one day working with a friend on eight math homework problems. He wasn't so much complaining as he was in awe that he could work so hard. 3

What's ironic about this glut of business majors is this: The students, often egged on by their parents, are pursuing their vocational degree because they assume that it's the ticket to a six-figure income. The evidence, however, suggests otherwise. 4

When PayScale conducted its latest annual survey of starting and mid-career salaries for college grads in dozens of college majors, business came in as the 60th best-paying college degree. It fared worse than such supposedly impractical degrees as history, political science and philosophy. 5

Why the lousy showing? Employers have repeatedly emphasized that they want to hire college graduates whose talents include writing. Ah, writing. Not something that biz majors are expected to do very often. After all, how can you require extensive writing in business classes when they can be packed with hundreds of students? Nobody would want to grade all those papers. Obviously this is a problem that business schools need to address. 6

In the meantime, if I was an employer who had to choose between a business major and a philosophy major, I'd pick the grad who could write well, and I know who that would likely be. 7

Professional Writing

Debt by Degrees

James Surowiecki

The protesters at Occupy Wall Street may not have put forth an explicit set of demands yet, but there is one thing that they all agree on: student debt is too damn high. Since the late nineteen-seventies, annual costs at four-year colleges have risen three times as fast as inflation, and, with savings rates dropping and state aid to colleges being cut, students have been forced to take on ever more debt in order to pay for school. The past decade has seen a student-loan binge, so that today Americans owe well over six hundred billion dollars in college debt. That's a burden that's hard to carry at a time when more than two million college graduates are unemployed and millions more are underemployed. 1

Some of the boom in student debt can be chalked up to demographics: in the past decade, the number of college-age Americans rose by more than three million and the proportion of eighteen-to-twenty-four-year-olds enrolled in college went from thirty-five percent to forty-one percent. Still, the piles of student loans are due largely to the fact that the cost of a college degree has been going up much faster than people's incomes. And that has raised the spectre that we might be living through a "higher-education bubble," in which Americans are irrationally borrowing money to spend more on college than it's actually worth. 2

We've just endured two huge bubbles, which sent the value of stocks and then homes to ridiculous levels, so the theory isn't implausible. Of course, a college-education bubble wouldn't look exactly like a typical asset bubble, because you can't flip a college degree the way you can flip a stock, or even a home. But what bubble believers are really saying is that young people today are radically overestimating the economic value of going to college, and that many of them would be better off doing something else with their time and money. After all, wages for college graduates actually fell over the past decade, and the unemployment rate for recent grads is close to ten percent. That's hardly a ringing endorsement of the economic value of education. 3

There's a big flaw in the bubble argument, though: things may look grim for college graduates, but they're much grimmer for people without a college degree. Though recent college grads are having a hard time finding a job, it's much harder for recent high school graduates, who have an unemployment rate of nearly twenty-two percent. And the overall unemployment rate for college grads is still, at 4.4 percent, very low. More striking, the college wage premium—how much more a college graduate makes than someone without a degree—is at an 4 all-time high. In fact, the spiralling cost of education has to some degree tracked the rising wage premium; as college has, in relative terms, become more valuable economically, people have become willing to pay more for it. It's telling, in this regard, that the one period in the past sixty years when college-tuition costs flatlined was during the seventies, which also happened to be the one period when the college wage premium fell.

This isn't to say that eighteen-year-olds are perfectly rational 5
economic actors. Most obviously, many of them borrow a lot of money and then don't finish college, ending up debt-laden and without a degree. But there's little evidence that kids are systematically overestimating the value of college, the way homeowners systematically overestimated the value of homes during the bubble. Nor is there much reason to think that a degree will matter less in the future: the demand for college grads in the workforce has been increasing steadily for sixty years.

The bubble analogy does work in one respect: education costs, 6
and student debt, are rising at what seem like unsustainable rates. But this isn't the result of collective delusion. Instead, it stems from the peculiar economics of education, which have a lot in common with the economics of health care, another industry with a huge cost problem. (Indeed, in recent decades the cost of both college education and health care has risen sharply in most developed countries, not just the U.S.) Both industries suffer from an ailment called Baumol's cost disease, which was diagnosed by the economist William Baumol back in the sixties. Baumol recognized that some sectors of the economy, like manufacturing, have rising productivity—they regularly produce more with less, which leads to higher wages and rising living standards. But other sectors, like education, have a harder time increasing productivity. Ford, after all, can make more cars with fewer workers and in less time than it did in 1980. But the average student-teacher ratio in college is sixteen to one, just about what it was thirty years ago. In other words, teachers today aren't any more productive than they were in 1980. The problem is that colleges can't pay 1980 salaries, and the only way they can pay 2011 salaries is by raising prices. And the Baumol problem is exacerbated by the arms-race problem: colleges compete to lure students by investing in expensive things, like high-profile faculty members, fancy facilities, and a low student-to-teacher ratio.

The college-bubble argument makes the solution to rising costs seem 7
simple: if people just wake up, the bubble will pop, and reasonable prices will return. It's much tougher to admit that there is no easy way out. Maybe we need to be willing to spend more and more of our incomes and taxpayer dollars on school, or maybe we need to be willing to pay educators and administrators significantly less, or maybe we need to find

...continued Debt by Degrees, **James Surowiecki**

ways to make colleges more productive places, which would mean radically changing our idea of what going to college is all about. Until America figures out its priorities, college kids are going to have to keep running just to stand still.

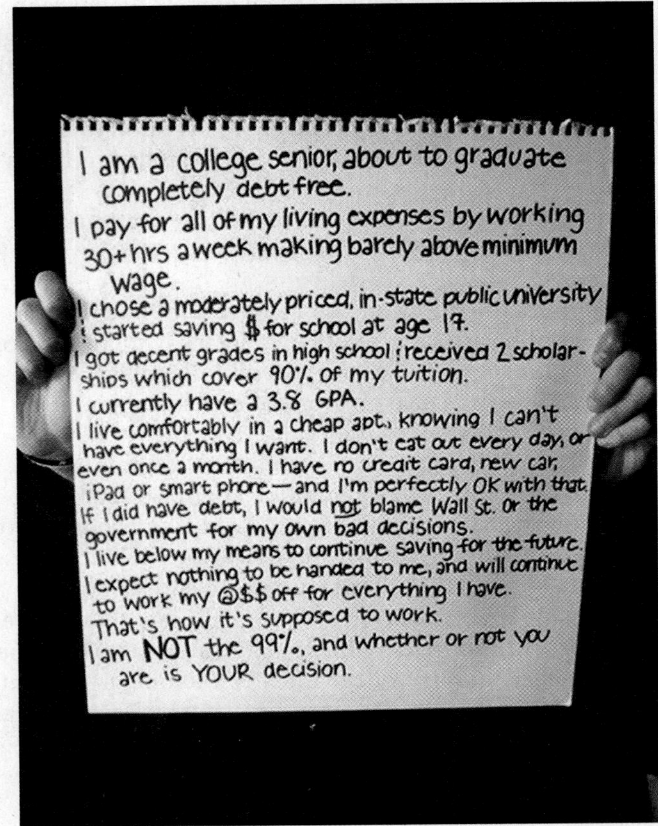
I am a college senior, about to graduate completely debt free.
I pay for all of my living expenses by working 30+ hrs a week making barely above minimum wage.
I chose a moderately priced, in-state public university
I started saving $ for school at age 17.
I got decent grades in high school & received 2 scholarships which cover 90% of my tuition.
I currently have a 3.8 GPA.
I live comfortably in a cheap apt., knowing I can't have everything I want. I don't eat out every day, or even once a month. I have no credit card, new car, iPad or smart phone—and I'm perfectly OK with that.
If I did have debt, I would not blame Wall St. or the government for my own bad decisions.
I live below my means to continue saving for the future.
I expect nothing to be handed to me, and will continue to work my @$$ off for everything I have.
That's how it's supposed to work.
I am NOT the 99%, and whether or not you are is YOUR decision.

"Graduating Debt Free"

Professional Writing

Even for Cashiers, College Pays Off

David Leonhardt

Almost a century ago, the United States decided to make high school nearly universal. Around the same time, much of Europe decided that 1 universal high school was a waste. Not everybody, European intellectuals argued, should go to high school.

It's clear who made the right decision. The educated American masses helped create the American century, as the economists Claudia Goldin and Lawrence Katz have written. The new ranks of high school graduates made factories more efficient and new industries possible. 2

Today, we are having an updated version of the same debate. Television, newspapers and blogs are filled with the case against college for the masses: It saddles students with debt; it does not guarantee a good job; it isn't necessary for many jobs. Not everybody, the skeptics say, should go to college. 3

The argument has the lure of counterintuition and does have grains of truth. Too many teenagers aren't ready to do college-level work. Ultimately, though, the case against mass education is no better than it was a century ago. 4

The evidence is overwhelming that college is a better investment for most graduates than in the past. A new study even shows that a bachelor's degree pays off for jobs that don't require one: secretaries, plumbers and cashiers. And, beyond money, education seems to make people happier and healthier. 5

"Sending more young Americans to college is not a panacea," says David Autor, an M.I.T. economist who studies the labor market. "Not sending them to college would be a disaster." 6

The most unfortunate part of the case against college is that it encourages children, parents and schools to aim low. For those families on the fence—often deciding whether a student will be the first to attend—the skepticism becomes one more reason to stop at high school. Only about 33 percent of young adults get a four-year degree today, while another 10 percent receive a two-year degree. 7

So it's important to dissect the anti-college argument, piece by piece. It obviously starts with money. Tuition numbers can be eye-popping, and student debt has increased significantly. But there are two main reasons college costs aren't usually a problem for those who graduate. 8

First, many colleges are not very expensive, once financial aid is taken into account. Average net tuition and fees at public four-year colleges this past year were only about $2,000 (though Congress may soon cut federal financial aid). 9

Second, the returns from a degree have soared. Three decades ago, full-time workers with a bachelor's degree made 40 percent more than those with only a high-school diploma. Last year, the gap reached 83 percent. College graduates, though hardly immune from the downturn, are also far less likely to be unemployed than nongraduates. 10

Skeptics like to point out that the income gap isn't rising as fast as it once was, especially for college graduates who don't get an advanced degree. But the gap remains enormous—and bigger than ever. 11

...continued Even for Cashiers, College Pays Off, **David Leonhardt**

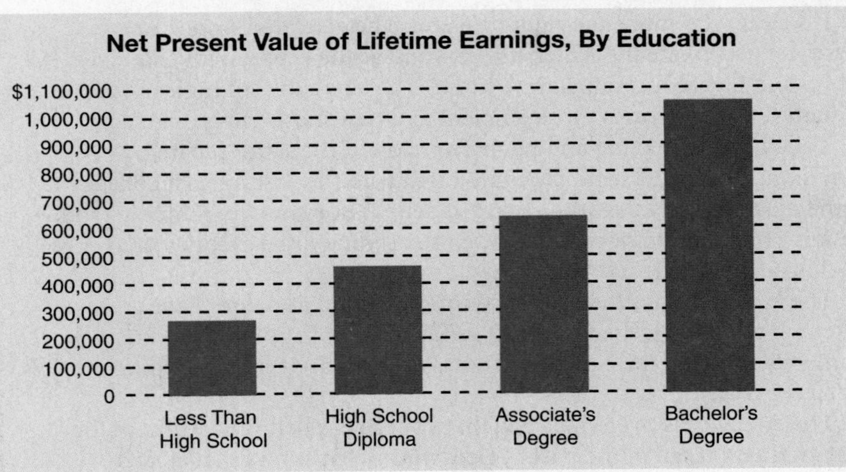

Skipping college because the pace of gains has slowed is akin to skipping your heart medications because the pace of medical improvement isn't what it used to be.

The Hamilton Project, a research group in Washington, has just 12
finished a comparison of college with other investments. It found that college tuition in recent decades has delivered an inflation-adjusted annual return of more than 15 percent. For stocks, the historical return is 7 percent. For real estate, it's less than 1 percent.

Another study being released this weekend—by Anthony Carnevale 13
and Stephen J. Rose of Georgetown—breaks down the college premium by occupations and shows that college has big benefits even in many fields where a degree is not crucial.

Construction workers, police officers, plumbers, retail salespeople 14
and secretaries, among others, make significantly more with a degree than without one. Why? Education helps people do higher-skilled work, get jobs with better-paying companies or open their own businesses.

This follows the pattern of the early 20th century, when blue- and 15
white-collar workers alike benefited from having a high-school diploma.

When confronted with such data, skeptics sometimes reply that 16
colleges are mostly a way station for smart people. But that's not right either. Various natural experiments—like teenagers' proximity to a campus, which affects whether they enroll—have shown that people do acquire skills in college.

Even a much-quoted recent study casting doubt on college educa- 17
tion, by an N.Y.U. sociologist and two other researchers [Richard Arum, Josipa Roksa, and Esther Cho], was not so simple. It found that only

55 percent of freshmen and sophomores made statistically significant progress on an academic test. But the margin of error was large enough that many more may have made progress. Either way, the general skills that colleges teach, like discipline and persistence, may be more important than academics anyway.

18 None of this means colleges are perfect. Many have abysmal graduation rates. Yet the answer is to improve colleges, not abandon them. Given how much the economy changes, why would a high school diploma forever satisfy most citizens' educational needs?

19 Or think about it this way: People tend to be clear-eyed about this debate in their own lives. For instance, when researchers asked low-income teenagers how much more college graduates made than nongraduates, the teenagers made excellent estimates. And in a national survey, 94 percent of parents said they expected their child to go to college.

20 Then there are the skeptics themselves, the professors, journalists and others who say college is overrated. They, of course, have degrees and often spend tens of thousands of dollars sending their children to expensive colleges.

21 I don't doubt that the skeptics are well meaning. But, in the end, their case against college is an elitist one—for me and not for thee. And that's rarely good advice.

Professional Writing

An Open Letter to George M. Philip, President of the State University of New York at Albany

Gregory Petsko

Dear President Philip,

1 Probably the last thing you need at this moment is someone else from outside your university complaining about your decision. If you want to argue that I can't really understand all aspects of the situation, never having been associated with SUNY Albany, I wouldn't disagree. But I cannot let something like this go by without weighing in. I hope, when I'm through, you will at least understand why.

2 Just 30 days ago, on October 1st, you announced that the departments of French, Italian, Classics, Russian and Theater Arts were being eliminated. You gave several reasons for your decision, including that "there are comparatively fewer students enrolled in these degree programs." Of course, your decision was also, perhaps chiefly,

...continued An Open Letter to George M. Philip..., **Gregory Petsko**

a cost-cutting measure—in fact, you stated that this decision might not have been necessary had the state legislature passed a bill that would have allowed your university to set its own tuition rates. Finally, you asserted that the humanities were a drain on the institution financially, as opposed to the sciences, which bring in money in the form of grants and contracts.

Let's examine these and your other reasons in detail, because I think if one does, it becomes clear that the facts on which they are based have some important aspects that are not covered in your statement. First, the matter of enrollment. I'm sure that relatively few students take classes in these subjects nowadays, just as you say. There wouldn't have been many in my day, either, if universities hadn't required students to take a distribution of courses in many different parts of the academy: humanities, social sciences, the fine arts, the physical and natural sciences, and to attain minimal proficiency in at least one foreign language. You see, the reason that humanities classes have low enrollment is not because students these days are clamoring for more relevant courses; it's because administrators like you, and spineless faculty, have stopped setting distribution requirements and started allowing students to choose their own academic programs—something I feel is a complete abrogation of the duty of university faculty as teachers and mentors. You could fix the enrollment problem tomorrow by instituting a mandatory core curriculum that included a wide range of courses. 3

Young people haven't, for the most part, yet attained the wisdom to have that kind of freedom without making poor decisions. In fact, without wisdom, it's hard for most people. That idea is thrashed out better than anywhere else, I think, in Dostoyevsky's parable of the Grand Inquisitor, which is told in Chapter Five of his great novel, *The Brothers Karamazov*. In the parable, Christ comes back to earth in Seville at the time of the Spanish Inquisition. He performs several miracles but is arrested by Inquisition leaders and sentenced to be burned at the stake. The Grand Inquisitor visits Him in his cell to tell Him that the Church no longer needs Him. The main portion of the text is the Inquisitor explaining why. The Inquisitor says that Jesus rejected the three temptations of Satan in the desert in favor of freedom, but he believes that Jesus has misjudged human nature. The Inquisitor says that the vast majority of humanity cannot handle freedom. In giving humans the freedom to choose, Christ has doomed humanity to a life of suffering. 4

That single chapter in a much longer book is one of the great works of modern literature. You would find a lot in it to think about. I'm sure your Russian faculty would love to talk with you about it—if only you had a Russian department, which now, of course, you don't. 5

Then there's the question of whether the state legislature's inaction gave you no other choice. I'm sure the budgetary problems you have to deal with are serious. They certainly are at Brandeis University, where I work. And we, too, faced critical strategic decisions because our income was no longer enough to meet our expenses. But we eschewed your draconian—and authoritarian—solution, and a team of faculty, with input from all parts of the university, came up with a plan to do more with fewer resources. I'm not saying that all the specifics of our solution would fit your institution, but the process sure would have. You did call a town meeting, but it was to discuss your plan, not let the university craft its own. And you called that meeting for Friday afternoon on October 1st, when few of your students or faculty would be around to attend. In your defense, you called the timing "unfortunate," but pleaded that there was a "limited availability of appropriate large venue options." I find that rather surprising. If the President of Brandeis needed a lecture hall on short notice, he would get one. I guess you don't have much clout at your university. 6

And do you really think even those faculty and administrators who may applaud your tough-minded stance (partly, I'm sure, in relief that they didn't get the axe themselves) are still going to be on your side in the future? I'm reminded of the fable by Aesop of the Travelers and the Bear: two men were walking together through the woods, when a bear rushed out at them. One of the travelers happened to be in front, and he grabbed the branch of a tree, climbed up, and hid himself in the leaves. The other, being too far behind, threw himself flat down on the ground, with his face in the dust. The bear came up to him, put his muzzle close to the man's ear, and sniffed and sniffed. But at last with a growl the bear slouched off, for bears will not touch dead meat. Then the fellow in the tree came down to his companion, and, laughing, said "What was it that the bear whispered to you?" "He told me," said the other man, "Never to trust a friend who deserts you in a pinch." 7

I first learned that fable, and its valuable lesson for life, in a freshman classics course. Aesop is credited with literally hundreds of fables, most of which are equally enjoyable—and enlightening. Your classics faculty would gladly tell you about them, if only you had a Classics department, which now, of course, you don't. 8

As for the argument that the humanities don't pay their own way, well, I guess that's true, but it seems to me that there's a fallacy in assuming that a university should be run like a business. I'm not saying it shouldn't be managed prudently, but the notion that every part of it needs to be self-supporting is simply at variance with what a university is all about. You seem to value entrepreneurial programs and practical subjects that might generate intellectual property more than you do "old-fashioned" courses of study. But universities aren't just about discovering and capitalizing on new knowledge; they are also about 9 preserving knowledge from being lost over time, and that requires a financial investment. There is good reason for it: what seems to be archaic today can become vital in the future. I'll give you two examples of that. The first is the science of virology, which in the 1970s was dying out because people felt that infectious diseases were no longer a serious health problem in the developed world and other subjects, such as molecular biology, were much sexier. Then, in the early 1990s, a little problem called AIDS became the world's number 1 health concern. The virus that causes AIDS was first isolated and characterized at the National Institutes of Health in the USA and the Institute Pasteur in France, because these were among the few institutions that still had thriving virology programs. My second example you will probably be more familiar with. Middle Eastern Studies, including the study of foreign languages such as Arabic and Persian, was hardly a hot subject on most campuses in the 1990s. Then came September 11, 2001. Suddenly we realized that we needed a lot more people who understood something about that part of the world, especially its Muslim culture. Those universities that had preserved their Middle Eastern Studies departments, even in the face of declining enrollment, suddenly became very important places. Those that hadn't—well, I'm sure you get the picture.

I know one of your arguments is that not every place should try to do everything. Let other institutions have great programs in classics or theater arts, you say; we will focus on preparing students for jobs in the real world. Well, I hope I've just shown you that the real world is pretty fickle about what it wants. The best way for people to be prepared for the inevitable shock of change is to be as broadly educated as possible, because today's backwater is often tomorrow's hot field. And interdisciplinary research, which is all the rage these days, is only possible if people aren't too narrowly trained. If none of that convinces you, then I'm willing to let you turn your institution into a place that focuses on the practical, but only if you stop calling it a university and yourself the President of one. You see, the word "university" derives from the Latin "universitas," meaning "the whole." You can't be a university without having a thriving humanities program. You will need to call SUNY Albany a trade school, or perhaps a vocational college, but not a university. Not anymore. 10

I utterly refuse to believe that you had no alternative. It's your job as President to find ways of solving problems that do not require the amputation of healthy limbs. Voltaire said that no problem can withstand the assault of sustained thinking. Voltaire, whose real name was François-Marie Arouet, had a lot of pithy, witty and brilliant things to say (my favorite is "God is a comedian playing to an audience that is 11 afraid to laugh"). Much of what he wrote would be very useful to you. I'm sure the faculty in your French department would be happy to introduce you to his writings, if only you had a French department, which now, of course, you don't.

12 I guess I shouldn't be surprised that you have trouble understanding the importance of maintaining programs in unglamorous or even seemingly "dead" subjects. From your biography, you don't actually have a PhD or other high degree, and have never really taught or done research at a university. Perhaps my own background will interest you. I started out as a classics major. I'm now Professor of Biochemistry and Chemistry. Of all the courses I took in college and graduate school, the ones that have benefited me the most in my career as a scientist are the courses in classics, art history, sociology, and English literature. These courses didn't just give me a much better appreciation for my own culture; they taught me how to think, to analyze, and to write clearly. None of my sciences courses did any of that.

13 One of the things I do now is write a monthly column on science and society. I've done it for over 10 years, and I'm pleased to say some people seem to like it. If I've been fortunate enough to come up with a few insightful observations, I can assure you they are entirely due to my background in the humanities and my love of the arts. . . .

14 Some of your defenders have asserted that this is all a brilliant ploy on your part—a master political move designed to shock the legislature and force them to give SUNY Albany enough resources to keep these departments open. That would be Machiavellian (another notable Italian writer, but then, you don't have any Italian faculty to tell you about him), certainly, but I doubt that you're that clever. If you were, you would have held that town meeting when the whole university could have been present, at a place where the press would be all over it. That's how you force the hand of a bunch of politicians. You proclaim your action on the steps of the state capitol. You don't try to sneak it through in the dead of night, when your institution has its back turned.

15 No, I think you were simply trying to balance your budget at the expense of what you believe to be weak, outdated and powerless departments. I think you will find, in time, that you made a Faustian bargain. Faust is the title character in a play by Johann Wolfgang von Goethe. It was written around 1800 but still attracts the largest audiences of any play in Germany whenever it's performed. Faust is the story of a scholar who makes a deal with the devil. The devil promises him anything he wants as long as he lives. In return, the devil will get—well, I'm sure you can guess how these sorts of deals usually go. If only you had a Theater department, which now, of course, you don't, you could ask them to perform the play so you could see what happens.

...continued An Open Letter to George M. Philip..., **Gregory Petsko**

It's awfully relevant to your situation. You see, Goethe believed that it profits a man nothing to give up his soul for the whole world. That's the whole world, President Philip, not just a balanced budget. Although, I guess, to be fair, you haven't given up your soul. Just the soul of your institution.

Disrespectfully yours,

Gregory A Petsko

Questions for Writing and Discussion

1. Choose one of the essays in this casebook and annotate it for the analysis of the problem and then for the proposed solution. Which paragraphs describe the problem and which the solution? Which parts are supported by specific evidence, statistics, or studies? Which parts need more explanation or more evidence? Be prepared to present your analysis in class.
2. Several of these essays seem to be in conversation with each other—that is, they discuss the same problems and in some cases cite similar evidence or research. Choose two or three of these essays or documents that discuss a common problem (academic achievement, high costs of college, student debt) and analyze where they agree and where they disagree. Explain how and where these authors' analyses of the problems or their solutions are similar or different.
3. Write a few paragraphs describing your own financial and academic experience in college. How have you dealt with the financial obligations? What courses have given you skills you may need for a future job? Then explain which of these articles speaks most directly to your own situation. Write a short response explaining which author's arguments, evidence, or analysis makes the most sense to you, based on your experience.
4. Examine this chapter's opening image. Then compare that document to the similar one in this casebook. Does the handlettering in each document make the testimony more believable? Is it possible for someone to put himself or herself through college without parental help or without incurring debt? What political statement is each writer making, and how does each statement connect to the goals of the Occupy movement?

Professional Writing

The Argument Culture

Deborah Tannen

A professor of linguistics at Georgetown University, Deborah Tannen is also a best-selling author of many books on discourse and gender, including You Just Don't Understand: Women and Men in Conversation *(1990),* The Argument Culture: Moving from Debate to Dialogue *(1998), and* You Were Always Mom's Favorite! *(2010). In the following essay, taken from* The Argument Culture, *Tannen tries to convince her readers that adversarial debates—which typically represent only two sides of an issue and thus promote antagonism—create problems in communication. But does Tannen persuade you that our "argument culture" really is a problem and that her solutions will help solve that problem?*

Balance. Debate. Listening to both sides. Who could question these noble American traditions? Yet today, these principles have been distorted. Without thinking, we have plunged headfirst into what I call the "argument culture." 1

The argument culture urges us to approach the world, and the people in it, in an adversarial frame of mind. It rests on the assumption that opposition is the best way to get anything done: The best way to discuss an idea is to set up a debate; the best way to cover news is to find spokespeople who express the most extreme, polarized views and present them as "both sides"; the best way to settle disputes is litigation that pits one party against the other; the best way to begin an essay is to attack someone; and the best way to show you're really thinking is to criticize. 2

More and more, our public interactions have become like arguing with a spouse. Conflict can't be avoided in our public lives any more than we can avoid conflict with people we love. One of the great strengths of our society is that we can express these conflicts openly. But just as spouses have to learn ways of settling their differences without inflicting real damage, so we, as a society, have to find constructive ways of resolving disputes and differences. 3

The war on drugs, the war on cancer, the battle of the sexes, politicians' turf battles—in the argument culture, war metaphors pervade our talk and shape our thinking. The cover headlines of both *Time* and *Newsweek* one recent week are a case in point: "The Secret Sex Wars," proclaims *Newsweek*. "Starr at War," declares *Time*. Nearly everything is framed as a battle or game in which winning or losing is the main concern. 4

The argument culture pervades every aspect of our lives today. Issues from global warming to abortion are depicted as two-sided arguments, when in fact most Americans' views lie somewhere in the middle. Partisanship makes gridlock in Washington the norm. Even in our 5 personal relationships, a "let it all hang out" philosophy emphasizes people expressing their anger without giving them constructive ways of settling differences.

Sometimes You Have to Fight

There are times when it is necessary and right to fight—to defend your country or yourself, to argue for your rights or against offensive or dangerous ideas or actions. What's wrong with the argument culture is the ubiquity, the knee-jerk nature of approaching any issue, problem or public person in an adversarial way. 6

Our determination to pursue truth by setting up a fight between two sides leads us to assume that every issue has two sides—no more, no less. But if you always assume there must be an "other side," you may end up scouring the margins of science or the fringes of lunacy to find it. 7

This accounts, in part, for the bizarre phenomenon of Holocaust denial. Deniers, as Emory University professor Deborah Lipstadt shows, have been successful in gaining TV air time and campus newspaper coverage by masquerading as "the other side" in a "debate." Continual reference to "the other side" results in a conviction that everything has another side—and people begin to doubt the existence of any facts at all. 8

The power of words to shape perception has been proved by researchers in controlled experiments. Psychologists Elizabeth Loftus and John Palmer, for example, found that the terms in which people are asked to recall something affect what they recall. The researchers showed subjects a film of two cars colliding, then asked how fast the cars were going; one week later they asked whether there had been any broken glass. Some subjects were asked, "How fast were the cars going when they bumped into each other?" Others were asked, "How fast were the cars going when they smashed into each other?" 9

Those who read the question with "smashed" tended to "remember" that the cars were going faster. They were also more likely to "remember" having seen broken glass. (There wasn't any.) This is how language works. It invisibly molds our way of thinking about people, actions and the world around us. 10

In the argument culture, "critical" thinking is synonymous with criticizing. In many classrooms, students are encouraged to read someone's life work, then rip it to shreds. 11

When debates and fighting predominate, those who enjoy verbal sparring are likely to take part—by calling in to talk shows or writing letters to the editor. Those who aren't comfortable with oppositional discourse are likely to opt out. 12

How High-Tech Communication Pulls Us Apart

One of the most effective ways to defuse antagonism between two groups is to provide a forum for individuals from those groups to get to know each other personally. What is happening in our lives, however, is just the opposite. More and more of our communication is not face to face, and not with people we know. The proliferation and increasing portability of technology isolates people in a bubble. 13

Along with the voices of family members and friends, phone lines bring into our homes the annoying voices of solicitors who want to sell something—generally at dinnertime. (My father-in-law startles phone solicitors by saying, "We're eating dinner, but I'll call you back. What's your home phone number?" To the nonplused caller, he explains, "Well, you're calling me at home; I thought I'd call you at home, too.") 14

It is common for families to have more than one TV, so the adults can watch what they like in one room and the kids can watch their choice in another—or maybe each child has a private TV. 15

E-mail, and now the Internet, are creating networks of human connection unthinkable even a few years ago. Though e-mail has enhanced communication with family and friends, it also ratchets up the anonymity of both sender and receiver, resulting in stranger-to-stranger "flaming." 16

"Road rage" shows how dangerous the argument culture—and especially today's technologically enhanced aggression—can be. Two men who engage in a shouting match may not come to blows, but if they express their anger while driving down a public highway, the risk to themselves and others soars. 17

The Argument Culture Shapes Who We Are

The argument culture has a defining impact on our lives and on our culture. 18

- **It makes us distort facts,** as in the Nancy Kerrigan-Tonya Harding story. After the original attack on Kerrigan's knee, news stories focused on the rivalry between the two skaters instead of portraying Kerrigan as the victim of an attack. Just last month, *Time* magazine called the event a "contretemps" between Kerrigan and Harding. And a recent joint TV interview of the two skaters reinforced that skewed image by putting the two on equal footing, rather than as victim and accused.
- **It makes us waste valuable time,** as in the case of scientist Robert Gallo, who co-discovered the AIDS virus. Gallo was the object of a groundless four-year investigation into allegations he had stolen the virus from another scientist. He was ultimately exonerated, but the toll was enormous. Never mind that, in his words, "These were the most painful and horrible years of my life." Gallo spent four years fighting accusations instead of fighting AIDS.

...continued The Argument Culture, **Deborah Tannen**

- **It limits our thinking.** Headlines are intentionally devised to attract attention, but the language of extremes actually shapes, and misshapes, the way we think about things. Military metaphors train us to think about, and see, everything in terms of fighting, conflict and war. Adversarial rhetoric is a kind of verbal inflation—a rhetorical boy-who-cried-wolf.
- **It encourages us to lie.** If you fight to win, the temptation is great to deny facts that support your opponent's views and say only what supports your side. It encourages people to misrepresent and, in the extreme, to lie.

End the Argument Culture by Looking at All Sides

How can we overcome our classically American habit of seeing issues in absolutes? We must expand our notion of "debate" to include more dialogue. To do this, we can make special efforts not to think in twos. Mary Catherine Bateson, an anthropologist at Virginia's George Mason University, makes a point of having her class compare three cultures, not two. Then, students are more likely to think about each on its own terms, rather than as opposites. 19

In the public arena, television and radio producers can try to avoid, whenever possible, structuring public discussions as debates. This means avoiding the format of having two guests discuss an issue. Invite three guests—or one. Perhaps it is time to re-examine the assumption that audiences always prefer a fight. 20

Instead of asking, "What's the other side?" we might ask, "What are the other sides?" Instead of insisting on hearing "both sides," let's insist on hearing "all sides." 21

We need to find metaphors other than sports and war. Smashing heads does not open minds. We need to use our imaginations and ingenuity to find different ways to seek truth and gain knowledge through intellectual interchange, and add them to our arsenal—or, should I say, to the ingredients for our stew. It will take creativity for each of us to find ways to change the argument culture to a dialogue culture. It's an effort we have to make, because our public and private lives are at stake. 22

Questions for Writing and Discussion

1. List three controversial topics currently in the news. Then choose one of those topics and explain the two "sides" of this argument. Now, imagine a

third point of view. How is it different from the first two positions? Does coming up with a third position help you think creatively about how to resolve this dispute? Explain.

2. In her essay, Tannen initially outlines the nature of the problem with the "argument culture" before she gives her solution. Which paragraphs most clearly demonstrate the problem? Which paragraphs explain her solution? Does she ignore aspects of the problem? Would her solution really solve the problem she describes? Why or why not?

3. Critically analyzing the social, political, or cultural context is an important strategy for solving a problem. Where does Tannen explain the context(s) for the problem? Where does she argue that her solution will help resolve social, political, or cultural problems? Are there contexts where her solution might not work? Explain.

4. According to Tannen, the language we choose and the metaphors we use affect our perceptions of the world. Where does Tannen discuss how words or metaphors shape our perceptions? What examples does she give? In her own argument, does Tannen herself avoid language or metaphors referring to war, violence, or conflict?

Problem Solving: The Writing Process

Assignment for Problem Solving

Select a problem that you believe needs a solution. Narrow and focus the problem and choose an appropriate audience. Describe the problem and, if necessary, demonstrate for your audience that it needs a solution. State your solution, and justify it with reasons and evidence. Where appropriate, weigh alternative solutions, examine the feasibility of your own solution, and answer objections to your solution.

The problem-solving assignment leads naturally to the genre of the proposal. Some proposals are long, formal documents addressed to knowledgeable readers, while others are short and informal, intended for general audiences. Review your assignment, and then use the following grid to brainstorm genres that would meet your purpose for your selected audience.

Audience	Possible Genres for Problem Solving
Personal Audience	Class notes, journal entry, blog, Web page
Academic Audience	Academic proposal, analysis, editorial, review, journal entry, forum entry on class site, multigenre document
Public Audience	Column, editorial, article, blog, or critique in a magazine, newspaper, online site, newsletter, or multigenre document

CHOOSING A SUBJECT

If one of your journal entries suggests a subject, try the collecting and shaping strategies below. If none of them leads to a workable subject, consider the following suggestions:

- Evaluating leads naturally to problem solving. Reread your journal entries and topic ideas for "evaluating." If your evaluation of your subject was negative, consider what would make your evaluation more positive. Based on your evaluation, write a proposal, addressed to the proper audience, explaining the problem and offering your solution.
- Organized groups are already trying to solve a number of national and international problems: illegal immigrants, acid rain, abuse of animals in scientific experiments, drug and alcohol abuse, and so forth. Read several current articles on one of these topics. Then narrow the problem to one aspect that students or residents of your town could help to resolve. Write an essay outlining the problem and proposing *specific and limited* actions that citizens could take.
- **Community Service Learning.** If you have a community-service-learning project in one of your classes, work collaboratively with the agency to assess the community's and/or the agency's needs as well as the knowledge and skills you might bring to the agency to contribute to a possible solution. Working with the agency, decide on a purpose, audience, and genre for your proposal.
- Every day the news media feature images that seem to suggest a problem that needs a solution. Choose one such image and investigate the issue. What problem does the image suggest? What does your research and investigation reveal about the rhetorical situation and cultural context surrounding this image and this issue? Choose a possible audience, genre, and context, and write your own problem-solving essay based on the issue raised by this image.

COLLECTING

With a possible subject and audience in mind, write out answers for each of the following topics. Not all of these approaches will apply to every subject; some topics will suggest very little, while others may prompt you to generate ideas or specific examples appropriate to your problem and solution. A hypothetical problem—large classes that hinder learning—illustrates how these topics may help you focus on your subject and collect relevant ideas and information.

9.2
Use collecting strategies to define a problem and develop solutions

Identify and Focus on the Specific Problem

Answer the first four "Wh" questions:

Who: A Psychology I professor; the Psychology Department
What: Psychology I class
When: Spring semester
Where: University of Illinois

You may want to generalize about large lecture classes everywhere, but begin by identifying the specific problem at hand.

Demonstrate That the Problem Needs a Solution

Map out the *effects* of a problem. (See the diagram.)

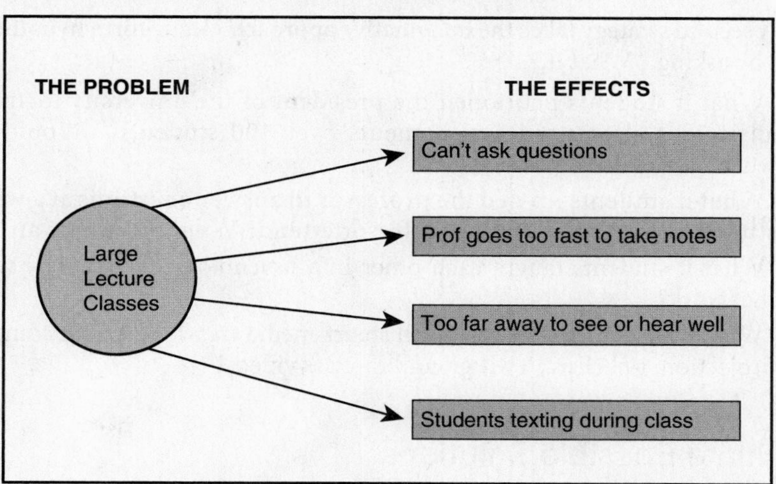

You may want to map out both *short-term effects* and *long-term effects.* Over the short term, large lecture classes prevent you from asking questions; over the long term, you may do poorly on examinations, get a lower grade in the class, lose interest in the subject, be unable to cope with your own and others' psychological problems, or end up in a different career or job.

Discover Possible Solutions

One strategy is to map out the history or the causes of the problem. If you can discover what caused the problem, you may have a possible solution. (See the diagram.)

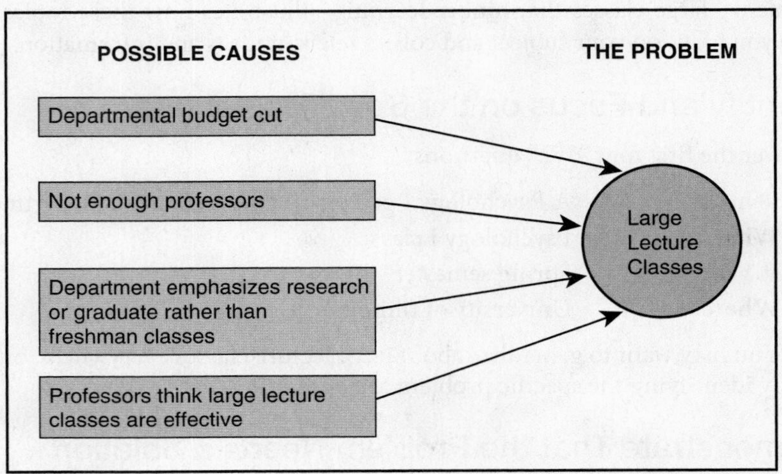

A second strategy takes the imaginative approach. Brainstorm hypothetical cases by asking, "What if…."

"What if students petitioned the president of the university to abolish all lecture classes with enrollments over 100 students?" Would that work?

"What if students invited the professor to answer questions at a weekly study session?" Would the professor attend? Would students attend?

"What if students taught each other in a psychology class?" How would that work?

"What if all lecture classes were in smart-media classrooms with computer projection, i-clickers, Twitter, and in-class videos?"

Evaluate Possible Solutions

Apply the "If … then …" test on each possible solution: Consider whether each proposal would:

A. actually solve the problem;

B. meet certain criteria, such as cost-effectiveness, practicality, ethicality, legality;

C. not create new problems.

"*If* classes were smaller, *then* students would learn more":

If classes were smaller, students might learn more, but a small class size does not necessarily guarantee greater learning.

Although students might learn more, do smaller classes meet other criteria? While they are legal and ethical, are they practical and cost-effective?

Would smaller classes create new problems? Smaller classes might mean fewer upper-level course offerings. Is that a serious new problem?

Convince Your Readers

Support your proposed solutions by stating *reasons* and providing supporting *evidence.*

Reason: Smaller classes are worth the additional expense because students engage the material rather than just memorize for exams.

Evidence: Data from studies comparing large and small classes; personal testimony by students, interviews, or questionnaires; testimony or evidence from authorities on teaching.

Answer Possible Objections to Your Proposal

Every solution has a down side or potential drawbacks. You need to respond to the most important objections.

List Drawbacks

Small classes cost more.

Small classes might reduce course offerings.

Small classes might mean less money for research.

List Your Responses

Good education does cost more. The University of Illinois has a reputation as an excellent undergraduate institution, and small classes would help it maintain quality education.

Perhaps some classes with low demand could be cut, but the necessary funds should not be taken out of upper-division classes for psychology majors or research projects.

List Possible Steps for Implementation

If appropriate, indicate the key steps or chronological sequence of your proposal.

1. Poll students and teachers in large lecture classes to confirm that the problem warrants attention.
2. Gather evidence from other colleges or universities to show how they reduced class sizes.
3. Present results of polls and other evidence to the state legislature to request more funds.

Observing

As you gather evidence and examples, use your observation skills. If the problem is large lecture classes, attend classes and *observe* the behavior of students and professors. Are students distracted by noise? Can they ask questions? Does the professor talk too softly to be heard in the back row? Remember that *repeated* observation is essential. If necessary, observe your subject over a period of several days or weeks.

> **"The best time for planning . . . is when you're doing the dishes."**
>
> —Agatha Christie, Mystery Writer

Remembering

Use *freewriting, looping,* or *clustering* to help you remember examples from your experience of the problem or of possible solutions. Brainstorm or freewrite about previous class sessions in Psychology I. Do looping or mapping on other small-enrollment classes: What made these classes effective or ineffective? What teaching strategies, projects, or activities were possible in these classes that would not be possible in a large class?

Reading and Investigating

Use the library to find books or articles about the problem. Other writers will have offered solutions to your problem that you could consider. Articles may even suggest objections to your proposed solution that you need to answer.

Interview participants or authorities on the problem. The professor who is teaching your Psychology I class may have ideas about a solution. Administration—department chairs, deans, even the president—may agree to answer your questions and react to your possible solutions.

Design a questionnaire that addresses aspects of your problem. Responses to questionnaires provide evidence that a problem is serious. If the results of a questionnaire show that 175 of the 200 people in Psychology I who returned it favor smaller sections, you can include those data in your letter to the head of the department and the dean of the college.

ResearchTips

As you begin researching your problem, don't spend all your time on the Internet or on the library's databases. Take the time to talk to people who may know about your problem. Use your investigating skills to locate local authorities and interview them in person, via e-mail, or on the telephone (see Chapter 6). Find out what other people think about this problem. How do they explain or define it? What are they already doing to solve the problem? Why are current solutions not working or not working effectively enough? Interview a teacher who knows about the problem, a student who has firsthand experience with the problem, an owner of a local business, or the coordinator of a community service or agency. Combining your online and library research with interviews makes your research more interesting, more local and current, and more effective.

SHAPING

As you think about ways to organize and develop your essay, be sure to reread your assignment and reconsider your purpose and audience. For your problem-solving essay, consider the following shaping strategies.

9.3
Shape your proposal

Shaping Strategies

Do you want to. . .	Consider using these rhetorical modes or strategies:
write for a particular audience or publication?	analyze genres for problem-solving (p. 315)
use an outline to help you organize?	outlines for problem-solving (pp. 316–317)
examine causes of your problem?	causal analysis (p. 317)
evaluate criteria for a solution?	criteria analysis (p. 318)
show how a solution could be implemented step by step?	chronological order (pp. 317–318)

Genres for Problem Solving

Initially, you need to consider genres appropriate for your issue and your particular rhetorical situation. Typical genres used for proposals include articles in magazines, letters to the editor, academic essays, self-help essays, political essays, and business proposals. Depending on the genre and audience, proposals often do the following.

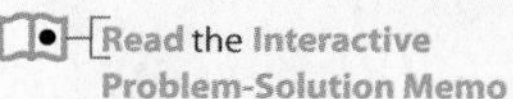
Read the Interactive Problem-Solution Memo

- Identify, analyze, and demonstrate the problem
- Describe and evaluate alternative solutions
- Make proposals
- Give reasons and evidence to support the proposal
- Answer objections; discuss feasibility problems
- Indicate implementation and call for action

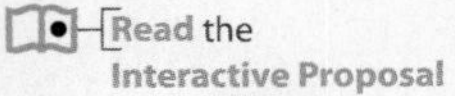

Not all problem-solving essays will have all six elements. Adam Richman's essay at the end of this chapter, for example, does not consider alternative solutions to the gradual demise of professional print journalism because his focus is on demonstrating that citizen journalism is a workable solution. Reconsidering your rhetorical situation and genre helps you decide how to shape your proposal.

Outlines for Problem Solving

The following patterns indicate four possible ways to organize a problem-solving essay.

Shaping Your Points: Problem-Solving Pattern

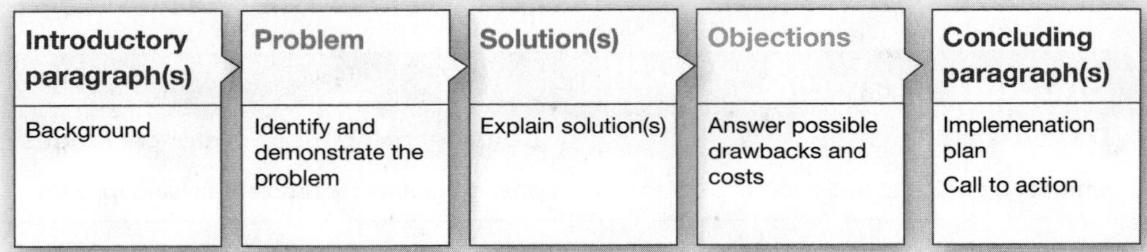

Shaping Your Points: Point-by-Point Pattern

Introductory paragraph(s)	Problem	One part of the problem	Second part of the problem, etc.	Concluding paragraph(s)
Background	Identify and demonstrate the problem	Explain first part of problem and its solution Provide evidence to support solution Respond to possible objections Explain why solution is feasible	Explain second part of problem and its solution, etc. Provide evidence to support solution Respond to possible objections Explain why solution is feasible	Implemenation plan Call to action

Shaping Your Points: Alternative Solution Pattern

Introductory paragraph(s)	Problem	Solutions 1, 2, etc., and objections	Best Solution	Concluding paragraph(s)
Background	Identify and demonstrate the problem	Explain solution 1 Explain why solution 1 is not satisfactory Do the same for solutions 2, 3, etc.	Explain and support best solution Explain objections Explain why best solution is feasible	Implemenation plan Call to action

Causal Analysis

Causal analysis can be used to organize some paragraphs of a proposal. In arguing the benefits or advantages of a proposed solution, you are explaining the *effects* of your solution.

- The effects or advantages of smaller class sections in Psychology I would be greater student participation, fewer distractions, more discussion during lectures, and more individual or small-group learning.
- Shortening the work week to thirty-two hours would increase the number of jobs, reduce tensions for working parents, and give employees time to learn new skills.

Shaping Your Points: Step-by-Step Pattern

Introductory paragraph(s)	Problem	Plan for implementing solution *or* how solution has worked in the past	Concluding paragraph(s)
Background	Identify and demonstrate the problem	Step 1 Step 2 Step 3 Provide reasons and evidence showing why each step is necessary and feasible.	Implementation plan Call to action

In each of these cases, each effect or advantage can become a separate point and, sometimes, a separate body paragraph.

Criteria Analysis

In some cases, the *criteria* for a good solution are quite clear. For example, cost-effectiveness, feasibility, and worker morale might be important criteria for a business-related proposal. If you work in a fast-food restaurant and are concerned about crime, for example, you might propose that your manager add a video surveillance system. In order to overcome the manager's resistance to the added expense, you could defend your proposal (and answer possible objections) by discussing relevant criteria.

Proposal: To reduce theft and protect the employees of the restaurant by installing a video surveillance system.

> "Vigorous writing is concise."
>
> —William Strunk, Jr.,
> Author and Teacher

- **Cost-effectiveness.** Citing evidence from other stores that have video cameras, you could prove that the equipment would pay for itself in less than a year.
- **Feasibility.** Installing a security system would not require extensive remodeling or significant training time for employees.
- **Employee morale**. Workers would feel more secure, they would feel that the management cares about them, and they would work more productively.

Chronological Order

If your proposal stresses the means of implementing your solution to a problem, you may organize several paragraphs or even an entire essay using chronological order or a step-by-step pattern.

A proposal to improve the reading skills of children might be justified by a series of coordinated steps: organizing seminars for teachers and PTA meetings to discuss possible solutions; establishing minimal reading requirements that teachers and parents agree on; offering reading prizes; and organizing media coverage of students who participate in reading programs.

DRAFTING

Using your examples, recorded observations, reading, interviews, results from questionnaires, or your own experience, make a sketch outline and begin writing. As you write, let your own proposal and your intended audience guide you. In your first draft, get as much as possible on paper. Don't worry about spelling or awkward sentences. If you hit a snag, stop and read what you have written so far or reread your collecting and shaping notes.

REVISING

When you have completed a draft and are ready to start revising your essay, get another member of your class to read and respond to it. Use the peer response guidelines that follow to get—and give—constructive advice.

Use the following revising guidelines to identify areas for improving your draft. Even at this point, don't hesitate to collect additional information, if necessary, or to reorganize your material. If a reader suggests changes, reread your draft to see if those changes will improve your essay.

PeerResponse

Writer: Provide the following information about your essay before you exchange drafts with a peer reader.

1. a. Audience and genre
   b. Statement of problem and context of problem
   c. Possible or alternative solutions
   d. Your recommended solution(s)
2. Write out one or two questions about your draft that you want your reader to answer.

Reader: Read the writer's entire draft. As you *reread* the draft, do the following.

1. Without looking at the writer's responses, describe (a) the essay's intended audience, (b) the main problem that the essay identifies, (c) the possible or alternative solutions, and (d) the writer's recommended solution. What feasibility problems or additional solutions should the writer consider? Why?
2. Indicate one paragraph in which the writer's evidence is strong. Then find one paragraph in which the writer needs more evidence. What additional *kinds* of evidence (personal experience, testimony from authorities, statistics, specific examples, etc.) might the writer use in this paragraph? Explain.
3. Number the paragraphs in the writer's essay and then describe, briefly, the purpose or main idea of each paragraph: paragraph 1 introduces the problem, paragraph 2 gives the writer's personal experience with the problem, and so on. Explain how the writer might improve the organization of the essay.

4. List the three most important things that the writer should focus on during revision.
5. Respond to the writer's questions in number 2.

Writer: When your essay is returned, read the comments by your peer reader(s) and do the following.

1. Compare your description of the audience, the problem, and the solutions with your reader's description. Where there are differences, try to clarify your essay.
2. Reconsider and revise your recommended solution(s).
3. What additional kinds of evidence will make your recommendations stronger?
4. Make a revision plan. List, in order, the three most important things that you need to do as you revise your essay.

Guidelines for Revision

- **Review your rhetorical situation.** How can you revise your genre to make it communicate your purpose more effectively to your intended audience?
- **Review to make sure you critically analyze the problem.** Don't assume that everyone will agree with your definition or representation of the problem. Investigate and describe those people who are affected by the problem.
- **Have a classmate or someone who might understand your audience read your draft and play devil's advocate.** Have your reader pretend to be hostile to your solution and ask questions about alternative solutions or weaknesses in your solution. Revise your proposal so that it answers any important objections.
- **Review your proposal for key elements.** If you are missing one of the following, would adding it make your proposal more effective for your audience? ***Remember:*** Proposals do not necessarily have to have all of these elements.
    - Develop the items that are most applicable to your proposal.
    - Show that a problem exists and needs attention.

- Evaluate alternative solutions.
- Propose your solution.
- Show that your solution meets certain criteria: feasibility, cost-effectiveness, legality.
- Answer possible objections.
- Suggest implementation or call for action.

- **Be sure that you *show* what you mean, using specific examples, facts, details, statistics, quotations from interviews or articles.** Don't rely on general assertions.
- **Signal the major parts of your proposal with key words and transitions.**
- **Avoid errors in logic and generalization.**

  Don't commit an "either-or" fallacy. For example, don't say that "*either* we reduce class sizes *or* students will drop out of the university." There are more than two possible alternatives.

  Don't commit an "ad hominem" fallacy by arguing "to the man" or "to the woman" rather than to the issue. Don't say, for example, that Deborah Tannen is wrong about argument because she is just another pushy woman who should stick to teaching linguistics.

  Test your proposal for "If ... then ..." statements. Does it really follow that "if we reduce class size, teaching will be more effective"?

  Avoid overgeneralizing your solution. If all your research concerns problems in large lecture classes in psychology, don't assume that your solution will apply to classes in physics or physical education.
- **When you provide data or quote sources, make sure that your material is accurately cited.**
- **Read your proposal aloud for flabby, wordy, or awkward sentences.** Revise your writing for clarity, precision, and forcefulness.
- **Edit your proposal for spelling, appropriate word choice, punctuation, usage, mechanics, and grammar.** Remember that, in part, your form and audience help determine what are appropriate usage and mechanics.

Postscript on the Writing Process

Before you turn in your essay, answer the following questions in your journal.

1. As you worked on your essay, what elements of the rhetorical situation did you revise? How did you change the purpose, audience, or genre elements as you drafted your essay? Cite specific sentences or paragraphs from your essay as examples.

2. List the skills you used in writing this paper: observing people, places, or events; remembering personal experience; using questionnaires and interviews; reading written material; explaining ideas; evaluating solutions. Which of these skills was most useful to you in writing this essay?
3. What was the most difficult problem you had to solve while writing this paper? Were you able to solve it yourself, or did your readers suggest a solution?
4. In one sentence, describe the most important thing you learned about writing while working on this essay.
5. What were the most successful parts of your essay?

Student Writing

Can Citizen Journalism Pick Up the Pieces?

Adam Richman

In a writing class focusing on the future of literacies, Adam Richman decided to write his essay on citizen journalism. Because many traditional newspapers were going bankrupt and ceasing publication, Richman wondered whether citizen journalism might fill the gap left by the disappearing traditional news sources. If citizen journalism could be a solution to the problem, he needed to know whether it was capable of meeting the responsibilities of professional journalism. After brainstorming his list of questions, he decided to design a questionnaire that would assess whether citizen journalism—as opposed to professional journalism—kept students informed and whether students thought citizen journalism was as reliable as professional journalism. Here are some of Richman's research questions, his survey questions, and his essay.

RESEARCH QUESTIONS

Overall Question: Is citizen journalism good for journalism as a whole?

- What percentage of journalism consumers read/watch/listen to (a) primarily professional journalism, (b) primarily citizen journalism, or (c) about an even mix?
- Which of the three groups is best informed on current events?
- Which of the three groups spends the most time consuming news?
- Which of the three groups is the best informed on current events?

- What percentage of journalism consumers says professional journalism has (a) more credibility than citizen journalism, (b) less credibility than citizen journalism, or (c) about the same credibility as citizen journalism?
- Which of these three groups is the best informed on current events?
- What percentage of journalism consumers fact-checks the news they consume?
- Which type of journalism gets fact-checked more: professional or citizen?
- What percentage of people considers citizen journalism to be journalism?
- Who is more informed on current events: those who say *yes* above or those who say *no* above?

QUESTIONNAIRE

This questionnaire is part of a research project conducted by Adam Richman. The topics to be covered include encyclopedias, media consumption and current events. Any information you provide will be kept entirely confidential, and your identity will not be requested.

1. **Which of the following do you use more often?**
   A. User-edited encyclopedias (Wikipedia, etc.)
   B. Staff-written encyclopedias (Encyclopedia Britannica, etc.)
2. **Which of the following statements best applies to you?**
   A. To get the news, I primarily use professional journalism (newspapers, TV news programs, news magazines, etc.).
   B. To get the news, I primarily use citizen journalism (weblogs, video logs, etc.).
   C. To get the news, I use an even mix of professional and citizen journalism.
3. **Which of the following has more credibility?**
   A. Professional journalism does.
   B. Citizen journalism does.
   C. They are about the same.
4. **Do you consider citizen journalism (weblogs, video logs, etc.) to be true journalism?**
   A. Yes
   B. No

...continued Can Citizen Journalism Pick Up the Pieces? **Adam Richman**

5. **When reading, watching, or listening to the news, which of the following do you prefer?**
   A. An attempt at objectivity
   B. A transparent bias

If you answered B, move on to question 6. If you answered A, skip to question 7.

6. **Which of the following statements best applies to you?**
   A. I primarily seek bias I agree with.
   B. I primarily seek bias I disagree with.
   C. I seek an even mix of bias I agree with and bias I disagree with.
7. **When reading, watching, or listening to the news, how often do you check facts?**
   1 (Never) 2 (Rarely) 3 (Sometimes) 4 (Often) 5 (Always)

ESSAY

Print journalism has recently seen historic cuts. In February, the *Rocky Mountain News* closed just weeks shy of its 150th anniversary. Also that month, Philadelphia Newspapers L.L.C., which owns the city's *Inquirer* and *Daily News,* filed for bankruptcy (Lieberman). Four years shy of its 150th anniversary, the *Seattle Post-Intelligencer* transferred 100 percent of its operations to the Internet (Richman and James). Most recently, Harrisburg's *Patriot-News* announced March 24 that all full-time employees must take 10 days off over the next five months ("Local Newspaper"). This alarming string of newspaper closings appears to be just the beginning of a fundamental change in journalism. We may well wonder how or if journalism—and our democratic way of life that depends on journalism—can survive these upheavals. 1

The problem is nothing less than the gradual demise of print journalism. But is there a solution? One possible solution could be the rise of citizen journalists, or "people without professional journalism training using the tools of modern technology and the global distribution of the Internet to create, augment or fact-check media on their own or in collaboration with others" (Glaser). User "djussila" of the citizen journalistic *NowPublic.com* defines journalism as one-third of the democratic equation: Politicians + Public + Publication = Democracy. The publication element is necessary, djussila argues, because direct democracy is obsolete. 2

"People do not really have a say in modern democracy, aside from their vote, unless they are a politician themselves," djussila says. "Journalism serves as a window."

Like a chemical reaction equation, each entity of a functioning democracy needs to remain balanced. But with the gradual reduction of print journalism, the equation becomes unstable. In a piece for the *Washington Post*, Marc Fisher quotes Warren Fiske of the *Virginia Pilot* lamenting the job cuts facing the newspaper industry: "When we had the larger bureaus, you could do the good investigative piece. Most sessions, somebody would find someone doing something wrong," Fiske said. "Now, we can only really cover the flow of legislation." 3

The number of citizen journalism sites that might replace print journalism has been growing dramatically in recent years. The most popular of these Web sites include the following: 4

- *NowPublic.com* said, "Nowhere are the merits of citizen journalism more apparent than at NowPublic.com" ("NowPublic Blog").
- CyberJournalist.net, one of Cnet's Top 100 Blogs. *USA Today* and the *Columbia Journalism Review* have both recommended the site ("About CyberJournalist.net").
- *Wanabehuman.blogspot.com,* a UK blog "founded on the principles of participatory or citizen journalism." Their site proudly declares, "We believe every citizen can be a journalist" (*Wanabehuman*: About Wanabehuman).

The growth of these news sources and many others like them raises a key question. Can citizen journalism pick up the pieces being left by professional journalism? To answer this, we first must answer other questions: (1) Can citizen journalism be considered real journalism? and (2) Does citizen journalism have the necessary characteristics to bridge the gap? 5

According to Mark Pearson's and Jane Johnston's *Breaking into Journalism*, news media serves "to inform . . . and to act as a public watchdog over government." If citizen journalism can accomplish these tasks to a degree that meets or exceeds the standards currently set by professional journalism, it can be considered real journalism. A survey I conducted of 100 York College students seems to suggest that citizen journalism may already be meeting the current standards. This survey included an eight-question current events quiz. Those who primarily used professional journalism to get the news answered an average of 3.98 questions correctly. Those who primarily used citizen journalism to get the news answered an average of 4.29 questions 6 correctly. Although it is difficult to generalize this data across the nation, it does suggest that citizen journalism at least has the potential to inform the public to a degree that meets or exceeds the standards set by professional journalism.

Because citizen journalism has shown the potential to inform to a degree that meets or exceeds the standards set by professional journalism, it can be considered real journalism. The next question is, "Can citizen journalism solve the problem by bridging the gap left by the fading of professional journalism?" 7

Professional journalism has three key functions: (1) to offer credible reporting of the news, (2) to report on the deliberations and decisions of state and local government, and (3) to do investigative work on public issues. Currently, there are already weaknesses in all of these areas. The *Columbia Journalism Review's* Web site laments the deterioration of credibility obvious in the media when CNN, Fox News, ABC News, and CNBC all focused heavily on a story revolving around a commercial being shot by Kevin Federline—better known as K-Fed or "Britney's ex," (Colby). Also, a *Washington Post* story explains, "as long as people buy property, look for jobs, send kids to school and pay taxes, they will need credible information about state government." Finally, Fiske says that professional journalism institutions no longer have the resources to commit to investigative reporting (qtd. in Fisher). 8

Although there are current weaknesses in professional journalism, both media critics and the public disagree about whether citizen journalism can serve these functions credibly. My survey of York College students suggested a lack of respect for citizen journalism. Seventy-nine percent of respondents said professional journalism is more credible, and fifty-three percent said that citizen journalism isn't even real journalism. Supporting that position, a Virginian politics blogger and maintainer of *RichmondSunlight.com*, Waldo Jaquith, admits an inability to cover local news as objectively as institutional journalists. "What I can't offer on my blogs is the relationships, the institutional memory, the why, the history that reporters who know the capital can bring to their stories," Jaquith said. "Newspapers can describe the candidates for governor in a more balanced, deeper way because you don't have a dog in the race. Webloggers do" (qtd. in Fisher). 9

On the other hand, many professionals do support the job that citizen journalists are doing. Dave Berlind, a blogger with *zdnet.com,* denies that blogs lack credibility. "Bloggers and so called 'citizen journalists' have to earn their credibility, and the community at large 10 does a good job of regulating the environment—quality will usually rise to the top." Providers of citizen journalism have earned praise from organizations like *Time, USA Today,* and the *Columbia Journalism Review*. In addition, the citizen journalistic *Chi-Town Daily News* covers Chicago's local happenings in depth, especially compared to the only eight local stories you may find in an average edition of the *Chicago Tribune* ("Investigative Journalism Done Better"): "We publish articles written by our team of seasoned beat reporters covering citywide topics like education, the environment, public housing and health," the site's About Us section reads. "Their work is supported by trained volunteer neighborhood reporters." Another Web site, the *Voice of San Diego,* operates similarly. Undeniably, citizen journalism has the ability to cover local news.

Because citizen journalism has shown the ability to adequately 11
accomplish these tasks, the potential exists for new media outlets to fill the vacuum being left by the downturn in professional journalism. Citizen journalism is able to pick up the pieces left by a fragmented and faltering print-based press. The fix will be neither immediate nor perfect, but a solid journalistic foundation supports the very capable field of citizen journalism. Potentially life-altering stories may go unnoticed, but for every one of those, another important story will see daylight that professional journalism alone could have never have shown. With every keystroke, with every click of the mouse on a button reading "post," citizen journalism is proving itself to the public. As accessibility to the Internet grows and as professional journalism continues to circle the drain, citizen journalism continues to grow stronger. Thanks to the brand-less brand of journalism that fosters independence, personal responsibility, and healthy skepticism, professional journalism's faltering need not throw the democratic equation off balance—if citizen journalism can meet its potential.

Works Cited

"About *CyberJournalist.net*." *CyberJournalist.net*. Jonathan Dube, 28 Mar. 2009. Web. 28 Mar. 2009.

Berlind, David. "Can Technology Close Journalism's Credibility Gap?" *ZDNet*. CBS Interactive, 19 Jan. 2005. Web. 28 Mar. 2009.

Chi-Town Daily News. Chi-Town Daily News, 28 Mar. 2009. Web. 28 Mar. 2009.

Colby, Edward B. "A Penny 'Saved' Is Media Credibility Burned." *Columbia Journalism Review*. Columbia Journalism Review, 23 June 2006. Web. 28 Mar. 2009.

djussila. "The Role of Journalism in a Democracy." *NowPublic.* NowPublic Technologies, 9 Mar. 2009. Web. 28 Mar. 2009.

Fisher, Marc. "Bloggers Can't Fill the Gap Left by a Shrinking Press Corps." *Washington Post.* Washington Post, 1 Mar. 2009. Web. 28 Mar. 2009.

Glaser, Mark. "MediaShift: Your Guide to Citizen Journalism." *PBS.* PBS, 27 Sept. 2006. Web. 25 Mar. 2009.

"Investigative Journalism Done Better, Faster and Cheaper without Newspapers." *techdirt.* Floor64, 18 Mar. 2009. Web. 28 Mar. 2009.

Lieberman, David. "Newspaper Closings Raise Fears about Industry." *USA Today.* Gannett, 19 Mar. 2009. Web. 28 Mar. 2009.

"Local Newspaper Announces Mandatory Furloughs." *WGAL News.* WGAL, Lancaster, 24 Mar. 2009. Television.

"NowPublic Blog." *NowPublic.com.* NowPublic News Coverages, 28 Mar. 2009. Web. 28 Mar. 2009.

Pearson, Mark, and Jane Johnston. *Breaking into Journalism.* Crow's Nest, Australia: Allen & Unwin, 1998. Print.

Richman, Dan, and Andrea James. "Seattle P-I to Publish Last Edition Tuesday." *Seattle Post-Intelligencer.* Seattle Post-Intelligencer, 16 Mar. 2009. Web. 28 Mar. 2009.

"*Wanabehuman:* About Wanabehuman." *Wanabehuman.* Wanabehuman, 28 Mar. 2009. Web. 28 Mar. 2009.

Questions for Writing and Discussion

1. Problem-solving essays need to demonstrate clearly an existing problem. According to Adam Richman, what is the problem facing journalism in America today? In what paragraphs does Adam Richman state this problem? Do you agree with his statement of the problem, or could other forces be creating the problem? Explain.

2. What solution to this problem does Richman propose? In what paragraphs does he state his solution most directly? What evidence does he present to convince you that his solution will work? Which pieces of evidence did you find most persuasive?

3. Richman presents one possible solution, but there are other solutions to the problem of declining print journalism. Some people say that newspapers can be saved by selling articles online. Others say that newspapers and other print journalism ought to have nonprofit status in order to pay professional journalists to protect our democratic way of life. In addition, critics of citizen journalism say that ordinary citizens are not trained to investigate and deliver news accurately and objectively. Should Richman consider these ideas in order to convince you that citizen journalism has the potential to replace traditional print journalism?
4. Richman is writing for an audience of fellow students at his college. Are the results of this study likely to convince them? Why or why not? If he were writing for an audience of Americans over the age of 50, would this study convince those readers? Why or why not?

Complete additional exercises and practice in your MyLab

For twelve swelteringly hot days in July 1925, the famous Scopes "Monkey Trial" in Dayton, Tennessee, tested a state law banning the teaching of evolution. The original debate between Clarence Darrow and William Jennings Bryan is recreated in this film version of the play *Inherit the Wind.* Written arguments sometimes recreate the pro–con debate style of a trial, but frequently, they represent multiple points of view, just as parents, teachers, administrators, and students might gather to recommend policy changes at a school or citizens get together to solve problems in the community. This chapter encourages you to imagine multiple situations for written argument as you adapt to different audiences, genres, and social contexts.

The Everett Collection

10

Arguing

What You Will Learn

In this chapter, you will learn to:

10.1 Use techniques for developing a claim

10.2 Use rhetorical appeals in argument

10.3 Use techniques for Rogerian argument

10.4 Use techniques for Toulmin argument

10.5 Use collecting strategies to develop an argument

10.6 Shape your argument

WHEN people argue with each other, they often become highly emotional or confrontational. Recall the last heated argument you had with a friend or family member: at the end of the argument, one of you stomped out of the room, slammed the door, and didn't speak to the other for days. In the aftermath of such a scene, you felt angry at the other person and at yourself. Neither of you came close to achieving what you wanted when you began the argument. Rather than understanding each other's point of view and working out your differences, you effectively closed the lines of communication.

When writers construct written arguments, however, they try to avoid the emotional outbursts that often turn arguments into displays of temper. Strong feelings may energize an argument—few of us make the effort to argue without an emotional investment in the subject—but written argument stresses the fair presentation of opposing or alternative arguments. Because written arguments are public, they take on a civilized manner. They implicitly say, Let's be reasonable. Let's look at the evidence on all sides. Before we argue for our position, let's put all the reasons and evidence on the table so everyone can see what's at stake.

As writers construct written arguments, they carefully consider the rhetorical situation:

- What is the social or cultural context for this issue?
- Where might this written argument appear or be published?

"Give me liberty to know, to utter, and to argue freely according to conscience, above all liberties."

—John Milton,
Poet

"Freedom of speech is established to achieve its essential purpose only when different opinions are expounded in the same hall to the same audience. . . . The opposition is indispensable."

—Walter Lippmann,
Journalist

- Who is the audience, and what do they already know or believe?
- Do readers hold an opposing or alternative viewpoint, or are they more neutral and likely to listen to both sides before deciding what to believe?

> **"All writing . . . is propaganda for something."**
> —Elizabeth Drew, Writer and Critic

A written argument creates an atmosphere of reason, which encourages readers to examine their own views clearly and dispassionately. When successful, such argument convinces rather than alienates an audience. It changes people's minds or persuades them to adopt a recommended course of action.

Techniques for Writing Arguments

A written argument is similar to a public debate between attorneys in a court of law or between members of Congress who represent different political parties. It begins with a debatable issue: Is this a good bill? Should we vote for it? In such debates, one person argues for a position or proposal, while the other argues against it. The onlookers (the judge, the jury, members of Congress, the public) then decide what to believe or what to do. The chapter-opening art, which shows a scene from *Inherit the Wind*, pictures the debate about evolution between Clarence Darrow and William Jennings Bryan during the 1925 Scopes trial. The judge in the picture makes sure the trial follows certain rules, and the audience (not in the picture) decides what or whom to believe.

Written argument, however, is not identical to a debate. *In a written argument, the writer must play all the roles.* The writer is above all the person arguing for the claim. But the writer must also represent what the opposition might say. In addition, the writer must think like the judge and make sure the argument follows appropriate rules. Perhaps certain arguments and evidence are inadmissible or inappropriate in this case. Finally, the writer needs to anticipate the responses of the audience and respond to them as well.

Written argument, then, represents several points of view, responds to them reasonably and fairly, and gives reasons and evidence that support the writer's claim. An effective written argument uses the following techniques.

Techniques for Arguing

Technique	Tips on How to Do It
Analyzing the *rhetorical situation*	Review your purpose, audience, genre, occasion, and context to understand how to write your essay. Pay particular attention to your *audience*. Knowing what your audience already knows and believes will help you persuade them.

Focusing on a *debatable* claim	Make this claim the *thesis of your paper.*
Representing and evaluating the *opposing points of view* on the issue fairly and accurately	The key to a successful arguing paper is *anticipating and responding* to the most important alternative or opposing positions.
Arguing reasonably *against opposing arguments* and *for your claim*	Respond to or refute alternate or opposing arguments. Present the best arguments supporting your claim. Argue reasonably and fairly.
Supporting your claims with sufficient *evidence*	Use firsthand observations; examples from personal experience; results of surveys and interviews; graphs, charts, and visuals; and statistics, facts, and quotations from your reading.

In an article titled "Active and Passive Euthanasia," James Rachels claims that active euthanasia may be defensible for patients with incurable and painful diseases. The following paragraphs from that article illustrate the key features of argument.

The distinction between active and passive euthanasia is thought to be crucial for medical ethics. The idea is that it is permissible, at least in some cases, to withhold treatment and allow a patient to die, but it is never permissible to take any direct action designed to kill the patient. This doctrine seems to be accepted by most doctors. . . . *[Opposing position]*

However, a strong case can be made against this doctrine. *[Claim]* In what follows I will set out some of the relevant arguments, and urge doctors to reconsider their views on this matter. *[Audience]*

To begin with a familiar type of situation, a patient who is dying of incurable cancer of the throat is in terrible pain, which can no longer be satisfactorily alleviated. *[Argument for claim]* He is certain to die within a few days, even if present treatment is continued, but he does not want to go on living for those days, since the pain is unbearable. So he asks the doctor for an end to it, and his family joins in the request. *[Example]*

Suppose the doctor agrees to withhold treatment, as the conventional doctrine says he may. *[Example]* The justification for his doing so is that the patient is in terrible agony, and since he is going to die anyway, it would be wrong to prolong his suffering needlessly. But now notice this. If one simply withholds treatment, it may take the patient longer to die, and so he may suffer more than he would if more direct action were taken and a lethal injection given. This fact provides strong reason for thinking that, once the initial decision not to prolong his agony has been made, active *[Argument against opposition]*

> euthanasia is actually preferable to passive euthanasia, rather than the reverse. To say otherwise is to endorse the option that leads to more suffering rather than less, and is contrary to the humanitarian impulse that prompts the decision not to prolong his life in the first place.

CLAIMS FOR WRITTEN ARGUMENT

10.1
Use techniques for developing a claim

The thesis of your argument is a *debatable claim*. Opinions on both sides of the issue must have some merit. Claims for a written argument usually fall into one of four categories: claims of fact, claims about cause and effect, claims about value, and claims about solutions and policies. A claim may occasionally fall into several categories or may even overlap categories.

Claims of Fact or Definition

Watch the Video on Types of Claims

These claims are about facts that are not easily determined or about definitions that are debatable. If I claim that a Lhasa apso was an ancient Chinese ruler, you can check a dictionary and find out that I am wrong. A Lhasa apso is, in fact, a small Tibetan dog. There is no argument. But people do disagree about some supposed "facts": Are polygraph tests accurate? Do grades measure achievement? People also disagree about definitions: Gender discrimination exists in the marketplace, but is it "serious"? What is discrimination, anyway? And what constitutes "serious" discrimination?

In "*American Gothic,* Pitchfork Perfect," a review of Grant Wood's famous painting, Paul Richard opens with a claim of fact and definition (the complete essay appears in Chapter 8). His claim is that "American Gothic" is an American emblem or icon. Although reviews typically contain claims of value, Richard begins his essay with a claim of fact or definition, arguing that the painting is a visual manifestation of the American dream.

> Is "American Gothic" America's best-known painting? Certainly it's one of them. Grant Wood's dual portrait—with its churchy evocations, its stiffness and its pitchfork—pierced us long ago, and got stuck into our minds. Now, finally, it's here.
>
> "American Gothic," which hasn't been in Washington in 40 years, goes on view today at the Renwick Gallery of the Smithsonian American Art Museum. By all means, take it in—although, of course, you have already.
>
> It should have gone all fuzzy—it's been parodied so often, and parsed so many ways—but the 1930 canvas at the Renwick is as sharp as ever. Its details are finer than its travesties suggest, its image more absorbing. . . .

> The picture with a pitchfork is an American unforgettable. Few paintings, very few, have its recognizability. Maybe Whistler's mother. Maybe Warhol's soup can. Maybe Rockwell's Thanksgiving turkey. They're national emblems, all of them, visual manifestations of the American dream.

Claims About Cause and Effect

- Testing in the schools improves the quality of education.
- Capital punishment does not deter violent crime.

Unlike the claim that grades affect admission to college—which few people would deny—the above claims about cause and effect are debatable. Do tests ultimately improve students' education, or do they just make students better test-takers? The deterrent effect of capital punishment is still an arguable proposition, with reasonable arguments on both sides.

In a selection from her book *The Plug-In Drug: Television, Children, and the Family,* Marie Winn argues that television has a negative effect on family life. In her opening paragraphs she sets forth both sides of the controversy and then argues that the overall effect is negative.

> Television's contribution to family life has been an equivocal one. For while it has, indeed, kept the members of the family from dispersing, it has not served to bring them *together*. By its domination of the time families spend together, it destroys the special quality that depends to a great extent on what a family does, what special rituals, games, recurrent jokes, familiar songs, and shared activities it accumulates.
>
> "Like the sorcerer of old," writes Urie Bronfenbrenner, "the television set casts its magic spell, freezing speech and action, turning the living into silent statues so long as the enchantment lasts. The primary danger of the television screen lies not so much in the behavior it produces—although there is danger there—as in the behavior it prevents: the talks, the games, the family festivities and arguments through which much of the child's learning takes place and through which his character is formed. Turning on the television set can turn off the process that transforms children into people."

Claims About Value

- Boxing is a dehumanizing sport.
- Internet pornography degrades children's sense of human dignity.

Claims about value typically lead to evaluative essays. All the strategies discussed in Chapter 8 apply here, with the additional requirement that you must anticipate and respond to alternative or opposing arguments. The essay that claims that boxing is dehumanizing must respond to the argument that boxing is merely another form of competition that promotes athletic excellence. The claim that pornography degrades children's sense of dignity must respond to the claim that restricting free speech on the Internet would cause greater harm.

In "College Is a Waste of Time and Money," teacher and journalist Caroline Bird argues that many students go to college simply because it is the "thing to do." For those students, Bird claims, college is not a good idea.

> Nowadays, says one sociologist, you don't have to have a reason for going to college; it's an institution. His definition of an institution is an arrangement everyone accepts without question; the burden of proof is not on why you go, but why anyone thinks there might be a reason for not going. The implication is that an 18-year-old . . . should listen to those who know best and go to college.
>
> I don't agree. I believe that college has to be judged not on what other people think is good for students, but on how good it feels to the students themselves.
>
> I believe that people have an inside view of what's good for them. If a child doesn't want to go to school some morning, better let him stay at home, at least until you find out why. Maybe he knows something you don't. It's the same with college. If high-school graduates don't want to go, or if they don't want to go right away, they may perceive more clearly than their elders that college is not for them.

Claims About Solutions or Policies

- Pornography on the Internet should be censored.
- Both texting and cell phone use while driving should be against the law.

Claims about solutions or policies sometimes occur *along with* claims of fact or definition, cause and effect, or value. Because grades do not measure achievement (argue that this is a fact), they should be abolished (argue for this policy). Boxing is a dehumanizing sport (argue this claim of value); therefore, boxing should be banned (argue for this solution). Claims about solutions or policies involve all the strategies used for problem solving (see Chapter 9), but with special emphasis on countering opposing arguments: "Although advocates of freedom of speech suggest that we cannot suppress pornography on the Internet, in fact, we already have self-monitoring devices in other media that could help reduce pornography on the Internet."

In *When Society Becomes an Addict,* psychotherapist Anne Wilson Schaef argues that our society has become an "Addictive System" that shares many characteristics with alcoholism and other addictions. Advertising becomes addictive, causing us to behave dishonestly; the social pressure to be "nice" can become addictive, causing us to lie to ourselves. Schaef argues that the solution for our social addictions begins when we face the reality of our dependency.

> We cannot recover from an addiction unless we first admit that we have it. Naming our reality is essential to recovery. Unless we admit that we are indeed functioning in an addictive process in an Addictive System, we shall never have the option of recovery. Once we name something, we own it. . . . Remember, to name the system as addict is not to condemn it: It is to offer it the possibility of recovery.
>
> Paradoxically, the only way to reclaim our personal power is by admitting our powerlessness. The first part of Step One of the AA [Alcoholics Anonymous] Twelve-Step Program reads, "We admitted we were powerless over alcohol." It is important to recognize that admitting to powerlessness over an addiction is not the same as admitting powerlessness as a person. In fact, it can be very powerful to recognize the futility of the illusion of control.

APPEALS FOR WRITTEN ARGUMENT

10.2 Use rhetorical appeals in argument

To support their claims and respond to opposing arguments, writers use *appeals* to the audience. Argument uses three important types of appeals: to *reason* (logic and evidence support the claim), to *character* (the writer's good character itself supports the claim), and to *emotion* (the writer's expression of feelings about the issue may support the claim). Effective arguments will emphasize the appeal to reason but may also appeal to character or emotion.

Appeal to Reason

An appeal to reason depends most frequently on *inductive logic,* which is sometimes called the *scientific method.* Inductive logic draws a general conclusion from personal observation or experience, specific facts, reports, statistics, testimony of authorities, and other data.

Watch the Video on Appeals to Reason

Inductive Logic In inductive logic, a reasonable conclusion is based on a *sufficient* quantity of accurate and reliable evidence that is selected in a *random* manner to reduce human bias or to take into account variation in the sample. The definition of *sufficient* varies, but generally the number must be large enough to convince your audience that your sample fairly represents the whole subject.

> "Mere knowledge of the truth will not give you the art of persuasion."
>
> —Plato, *Phaedrus*

Let's take an example to illustrate inductive reasoning. Suppose you ask a student, one of fifty in a Psychology I class, a question of value: "Is Professor X a good teacher?" If this student says, "Professor X is the worst teacher I've ever had!" what conclusion can you draw? If you avoid taking the class based on a sample of one, you may miss an excellent class. So you decide to gather a *sufficient sample* by polling twenty of the fifty students in the class. But which twenty do you interview? If you ask the first student for a list of students, you may receive the names of twenty other students who also hate the professor. To reduce human or accidental bias, then, you choose a random method for collecting your evidence: As the students leave the class, you give a questionnaire to two out of every five students. If they all fill out the questionnaires, you probably have a *sufficient* and *random* sample.

Finally, if the responses to your questionnaire show that fifteen out of twenty students rate Professor X as an excellent teacher, what *valid conclusion* should you draw? You should not say, categorically, "X is an excellent teacher." Your conclusion must be restricted by your evidence and the method of gathering it: "Seventy-five percent of the students polled in Psychology I believe that Professor X is an excellent teacher."

Claim	Professor X is an excellent psychology teacher
Reason #1:	Professor X is an excellent teacher because she gives stimulating lectures that students rarely miss. ***Evidence:*** Sixty percent of the students polled said that they rarely missed a lecture.
Reason #2:	Professor X is an excellent teacher because she gives tests that encourage learning rather than sheer memorization. ***Evidence:*** Seventy percent of the students polled said that Professor X's essay tests required thinking and learning rather than memorization.

Most arguments use a shorthand version of the inductive method of reasoning. A writer makes a claim and then supports it with *reasons* and representative *examples* or *data*.

Appeal to Character

Watch the **Video** on Appeals to Character

An appeal based on your good character as a writer can also be important in argument. (The appeal to character is frequently called the *ethical appeal* because readers make a value judgment about the writer's character.) In a written argument, you show your audience—through your reasonable persona, voice, and tone—that you are a person who abides by moral standards that your audience shares: You have a good reputation, you are honest and trustworthy, and you argue "fairly."

A person's reputation often affects how we react to a claim, but *the argument itself* should also establish the writer's trustworthiness. You don't have to be a Mahatma Gandhi or a Mother Teresa to generate a strong ethical appeal for your claim. Even if your readers have never heard your name before, they will feel confident about your character if you are knowledgeable about your subject, present opposing arguments fairly, and support your own claim with sufficient, reliable evidence.

At the most basic level, your interest in the topic and willingness to work hard can improve your ethical appeal. Readers can sense when a writer cares about his or her subject, when a writer knows something about the topic, about the rhetorical or cultural context, and about the various viewpoints on a topic. Show your readers that you care about the subject, and they will find your arguments more convincing. Show you care by

- using sufficient details and specific, vivid examples.
- including any relevant personal experience you have on the topic.
- including other people's ideas and points of view and by responding to their views with fairness and tact.
- organizing your essay so your main points are easy to find and transitions between ideas are clear and logical.
- revising and proofreading your essay.

Readers know when writers care about their subjects, and they are more willing to listen to new ideas when the writer has worked hard and is personally invested in the topic.

Appeal to Emotion

Appeals to emotion can be tricky because, as we have seen, when emotions come in through the door, reasonableness may fly out the window. Argument emphasizes reason, not emotion. Emotional appeals designed to *deceive* or *frighten* people or to *misrepresent* the virtues of a person, place, or object have no place in rational argument. But emotional appeals that illustrate a truth or movingly depict a reality are legitimate and effective means of convincing readers.

Watch the **Video** on Appeals to Emotion

Combined Appeals

Appeals may be used in combination. Writers may appeal to reason and, at the same time, establish trustworthy characters and use legitimate emotional appeals. The following excerpt from Martin Luther King, Jr.'s *Letter from Birmingham Jail* illustrates all three appeals. (See Chapter 4 for an extended analysis of King's use of rhetorical appeals.) He appeals to reason, arguing that, historically, civil rights reforms are rarely made without political pressure. He establishes his integrity and good character by treating the opposition (in this case, the Birmingham clergy) with respect and by showing moderation and restraint. Finally, he uses emotional appeals, describing his six-year-old daughter in tears and recalling his own humiliation at being refused a place to sleep. King uses these emotional appeals legitimately; he is not misrepresenting reality or deceiving his readers.

Appeals to character and reason

One of the basic points in [the statement by the Birmingham clergy] is that the action that I and my associates have taken in Birmingham is untimely. Some have asked: "Why didn't you give the new city administration time to act?" The only answer that I can give to this query is that the new Birmingham administration must be prodded about as much as the outgoing one, before it will act. We are sadly mistaken if we feel that the election of Albert Boutwell as mayor will bring the millennium to Birmingham. While Mr. Boutwell is a much more gentle person than Mr. Connor, they are both segregationists, dedicated to the maintenance of the status quo. I have hoped that Mr. Boutwell will be reasonable enough to see the futility of massive resistance to desegregation. But he will not see this without pressure from devotees of civil rights. My friends, I must say to you that we have not made a single gain in civil rights without determined legal and nonviolent pressure. Lamentably, it is an historical fact that privileged groups seldom give up their privileges voluntarily. Individuals may see the moral light and voluntarily give up their unjust posture; but, as Reinhold Niebuhr has reminded us, groups tend to be more immoral than individuals.

Appeal to reason

Evidence

Appeals to character and reason

We know through painful experience that freedom is never voluntarily given by the oppressor; it must be demanded by the oppressed. Frankly, I have yet to engage in a direct-action campaign that was "well timed" in the view of those who have not suffered unduly from the disease of segregation. For years now I have heard the word "Wait!" It rings in the ear of every Negro with piercing familiarity. This "Wait" has almost always meant "Never." We must come to see, with one of our distinguished jurists, that "justice too long delayed is justice denied."

Appeal to emotion

We have waited for more than 340 years for our constitutional and God-given rights. . . . Perhaps it is easy for those who have never felt the stinging darts of segregation to say, "Wait." But when you have seen vicious mobs lynch your mothers and fathers at will and drown your sisters and brothers at whim; when you have seen hate-filled policemen curse, kick, and even kill your black brothers and sisters; when you see the vast majority of your twenty million Negro brothers smothering in an airtight cage of poverty in the midst of an affluent society; when you suddenly find your tongue twisted and your speech stammering as you seek to explain to your six-year-old daughter why she can't go to the public amusement park that has just been advertised on television, and

Appeal to emotion

see tears welling up in her eyes when she is told that Funtown is closed to colored children . . . when you take a cross-country drive and find it necessary to sleep night after night in the uncomfortable corners of your automobile because no motel will accept you; when you are humiliated day in and day out by nagging signs reading "white" and "colored"; when your first name becomes "nigger," your middle name becomes "boy" (however old you are) and your last name becomes "John" . . . —then you will understand why we find it difficult to wait. There comes a time when the cup of endurance runs over, and men are no longer willing to be plunged into the abyss of despair. I hope, sirs, you can understand our legitimate and unavoidable impatience.

Appeal to emotion

Appeals to character and reason

ROGERIAN ARGUMENT

10.3
Use techniques for Rogerian argument

Traditional argument assumes that people are most readily convinced or persuaded by a confrontational "debate" on the issue. The argument becomes a kind of struggle or "war" as the writer attempts to "defeat" the arguments of the opposition. The purpose of a traditional argument is thus to convince an undecided audience that the writer has "won a fight" and emerged "victorious" over the opposition.

In fact, there are many situations in which a less confrontational and adversarial approach is more effective. Particularly when the issues are highly charged or when the audience is the opposition, writers may more effectively use negotiation rather than confrontation. *Rogerian argument*—named after psychologist Carl Rogers—is a kind of negotiated argument where understanding and compromise replace the traditional, adversarial approach. Rogerian, or *nonthreatening,* argument opens the lines of communication by reducing conflict. When people's beliefs are attacked, they instinctively become defensive and strike back. As a result, the argument becomes polarized: The writer argues for a claim, the reader digs in to defend his or her position, and no one budges.

To avoid this polarization, Rogerian arguments work toward a compromise. As Rogers says, "This procedure gradually achieves a mutual communication. Mutual communication tends to be pointed toward solving a problem rather than toward attacking a person or group." Rogerian argument, then, imitates not a courtroom debate but the mutual communication that may take place between two people. Whereas traditional argument intends to change the actions or the beliefs of the opposition, Rogerian argument works toward changes *in both sides* as a means of establishing common ground and reaching a solution.

Rogerian argument is appropriate in a variety of sensitive or highly controversial situations. You may want to choose Rogerian argument if you are an employer requesting union members to accept a pay cut to help the company avoid bankruptcy. Similarly, if you argue to husbands that they should assume responsibility for half the housework, or if you argue to Anglo-Americans that Spanish language and culture should play a larger role in public education, you may want to use a Rogerian strategy. By showing that you empathize with the opposition's position and are willing to compromise, you create a climate for mutual communication.

Rogerian argument makes a claim, considers the opposition, and presents evidence to support the claim, but in addition, it avoids threatening or adversarial language and promotes mutual communication and learning. A Rogerian argument uses the following strategies.

- **Avoiding *a confrontational stance.*** Confrontation threatens your audience and increases their defensiveness. Threat hinders communication.
- **Presenting your *character* as someone who understands and can empathize with the opposition.** Show that you understand by restating the opposing position accurately.
- **Establishing *common ground* with the opposition.** Indicate the beliefs and values that you share.
- **Being willing *to change your views.*** Show where your position is not reasonable and could be modified.
- **Directing your argument toward *a compromise or workable solution.***

Note: An argument does not have to be either entirely adversarial or entirely Rogerian. You may use Rogerian techniques for the most sensitive points in an argument that is otherwise traditional or confrontational.

In his essay "Animal Rights Versus Human Health," biology professor Albert Rosenfeld illustrates several features of Rogerian argument. Rosenfeld argues that animals should be used for medical experiments, but he is aware that the issues are emotional and that his audience is likely to be antagonistic. Rosenfeld avoids threatening language, represents the opposition fairly, grants that he is guilty of *speciesism,* and says that he sympathizes with the demand to look for alternatives. He indicates that his position is flexible and grants that there is some room for compromise, but he is firm in his position that some animal experimentation is necessary for advancements in medicine.

States opposing position fairly and sympathetically

> It is fair to say that millions of animals—probably more rats and mice than any other species—are subjected to experiments that cause them pain, discomfort, and distress, sometimes lots of it over long periods of time. . . . All new forms of medication or surgery are tried out on animals first. Every new substance that is released into the environment, or put on the market, is tested on animals. . . .

In 1975, Australian philosopher Peter Singer wrote his influential book called *Animal Liberation,* in which he accuses us all of "speciesism"—as reprehensible, to him, as racism or sexism. He freely describes the "pain and suffering" inflicted in the "tyranny of human over nonhuman animals" and sharply challenges our biblical license to exercise "dominion over the fish of the sea, and over the fowl of the air, and over every living thing that moveth upon the Earth."

States opposing position fairly

Well, certainly we are guilty of speciesism. We do act as if we had dominion over other living creatures. But domination also entails some custodial responsibility. And the questions continue to be raised: Do we have the right to abuse animals? To eat them? . . . To keep them imprisoned in zoos—or, for that matter, in our households? Especially to do experiments on these creatures who can't fight back?

Acknowledges common ground

Sympathetic to opposing position

Hardly any advance in either human or veterinary medicine—cure, vaccine, operation, drug, therapy—has come about without experiments on animals. . . . I certainly sympathize with the demand that we look for ways to get the information we want without using animals. Most investigators are delighted when they can get their data by means of tissue cultures or computer simulations. But as we look for alternative ways to get information, do we meanwhile just do without?

Suggests compromise position

THE TOULMIN METHOD OF ARGUMENT

10.4
Use techniques for Toulmin argument

In *The Uses of Argument* (1958), British philosopher Stephen Toulmin identified six concepts that can be helpful as we analyze the logic of an argument.

- **Data:** The evidence gathered to support a particular claim.
- **Claim:** The overall thesis the writer hopes to prove. This thesis may be a claim of fact or definition, of cause and effect, of value, or of policy.
- **Warrant:** The statement that explains why or how the data support the writer's claim.
- **Backing:** The additional logic or reasoning that, when necessary, supports the warrant.
- **Qualifier:** The short phrases that limit the scope of the claim, such as "typically," "usually," or "on the whole."
- **Exceptions:** Those particular situations in which the writer does not or would not insist on the claim.

Example of a Toulmin Analysis

We can illustrate each of these six concepts using Cathleen A. Cleaver's argument against Internet pornography in her essay, "The Internet: A Clear and

Present Danger?" that appears later in this chapter. The relationship of the data, warrant, and claim are shown here.

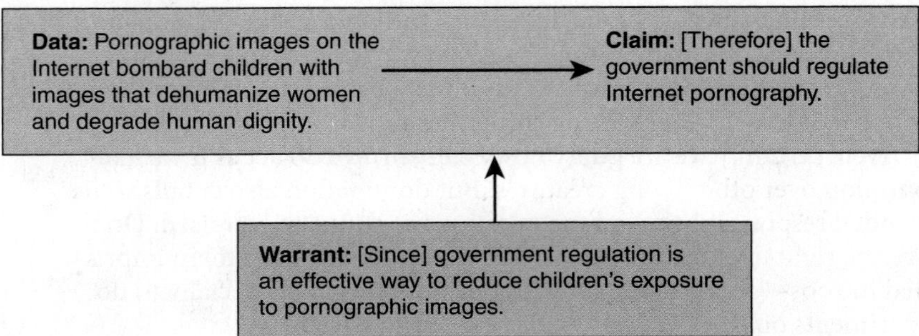

- **Backing:** Government regulation already exists in print, radio, and television media, so it should be extended to the Internet.
- **Qualifier:** *In most cases,* the government should regulate pornography on the Internet. (Cleaver does not use a qualifier for her claim; this is a qualifier she might use.)
- **Exceptions:** Government regulations must protect children, but *where children are not involved, regulation may not be as urgent.* (Cleaver implies this exception, since she focuses her argument only on pornography's effect on children.)

Using the Toulmin Model

Applying the Toulmin model of argument to written texts can help us as readers and writers if we follow a few guidelines. First, the Toulmin model is especially helpful as we critically read texts for their logical strengths and weaknesses. As we become better critical readers, we are likely to make our own arguments more logical and thus more persuasive. Second, as we critically read texts, not all of us find the same warrant statements because there can be several ways of explaining a logical connection between the data and the stated claim. Third, applying the Toulmin model and using warrants, backing, qualifiers, and exceptions becomes more important when our readers are likely to disagree with the claim.

Just as Rogerian argument tries to reduce conflict in adversarial situations through mutual communication and a strong appeal to character, the Toulmin model helps communicate in adversarial contexts by being especially reasonable and logical. If our readers already agree that pornography on the Internet is a bad thing, we need to give only a few examples and go straight to our claim. But if readers have a strong belief in free speech on the Internet, we need to qualify our claim and make our warrants—the connections between the data and the claim—as explicit and logical as possible. We may also need to state backing for the warrant and note the exceptions where we don't want to press

> "A society which is clamoring for choice [is] filled with many articulate groups, each arguing its own brand of salvation."
>
> —Margaret Mead, Anthropologist

our case. The more antagonistic our readers are, the more we need to be as logical as possible. The Toulmin model is just one approach that can help bolster the logic of our argument.

WARMING UP: Journal Exercises

The following exercises ask you to practice arguing. Read all of the exercises and then write on three that interest you. If another idea occurs to you, write about it.

1. From the list of "should" statements, choose one that relates to your experience and freewrite for ten minutes. When you finish your freewriting, state a claim and list arguments on both sides of the issue.
   - Handguns should not be permitted on college campuses.
   - Using a cell phone or texting while driving should be outlawed.
   - Bicyclists should be subject to regular traffic laws, including DWI.
   - High-quality child care should be available to all working parents at employer's expense.
   - NCAA football should have playoffs.
   - Punishments for plagiarism in college courses need to be more strict.
   - Organic foods need to meet a single, national standard.
   - Every adult citizen in the United States should be required to purchase health insurance.
2. Controversial subjects depend as much on the audience as they do on the issue itself. Make a short list of your everyday activities: eating, reading, socializing, discussing ideas. For one of these activities, imagine people who might find what you do immoral, illogical, unjust, or unhealthy. What claim might they make about your activity? What reasons or evidence might they use to argue that your activity should be abolished, outlawed, or changed? Write for five minutes arguing *their* point of view.
3. **Writing Across the Curriculum.** Grades are important, but in some courses they get in the way of learning. Choose a course that you have taken and write an open letter to the school administration, arguing for credit/no-credit grading in that course. Assume that you intend to submit your letter to the campus newspaper.
4. Arguments for academic or public audiences should focus on a *debatable* claim—that is, a claim about which knowledgeable people might disagree. Sometimes, however, even the notion of what constitutes a "debatable claim" is debated. Read and analyze the Doonesbury cartoon reprinted on the next page. What controversies does the cartoon suggest are not really controversies? How does Garry Trudeau use irony to make his point?

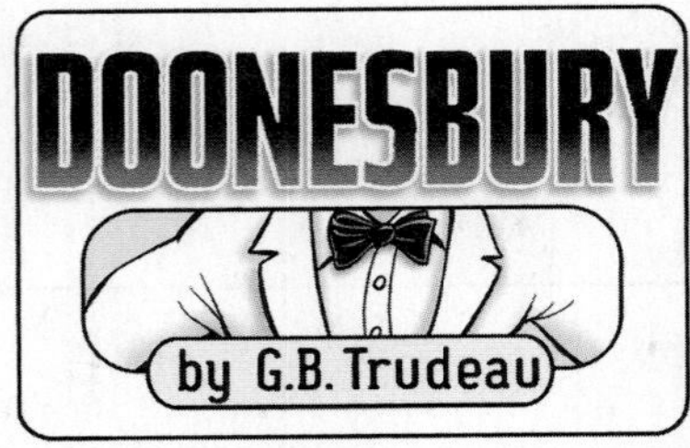

Professional Writing

The Internet: A Clear and Present Danger?

Cathleen A. Cleaver

Cathleen Cleaver has published extensively on issues relating to children and the Internet, in newspapers and magazines such as *USA Today, Newsday,* and the *Congressional Quarterly Researcher.* The following essay was originally a speech given at Boston University as part of a College of Communication Great Debate. In this speech, she argues that some industry and government regulation of the Internet is necessary.

- Someone breaks through your firewall and steals proprietary information from your computer systems. You find out and contact a lawyer who says, "Man, you shouldn't have had your stuff online." The thief becomes a millionaire using your ideas, and you go broke, if laws against copyright violation don't protect material on the Internet. 1

- You visit the Antiques Anonymous Web site and decide to pay their hefty subscription fee for a year's worth of exclusive estate sale previews in their private online monthly magazine. They never deliver and, in fact, never intended to—they don't even have a magazine. You have no recourse, if laws against fraud don't apply to online transactions. 2
- Bob Guccione decides to branch out into the lucrative child porn market and creates a Teen Hustler Web site featuring nude adolescents and preteens. You find out and complain, but nothing can be done, if child pornography distribution laws don't apply to computer transmissions. 3
- A major computer software vendor who dominates the market develops his popular office software so that it works only with his browser. You're a small browser manufacturer who is completely squeezed out of the market, but you have to find a new line of work, if antitrust laws don't apply online. 4
- Finally, a pedophile e-mails your son, misrepresenting himself as a twelve-year-old named Jenny. They develop an online relationship and one day arrange to meet after school, where he intends to rape your son. Thankfully, you learn in advance about the meeting and go there yourself, where you find a forty-year-old man instead of Jenny. You flee to the police, who'll tell you there's nothing they can do, if child-stalking laws don't apply to the Internet. 5

The awesome advances in interactive telecommunication that we've witnessed in just the last few years have changed the way in which many Americans communicate and interact. No one can doubt that the Internet is a technological revolution of enormous proportion, with outstanding possibilities for human advancement. 6

As lead speaker for the affirmative, I'm asked to argue that the Internet poses a "clear and present danger," but the Internet, as a whole, isn't dangerous. In fact, it continues to be a positive and highly beneficial tool, which will undoubtedly improve education, information exchange, and commerce in years to come. In other words, the Internet will enrich many aspects of our daily life. Thus, instead of defending this rather apocalyptic view of the Internet, I'll attempt to explain why some industry and government regulation of certain aspects of the Internet is necessary—or, stated another way, why people who use the Internet should not be exempt from many of the laws and regulations that govern their conduct elsewhere. My opening illustrations were meant to give examples of some illegal conduct which should not become legal simply because someone uses the Internet. In looking at whether Internet regulation is a good idea, I believe we should consider whether regulation is in the public interest. In order to do that, we have to ask the question: 7

Who is the public? More specifically, does the "public" whose interests we care about tonight include children?

CHILDREN AND THE INTERNET

Dave Barry describes the Internet as a "worldwide network of university, government, business, and private computer systems, run by a thirteen-year-old named Jason." This description draws a smile precisely because we acknowledge the highly advanced computer literacy of our children. Most children demonstrate computer proficiency that far surpasses that of their parents, and many parents know only what their children have taught them about the Internet, which gives new relevance to Wordsworth's insight: "The child is father of the man." In fact, one could go so far as to say that the Internet is as accessible to many children as it is inaccessible to many adults. This technological evolution is new in many ways, not the least of which is its accessibility to children, wholly independent of their parents. *8*

When considering what's in the public interest, we must consider the whole public, including children, as individual participants in this new medium. *9*

PORNOGRAPHY AND THE INTERNET

This new medium is unique in another way. It provides, through a single avenue, the full spectrum of pornographic depictions, from the more familiar convenience store fare to pornography of such violence and depravity that it surpasses the worst excesses of the normal human imagination. Sites displaying this material are easily accessible, making pornography far more freely available via the Internet than from any other communications medium in the United States. Pornography is the third largest sector of sales on the Internet, generating $1 billion annually. . . . *10*

There is little restriction of pornography-related activity in cyberspace. While there are some porn-related laws, the specter of those laws does not loom large in cyberspace. There's an implicit license there that exists nowhere else with regard to pornography—an environment where people are free to exploit others for profit and be virtually untroubled by legal deterrent. Indeed, if we consider cyberspace to be a little world of its own, it's the type of world for which groups like the ACLU have long fought but, so far, fought in vain. *11*

I believe it will not remain this way, but until it changes, we should take the opportunity to see what this world looks like, if for no other reason than to reassure ourselves that our decades-old decisions to control pornography were good ones. *12*

With a few clicks of the mouse, anyone, any child, can get graphic and often violent sexual images—the kind of stuff it used to be difficult to *13* find without exceptional effort and some significant personal risk. Anyone with a computer and a modem can set up public sites featuring the perversion of their choice, whether it's mutilation of female genitals, eroticized urination and defecation, bestiality, or sites featuring depictions of incest. These pictures can be sold for profit, they can be sent to harass others, or posted to shock people. Anyone can describe the fantasy rape and murder of a specific person and display it for all to read. Anyone can meet children in chat rooms or via e-mail and send them pornography and find out where they live. An adult who signs onto an AOL chat room as a thirteen-year-old girl is hit on thirty times within the first half hour.

All this can be done from the seclusion of the home, with the feeling of near anonymity and with the comfort of knowing that there's little risk of legal sanction. . . . 14

Beyond the troubling social aspects of unrestricted porn, we face the reality that children are accessing it and that predators are accessing children. We have got to start considering what kind of society we'll have when the next generation learns about human sexuality from what the Internet teaches. What does unrestricted Internet pornography teach children about relationships, about the equality of women? What does it teach little girls about themselves and their worth? 15

Opponents of restrictions are fond of saying that it's up to the parents to deal with the issue of children's exposure. Well, of course it is, but placing the burden solely on parents is illogical and ineffective. It's far easier for a distributor of pornography to control his material than it is for parents, who must, with the help of software, search for and find the pornographic sites, which change daily, and then attempt to block them. Any pornographer who wants to can easily subvert these efforts, and a recent Internet posting from a teenager wanting to know how to disable the filtering software on his computer received several effective answers. Moreover, it goes without saying that the most sophisticated software can only be effective where it's installed, and children will have access to many computers that don't have filtering software, such as those in libraries, schools, and at neighbors' houses. 16

INTERNET TRANSACTIONS SHOULD NOT BE EXEMPT

Opponents of legal restrictions often argue simply that the laws just cannot apply in this new medium, but the argument that old laws can't apply to changing technology just doesn't hold. We saw this argument last in the early '80s with the advent of the videotape. Then, certain groups tried to argue that, since you can't view videotapes without a VCR, you can't make the sale of child porn videos illegal, because, after all, they're just plastic boxes with magnetic tape inside. Technological change mandates legal change only insofar as it affects the justification for a law. It just doesn't make sense that the government may take steps to restrict 17 illegal material in *every* medium—video, television, radio, the private telephone, *and* print—but that it may do nothing where people distribute the material by the Internet. While old laws might need redefinition, the old principles generally stand firm.

The question of enforcement usually is raised here, and it often comes in the form of: "How are you going to stop people from doing it?" Well, no law stops people from doing things—a red light at an intersection doesn't force you to stop but tells you that you should stop and that there could be legal consequences if you don't. Not everyone who runs a red light is caught, but that doesn't mean the law is futile. The same concept holds true for Internet laws. Government efforts to temper harmful conduct online will never be perfect, but that doesn't mean they shouldn't undertake the effort at all. *18*

There's clearly a role for industry to play here. Search engines don't have to run ads for porn sites or prioritize search results to highlight porn. One new search engine even has sex as the default search term. Internet service providers can do something about unsolicited e-mail with hotlinks to porn, and they can and should carefully monitor any chat rooms designed for kids. *19*

Some charge that industry standards or regulations that restrict explicit pornography will hinder the development of Internet technology. But that is to say that its advancement depends upon unrestricted exhibition of this material, and this cannot be true. The Internet does not belong to pornographers, and it's clearly in the public interest to see that they don't usurp this great new technology. We don't live in a perfect society, and the Internet is merely a reflection of the larger social community. Without some mitigating influences, the strong will exploit the weak, whether a Bill Gates or a child predator. *20*

CONCLUSION: TECHNOLOGY MUST SERVE MAN

To argue that the strength of the Internet is chaos or that our liberty depends upon chaos is to misunderstand not only the Internet but also the fundamental nature of our liberty. It's an illusion to claim social or moral neutrality in the application of technology, even if its development may be neutral. It can be a valuable resource only when placed at the service of humanity and when it promotes our integral development for the benefit of all. *21*

Guiding principles simply cannot be inferred from mere technical efficiency or from the usefulness accruing to some at the expense of others. Technology by its very nature requires unconditional respect for the fundamental interests of society. *22*

> Internet technology must be at the service of humanity and of our inalienable rights. It must respect the prerogatives of a civil society, among which is the protection of children. 23

Questions for Writing and Discussion

1. The rhetorical occasion for Cleaver's argument was a debate sponsored by the College of Communication at Boston University. In her essay, can you find evidence (word choice, vocabulary, sentence length, tone, use of evidence, use of appeals) that suggests that her original *genre* was a speech and that her *audience* was college students, college faculty, and members of the community? Cite evidence from the essay showing where Cleaver uses debate elements appropriate for this genre and makes appeals to this audience.
2. Cleaver states her case for government regulation of pornography on the Internet, but who is against regulation, and what are their arguments? What arguments opposing Internet regulation does Cleaver cite? (Are there other opposing arguments that Cleaver does not consider?) How well does Cleaver answer these opposing arguments?
3. Arguing essays make appeals to reason, to character, and to emotion. Find examples of each type of appeal in Cleaver's essay. Which type of appeal does she use most frequently? Which appeals are most or least effective? Does she rely too much on her emotional appeals (see paragraph 13, for example)? For her audience and her context (a debate), should she bolster her rational appeals with more evidence and statistics? Why or why not?
4. Imagine that you are at this debate on the Internet and that your side believes that there should be very little or no regulation of the Internet. What arguments might you make in response to Cleaver? Make a list of the possible pro–con arguments on this topic and explain which ones you will focus on as you respond to Cleaver.

MULTIGENRE CASEBOOK ON WEB 2.0

Contents

> "The way today's students will do science, politics, journalism, and business next year and a decade from now will be shaped by the skills they acquire in using social media and by the knowledge they gain of the important issues of privacy, identity, community, and the role of citizen media in democracy."
>
> —Howard Rheingold, Author of *Smart Mobs*

Contents *(continued)*

The texts in this casebook represent a snapshot of the ongoing conversation and debate about the uses and abuses of social media and the Internet. These texts raise many questions about how social media and the Internet are affecting our lives:

- Are social networking sites such as Facebook really bringing us closer to our friends?
- Is social media responsible for cyberbullying?
- What are the most effective responses to cyberbullying?
- Should speech on the Internet and social networking sites be censored?
- Is the information on Wikipedia reliable?
- Is the Internet changing how we read, reflect, or remember?

These texts are meant to open the conversation about contemporary Internet and social media sites, to start you thinking critically about your own online habits and the effects of Internet use on people throughout the world.

In addition to thinking critically about the arguments in each of the texts, analyze the texts rhetorically. Are the authors making claims of fact or definition, cause-and-effect, value, or policy? Does each document make an argument and consider alternative points of view? (Are any of these texts simply informative without making an argument?) What appeals—to reason, to character, or to emotion—do the authors make? Consider also how these writers construct or address their audience: Who do they think their reader is? What do they believe their readers already know or believe? What strategies do they think will convince or persuade their readers?

> "The popularity of Web 2.0 is evidence of a tide of credulity and misinformation that can only be countered by a culture of respect for authenticity and expertise in all scholarly, research, and educational endeavors."
>
> —Michael Gorman, "Web 2.0: The Sleep of Reason"

Finally, after you have read these texts, consider how the genre of the document—essay or article in a journal or magazine, blog on a Web site, visual, or graphic—affects the argument of the document. Do the visuals or graphics make appeals as strong—or stronger—than the written texts? If your own assignment is to create a multigenre document for a specific audience, or if you want to integrate visuals or graphs in your document, consider how each genre will contribute to your goal of convincing or persuading your audience.

Professional Writing

You Have No Friends

Farhad Manjoo

At 1:37 A.M. on Jan. 8, Mark Zuckerberg, the 24-year-old founder and CEO of Facebook, posted a message on the company's blog with news of a milestone: The site had just added its 150-millionth member. Facebook now has users on every continent, with half of them logging in at least once a day. "If Facebook were a country, it would be the eighth most populated in the world, just ahead of Japan, Russia and Nigeria," Zuckerberg wrote. This People's Republic of Facebook would also have a terrible population-growth problem. Like most communications networks, Facebook obeys classic network-effects laws: It gets better—more useful, more entertaining—as more people join it, which causes it to grow even faster still. It was just last August that Facebook hit 100 million users. Since then, an average of 374,000 people have signed up every day. At this rate, Facebook will grow to nearly 300 million people by this time next year. 1

If you're reading this article, there's a good chance you already belong to Facebook. There's a good chance everyone you know is on Facebook, too. Indeed, there's a good chance you're no longer reading this article because you just switched over to check Facebook. That's fine—this piece is not for you. Instead I'd like to address those readers who aren't on Facebook, especially those of you who've consciously decided to stay away. 2

Though your ranks dwindle daily, there are many of you. This is understandable—any social movement that becomes so popular so fast engenders skepticism. A year ago, the *New York Observer* interviewed a half-dozen or so disdainful Facebook holdouts. "I don't see how having hundreds or thousands of 'friends' is leading to any kind of substantive friendships," said Cary Goldstein, the director of publicity at Twelve Publishers. "The whole thing seems so weird to me. Now you really have to turn off your computer and just go out to live real life and make real connections with people that way. I don't think it's healthy. . . ." 3

Friends—can I call you friends?—it's time to drop the attitude: There is no longer any good reason to avoid Facebook. The site has crossed a threshold—it is now so widely trafficked that it's fast becoming a routine aide to social interaction, like e-mail and antiperspirant. It's only the most recent of many new technologies that have crossed over this stage. For a long while—from about the late '80s to the late-middle '90s, *Wall Street* to *Jerry Maguire*—carrying a mobile phone seemed like a haughty affectation. But as more people got phones, they became more useful for everyone—and then one day enough people had cell phones that everyone began to assume that you did, too. Your friends stopped prearranging where they 4 would meet up on Saturday night because it was assumed that everyone would call from wherever they were to find out what was going on. From that moment on, it became an affectation *not* to carry a mobile phone; they'd grown so deeply entwined with modern life that the only reason to be without one was to make a statement by abstaining. Facebook is now at that same point—whether or not you intend it, you're saying something by staying away.

I use Facebook every day, and not always to waste time. Most of my extended family lives in South Africa, and though I speak to them occasionally on the phone, Facebook gives me an astonishingly intimate look at their lives—I can see what they did yesterday, what they're doing tomorrow, and what they're doing right now, almost like there's no distance separating us. The same holds true for my job: I live on the West Coast, but I work in an industry centered on the East Coast; Facebook gives me the opportunity to connect with people—to "network," you might say—in a completely natural, unaggressive manner. More than a dozen times, I've contacted sources through Facebook—searching for them there is much easier than searching for a current e-mail or phone number. 5

In fact, Facebook helped me write this story. The other day I posted a status update asking my Facebook friends to put me in touch with people who've decided against joining. The holdouts I contacted this way weren't haughty—they were nice, reasonable people with entirely rational-sounding explanations for staying off the site. Among the main reasons people cited was that Facebook looked like it required too much work. Chad Retelle, a network systems administrator in Madison, Wis., said he'd seen how his wife—my friend Katie—had taken to the site. But at the same time, it had changed her: "Now she's obligated to spend time maintaining her Facebook page. She's got to check it every morning. I have no desire to do that." 6

Retelle and other Facebook holdouts also protested that the site presents numerous opportunities for awkwardness—there's the headache of managing which people to friend and which to forget, the fear that one of your friends might post something on your wall that will offend everyone else, the worry that someone will find something about you that you didn't mean to share. Naomi Harris, a magazine photographer in New York, says that, for all that trouble, Facebook seems to offer little in return. "Why?" she asks. "I'm on the computer enough as it is for work. I don't really want to be there for recreation purposes, too. I have no interests in someone from fifth grade contacting me and saying, 'Hey, I sat behind you in class—wanna chat?'" 7

Finally, I heard what must be the most universal concern about Facebook—*I don't want people knowing my business!* Kate Koppelman is a 23-year-old New Yorker who works in the fashion industry. She was on Facebook all through college, and she concedes that the site has many benefits. And yet, the whole thing creeped her out: "I had friends from 8 back home knowing what was going on with my friends from college—people they had never met—which was weird," she told me. "I found friends knowing things about what was on my 'wall' before I'd had a chance to see it—which was also weird." Koppelman quit Facebook last year. She still uses it by proxy—her roommates look people up for her when she's curious about them—but she says she'll never sign up again.

Yet of the many concerns about Facebook, Koppelman's is the most easily addressed. Last year, the site added a series of fine-grained privacy controls that let you choose which friends see what information about you. Your college friends can see one version of your profile, your high-school friends another, and your family yet another; if you want, you can let everyone see essentially nothing about you. 9

Retelle's worry that Facebook demands a lot of work is also somewhat misguided. It's true that some people spend a lot of time on it, but that's because they're having fun there; if you're not, you can simply log in once or twice a week just to accept or reject friends. Even doing nothing and waiting for others to friend you is enough: You're establishing a presence for other people to connect with you, which is the site's main purpose. 10

That brings us to Harris' argument: What's the social utility to Facebook—why should you join? Like with e-mail and cell phones, there are many, and as you begin to use it, you'll notice more and different situations in which it proves helpful. In general, Facebook is a lubricant of social connections. With so many people on it, it's now the best, fastest place online to find and connect with a specific person—think of it as a worldwide directory, or a Wikipedia of people. As a result, people now expect to find you on Facebook—whether they're contacting you for a job or scouting you out for a genius grant. 11

True, you might not want people to be able to follow your life—it's no great loss to you if your long-lost college frenemy can't find you. But what about your old fling, your new fling, your next employer, or that friend-of-a-friend you just met at a party who says he can give you some great tips on your golf swing? Sure, you can trade e-mail addresses or phone numbers, but in many circles Facebook is now the expected way to make these connections. By being on Facebook, you're facilitating such ties; without it, you're missing them and making life difficult for those who went looking for you there. 12

Skeptics often suggest that online social networks foster introverted, anti-social behavior—that we forge virtual connections at the expense of real-life connections. But only someone who's never used Facebook would make that argument. Nobody avoids meeting people in real life by escaping to the Web. In fact, the opposite seems true: Short, continuous, low-content updates about the particulars of your friends' lives—Bob has the flu, Barbara can't believe what just happened on *Mad Men*, Sally and Ned are no longer on speaking terms—deepen your bonds with them. . . . 13

...continued You Have No Friends, **Farhad Manjoo**

It's this benefit of Facebook that seems to hook people in the end: Their 14
friendships seem to demand signing up. Last year, Darcy Stockton, a fashion photographer in New York, held nothing back in describing her hatred of Facebook to the *Observer*. "If you have time to network through a site like that, you aren't working enough," she said. "I just don't have the *time* or the *ability* to keep up with yet another social networking site in my free time. I feel there's other things and real experiences I could be having in real life instead of wasting my free time on Facebook."

Stockton now has 250 Facebook friends. In an e-mail, she explained 15
that she'd decided to join the site when her friends migrated over from MySpace. She added, "Thank you for making me eat my words!"

Social Networking Gets Most Online Time

Americans spend nearly a quarter of their time online on social networking sites and blogs—up from 15.8 percent a year ago. That is far more than any other sector and also more time than is spent on e-mail and online games combined.

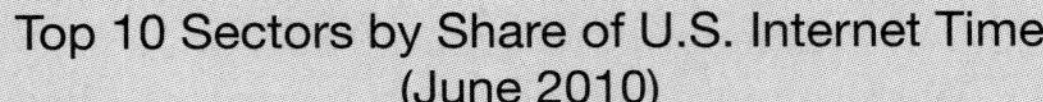

Top 10 Sectors by Share of U.S. Internet Time
(June 2010)

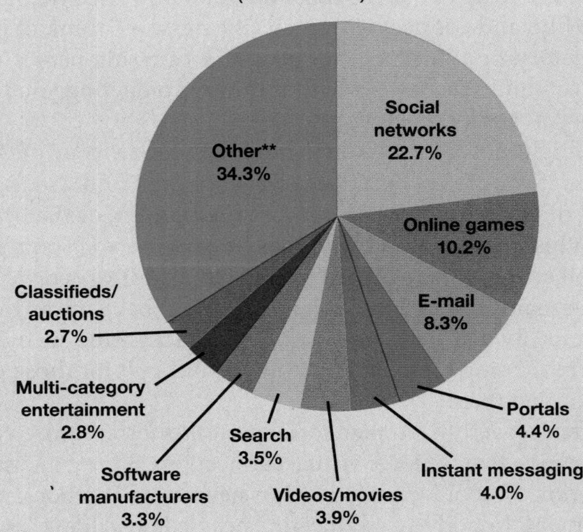

*Figures do not total 100 due to rounding

**74 remaining online categories visited from PCs/laptops

Source: "What Americans Do Online: Social Media and Games Dominate Activity," Nielsen, August 2010.

Professional Writing

. . . And Why I Hate It

Sarah Kliff

The site nurses my worst self-indulgent instincts. Does anyone really care that I love penguins?

I have no idea how many hours of my life I've wasted on Facebook. When I wake up each morning, with my laptop sitting on the edge of my futon, I check it. Before I've thought about brushing my teeth, I have already seen the photographs of my brother's new apartment in San Francisco and discovered the evidence of my friend's tumultuous breakup: she changed her relationship status from "In a Relationship" to "Single" to "It's Complicated," all while I was sleeping. As best I can figure, since joining the site in 2004 when I was a freshman at Washington University in St. Louis, I've been logging on a dozen times a day. When I should have been studying or working, I found myself instead doing tasks like flipping through 400 photos of myself online, debating whether I wanted the picture where I have food in my hair to be on display to the world. (I decided to leave it: while it's not the most attractive pose, I think it indicates that I am a laid-back, good-humored person.) 1

I spend an inordinate amount of time like this, worrying about what's in my online profile. When I graduated from college this May, I decided it was time for a Facebook makeover. Looking to present a more "professional" image, I stripped my profile of many of my collegiate interests—you'll no longer know from Facebook that I'm obsessed with penguins—and I purged my membership in questionable Facebook groups such as "Scotland? Sounds more like Hotland" (tamer than it sounds). I know I'm not the only one constantly revamping my cyber-image: according to my Facebook account, 109 of my friends have changed something over the past two days. One friend added "goofy dads" to her interests, and another let it be known that he "falls asleep easily" and "loses things all the time." 2

What is with all this time we've spent, thinking about ourselves and creating well-planned lists of our interests? Facebook is much worse than e-mail, cell phones, instant messaging and the other devices that keep me constantly connected. It nurses every self-indulgent urge I could possibly have. I hate that Facebook encourages me to home in on each of my idiosyncrasies—that I like running in Central Park, for example, or that my favorite forms of punctuation are the dash and semicolon—and broadcast them to a largely uninterested world. . . . The network is as much about obsessing over the dull details of my life as it as about connecting with others. 3

As a recent college graduate, with my friends scattered across the globe, I understand the communicative value of Facebook. Right now, 4

...continued . . . And Why I Hate It, **Sarah Kliff**

I have 469 “friends”—though I admit many of these virtual relationships are tenuous at best. Still, I would be hard-pressed to give up my four-year-long membership or leave Facebook out of my early morning routine. But who knows what I’m missing out on in the real world while sitting at my laptop, debating whether penguins or bagels are more respectable?

Professional Writing

Cyberbullying

Jennifer Holladay

Phoebe Prince is loved by her peers. At least, now she is. Hundreds of people have supported her on Facebook. Taylor Gosselin wrote, “Your story touched my heart.” Dori Fitzgerald Acevedo added, “I am so glad we are not letting this get swept under the carpet.” 1

“This” is what some might call bullicide—suicide by bullying. 2

Before Phoebe Prince hanged herself, she was a new student at South Hadley (MA) High School. She reportedly dared to date boys whom others thought should be off limits to her. 3

Girls at Phoebe’s school reportedly called her a “whore” and a “bitch,” viciously harassing her in person and on Facebook. At least one student gloated after Phoebe took her own life, “I don’t care that she’s dead.” 4

Phoebe’s tormentors have since been dubbed the “Mean Girls,” after the clique in the 2004 Tina Fey–scripted movie. And for the Mean Girls of South Hadley, the consequences of their purported actions have been severe. They are now maligned across the Internet, from postings on Facebook to the comment areas of news websites worldwide. 5

The Mean Girls, along with two male students, also face criminal charges for allegedly bullying Phoebe. Since then, it’s become clear that Phoebe’s reasons for taking her own life were complicated. She struggled with depression and had even attempted suicide once before. But the bullying she endured definitely had an impact. 6

NEW TERM, OLD CONCEPT

The word cyberbullying didn’t even exist a decade ago, yet the problem is pervasive today. Simply put, cyberbullying is the repeated use of technology to harass, humiliate, or threaten. When people take to the keyboard or cell phone and craft messages of hate or malice about a specific person, cyberbullying is emerging. And unlike traditional bullying, it comes with a wide audience. 7

"You can pass around a note to classmates making fun of a peer, and it stays in the room," said Sheri Bauman, director of the school counseling master's degree program at the University of Arizona. "But when you post that same note online, thousands can see it. The whole world becomes witness and is invited to participate." 8

Anywhere from one-third to one-half of youths have been targeted by cyberbullies. And those experiences produce damaging consequences—from a decline in academic performance to suicide. 9

"Our study of upwards of 2,000 middle school students revealed that cyberbullying victims were nearly twice as likely to attempt suicide compared with students not targeted with online abuse," said Sameer Hinduja, study co-author and founder of the Cyberbullying Research Center. "Cyberbullying clearly heightens instability and hopelessness in adolescents' minds." 10

Findings like these lend a sense of urgency to anti-cyberbullying efforts. Legally speaking, those efforts can be tricky for school administrators. The judiciary has long struggled to balance freedom of speech against the darker side of digital communication. 11

More and more though, courts and law enforcement send the message that cyberbullying will not be tolerated. For instance, in March 2010, California's Second Appellate District concluded that online threats against a student were not protected speech and allowed a civil lawsuit against the alleged perpetrators, their parents, and school officials to proceed. 12

The notion that schools must respond to behavior that takes place off campus and online may seem a tall order. But schools are coming to understand that bullies don't just attack in the cafeteria or on the playground. "Wherever kids go with their computers or phones, which is nearly everywhere, the bullies come with them," said Bauman. 13

A 2010 study by the Henry J. Kaiser Family Foundation found that technology access among children has skyrocketed since 1999. Today, 93% of children ages 8 to 18 have computers at home, 66% have cell phones, and 76% own another multimedia device, such as an iPod. 14

These tools give them access to a dizzying array of social media. Some, such as Twitter and Facebook, are well known among parents and teachers. Others, such as Formspring, fly well below the radar of most adults. Yet sites like Formspring can create the biggest headaches. Formspring offers its users total anonymity. That makes it at once a huge draw for curious teenagers and a nearly perfect medium for cyberbullies. 15

Is Cyberbullying Largely a Problem for Girls?

Conventional wisdom suggests that boys are more likely to bully in person and girls to bully online. But Sheri Bauman notes that "cyberbullying is a new area of inquiry, and it's just hard to draw definitive conclusions from the research that's currently available," she said.

What is clear is that cyberbullying, like traditional bullying, is about power. "Students attempt to gain social status through cyberbullying," said Bauman. Sameer Hinduja says that gaining social status often means tearing someone else down, and boys and girls often do that differently.

"Girls tend to target each other with labels that carry particular meanings for them," said Hinduja. Labels like "slut," "whore," and "bitch" are common within girl-to-girl cyberbullying. The main tactic of boy cyberbullies who attack other boys is to accuse them of being gay. "The amount of abuse boys encounter because of real or perceived sexual orientation is pronounced," Bauman said.

...continued Cyberbullying, **Jennifer Holladay**

RELIEVING THE DRAMA

The ostensible boundary between off-campus behavior and school life evaporated for Highline Academy, a K-8 charter in Denver, last spring when a conflict fueled by Facebook posts ultimately led to a physical altercation. In the wake of the incident, Highline officials spoke with students in meetings and issued a packet of information to parents and guardians about cyberbullying and Internet safety. Still, a new Facebook page soon appeared, with a growing stream of posts about a student involved in the altercation. 16

"As a community, we needed to step back from the incident and relieve some of the drama," principal Greg Gonzales said. He asked every parent to support a 48-hour moratorium on Facebook activity at home and to discuss the use of the social networking site with their children. 17

Gonzales and colleagues also placed personal phone calls to parents of students who had engaged in the online conversations. "It may be outside our jurisdiction to dictate what students do on their own time, but it was important to let parents know we'd discovered their child had engaged in cyberbullying or inappropriate conversations about the incident," Gonzales said. "Numerous parents came back to us and said, 'I had no idea'—no idea what their child was doing online, or even that they had a Facebook page." 18

A 2009 study from Common Sense Media found that parents nationally underestimate children's use of social networking sites and often are unaware of how they are used. Thirty-seven percent of students, for example, admitted they'd made fun of a peer online, but only 18% of parents thought their child would do so. 19

GETTING IN FRONT OF THE PROBLEMS

The Seattle Public School District took a proactive stance last year when it launched a pilot curriculum to prevent cyberbullying in junior high and middle schools. 20

Mike Donlin, senior program consultant who led the curriculum's development, says the district created its own resources rather than use off-the-shelf products, ensuring that the resources would be easy to use and integrate into existing curricula. "There also was the issue of cost," he said. "We believed we could create something great with far less expense." 21

Unlike many programs that address **cyberbullying** piecemeal—focusing only on Internet safety skills, for example—the Seattle curriculum attacked the entire problem by using the four most promising prevention practices: 22

- Debunking misperceptions about digital behavior,
- Building empathy and understanding,

- Teaching online safety skills, and
- Equipping young people with strategies to reject digital abuse in their lives.

The Seattle curriculum also recognizes the importance of parental engagement by offering take-home letters and activities. 23

Academically, the curriculum focuses on writing, which boosts student skills in a tested area, while allowing the program to discard common, ineffective practices. Instead of asking students to sign a pre-crafted pledge, for example, the curriculum prompts them to write personal contracts for themselves about their online behavior. 24

The curriculum also educates teachers about cyberbullying and introduces language they can share with students. "We couch lessons in a way that resonates for teachers, too," said Donlin. "So, we use the Golden Rule. We use the old-fashioned mantra 'don't kiss and tell' to address sexting." 25

Still, some information requires repeated explanation. Some might wonder, for example, why the curriculum prompts students to try to see things from the bully's perspective. "A student can be a victim, a bystander, and a bully in different moments," Donlin explained. "Maybe a child was bullied at school this morning, but gets online later and bullies back. Roles shift. Technology gives them tremendous freedom and power to reach out and touch in nearly every moment, for good or evil." 26

Learning to resist the urge to "bully back" is important, as is unlearning some common myths about being online. Kids often think they can be anonymous, or that what they do on the Internet is fleeting. Both ideas are mistaken. The Library of Congress, for example, is archiving all Twitter messages sent from March 2006 forward. Even the "mean tweets" will be immortalized for future generations. "Everything students do online reflects on them, permanently," says Donlin. 27

For teachers, a common stumbling block revolves around First Amendment protections and discomfort about corralling students' speech. Donlin believes that should not be a problem. "We have Second Amendment rights to possess weapons, but that doesn't mean we allow children to bring guns to school," he observed. "When it comes to cyberbullying, we're still talking about school safety." 28

Professional Writing

Bullying as True Drama

Danah Boyd and Alice Marwick

The suicide of Jamey Rodemeyer, the 14-year-old boy from western New York who killed himself last Sunday after being tormented by his classmates 1 for being gay, is appalling. His story is a classic case of bullying: he was aggressively and repeatedly victimized. Horrific episodes like this have sparked conversations about cyberbullying and created immense pressure on regulators and educators to do something, anything, to make it stop. Yet in the rush to find a solution, adults are failing to recognize how their conversations about bullying are often misaligned with youth narratives. Adults need to start paying attention to the language of youth if they want antibullying interventions to succeed.

Jamey recognized that he was being bullied and asked explicitly for help, but this is not always the case. Many teenagers who are bullied can't emotionally afford to identify as victims, and young people who bully others rarely see themselves as perpetrators. For a teenager to recognize herself or himself in the adult language of bullying carries social and psychological costs. It requires acknowledging oneself as either powerless or abusive. 2

In our research over a number of years, we have interviewed and observed teenagers across the United States. Given the public interest in cyberbullying, we asked young people about it, only to be continually rebuffed. Teenagers repeatedly told us that bullying was something that happened only in elementary or middle school. "There's no bullying at this school" was a regular refrain. 3

This didn't mesh with our observations, so we struggled to understand the disconnect. While teenagers denounced bullying, they—especially girls—would describe a host of interpersonal conflicts playing out in their lives as "drama." 4

At first, we thought drama was simply an umbrella term, referring to varying forms of bullying, joking around, minor skirmishes between friends, breakups and makeups, and gossip. We thought teenagers viewed bullying as a form of drama. But we realized the two are quite distinct. Drama was not a show for us, but rather a protective mechanism for them. 5

Teenagers say drama when they want to diminish the importance of something. Repeatedly, teenagers would refer to something as "just stupid drama," "something girls do," or "so high school." We learned that drama can be fun and entertaining; it can be serious or totally ridiculous; it can be a way to get attention or feel validated. But mostly we learned that young people use the term drama because it is empowering. 6

Dismissing a conflict that's really hurting their feelings as drama lets teenagers demonstrate that they don't care about such petty concerns. They can save face while feeling superior to those tormenting them by dismissing them as desperate for attention. Or, if they're the instigators, the word drama lets teenagers feel that they're participating in something 7 innocuous or even funny, rather than having to admit that they've hurt someone's feelings. Drama allows them to distance themselves from painful situations.

Adults want to help teenagers recognize the hurt that is taking place, which often means owning up to victimhood. But this can have serious consequences. To recognize oneself as a victim—or perpetrator—requires serious emotional, psychological and social support, an infrastructure unavailable to many teenagers. And when teenagers like Jamey do ask for help, they're often let down. Not only are many adults ill-equipped to help teenagers do the psychological work necessary, but teenagers' social position often requires them to continue facing the same social scene day after day. *8*

Like Jamey, there are young people who identify as victims of bullying. But many youths engaged in practices that adults label bullying do not name them as such. Teenagers want to see themselves as in control of their own lives; their reputations are important. Admitting that they're being bullied, or worse, that they are bullies, slots them into a narrative that's disempowering and makes them feel weak and childish. *9*

Antibullying efforts cannot be successful if they make teenagers feel victimized without providing them the support to go from a position of victimization to one of empowerment. When teenagers acknowledge that they're being bullied, adults need to provide programs similar to those that help victims of abuse. And they must recognize that emotional recovery is a long and difficult process. *10*

But if the goal is to intervene at the moment of victimization, the focus should be to work within teenagers' cultural frame, encourage empathy and help young people understand when and where drama has serious consequences. Interventions must focus on positive concepts like healthy relationships and digital citizenship rather than starting with the negative framing of bullying. The key is to help young people feel independently strong, confident and capable without first requiring them to see themselves as either an oppressed person or an oppressor. *11*

Professional Writing

Facebook Wrestles with Free Speech and Civility

Miguel Helft

Palo Alto, Calif.—Mark Zuckerberg, the co-founder and chief executive of Facebook, likes to say that his Web site brings people together, helping to make the world a better place. But Facebook isn't a utopia, and when it comes up short, Dave Willner tries to clean up. *1*

Dressed in Facebook's quasi-official uniform of jeans, a T-shirt and flip-flops, the 26-year-old Mr. Willner hardly looks like a cop on the beat. Yet he and his colleagues on Facebook's "hate and harassment team" are part of a virtual police squad charged with taking down content that is illegal or violates Facebook's terms of service. That puts them on the front line of the debate over free speech on the Internet. 2

"Facebook has more power in determining who can speak and who can be heard around the globe than any Supreme Court justice, any king or any president," said Jeffrey Rosen, a law professor at George Washington University who has written about free speech on the Internet. "It is important that Facebook is exercising its power carefully and protecting more speech rather than less." 3

But Facebook rarely pleases everyone. Any piece of content—a photograph, video, page or even a message between two individuals—could offend somebody. Decisions by the company not to remove material related to Holocaust denial or pages critical of Islam and other religions, for example, have annoyed advocacy groups and prompted some foreign governments to temporarily block the site. 4

Some critics say Facebook does not do enough to prevent certain abuses, like bullying, and may put users at risk with lax privacy policies. They also say the company is often too slow to respond to problems. 5

For example, a page lampooning and, in some instances, threatening violence against an 11-year-old girl from Orlando, Fla., who had appeared in a music video, was still up last week, months after users reported the page to Facebook. The girl's mother, Christa Etheridge, said she had been in touch with law enforcement authorities and was hoping the offenders would be prosecuted. 6

"I'm highly upset that Facebook has allowed this to go on repeatedly and to let it get this far," she said. 7

A Facebook spokesman said the company had left the page up because it did not violate its terms of service, which allow criticism of a public figure. The spokesman said that by appearing in a band's video, the girl had become a public figure, and that the threatening comments had not been posted until a few days ago. Those comments, and the account of the user who had posted them, were removed after the *New York Times* inquired about them. 8

Facebook says it is constantly working to improve its tools to report abuse and trying to educate users about bullying. And it says it responds as fast as it can to the roughly two million reports of potentially abusive content that its users flag every week. 9

"Our intent is to triage to make sure we get to the high-priority, high-risk and high-visibility items most quickly," said Joe Sullivan, Facebook's chief security officer. 10

In early October, Mr. Willner and his colleagues spent more than a week dealing with one high-risk, highly visible case; rogue citizens of Facebook's world had posted antigay messages and threats of violence on a page inviting people to remember Tyler Clementi and other gay teenagers who have committed suicide, on so-called Spirit Day, Oct. 20. 11

Working with colleagues here and in Dublin, they tracked down the accounts of the offenders and shut them down. Then, using an automated technology to tap Facebook's graph of connections between members, they tracked down more profiles for people, who, as it turned out, had also been posting violent messages. 12

"Most of the hateful content was coming from fake profiles," said James Mitchell, who is Mr. Willner's supervisor and leads the team. He said that because most of these profiles, created by people he called "trolls," were connected to those of other trolls, Facebook could track down and block an entire network relatively quickly. 13

Using the system, Mr. Willner and his colleagues silenced dozens of troll accounts, and the page became usable again. But trolls are repeat offenders, and it took Mr. Willner and his colleagues nearly 10 days of monitoring the page around the clock to take down over 7,000 profiles that kept surfacing to attack the Spirit Day event page. 14

...continued Facebook Wrestles with Free Speech and Civility, **Miguel Helft**

Most abuse incidents are not nearly as prominent or public as the defacing of the Spirit Day page, which had nearly 1.5 million members. As with schoolyard taunts, they often happen among a small group of people, hidden from casual view. 15

On a morning in November, Nick Sullivan, a member of the hate and harassment team, watched as reports of bullying incidents scrolled across his screen, full of mind-numbing meanness. "Emily looks like a brother." (Deleted) "Grady is with Dave." (Deleted) "Ronald is the biggest loser." (Deleted) Although the insults are relatively mild, as attacks on specific people who are not public figures, these all violated the terms of service. 16

"There's definitely some crazy stuff out there," Mr. Sullivan said. "But you can do thousands of these in a day." 17

Facebook faces even thornier challenges when policing activity that is considered political by some, and illegal by others, like the controversy over WikiLeaks and the secret diplomatic cables it published. 18

Last spring, for example, the company declined to take down pages related to "Everybody Draw Muhammad Day," an Internetwide protest to defend free speech that surfaced in repudiation of death threats received by two cartoonists who had drawn pictures of Muhammad. A lot of the discussion on Facebook involved people in Islamic countries debating with people in the West about why the images offended. 19

Facebook's team worked to separate the political discussion from the attacks on specific people or Muslims. "There were people on the page that were crossing the line, but the page itself was not crossing the line," Mr. Mitchell said. 20

Facebook's refusal to shut down the debate caused its entire site to be blocked in Pakistan and Bangladesh for several days. 21

Facebook has also sought to walk a delicate line on Holocaust denial. The company has generally refused to block Holocaust denial material, but has worked with human rights groups to take down some content linked to organizations or groups, like the government of Iran, for which Holocaust denial is part of a larger campaign against Jews. 22

"Obviously we disagree with them on Holocaust denial," said Rabbi Abraham Cooper, associate dean of the Simon Wiesenthal Center. But Rabbi Cooper said Facebook had done a better job than many other major Web sites in developing a thoughtful policy on hate and harassment. 23

The soft-spoken Mr. Willner, who on his own Facebook page describes his political views as "turning swords into plowshares and spears into pruning hooks," makes for an unlikely enforcer. An archaeology and anthropology major in college, he said that while he loved his job, he did not love watching so much of the underbelly of Facebook. 24

"I handle it by focusing on the fact that what we do matters," he said. 25

Professional Writing

Why You Can't Cite Wikipedia in My Class

Neil L. Waters

The case for an online opensource encyclopedia is enormously appealing. What's not to like? It gives the originators of entries a means to publish, albeit anonymously, in fields they care deeply about and provides editors the opportunity to improve, add to, and polish them, a capacity not afforded to in-print articles. Above all, open sourcing marshals legions of unpaid, eager, frequently knowledgeable volunteers, whose enormous aggregate labor and energy makes possible the creation of an entity—Wikipedia, which today boasts more than 1.6 million entries in its English edition alone—that would otherwise be far too costly and labor-intensive to see the light of day. In a sense it would have been technologically impossible just a few years ago; open sourcing is democracy in action, and Wikipedia is its most ubiquitous and accessible creation. *1*

Yet I am a historian, schooled in the concept that scholarship requires accountability and trained in a discipline in which collaborative research is rare. The idea that the vector-sum products of tens or hundreds of anonymous collaborators could have much value is, to say the least, counterintuitive for most of us in my profession. We don't allow our students to cite printed general encyclopedias, much less open-source ones. Further, while Wikipedia compares favorably with other tertiary sources for articles in the sciences, approximately half of all entries are in some sense historical. Here the qualitative record is much spottier, with reliability decreasing in approximate proportion to distance from "hot topics" in American history [1]. For a Japan historian like me to perceive the positive side of Wikipedia requires an effort of will. *2*

I made that effort after an innocuous series of events briefly and improbably propelled me and the history department at Middlebury College into the national, even international, spotlight. While grading a set of final examinations from my "History of Early Japan" class, I noticed that a half-dozen students had provided incorrect information about two topics—the Shimabara Rebellion of 1637–1638 and the Confucian thinker Ogyu Sorai—on which they were to write brief essays. Moreover, they used virtually identical language in doing so. A quick check on Google propelled me via popularity-driven algorithms to the Wikipedia entries on them, and there, quite plainly, was the erroneous information. To head off similar events in the future, I proposed a policy to the history department it promptly adopted: "(1) Students are responsible for the accuracy of information they provide, and they cannot point to Wikipedia or any similar source that may appear in the future to escape the consequences of errors. (2) Wikipedia is not an acceptable citation, even though it may lead one to a citable source." *3*

...continued Why You Can't Cite Wikipedia in My Class, **Neil L. Waters**

The rest, as they say, is history. The Middlebury student newspaper ran a story on the new policy. That story was picked up online by *The Burlington Free Press,* a Vermont newspaper, which ran its own story. I was interviewed, first by Vermont radio and TV stations and newspapers, then by the *New York Times,* the *Asahi Shimbun* in Tokyo, and by radio and TV stations in Australia and throughout the U.S., culminating in a story on NBC Nightly News. Hundreds of other newspapers ran stories without interviews, based primarily on the *Times* article. I received dozens of phone calls, ranging from laudatory to actionably defamatory. . . . 4

In the wake of my allotted 15 minutes of Andy Warhol-promised fame I have tried to figure out what all the fuss was about. There is a great deal of uneasiness about Wikipedia in the U.S., as well as in the rest of the computerized world, and a great deal of passion and energy have been spent in its defense. It is clear to me that the good stuff is related to the bad stuff. Wikipedia owes its incredible growth to open-source editing, which is also the root of its greatest weakness. Dedicated and knowledgeable editors can and do effectively reverse the process of entropy by making entries better over time. Other editors, through ignorance, sloppy research, or, on occasion, malice or zeal, can and do introduce or perpetuate errors in fact or interpretation. The reader never knows whether the last editor was one of this latter group; most editors leave no trace save a whimsical cyber-handle. 5

Popular entries are less subject to enduring errors, innocent or otherwise, than the seldom-visited ones, because, as I understand it, the frequency of visits by a Wikipedia "policeman" is largely determined, once again, by algorithms that trace the number of hits and move the most popular sites to a higher priority. The same principle, I have come to realize, props up the whole of the Wiki-world. Once a critical mass of hits is reached, Google begins to guide those who consulted it to Wikipedia before all else. A new button on my version of Firefox goes directly to Wikipedia. Preferential access leads to yet more hits, generating a still higher priority in an endless loop of mutual reinforcement. 6

It seems to me that there is a major downside to the self-reinforcing cycle of popularity. Popularity begets ease of use, and ease of use begets the "democratization" of access to information. But all too often, democratization of access to information is equated with the democratization of the information itself, in the sense that it is subject to a vote. That last mental conflation may have origins that predate Wikipedia and indeed the whole of the Internet. 7

The quiz show "Family Feud" has been a fixture of daytime television for decades and is worth a quick look. Contestants are not rewarded for guessing the correct answer but rather for guessing the answer that the largest number of people have chosen as the correct answer. The show must tap into some sort of popular desire to democratize information. Validation is not conformity to verifiable facts or weighing of interpretations and evidence but conformity to popular opinion. Expertise plays practically no role at all. 8

Here is where all but the most hopelessly postmodernist scholars bridle. "Family Feud" is harmless enough, but most of us believe in a real, external world in which facts exist independently of popular opinion, and some interpretations of events, thoroughly grounded in disciplinary rigor and the weight of evidence, are at least more likely to be right than others that are not. I tell my students that Wikipedia is a fine place to search for a paper topic or begin the research process, but it absolutely cannot serve subsequent stages of research. Wikipedia is not the direct heir to "Family Feud," but both seem to share an element of faith—that if enough people agree on something, it is most likely so. 9

What can be done? The answer depends on the goal. If it is to make Wikipedia a truly authoritative source, suitable for citation, it cannot be done for any general tertiary source, including the *Encyclopaedia Britannica.* For an anonymous open-source encyclopedia, that goal is theoretically, as well as practically, impossible. If the goal is more modest—to make Wikipedia more reliable than it is—then it seems to me that any changes must come at the expense of its open-source nature. Some sort of accountability for editors, as well as for the originators of entries, would be a first step, and that, I think, means that editors must leave a record of their real names. A more rigorous fact-checking system might help, but are there enough volunteers to cover 1.6 million entries, or would checking be in effect reserved for popular entries? 10

Can one move beyond the world of cut-and-dried facts to check for logical consistency and reasonableness of interpretations in light of what is known about a particular society in a particular historical period? Can it be done without experts? If you rely on experts, do you pay them or depend on their voluntarism? 11

I suppose I should now go fix the Wikipedia entry for Ogyu Sorai (en.wikipedia.org/wiki/Ogyu_Sorai). I have been waiting since January to see how long it might take for the system to correct it, which has indeed been altered slightly and is rather good overall. But the statement that Ogyu opposed the Tokugawa order is still there and still highly misleading [2]. Somehow the statement that equates the samurai with the lower class in Tokugawa Japan has escaped the editors' attention, though anyone with the slightest contact with Japanese history knows it is wrong. One down, 1.6 million to go. 12

...continued Why You Can't Cite Wikipedia in My Class, **Neil L. Waters**

References

1. Rosenzweig, R. Can history be open source? *Journal of American History 93,* 1 (June 2006), 117–146.
2. Tucker, J. (editor and translator). *Ogyu Sorai's Philosophical Masterworks.* Association for Asian Studies and University of Hawaii Press, Honolulu, 2006, 12–13, 48–51; while Ogyu sought to redefine the sources of Tokugawa legitimacy, his purpose was clearly to strengthen the authority of the Tokugawa shogunate.

Professional Writing

Professors Should Embrace Wikipedia

Mark Wilson

When the online, anyone-can-edit Wikipedia appeared in 2001, teachers, especially college professors, were appalled. The Internet was already an apparently limitless source of nonsense for their students to eagerly consume—now there was a Web site with the appearance of legitimacy and a dead-easy interface that would complete the seduction until all sense of fact, fiction, myth and propaganda blended into a popular culture of pseudointelligence masking the basest ignorance. . . . 1

Now the English version of Wikipedia has over 2 million articles, and it has been translated into over 250 languages. It has become so massive that you can type virtually any noun into a search engine and the first link will be to a Wikipedia page. After seven years and this exponential growth, Wikipedia can still be edited by anyone at any time. A generation of students was warned away from this information siren, but we know as professors that it is the first place they go to start a research project, look up an unfamiliar term from lecture, or find something disturbing to ask about during the next lecture. In fact, we learned too that Wikipedia is indeed the most convenient repository of information ever invented, and we go there often—if a bit covertly—to get a few questions answered. Its accuracy, at least for science articles, is actually as high as the revered *Encyclopedia Britannica,* as shown by a test published in the journal *Nature.* 2

It is time for the academic world to recognize Wikipedia for what it has become: a global library open to anyone with an Internet connection and a pressing curiosity. The vision of its founders, Jimmy Wales and Larry Sanger, has become reality, and the librarians were right: the world has not been the same since. If the Web is the greatest information 3 delivery device ever, and Wikipedia is the largest coherent store of information and ideas, then we as teachers and scholars should have been on this train years ago for the benefit of our students, our professions, and that mystical pool of human knowledge.

What Wikipedia too often lacks is academic authority, or at least the perception of it. Most of its thousands of editors are anonymous, sometimes known only by an IP address or a cryptic username. Every article has a "talk" page for discussions of content, bias, and organization. "Revert" wars can rage out of control as one faction battles another over a few words in an article. Sometimes administrators have to step in and lock a page down until tempers cool and the main protagonists lose interest. The very anonymity of the editors is often the source of the problem: how do we know who has an authoritative grasp of the topic? 4

That is what academics do best. We can quickly sort out scholarly authority into complex hierarchies with a quick glance at a vita and a sniff at a publication list. We make many mistakes doing this, of course, but at least our debates are supported with citations and a modicum of civility because we are identifiable and we have our reputations to maintain and friends to keep. Maybe this academic culture can be added to the Wild West of Wikipedia to make it more useful for everyone? 5

I propose that all academics with research specialties, no matter how arcane (and nothing is too obscure for Wikipedia), enroll as identifiable editors of Wikipedia. We then watch over a few wikipages of our choosing, adding to them when appropriate, stepping in to resolve disputes when we know something useful. We can add new articles on topics which should be covered, and argue that others should be removed or combined. This is not to displace anonymous editors, many of whom possess vast amounts of valuable information and innovative ideas, but to add our authority and hard-won knowledge to this growing universal library. 6

The advantages should be obvious. First, it is another outlet for our scholarship, one that may be more likely to be read than many of our journals. Second, we are directly serving our students by improving the source they go to first for information. Third, by identifying ourselves, we can connect with other scholars and interested parties who stumble across our edits and new articles. Everyone wins. 7

I have been an open Wikipedia editor now for several months. I have enjoyed it immensely. In my teaching I use a "living syllabus" for each course, which is a kind of academic blog. (For example, see my History of Life course online syllabus.) I connect students through links to outside sources of information. Quite often I refer students to Wikipedia articles that are well-sourced and well written. Wikipages that are not so good are easily fixed with a judicious edit or two, and many pages become more useful with the addition of an image from my collection (all donated to 8

...continued Why You Can't Cite Wikipedia in My Class, **Neil L. Waters**

the public domain). Since I am open in my editorial identity, I often get questions from around the world about the topics I find most fascinating. I've even made important new connections through my edits to new collaborators and reporters who want more background for a story.

9 For example, this year I met online a biology professor from Centre College who is interested in the ecology of fish on Great Inagua Island in the Bahamas. He saw my additions and images on that Wikipedia page and had several questions about the island. He invited me to speak at Centre next year about evolution–creation controversies, which is unrelated to the original contact but flowed from our academic conversations. I in turn have been learning much about the island's living ecology I did not know. I've also learned much about the kind of prose that is most effective for a general audience, and I've in turn taught some people how to properly reference ideas and information. In short, I've expanded my teaching.

10 Wikipedia as we know it will undoubtedly change in the coming years as all technologies do. By involving ourselves directly and in large numbers now, we can help direct that change into ever more useful ways for our students and the public. This is, after all, our sacred charge as teacher-scholars: to educate when and where we can to the greatest effect.

Professional Writing

Does the Internet Make You Dumber?

Nicholas Carr

1 The Roman philosopher Seneca may have put it best 2,000 years ago: "To be everywhere is to be nowhere." Today, the Internet grants us easy access to unprecedented amounts of information. But a growing body of scientific evidence suggests that the Net, with its constant distractions and interruptions, is also turning us into scattered and superficial thinkers.

2 The picture emerging from the research is deeply troubling, at least to anyone who values the depth, rather than just the velocity, of human thought. People who read text studded with links, the studies show, comprehend less than those who read traditional linear text. People who watch busy multimedia presentations remember less than those who take in information in a more sedate and focused manner. People who are continually distracted by emails, alerts and other messages understand less than those who are able to concentrate. And people who juggle many tasks are less creative and less productive than those who do one thing at a time.

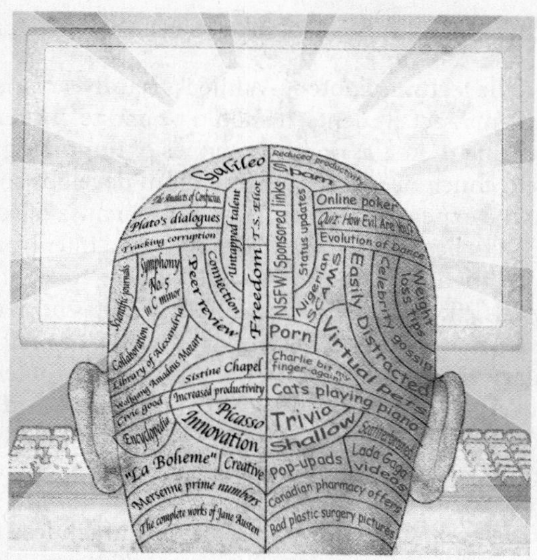

The common thread in these disabilities is the division of attention. The richness of our thoughts, our memories and even our personalities hinges on our ability to focus the mind and sustain concentration. Only when we pay deep attention to a new piece of information are we able to associate it "meaningfully and systematically with knowledge already well established in memory," writes the Nobel Prize–winning neuroscientist Eric Kandel. Such associations are essential to mastering complex concepts. *3*

When we're constantly distracted and interrupted, as we tend to be online, our brains are unable to forge the strong and expansive neural connections that give depth and distinctiveness to our thinking. We become mere signal-processing units, quickly shepherding disjointed bits of information into and then out of short-term memory. *4*

In an article published in *Science* last year, Patricia Greenfield, a leading developmental psychologist, reviewed dozens of studies on how different media technologies influence our cognitive abilities. Some of the studies indicated that certain computer tasks, like playing video games, can enhance "visual literacy skills," increasing the speed at which people can shift their focus among icons and other images on screens. Other studies, however, found that such rapid shifts in focus, even if performed adeptly, result in less rigorous and "more automatic" thinking. *5*

In one experiment conducted at Cornell University, for example, half a class of students was allowed to use Internet-connected laptops during a lecture, while the other had to keep their computers shut. Those who browsed the Web performed much worse on a subsequent test of how *6* well they retained the lecture's content. While it's hardly surprising that Web surfing would distract students, it should be a note of caution to schools that are wiring their classrooms in hopes of improving learning.

Ms. Greenfield concluded that "every medium develops some cognitive skills at the expense of others." Our growing use of screen-based media, she said, has strengthened visual-spatial intelligence, which can improve the ability to do jobs that involve keeping track of lots of simultaneous signals, like air traffic control. But that has been accompanied by "new weaknesses in higher-order cognitive processes," including "abstract vocabulary, mindfulness, reflection, inductive problem solving, critical thinking, and imagination." We're becoming, in a word, shallower. *7*

In another experiment, recently conducted at Stanford University's Communication Between Humans and Interactive Media Lab, a team of researchers gave various cognitive tests to 49 people who do a lot of media multitasking and 52 people who multitask much less frequently. The heavy multitaskers performed poorly on all the tests. They were more easily distracted, had less control over their attention, and were much less able to distinguish important information from trivia. *8*

The researchers were surprised by the results. They had expected that the intensive multitaskers would have gained some unique mental advantages from all their on-screen juggling. But that wasn't the case. In fact, the heavy multitaskers weren't even good at multitasking. They were considerably less adept at switching between tasks than the more infrequent multitaskers. "Everything distracts them," observed Clifford Nass, the professor who heads the Stanford lab. *9*

It would be one thing if the ill effects went away as soon as we turned off our computers and cellphones. But they don't. The cellular structure of the human brain, scientists have discovered, adapts readily to the tools we use, including those for finding, storing and sharing information. By changing our habits of mind, each new technology strengthens certain neural pathways and weakens others. The cellular alterations continue to shape the way we think even when we're not using the technology. *10*

The pioneering neuroscientist Michael Merzenich believes our brains are being "massively remodeled" by our ever-intensifying use of the Web and related media. In the 1970s and 1980s, Mr. Merzenich, now a professor emeritus at the University of California in San Francisco, conducted a famous series of experiments on primate brains that revealed how extensively and quickly neural circuits change in response to experience. When, for example, Mr. Merzenich rearranged the nerves in a monkey's hand, the nerve cells in the animal's sensory cortex quickly reorganized themselves to create a new "mental map" of the hand. In a conversation late last year, he said that he was profoundly worried about the cognitive consequences of the constant distractions and interruptions *11* the Internet bombards us with. The long-term effect on the quality of our intellectual lives, he said, could be "deadly."

What we seem to be sacrificing in all our surfing and searching is our capacity to engage in the quieter, attentive modes of thought that underpin contemplation, reflection and introspection. The Web never encourages us to slow down. It keeps us in a state of perpetual mental locomotion. 12

It is revealing, and distressing, to compare the cognitive effects of the Internet with those of an earlier information technology, the printed book. Whereas the Internet scatters our attention, the book focuses it. Unlike the screen, the page promotes contemplativeness. 13

Reading a long sequence of pages helps us develop a rare kind of mental discipline. The innate bias of the human brain, after all, is to be distracted. Our predisposition is to be aware of as much of what's going on around us as possible. Our fast-paced, reflexive shifts in focus were once crucial to our survival. They reduced the odds that a predator would take us by surprise or that we'd overlook a nearby source of food. 14

To read a book is to practice an unnatural process of thought. It requires us to place ourselves at what T. S. Eliot, in his poem "Four Quartets," called "the still point of the turning world." We have to forge or strengthen the neural links needed to counter our instinctive distractedness, thereby gaining greater control over our attention and our mind. 15

It is this control, this mental discipline, that we are at risk of losing as we spend ever more time scanning and skimming online. If the slow progression of words across printed pages damped our craving to be inundated by mental stimulation, the Internet indulges it. It returns us to our native state of distractedness, while presenting us with far more distractions than our ancestors ever had to contend with. 16

Questions for Writing and Discussion

1. A key strategy for persuading or convincing your readers is to directly engage them in the topic. For example, Farhad Manjoo in "You Have No Friends" directly addresses his readers in paragraph four: "Friends—can I call you friends?—it's time to drop the attitude: There is no longer any good reason to avoid Facebook." Find two other places in his article where Manjoo directly addresses his readers. Explain why you think this strategy is or is not effective for his readers on Slate.com.

2. In ". . . And Why I Hate It," Sarah Kliff explains the disadvantages of Facebook. What does she dislike about using her Facebook page? Which of her objections has Manjoo already anticipated and responded to? After reading both essays, make your own list of the reasons you both like and dislike Facebook.

3. Both Jennifer Holladay in "Cyberbullying" and Danah Boyd and Alice Marwick in "Bullying as True Drama" make recommendations for responding to cyberbullying. Explain how their recommendations are similar and how they differ. Based on your own experience with social networking and cyberbullying, explain which of their recommendations would be most effective and why.

4. Although the First Amendment to the Constitution says that "Congress shall make no law . . . abridging freedom of speech," certain kinds of speech are not permitted, including speech that incites actions that cause harm to others (shouting "fire" in a crowded arena). Based on Miguel Helft's "Facebook Wrestles with Free Speech and Civility," explain how Facebook's policies do or do not meet First Amendment guidelines. (Check a U. S. government site such as http://www.uscourts.gov for specific cases related to free speech in social media.) Just because Facebook users agree to a contract, can Facebook still censor language that it believes constitutes "hate or harassment"?

5. Neil Waters in "Why You Can't Cite Wikipedia in My Class" and Mark Wilson in "Professors Should Embrace Wikipedia" represent nearly opposing points of view. According to each author, what are the proper uses and limitations of Wikipedia? Citing examples from both articles, explain what uses of Wikipedia they agree on and then exactly how their recommendations differ.

6. Review Chapter 4 on strategies for doing a rhetorical analysis. Then analyze Nicholas Carr's "Does the Internet Make You Dumber?" for its key rhetorical strategies. How effectively does Carr state his purpose for his selected audience? What appeals to logos, ethos, or pathos does Carr make? Which of his

appeals are most or least effective? Are his conclusions logically supported by his review of the research?

7. Analyze the cartoon on the previous page, "The Evolution of Communication," by Mike Keefe. What argument about the Internet or social media does this cartoon make? How do the cartoon's elements (composition, focal points, and narrative) help make this argument? Explain how this argument is similar to or different from Nicholas Carr's argument.

Arguing: The Writing Process

Assignment for Arguing

For this assignment, choose a controversial and debatable topic that catches your interest or relates to your own personal experience. (Avoid ready-made pro–con subjects such as abortion or drugs unless you have personal experience that can bring a fresh perspective to the subject.) Then examine the topic for possible claims of fact or definition, value, cause and effect, or policy. If the claim is debatable, you may have a focus for your arguing assignment. Next, think about your possible audience. Who needs to be convinced about your argument? Who has the power to change the status quo? Are there multiple perspectives or stakeholders involved in this issue? Is there a compromise position you should argue for? (How might your understanding of your audience change your claim?) If possible, narrow your audience to a local group that might be influential. Finally, choose a genre or set of genres that best fits your purpose and audience. Use the following grid to help brainstorm combinations of audience and genre that would be most effective for your purpose and topic.

Audience	Possible Genres for Arguing
Personal Audience	Class notes, journal entry, blog, scrapbook, social networking page
Academic Audience	Academic essay, researched argument, examination essay, debate script, forum entry on class site, journal entry, Web site, or multigenre document
Public Audience	Letter to the editor, column, editorial, blog, article, or critique in a newspaper, online site, magazine, newsletter, graphic novel, Web site, or multigenre document

CHOOSING A SUBJECT

"You can write about anything, and if you write well enough, even the reader with no intrinsic interest in the subject will become involved."

—Tracy Kidder, Novelist

If a journal entry suggests a possible subject, do the collecting and shaping strategies. Otherwise, consider the following ideas.

- Review your journal entries and the papers you have already written for this class. Test these subjects for an arguable claim that you could make, opposing arguments you could consider, and an appropriate audience for an argumentative piece.
- **Writing Across the Curriculum.** Brainstorm ideas for argumentative subjects from the other courses you are currently taking or have taken. What controversial issues have you discussed in your classes? Ask current or past instructors for controversial topics relating to their courses.
- Newspapers and magazines are full of controversial subjects in sports, medicine, law, business, and family. Browse current issues or online magazines, looking for possible subjects. Check news items, editorials, and cartoons. Look for subjects related to your own interests, your job, or your experiences.
- Interview friends, family, or classmates. What controversial issues affect their lives most directly? What would they most like to change about their lives? What has irritated or angered them most in the recent past?
- **Community Service Learning.** If you are doing a community-service-learning project, consider one of these topics: (1) Which of the agency's activities best meet the goals of the agency? Write an essay to the agency coordinator recommending a reallocation of resources to the most effective activities. (2) How might agency volunteers more usefully serve the agency in future projects? Write to your project coordinator recommending improvements that would better meet the dual goals of academic learning and agency service.

COLLECTING

10.5
Use collecting strategies to develop an argument

Narrowing and Focusing Your Claim

Narrow your subject to a specific topic, and sharpen your focus by applying the "Wh" questions. If your subject is "grades," your responses might be as follows.

Subject: Grades

Watch the Video on Topics for Argument

- **Who:** College students
- **What:** Letter grades
- **When:** In freshman and sophomore years
- **Where:** Especially in nonmajor courses
- **Why:** What purpose do grades serve in nonmajor courses?

Determine what claim or claims you want to make. Make sure that your claim is *arguable.* (Remember that claims can overlap; an argument may combine several related claims.)

Claim of Fact or Definition

- Letter grades exist. (not arguable)
- Employers consider grades when hiring. (slightly more arguable, but not very controversial)
- Grades do not measure learning. (very arguable)

Claim About Cause or Effect

- Grades create anxiety for students. (not very arguable)
- Grades prevent discovery and learning. (arguable)

Claim About Value

- Grades are not fair. (not very arguable: "fairness" can usually be determined)
- Grades are bad because they discourage individual initiative. (arguable)
- Grades are good because they give students an incentive to learn. (arguable)

Claim About a Solution or Policy

- Grades should be eliminated altogether. (arguable—but difficult)
- Grades should be eliminated in humanities courses. (arguable)
- Grades should change to pass/fail in nonmajor courses. (arguable—and more practical)

Focusing and narrowing your *claim* helps determine what evidence you need to collect. Use your observing, remembering, reading, and investigative skills to gather the evidence. ***Note:*** An argumentative essay should not use only abstract and impersonal evidence. *Your experience* can be crucial to a successful argumentative essay. Start by doing the *remembering* exercises. Your audience wants to know not only why you are writing on this particular *topic,* but also why it is of interest to *you.*

Remembering

Use *freewriting, looping, branching,* or *clustering* to recall experiences, ideas, events, and people who are relevant to your claim. If you are writing about grades, brainstorm about how *your* teachers used grades, how you reacted to specific grades in one specific class, how your friends or parents reacted, and what you felt or thought. These prewriting exercises will help you understand your claim and give you specific examples that you can use for evidence.

Analyzing Statistics

Whether you are evaluating statistical sources in an essay that you are reading or choosing statistical data to use as evidence for a claim in your own essay, use the following questions to help you determine the relevance, validity, and bias of the statistics.

- Who is the author or the group responsible for gathering or presenting the information? Do they have a bias or point of view?
- What is the date of the study or survey? Are the data still relevant?
- For a survey or poll, what is the sample size (number of respondents) and sample selection (demographic group selected)? Is the sample large enough to give reliable results? Was the group randomly selected? Are certain key groups not included?
- Analyze the wording of the questions asked in the poll or survey. Are the questions relatively neutral? Do the questions lead respondents to a certain conclusion?
- Are the conclusions drawn justified by the data? Are the conclusions exaggerated or overgeneralized?

Observing

If possible for your topic, collect data and evidence by observing, firsthand, the facts, values, effects, or possible solutions related to your claim. *Repeated* observation will give you good inductive evidence to support your argument.

Investigating

For most argumentative essays, some research or investigation is essential. Because it is difficult to imagine all the valid counterarguments, interview friends, classmates, family, coworkers, and authorities on your topic. From the library, gather books and articles that contain arguments in support of your claim. ***Note:*** As you do research in the library, print out articles or make photocopies of key passages from relevant sources to hand in with your essay. If you cite sources, list them on a Works Cited page following your essay. (See Chapter 13 for the proper format.)

SHAPING

10.6
Shape your argument

As you plan your organization, reconsider your rhetorical situation. Will the *genre* you have selected (letter, researched essay, letter to the editor, blog, Web site, brochure, PowerPoint presentation) help carry out your *purpose* for your intended audience? Is there a relevant *occasion* (meeting, anniversary, or response to news item) that your writing might focus on? What is the *cultural, social,* or *political context* for your writing? Finally, reconsider your *audience.* Try imagining one real person who might be among your readers. Is this person open-minded and likely to be convinced by your evidence? Does this person represent the opposing position? If you have several alternative positions, are there individual people who represent each of these positions? After reconsidering your rhetorical situation, try the shaping strategies that follow.

Shaping Strategies

Do you want to . . .	Consider using these rhetorical modes or strategies:
write an argument with just one opposing position?	list "pro" and "con" arguments in two columns (pp. 381–382)
write an argument with several alternative positions or solutions?	draw a circle of alternative positions (p. 382)
outline your argument using classical structure?	organizing arguments (p. 383)
develop your argument with several supporting reasons?	developing arguments (p. 385)

List "Pro" and "Con" Arguments

Write out your *claim,* then list the arguments for your position (pro) and the arguments for the opposing positions (con). After you have made the list, match up arguments by drawing lines, as indicated in this lists below.

Listen to the **Audio** on Constructing an Argument

When pro and con arguments match, you will be able to argue against the con and for your claim at the same time. When arguments do not match, you will need to consider them separately.

Claim: Grades should be changed to pass/fail in nonmajor courses.

Pro		Con
Grades inhibit learning by putting too much emphasis on competition.	———	Grades actually promote learning by setting students to study as hard as possible.
Grade competition with majors in the field can be discouraging.	——	Students should be encouraged to compete with majors. They may want to change majors and need to know if they can compete.

Pass/fail grading encourages students to explore nonmajor fields. — If students don't have traditional grading, they won't take nonmajor courses seriously.

Some students do better without the pressure of grades; they need to find out if they can motivate themselves without grades, but they shouldn't have to risk grades in their major field to discover that.

Draw a Circle of Alternative Positions

If you are considering multiple alternative positions, put your claim in the middle of a circle and indicate the various positions or stakeholders outside the circle. This diagram will help you identify the most important positions in the debate and will help you organize your writing.

Once you have a diagram for all the major alternative positions or stakeholders, decide the focus of your argument. For your purpose, audience, and context, you may want to focus on the different goals of teachers, students, and parents. Or you may want to suggest how teachers, students, and parents should organize and force legislators to change the standardized tests or change how schools are funded based on test results.

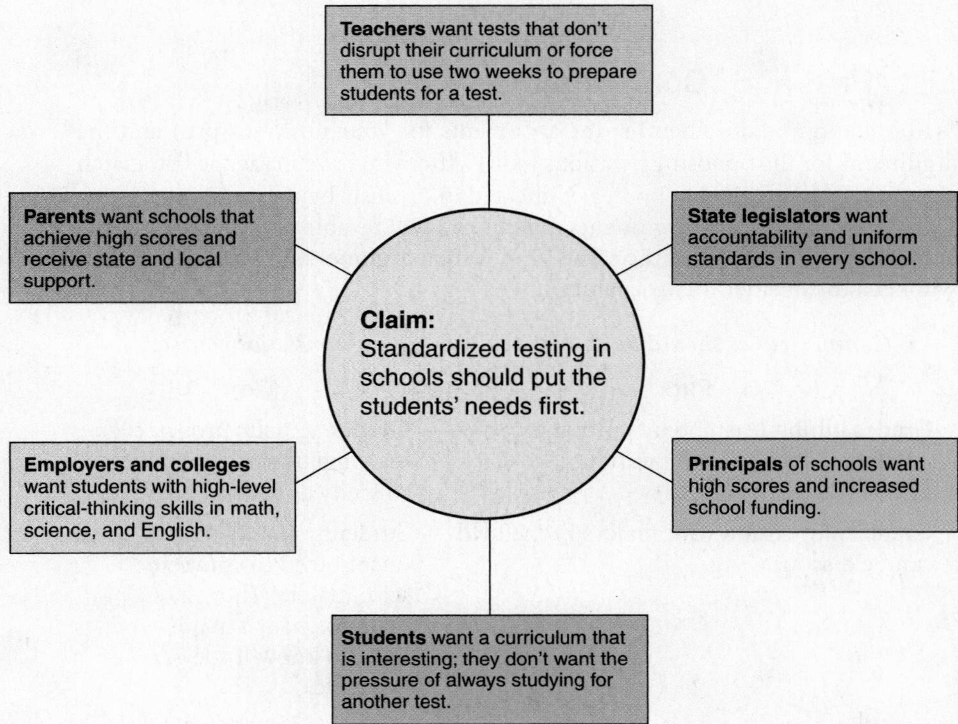

Organizing Arguments

For more than two thousand years, writers and speakers have been trying to determine the most effective means to persuade audiences. One of the oldest outlines for a successful argument comes from classical rhetoric. The six-part outline is intended as a guideline rather than a rigid list; test this outline to see if it will work for *your* argument.

Shaping Your Points: Classical Argument

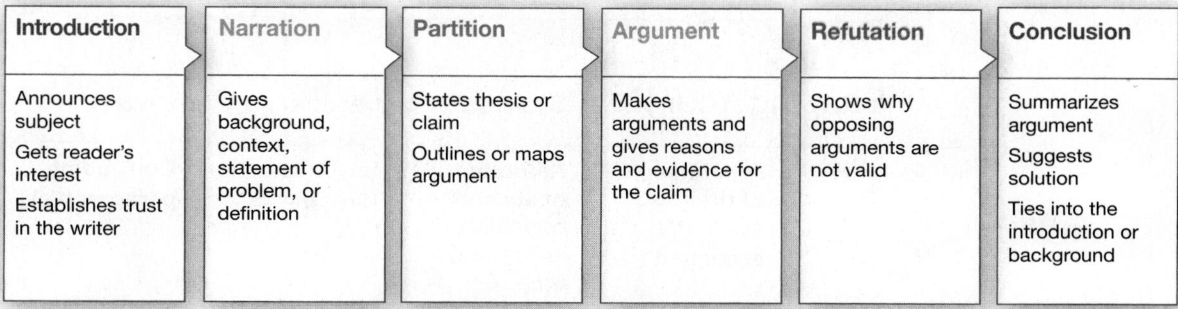

Introduction
Announces subject
Gets reader's interest
Establishes trust in the writer
Narration
Gives background, context, statement of problem, or definition
Partition
States thesis or claim
Outlines or maps argument
Argument
Makes arguments and gives reasons and evidence for the claim
Refutation
Shows why opposing arguments are not valid
Conclusion
Summarizes argument
Suggests solution
Ties into the introduction or background

Most arguments have these features, but not necessarily in this order. Some writers prefer to respond to or refute opposing arguments before giving the reasoning in support of their claims. When con and pro arguments match, refuting an argument and then arguing for your claim may work best. As you organize your own arguments, put your strongest argument last and your weakest argument either first or in the middle.

Because most short argumentative essays contain the introduction, narration, and partition all in a few introductory paragraphs, you may use the following abbreviated outlines for argument.

Shaping Your Points: Abbreviated Argument Pattern 1

Introductory paragraph(s)	Your arguments	Refutation of opposing arguments	Concluding paragraph(s)
Attention getter Background Claim or thesis	Gives arguments and reasons and evidence to support them	Shows why opposing arguments are not valid	Summarizes argument Ties into the introduction or background

Shaping Your Points: Abbreviated Argument Pattern 2

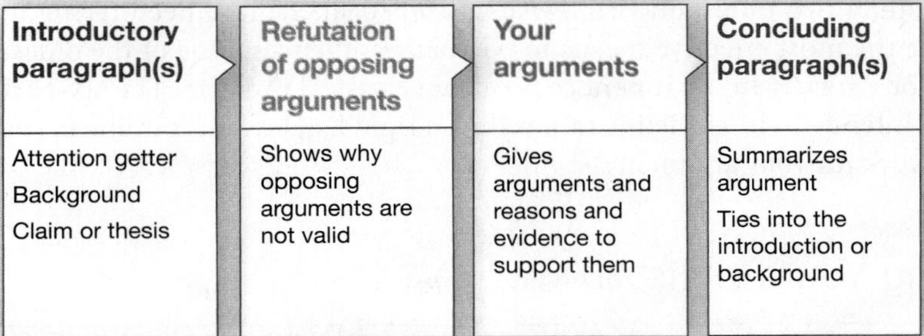

Introductory paragraph(s)	Refutation of opposing arguments	Your arguments	Concluding paragraph(s)
Attention getter Background Claim or thesis	Shows why opposing arguments are not valid	Gives arguments and reasons and evidence to support them	Summarizes argument Ties into the introduction or background

Shaping Your Points: Abbreviated Argument Pattern 3

Introduction	Refutation of first opposing argument	Refutation of second opposing argument, etc.	Additional arguments	Concluding paragraph(s)
Attention getter Background Claim or thesis	Refutes first opposing argument that matches your first argument	Refutes second opposing argument that matches your second argument, etc.	Makes arguments and gives reasons and evidence for each claim	Summarizes argument Ties into the introduction or background

For Rogerian arguments, you can follow one of the above outlines, but the emphasis, tone, and attitude will be different.

Shaping Your Points: Rogerian Argument

Introduction	Opposing arguments	Your arguments	Concluding paragraph(s)
Attention getter and background Claim or thesis (often downplayed to reduce threat) Appeal to character (crucial)	States opposing arguments fairly Shows where, how, or when those arguments may be valid Establishes common ground	States your position fairly Shows where, how, or when your arguments are valid	Presents compromise position States solution to the problem Shows its advantages to both sides

Developing Arguments

Think of your argument as a series of *because* statements, each supported by evidence, statistics, testimony, expert opinion, data, specific examples from your experience, or a combination of these.

THESIS OR CLAIM: Grades should be abolished in nonmajor courses.

Reason 1	Because they may keep a student from attempting a difficult nonmajor course *Statistics, testimony, data, and examples*
Reason 2	Because competition with majors in the field can be discouraging *Statistics, testimony, data, and examples*
Reason 3	Because grades inhibit students' learning in nonmajor fields *Statistics, testimony, data, and examples*

You can develop each reason using a variety of strategies. The following strategies may help you generate additional reasons and examples.

Definition	Define the crucial terms or ideas. (What do you mean by *learning?*)
Comparison	Compare the background, situation, and context with similar context. (What other schools have tried pass/fail grading for nonmajor courses? How has it worked?)
Process	How does or should a change occur? (How do nonmajors become discouraged? How should a school implement pass/fail in grading?)

These strategies may help you develop an argument coherently and effectively. If several strategies are possible, consider which would be most effective for your audience.

Research Tips

When you draft an arguing essay, don't let citations or direct quotations overpower your own argument. Two tactics will keep you in control of your argument:

First, always avoid "unidentified flying quotations" by *sandwiching* your quotations. *Introduce* quotations by referring to the author, the source, and/or the author's study. *Follow* quotations with a sentence explaining how the author's evidence supports your argument. For examples, see paragraphs 4 and 5 in the essay by student writer Crystal Sabatke at the end of this chapter.

Second, keep your direct quotations *short*. If possible, reduce a long passage to one sentence and incorporate the quoted material in the flow of your own language. For example, in her essay at the end of this chapter, Sabatke writes:

> According to Ruth Conniff, author of "Big Bad Welfare: Welfare Reform, Politics, and Children," the welfare reform discussion "indicates that what happens to children doesn't matter to Americans, so long as mothers are forced to work" (8).

DRAFTING

> "No one can write decently who is distrustful of the reader's intelligence, or whose attitude is patronizing."
>
> —E. B. White, Essayist

You will never really know "enough" about your subject or have "enough" evidence. At some point, however, you must stop collecting and start your draft. The most frequent problem in drafting an argumentative essay is delaying the actual writing too long, until the deadline is close.

For argumentative essays, start with a working order or sequence and sketch an outline on paper or in your head. Additional examples and appeals to reason, character, or emotion may occur to you as you develop your argument or refute opposing arguments. In addition, if you have done some research, have your notes, photocopies of key data, statistics, quotations, and citations of authorities close at hand. As you write, you will discover that some information or arguments don't fit into the flow of your essay. Don't force arguments into your draft when they no longer belong.

PeerResponse

Writer: Before you exchange drafts with a peer reader, provide the following information about your essay.

1. **a.** Intended audience and genre
   b. Primary claim or thesis
   c. Opposing arguments that you refute
   d. Arguments supporting your claim

2. Write out one or two questions about your draft that you want your reader to answer.

Reader: Read the writer's entire draft. As you reread, answer the following questions.

1. **Arguments.** Without looking at the writer's responses above, describe the essay's (a) target audience, (b) primary claim, (c) opposing arguments that are refuted, (d) arguments supporting the claim. Which of these did you have trouble identifying? What additional pro or con arguments should the writer consider?
2. **Organization.** Identify the following parts of the writer's draft: introduction, narration, partition, argument, refutation, and conclusion. Does the writer need all of these elements for his or her subject and audience? Why or why not? Where could the writer clarify transitions between sections? Explain.
3. **Appeals.** Identify places where the writer appeals to reason, to character, and to emotion. Where could these appeals be stronger? Identify sentences where the writer is overly emotional or illogical (see the section "Revising Fallacies in Logic" on pages 389–391).
4. **Evidence.** Identify at least one paragraph in which the supporting evidence is strong. Then identify at least one paragraph in which the writer makes assertions without sufficient supporting evidence. What kind of evidence might the writer use—first-hand observation, personal examples, testimony from experts, interviews, statistics, or other? Explain.
5. **Revision plan.** List three key changes that the writer should make during the revision.
6. Answer the writer's questions.

Writer: When your essay is returned, read the comments by your peer reader(s) and do the following.

1. Compare your descriptions of the audience, genre, claim, and pro and con arguments with your reader's descriptions. Where there are differences, clarify your essay.
2. Read all of your peer reader's responses. List revisions that you intend to make in each of the following areas: *audience, genre, arguments, organization, appeals, and supporting evidence.*

REVISING

Argumentation is the most public of the purposes for writing. The rhetorical situation (purpose, audience, genre, occasion, and cultural context) plays a crucial role. As you revise, look at this larger context, not just at phrasing, words, or

Read the Paper on Revising the Declaration of Independence

sentences. Test your argument by having friends or classmates read it. Explain your claim, your focus, and your intended audience, genre, and context. Ask them to look for counterarguments that you have omitted or for weaknesses, omissions, or fallacies in logic. But don't automatically change your draft in response; follow only the advice that makes your overall purpose more effective for your audience.

Guidelines for Revision

- **When you finish your draft, reconsider the elements of the rhetorical situation** (writer, purpose, audience, genre, occasion, cultural context). Look at the big picture. What needs changing? What needs to be added? What parts are repetitious or ineffective?
- **Ask a class member or friend to read your draft to determine the intended audience for your argument.** See which arguments your reader thinks would not be effective for your audience.
- **Use the Toulmin model to evaluate your essay.** Is your claim clearly stated? Does your claim have a qualifier? Do you note exceptions to your claim? Do you have warrant statements explaining how your data support your reasons and claim?
- **Which of your *because* arguments are most effective?** Least effective? Should you change the outline or structure that you initially chose?
- **Revise your draft to avoid fallacies or errors in reasoning.** Errors in logic create two problems: They can destroy your rational appeal and open your argument to a logical rebuttal, and they can weaken your credibility—and thus reduce your appeal to your character. (Review the list of fallacies below.)
- **Support your reasons with evidence: *data, facts, statistics, quotations, observations, testimony, statistics, or specific examples from your experience.*** Check your collecting notes once again for further evidence to add to your weakest argument. Is there a weak or unsupported argument that you should omit?
- **Signal the major arguments and counterarguments in your partition or map.** Between paragraphs, use clear transitions and paragraph hooks.
- **Could your essay be improved by visuals or special formatting?** Reconsider your genre and audience. If visuals might make your essay more effective, do a search on the computer. If you need help formatting your essay, check with a peer, a computer lab assistant, or your instructor.

- **If you cite sources in your essay, check the *accuracy* of your statistics, quotations, and source references.** (See Chapter 13 for the proper format of in-text documentation and the Works Cited page.)
- **Revise sentences to improve conciseness and clarity.**
- **Edit sentences for grammar, punctuation, and spelling.**

Revising Fallacies in Logic

Be careful to avoid using any of the common fallacies in logic described here. Reread your draft or your peer's draft and revise as appropriate to eliminate these illogical forms of argument.

[**Watch** the **Video** on Logical Fallacies

- **Hasty generalization:** Conclusion not justified by sufficient or unbiased evidence. If Mary tells you that Professor Paramecium is a hard grader because he gave her 36 percent on the first biology test, she is making a hasty generalization. It may be *true*—Prof P. may *be* a difficult grader—but Mary's logic is not valid because she cannot logically draw that conclusion from a sample of one.
- **Post hoc ergo propter hoc:** Literally, "after this, therefore because of this." Just because B *occurred after* A does not mean that A *necessarily caused* B. You washed your car in the morning, and it rained in the afternoon. Though we joke about how it always rains after we wash the car, there is, of course, no causal relationship between the two events.
- **Genetic fallacy:** Arguing that the origins of a person, object, or institution determine its character, nature, or worth. Like the post hoc fallacy, the genetic fallacy is an error in causal relationships.

  This automobile was made in Detroit. It'll probably fall apart after 10,000 miles.

  He speaks with a funny German accent. He's really stupid, you know.

  He started Celestial Seasonings Herb Teas just to make a quick buck; it's just another phony yuppie product.

  The second half of each statement *may* or *may not* be true; the logical error is in assuming that the origin of something will determine its worth or quality. Stereotyping is frequently caused by a genetic fallacy.
- **Begging the question:** Loading the conclusion in the claim. Arguing that "pornography should be banned because it corrupts our youth" is a logical claim. However, saying that "filthy and corrupting pornography should be banned" is begging the question: The conclusion that the writer should *prove* (that pornography corrupts) is assumed in the claim. Other examples: "Those useless psychology classes should be dropped from the curriculum"; "Everyone knows that our ineffective drug control program is a miserable

failure." The writers must *prove* that the psychology classes are useless and that the drug program is a failure.

- **Circular argument:** A sentence or argument that restates rather than proves. Thus, it goes in a circle: "President Reagan was a great communicator because he had that knack of talking effectively to the people." The terms in the beginning of the sentence (*great communicator*) and the end of the sentence (*talking effectively*) are interchangeable. The sentence ends where it started.
- **Either/or:** An oversimplification that reduces the alternatives to only two choices, thereby creating a false dilemma. Statements such as "Love it or leave it" attempt to reduce the alternatives to two. If you don't love your school, your town, or your country, you don't have to leave: A third choice is to change it and make it better. Proposed solutions frequently have an either/or fallacy: "Either we ban boxing or hundreds of young men will be senselessly killed." A third alternative might be to change boxing's rules or equipment.
- **Faulty comparison or analogy:** Basing an argument on a comparison of two things, ideas, events, or situations that are similar but not identical. Although comparisons or analogies are often effective in argument, they can hide logical problems. "We can solve the meth problem the same way we reduced the DWI problem: Attack it with increased enforcement and mandatory jail sentences." Although the situations are similar, they are not identical. The DWI solution will not necessarily work for drugs. An analogy is an extended comparison that uses something simple or familiar to explain something complex or less familiar. "Solving a mathematics problem is like baking a cake: You have to take it one step at a time. First, you assemble your ingredients or your known data. . . ." Like baking, solving a problem does involve a process; unlike baking, however, mathematics is more exact. Changing the amount of flour in a recipe by 1 percent will not make the cake fall; changing a numeric value by 1 percent, however, will ruin the whole problem. The point, however, is not to avoid comparisons or analogies. Simply make sure that your conclusions are qualified; acknowledge the *differences* between the two things compared as well as the similarities.
- **Ad hominem (literally, "to the man"):** An attack on the character of the individual or the opponent rather than his or her opinions, arguments, or qualifications: "Susan Davidson, the prosecuting attorney, drinks heavily. There's no way she can present an effective case." This is an attack on Ms. Davidson's character rather than an analysis of her legal talents. Her record in court may be excellent.
- **Ad populum (literally, "to the people"):** An emotional appeal to positive concepts (God, mother, country, liberty, democracy, apple pie) or negative concepts (fascism, atheism) rather than a direct discussion of the real

issue: "If you are a true American, you should be in favor of tariffs to protect the garment industry."

- **Red herring:** A diversionary tactic designed to avoid confronting the key issue. *Red herring* refers to the practice of dragging a smelly fish across the trail to divert tracking dogs away from the real quarry. A red herring occurs when writers avoid countering an opposing argument directly: "Of course equal pay for women is an important issue, but I wonder whether women really want to take the responsibility that comes with higher paying jobs. Do they really want the additional stress?"

Postscript on the Writing Process

Writing in your journal, answer the following questions.

1. How did your beliefs about your subject change from the time you decided on your claim to when you revised your essay? What caused the change in your views?
2. What opposing argument was most difficult to counter? Explain how you handled it.
3. Which was your strongest argument? Did you use logical appeals and evidence, or did you rely more on appeals to character or emotion? Explain.
4. How did your writing process for the argumentative essay change from the process for your previous essays? What steps or stages took longer? What stages did you have to go back and rework?

Student Writing

Welfare Is Still Necessary for Women and Children in the U.S.

Read the Argument on Wolf Reintroduction

Crystal Sabatke

Crystal Sabatke decided to write her arguing essay about changes in the welfare system that require women to work in order to receive benefits. She decided to focus particularly on readers who believe that welfare mothers will only become lazy if they don't have to earn the money to support their families. She hopes that "by showing examples of positive welfare stories, I can show that mothers and their children are more important than saving a few cents per dollar." Reproduced below are Sabatke's notes for her audience analysis, her rough draft, the responses from her peer review workshop, and her final, revised draft.

...continued Welfare Is Still Necessary for Women..., **Crystal Sabatke**

AUDIENCE ANALYSIS: READERS' BELIEFS

My readers will assume that women on welfare who have children can go out and get jobs. That they should get jobs for the betterment of themselves and their children. That when they do get a job, their financial problems will be solved and that welfare will be a thing of the past. In order to shake these assumptions, I believe that emotional appeals should be used. Examples of factual women on welfare in negative situations that prevent them from getting jobs—children, low-income wage jobs, etc.

My readers also believe in the principle of a strong work ethic. I do feel that I should show how this principle is not applicable in certain situations—ones that my readers probably do not take into strong consideration.

Finally, I feel that my readers blindly value getting jobs more than taking care of children (even though these are the same people who hypocritically focus on family values). I think that family values should be focused on because this is something that is held in high regard by nearly every human being.

Welfare in the United States—Necessity Without Programming

FIRST DRAFT

What defines an American woman? Women in the United States play numerous roles; many are successful executives, mothers, wives, and scholars. Women have broken many barriers throughout U.S. history and have become, in general, a very successful group in society. But what about the women who haven't broken the barriers? What about the women who had children at a young age with a boyfriend or husband who left them alone soon after? What about the women who can't find a job because their education level hinders their prosperity? What about the women who can't seem to find their way above the poverty level and have to seek help from the government?

Throughout the United States, poverty is not abnormal—especially for women and children. With "44.6 percent of the children who lived in [female-headed households] poor in 1994, and almost half of all children who are poor living in female-headed households," (A) doesn't it seem ironic that the government is cutting welfare expenditures for women and children? Many government officials believe that "the welfare system and its recipients are the cause of the problem." (B) What the lawmakers aren't considering, however, is that poverty is essentially the catalyst in a circle of controversy, and that the only way out of the problems is to provide adequate educational opportunities for welfare recipients, along with ample child care programs and options and a sufficient minimum wage for all citizens. The answer is not ending welfare, but dealing with the problems of poverty in a realistic manner.

In contrast to opposing arguments, most women aren't poor and having children because they want more welfare money or because they are lazy, but because they don't have a sufficient education. As Nicholas Zill, a writer for *Public Health Reports,* states, "Girls and boys who become parents while they are still of school age are . . . predominantly those with low test scores and grades, who are disengaged from school or in active conflict with parents, teachers, or school authorities." (C) The government needs to provide for all Americans an education system that works not only for the successful student, but also for the students that are not doing well. Female students, especially, should be educated about birth control and negative outcomes of having children at younger ages. Welfare is indispensable for uneducated women and their children until a system of education and support can be initiated and proven successful.

For people opposing government assistance of the poor, another popular argument is that welfare needs to be ended in all forms, and women with children need to get jobs. According to Charles Murray, a strong oppressor of the welfare system in America and an advocate of family values, a "strict job program" needs to be established that will force women to "drop out of a welfare program altogether." (D) Essentially, to the opposition, "the welfare-reform discussion indicates that what happens to children doesn't matter to Americans, so long as mothers are forced to work." (E) Unfortunately, however, for women with children who either decide to go into or are forced into the job market, there isn't a child care system that works with mothers to make a "strict job program" successful. The truth is, there is a scarcity of child care options in this country, and the ones that are available are generally out of the price range of a welfare mother. Welfare is essential in providing a means for women to provide not only adequate care for their children, but positive values for their future.

Another category of women on welfare who are quite often overlooked are those mothers who have minimum-wage jobs and who still need government assistance. The current method of getting women into the workplace is the Job Training Partnership Act, or "the Government's biggest training program." (E) According to *The Wall Street Journal,* however, this program, which offers low-wage jobs such as fast food "is a sham" (E) and "actually led to lower wages for poor young women compared with a control group." (E) Once a woman is in the workplace, it is easy to assume that she will be removed from welfare. What is not taken into consideration, however, is that a minimum wage can hardly keep up with the needs of a single mother. "The average [welfare] recipient who gets a full-time job . . . makes $6.74 an hour—about $14,000 a year. Daycare for two children can easily cost $12,000." (E) Until Washington can come up with a solution that involves education and child care assistance and has raised the minimum wage enough to support a mother with children, a welfare system still needs to be provided.

The answer is not ending welfare, but providing supplemental programs that can realistically assist a single mother. With the minimum wage being too low, child care costs being impractical, and education programs virtually nonexistent, it is not fair to assume that welfare can be abolished. Of course, there are problems with the current welfare system, but supplemental programming is the only way to effectively change these glitches.

ARGUING ESSAY: PEER-RESPONSE WORKSHEET

To the Writer: Briefly describe the audience for this paper. (Be sure to include your audience's position on the issue you're writing about.) Also note what you want your readers to focus on as they read.

My audience is white, conservative males who are against any welfare. Please comment on my development—and I kind of gave up on my conclusion. How can I make it better?

To the Reader: Answer the following questions.

1. Underline the *claim/thesis.* Is it clear? Make suggestions for improvement.

   Bev: Good thesis. It is clear and placed in a good spot, just after enough background and before the bulk of the paper. However, I would elaborate more on the "realistic manner" either in your thesis sentence or a separate sentence.

   Amy: *The thesis is very clear—however, the sentence after it confused me.*

2. Is the claim adequately *focused*—narrow within manageable/defensible limits? Why or why not? Explain.

   Bev: The claim is well focused and clear.

   Amy: *Possibly even too focused. Reads more like an essay map than a thesis.*

3. **Do you feel the writer needs to add any *qualifiers* or exceptions in order to avoid overgeneralizing? If yes, explain.**

Bev: You sort of overgeneralize about women on welfare, but not too noticeably. Maybe some statistics concerning these women would help.

Amy: *Possibly qualify for 2 parent and singles—see paragraph 5.*

4. **Does the paper deal with *opposing arguments?* How successful do you feel the paper is in conceding and/or refuting opposing arguments? Explain.**

Bev: Good job of laying out the opposing sides of the argument.

Amy: *Opposition clearly stated each time and then refuted. No work needed on the ones you have stated. Does not take into consideration two-parent welfare families or singles. Will some of your claims work for them as well?*

5. **Does the *evidence* support the reasons? Where is more evidence needed? What kind of evidence is needed?**

Bev: Your use of evidence is effective. However, I would suggest more evidence in the first body paragraph. You only have one quotation—maybe throw another one in there.

Amy: *More statistics would be helpful, for example, test scores as related to teen pregnancy.*

6. **What are *one* or *two* areas that you feel the writer should address *first* in revising this paper? What suggestions can you make for conducting those revisions?**

Bev: Good organization of the paper. You follow a clear layout and it is easy to follow. I would develop your quotations more in paragraph 2. You use good evidence. Just develop it more. In your conclusion, maybe if you tied it into the intro, it would help you out. Restate arguments that you made in the introduction.

Amy: *The lead paragraph seems to give an essay map but doesn't. Possibly phrase some of the questions to relate to the paragraphs? Conclusion: Instead of summing up what you said, try an analysis of the problem and its solutions.*

7. **Return the paper to the writer and discuss your comments.**

FINAL DRAFT

Welfare Is Still Necessary for Women and Children in the U.S.

What defines an American woman? Women in the United States *1*
play numerous roles; many are successful executives, mothers, wives,

and scholars. Women have broken many barriers throughout U.S. history and have become, in general, a very successful group in society. But what about the women who haven't broken the barriers? What about the women who had children at a young age with a boyfriend or husband who left them soon after? What about the women who can't find a job because their education level hinders their prosperity? What about the women who can't seem to find their way above the poverty level and have to seek help from the government?

In the United States, poverty is not abnormal—especially for women and children. With "44.6 percent of the children who lived in [female-headed households] in 1994, and almost half of all children who are poor living in female-headed households," doesn't it seem ironic that the government continues to cut welfare expenditures for women and children? (Wellstone 1). Many government officials believe that "the welfare system and its recipients are the cause of the problem" (Rank 1). What these lawmakers aren't considering, however, is that poverty is essentially the catalyst in a circle of controversy, and that the only way out of the problem is to provide adequate educational opportunities for welfare recipients, ample child care programs and options, and a sufficient minimum wage for all citizens. Until methods such as these are instituted, it is necessary for the government to maintain a supportive welfare system for the women and children of our country. *2*

In refutation of opposing arguments, most women aren't poor and having children because they want more welfare money or because they are lazy, but because they don't have a sufficient education. As Nicholas Zill, a writer for Public Health Reports, states, "Girls and boys who become parents while they are still of school age are . . . predominantly those with low test scores and grades, who are disengaged from school or in active conflict with parents, teachers, or school authorities" (6). Recent studies by the National Center for Health Statistics show that "nearly one in every four children in the U.S. is born to a mother who has not finished high school" (Zill 2). The government needs to provide an educational system that focuses not only on the successful student, but also on the student who is performing poorly. Because "parent education is linked to children's economic well-being," positive programs need to be created that provide support and alternatives to mainstream education for students who are "high risk" or are not college-bound (Zill 3). Female students, specifically, should be educated about birth control and the negative consequences of having children at younger ages. Until our nation takes active measures to improve the educational system, welfare is *3* necessary to support the children who are born because of the inadequacies of our schools. Welfare is indispensable for uneducated women and their children until a better system of education and support can be initiated and proven successful.

Another popular argument given by people who oppose welfare is that single women with children should be working, not accepting welfare. According to Charles Murray, a strong critic of the welfare system, we need to institute a "strict job program" that will force women to "drop out of welfare altogether" (285). According to Ruth Conniff, author of "Big Bad Welfare: Welfare Reform Politics and Children," the welfare reform discussion "indicates that what happens to children doesn't matter to Americans, so long as mothers are forced to work" (8). Unfortunately, however, for single women with children who either decide to work or are forced into the job market, there isn't a child care system that could make a "strict job program" successful (Murray 285). With child care costing "about $116 a week for a toddler and $122 for an infant," not only is American day care economically insensitive, but day care options are limited as well (Conniff 8). According to Mark Robert Rank, author of "Winners and Losers in the Welfare Game," the "scarcity of affordable child care for low-income families" makes the current welfare system in this country a "losing game" (1). How can women be expected to get jobs when there aren't sufficient means to care for their children? Ruth Conniff wonders that if our country "is so concerned about family values, wouldn't it make sense to let mothers stay home with their young children?" (8). Welfare is essential to provide means for women to supply not only adequate care for their children but also positive values for their children's future. 4

Another category of women on welfare who are quite often overlooked are those mothers who have minimum-wage jobs and who still need government assistance. The current method of getting women into the workplace is the Job Training Partnership Act, or "the Government's biggest training program" (Conniff 5). According to the *Wall Street Journal,* however, this program—which offers low-wage jobs such as fast-food work—has "actually led to lower wages for poor young women compared with a control group" (Conniff 5). Once a woman is in the workplace, many people assume that she will be removed from welfare and become an independent member of society. What is not considered, however, is that the minimum wage can scarcely keep up with the needs of a single mother. According to a survey done of welfare recipients in Dane County, Wisconsin, "the average [welfare] recipient who gets a full-time job . . . makes $6.74 an hour—about $14,000 a year. Day care for two children can easily cost $12,000" (Conniff 7). It is obvious that 5 after subtracting child care costs, this equation leaves a mother with virtually nothing left to provide herself and her children with necessities such as food, clothing, and shelter—making it necessary to stay on government assistance. Until the minimum wage has been raised to keep up with these strenuous living situations, Washington needs to continue providing welfare to help single mothers and their children survive.

One of the many roles that American women assume is often that of a poverty-stricken single mother. With current education programs that are not effective for "high-risk" women students, with child care costs that are overwhelming, and with a minimum wage so low that it can't keep up with the needs of single mothers, it is not fair to assume that welfare can be abolished. As Michelle Tingling Clement of National Public Radio states, "What [women] truly need is . . . education, skills development . . . and not just any job but jobs that pay living wages with family health benefits and child care" (2). Until programs that can realistically assist women and children are created, welfare is still a definite necessity. 6

Works Cited

Clement, Michelle T. "Republicans Finalize Welfare Reform Package." *All Things Considered*. Natl. Public Radio, 15 Nov. 1998. Print. Transcript.

Conniff, Ruth. "Big Bad Welfare: Welfare Reform Politics and Children." *Progressive* 84 (1994): 1-10. Print.

Murray, Charles. "Keeping Priorities Straight on Welfare Reform." *The Aims of Argument*. Ed. Timothy W. Crucius and Carolyn E. Channell. Mountain View: Mayfield, 1998. 285-88. Print.

Rank, Mark Robert. "Winners and Losers in the Welfare Game." Editorial. *St. Louis Post-Dispatch* 15 Sept. 1994: 1-2. Print.

Wellstone, Paul. "If Poverty Is the Question." *Nation*. The Nation, 4 Apr. 1997. Web. 10 Oct. 1998.

Zill, Nicholas. "Parental Schooling and Children's Health." *Public Health Reports* 111 (1996): 1-10. Print.

Questions for Writing and Discussion

1. Sabatke says that her audience consists of white, conservative males who believe that everyone should have a job and no one should be on welfare. Where in her essay does she address this audience? Could she revise her essay to focus on this audience even more specifically? Explain.

2. Read Sabatke's first draft and then the responses by Bev and Amy on the peer-response sheet. Which of Bev's and/or Amy's suggestions do you agree with? What other suggestions might you give Sabatke? Which of the peer-response suggestions does Sabatke take or ignore in her final draft? How might Sabatke have improved her final version even more? Explain.

3. What opposing arguments does Sabatke consider? Choose one of her responses, and explain why you think the counterargument is or is not effective. Think of one additional counterargument that she might consider. Should she address that argument? Why or why not?

Complete additional exercises and practice in your MyLab

The Vietnam Veterans Memorial in Washington, DC, bears the names of more than 58,000 Americans killed in the Vietnam War, which ended in 1973. In this chapter a poem by Yusef Komunyakaa, "Facing It," deals with the experience of visiting the memorial. You may find that lines or images in the poem seem to be captured in this photograph.

Steve Raymer/Corbis

11 Responding to Literature

What You Will Learn
In this chapter, you will learn to:

11.1 Use techniques for responding to literature

11.2 Use collecting strategies to develop your response to literature

11.3 Shape your response to literature essay

RESPONDING to poems and short stories requires both imagination and critical-reading skill. As readers, we anticipate, imagine, feel, worry, analyze, and question. A story or poem is like an empty balloon that we inflate with the warm breath of our imagination and experience. Our participation makes us partners with the author in the artistic recreation.

Readers must *imagine* and recreate that special world described by the writer. The first sentences of a short story, for example, throw open a door to a world that—attractive or repulsive—tempts our curiosity and imagination. Like Alice in *Alice in Wonderland,* we cannot resist following a white rabbit with pink eyes who mutters to himself, checks his watch, and then zips down a rabbit hole and into an imaginary world.

Here are three opening sentences of three very different short stories.

> Young Goodman Brown came forth at sunset into the street at Salem village; but put his head back, after crossing the threshold, to exchange a parting kiss with his young wife.
>
> —Nathaniel Hawthorne, "Young Goodman Brown"

> As Gregor Samsa awoke one morning from uneasy dreams he found himself transformed in his bed into a gigantic insect.
>
> —Franz Kafka, "The Metamorphosis"

> The morning of June 27th was clear and sunny, with the fresh warmth of a full-summer day; the flowers were blossoming profusely and the grass was green.
>
> —Shirley Jackson, "The Lottery"

> **"I hungered for new books, new ways of looking and seeing. It was not a matter of believing or disbelieving what I read, but of feeling something new, of being affected by something that made the look of the world different."**
>
> **—Richard Wright**
> Author of *Black Boy*

> **"No one else can read a literary work for us. The benefits of literature can emerge only from creative activity on the part of the reader."**
>
> —Louise Rosenblatt
> Author of *Literature as Exploration*

Whether our imaginations construct the disturbing image of a "gigantic insect" or the seemingly peaceful picture of a perfect summer day, we actively recreate each story.

In a similar way, poems invite the reader to participate in actively creating characters, images, places, feelings, and reflections. Here are lines from several poems, each creating its own characters, places, images, and themes.

Because I could not stop for Death—
He kindly stopped for me—
The Carriage held but just Ourselves—
And Immortality.

—Emily Dickinson, "Because I could not stop for Death"

anyone lived in a pretty how town
(with up so floating many bells down)
spring summer autumn winter
he sang his didn't he danced his did.

—e. e. cummings, "anyone lived in a pretty how town"

Tyger! Tyger! burning bright
In the forests of the night,
What immortal hand or eye
Could frame thy fearful symmetry?

—William Blake, "The Tyger"

Two roads diverged in a yellow wood,
And sorry I could not travel both
And be one traveler, long I stood
And looked down one as far as I could
To where it bent in the undergrowth

—Robert Frost, "The Road Not Taken"

Responding to literature also requires that readers *reread.* First, you reread for yourself—that is, reread to write down your ideas, questions, feelings, and reactions. To heighten your role in re-creating a story or poem, you should note in the margins your questions and responses to main characters, places, metaphors and images, and themes that catch your attention: "Are the names of Hawthorne's characters significant? Is Young Goodman Brown really good? Is his wife, Faith, really faithful?" "Why does Emily Dickinson have her speaker personify Death as the driver of a carriage? Why does her speaker say that 'he *kindly* stopped for me'? What action is taking place?" Don't just underline or highlight passages. *Write* your questions and responses in the margins.

Second, you reread with a writer's eye. In fiction, identify the major and minor characters. Look for conflicts between characters. Mark passages that contain foreshadowing. Pinpoint sentences that reveal the narrative point of view. Use the appropriate critical terms (*character, plot, conflict, point of view, setting, style,* and *theme*) to help you reread with a writer's eye and see how the parts of a story relate to the whole. Similarly, in poetry, look for character, key events, and setting, and *always* pay attention to images and metaphors, to voice and tone, to word choice, and to rhythm and rhyme. Each critical term is a tool—a magnifying glass that helps you understand and interpret the literary work more clearly.

In addition to rereading, responding to literature requires that readers *share* ideas, reactions, and interpretations. Sharing usually begins in small-group or class discussions, and it continues as you explain your interpretation in writing. A work of literature is not a mathematical equation with a single answer. Great literature is worth interpreting precisely because each reader responds to it differently. One purpose of literature is to encourage you to reflect on your life and the lives of others—to look for new ways of seeing and understanding your world—and ultimately to expand your world. Sharing is crucial to appreciating literature.

Responding to a Short Story

Read and respond to Kate Chopin's "The Story of an Hour." Use your imagination to help create the story as you read. Then *reread* the story, noting in the margin your questions and responses. When you finish rereading and annotating your reactions, write your interpretation of the last line of the story.

Professional Writing

The Story of an Hour

Kate Chopin

Kate O'Flaherty Chopin (1851–1904) was an American writer whose mother was French and Creole and whose father was Irish. In 1870, she moved from St. Louis to New Orleans with her husband, Oscar Chopin, and over the next ten years she gave birth to five sons. After her husband died in 1882, Chopin returned to St. Louis to begin a new life as a writer.

Knowing that Mrs. Mallard was afflicted with a heart trouble, great care was taken to break to her as gently as possible the news of her husband's death. *1*

...continued The Story of an Hour, **Kate Chopin**

It was her sister Josephine who told her, in broken sentences, veiled hints that revealed in half concealing. Her husband's friend Richards was there, too, near her. It was he who had been in the newspaper office when intelligence of the railroad disaster was received, with Brently Mallard's name leading the list of "killed." He had only taken the time to assure himself of its truth by a second telegram, and had hastened to forestall any less careful, less tender friend in bearing the sad message. 2

She did not hear the story as many women have heard the same, with a paralyzed inability to accept its significance. She wept at once, with sudden, wild abandonment, in her sister's arms. When the storm of grief had spent itself she went away to her room alone. She would have no one follow her. 3

There stood, facing the open window, a comfortable, roomy armchair. Into this she sank, pressed down by a physical exhaustion that haunted her body and seemed to reach into her soul. 4

She could see in the open square before her house the tops of trees that were all aquiver with the new spring life. The delicious breath of rain was in the air. In the street below a peddler was crying his wares. The notes of a distant song which someone was singing reached her faintly, and countless sparrows were twittering in the eaves. 5

There were patches of blue sky showing here and there through the clouds that had met and piled one above the other in the west facing her window. 6

She sat with her head thrown back upon the cushion of the chair quite motionless, except when a sob came up into her throat and shook her, as a child who has cried itself to sleep continues to sob in its dreams. 7

She was young, with a fair, calm face, whose lines bespoke repression and even a certain strength. But now there was a dull stare in her eyes, whose gaze was fixed away off yonder on one of those patches of blue sky. It was not a glance of reflection, but rather indicated a suspension of intelligent thought. 8

There was something coming to her and she was waiting for it, fearfully. What was it? She did not know; it was too subtle and elusive to name. But she felt it, creeping out of the sky, reaching toward her through the sounds, the scents, the color that filled the air. 9

Now her bosom rose and fell tumultuously. She was beginning to recognize this thing that was approaching to possess her, and she was striving to beat it back with her will—as powerless as her two white slender hands would have been. 10

When she abandoned herself a little whispered word escaped her slightly parted lips. She said it over and over under her breath: "Free, free, free!" The vacant stare and the look of terror that had followed it went 11 from her eyes. They stayed keen and bright. Her pulses beat fast, and the coursing blood warmed and relaxed every inch of her body.

She did not stop to ask if it were not a monstrous joy that held her. 12
A clear and exalted perception enabled her to dismiss the suggestion as trivial.

She knew that she would weep again when she saw the kind, tender 13
hands folded in death; the face that had never looked save with love upon her, fixed and gray and dead. But she saw beyond that bitter moment a long procession of years to come that would belong to her absolutely. And she opened and spread her arms out to them in welcome.

There would be no one to live for during those coming years; she 14
would live for herself. There would be no powerful will bending her in that blind persistence with which men and women believe they have a right to impose a private will upon a fellow creature. A kind intention or a cruel intention made the act seem no less a crime as she looked upon it in that brief moment of illumination.

And yet she had loved him—sometimes. Often she had not. What 15
did it matter! What could love, the unsolved mystery, count for in face of this possession of self-assertion which she suddenly recognized as the strongest impulse of her being.

"Free! Body and soul free!" she kept whispering. 16

Josephine was kneeling before the closed door with her lips to the 17
keyhole, imploring for admission. "Louise, open the door! I beg; open the door—you will make yourself ill. What are you doing, Louise? For heaven's sake open the door."

"Go away. I am not making myself ill." No; she was drinking in a very 18
elixir of life through that open window.

Her fancy was running riot along those days ahead of her. Spring 19
days, and summer days, and all sorts of days that would be her own. She breathed a quick prayer that life might be long. It was only yesterday she had thought with a shudder that life might be long.

She arose at length and opened the door to her sister's importuni- 20
ties. There was a feverish triumph in her eyes, and she carried herself unwittingly like a goddess of Victory. She clasped her sister's waist, and together they descended the stairs. Richards stood waiting for them at the bottom.

Someone was opening the front door with a latchkey. It was Brently 21
Mallard who entered, a little travel-stained, composedly carrying his grip-sack and umbrella. He had been far from the scene of accident, and did not even know there had been one. He stood amazed at Josephine's piercing cry; at Richards's quick motion to screen him from the view of his wife.

But Richards was too late. 22

When the doctors came they said she had died of heart disease—of 23
joy that kills.

Responding to a Poem

Read and respond to W. H. Auden's "Musée des Beaux Arts." Begin by examining the painting by Pieter Brueghel, *Landscape with the Fall of Icarus,* reproduced below. Carefully read and reread the poem, comparing it with details in the painting. Then go online to find the description of Daedalus and Icarus in the Roman poet Ovid's *Metamorphoses.* As you reread Auden's poem, pay particular attention to the detail in the description, to Auden's references to scenes not depicted in the painting, and to the language and word choice.

Professional Writing

Musée des Beaux Arts

W. H. Auden

W. H. Auden (1907–1973) was born in England, went to college at Oxford, and moved to the United States in 1939. In this poem, Auden reflects on the art and the theme of Pieter Brueghel's famous painting, *Landscape with the Fall of Icarus* (c. 1558). Auden describes and interprets Brueghel's vision of the Fall of Icarus, and Brueghel in turn visualizes and interprets the Roman poet Ovid's version of the story of Daedalus and his son, Icarus. In this Greek myth, according to Ovid, Daedalus fashions wings made out of feathers and wax in order to help them escape the island of Crete. Daedalus cautions his son not to fly too near the heat of the sun, but Icarus ignores his father's advice. When Icarus soars too high, the sun melts the wax in his wings, and he plunges into the ocean. In Brueghel's painting, only the white legs of Icarus are visible (in the lower right-hand corner of the painting) as he disappears into the water.

Pieter Brueghel, *Landscape with the Fall of Icarus*

About suffering they were never wrong,
The old Masters: how well they understood
Its human position: how it takes place
While someone else is eating or opening a window or
just walking dully along;
How, when the aged are reverently, passionately waiting
For the miraculous birth, there always must be
Children who did not specially want it to happen, skating
On a pond at the edge of the wood:
They never forgot
That even the dreadful martyrdom must run its course
Anyhow in a corner, some untidy spot
Where the dogs go on with their doggy life and the
torturer's horse
Scratches its innocent behind on a tree.
In Brueghel's Icarus, for instance: how everything
turns away
Quite leisurely from the disaster; the ploughman may
Have heard the splash, the forsaken cry,
But for him it was not an important failure; the sun shone
As it had to on the white legs disappearing into the green
Water, and the expensive delicate ship that must have seen
Something amazing, a boy falling out of the sky,
Had somewhere to get to and sailed calmly on.

Techniques for Responding to Literature

As you read and respond to a work of literature, keep the following techniques in mind.

Techniques for Responding to Literature

Technique	Tips on How to Do It
Understanding the assignment and selecting a possible purpose and audience	Unless stated otherwise in your assignment, your purpose is to *interpret* a work of literature. Your audience will often be other members of your class, including the teacher.
Actively reading, annotating, and discussing the literary work	Remember that literature often contains *highly condensed experiences*. In order to interpret literature, you need to reread patiently both the major events and the seemingly insignificant passages. In discussions, look for the differences between your responses and other readers' ideas.

Focusing your essay on a single, clearly defined interpretation	State your *main idea or thesis,* focusing on a single idea or aspect of the piece of literature. *Your thesis should* not *be a statement of fact.* Whether you are explaining, evaluating, or arguing, your interpretation must be clearly stated.
Supporting your interpretation with evidence	Because your readers will probably have different interpretations, you must show which specific characters, events, scenes, conflicts, images, metaphors, or themes prompted your response, and you must use details to support your interpretation. *Do **not** merely retell the major events of the story or describe the main images in the poem.* Assume that your readers have read the story or poem.

Warming Up: Journal Exercises

Read all of the following questions and then write for five minutes on two or three. These questions should help clarify your perceptions about literature or develop your specific responses to "The Story of an Hour" or to "Musée des Beaux Arts."

1. Write out the *question* that "The Story of an Hour" seems to ask. What is your answer to this question? What might have been Kate Chopin's answer?
2. The words *heart, joy, free, life,* and *death* appear several times in "The Story of an Hour." Underline these words (or their synonyms) each time they appear. Explain how the meaning of each of these words seems to change during the story. Is each word used ironically?
3. Write out a dictionary definition of the word *feminism.* Then write out your own definition. Is Mrs. Mallard a feminist? Is Kate Chopin a feminist? What evidence in the story supports your answers?
4. In Ovid's account of the myth of Daedalus and Icarus, the fisherman, shepherd, and plowman are "astonished" as they observe Icarus flying, and Ovid suggests that they might worship Icarus and Daedalus as gods. In what way does Brueghel revise Ovid's account? Explain how and why Brueghel changes this part of the myth.
5. Auden suggests that one theme of Brueghel's painting is that suffering is largely ignored by the general populace. Study Brueghel's painting again. What other themes or ideas are present in the painting that Auden does not mention? Explain another possible interpretation of the painting based on specific images or points of focus in the painting.

6 Auden says that the theme of Brueghel's painting is about suffering, but he also includes a description of "the miraculous birth" and children who "did not specially want it to happen." Does this image distract from Auden's main point, or is the idea of the miraculous birth related to Auden's theme? Explain.

PURPOSES FOR RESPONDING TO LITERATURE

11.1
Use techniques for responding to literature

Watch the Animation on Literary Analysis

In responding to literature, you should be guided by the purposes that you have already followed in previous chapters. Begin by writing *for yourself.* Your purposes are to observe, feel, remember, understand, and relate the work of literature to your own life: What is happening? What memories does it trigger? How does it make you feel? Why is this passage confusing? Why do you like or dislike this character? Literature has special, personal value. You should write about literature initially in order to discover and understand its importance in your life.

When you write an interpretive essay, however, you are writing *for others.* Your purposes will often be mixed, but an interpretive essay often contains elements of *explaining, evaluating, problem solving,* and *arguing.*

- **Explaining.** Interpretive essays about literature explain the *what, why,* and *how* of a piece of literature. What is the key subject? What is the most important line, event, or character? What are the major conflicts or the key images? What motivates a character? How does a character's world build or unravel? How does a story or poem meet or fail to meet our expectations? How did our interpretations develop? Each of these questions might lead to an interpretive essay that explains the *what, why,* and *how* of your response.
- **Evaluating.** Readers and writers often talk about "appreciating" a work of literature. *Appreciating* means establishing its value or worth. It may mean praising the work's literary virtues; it may mean finding faults or weaknesses. Usually, evaluating essays measure *both strengths and weaknesses,* according to specific criteria. What important standards for literature do you wish to apply? How does the work in question measure up? What kinds of readers might find this story worth reading? An evaluative essay cites evidence to show why a story is exciting, boring, dramatic, puzzling, vivid, relevant, or memorable.
- **Problem solving.** Writers of interpretive essays occasionally take a problem-solving approach, focusing on how the reader overcomes obstacles in understanding the work, or on how the author solved problems in writing key scenes, choosing images and language, developing character, and creating and resolving conflicts. Particularly if you like to write fiction or poetry yourself, you may wish to take the writer's

point of view: how did the writer solve (or fail to solve) problems of image, metaphor, character, setting, plot, or theme?

- **Arguing.** As readers share responses, they may discover that their interpretations diverge sharply. Does "The Story of an Hour" have a feminist theme? Is it about women or about human nature in general? Is the main character admirable or selfish? Is Auden's interpretation of Brueghel's painting faithful to Brueghel's conception? Is Auden's the only way to interpret Bureghel's painting? In interpretive essays, writers sometimes argue for their beliefs. They present evidence that refutes an opposing or alternative interpretation and supports their own reading.

Most interpretive essays about literature are focused by these purposes, whether used singly or in combination. Writers should *select* the purpose(s) that are most appropriate for the work of literature and their own responses.

RESPONDING TO SHORT FICTION

Watch the Video on Reading a Short Story

Begin by noting your reactions at key points. *Summarize* in your own words what is happening in the story. Write down your *observations* or *reactions* to striking or surprising passages. Ask yourself *questions* about ambiguous or confusing passages.

After you respond initially, use the following basic elements of fiction to help you analyze how the parts of a short story relate to the whole. Pay attention to how setting or plot affects the character, or how style and setting affect the theme. Because analysis artificially separates plot, character, and theme, look for ways to *synthesize* the parts: Seeing how these parts relate to each other should suggest an idea, focus, or angle to use in your interpretation.

Character

Watch the Video on Character

In short fiction, typically both *major* and *minor* characters contribute to the story as a whole. As you analyze the characters, consider these questions:

- How does the main character face *conflicts*, undergo *changes*, or reveal his or her personality?
- Which characters are *flat*, *one-dimensional*, or *stereotyped*?
- How are characters *motivated*? Are there *internal* or *external* forces at work?
- How do characters reveal themselves—by their *own actions and choices*, through what *others* say or do, or by both?

Plot

Plot is the sequence of events in a story, but it is also the cause-and-effect relationship of one event with another. Use the following critical terms to understand and analyze the story.

- *Exposition.* Exposition is the information given to the reader early in the story about what has happened before the story begins.

- *Foreshadowing.* Writers often give readers clues or hints about what will occur, before it actually happens.
- *Conflicts.* Frequently, stories set up conflicts within a character, between characters, and/or between characters and their environment. These conflicts often keep the plot in motion.

Watch the Video on Conflict

- *Climax.* The climax is the high point, the point of no return, or the most dramatic moment of the story. At the climax of a story, often the characters—and the readers as well—discover something important about themselves or their world.
- *Denouement.* At or near the end of a story, sometimes the complications and conflicts are resolved or "unraveled." In "The Story of an Hour," the climax and denoument occur almost at the same time, in the last lines of the story.

Narrative Point of View

Fiction is usually narrated from either the first-person or the third-person point of view.

Watch the Video on Point of View

- *A first-person narrator* is a character who tells the story from his or her point of view. This person may be a minor or a major character and may be relatively *reliable* (trustworthy) or *unreliable* (naïve or misleading). *Reliable* first-person narrators often invite the reader to identify with their perspectives or predicaments, while *unreliable* narrators may cause readers to be wary of their judgments or their states of mind.
- A *third-person omniscient narrator* is not a character or participant in the story. Omniscient narrators are assumed to know everything about the characters and events. They move through space and time, giving readers necessary information throughout the story. Omniscient narrators may be *intrusive,* jumping into the story to give their editorial judgments, or they may be *objective,* removing themselves from the action and the minds of characters.
- A *selective omniscient narrator* usually limits his or her focus to a single character's experiences and thoughts, as Kate Chopin's narrator focuses on Mrs. Mallard in "The Story of an Hour."
- *Stream-of-consciousness narration* occurs when an omniscient narrator presents the thoughts, memories, and associations of a character in the story.

Setting

Setting is the physical place, scene, and time of the story. It includes the social or historical context of the story. The setting in "The Story of an Hour" is the house and the room in which Mrs. Mallard waits, but it is also the social and historical time frame. *Setting is usually important for what it reveals about the characters,*

Watch the Video on Setting

the plot, or the theme of the story. Does the setting reflect a character's personality or state of mind? Is the setting or environment a source of conflict or tension in the story? Do environmental details of sight, touch, smell, hearing, or taste affect or reflect the characters' personality, predicaments, shortcomings, or desires?

Style

Style is a general term that may refer to sentence structure, figurative language, and symbols, as well as to the author's tone or use of irony.

- *Sentence structure* may be long and complicated or relatively short and simple. It may reflect the narrator's style or even a character's manner of thinking or speaking.
- *Figurative language,* such as similes and metaphors, often helps to depict a setting or describe a character. Mrs. Mallard, for example, is described as sobbing, "as a child who has cried itself to sleep continues to sob in its dreams."
- A *symbol* is a person, place, thing, or event that suggests or signifies something beyond itself. In "The Story of an Hour," the open window and the new spring life suggest or represent Mrs. Mallard's new freedom.
- *Tone* is the author's attitude toward the characters, setting, or plot. Tone may be sympathetic, humorous, serious, detached, or critical.
- *Irony* occurs when the author or a character says or does one thing but means the opposite or something altogether different. The ending of "The Story of an Hour" is ironic: The doctors say Mrs. Mallard has died "of joy that kills." In fact, she has died of killed joy.

Watch the **Video** on Figures of Speech

Theme

Watch the **Video** on Theme

The focus of an interpretive essay is often on the *theme* of a story. In arriving at a theme, ask how the characters, plot, point of view, setting, and style *contribute* to the main ideas or point of the story. The theme of a story depends, within limits, on your reactions as a reader. "The Story of an Hour" is *not* about relationships between sisters, nor is it about medical malpractice. It is an ironic story about love, personal freedom, and death, but what precisely is the *theme*? Does "The Story of an Hour" carry a feminist message, or is it more universally about the repressive power of love? Is Mrs. Mallard to be admired or criticized for her impulse to free herself? Do not trivialize the theme of a story by looking for some simple "moral." In describing the theme, deal with the complexity of life recreated in the story.

Professional Writing

The Lesson

Toni Cade Bambara

Toni Cade Bambara (1939–1995) was an activist for the African-American community. She worked for political and social causes in urban communities, taught African-American studies at half a dozen colleges and universities, and was the author of several collections of short stories and novels. "The Lesson" dramatizes the gradual awakening of several children to the political and economic realities of contemporary urban life. As you read the story, pay attention to the narrator, Sylvia. What is the lesson, and what does Sylvia learn?

Back in the days when everyone was old and stupid or young and foolish and me and Sugar were the only ones just right, this lady moved on our block with nappy hair and proper speech and no makeup. And quite naturally we laughed at her, laughed the way we did at the junk man who went about his business like he was some big-time president and his sorry-ass horse his secretary. And we kinda hated her too, hated the way we did the winos who cluttered up our parks and pissed on our handball walls and stank up our hallways and stairs so you couldn't halfway play hide-and-seek without a goddamn gas mask. Miss Moore was her name. The only woman on the block with no first name. And she was black as hell, cept for her feet, which were fish-white and spooky. And she was always planning these boring-ass things for us to do, us being my cousins, mostly, who lived on the block cause we all moved North the same time and to the same apartment then spread out gradual to breathe. And our parents would yank our heads into some kinda shape and crisp up our clothes so we'd be presentable for travel with Miss Moore, who always looked like she was going to church, though she never did. Which is just one of the things the grownups talked about when they talked behind her back like a dog. But when she came calling with some sachet she'd sewed up or some gingerbread she'd made or some book, why then they'd all be too embarrassed to turn her down and we'd get handed over all spruced up. She'd been to college and said it was only right that she should take responsibility for the young ones' education, and she not even related by marriage or blood. So they'd go for it. Specially Aunt Gretchen. She was the main gofer in the family. You got some ole dumb shit foolishness you want somebody to go for, you send for Aunt Gretchen. She been screwed into the go-along for so long, it's a blood-deep natural thing with her. Which is how she got saddled with me and Sugar and Junior in the first place while our mothers were in a la-de-da apartment up the block having a good ole time. 1

So this one day Miss Moore rounds us all up at the mailbox and it's puredee hot and she's knockin herself out about arithmetic. And school suppose to let up in summer I heard, but she don't never let up. And the 2

...continued The Lesson, **Toni Cade Bambara**

starch in my pinafore scratching the shit outta me and I'm really hating this nappy-head bitch and her goddamn college degree. I'd much rather go to the pool or to the show where it's cool. So me and Sugar leaning on the mailbox being surly, which is a Miss Moore word. And Flyboy checking out what everybody brought for lunch. And Fat Butt already wasting his peanut-butter-and-jelly sandwich like the pig he is. And Junebug punchin on Q.T.'s arm for potato chips. And Rosie Giraffe shifting from one hip to the other waiting for somebody to step on her foot or ask her if she from Georgia so she can kick ass, preferably Mercedes's. And Miss Moore asking us do we know what money is, like we a bunch of retards. I mean real money, she say, like it's only poker chips or monopoly papers we lay on the grocer. So right away I'm tired of this and say so. And would much rather snatch Sugar and go to the Sunset and terrorize the West Indian kids and take their hair ribbons and their money too. And Miss Moore files that remark away for next week's lesson on brotherhood, I can tell. And finally I say we oughta get to the subway cause it's cooler and besides we might meet some cute boys. Sugar done swiped her mama's lipstick, so we ready.

So we heading down the street and she's boring us silly about what 3
things cost and what our parents make and how much goes for rent and how money ain't divided up right in this country. And then she gets to the part about we all poor and live in the slums, which I don't feature. And I'm ready to speak on that, but she steps out in the street and hails two cabs just like that. Then she hustles half the crew in with her and hands me a five-dollar bill and tells me to calculate 10 percent tip for the driver. And we're off. Me and Sugar and Junebug and Flyboy hangin out the window and hollering to everybody, putting lipstick on each other cause Flyboy a faggot anyway, and making farts with our sweaty armpits. But I'm mostly trying to figure how to spend this money. But they all fascinated with the meter ticking and Junebug starts laying bets as to how much it'll read when Flyboy can't hold his breath no more. Then Sugar lays bets as to how much it'll be when we get there. So I'm stuck. Don't nobody want to go for my plan, which is to jump out at the next light and run off to the first bar-b-que we can find. Then the driver tells us to get the hell out cause we there already. And the meter reads eighty-five cents. And I'm stalling to figure out the tip and Sugar say give him a dime. And I decide he don't need it bad as I do, so later for him. But then he tries to take off with Junebug foot still in the door so we talk about his mama something ferocious. Then we check out that we on Fifth Avenue and everybody dressed up in stockings. One lady in a fur coat, hot as it is. White folks crazy.

"This is the place," Miss Moore say, presenting it to us in the voice she uses at the museum. "Let's look in the windows before we go in." 4

"Can we steal?" Sugar asks very serious like she's getting the ground rules squared away before she plays. "I beg your pardon," say Miss Moore, and we fall out. So she leads us around the windows of the toy store and me and Sugar screamin, "This is mine, that's mine, I gotta have that, that was made for me, I was born for that," till Big Butt drowns us out. 5

"Hey, I'm goin to buy that there." 6

"That there? You don't even know what it is, stupid." 7

"I do so," he say punchin on Rosie Giraffe. "It's a microscope." 8

"Whatcha gonna do with a microscope, fool?" 9

"Look at things." 10

"Like what, Ronald?" ask Miss Moore. And Big Butt ain't got the first notion. So here go Miss Moore gabbing about the thousands of bacteria in a drop of water and the somethinorother in a speck of blood and the million and one living things in the air around us is invisible to the naked eye. And what she say that for? Junebug go to town on that "naked" and we rolling. Then Miss Moore ask what it cost. So we all jam into the window smudgin it up and the price tag say $300. So then she ask how long'd take for Big Butt and Junebug to save up their allowances. "Too long," I say. "Yeh," adds Sugar, "outgrown it by that time." And Miss Moore say no, you never outgrow learning instruments. "Why, even medical students and interns and," blah, blah, blah. And we ready to choke Big Butt for bringing it up in the first damn place. 11

"This here costs four hundred eighty dollars," say Rosie Giraffe. So we pile up all over her to see what she pointin out. My eyes tell me it's a chunk of glass cracked with something heavy, and different-color inks dripped into the splits, then the whole thing put into a oven or something. But for $480 it don't make sense. 12

"That's a paperweight made of semi-precious stones fused together under tremendous pressure," she explains slowly, with her hands doing the mining and all the factory work. 13

"So what's a paperweight?" asks Rosie Giraffe. 14

"To weigh paper with, dumbbell," say Flyboy, the wise man from the East. 15

"Not exactly," say Miss Moore, which is what she say when you warm or way off too. "It's to weigh paper down so it won't scatter and make your desk untidy." So right away me and Sugar curtsy to each other and then to Mercedes who is more the tidy type. 16

"We don't keep paper on top of the desk in my class," say Junebug, figuring Miss Moore crazy or lyin one. 17

"At home, then," she say. "Don't you have a calendar and a pencil case and a blotter and a letter-opener on your desk at home where you do your homework?" And she know damn well what our homes look like cause she nosys around in them every chance she gets. 18

...continued The Lesson, **Toni Cade Bambara**

"I don't even have a desk," say Junebug. "Do we?" 19

"No. And I don't get no homework neither," says Big Butt. 20

"And I don't even have a home," say Flyboy like he do at school to 21
keep the white folks off his back and sorry for him. Send this poor kid to camp posters, is his specialty.

"I do," says Mercedes. "I have a box of stationery on my desk and a 22
picture of my cat. My godmother bought the stationery and the desk. There's a big rose on each sheet and the envelopes smell like roses."

"Who wants to know about your smelly-ass stationery," say Rosie 23
Giraffe fore I can get my two cents in.

"It's important to have a work area all your own so that. . . ." 24

"Will you look at this sailboat, please," say Flyboy, cuttin her off and 25
pointin to the thing like it was his. So once again we tumble all over each other to gaze at this magnificent thing in the toy store which is just big enough to maybe sail two kittens across the pond if you strap them to the posts tight. We all start reciting the price tag like we in assembly. "Handcrafted sailboat of fiberglass at one thousand one hundred ninety-five dollars."

"Unbelievable," I hear myself say and am really stunned. I read it 26
again for myself just in case the group recitation put me in a trance. Same thing. For some reason this pisses me off. We look at Miss Moore and she lookin at us, waiting for I dunno what.

"Who'd pay all that when you can buy a sailboat set for a quarter 27
at Pop's, a tube of glue for a dime, and a ball of string for eight cents? It must have a motor and a whole lot else besides," I say. "My sailboat cost me about fifty cents."

"But will it take water?" say Mercedes with her smart ass. 28

"Took mine to Alley Pond Park once," say Flyboy. "String broke. Lost 29
it. Pity."

"Sailed mine in Central Park and it keeled over and sank. Had to ask 30
my father for another dollar."

"And you got the strap," laugh Big Butt. "The jerk didn't even have a 31
string on it. My old man wailed on his behind."

Little Q.T. was staring hard at the sailboat and you could see he 32
wanted it bad. But he too little and somebody'd just take it from him. So what the hell. "This boat for kids, Miss Moore?"

"Parents silly to buy something like that just to get all broke up," say 33
Rosie Giraffe.

"That much money it should last forever," I figure. 34

"My father'd buy it for me if I wanted it." 35

"Your father, my ass," say Rosie Giraffe getting a chance to finally 36
push Mercedes.

"Must be rich people shop here," say Q.T. 37

"You are a very bright boy," say Flyboy. "What was your first clue?" And he rap him on the head with the back of his knuckles, since Q.T. the only one he could get away with. Though Q.T. liable to come up behind you years later and get his licks in when you half expect it. 38

"What I want to know is," I says to Miss Moore though I never talk to her, I wouldn't give the bitch that satisfaction, "is how much a real boat costs? I figure a thousand'd get you a yacht any day." 39

"Why don't you check that out," she says, "and report back to the group?" Which really pains my ass. If you gonna mess up a perfectly good swim day least you could do is have some answers. "Let's go in," she say like she got something up her sleeve. Only she don't lead the way. So me and Sugar turn the corner to where the entrance is, but when we get there I kinda hang back. Not that I'm scared, what's there to be afraid of, just a toy store. But I feel funny, shame. But what I got to be shamed about? Got as much right to go in as anybody. But somehow I can't seem to get hold of the door, so I step away for Sugar to lead. But she hangs back too. And I look at her and she looks at me and this is ridiculous. I mean, damn, I have never ever been shy about doing nothing or going nowhere. But then Mercedes steps up and then Rosie Giraffe and Big Butt crowd in behind and shove, and next thing we all stuffed into the doorway with only Mercedes squeezing past us, smoothing out her jumper and walking right down the aisle. Then the rest of us tumble in like a glued-together jigsaw done all wrong. And people lookin at us. And it's like the time me and Sugar crashed into the Catholic church on a dare. But once we got in there and everything so hushed and holy and the candles and the bowin and the hand-kerchiefs on all the drooping heads, I just couldn't go through with the plan. Which was for me to run up to the altar and do a tap dance while Sugar played the nose flute and messed around in the holy water. And Sugar kept givin me the elbow. Then later teased me so bad I tied her up in the shower and turned it on and locked her in. And she'd be there till this day if Aunt Gretchen hadn't finally figured I was lyin about the boarder takin a shower. 40

Same thing in the store. We all walkin on tiptoe and hardly touch-in the games and puzzles and things. And I watched Miss Moore who is steady watchin us like she waitin for a sign. Like Mama Drewery watches the sky and sniffs the air and takes note of just how much slant is in the bird formation. Then me and Sugar bump smack into each other, so busy gazing at the toys, 'specially the sailboat. But we don't laugh and go into our fat-lady bump-stomach routine. We just stare at that price tag. Then Sugar run a finger over the whole boat. And I'm jealous and want to hit her. Maybe not her, but I sure want to punch somebody in the mouth. 41

"Watcha bring us here for, Miss Moore?" 42

...continued The Lesson, **Toni Cade Bambara**

"You sound angry, Sylvia. Are you mad about something?" Givin me one of them grins like she tellin a grown-up joke that never turns out to be funny. And she's lookin very closely at me like maybe she plannin to do my portrait from memory. I'm mad, but I won't give her that satisfaction. So I slouch around the store bein very bored and say, "Let's go." 43

Me and Sugar at the back of the train watchin the tracks whizzin by large then small then gettin gobbled up in the dark. I'm thinkin about this tricky toy I saw in the store. A clown that somersaults on a bar then does chin-ups just cause you yank lightly at his leg. Cost $35. I could see me askin my mother for a $35 birthday clown. "You wanna who that costs what?" she'd say, cocking her head to the side to get a better view of the hole in my head. Thirty-five dollars could buy new bunk beds for Junior and Gretchen's boy. Thirty-five dollars and the whole household could go visit Granddaddy Nelson in the country. Thirty-five dollars would pay for the rent and the piano bill too. Who are these people that spend that much for performing clowns and $1,000 for toy sailboats? What kinda work they do and how they live and how come we ain't in on it? Where we are is who we are, Miss Moore always pointin out. But it don't necessarily have to be that way, she always adds then waits for somebody to say that poor people have to wake up and demand their share of the pie and don't none of us know what kind of pie she talkin about in the first damn place. But she ain't so smart cause I still got her four dollars from the taxi and she sure ain't gettin it. Messin up my day with this shit. Sugar nudges me in my pocket and winks. 44

Miss Moore lines us up in front of the mailbox where we started from, seem like years ago, and I got a headache for thinkin so hard. And we lean all over each other so we can hold up under the draggy-ass lecture she always finishes us off with at the end before we thank her for borin us to tears. But she just looks at us like she readin tea leaves. Finally she say, "Well, what did you think of F. A. O. Schwarz?" 45

Rosie Giraffe mumbles, "White folks crazy." 46

"I'd like to go there again when I get my birthday money," says Mercedes, and we shove her out the pack so she has to lean on the mailbox by herself. 47

"I'd like a shower. Tiring day," say Flyboy. 48

Then Sugar surprises me by sayin, "You know, Miss Moore, I don't think all of us here put together eat in a year what that sailboat costs." And Miss Moore lights up like somebody goosed her. "And?" she say, urging Sugar on. Only I'm standin on her foot so she don't continue. 49

"Imagine for a minute what kind of society it is in which some people can spend on a toy what it would cost to feed a family of six or seven. What do you think?" 50

"I think," say Sugar pushing me off her feet like she never done 51
before, cause I whip her ass in a minute, "that this is not much of a
democracy if you ask me. Equal chance to pursue happiness means an
equal crack at the dough, don't it?" Miss Moore is besides herself and I am
disgusted with Sugar's treachery. So I stand on her foot one more time to
see if she'll shove me. She shuts up, and Miss Moore looks at me, sorrow-
fully I'm thinkin. And somethin weird is goin on, I can feel it in my chest.

"Anybody else learn anything today?" lookin dead at me. I walk away 52
and Sugar has to run to catch up and don't even seem to notice when I
shrug her arm off my shoulder.

"Well, we got four dollars anyway," she says. 53

"Uh hunh." 54

"We could go to Hascombs and get half a chocolate layer and then go 55
to the Sunset and still have plenty money for potato chips and ice cream
sodas."

"Uh hunh." 56

"Race you to Hascombs," she say. 57

We start down the block and she gets ahead which is O.K. by me 58
cause I'm going to the West End and then over to the Drive to think
this day through. She can run if she want to and even run faster. But
ain't nobody gonna beat me at nuthin.

Questions for Writing and Discussion

1. Reread the opening sentence of the story. What does the first half of that sentence reveal about the character of the narrator? Does the rest of the story confirm that initial impression? Explain.
2. Locate at least one sentence or passage describing the reactions of each of the following children to the merchandise at F. A. O. Schwarz: Sylvia (the narrator), Sugar, Flyboy, Mercedes, Big Butt, Junebug, Rosie Giraffe, and Q.T. How do their reactions to the toys and their prices affect the narrator? Why does Bambara include all of these children in the story rather than tell it using just Miss Moore, Sylvia, and Sugar?
3. What exactly is the lesson that Miss Moore tries to teach her students? Find the sentences that express what Miss Moore wants her students to learn. Does Sugar learn this lesson? Does the narrator? How is this lesson similar to or different from the goals of the Occupy Wall Street movement?
4. What evidence (cite specific sentences) suggests that Sylvia is learning more from this lesson than she wants to? What exactly is she learning? Describe what she might do in the future as a result of what she learns.

5 Write two paragraphs comparing and contrasting the "awakenings" of Mrs. Mallard in "The Story of an Hour" and Sylvia in "The Lesson." What—and how—does each character learn? How do they react to what they learn? What do we, as readers, learn?

RESPONDING TO POETRY

Watch the Video on Reading a Poem

Poems often have characters, setting, and point of view, but they also have other features that are important to reading imaginatively and critically. Use the following literary terms to focus your reading and response to poems.

Voice and Tone

The speaker in a poem is not necessarily the same as the author of the poem. When Robert Frost says in "The Road Not Taken," "Two roads diverged in a yellow wood, /And sorry I could not travel both," the "I" in the poem is not directly equivalent to Robert Frost. The "I" represents a speaker faced with this particular choice. *Tone,* the speaker's attitude toward the subject matter, is also important in the poem. A speaker's tone might be happy or sad, delighted or angry, serious or humorous, spontaneous or reflective, straightforward or ironic. In Frost's poem, the speaker's tone is serious and reflective when he says, in conclusion, "I took the one less traveled by, /And that has made all the difference." In Auden's poem, the speaker is a person explaining or interpreting a painting. Phrases such as "how well they understood its human position" or "In Brueghel's Icarus, for instance" reveal the speaker as knowledgeable and perhaps slightly academic. The speaker's tone is serious and reflective: he is praising the virtues of a painting by one of the Old Masters.

Word Choice

In poetry, diction and word choice are especially important. A poet might use academic language and formal phrasing or street language and slang. A poet might use short, emphatic words, or longer, more flowing language. Sometimes a poem juxtaposes formal and informal language. Auden deliberately contrasts a more formal diction ("About suffering they were never wrong, /The Old Masters") with more informal and colloquial (spoken) language ("Anyhow in a corner, some untidy spot / Where the dogs go on with their doggy life and the torturer's horse / Scratches its innocent behind on a tree").

Figures of Speech

Figures of speech enable poets to compress experience, add emotional impact, and make an experience vivid, dramatic, or memorable.

- A *simile* is a comparison using *like* or *as*: "My love is like a red, red rose."

- A *metaphor* creates a direct equivalency between two things without using *like* or *as*: "My love is a red, red rose." William Blake uses metaphor when he writes, "Tyger! Tyger! Burning bright / In the forests of the night." The tiger is not literally burning, but the colors of his coat and his potentially violent spirit are seen as a fire.
- A *symbol* is a word or concept that represents something larger or more abstract than its literal meaning. The tiger in Blake's poem becomes a symbol because it represents something larger than its literal self: the potential for violence and perhaps natural evil in the world.
- *Personification* occurs when poets give human qualities to an inanimate object or an abstraction. Death, in Emily Dickinson's poem, is personified: like the driver of a carriage, Death stops to pick up the speaker and carry her on toward eternity.

Rhythm, Rhyme, and Sound

Poets use the natural rhythm of spoken words and the sounds of words to create forms and patterns for poetry that add dramatic impact to language and enhance a reader's or a listener's ability to remember words and lines.

- *Rhythm* is the cadence established by words and lines in a poem. Poets often use patterns of stressed and unstressed syllables to support their meaning. Two common patterns are *iambic* and *trochaic*. Emily Dickinson's poem uses an iambic pattern (one unstressed syllable followed by a stressed syllable) to create a regular rhythm: "Because I could not stop for death— / He kindly stopped for me." William Blake uses a trochaic pattern (a stressed syllable followed by an unstressed syllable): "Tyger! Tyger! Burning bright / In the forests of the night."
- *Rhyme* is the patterned repetition of the sound of a word, typically at the end of a line: "Tyger! Tyger! Burning *bright* / In the forests of the *night*."
- The *sounds* of words are carefully chosen by poets to enhance meaning and add a musical quality. In addition to the sounds of rhyming words, poets use alliteration and assonance. *Alliteration* is the repetition of consonant sounds, and *assonance* is the repetition of vowel sounds. "Tyger! Tyger! Burning bright" uses the *alliteration* of the "t's" and "g's" in "Tyger! Tyger!" and the repeated "b's" and "r's" in "burning bright" to give emphasis and power to the lines. In "anyone lived in a pretty how town," e. e. cummings uses *assonance* when he repeats the /o/ sound in several successive words to give a smooth, easy flow to the language.

Professional Writing

Five Contemporary Poems

Aurora Levins Morales

Born in Puerto Rico in 1954, Aurora Levins Morales moved with her family to the United States in 1967. She has published a collection of short stories and written collaboratively with her mother, Rosario Morales, a book containing short stories, essays, and poetry, *Getting Home Alive* (1986). She currently lives near San Francisco.

Child of the Americas

I am a child of the Americas,
a light-skinned mestiza of the Caribbean,
a child of many diaspora,[1] born into this continent at a crossroads.

I am a U.S. Puerto Rican Jew
a product of the ghettos of New York I have never known.
An immigrant and the daughter and granddaughter of
    immigrants.
I speak English with passion: it's the tongue of my
    consciousness,
a flashing knife blade of crystal, my tool, my craft.

I am Caribeña,[2] island grown. Spanish is in my flesh,
ripples from my tongue, lodges in my hips:
the language of garlic and mangoes,
the singing in my poetry, the flying gestures of my hands.

I am of Latinoamerica, rooted in the history of my
    continent:
I speak from that body.
I am not african. Africa is in me, but I cannot return.
I am not taína.[3] Taíno is in me, but there is no way back.
I am not european. Europe lives in me, but I have no
    home there.

I am new. History made me. My first language was spanglish.[4]
I was born at the crossroads
and I am whole.

---

[1]**diaspora** "a scattering," referring to the dispersion of Jews from Israel.
[2]**Caribeña** Carribean woman
[3]**taína** a native Indian tribe in Puerto Rico
[4]**spanglish** a mixture of Spanish and English

Taylor Mali

Taylor Mali was born in New York City in 1965. He earned degrees in English and creative writing from Bowdoin College and Kansas State University. After teaching for nine years in middle school, high school, and college, he turned to slam poetry. He is the author of two books of poetry, *What Learning Leaves* (2002) and *The Last Time As We Are* (2009). The goal of his Quest for New Teachers Project, to create 1,000 new teachers through "poetry, persuasion, and perseverance," was met on April 7, 2012.

Miracle Workers

Sunday nights I lie awake—
as all teachers do—
and wait for sleep to come
like the last student in my class to arrive.
My grading is done, my lesson plans are in order,
and still sleep wanders the hallways like Lower School
  music.
I'm a teacher. This is what I do.

Like a builder builds, or a sculptor sculpts,
a preacher preaches, and a teacher teaches.
This is what we do.
We are experts in the art of explanation:
I know the difference between questions
to answer and questions to ask.

That's an excellent question.
What do you think?

If two boys are fighting, I break it up.
But if two girls are fighting, I wait until it's over and
  then drag what's left to the nurse's office.
I'm not your mother, or your father,
or your jailer, or your torturer,
or your biggest fan in the whole wide world
even if sometimes I am all of these things.
I know you can do these things I make you do.
That's why I make you do them.
I'm a teacher. This is what I do.

Once in a restaurant, when the waiter asked me
if I wanted anything else, and I said,
"No, thank you, just the check, please,"
and he said, "How about a look at the dessert menu?"

...continued Miracle Workers, **Taylor Mali**

I knew I had become a teacher when I said,
"What did I just say?
Please don't make me repeat myself!"

In the quiet hours of the dawn
I write assignment sheets and print them
without spell checking them. Because I'm a teacher,
and teachers don't make spelling mistakes.
So yes, as a matter of fact, the new dress cod
will apply to all members of the 5th, 6th, and 78th grades;
and if you need an extension on your 55-paragraph essays
examining The Pubic Wars from an hysterical perspective
you may have only until January 331st.
I trust that won't be a problem for anyone?

I like to lecture on love and speak on responsibility.
I hold forth on humility, compassion, eloquence, and
honesty.
And when my students ask,
"Are we going to be responsible for this?"
I say, If not you, then who?
You think my generation will be responsible?
We're the ones who got you into this mess,
now you are our only hope.
And when they say, "What we meant
was, 'Will we be tested on this?'"
I say Every single day of your lives!

Once, I put a pencil on the desk of a student
who was digging in her backpack for a pencil.
But she didn't see me do it, so when I walked
to the other side of the room and she raised her hand
and asked if she could borrow a pencil,
I intoned, In the name of Socrates and Jesus,
and all the gods of teaching,
I declare you already possess everything you will ever need!
Shazzam!
"You are the weirdest teacher I have ever—"
Then she saw the pencil on her desk and screamed.
"You're a miracle worker! How did you do that?"

I just gave you what I knew you needed
before you had to ask for it.

Education is the miracle, I'm just the worker.
But I'm a teacher.
And that's what we do.

Joy Harjo

A prolific writer of poems and songs, Joy Harjo was born in Tulsa, Oklahoma, in 1951. Her books of poetry include She Had Some Horses (1983), The Woman Who Fell from the Sky (1994), and How We Became Human: New and Selected Poems (2002).

Perhaps the World Ends Here

The world begins at a kitchen table. No matter what,
we must eat to live.

The gifts of earth are brought and prepared, set on the
table. So it has been since creation, and it will go on.

We chase chickens or dogs away from it. Babies teethe
at the corners. They scrape their knees under it.

It is here that children are given instructions on what
it means to be human. We make men at it,
we make women.

At this table we gossip, recall enemies and the ghosts
of lovers.

Our dreams drink coffee with us as they put their arms
around our children. They laugh with us at our poor
falling-down selves and as we put ourselves back
together once again at the table.

This table has been a house in the rain, an umbrella in
the sun.

Wars have begun and ended at this table. It is a place
to hide in the shadow of terror. A place to celebrate the
terrible victory.

We have given birth on this table, and have prepared
our parents for burial here.
At this table we sing with joy, with sorrow.
We pray of suffering and remorse.
We give thanks.

...continued Perhaps the World Ends Here, **Joy Harjo**

Perhaps the world will end at the kitchen table,
while we are laughing and crying,
eating of the last sweet bite.

Wislawa Szymborska

Wislawa Szymborska (1923–2012) was born in Poland. She was the author of many books of poetry, including two that are translated into English: Sounds, Feelings, Thoughts: Seventy Poems by Wislawa Szymborska (1981) and View with a Grain of Sand: Selected Poems (1995).

End and Beginning

Translated by Joseph Brodsky

After each war
somebody has to clear up
put things in order
by itself it won't happen.

Somebody's got to push
rubble to the highway shoulder
making way
for the carts filled up with corpses.

Someone might trudge
through muck and ashes,
sofa springs,
splintered glass
and blood-soaked rugs.

Somebody has to haul
beams for propping a wall,
another put glass in a window
and hang the door on hinges.

This is not photogenic
and takes years.
All the cameras have left already
for another war.

Bridges are needed
also new railroad stations.
Tatters turn into sleeves
for rolling up.

Somebody, broom in hand,
still recalls how it was,
Someone whose head was not
torn away listens nodding.
But nearby already
begin to bustle those
who'll need persuasion.

Somebody still at times
digs up from under the bushes
some rusty quibble
to add it to burning refuse.

Those who knew
what this was all about
must yield to those
who know little
or less than little
essentially nothing.

In the grass that has covered
effects in causes
somebody must recline,
a stalk of rye in the teeth,
ogling the clouds.

Yusef Komunyakaa

Born in 1947 in Bogalusa, Louisiana, Yusef Komunyakaa served in Vietnam before returning to earn degrees at the University of Colorado, Colorado State University, and the University of California, Irvine. He has published many books of poetry, including Thieves of Paradise (1998), Pleasure Dome: New Collected Poems, 1975–1999 (2001), and Dien Cai Dau (1988), in which the poem "Facing It" appears. The photograph of the Vietnam Veterans Memorial at the beginning of this chapter was selected to appear with this poem. After you read the poem, consider how effectively the photograph illustrates the themes and images in the poem.

Facing It

My black face fades,
hiding inside the black granite.
I said I wouldn't,
dammit: No tears.

...continued End and Beginning, **Wislawa Szymborska**

I'm stone. I'm flesh.
My clouded reflection eyes me
like a bird of prey, the profile of night
slanted against morning. I turn
this way—the stone lets me go.
I turn that way—I'm inside
the Vietnam Veterans Memorial
again, depending on the light
to make a difference.
I go down the 58,022 names,
half-expecting to find
my own in letters like smoke.
I touch the name Andrew Johnson;
I see the booby trap's white flash.
Names shimmer on a woman's blouse
but when she walks away
the names stay on the wall.
Brushstrokes flash, a red bird's
wings cutting across my stare.
The sky. A plane in the sky.
A white vet's image floats
closer to me, then his pale eyes
look through mine. I'm a window.
He's lost his right arm
inside the stone. In the black mirror
a woman's trying to erase names:
No, she's brushing a boy's hair.

Questions for Writing and Discussion

1. In "Child of the Americas," Aurora Levins Morales compares the mixture of languages and cultures within her to geographical mixtures and crossroads. Find several places in the poem where Levins Morales makes this comparison. What kinds of figurative language does she use (simile, metaphor, or image)? Explain how these images help construct one of Levins Morales's themes in the poem.

2. Taylor Mali's poetry mixes humorous observations with serious statements. Where in the poem is Mali being most direct and serious about education? Where is his humor most obvious? How do his serious points develop out of his humor? Explain.

3. Although Joy Harjo titles her poem "Perhaps the World Ends Here," the poem is about both beginnings and endings. What images or examples of figurative language illustrate the beginnings, and which refer to endings? In your own words, explain how Harjo does or does not resolve the conflicts between beginnings and endings.
4. Wislawa Szymborska's poem "End and Beginning" echoes Harjo's theme of beginnings and endings in a poem about the aftermath of war. The end of war, Szymborska says, "is not photogenic / and takes years. / All the cameras have left already / for another war." What images in the poem suggest the hard, dirty, and thankless work required to rebuild a civilization? How do these images fit into Szymborska's overall theme in the poem?
5. In "Facing It," Yusef Komunyakaa contrasts the realities outside the memorial wall with the reflections and images inside the wall. What does Komunyakaa describe that is outside the wall? What does he see in the wall or in the reflections of the wall? What do you think Komunyakaa means when he says of a white vet, "He's lost his right arm / inside the stone"? Explain how these images or reality and reflection help explain a major theme of the poem.

Responding to Literature: The Writing Process

Assignment for Responding to Literature

Choose one of the poems or short stories from this chapter (or a work of literature assigned in your class), reread and annotate the work, and share your responses with others in the class. Then write an interpretation of the literary work. Unless stated otherwise in your assignment, assume that you are writing for other members of your class (including the instructor) who have read the work but who may not understand or agree with your interpretation.

Audience	Possible Genres for Responding to Literature
Personal Audience	Class notes, journal entry, blog, scrapbook, social networking page
Academic Audience	Academic analysis, critique, interpretation, journal entry, forum entry on class site, or multigenre document
Public Audience	Literary interpretation, article, or critique in a magazine, newspaper, online site, newsletter, or multigenre document

COLLECTING

11.2
Use collecting strategies to develop your response to literature

In addition to reading, rereading, annotating, and sharing your responses, try the following collecting strategies.

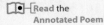

- **Collaborative annotation.** Working in small groups, choose a work of literature or select a passage that you have already annotated. In the group, read each other's annotations. Then discuss each annotation. Which annotations does your group agree are the best? Have a group recorder record the best annotations.

Read the Annotated Poem

- **Elements of poetry analysis.** Reread the paragraphs in this chapter on voice and tone, word choice, figures of speech, and sound, rhyme, and rhythm. Focus on the elements that seem most important for the poem you have selected. After you have finished annotating, freewrite a paragraph explaining how these elements work together to create the theme or overall effect of the poem.
- **Elements of fiction analysis.** Reread the paragraphs defining *character, plot, point of view, setting,* and *style.* Choose three of these elements that seem most important in the story that you are reading. Reread the story, annotating for these three elements. Then freewrite a paragraph explaining how these three elements are interrelated or how they explain the theme.
- **Time line.** In your journal, draw a time line for the story. List above the line everything that happens in the story. Below the line, indicate where the story opens, when the major conflicts occur, and where the climax and the denouement occur. For "The Story of an Hour," student writer Karen Ehrhardt drew this time line:

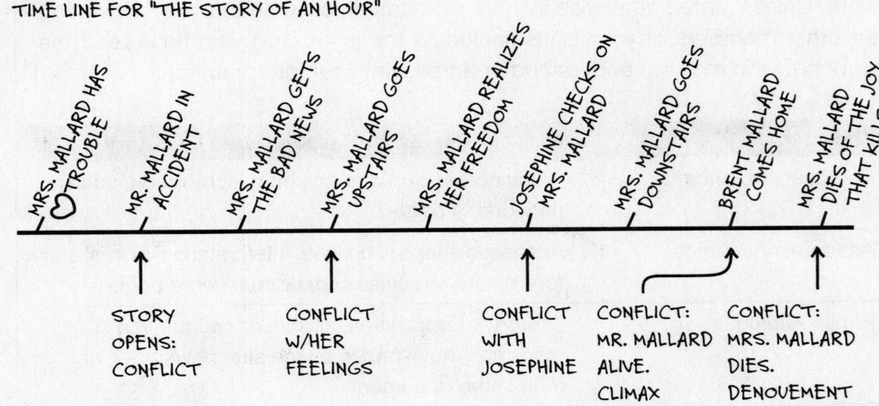

- **Feature list.** Choose a character trait, repeated image, or idea that you wish to investigate in the poem or story. List, in order of appearance, every word, image, or reference that you find.
- **Scene vision or revision.** Write a scene for this story in which you change some part of it. You may *add* a scene to the beginning, middle, or end of the story. You may *change* a scene in the story. You may write a scene in the story from a different character's point of view. You may change the style of the story for your scene. How, for example, might Toni Cade Bambara have described the opening scene of "The Story of an Hour"?
- **Draw a picture.** For your poem or short story, draw a picture based on images, characters, conflicts, or themes in the work of literature. Student writer Lori Van Sike drew the following picture for "The Story of an Hour" that shows how the rising and falling action of the plot parallels Mrs. Mallard's ascent and descent of the stairs.

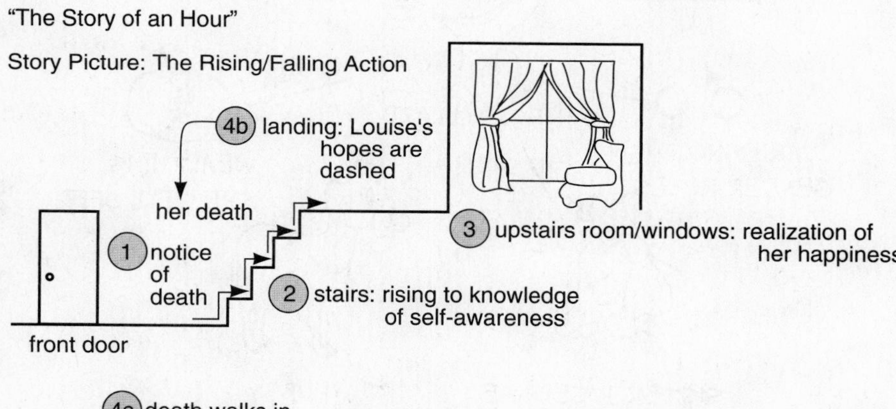

- **Background investigation.** Investigate the biographical, social, or historical context of the poem or story. Find biographical information or other stories or poems by the same author. How does this information increase your understanding or appreciation of the poem or story?
- **Character conflict map.** Start with a full page of paper. Draw a main character in the center of the page. Locate the other major characters, internal forces, and external forces (including social, economic, and environmental pressures) in a circle around the main character. Draw a line between each of these peripheral characters or forces and the main character. For his character conflict map for "The Story of an Hour," student writer Darren Marshall used

images from his computer program to surround his picture of Mrs. Mallard.

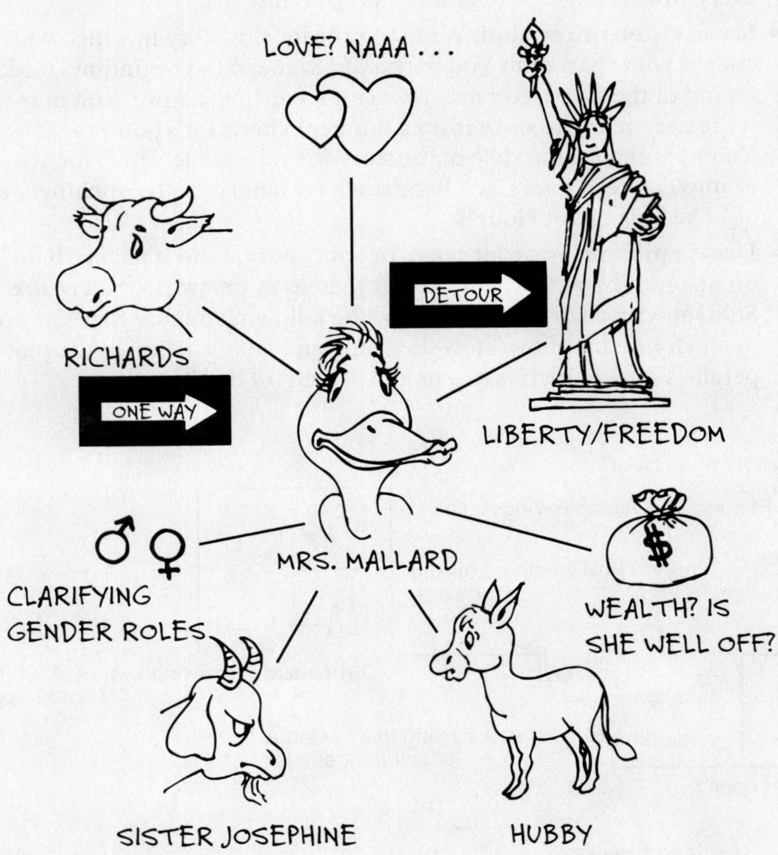

- **Reconsideration of purposes.** What idea, theme, or approach most interests you? Will you be explaining, evaluating, problem solving, or arguing? Are you combining purposes? Do these purposes suggest what kinds of information you might collect?

SHAPING

11.3
Shape your response to literature essay

Test each of the following possible shapes against your ideas for your essay. Use or adapt the shape or shapes that are most appropriate for your own interpretation.

Shaping Strategies

Do you want to ...	Consider using these rhetorical modes or strategies:
show how the parts of a poem or story relate to the whole?	explaining relationships (p. 433)
demonstrate how and why a poem or a short story is effective?	evaluating (pp. 433–434)
convince your readers that your interpretation is more accurate than another response?	arguing (p. 434)
explain how your interpretation changed from your initial reaction?	investigating changes in interpretation (p. 434)

Explaining Relationships

Interpretative essays often analyze how the parts of a poem or story relate to the whole. As you explain these relationships, you should show how key images, lines, or scenes contribute to the overall theme or idea of the poem or story.

Introduction and thesis:	The details and images in the work reveal that the theme is X.
First scene, stanza, or group of lines:	How details and images establish the theme.
Second scene or group of lines:	How details and images relate to or build on previous images and contribute to the theme.
Third scene or group of lines:	How details and images continue building the theme.
Conclusion:	How the author highlights the key images or themes.

Evaluating

If your response suggests an evaluating purpose, you may wish to set up criteria for an effective poem or short story and then provide evidence showing how this poem or story does or does not measure up to your standards. Using criteria for a story, you might base your essay on the following outline.

Introduction and thesis:	Story X is highly dramatic.
Criterion 1:	A dramatic short story should focus on a character who changes his or her behavior or beliefs. Judgment and evidence for Criterion 1.

Criterion 2:	A dramatic story must have striking conflicts that lead to a crisis or a predicament. Judgment and evidence for Criterion 2.
Criterion 3:	A dramatic story should have a theme that makes a controversial point. Judgment and evidence for Criterion 3.
Conclusion:	Reinforces thesis.

Arguing

During class discussion, you may disagree with another person's response. Your thesis may then take the form, "Although some readers believe this poem or story is about X, the poem or story can also be about Y."

Introduction and thesis:	Although some readers suggest the poem or story is about X, it is really about Y.
Body paragraphs:	State the opposing interpretation and give evidence for that interpretation. Then state your interpretation and give evidence (images, characters, events, points of conflict) supporting your interpretation.
Conclusion:	Clarify and reinforce thesis.

Investigating Changes in Interpretation

Often, readers *change* interpretations during the course of responding to a piece of literature. Thus, your main point might be, "Although I initially believed X about the poem or story, I gradually realized the theme of the poem or story is Y." If that sentence expresses your main idea, you may wish to organize your essay following the chronology or the steps in the changes in your interpretation.

Introduction and thesis:	Although I initially thought X, I now believe Y.
Body paragraphs:	First step (your original interpretation of the story or poem and supporting evidence).
	Second step (additional or contradictory ideas and evidence that made you reconsider your interpretation).
	Third step (your final interpretation and supporting evidence).
Conclusion:	Show how steps lead to thesis.

Note: One strategy you should *not* use is to retell the key parts of a poem or the plot of the story. Your audience has already read the poem or story. They want you to state your interpretation and then use details to show how and why your interpretation is credible. Although you will cite key characters, images, or events in the poem or story, you must explain how or why each of these details supports your interpretation.

DRAFTING

To prepare to draft your essay, read through your annotations and gather your collecting and shaping notes. Some writers prefer to write one-sentence statements of their main ideas at the top of the page to keep them focused as they write. Other writers prefer to make rough outlines to follow, based on their adaptations of one of the preceding shaping strategies. When you begin drafting, you may wish to skip your introduction and start with the body of your essay. You can fill in the introduction after you have written a draft.

Once you start writing, keep your momentum going. If you draw a blank, reread what you have already written or look at your notes. If you cannot think of a particular word or are unsure about a spelling, draw a line______ and keep on writing.

REVISING

Use the following guidelines as you read your classmates' drafts and revise your own essay. Be prepared to make changes in your ideas, organization, and evidence, as well as to fix problems in sentences and word choice.

Guidelines for Revision

- **Clarify your main idea or interpretation.** Ask your readers to write, in one sentence, the main point of your interpretation. If their statements do not exactly match your main point, clarify your thesis. Your interpretation should be clearly stated early in your essay.
- **Do not just summarize the poem or story.** Start with your interpretation; cite key images, metaphors, or lines that support your interpretation; and then explain why these images or key words are important.
- **Support each part of your interpretation with references to specific passages from the text.** Do not be satisfied with one piece of evidence. Find as many bits of evidence as possible. The case for your interpretation grows stronger with each additional piece of evidence.
- **Explain how each piece of evidence supports your interpretation.** Do not just cite several pieces of evidence and go on to your next point. Explain for your readers *how* the evidence supports your interpretation.

- **Define key terms in your essay.** If you are writing about the hero in a story, define what you mean by *hero* or *heroine.* If you are arguing that "The Story of an Hour" has a *feminist* theme, define *feminism.*
- **Signal the major parts of your interpretation.** Let your readers know when you shift to a new point. Use transitions and paragraph hooks at the beginning of body paragraphs.
- **Use the present tense as you describe the events in the story.** If you are describing the end of "The Story of an Hour," write, for example, "Mrs. Mallard descends the stairs and learns the 'good news' about her husband."
- **Quote accurately and cite page numbers for each reference.** Double-check your quotations to make sure they are accurate, word-for-word transcriptions. Following each direct quotation, cite page references:

  In the first sentence, Kate Chopin says, "Mrs. Mallard was afflicted with a heart trouble" (479).

  In "Child of the Americas," the author states the central idea of the poem when she says, "I am of Latinoamerica, rooted in the history of my continent" (line 13).

  Note: The period goes outside the parentheses. See Chapter 13 for correct documentation style.
- **Revise your essay for sentence clarity and conciseness.** Read your essay aloud or have a classmate read it. Reduce unnecessary repetition. Use active verbs. Rework awkward or confusing sentences.
- **Edit your essay.** Check your essay for correct spelling, word choice, punctuation, and grammar.

Postscript on the Writing Process

Before you turn in your essay, answer the following questions in your journal.

1. Explain what part of this essay (collecting ideas and evidence, focusing on your interpretation, shaping your essay, drafting, or revising) was most difficult for you. How did you work around the problems?
2. What do you like best about your essay? Refer to specific places in the essay (lead-in, thesis, pieces of evidence, ideas, conclusion). Which specific paragraphs do you like best? Why?
3. What did you learn about the story by writing your interpretation? What do you realize now that you did not understand when you first read the story?
4. If you had two more hours to work on this essay, what would you change? Why?

Student Writing

Facing It: Reflections on War

Grace Rexroth

Grace Rexroth was assigned to write an explication of "Facing It," a Vietnam War poem by Yusef Komunyakaa. (This poem appears on page 427.) After reading the poem several times, she noticed that the key images seemed to evoke recurring themes of the painful consequences of the Vietnam War, the war's impact on memory, and the importance of facing the truth and honoring the past. Before you read her essay, read Komunyakaa's poem and take notes on its themes and key images. Decide what "Facing It" means to you before you read Rexroth's essay.

Yusef Komunyakaa's poem "Facing It" illustrates his difficulty facing the Vietnam Veterans Memorial and the memories of his past as a soldier. The fleeting images he recounts show the tangible aspects of his experience but also mirror his own emotional struggle to reconcile the past with the present moment. In "facing" the memorial, he wrestles with confronting grief and attempting to evade it. The portrayal of his experience illuminates several interconnected themes: the painful consequences of war, its scarring impact upon memory, and the importance of remembering and honoring the past. *1*

Komunyakaa begins his poem by focusing on the tangible stone of the memorial: "My black face fades / hiding inside the black granite" (lines 1–2). When he describes his face "fading" into the black granite, it is a physical image as well as a symbolic one. The black granite can be seen as representing the Vietnam War as a whole and Komunyakaa fades into it, connoting the magnitude of the war and the way it consumes him. Yet he is also "hiding" in the granite, focusing on the polished stone as opposed to the meaning of the memorial; he is evading grief and memory. This suggests that it is his first time really "facing" the consequences of the Vietnam War, substantiated by his next lines; "I said I wouldn't / damnit: No tears / I'm stone. I'm flesh." He had a preconceived idea of how he would endure this experience: no tears. Komunyakaa is wrestling with himself; the "stone" represents the repression of his memory and emotion, and the "flesh" represents his pain and grief which need an outlet through tears. *2*

Having given in to tears, Komunyakaa focuses again on the stone of the memorial and his tangible reflection. He says "my clouded reflection eyes me / like a bird of prey, the profile of night / slanted against morning" (lines 6–8). His "clouded reflection" could represent his vision, clouded by tears, which means that he is also seeing his "emotional" reflection. His clouded vision may also mean that his visions of the past *3*

...continued Facing It: Reflections on War, **Grace Rexroth**

and the present are distorted, hinting that he feels stranded in a place of emotional and intellectual uncertainty. The idea that it "eyes" him like a "bird of prey" insinuates a sense of fear. He is afraid of his emotions; afraid of being devoured or overcome by grief. It is interesting that he then turns away from the memorial saying "the stone lets me go," symbolizing an emotional reprieve (line 9). Yet, he finally turns back to face the stone rather than the reality behind him.

Komunyakaa transitions back to the meaning of the memorial 4
saying, "I go down the 58,022 names / half-expecting to find / my own in letters like smoke" (lines 14–16). His use of the specific number "58,022" references the fact that each one has meaning; each name represents a life. The idea that he "half-expects" to find his own name connotes the surreal nature of life and death; the absurdity that he is still alive though he took the same risk as those who died. The image of "letters like smoke" suggests that the bare names seem like a ghostly representation of so many vibrant lives.

Finding a specific name, "Andrew Johnson," Komunyakaa is briefly 5
pulled into his violent memories of the war. He sees "the booby trap's white flash," suggesting that he witnessed Johnson's death (line 18). This image is quickly followed by an image of the present; "names shimmer on a woman's blouse/ but when she walks away / the names stay on the wall" (line 19). This juxtaposition depicts Komunyakaa's harsh struggle to deal with the images in his memory and the images of the present. He is desperately trying to reconcile the pain of the past with the odd serenity of the current moment. The image of the woman walking can be construed as an absurd transient image of life amidst the finality of death.

Komunyakaa returns to focusing on the stone of the memorial, 6
once more seeking a reprieve from his grief. He despondently mentions "a red bird's wings," "the sky," and "a plane in the sky," each a reflection in the black granite mirror of the memorial (lines 22–24). He still cannot turn to face the reality of the life behind him; everything is filtered through the memorial, which suggests that he is seeing through his grief. Then, he says "a white vet's image floats / closer to me, then his pale eyes / look through mine. I'm a window" (lines 25–27). The fact that Komunyakaa makes the distinction that it is a "white" veteran who moves towards him, further proves that it is Komunyakaa speaking and recognizing the difference between the white veteran's reflection and his own dark image.

The description of the "white vet" is almost ghost-like, seemingly 7
stranded between the speaker's world of memory and the world of the present. The image "his pale eyes / look through mine" is a symbol of

communion, representing the bond of pain and uncertainty shared by veterans. It is interesting that Komunyakaa switches to describing himself as "a window" for the other veteran when he has been viewing the world through the "window" of the memorial. As they look at each other they interact only as reflections in the memorial which adds to the surreal experience of "facing the memorial"—trying to understand life in the midst of death. When Komunyakaa says "he's lost his right arm inside the stone," the reader cannot be certain if the white vet is really handicapped or simply standing at an odd angle (lines 28–29). In the memorial, just as in war, everything is blurred and indistinct.

Komunyakaa ends his poem with the image of a woman "trying to 8
erase names" but then qualifies that statement, "No, she's brushing a boy's hair" (lines 30–31). The provocative image of someones trying to erase names could symbolize the country's desire to erase the memory of an unpopular war, perhaps even to shield the public from the pain of its atrocities. The image of the little boy, however, could also represent another generation of young men being groomed for future wars. It is precisely for the benefit of the next generation, Komunyakaa seems to imply, that we must face the consequences of war with truth and integrity.

Questions for Writing and Discussion

1. If you read and took notes on Komunyakaa's poem before you read Rexroth's explication of "Facing It," explain how your interpretation of the poem was similar to but also different from Rexroth's explication. Cite specific images or passages from the poem to illustrate the similarities and differences between your reading and Rexroth's explication of the poem.
2. At the end of the first paragraph, Rexroth identifies three key themes that she found in the poem. What are those themes? In which paragraphs does she illustrate each of these themes? Explain your choices.
3. Rexroth supports her explication of the themes in this poem by analyzing key passages and images. Reread her essay and *list* the specific images that she comments on. Then compare your list with the poem. Does Rexroth refer to or analyze every key image or relevant passage? Are there other images that she might also analyze? Explain.
4. Does Rexroth interpret Komunyakaa's poem as a war protest poem or as a poem that honors the sacrifices of war? Does Rexroth do both at the same time? Reread Rexroth's final paragraph and explain, as clearly as you can, how she handles this ambiguous or contradictory portrayal of war.

Student Writing

Death: The Final Freedom

Pat Russell

Following a class discussion of the feminist theme in Kate Chopin's "The Story of an Hour," Pat Russell wrote in his journal, "Is the story a feminist one? No. It is not just about feminism but about how people stifle their own needs and desires to accommodate those of their mate." In his essay, Russell argues that the traditional feminist reading limits the universal theme of the story. As you read his essay, see if you are persuaded by his argument.

The poor treatment of women and their struggle for an individual identity make up a major underlying theme of Kate Chopin's stories. Although many regard Chopin's "The Story of an Hour" as a feminist story, today a more universal interpretation is appropriate. This story is not about the oppression of a woman, but about how people strive to maintain the normality and security of their relationships by suppressing their own individual wants and needs. 1

Evidence in favor of the feminist argument begins with the period the story was written in, sometime around the turn of the century. Society prevented women from coming out of the household. Most women weren't allowed to run a business, and for that matter, they couldn't even vote. Their most important jobs were wife and mother. This background sets the tone for the main character's life. In the beginning we are told Mrs. Mallard has a "fair, calm face whose lines be-spoke repression" (Chopin 414). There is also evidence that suggests her husband is ignorant of her ideas and forceful with his own. Chopin writes: "There would be no powerful will bending her in that blind persistence with which men and women believe they have a right to impose a private will upon a fellow creature" (415). In addition, Mrs. Mallard is described early as fearful and powerless, and later as a triumphant "goddess of Victory," indicating her rebirth. These citations suggest that this is a feminist story, but this label limits the meaning behind the story. 2

Many people who are unhappy with their marriages either fail to recognize their unhappiness or refuse to accept responsibility for it. I feel sorry for those who don't recognize their unhappiness. However, it is pathetic to see someone such as Mrs. Mallard hold onto a relationship simply because she doesn't know how to let go. "And yet she had loved him—sometimes. Often she had not" (415). She continuously fell in and out of love with her husband until he "died," at which point she told herself that love didn't matter compared to the self-assertion "which she suddenly recognized as the strongest impulse of her being" (415). It is as if she has waited for all of her life for this moment; she prays for a long 3 life, when only the day before she dreaded it. She weeps for him but at the same time compares her husband to a criminal, a man whom she has lived her life for, never once thinking of herself. But now "there would be no one to live for during those coming years; she would live for herself" (415). She is lucky in that she feels "free." Her emotional suppression is over, and she will no longer have anyone to blame for her unhappiness.

It is important not only to try to interpret the author's intended meaning of the story, but also to think about what message "The Story of an Hour" has for us today. As a feminist story, the lesson "The Story of an Hour" teaches is one-dimensional. Interpreting it as a story about the struggle of all people opens up the possibility of teaching others that selfishness and selflessness are both good, when used in moderation. In Mrs. Mallard's case, correcting this balance becomes a matter of life and death. In the face of her suppressor, her desperation for freedom forces her to choose death. 4

Work Cited

Chopin, Kate. "The Story of an Hour." *The Awakening and Selected Stories.* New York: Penguin, 1984. 413–16. Print.

Questions for Writing and Discussion

1. With what parts of Russell's interpretation do you agree? What additional evidence from the story might Russell cite in support of his interpretation? What ideas or sentences might you challenge? What evidence from the story might refute those statements?
2. Write out your definition of *feminism.* Where does or should Russell explain his definition? How should Russell clarify his definition?
3. Write out Russell's main idea or thesis. Explain why his thesis is an interpretation and not just a statement of fact.
4. What shaping strategy does Russell use to organize his essay?
5. Write out two other possible titles for Russell's essay. Explain why your alternative titles are (or are not) better than Russell's title.

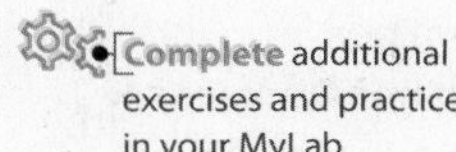
Complete additional exercises and practice in your MyLab

The acclaimed 2004 movie *Hotel Rwanda* depicts the effects of the 1994 genocide in Rwanda that resulted in the deaths of 800,000 people. The student research project in this chapter and Chapter 13 examines whether films like this one accurately portray the genocide.

Everett Collection

12 Researching

What You Will Learn

In this chapter, you will learn to:

12.1 Keep purpose and audience in mind when developing a research topic

12.2 Use techniques for planning your research and choosing appropriate sources

12.3 Use techniques to evaluate sources

12.4 Write a research proposal and annotated bibliography

THE impulse to learn more—especially about complex topics—is a key motivation for doing research. As a college student, you will encounter many such topics that will challenge what you already know and believe. While the techniques discussed in the previous chapters of this book all involve forms of research, there will be occasions when you need to build a substantial piece of writing that carefully documents the supporting information you discovered by doing research. This is when your initial interest in a topic becomes a set of research questions—questions that you seek to answer by reading a large variety of sources and/or doing sustained and deliberate field research. This chapter will help you to build on and satisfy that natural curiosity, offering you techniques and processes for becoming an informed and credible writer.

"Research is to see what everybody else has seen and to think what nobody else has thought."

—Albert Szent-Gyoergyi,
1937 Nobel Laureate

HABITS OF MIND LEAD TO EFFECTIVE RESEARCH

Developing a credible voice begins with the habits of mind you bring to your research—the attitudes that help you propose, plan, and see a project through to completion. Writing experts agree that certain attitudes and abilities are most likely to lead to success in college writing. In *A Framework for Success in Postsecondary Writing*, the National Council of Teachers of English, Council of Writing Program Administrators and National Writing Project propose that eight habits of mind are essential for success:

- *Curiosity*—the desire to know more about the world.
- *Openness*—the willingness to consider new ways of being and thinking in the world.

- *Engagement*—a sense of investment and involvement in learning.
- *Creativity*—the ability to use novel approaches for generating, investigating, and representing ideas.
- *Persistence*—the ability to sustain interest in and attention to short- and long-term projects.
- *Responsibility*—the ability to take ownership of one's actions and understand the consequences of those actions for oneself and others.
- *Flexibility*—the ability to adapt to situations, expectations, or demands.
- *Metacognition*—the ability to reflect on one's own thinking as well as on the individual and cultural processes used to structure knowledge.

These habits of mind are crucial for success in the research process. When you approach a research project with *curiosity* and *openness,* when you *engage* with the learning necessary to gain expertise in your topic and *persist* in a desire to learn over the long haul, you are likely to produce rich, useful research. When you exercise *creativity* in your approach to a question or problem, and when you are *flexible* and *responsible* enough to follow the research where it leads you, your project will be more authentic and interesting. And when you exercise *metacognition*—which simply means that you continually reflect on your own research processes—you are more likely to develop the most effective methods, both for a particular project and for future ones.

Research projects can arise from almost any impulse—a movie you watch, a blog entry you see, a natural phenomenon you observe. For example, in high school, Carrie Gingrich watched a film, *Hotel Rwanda*, that depicted the story of Paul Rusesabagina, manager of a hotel that housed over a thousand refugees during the period of genocide in the African country of Rwanda. Later, as a college student, Gingrich heard a professor refer to this event. During the class discussion, she recalled the film and wondered how people learn about such historical events as the genocide. Some of the new things she learned, and the lack of awareness about the genocide she saw in fellow students (including those who had seen the film), made her wonder whether that film—and films more generally—preserve the truth about historical events.

Gingrich's new interest in the Rwandan genocide, added to her limited understanding of it that came from the film she saw in high school, made her *curious* and *open* to learning more. But just being curious and open isn't enough. The next step calls for commitment—a commitment to *engage* with the material and to *persist* in a sometimes messy process, since a researched writing project can take weeks or a month to complete.

> **"Research is formalized curiosity. It is poking and prying with a purpose."**
>
> —Zora Neale Hurston

Doing research is not as simple as following a set of steps. You will often need to use *metacognition*, to stop and revise your research questions, collect new information, rethink your evaluation of sources when you find contrary perspectives, add to or subtract from your annotated bibliography, and revise the goal of your research project. But having a clear plan—even one that you may revise several times—is still central to a successful project.

To illustrate these techniques, you will find Carrie Gingrich's notes, drafts, and documentation throughout this chapter and the next, where you will find the product of her work. Her paper,"Learning about the Rwandan Genocide: Misconceptions and Film," illustrates important features of a source-based paper in Modern Language Association (MLA) style. By following the development of Gingrich's paper, and by adapting its stages to a project of your own, you can develop your own research techniques and processes.

Techniques for Researching

Because research projects differ from other writing in process and in the end product—and because much of the writing you do in college will involve research—you need techniques specific to this basic form of writing. Here are essential techniques to keep in mind.

Techniques for Researching

Technique	Tips on How to Do It
Use purpose and audience as a guide for finding useful information. Choose relevant sources that help you to make *your* point to *your* audience.	Choose the pieces of information that are most applicable to your own rhetorical situation. Annotate your sources for key ideas and note each source's relevance to your purpose and audience.
Use your physical and electronic library, as well as the open Web, to find information.	Know what databases and search engines are available to you, what types of information they can best provide, and the techniques for limiting and focusing your search.
Choose reliable and current sources. Critically evaluate your sources for accuracy, reliability, and bias.	Consider the author's expertise, the place of publication, and potential biases. Be especially careful about Internet sources, which may represent people or organizations with a pronounced bias.
Keep careful track of your sources.	Because you will need to document your sources, why they are reliable, and their relevance to your topic, keep careful notes throughout the research process. Having electronic or paper copies of each article you use can help you avoid inadvertent plagiarism.
Develop a topic proposal and an annotated bibliography.	In your topic proposal, explain your intended topic, purpose, and audience and show why the project is important. As you work, keep an annotated bibliography that lists all sources and explains the relevance and credibility of each source.

DEVELOPING A TOPIC, PURPOSE, AND AUDIENCE

12.1
Keep purpose and audience in mind when developing a research topic

In the early stages of your research process, it is natural to feel overwhelmed by the amount of information that you encounter. But remember that you aren't looking for *any* information you can find on a given topic. You are looking for information that can help you **engage** with the topic—information that helps you invest in the topic and that will serve a specific purpose when you address a particular group of readers.

Know Your Purpose

Like any other kind of writing, researched papers have a *purpose.* To decide whether a source of information is worth reading and including in your list of sources, ask whether the piece is relevant to the purpose of your project. Since student author Carrie Gingrich was specifically seeking information about whether media like films portray the history of an event adequately and accurately, not all articles about the Rwandan genocide were useful to her purpose. A glance at her annotated working bibliography on page 480 will indicate how each source was chosen to support that purpose.

Accommodate Your Audience

Research papers have a defined *audience,* too. In choosing sources, you'll want to consider what your audience already knows, and what they will need to know to accomplish your purpose. You'll also want to gauge what *attitudes and opinions* they seem to hold about your topic before they read what you write, and how you want to change, reinforce, or influence those attitudes. And you'll want to gauge the *level of complexity and types of evidence* most likely to engage your audience.

Asking questions about your potential audience can help you choose relevant sources.

- What does my audience already know about this topic? What opinions are they likely to have?
- What information can I find that will add to my audience's knowledge? To change or clarify their opinions?
- What types of information are they most likely to accept as valid?
- What kinds of evidence will match my audience's understanding of this topic? What is too simple? Too complex?
- Where can I find these types of information? How can I use this information to find my own thesis or main argument?

"There is nothing like looking, if you want to find something. You certainly usually find something, if you look, but it is not always quite the something you were after."

—J. R. R. Tolkien, *The Hobbit*

PLANNING RESEARCH

12.2
Use techniques for planning your research and choosing appropriate sources.

Research is messy, so you'll need *persistence, flexibility,* and *creativity* throughout the process. You will continually be asking new questions, finding new focal points, and adding and removing source material. (This self-reflection is what we mean by *metacognition.*) If you expect those complications, you'll feel less frustrated when you reach what seems like a dead end and also readier to appreciate valuable information when you discover it.

However—and this is a *big* however—*planning is still an important part of successful research processes.* Being *flexible* is not the same thing as being disorganized! To search productively, you will need techniques for planning focused research questions.

"Research is the process of going up alleys to see if they are blind."
—Marston Bates

Brainstorm Available Sources

One technique that can help you plan is brainstorming the types of research you might do. For example, consider the early brainstorming that Carrie Gingrich performed to focus her early research:

Watch the **Animation** on Planning Research

To better understand whether media depictions are an accurate way to teach students about the Rwandan genocide, I could:

- *Interview students, set up discussion groups, or distribute a survey about knowledge of this event.*
- *Visit high schools and sit in on some classes and maybe interview teachers.*
- *Look for recent reference sources or journal articles that provide the most current and reliable information on the events. (To do this, I might want to find out which sources and journals are most respected by experts.)*
- *Recall my own experiences, and the experiences of my classmates, in watching the film Hotel Rwanda.*
- *Watch the film again as well as other films on the topic to compare them with the research historians have done and to analyze their purposes.*
- *Read reviews and analyses of the films and interviews with the filmmakers to better understand the films' purposes and reactions to them.*
- *Read some background information on how media influences our understanding of history.*
- *Interview professors on this topic.*

Brainstorming like this can help you plan focused searches. Looking back over your list will also help you rule out strategies not directly related to your audience and purpose.

Use Question Analysis

Another way to plan for effective research is to consider the *who, what, when, where,* and *why* questions that you might ask:

Who: What group of people is affected or interested—or should be?
What: What important information and key terms should my audience know? What academic disciplines are involved?
When: What time period is covered by this question?
Where: What continent, country, state, or town is most relevant?
Why: Why is my topic important—what are its possible effects or implications?

Answering questions such as these—by yourself, in a group, or with a reference librarian—may suggest new angles, new avenues for research, or subtopics that could lead to a focus for your research.

Warming Up: Journal Exercises

No matter your field or major, formulating good questions and then considering the types of resources that can help you answer those questions is an important part of the research process. The exercises below present you with some scenarios through which you can practice this important early stage in the research process.

Following the model on page 447, consider the following rhetorical situations and use *brainstorming* and *question analysis* to identify the types of research you might do to complete each research project. Then decide which items on the list are most useful in serving your audience and purpose.

1. As an engineering major interested in sustainability, you wonder whether the public has enough knowledge about biofuels. You want to write an article for a publication such as *Discover* magazine to inform readers about some problems related to biofuels, but you need to present the information in a way that is understandable to the general public. What kinds of research would be best for this rhetorical situation?
2. You are a nursing major, and you believe that a lack of understanding of how viruses are spread is a serious problem that could keep the public from behaving in responsible ways should a pandemic occur. You would like to produce both an informational pamphlet that could be distributed in doctors' offices and a Web site for further information. What kinds of research might you do to (1) find out what the public perceptions/misperceptions are and (2) find accurate information and translate it into understandable terms?
3. You are a psychology major, and you wonder about the effects of the recent economic crisis on the mental health of unemployed workers.

You would like to research how mental health professionals react to specific social challenges like this one in order to produce a set of resources for individuals who are struggling with this situation. What kinds of reading might you do to learn about the ways psychologists adapt their methods to current problems? What field research could you do to see the effects of these stress factors on unemployed workers? How could you use that information to help those who need help to find it?

TYPES OF SOURCES

The librarian is the first and perhaps the most valuable resource for your background research. Asking for help can be intimidating, so try to have focused questions (like those listed above) prepared in advance. After you've talked with the librarian once, it will be easier to return and ask a question when you hit a snag. Once you've talked to the librarian about your topic, it's time to look for specific sources of information. They will fall into four major categories: general reference materials, primary sources, secondary sources, and field research.

General Reference Materials

Early in the process, it may be useful to obtain an overview of your subject by consulting one or more *general reference* materials:

- encyclopedias, including online encyclopedias and wikis such as Wikipedia, which are discussed in the section on Web 2.0 sources below
- dictionaries
- almanacs
- biographies

Although general reference sources do not provide the depth of knowledge you seek, they are an excellent source of basic information and terminology that may help you focus, narrow, and define your subject. These sources can also help you develop search terms for deeper research. *Use them as background reading,* however, not as major sources.

Primary and Secondary Sources

Research sources you might seek in the initial stages of a project fall into two general categories: *primary* and *secondary.*

- *Primary sources* include accounts of scientific experiments, transcripts of speeches or lectures, questionnaires, interviews, private documents. They contain original, firsthand information.
- *Secondary sources* include reports, analyses, and descriptions based on primary sources. Secondary sources may contain the same information as primary sources, but they are once-removed.

For example, a lecture or experiment by an expert in food irradiation is a primary source; the newspaper report of that lecture or experiment is a secondary source. A letter from a president to his secretary of state is a primary source; a history paper about that letter is a secondary source.

The distinction between primary and secondary sources is important to assure *reliability*. Secondary sources may contain errors. The newspaper account, for example, may misquote the expert or misrepresent the experiment. If possible, therefore, find the primary source—a copy of the actual lecture or a published article about the experiment. Not only does uncovering the primary data make your research more accurate, but your additional effort makes all your data and arguments more credible.

Warming Up: Journal Exercise

Understanding how both primary and secondary sources can help you to gain knowledge and expertise on a topic is crucial to becoming a better writer of research projects. Determining the types of sources that are most useful, and most reliable, is accomplished by considering carefully the needs of each situation in which you write. The scenarios below can help you to practice those processes.

1. You are doing research on the civil rights movement of the 1960s and 1970s in order to compare the goals of activists then to those of current activist movements like the Tea Party and Occupy Wall Street. Use your library's Web site to discover primary sources that will tell you more about that period or about current activism.
2. You read in the newspaper that a new drug being tested has the potential to cure breast cancer. Since you have family members who are affected by the disease, you are excited about this possibility. But the newspaper account is sketchy. What further primary or secondary sources might you seek to learn more about these drug trials? Where might you seek it, or what information might you take from the newspaper article that could help you ask good questions of a librarian?
3. You have read several recent novels by a favorite author and would like to write a paper on her work for your literature class. But you are not sure what experts or ordinary readers think of her work. What kinds of secondary sources would you seek to learn more about the reception of this author's work?

Field Research

Brainstorming and question analysis not only help you identify published research sources but also suggest opportunities for generating information on your own through *field research*. Field research can be accomplished by means of interviews, surveys, experiments, observing field sites, and so forth (see Chapter 6). Field research allows you to develop information first-hand and to focus that research on precisely the purpose you have in mind. For example, while much of Carrie Gingrich's research involved such sources as publications and film, she also wanted to know more about the attitudes and experiences of students of her generation. So she planned and executed field research through interviews with students and faculty. She also visited classes to observe how students learned about the genocide. While some projects will not require field research, in the early stages of your research you should consider whether it would enrich your understanding.

The chart below lists the sources and techniques Carrie Gingrich used for primary, secondary, and field research. Note that researching often combines many different techniques.

Overview of Gingrich's Research Sources and Techniques

Field Research Sources	Key Questions	Research Technique	Places in This Book to Review
Interview high school students	What do you know about the Rwandan genocide? Have you seen films about this event? Did you study it in school?	Field research: Interviewing	Guidelines for interviewing in Chapter 6
Visit high school classes as they watch films about the genocide	How is the genocide presented? What films are students viewing? Is it covered in other ways?	Field research: Observing	Chapter 3
Interview professors	What attitudes and goals do professors hold toward teaching history through film? Do high school teachers have similar or different attitudes?	Field research: interviewing	Guidelines for interviewing in Chapter 6
Primary Research Sources	**Key Questions**	**Research Technique**	**Places in This Book to Review**
View and analyze films	What perspective on history do the films present? Are they accurate, based on what I have read? What seems to be stressed in the visual presentation? What is missing?	Primary research: analyzing media and visuals	Techniques for analyzing rhetorical appeals of visuals in Chapter 5

(continued)

Overview of Gingrich's Research Sources and Techniques *(continued)*

Remember past experiences	What can I recall about my own and my classmates' reactions to viewing films about this event?	Primary research: remembering	Techniques for remembering and incorporating past experiences in Chapter 3
Examine course materials from high school classes	What can I learn about how genocides are taught by looking at class and curriculum plans?	Primary research: explaining and evaluating	Use techniques for explaining and evaluating these materials from Chapters 7 and 8
Secondary Research Sources	**Key Questions**	**Research Technique**	**Places in This Book to Review**
Read reference sources	What are the generally accepted facts about this event?	Secondary research: using general reference sources	Section on general reference sources in this chapter and reading rhetorically in Chapter 4
Read journal articles	What concepts and facts are disputed? How do historians write about these events? What evidence do they use? What do film and media studies experts suggest about the effect of films on our understanding of history?	Secondary research: evaluating journal sources	Section on evaluating journal sources in this chapter and reading rhetorically in Chapter 4
Read reviews	How do film reviewers see the purpose and effects of these films? What expertise do they bring to these sources? Are the reviews written by experts or the general public?	Secondary research and active reading	Sections on evaluating peer-reviewed and open Web sources in this chapter and reading rhetorically in Chapter 4; techniques for analyzing literature in Chapter 11

FINDING RELIABLE SECONDARY SOURCES

Early planning can help you form pertinent questions, identify a variety of sources of information, and become more informed about your topic. The next step is to add depth to that preliminary knowledge. Even projects that are largely based on field research or experiments will begin with secondary sources; by reviewing the literature, you learn what experts have already written on the topic. This is where the habits of mind of *responsibility* and *persistence* become crucial.

Electronic tools make it easy to find information on any topic quickly. But finding authoritative sources, and deciding which sources are reliable and appropriate for your audience and purpose, can be more challenging. And because researched essays are often meant for scholarly purposes and audiences, you will need to follow some strict conventions that help readers check the validity of your argument—conventions that we call *documenting* sources (see Chapter 13). If you pay attention to these needs as you do your research, you will save a great deal of time later.

“The outcome of any serious research can only be to make two questions grow where only one grew before.”

—Thorstein Veblen

As a twenty-first-century student, you have access to two types of interconnected libraries: the physical library and the online library. The physical space that contains books, journals, and library staff is still an essential research location. If you have not already done so, inquire about library tours, or walk through the library with a friend or classmate. But just as it is a good idea to acquaint yourself with the physical library, it is also important to learn how to access sources from your library's Web page.

Watch the Animation on Finding Sources

Your library most likely provides access to many bibliographic *databases*, which allow you to search and in many cases retrieve the full text of periodical articles and other research materials. Academic Search Premier, LexisNexis Academic, and InfoTrac are three popular databases that span academic disciplines. Since in some cases your academic research will focus on a particular discipline, such as biology, history, or film studies, you may want to limit your search to publications within one field. Databases such as ERIC, which focuses on education topics, or PsycINFO, on psychology, specialize in materials from particular disciplines. Learn the advantages and disadvantages of each so that you can choose which tool fits your purpose.

While library databases usually turn up relatively reliable sources, it is still important for you to consider point of view, currency, and relevance to your project. Note how the citation information provided on the library page on page 454 can tell you a great deal about the value and credibility of a source and help you to find other search terms.

If you examine Carrie Gingrich's working annotated bibliography at the end of this chapter, and the more developed Works Cited page in her full paper at the end of Chapter 13, you can reconstruct the strategy and thought process she used in her research. She included popular sources such as film reviews and academic journals from several fields. Each of these sources had a specific purpose: to provide background on the historical event, to show how media influences our views of historical events, and to explain how historical films are received by viewers. She found that relevant information by limiting her searches with good questions and by using the specific tools included in her library database.

EVALUATING SOURCES: RELEVANCE, CURRENCY, AND RELIABILITY

12.3 Use techniques to evaluate sources.

It goes without saying that you want the “best” sources that you can find. But what makes a “best” source? For each source you turn up, ask yourself: Does this contribute directly or indirectly to accomplishing my purpose with this specific

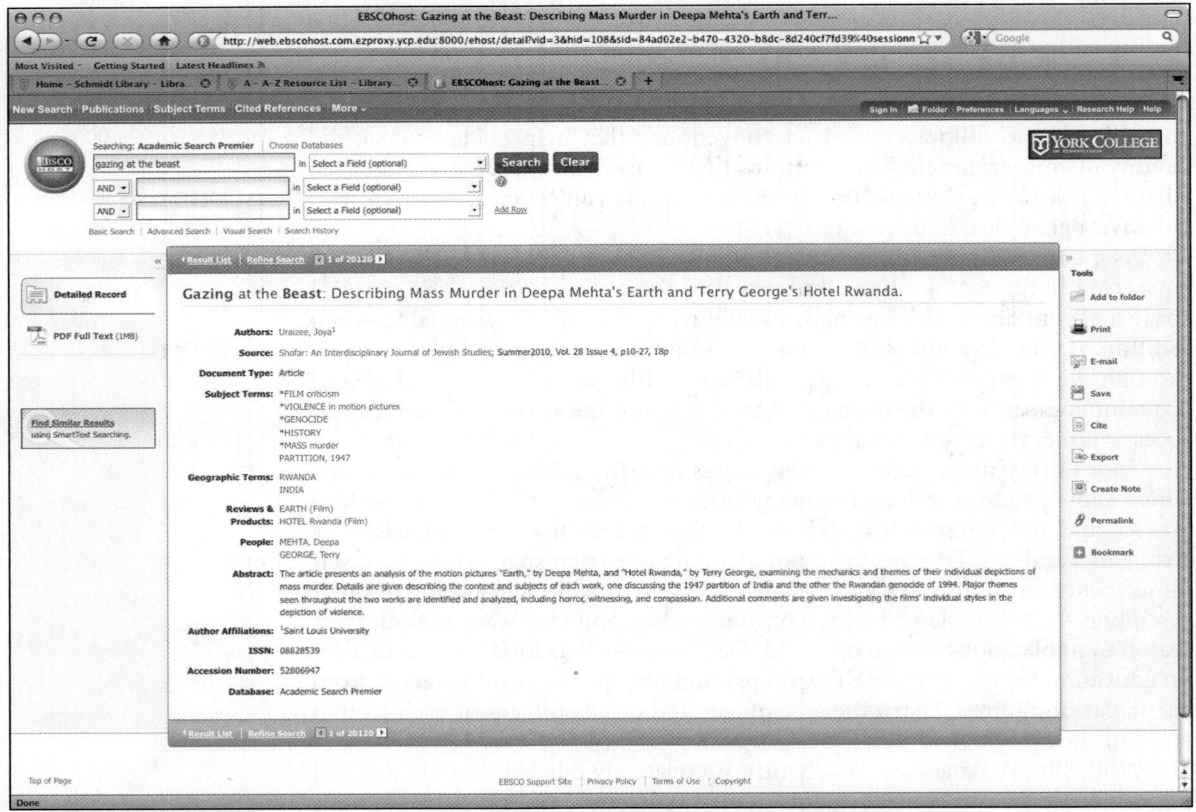

A journal article accessed through a library database. The interconnected (and often hyperlinked) information provided on this page can make your searches much more rich and productive.

audience? That is, is this source *relevant* to my specific purpose and audience? To determine this, you will need to consider two additional factors: *currency* and *reliability*.

- ***Relevance to topic, purpose, and audience***: Does the article's title and description suggest that it will be useful for your particular project? Why or why not?
- ***Currency***: When was the article published? Is the article recent enough to take into account the most up-to-date data and research? How important is it that the article was published recently, considering your topic?
- ***Reliability***: Is the author an authority? Was the article peer-reviewed—that is, was it checked for accuracy by other experts? What topics does it cover? Who would be likely to write for such a journal? Is the author biased?

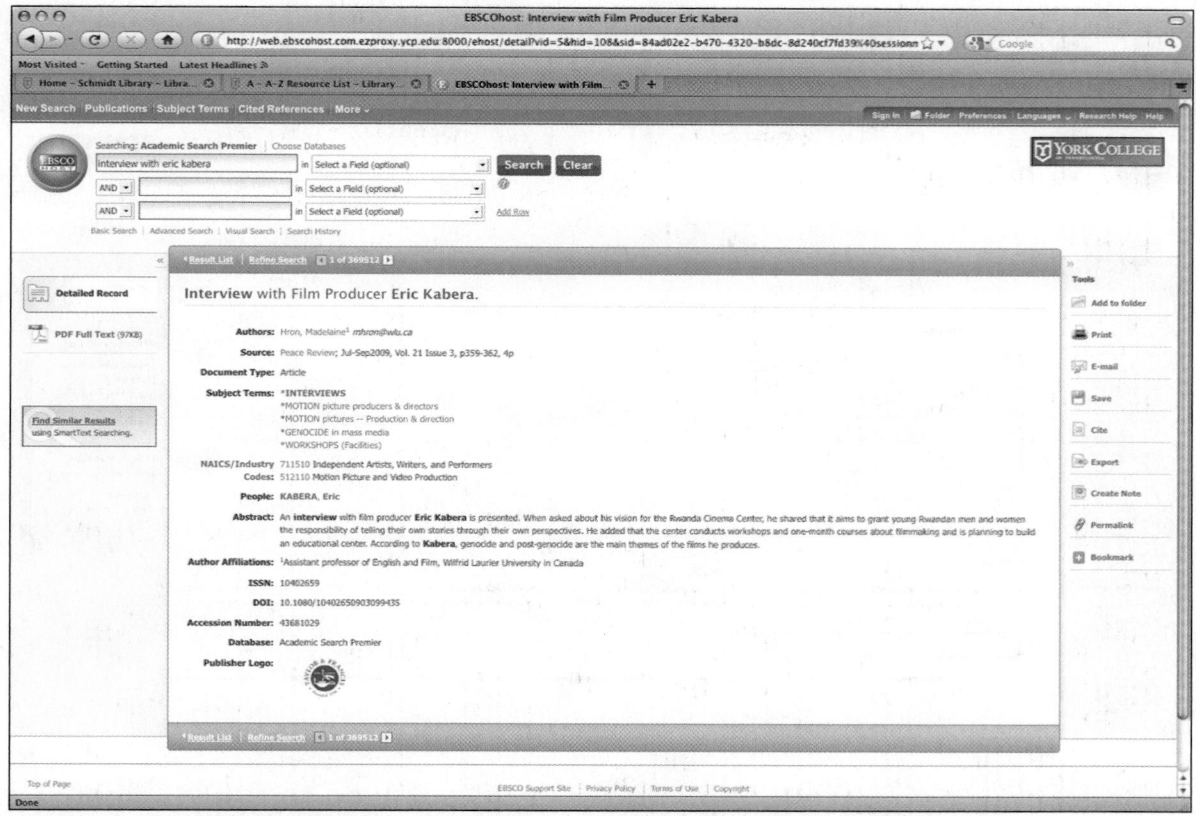

A citation in a library database contains useful information that can help you make good choices as you develop your working bibliography. Note all the parts of this page that can aid you in considering relevance, currency, and reliability.

For example, during her research, Gingrich came across an interview with a film director (see the library database page above). She first needed to consider its relevance to her topic by reading the abstract and other information on the page. All the information found there can help you decide whether the source is truly relevant to your purpose and audience, whether it is likely to contain current enough information, and whether the author and the publication are likely to provide reliable, unbiased information.

But to consider reliability, Gingrich also needed to consider the credibility and potential biases of the publication itself. Especially authoritative sources are published through a process called *peer review.* This means that before an article is published, the manuscript is reviewed by experts in the field, who check it for accuracy, use of reliable methods, potential biases, and inclusion of pertinent and current information. Just a few more clicks led this student writer to a description

Watch the Video on Evaluating Sources

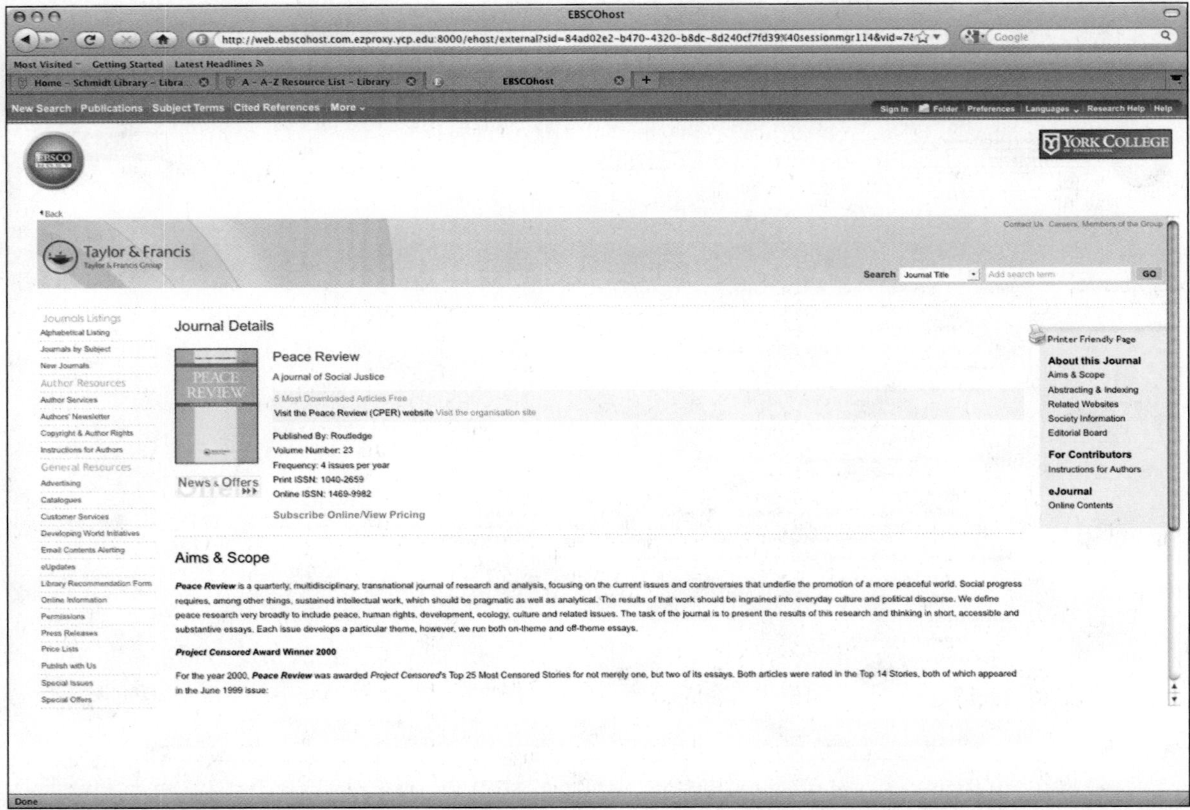

Description of a journal. What does this description tell you about the journal, its purposes, its editorial procedures, and any likely bias? Does it make you more or less comfortable about the relevance and reliability of an article published in this journal? What other features of the page could lead you to pertinent information about the publication?

of the journal in which it appeared, giving her a better sense of the reliability of the source and any potential bias (see the Journal Details page above).

Because the audience for your paper will want evidence that you based your argument on credible sources, it is important to articulate the reasons a particular source is reliable (and why your audience will consider it so). Taking notes about the reliability of each source and any potential biases will be very useful later in the process. Although there are slightly different criteria for evaluating each kind of source, some questions apply to all sources of information.[1]

[1]These criteria are adapted from guidelines designed by Elizabeth E. Kirk, the library instruction coordinator for the Milton S. Eisenhower Library at Johns Hopkins University, and are available at www.library.jhu.edu/researchhelp/general/evaluating.

Evaluating the Reliability of Sources

Clues to Reliability	Questions to Ask	Notes on Choosing Sources
Authorship	Who is the author? Is the author well known? Are the author's credentials or biographical information available on the Internet or elsewhere? Does the author have a reason to be biased?	The less you know about the author, the more cautious you need to be about using the source. *If you decide to include a document by a questionable authority, indicate exactly what you know or don't know about the author's credentials.*
Publishing organization	Is the article in a peer-reviewed journal? Is there information about the publication, or in the case of an electronic publication, the organization, Webmaster, or designer of the page? Is this organization recognized in its field?	It is best to use information from sources that are published by reliable, unbiased sources. However, in some cases you may wish to include information from other types of sources to show popular opinions or to illustrate that biases exist. *If you know the source is not authoritative or has a commercial basis, indicate the organization's identity if you quote from the site, and offer your own critique.*
Point of view or bias	Every document or text has a point of view or bias—but some biases may mean that the site's information is not reliable or accurate. Does the author or organization have a commercial, political, philosophical, religious, environmental, or even scientific agenda? Is the organization selling something?	*When you use a source with highly selective or biased information or perspectives, indicate the author's probable bias or agenda when you cite the text.*
Reliability and knowledge of the literature	Reliable sources refer to other texts in that discipline or field. Look for documents that have in-text citations or references to other sources, a fair and reasonable appraisal of alternative points of view, and a bibliography.	*Any source that has no references to other key works may be one writer's opinion and may contain erroneous information. If you have reason to believe the source is not reliable or accurate, find another source.*

EVALUATING SPECIFIC TYPES OF SOURCES

While the evaluation techniques described in the chart above apply to all secondary sources, certain techniques are helpful for evaluating specific types of sources.

Evaluating Academic Journals

Academic or *peer-reviewed* journals, sometimes called *refereed* journals, publish articles that have been evaluated by other experts in the field. But you will still need to consider the reliability of each article by asking these questions:

- Who is the author? What can you find out about this individual or group?
- What is the publication or who is the publisher? What is the purpose?
- What point of view or biases might that purpose suggest?
- Does the article draw on accurate, current, and reliable research, citing literature from the field, or just opinions?
- Does the information fit your purpose and audience? How?

Evaluating Open Web Sources

Choosing relevant sources from the open Web requires the same care and attention that is required when judging library sources. This too requires the *persistent,* yet *flexible,* habits of mind that inform good research. You will want to be *open* and *creative* enough to consider all types of sources; sometimes including information from unusual sources can be quite effective. But you also want to be *responsible* enough to use only information that you deem to be reliable—or to be honest and thoughtful about the source's shortcomings. Information from a biased blog or Web site may help you demonstrate a range of opinions, but you would also want to acknowledge the biases, show why the biases exist, and critique those opinions.

The first problem you face when doing a search on the open Web is the sheer mass of data that an unfocused search will yield. The second problem is the mixture of source types. Unlike library databases, the open Web may offer few context cues to help you judge what you are reading, so it requires your persistence to ensure that the information you find has been carefully reviewed and the source's shortcomings revealed. A single Google search may turn up scholarly sources, commercial sites, blogs, wikis, personal pages, and Facebook pages. This means that you must be especially vigilant as you evaluate the reliability and relevance of the sources you find.

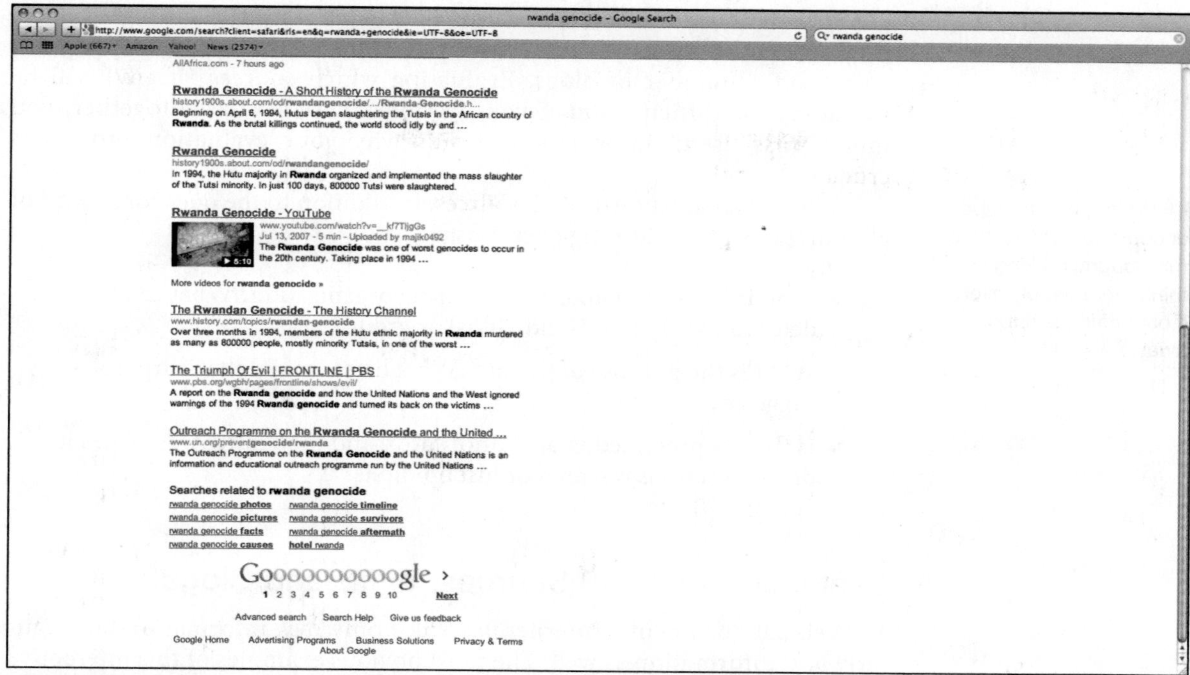

Google search results. Some little-known Google features can help you find the most useful and authoritative sources on the open Web.

For example, a Google search on "Rwanda genocide" will yield over one million results. But if you scroll through the pages, and look closely, you'll find tools to help you limit your search:

- A link for "more" helps you limit a search to particular types of material, such as blogs, images, or videos. This will lead you to Google Scholar, a fine open Web search engine that is limited to academic sources.
- A series of related searches can help you limit a search.
- Adding limiting terms to your search—terms such as "film," "education," "effects or impact"—produces a more focused result. Look back at your purpose and audience to develop those search terms, and try them in various combinations.
- Specific links can lead you to more authoritative sources or educational or organizational Web sites that have already collected and organized information for you.

On the right side of the page, you'll find commercial sites that offer products and services; as you scroll, you'll find the ubiquitous Wikipedia entry and a number of blogs. Evaluating which sources (if any) will be useful can be difficult. But if you overlook these sources altogether, you might miss useful information. That's why your evaluation process is crucial.

> **"Putting pen to paper encourages us to pause for thought, making us think more deeply even if our writing is thrown away."**
> —Norbet Platt

When evaluating open Web sources, in addition to the questions asked of all sources, ask the following questions:

- Who is the author and/or sponsoring organization? What can be determined about this individual or group?
- What is the purpose of the site? What biases might that purpose suggest?
- Is the site presented in an authoritative and thoughtful way? Does it draw on serious research or just opinions?

Evaluating Web 2.0 Sources: Wikis and Blogs

In Web 2.0 documents, Internet users not only *seek* information but regularly *post* information as well. The most obvious examples of this interactive Web are wikis and blogs, both of which consist of a constant stream of postings by all types of individuals, from top-notch experts to novices, from those who value objective research to those with their own agendas—and those who just like to subvert the process. Wikis like Wikipedia, for example, allow editing by the users. In some cases, Wikipedia and other wikis provide excellent bibliographies that can guide your further research, help you discover other useful sources, and help you check the reliability of the entry itself. But you should also be wary of sources like Wikipedia—be sure to check with your instructor to see if he or she allows the (careful) use of this source.

One way to check a wiki's reliability is to consider the changes that users have made to an entry. The "history" tab of Wikipedia allows you to trace and evaluate the edits made to a page over time.

Blogs are another form of Web 2.0 source; they began as open, personal journals (Weblogs), and they are now often sites of public debate. They offer a voice to anyone who wishes to post, without regard to expertise (though many blog authors *are* experts) and without the refereeing and editing that articles published in academic journals must undergo. Therefore, you should consider carefully not only which blogs to select but also how to use them. Using blogs to show the wide range of opinions on a topic can be useful; citing information from a blog (or a wiki) as authoritative is usually not advisable.

When evaluating a blog, add these questions to your inquiry:

- Who is the author and who is the sponsoring organization? Who contributes to this blog? Why do they contribute, and from what point of view?
- What is the purpose of the site? What biases does that suggest?
- Does the owner of the blog manage and vet the postings? Does he or she provide expert commentary?
- How current are the postings? How active is the blog? Is there an archive of past postings?

Some blogs, like that found on Rwandan Survivors site (http://rwandansurvivors.blogspot.com/), promote a specific agenda. That blog, according to its founder, was created to "be a voice and a platform for survivors of the Rwandan genocide." It provides survivors' stories and asks for "views on how we can prevent these atrocities happening again," providing a clear sense of its purpose. Other blogs are maintained by experts who provide running commentary on the ideas that are discussed on the site. For example, in her research, Carrie Gingrich found a blog sponsored by the *New York Times* that combines visual depictions of the Rwanda genocide with stories about and interviews with survivors. This blog features the work of trained journalists and links to authoritative information on the incident. It also allows readers to respond with their own thoughts, comments, and information. Readers' comments include emotional responses ("May the Lord have mercy on all of you") as well as perspectives on history, the U.S. Constitution, and the United Nations that could be useful both in themselves and as leads for seeking further sources.

As a researcher, you could use this information from a blog in a number of ways:

- Read the opinions in light of other information you have found, and make note of the readers' comments as you consider what others know about this topic and their reaction to this media source (in the case of Carrie Gingrich, this is one of the key purposes of her essay).
- Follow the links from the site to learn more about the topic and find additional sources.
- Post your own comments and queries as a way of gathering primary source information. Reading responses gives you a variety of perspectives and informs you about the ongoing conversation on this issue.

If you combine Web sources with library sources and primary information, you will likely produce well-rounded and innovative research. And when you use Web sources much as you use general reference sources—as a starting point to drive other research—they can be particularly useful.

Researching: The Writing Process

12.4
Write a research proposal and annotated bibliography.

This section of the chapter will help you use the research techniques you have learned to move from your general research goals to a specific *research proposal* and a *working annotated bibliography*. A strong research proposal and annotated bibliography can help you to:

- be creative in making the case that the project is worth doing and that you are capable of completing it within a specific time frame (something your instructor will want to know).
- maintain your flexibility and curiosity in seeking areas for further research that will enhance your project.
- be persistent enough to use your early research to develop a clear plan for completing the project.
- be open enough to invite the feedback of others (your teacher and peers) who might suggest ways to enhance the project.

Assignment for Researching: Research Proposal and Annotated Bibliography

Choose a subject that strongly interests you, about which both you *and a specific audience* would like to learn more. It may be a subject that you have already written about in this course (or, with your teacher's approval, in another course) and which would be enriched by more sustained research. **Using techniques described in this chapter, make sure that your research plan goes beyond *finding* information on your topic and becomes a process of *discovering* a focused purpose and audience for your researched essay.** As you consider library resources (both paper and online), field research (such as questionnaires, interviews, and field studies), electronic sources (Web sites, blogs, wikis, organizational databases), and unpublished sources, your goal will be to move from a generic topic to a specific stance that articulates what you can add to the ongoing conversation on that topic. This statement of your topic, purpose, and audience will take the form of a hypothesis or "working thesis"—your best educated guess as to the focused point that your project will forward to a particular audience, and the purpose that your research will serve. Check with your instructor for suggested length, appropriate number or kinds of sources, and additional format requirements. Do your initial research and—using techniques for choosing, annotating, and keeping track of your source information—**develop a detailed research proposal and annotated bibliography to present to your teacher for approval.** The proposal should argue that your project has a clear purpose and audience, and that you have the resources and time to complete this project well. Be sure to choose the documentation style appropriate for your subject, purpose, and audience, and to keep careful bibliographic records.

While some features of academic research and writing apply to all papers you will write in college courses, genre conventions are determined by the specific purposes and guidelines of specific courses. At the end of Chapter 13, you will learn more about other public purposes for academic research as well.

Audience	Possible Purposes and Genres for Academic Research
Non-Expert Audience	• A wiki entry that uses your research to inform readers about a current topic like racism or energy sustainability. • An editorial or letter to the editor that uses academic research to help the larger public to better understand a current issue. • A position paper that uses research to pose a solution to a local problem such as juvenile crime.
Discipline-based Audience	• A psychology paper that makes use of survey research or a business administration paper that uses case studies. • A science report that reviews the literature on a topic and uses experimental methods to employ or test other experiments. • A literary analysis that uses a specific literary theory to examine a novel or poem. • A comment posted to a listserv or blog sponsored by an organization such as the American Psychological Association
Interdisciplinary Audience	• A paper that applies sociological theories to an analysis of an historical incident. • An analysis that shows the impact of a film on historical events or perspectives. • A paper on healthcare policy that uses research from the nursing field.

Because a research project takes a good deal of time and energy, your teacher will want to feel comfortable that your project has a reasonable chance of success before approving it. Writing a detailed research proposal can demonstrate that your project is worth doing and that you have done sufficient inquiry and research to ensure success. Writing a proposal has several important steps that will help you refine your thoughts on the topic, purpose, and audience.

CHOOSING: NARROWING AND FOCUSING YOUR TOPIC

Watch the **Animation** on Narrowing a Topic

Narrowing and focusing your topic to arrive at a working thesis statement is a process of choosing from among the possibilities suggested by your preliminary research. Though your thesis statement won't be final until you've completed your research, it is useful to start with a working thesis or hypothesis. Carrie Gingrich began her research because of her personal concern that the world had not learned from the mistakes made during the Rwanda genocide. But claiming that her topic is "the Rwanda Genocide" or that her purpose is to "stop future genocides" was far too broad.

To propose a research project that you will be able to complete, you need to carve out a niche, a focused sense of what you can promise to deliver. To do this, ask yourself these basic questions:

1. **What is my main idea?** Answer this question as specifically as you can, revising again and again until your topic statement clearly expresses your hypothesis or working thesis based on what you have learned so far. Write out your working thesis several times, let it sit awhile, show it to others, and then return to it each time you learn more, revising it based on your changing perspective on the topic. This will ensure that by the time you articulate your working thesis in your topic proposal, it expresses accurately what you are promising to do.
2. **Based on my early research, in what ways have authors addressed this topic?** Articulate the approaches others have taken on this topic: Have they made comparative analyses? Have they used emotional arguments? Have they tried to supply scientific facts? What kinds of evidence seem to be most effective in making the kinds of argument that you would like to make? The answers to these questions will help you state to your teacher (and yourself) precisely what you need to accomplish in the research stage to defend your thesis.
3. **What kinds of audiences might be most interested in this topic?** Why are they stakeholders, and how can I show them that they do indeed have a vested interest in it? Remember, a "general" audience is the hardest audience to address because it has such a diversity of knowledge, beliefs, and experience. Even if you believe that just about everyone should be interested in the topic, it will still be best to focus on a specific group, such as those who disagree or those who want to know more. Imagine what perspective this group already holds, how you want to change or advance that perspective, and what strategies are most likely to do so. Make a list of likely characteristics and opinions of your audience. What resistance must you overcome? What views or characteristics can you build on? If you can't answer these questions with some confidence, your conceived audience might be too broad.

4. **How much can I reasonably expect to learn about my topic in the allotted time?** To write confidently on any topic, you need to become an expert. List the things you'll need to learn if you are to write with authority and to address your audience's questions. It also helps to note explicitly those aspects of the topic you will *not* address, to keep you from going off on tangents.
5. **What will my final project look like?** Consider the possible genres, structures, and organizational patterns that are most likely to create a coherent treatment of the topic. To do so, you might review the types of writing that are discussed throughout the chapters of this book.

Allowing yourself time to reflect on these questions early in the process can save you a great deal of time later on. As Carrie Gingrich developed her proposal, she considered what small piece of her larger purpose she could reasonably address, and she developed this working thesis:

> Although media depictions of the Rwanda tragedy seem to be an effective way to teach students, using films in the classroom without supplementary discussions and materials will not adequately inform these future citizen leaders about the tragedy or how to avoid future tragedies.

While this working thesis would develop further as she completed her research, it did start to define a particular audience (instructors), a purpose (to suggest better teaching methods and materials), a scope (use of films in the classroom), and an approach (arguing and informing).

Even after you have developed a narrow working thesis, you'll still need to see if your research supports that hypothesis. (Be willing to change your mind as the research warrants it.) But having that working version of your thesis will help you find and assess the research sources necessary to test the validity of your claim.

Warming Up: Journal Exercises

Developing a thoughtful working thesis, and using that initial thesis as a jumping-off point for further research, can help you to enrich your researched writing. The scenarios below walk you through some of the key processes of using a working thesis as a way to structure and focus your searches for further information.

1. As a political science major, you are concerned that your generation is not engaging in important national issues. As you plan your research, you

hypothesize about the reasons why this may be true. Write several versions of a working thesis that captures possible reasons why young people are failing to engage in politics, and then consider forms of research that you could propose to test that working thesis. Be sure to consider who your audience is and to list the characteristics of this audience that you must consider to accomplish your purpose.

2 As a major in business administration interested in starting your own business, you are concerned about the high failure rate of start-up companies. You wish to learn more about the factors that influence a business' success or failure and pass that information along to other business majors. But you also know that this topic is quite broad. Try writing a series of working theses that are increasingly focused and narrow and then suggest ways to begin research on the most focused topic. Be sure to consider primary, secondary, and field research sources. Consider how you will express to this audience the reasons why they are stakeholders.

3 As a future educator, you are interested in how science is taught in the secondary schools, especially in the differences between high school and college teaching. You decide to do a research project that will help you—and other current and future teachers—consider innovative teaching methods. What form or genre might this project take? What kinds of writing will be central? Consider at least four ways that you might present this information to your audience, and list the advantages and disadvantages of each. Consider both traditional and new media genres and how each can serve your audience and purpose.

COLLECTING AND NOTETAKING

Once you have developed a working thesis, a strategy for beginning your research (which will continue to evolve), and an initial sense of the genre you will use, the process of learning about that focused topic begins. This is the longest part of the research process, so it will require persistence, engagement, and flexibility. Because this process will take at least several weeks, it is important that you be conscientious about keeping good notes. Otherwise you will waste time and effort in going back to recover lost information, search for proper documentation, and reread materials. If done properly, however, these processes will provide a running log of the ways that your thoughts on the topic progress.

Three techniques will help you make the most of your research as you develop a research proposal: annotating sources and notetaking, summarizing sources, and recording bibliographic notes.

Annotating Sources and Notetaking

The process of *annotating* the material you read is crucial to effective, efficient reading. Annotating means making notes in the margin of a text. When you annotate a text, several things happen:

1. You become a more *active* reader. While you make notes, you do not just passively experience a text. Instead, you ask questions of it, try to bring together its various points, come to grips with its thesis and forms of evidence, and better understand its rhetorical and stylistic elements—how the author is attempting to make her case and to persuade you. (See Chapter 4 for processes of active, rhetorical reading.)
2. Sources become more valuable. Annotating helps you read with specific intentions. For example, as you read, you will highlight the most important concepts; evaluate the currency and reliability of the material; link the material to your own topic, purpose, and audience; and generate key questions for your project.

To make full use of the annotation process, you can use several types of annotation.

Types of Annotation

Annotation Purposes	Type of Annotation	How to Do It
To understand the main point or thesis	Thesis identification	Mark and comment on those places *where the author attempts to crystallize the main point*, and paraphrase that point in your own words.
To understand the main concepts in order to follow the piece's topic and argument	Concepts and terms	Underline or highlight *key words* and *concepts* and explain their meaning. Either use context clues—explanations in the text itself—or look outside the text for further definitions and details.
To help you engage in active reading	Questions	As you read, keep a running list of questions. Is the piece reliable? Has the author proven her point? What questions does the piece raise about your topic, purpose, and audience?
To better understand the ways that other authors build arguments	Rhetorical and stylistic elements	Mark spots where an author is trying to persuade you, and note in the margin how this author uses a particular technique to build her argument. Evaluate whether that technique is useful, viable, and credible.

(continued)

Types of Annotation *(continued)*

To note the evidence (or lack of evidence) for claims that are made	Elements of proof	Whenever you see an element of proof—statistics, citing other authors, experiments, anecdotes—highlight it and note the value of the evidence, its credibility, and how it might help you to support your argument (or, in some cases, what counterarguments you should address).
To map out the way an argument develops throughout a piece	Organization	Point out the places where an author transitions among ideas, builds on ideas, and uses specific techniques to help the reader follow the argument.

Below is a text that has been annotated using these techniques, and through which you can see the thought processes that are developing toward a more focused research proposal. *Photocopy or download important sources for later rereading and reference.* Make sure that your copies clearly show authors, titles, and page numbers. Electronic downloads can be annotated using either the Review function of software like Microsoft Word, or sticky notes for PDFs.

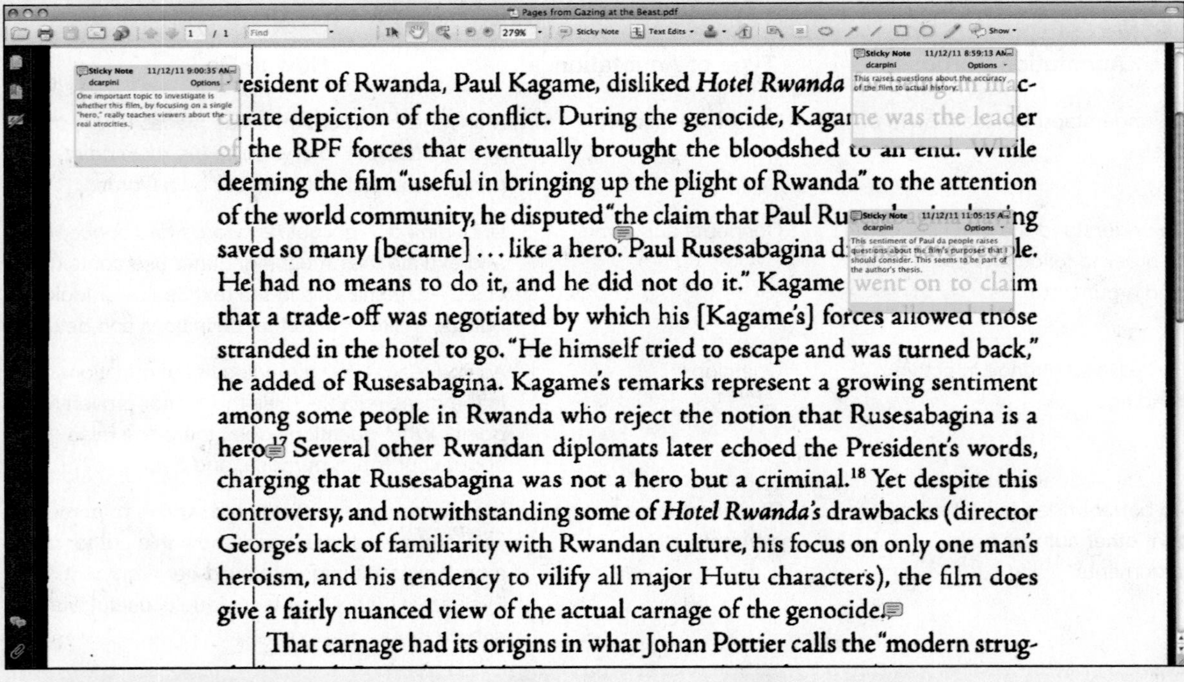

resident of Rwanda, Paul Kagame, disliked *Hotel Rwanda* … c-urate depiction of the conflict. During the genocide, Kagame was the leader of the RPF forces that eventually brought the bloodshed to an end. While deeming the film "useful in bringing up the plight of Rwanda" to the attention of the world community, he disputed "the claim that Paul Ru… ng saved so many [became] . . . like a hero. Paul Rusesabagina d… le. He had no means to do it, and he did not do it." Kagame went on to claim that a trade-off was negotiated by which his [Kagame's] forces allowed those stranded in the hotel to go. "He himself tried to escape and was turned back," he added of Rusesabagina. Kagame's remarks represent a growing sentiment among some people in Rwanda who reject the notion that Rusesabagina is a hero.[17] Several other Rwandan diplomats later echoed the President's words, charging that Rusesabagina was not a hero but a criminal.[18] Yet despite this controversy, and notwithstanding some of *Hotel Rwanda's* drawbacks (director George's lack of familiarity with Rwandan culture, his focus on only one man's heroism, and his tendency to vilify all major Hutu characters), the film does give a fairly nuanced view of the actual carnage of the genocide.

That carnage had its origins in what Johan Pottier calls the "modern strug-

Annotating and Notetaking. Electronic annotations and notes using the Sticky Note function in a pdf file.

Summarizing a Text

While annotating a text can help you focus on the useful parts, it is helpful to stand back and assess the message and purpose of the piece as a whole. Summarizing the thesis, purpose, audience, and main points of evidence of each piece that seems useful can greatly advance your thinking on a topic. It can also provide you with material in your own words to use in your proposal and, later, in drafting your paper.

Be careful as you summarize to use your own words. Do not allow the language of the original author to slip into your summary and then into your paper, which would result in inadvertent plagiarism. As you read, however, you will likely find wording that captures some facet of your topic in a particularly compelling way. Write or paste these words into your summary, placing quotation marks around them and carefully noting the page number.

Carrie Gingrich wrote this summary of the article "Gazing at the Beast":

> By comparing two films about genocides, one in India and one in Rwanda, this article examines the accuracy of the films in portraying these tragic events. The article uses responses to the films by people in India and Rwanda to suggest that there may be inaccuracies, and in the case of Hotel Rwanda, that there is a real debate about whether the "hero," Paul Rusesabagina, was really a hero (or even a "criminal") and also whether by focusing on one man's action, the film ignores the bigger issues of the genocide and tends to portray all Hutus as evil. This analysis can help me to show some of the complications in the way media is used to portray complex historical events. There are important historical questions raised that I can examine further, including the main character's actual history. A key quote from page 17 comes from the Rwandan president, Paul Kagame, who acknowledged that the film was useful "in bringing up the plight of Rwanda," but said "Paul Rusesabagina did not save people. He had no means to do it, and he did not do it" (17).

The process of collecting sources provides an important chance for you to focus your argument. After reading and summarizing each new piece, take a moment to jot down your thoughts about what you have learned *and how it confirms, contradicts, or expands on the ideas in other sources you have read.* This is a portion of the process that is *recursive*—that is, you return to your earlier notes on sources and add the new insights and information you have found. By cross-referencing the pieces you read, you will see how the various sources of information speak to one another and how you can synthesize their ideas to understand the bigger picture. In this way, Carrie Gingrich might return to her notes above after reading more about Paul Rusesabagina. She might supplement the quotation from President Kagame or the author's perspective on the value of this film after consulting the Web source "Was Hotel Rwanda's Paul Rusesabagina a Hero or an Opportunist?" an article that raises similar questions and provides two contradictory quotations:

> Dorcas Komo notes that two Rwanda citizens sent out a mass email that called Rusesabagina "'a heartless imposter'. . . who was taking advantage of horrible situations to do business and earn a living." Another citizen suggested that "the Rwandan government had rewarded certain people to make those [negative] claims." [source: (http://minneafrica.wordpress.com/2008/12/05/was-hotel-rwandas-paul-rusesabagina-a-hero-or-opportunist/).]

Adding information from these sources to her notes can help Carrie identify a key point of debate as she considers the truth of the story told by *Hotel Rwanda*.

Recording Careful Bibliographic Notes

Rather than waste time later trying to reconstruct the information you will need to cite sources and prepare an annotated bibliography, list of references, or works cited list, keep careful notes from the start. Even though you will not complete your Works Cited or References page until the final stages of writing, selecting a documentation style **before** you begin is crucial. The documentation style you choose will tell you what bibliographic information you must collect.

If you are writing a paper in the humanities, follow the Modern Language Association (MLA) style set forth in the *MLA Handbook for Writers of Research Papers* (seventh edition, 2009). If you are writing a paper in the behavioral sciences, use the American Psychological Association (APA) style as described in the *Publication Manual of the American Psychological Association* (sixth edition, 2009). This chapter illustrates both MLA and APA styles, and the chart below is comprehensive. It is always a good idea to check the preferences of your teacher.

Bibliographic Information to Collect on Each Source

Item	Journal Article Example
Author(s), if Known	Joya Uraizee
Full title and subtitle of the source • For an **article**, list both title and subtitle from the opening page. • For a **book**, list the title and any subtitle as shown on the title page; if you are using only one section or chapter, list that title as well. • For a **Web page**, list title and subtitle of the specific page on a site.	"Gazing at the Beast: Describing Mass Murder in Deepa Mehta's *Earth* and Terry George's *Hotel Rwanda*"

Publication information • For an **article**, list the name of the periodical, the volume, issue number, date, and if you are using APA style, the digital object identifier (doi) if any. If you accessed the article through a database, note the database name (MLA). • For a **book**, list the city, state, publisher, and year of publication. • For a **Web page**, list the sponsoring organization or individual who maintains the site, and list the date of last revision, usually at the bottom of a Web page. • For an **online source**, list the URL (you can cut and paste this into your bibliographic file and even make it a hyperlink). For an online article cited in APA style, note the URL of the journal's home page when there is no doi.	*Shofar: An Interdisciplinary Journal of Jewish Studies* Volume 28, Number 4, 2010 Academic Search Premier
Date you accessed the source	November 17, 2012
Medium of publication • List the **medium** (Print, Web, DVD, Tweet, iPad, Kindle, etc.) of the source.	Web
Beginning and ending page numbers (if available) • For a **journal article**, list the page numbers of the entire article. • For a **book**, list the page numbers of the portion that you are citing or referencing. • For an **online source**, list page numbers only if they are stable (as in a PDF) or the page numbers from the print source are identified.	10–27

Rethinking and Revising Your Working Thesis

Pause at times as you do your research to see how new pieces of information affect your original hypothesis. If you make this procedure a regular part of your notetaking, you will have a rich resource when you start the writing processes of shaping and drafting your paper. As you learn more, you are continually likely to revise your thesis. Recall that Carrie Gingrich's working thesis was this:

> Although the use of media depictions of the Rwanda tragedy seem to be an effective way to teach students about this event, they may not be completely successful in raising awareness.

Based on the questions raised about Paul Rusesabagina, she might now revise that thesis to look like this:

> Although media depictions of the Rwanda tragedy seem to be an effective way to teach students about this event, they may not be completely successful in raising awareness, and in fact may be considered inaccurate or counterproductive.

SHAPING YOUR RESEARCH PROPOSAL

A research proposal, like any form of writing, has a specific topic, purpose, and audience. It describes your project and what you intend to accomplish by completing it. Its central purpose is to convince your instructor that your project is well thought out and has a good chance of succeeding. As you consider each of the following shaping strategies, refer to Carrie Gingrich's research proposal on page 477 for examples.

To shape your proposal, you will use your notes, your annotated source materials, and the summaries you have written to synthesize what you have learned into a strong working thesis. The following questions can help you to complete this synthesis and demonstrate the value of your project.

Questions for Shaping Your Research Proposal

- What is your specific topic? Is it limited and focused enough to allow you to explore the topic in some depth?
- What are your goals and purpose for the completed project? What do you want it to accomplish?
- Who is the specific audience, and why will they be—or should they be—concerned about this topic? How will you address their concerns and demonstrate the value of your project?
- What research have you completed? How has it influenced your thinking on this topic so far? How has this early research substantiated or changed your working thesis?

Planning

Planning your research proposal provides the opportunity for you to look again at your project globally and to determine how your thoughts on your topic and purpose have changed through your early research. Use these strategies:

- Look over your original brainstorming and your notes, and capture in a few clear statements your central goals for the project and why it is worthwhile.
- Reread your notes and annotations, and highlight the most compelling evidence for the project's worth that you have collected.
- Explain to a friend or classmate the overall purpose and working thesis for your project.
- List the main points that you want your finished paper to make and an order of presentation that will best develop that case.

Recall that the purpose of a research proposal is to gain the permission of your teacher to proceed with the project. At this point your goal is not to develop the full argument of your paper—you still have work to do—but to develop a shape for your proposal that demonstrates that you have a clear plan for moving forward.

Organizing

If you keep the purpose of a research proposal in mind, a structure for the proposal will start to take shape. Though research proposals can take many forms, usually the following parts of a proposal are necessary to building that case. Check with your instructor about his or her specific requirements.

Shaping Your Points: Research Proposal and Annotated Bibliography

Introduction	Audience	Genre, Style, Medium	Overall Project Plan	Research Plan	Annotated Bibliography
States a limited and focused topic Explains your interest in the topic	Describes your intended audience Explains why they would be interested	Describes how the genre, style, and medium of delivery fit the rhetorical situation	Describes the plan for further research and writing Includes a schedule showing you can complete the project on time	Describes your research plan, both what you have accomplished so far and what you will do in the future	Shows that you have already gathered some useful information

DRAFTING AN ANNOTATED WORKING BIBLIOGRAPHY

An annotated bibliography is a list of sources much like a Works Cited or References list (see page 480). However, since you prepare it before you have completed your research, it has two substantial differences:

- **It is a working draft of your source list.** You will add further sources as you continue your project. Also, since you may not yet have read all the sources carefully, you may delete sources that you decide do not fit your topic, purpose, and audience.
- **It is annotated.** You have added notes on the reliability, credibility, and currency of each source and on how each source might be useful and relevant to your project.

The process of writing your annotations has two steps.

1. Provide all necessary information for each source in correct MLA or APA style.

2. State why you have chosen each source. In other words, demonstrate that the source passes the tests for reliability, currency, and relevance discussed in this chapter. Each annotation should include:
   - a summary of the main ideas and arguments of the source
   - a statement about the relevance of these arguments and information to your audience and purpose
   - an explanation of the currency, credibility, and reliability of the source, including any potential bias of the author

Guidelines for Revision

- **Take the perspective of your audience.** If you were the instructor, what would make you confident that the project will succeed? What concerns might you have?
- **Be sure that you have shown the need for this project.** A good proposal not only describes what you will research and write about; it also answers the "so what" question: Why would a specific audience want to read about this?
- **Check your working thesis.** Does this statement capture the main point that you wish to make in the clearest possible terms? Is there room for misinterpretation? Is it sufficiently focused and limited in terms of topic, purpose, audience, and scope?
- **What does the proposal say about the final project's shape or genre?** Remember that a proposal not only lays out the topic, it predicts the "deliverable"—what you are promising to produce. While there is still time to alter your plans, check to see that your proposal accurately states what you believe you can deliver.
- **Check your annotated bibliography.** Are the sources you have listed sufficient resources, and do you have good leads on how to become well informed on this topic? Are your sources directly relevant to your purpose and audience, and will your audience accept them as reliable and current?

PeerResponse

The questions that follow will help you give and receive constructive advice about the rough draft of your proposal and annotated bibliography. You may use these guidelines for an in-class workshop, a take-home review, or a computer e-mail response.

Writer: Before you exchange drafts with another reader, write out the following information about your own rough draft.

1. On the draft, label the working thesis and the description of the purpose and audience for your proposed project.
2. Underline or highlight what you take to be the best arguments for this project to be approved.
3. On your annotated bibliography, label the places where you have shown the relevance and credibility of each source.
4. Write a brief note to your reviewers that describes three major concerns about your ability to complete this project, and ask for suggestions on how they might be overcome.

Reader: Without making any comment, read the entire draft from start to finish. As you *reread* the draft, answer the following questions.

1. Review the purposes and goals for a topic proposal. Putting yourself in the role of the instructor, note those parts of the draft that make you comfortable in approving the project.
2. Still acting from the point of view of the instructor, note any shortcomings or concerns about the writer's ability to complete the project.
3. Comment on the likelihood that the proposed audience will be interested in reading this project. What is most likely to create interest? What is least likely? What suggestions do you have for increasing the project's audience appeal?
4. Look over the annotated bibliography and assess the reliability and relevance of each source. Are you convinced that the writer is on his or her way to providing a solid base of evidence? What suggestions do you have for seeking additional evidence?
5. Address the writer's concerns from number 4, above.

Postscript on the Writing Process

1. Because researched essays must be clearly focused and directed to a specific audience, indicate where in the proposal you clearly state your purpose and its relevance to the audience for your paper.
2. Since researched essays are usually meant for academic audiences, be sure that you have carefully documented any information that you have taken from another source. Indicate other places in your proposal where you have been *responsible* in giving credit where it is due.
3. In some cases, a topic proposal can jump too far ahead and start drawing conclusions that are best left until you have completed

your project. Cite one sentence that shows that you have remained *open* and *flexible* enough to consider any future evidence you collect.

4. Reflect on your proposal and your purposes in writing it. Then, using techniques of *metacognition*, read it as objectively as you can, reflecting both on the proposal itself and the processes you used to develop it. Are there alternative, *creative* ways to further this project's goals? Explain.
5. Reflect also on your level of *engagement*: Do you still have the same level of interest in the project that you had at the start? What parts of this proposal most energize and intrigue you?
6. Recall that a topic proposal is at its heart an argument that your project is worthwhile. After reviewing your peer's response, have you adequately made that case? What is the best argument you have formed?

An example of a research proposal and an annotated bibliography that accomplishes these important purposes follows. Use it as a guide as you prepare a proposal for your own project.

1"

A Research Proposal and Annotated Bibliography
on the Rwanda Genocide and the Media

/double space

The general topic of my research is the Rwandan genocide. More specifically, I will examine how the media portrayed the genocide, and how those portrayals affected the perceptions of people my age. Since much of our knowledge about historical events comes from the media, I want to know more about whether the media portrayals—especially films—were useful ways to raise awareness about this atrocity, especially in people of my age, who are too young to remember these events first hand. I will compare and contrast historical and media accounts of the genocide to the ways that this event has been recounted in more recent films.

Gingrich goes beyond the general topic to her particular spin on that topic.

Gingrich shows why she is interested in the topic, which helps to argue that she is ready to do this work.

My Goals

- to understand the causes of the Rwanda genocide, and how this kind of evil event can happen
- to understand why and how humans can turn away and ignore such suffering
- to comprehend the effect of the media's influence on and in society, and specifically, upon my generation's understanding (or lack of understanding) of events such as this one
- to present what I have learned through the process of writing this paper to a specific audience in way that is likely to help them gain a more accurate understanding

1" 1"

Gingrich's goals combine her personal interests and the objectives she anticipates meeting with her finished product.

Audience

Because the events of the Rwanda genocide took place when we were young children—too young to be aware of what was happening but during our lifetime—I would like to trace how media portrayals in film (and perhaps other sources) influenced the way today's college students learned about what happened during this awful historical event. By making my fellow students my audience, I can help them better understand the ways that they learn about history, and perhaps help them to pay more attention to the accuracy of those portrayals. A secondary audience could also be high school

1"

Gingrich explains why the audience she has chosen should be interested in her topic.

Many projects have both primary and secondary audiences.

social studies teachers, also making them aware of the strengths and weaknesses of using historical films to teach history.

Purpose

This sense of personal interest and commitment shows that Gingrich has the habits of mind to complete the project.

I have both personal and public reasons for examining this topic. Though I will never completely understand human nature and how such awful things can happen, I choose to continue researching this topic because I want to understand human nature.

This paragraph links her purposes with the methods she will use to achieve them.

My public purpose comes from what a reporter in the film *Hotel Rwanda* says: people will see what's happening and say "oh my god that's horrible, and then go on eating their dinners." It is terrible to think, but in reality that is what happens. People are affected while seeing the movie and maybe for the next hour; yet the situation is so far removed from them that it is not tangible and their lives keep going largely unaffected. By researching and studying the Rwandan genocide and how media influenced the way it was/is portrayed, I can also help them understand how crucial the media's interpretation and assessment of a situation is in helping to stop violence and prevent violence—and/or how it might fail to accomplish that. This topic matters to my audience because whether they like it or not, media affects them. Media decides for the most part what they know and what they come to believe about everything the media broadcasts.

Early Research

In a proposal, it is important to demonstrate that the writer has already devoted time and effort to the project.

I have already begun several parts of my research. As I had already seen *Hotel Rwanda*, I have viewed other films about the Rwanda genocide and begun reading reviews and articles about those films. So far, the films all seem to agree that the western world should have intervened, they all exalt those people who helped, and they all try to get the truth of the genocide to the masses.

Looking at both films and historical accounts can give the author a good basis for comparison.

To become better informed about the accuracy of the films, I have begun studying other historical documents about the event. This will help me compare the film versions (and perhaps other media accounts) with the version of the event that is accepted by historians. I may also seek articles that can better help me understand the influence of media on our perceptions more generally.

Because I am interested specifically in the effects of the media upon people of my generation, and how they learned about these events, I will also do some field research. I have scheduled interviews with college students about what they know about the Rwanda genocide and the ways that film versions may have influenced their understanding (or misunderstanding) and if they had any effect upon their desire to do something about these atrocities.

Gingrich shows commitment in already having begun the planning of research—in this case, field research.

Genre

There are several genres that I think will be effective in serving my purpose. First, I intend to write a formal academic paper because part of my goal is to supplement the sometimes superficial understanding of the Rwanda genocide with reliable historical information. But that will not be enough to reach my audience, so I could use a more popular genre as well—perhaps a story about the event that makes my case but that portrays the events accurately. I could create an informative Web page or wiki. Or I could start a blog and invite classmates to comment upon their understanding of what happened in Rwanda. I could even post pieces of my research paper for others to read and blog about.

Gingrich explores the value of several types of genres, what each can best accomplish, and how each can reach a specific audience.

Schedule

In Progress:	Schedule interviews with students; locate historical source information to overview the events; watch films about Rwanda
Week 1:	Compile and submit annotated working bibliography of sources; begin interviews
Weeks 2-3:	Read and annotate articles, and seek more articles as needed, adding to working bibliography
Week 4:	Review annotations and notes, and develop an outline of my paper; visit Writing Center
Week 5:	Review of the literature completed; reconsider the focus of my paper
Week 6:	Complete first draft for peer review; meet with Professor to discuss, and perhaps visit Writing Center. Seek additional information as necessary, and begin revision process

A schedule serves two purposes: It shows the reader that the project can be completed on time, and it gives the researcher specific deadlines and benchmarks.

This annotated working bibliography demonstrates that the work is under way, and it helps the writer begin to compare and synthesize sources, developing a focus and a thesis.

Week 7: Peer Review workshop on revised draft; visit Writing Center

Week 8: Complete revised draft and work on editing and proof-reading; compile full Works Cited pages; visit writing center and complete peer reviews

Week 9: Final paper due

Annotated Working Bibliography

Citations are in MLA style.

Brooks, Richard. "Atrocities against the Tutsis in Rwanda." *Sunday Times*. Times Newspapers, 20 Feb. 2005. Web. 2 Oct. 2012. This short review illustrates some of the emotional responses to three films about the Rwanda genocide that were released within a year (*Hotel Rwanda*, *Shooting Dogs*, and *Sometimes in April*). More specifically, it makes the case that the purpose of the three films is the same: to remind the world not to let such atrocities occur again. This addresses similar questions as I have. The article is credible and current because it was published in a respected newspaper soon after the films were released, but since reviews are subjective, potential biases should be noted.

Gingrich connects the review to her own purposes for writing.

Gingrich identifies potential biases in the source.

Caton-Jones, Michael, dir. *Shooting Dogs*. Perf. John Hurt, Hugh Dancy, and Claire-Hope Ashitey. BBC Films, 2005. DVD. This film tells the story of the Rwandan genocide from the perspective of two men: a late-middle-aged priest and a young teacher. This is a primary sources for my analysis, and it offers an important link between what scholarly journals say and what mass media (newspapers and magazines) tell the public. I plan on using this film as an example of how some forms of media are capable of telling mostly true stories, but still focus on only a small part of history.

Gingrich notes that the films are primary sources—direct sources that she will analyze herself—as opposed to the reviews, which are secondary sources.

Clarke, Donald. "A Tale of Two Movies." *Irishtimes.com*. Irish Times, 17 Mar. 2006. Web. 2 Oct. 2012. This article focuses on the director of *Shooting Dogs*, Michael Caton-Jones, who claims to have chosen the project because he was no longer satisfied with what Hollywood had to offer. It is current and credible because it was published soon after the film was released. Caton-Jones also explains that contrary to some people's belief, the

Gingrich indicates why this source is relevant to her focus.

Gingrich addresses currency; though the article is several years old, it was published in the midst of the debate about these films.

survivors were not re-traumatized through the process of recreating their story, so this article gives me perspectives on the effects of media.

Gingrich considers how the source relates to her own question.

Dwyer, Michael. "Darkness Falls." *Irishtimes.com*. Irish Times, 31 Mar. 2006. Web. 2 Oct. 2012. This article, published in a well-respected newspaper soon after the film was released, compares and contrasts *Shooting Dogs* and *Hotel Rwanda*. Dwyer claims that even though *Shooting Dogs* is shown from the perspective of two white men, there is still legitimacy in its tale. This can help me consider the role of race in how we perceive this genocide.

George, Terry, dir. *Hotel Rwanda*. Perf. Don Cheadle. 2004. United Artists, 2005. DVD. This film tells the story of the Rwandan genocide from the perspective of Paul Rusesabagina, a Hutu hotel house manager who offers a safe haven for both Hutus and Tutsis. The film focuses on his struggle to keep his Tutsi wife and three children alive, along with the 1,268 people taking refuge in the hotel. While this film is based on a true story, I can compare it with the historical record and with those who suggest that Rusesabagina was not really a hero. I will use this primary source to analyze whether the media produces what it thinks society wants to hear by manipulating and filtering the story till the information being portrayed is deemed palatable for the public.

Another possible angle on the topic is emerging here as Gingrich considers relevance.

Gingrich is starting to compare alternative perspectives as she brings sources together in her mind.

Nelima. "Was Hotel Rwanda's Paul Rusesabagina a Hero or Opportunist." *MinneAfrica*. N.p. 5 Dec. 2008. Web. 7 Oct. 2012. This Weblog or "online community" is designed to bring African-Americans in Minnesota together on issues related to their heritage as well as to support each other. The site hosted an online conversation about the role of Rusesabagina in the Rwanda genocide; the comments give me some insight into perceptions of African-Americans surrounding both the genocide and the "hero" of the film. While this is not all authoritative information, it can be useful in gauging public sentiment.

Gingrich acknowledges both the usefulness as well as the possible limitations of this open Web source.

Puig, Claudia. "Haunting *Hotel Rwanda*." *USA Today.* Gannett, 22 Dec. 2004. Web. 7 Oct. 2012. This article was published the day *Hotel Rwanda* was released in New York, Los Angeles, and

Gingrich considers currency as related to the timeliness of the piece as the films were released.

Gingrich shows the limitations of the source as well as why she chose to include it.

These points address the qualifications of the authors and editors and the currency of the source.

General reference sources can provide "generally accepted facts," a useful starting point. For more depth, other kinds of sources are necessary.

Currency is related to the frequency of revision in online sources.

Peer-reviewed journals are useful because they have been vetted by other experts.

Gingrich took time to learn more about the author of this piece—information that is usually just a click or two away. This helps gauge credibility.

Chicago, giving it currency. Since it was published in a popular press source, I will treat it not as authoritative, but as an example of the popular opinions. Although there was not much new information in this article, I found it striking that Puig compared the film to *Schindler's List*, saying it was an African version. This can help me compare the treatment of two different historical genocides to see if there are similarities in media treatments, since both films focus on one individual.

"Rwanda Genocide." *Encyclopedia of Race and Racism*. 2008. 52-59. Web. 5 Oct. 2012. The *Encyclopedia of Race and Racism* is a general reference source that "examines the anthropological, sociological, historical, and scientific theories of race and racism in the modern era." This article on the genocide is credible because the encyclopedia is edited by academic experts in these fields and current because it was revised in 2009. It will give me background on the historical events, and provide me with a racial perspective on the Rwanda genocide, helping me to consider if Americans' ignoring of the event was influenced by cultural issues.

"Rwanda Genocide of 1994." *Encyclopaedia Britannica Academic Edition.* 2010. Web. 2 Oct. 2012. This article from a well-respected encyclopedia's "academic edition" will provide me with some generally accepted historical facts about the events of the 1994 genocide which I can compare to the film versions and students' knowledge. Since this is an online version, it is kept up-to-date with new information.

Uraizee, Joya. "Gazing at the Beast: Describing Mass Murder in Deepa Mehta's *Earth* and Terry George's *Hotel Rwanda*." *Shofar* 28.4 (2010): 10-27. Print. This article analyzes the similarities and differences between two films about genocides—one about the Indian "partition" and the other *Hotel Rwanda*. It was published in a peer-reviewed academic journal, and was written by a professor of postcolonial literature at St. Louis University who has published other articles on similar topics. This article can help me compare the approach to another genocide that the film *Earth* takes with those on the Rwandan genocide. It can also help me understand how academic journals approach this kind of analysis.

Questions for Writing and Discussion

1. What are the most important goals for Carrie Gingrich's proposed project? What stands out as the best argument for allowing her to proceed? What questions are left unanswered?
2. Looking over the annotated bibliography, what sources seem to be most useful to her intended research? Which seem less useful?
3. Do the annotations for each source clearly explain the relevance and reliability of the source? Which annotations seem incomplete?
4. What further research do you think will be most important for Gingrich to complete this project effectively? Make a list of potential forms of primary, secondary, and field research that she has not yet considered.
5. What biases seem to exist in the writer's perspectives? In what ways might she work to overcome those biases through further research? What suggestions would you make to her if you were a peer reviewer of her proposal?

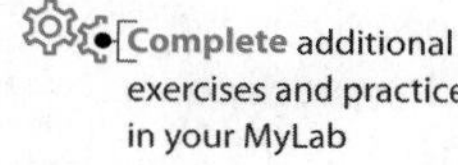
Complete additional exercises and practice in your MyLab

Research can be used to produce many different genres of writing that address diverse audiences. Carrie Gingrich, whose research into the causes and media presentation of the Rwanda genocide is presented in this chapter and Chapter 12, created this Web page and wrote the research paper that concludes this chapter. What audiences does each genre allow her to reach?

Everett Collection

Remembering Rwanda:
USING GENOCIDE FILMS MORE EFFECTIVELY IN THE CLASSROOM

About this Site: This site is designed for educators and students who want to go beyond the limited understanding of the Rwanda genocide offered by films to better understand the causes and effects of this horrific event. Read more

The Case for More Effective Methods: Read Carrie Gingrich's essay about the need for new and more effective methods for teaching about the Rwanda genocide. Full Essay

About the Author: Carrie Gingrich is a student majoring in English at York College of Pennsylvania. Full Bio

Resources for Teachers: Want to learn effective methods for using film to teach history and spur critical thinking? Links

Resources for Students: Go beyond the story told in the films to learn more about the Rwanda genocide. Links

Selected Bibliography: Many historians, survivors, and political figures have analyzed the events leading to the Rwanda genocide. This selected bibliography can help you find credible articles and books on this topic. Bibliography

Blog: These blogs can help connect you with other teachers and students interested in this topic. Teacher Blog

Beginning in April, 1994, and continuing for 100 days, more than 800,000 Rwandans were slaughtered, an average of 10,000 people per day.

"**Will the world remember? Will we say never again?**"

Educators and their students have a responsibility to help correct misconceived understandings.

Links to Film Clips about the Rwanda Genocide

One of the most effective and powerful ways students learn about the past is through film. Films about this genocide were meant to portray and preserve what happened; the stated goal of many of these filmmakers was to help viewers learn from its cruel mistakes. **In the end, though, films like these squeeze into one drop the ocean of what happened.** They focus on one story. In doing so, they lose the fact that the genocide was more than just one story, more than one drop. This site can help teachers and students learn the full story.

This site provides resources for teachers to go beyond the emotional impact of film and help students think more deeply about the past—and so help to create a less violent future.

Site Created and Maintained by Carrie Gingrich. She is interested in working with others who share this goal. **Contact her**

13

Researched Writing

What You Will Learn
In this chapter, you will learn to:

13.1 Use techniques for writing a working thesis statement

13.2 Use techniques for establishing claims

13.3 Use sources to support your claims

13.4 Use techniques for synthesizing sources

13.5 Avoid plagiarism by quoting, paraphrasing, summarizing, and citing sources properly

13.6 Shape your researched essay

13.7 Use proper MLA or APA documentation

WHILE most writing requires some form of supporting evidence, the standard is higher in a documented researched essay because this genre addresses an audience that is more knowledgeable, more demanding, and more critical (in the positive sense of the word). To build the substantive arguments that this audience will expect, you need to *document* the validity of your evidence—that is, to demonstrate that the information you present is credible by the standards of your audience. This can be accomplished by:

- revising your research proposal into a clear, succinct *thesis* statement.
- *organizing* your essay to move your readers through a series of claims and supporting documentation.
- *smoothly integrating* the information you have found in sources into your own writing.
- *citing sources* in the body of your paper and in a Works Cited (MLA) or References (APA) page.
- *revising* your ideas *and* your writing to sharpen and focus your essay.

This chapter uses student writer Carrie Gingrich's research paper on the Rwanda genocide to illustrate these steps. Throughout the chapter you will see Carrie's notes, drafts, and documentation, culminating in her completed paper.

"Facts are stubborn things; and whatever may be our wishes, our inclinations, or the dictates of our passions, they cannot alter the state of facts and evidence."

—John Adams

Techniques for Writing a Researched Essay

Because documented essays depend on materials that you collect from other sources, you need techniques for using those materials effectively and ethically. The techniques described in this section will help you write the kinds of academic essays that many of your classes will require.

Techniques for Researched Essays

Technique	Tips on How to Do It
Developing a working thesis	Based on your research and the needs of your audience, write out your working thesis. Indicate if your primary purpose is to inform, explain, propose a solution, argue a specific claim, or a combination of those purposes.
Establishing claims	Develop specific claims and reasons that support your main thesis.
Supporting your claims with evidence	Give relevant and credible supporting information for each claim. Explain the logical connection between the claim and the supporting evidence. Provide information that supports each claim in ways that show the claim's relevance to the topic, credibility, and the logical connection between the claim and the evidence that supports it.
Citing your sources	**Provide in-text citations for each source you use,** distinguishing direct quotations from summaries and paraphrases. These citations refer readers to your list of works cited or references at the end of the paper.

As you practice these techniques, remember that your goal is not only to present the work of other writers fairly but also to develop and offer your own unique perspective.

WRITING A WORKING THESIS

13.1
Use techniques for writing a working thesis statement

After you have done your initial research and written your research proposal, write out your *working thesis*—an initial statement of the main claims you want to make in your paper. While you will likely revise it as you work, having a working thesis will help you avoid two dangers: losing sight of your original purpose, and letting the source material control your own thoughts. This technique can also help you later as you decide on the genre or mode of presentation that would best help you to support the claims you want to make for your selected audience.

Consider how Carrie Gingrich, in writing her paper about the Rwanda genocide, might have framed her working thesis, as shown in the chart below. Note that different purposes may be combined: you might inform *and* argue, argue *and* problem-solve, or explain, evaluate, *and* argue to support your thesis. The italicized phrases illustrate how these purposes are expressed to readers.

"It is wrong always, everywhere, and for everyone, to believe anything upon insufficient evidence."

—William James

Framing a Working Thesis Statement

Purpose	Sample Working Thesis
Informing	This essay will help college students to *learn more* about the facts surrounding the Rwandan genocide.
Explaining	In this essay, I will *explain* to history majors the theories surrounding genocide that have been offered by historians and their connection to the events of 1994 in Rwanda.
Evaluating	This essay will demonstrate to teachers that the films depicting the Rwandan genocide *are inadequate* to teach students about the facts of this horrific historical event.
Problem-solving	In this essay, I will demonstrate to prospective teachers the reasons why just showing films about historical events such as the Rwandan genocide is not a useful teaching technique, and I will *propose some better teaching techniques* for helping students become more critical of media depictions of history.
Arguing	In this essay, I will *argue* that film critics who believe that popular films like *Hotel Rwanda* raise awareness about the horrors of genocide *have ignored evidence* that such films misinform and desensitize the audience to the realities of historical events.

ESTABLISHING CLAIMS

13.2
Use techniques for establishing claims

To support your main thesis, you need to establish smaller points along the way. For example, to propose a solution, you may first need to demonstrate that there is a problem—and that it is large enough to warrant action. Or to develop your central argument, you might first need to win your readers over on several smaller points. The following questions can help you to determine the specific information you will need to build your case from your source material. Asking these questions both from your perspective and from that of your potential audience will help you to gather the information most useful for your essay.

Types of Claims and Questions to Answer

Types of Claims	What These Claims Can Help My Audience Understand	Sample Questions
Claims of Fact	The established or generally accepted knowledge about the topic that can inform you and your audience.	What constitutes a genocide? How many Rwandans were killed during the 1994 genocide? Who were the principal persons involved? What films were made about this?
Claims of Cause and Effect	Whether a link between specific causes and effects exists, and if so, what it is.	What conditions allowed the genocide to happen? What was the immediate cause or catalyst? What effect did the media reports have on the genocide? What effect do films have on student understanding?
Claims of Value or Importance	Whether the facts, even if they are generally accepted, are important enough to support your claims—why your audience should care.	*To what degree* did the media affect the outcomes? *How important* is understanding the causes of genocide in avoiding future ones? Which actions were *most instrumental* in allowing the genocide to continue?
Claims of Policy	Whether any action is called for, and if so, why your proposal can help alleviate a problem.	How can the international community come together to avoid future tragedies? What guidelines might the media follow to serve positive change? How can teachers create a more effective curriculum?

USING SOURCES TO SUPPORT YOUR CLAIMS

13.3
Use sources to support your claims

As a student, you may have come to think of *documenting* sources as merely a matter of adding in-text citations and a works cited page. While those are indeed important elements, thinking about the purpose and audience for this documentation can help you to develop habits of mind such as flexibility and metacognition. Because academic audiences value arguments based on established evidence, your job as a writer is to show that your conclusions follow from substantive evidence. By *documenting* each step in your reasoning, you show the connection between your claims and reliable evidence. The chart below shows how to consider the purpose and audience expectations for a documented essay. Be sure that you look at Carrie Gingrich's essay at the end of this chapter to see how these audience needs are addressed.

Purpose and Audience Expectations

Technique	Purpose and Audience Expectations	How to Do It
Establishing your main point	The academic audience expects a clear, focused, and well thought out introduction that describes what you will accomplish and the evidence you will draw on.	State your main ideas and describe the methods you will use to prove them.
Demonstrating the reliability of your evidence	The academic audience expects explicit methods of proof that are acceptable in that discipline. Literature experts value close reading of primary texts; scientists value results of well-constructed experiments; business experts value valid case studies, historians expect the use of primary sources.	Create in-text citations and a works cited page that allows readers to verify your evidence. And as you introduce quotations, paraphrases, or summaries, explain why the evidence is reliable.
Showing that your evidence is current and reliable	Your audience expects evidence that is current, reliable, and credible.	Demonstrate the expertise of the authors you cite and describe how those sources used accepted and current methods to reach their conclusions.
Showing that your conclusions are reasonable	Your audience expects a clear line of reasoning between the claims you make and the evidence that supports them.	After presenting each piece of evidence, explain *why* and *how* the evidence supports your claim.

Warming Up: Journal Exercises

1. You have been researching the advantages and disadvantages of using interactive Web resources to teach classic literary texts. You have learned that there is a good deal of debate on this topic, and you want to write a documented essay for current and future teachers on this topic. Write a working thesis for each of these purposes:
   - An essay that informs your audience.
   - An essay that explains techniques for using interactive Web sites.
   - An essay that evaluates the use of interactive Web sites.
   - An essay that argues for limited use of Web sources.
   - An essay that argues against what most people think about this topic.

> "Facts are stupid things until brought into connection with some general law."
> —Samuel Scudder

Then brainstorm the kinds of evidence you might need to support each working thesis for specific audiences. Be sure to consider the various attitudes teachers might hold.

2. You are writing an essay for your world civilizations class about how contemporary society was influenced by Roman laws. Considering the kinds of evidence that your instructor is likely to find most credible and reliable, create a list of at least five library databases, journals, and Web sources that you believe would be acceptable to that audience. Then, write a brief description of each source that you might use to demonstrate its credibility for your audience. You might also make notes about sources that you think would *not* be acceptable.

3. In order to build your case in a documented essay, you need to show explicitly the logic that holds together claims and evidence. Imagine that you are trying to make the claim that men suffering from depression because of job losses are less likely to seek psychological help than women. Try writing a sentence that shows how each of the following pieces of evidence might support your claim:

   - 75% of psychologists' patients are women.
   - Male role models tend to stress self-reliance as a sign of strength.
   - Men still tend to think of themselves as the primary breadwinner.
   - Most media depictions of men relate success to job performance.
   - Men tend to be more introverted than women.
   - Men talk less with their friends about personal problems than women do.

SYNTHESIZING SOURCES

13.4
Use techniques for synthesizing sources

Completing an effective research project requires more than *finding* reliable and relevant sources; you must also effectively *synthesize* those sources and incorporate them into your own writing without losing sight of your own purpose. Use these three techniques:

Choose sources carefully Your job as a writer is to determine which sources are both reliable and *relevant to your discussion*—whether they support your position or not. Incorporating reliable and relevant information shows that you are well-informed on the subject.

> "Everything must be taken into account. If the fact will not fit the theory, let the theory go."
> —Agatha Christie

Link source information to your own central point Sometimes, in the process of presenting the ideas of others, your voice can be muted and your purpose deemphasized. *Write your own paper; don't let your sources write it for you.* Introduce each source by telling your readers how it relates to a claim *you* are making.

Synthesize source material into your own argument After looking back over your notes and annotations, jot down what you have learned from each source and how it confirms, contradicts, or expands on the ideas in other sources. By cross-referencing the pieces you read, you will see how the various sources speak to one another and how you can synthesize them to see the bigger picture. For example, Carrie Gingrich found a number of sources that helped her to better understand the ethnic groups that were in conflict:

"Nearly all scholars agree that populations having the designations Hutu, Tutsi, and Twa existed in the pre-colonial Rwanda state (prior to 1895); however, the exact historic and demographic meanings of these designations remain contested" (Longman).

"In Rwanda before colonialism, prosperous Hutu became Tutsi over a period of generations. . . . Belgian colonialism did not invent Tutsi privilege. What was new with the Belgian colonialism was the justification for it" (Genocide in Rwanda).

"It was also the Belgians who (in 1933) instituted the identity-card system that designated every Rwandan as Hutu, Tutsi, or Twa" (Case Study: Genocide in Rwanda 1994).

"For the first time in the history of Rwanda, the terms 'Hutu' and 'Tutsi' came to identify two groups, one branded indigenous, the other exalted as alien" (Encyclopedia of Race and Racism).

To synthesize these four quotations into a reliable explanation of how ethnic conflicts contributed to the genocide, Gingrich needed to find the common facts in each source. This allowed her to determine some key, accepted facts: that tribal divisions had existed for a long time, and that most experts agree that the Belgian colonists seemed to have created a large part of the problem.

Her synthesis thus came to look like this:

For example, to better understand the reasons for the Rwandan genocide, students should know more about three ethnic groups that settled in the country: the Twa, the Hutu, and the Tutsi. . . . A caste system of rank developed in which the majority of Tutsi tended to be in the higher class. While some might see the conflicts between these tribes as the cause of the genocide, most experts agree this alone was not the cause. Instead, they suggest that the Belgian colonists made ethnic conflicts more severe by using identity cards. The identity cards said one of three things: Twa, Hutu, or Tutsi, and as noted in *The Encyclopedia of Race and*

"A wise man proportions his belief to the evidence."

—David Hume

> *Racism*, "for the first time in the history of Rwanda, the terms 'Hutu' and 'Tutsi' came to identify two groups, one branded indigenous, the other exalted as alien" (Longman 925; "Genocide in Rwanda", 54–57; "Case Study: Genocide in Rwanda, 1994").

At the same time, Gingrich also wanted to note the points of disagreement that emerge in the different film versions of the genocide. For example, one key point of debate about the Rwanda genocide involves the shooting down of President Habyrimana's plane, an event seen by many as the catalyst of the genocide. In her paper (see page 531), she lists five different theories about this event. Bringing together information from various sources in this way allows a writer to keep the focus on her own purpose, while illustrating the points of agreement and disagreement in the source materials.

AVOIDING PLAGIARISM

13.5
Avoid plagiarism by quoting, paraphrasing, summarizing, and citing sources properly

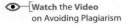

Watch the Video on Avoiding Plagiarism

Plagiarism occurs when you use the language, ideas, or visual materials from another person or text without acknowledging the source—even if you do this unintentionally. Writing a documented essay involves spending considerable time reading and studying your topic, and you may well have difficulty remembering the source of some of your ideas. This can lead to your unintentionally failing to acknowledge them. To avoid this kind of inadvertent plagiarism, observe the following guidelines:

- Do not use language, ideas, or graphics from any essay, text, or visual image that you find *online*, in the *library*, or from *commercial sources* without acknowledging the source.
- Do not use language, ideas, or visuals from *any other student's essay* without acknowledging the source.

Students who plagiarize—even unintentionally—typically fail the course and face disciplinary action by the college or university.

Citing Sources Accurately

Watch the Video on Citing Sources

What sources do you need to cite? You must cite a source for any fact or bit of information that is not *general knowledge*. Obviously, what is "general knowledge" will vary from one writer and audience to another. **As a rule, document any information or fact that you did not know before you began your research.** It might be common knowledge, for example, that thousands of Rwandans were slaughtered during the 1994 genocide. However, when Gingrich reports that "beginning in April 1994, and continuing for 100 days, more than 800,000 Rwandans were slaughtered, an average of 10,000 people per day," she needs to include a citation to the two sources that provide these specific facts.

Citing sources accurately as you develop your argument builds your credibility or ethos as a writer. Be sure to include in-text citations *as you incorporate materials into your draft*; this will help you avoid inadvertent plagiarism.

Developing proper in-text citations can be accomplished through two techniques:

- **Use the notes you have been taking as a guide as you incorporate information.** As explained in Chapter 12, notetaking includes two parts: (1) recording the bibliographic information you will need to document your sources later, and (2) digesting the specific information from each piece that is relevant to your topic, purpose, and audience.
- **As you incorporate source material into your own argument during the writing process, include in-text citations to identify that source for your readers.** The in-text citations signal to your readers that complete information can be found at the end of your paper; guidelines for creating that References or Works Cited page appear later in this chapter.

Quoting, Paraphrasing, and Summarizing

Sometimes, however, you can run into problems by rushing or by not knowing how to quote or paraphrase accurately and fairly. You can avoid this inadvertent plagiarism by quoting accurately from your sources, by paraphrasing using your own words, and by citing your sources carefully and precisely.

Watch the Animation on Integrating Sources

Assume that you are working with the following passage, taken from the opening paragraph of an article by Charles Murigande:

Original So the first lesson we learn from the 1994 Rwanda genocide is that silence and indifference in the face of such horrific crimes only emboldens the killers and makes even worse crimes possible. The 1994 genocide would not have been possible or even contemplated had the international community responded more decisively to prevent or stop the crimes of 1959, the 1960s, and the 1970s. These crimes took place despite the pledges of "never again" following the Holocaust. They took place despite the obligations to prevent such crimes under the 1948 Genocide Convention as well as other international instruments including the UN Charter. Therefore, the first lesson is quickly followed by a second, namely, that international law and other political commitments are only as good as our political will to implement or enforce them. Without political will, international law and other commitment are impotent.

Plagiarism Though genocide has many causes, one of them is clearly silence and indifference in the face of horrific crimes. These crimes were allowed to happen despite obligations to prevent crimes like this under the 1948 Genocide Convention as well as other international instruments that had been established.

This writer uses several phrases lifted directly from the source (see highlighted text) without using quotation marks or acknowledging the source.

Proper Quotation and Citation The media has an obligation to present the facts about international crimes such as genocide to the public. As Murigande suggests, it is clear that "silence and indifference in the face of such crimes only emboldens the killers and makes even worse crimes possible" (6).

In this passage, the writer cites the author before introducing the quotation, uses quotation marks for words and phrases that appear in the article, and uses the proper citation format (parentheses with page citation) at the end of the sentence. Note also how the author fits the quotation into her own purpose—to show the responsibility of the media to report the truth. This article would also be listed on the Works Cited page.

Proper Paraphrase and Citation The media has an obligation to present the facts about international crimes such as genocide to the public. As Murigande suggests, it is clear that ignoring genocide leads to more genocide (6).

In this passage, the writer cites the author, Murigande, before paraphrasing his point. Just as she did when she quoted Murigande's exact words, she uses the proper citation format (parentheses with page citation) at the end of the sentence to indicate where the information came from.

Proper Summary and Citation The media has an obligation to present the facts about international crimes such as genocide to the public. Murigande discusses these obligations in his essay, which argues that many countries shirked their responsibility to react quickly to these events (6–10). I would suggest that the media, similarly, did not live up to this obligation.

Rather than quote directly or paraphrase a short section, the writer gives credit for the idea to the original author by summarizing the article and connecting Murigande's points to the related, but different, point that she is making. Despite the lack of direct quotation, because the author is summarizing Murigande's piece in her own words, she is careful to cite his work accurately.

As these examples illustrate, citations serve three purposes: they give due credit, they allow you to show that you are aware of other credible research—giving you more credibility as well—and they allow you to distinguish your own points from those of other authors. If at any point you have a question about how to cite your sources accurately, recheck the sections in this chapter or ask your instructor.

Warming Up: Journal Exercises

You are writing a paper that is meant to inform men about the dangers of depression should they lose their jobs. In your research, you find the following information on a Web site of the Royal College of Psychiatrists (http://www.rcpsych.ac.uk/mentalhealthinfoforall/problems/depression/mendepression.aspx):

> After relationship difficulties, unemployment is the thing most likely to push a man into a serious depression. Recent research has shown that up to 1 in 7 men who become unemployed will develop a depressive illness in the next 6 months. Your work may be a large part of what makes you feel good about yourself. If you lose your job, you may lose other things that are important to you, such as a company car. It can be hard to adjust to being at home and looking after the children while your wife or partner becomes the bread-winner. From a position of being in control, you may face a future over which you have little control, especially if it takes a long time to find another job. And depression itself can make it harder to get another job.

Based on this quotation, do the following:

1. Write a sentence that effectively captures your own thesis, but which also accurately and correctly incorporates a quotation from this passage. Choose what you consider to be a particularly important part of the larger quotation for your purpose, but limit its length and keep your own voice central.
2. Summarize the quotation, being careful to avoid unintentional plagiarism: be sure to use your own words and to distinguish between your ideas and those of the author.
3. Write a sentence that cites a statistic from this source (or another that you might find). Be sure to put the information in your own words and make the source of the information clear.
4. Look for more information on this topic, and write a brief synthesis of what you find in at least three sources. Doing this can help you check the accuracy of your information.

USING MLA OR APA CITATIONS

Knowing *what* to cite and how to distinguish your ideas from those of others is the first step in documenting sources. But you also need to know *how* to cite your sources in a form that your audience will recognize and be able to use easily. In the text of your paper, you will usually need to cite your sources according to either Modern Language Association (MLA) style for the humanities or American Psychological Association (APA) style for the social sciences. Both styles use a system of in-text citations in the body of a paper that correspond to full bibliographical entries in a complete list of sources at the end of the paper.

- In MLA style, the in-text citation contains the author's name and page number of your source: (Torres 50). No comma appears between name and page number. (If the author is unknown, give the title and page number of your source. Italicize book titles; place quotation marks around article titles.) A complete citation appears at the end of the paper in a Works Cited list.
- In APA style, the in-text citation contains author's name and date of publication (Murigande, 2007). Use a comma between name and year. If you are quoting, include a page number after the name and year: (Torres, 2007, p. 6). Use *p.* (or *pp.* for more than one page) before the page number(s). A complete citation appears at the end of the paper in a References list.

See the "Documenting Sources" section (pp. 509–530) for examples of both APA and MLA styles of in-text and end-of-paper citations.

Introducing and Citing Sources

Once you have decided that a fact, a paraphrase, or a direct quotation contributes to your thesis, use the following guidelines for preparing the in-text citation. These examples show MLA style.

Identify in the text the persons or source for the fact, paraphrased idea, or quotation.

> As one philosopher noted, "The literal meaning of 'genocide,' after all, is the killing of a kind" (Lee 336).

Note: The parentheses and the period *follow* the final quotation mark.

If you cite the author in your sentence, the parentheses will contain only the page reference.

> According to Charles Murigande, a Rwandan minister of foreign affairs, "indifference has always characterized the response of the international community to our cries for help" (6).

Use block format (beginning on a new line, indented one inch from the left margin, and double-spaced) for quotations of five lines or more.

> Historian Alan J. Kuperman suggests that there are several explanations for the actions of the Rwandan Patriotic Front (RPF) during the genocide:
>
> > There are four potential explanations for the RPF pursuing a violent challenge that provoked such tragic consequences. One possibility is

> that the Tutsi rebels did so irrationally, without thinking of expected consequences. . . . The final possibility is that the rebels expected their challenge to provoke genocidal retaliation but viewed this as an acceptable cost of achieving their goal of attaining power in Rwanda. (63)

Note: In block quotations, the final punctuation mark comes *before* the parentheses, and no quotation marks are used to set off the cited material.

Vary your introductions to quotations.

> Philosopher Steven P. Lee claims that "the belief that genocide is due to special moral condemnation is widespread" (335).

> While some might question whether genocide has been treated as a crime against humanity that has received adequate moral outrage, it is clear that "the belief that genocide is due special moral condemnation is widespread" (Lee 335).

Edit quotations when necessary to condense or clarify. Use an ellipsis mark, which is three points preceded and followed by a space (. . .), when you omit words from the middle of a quoted sentence.

> As one historian noted, "the RPF persisted in its military offensive . . . refusing to make compromises with the Hutu government that might have averted massive retaliation" (Kuperman 61).

If you omit words from the end of a quoted sentence or omit sentences from a long quoted passage, place a period after the last word quoted before the omission; follow it with an ellipsis mark—for a total of four periods. Be sure that you have a complete sentence both before and after the four points.

> Steven Lee helps us to see the distinctive nature of genocide:
>
>> Initially, a collectivist account of genocide may seem more appealing than an individualist account. The literal meaning of "genocide," after all, is the killing of a kind. . . . A non-genocidal mass murder lacks the special harm to the group (or the intention to do such) that characterizes genocide on a collectivist account. (336)

Note: The first line would be indented an additional half-inch if more than one paragraph is cited from the original source.

In some cases you may want to change the wording of a quotation or add explanatory words of your own to clarify your quotation. If you do so, clearly indicate your changes or additions by placing them within square brackets.

> As Kuperman suggests, "There are four potential explanations for the RPF [Rwandan Patriotic Front] pursuing a violent challenge that provoked such tragic consequences" (63).

Knowing the variety of citation techniques not only allows you to write citations correctly but also gives you a range of ways to incorporate sources that suit your specific purposes.

Researched Essay: The Writing Process

Assignment for Writing a Researched Essay

In Chapter 12, you were asked to develop a research proposal for a possible research project on a subject that would interest both you *and a specific audience*. You were also given techniques and processes for collecting and keeping track of information on that topic. Earlier in this chapter, you learned techniques that can help you develop a documented academic essay. Now your assignment is to move forward with that essay: to establish a clear thesis, provide ample evidence to defend that thesis, and organize your essay to help your readers see the reasoning that led you to your conclusions. Be sure to use proper methods for citing sources and creating a Works Cited (MLA) or References (APA) list. Check with your instructor for specific guidelines on your project.

While the academic essay is a crucial format for you to master for your college studies, the research you do and the conclusions you draw can also be translated into other styles or genres of writing. After all, many audiences will be moved effectively by styles of writing that do not follow the conventions of a scholarly paper. As a result, while many research projects culminate in a formal, documented paper, other genres might sometimes suit your purpose and audience. Choosing the right genre depends on considering the audience to whom you will be writing (and the parameters of the assignment).

Audience	Sample Genres and Purposes for Researched Writing
Personal Audience	• A blog on your experiences with languages on a trip abroad, in order to collect others' similar experiences • A journal describing your experiences with standardized testing under No Child Left Behind, meant to show teachers the pressures it creates on students • A personal essay that combines research on attention deficit disorder with your own experiences with the disorder, which you hope will help others in similar situations

Academic Audience	• A humanities-based essay that joins the debate among ethicists about the effects of technology on our lives • A social sciences study based on survey information about student attitudes toward plagiarism • A natural sciences study of the effects of industry on a local creek, based on field research and published studies of water pollution • A study that explores the challenges of start-up ventures, based on recent legislation regulating business operations and meant for other students in the entrepreneurship program at your college
Public Audience	• A wiki, or an entry in an existing wiki, about your use of a genetic testing service, in order to correct erroneous public opinions • A Facebook page that encourages young people to pay more attention to political debates • A letter to the editor arguing that standardized testing is important for teacher accountability • A report for your local community on why public spaces for recreation are needed to revitalize the community • A Web site outlining alternative energies for consumers shopping for a new car

After Carrie Gingrich completed her research project on the need to find better methods to inform students about the Rwandan genocide, she decided to use what she had learned to create an informative Web site that teachers could use to supplement films in teaching about this topic. Drawing on the research she had done, she created a rich Web site of important facts about the genocides, links to sources for further reading, links to sites that provide stories of genocide survivors, and links to various blogs and other Web 2.0 sources. The home page of that site appears on the first page of this chapter.

"Out of clutter, find Simplicity. From discord, find Harmony. In the middle of difficulty lies opportunity."
—Albert Einstein

SHAPING

13.6
Shape your researched essay

If you have written a research proposal, you will have already collected and assessed a good deal of information. As you begin the drafting process, you may be tempted simply to present that information in the order you found it, *accumulating* information rather than using it in a purposeful way. To shape your essay more effectively, consider the expectations of your audience and the genre of writing that you want to produce, using the strategies listed below.

Questions for Shaping Your Researched Essay

To begin shaping the information that you have collected into a draft, ask yourself the following questions.

Reevaluating Your Researched Essay

Purpose	How has my purpose changed now that I have completed the bulk of my research?
Revised Thesis	Based on my research, should I adjust my thesis? Is my working thesis still arguable and valid? Can it be expressed more clearly and directly? Can I narrow and focus it further?
Research	Does my research include a variety of perspectives? Is the evidence I have selected reliable and corroborated by other sources? Is it the type of evidence likely to be accepted by an academic audience? Is there ample evidence to support both my thesis and the claims that I must make to lead to that thesis?
Audience	What specific information that I have found will most interest my audience? What values or beliefs can I build on or argue against with the research I have collected? What concessions should I make to my audience?
Genre	What conventions of academic writing are most useful for the specific audience or field of study? Does this genre tend to use graphics, images, long quotations, primary texts? What parts of my research can be used within those conventions?

Questions like these can help you to incorporate your researched materials in the most effective order, and to identify any weak spots in your body of research. As you plan, outline, draft, and revise your essay, return to these questions frequently to keep yourself on track. In some cases, answering these questions might require a bit more research to defend your claims, support your thesis, and accommodate the audience that you are addressing.

Planning a Line of Reasoning

The audience of a researched paper will expect to be able to trace your claims back to their source and to see the logic that links claim to evidence. **Develop a line of reasoning that moves readers from their *present* understanding of the topic to the *new* understanding you want them to have.**

> "The fact that an opinion has been widely held is no evidence whatever that it is not utterly absurd."
> —Bertrand Russell

Below, you can see Carrie Gingrich's developing line of reasoning—and more important, the steps she wants her readers to take to follow her major points. Her ideas have developed into an order of presentation that will help her do two essential things: *create an outline* and *decide when and where to use specific information.* If you attempt to write an outline without considering the logical connections that lead from one point to the next, you will find it difficult to form transitions, and your essay will tend to drift off on tangents.

Shaping Your Points: Developing a Line Reasoning

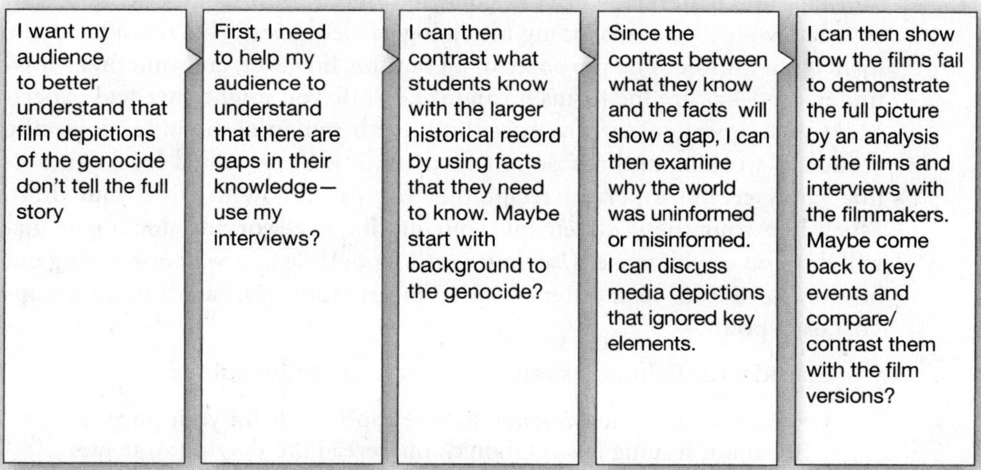

I want my audience to better understand that film depictions of the genocide don't tell the full story
First, I need to help my audience to understand that there are gaps in their knowledge—use my interviews?
I can then contrast what students know with the larger historical record by using facts that they need to know. Maybe start with background to the genocide?
Since the contrast between what they know and the facts will show a gap, I can then examine why the world was uninformed or misinformed. I can discuss media depictions that ignored key elements.
I can then show how the films fail to demonstrate the full picture by an analysis of the films and interviews with the filmmakers. Maybe come back to key events and compare/contrast them with the film versions?

After you have established a line of reasoning, ask yourself which pieces of evidence support each logical step. This in turn will show you whether there are gaps in your research that need to be filled with further research.

Another step in planning your essay is to consider what rhetorical strategies would serve your main purposes. These strategies can be applied *to the whole of your essay and/or to specific parts of the essay or specific claims you need to establish.*

Shaping Strategies

Is your purpose to . . .	Consider using this rhetorical strategy
Explain a key term or establish an important concept	Definition (p. 200)
Argue against a common perspective	Refutation (p. 383)
Show a better way to accomplish something	Process analysis (p. 202)
Show the reasons for a phenomenon	Causal analysis (p. 204)
Show why one solution is better than another	Comparison and contrast (p. 271) or division and classification (p. 224)

DEVELOPING A WORKING OUTLINE

To shape the materials you have collected into a draft, your next step is to translate your line of reasoning into a logical sequence. This often takes the form of an outline. The purposes of an outline, however, are sometimes misunderstood—as are the forms it can take. While you might have had experiences with a particular form of outline—with roman numerals and specific sections—working outlines do not always follow a prescribed form. An outline rarely creates a perfect recipe that you can follow to write your draft. Much like your thesis statement, your outline is a working document that will develop as you write. Use your working outline as a way of figuring out how one idea leads to another and what information you can draw on to support each point.

Consider the following strategies for developing an outline:

- *Review strategies for shaping* that are appropriate for your purpose. If you are arguing for a certain claim, reread the shaping strategies discussed in Chapter 10. If you are evaluating something or analyzing a problem and proposing a solution, review the strategies discussed in Chapters 8 and 9.
- *Explain to a friend or classmate your purpose, audience, and working thesis.* As you describe your project to others, the reasoning you will need to accomplish that purpose or defend that thesis often emerges. Have your partner ask questions and make notes as you describe the project. Then use those notes to develop an outline, filling in the missing pieces alone or collaboratively.

- *Reread your summaries of the sources you found and look for recurring ideas.* From this, you can create a list of key subtopics that can be put into a reasonable order.
- *Connect claims to evidence.* Create or look over the sequence of claims you want to establish. Clearly state each claim, then list the evidence you have accumulated to support it.
- *Take a break.* Let your ideas simmer for a while. Go for a walk. Work on an assignment for another course. Go jogging or swimming. Let your mind run on automatic pilot—the information and ideas may begin organizing themselves into a sketch outline without your conscious effort.

As Carrie Gingrich developed her outline, she considered what part of her argument she could cover in each section. Although she modified it considerably as her argument developed, the working outline helped her organize the claims she was making and the source material that would support each claim. Note how this outline shows the purpose and reasoning in each section, *as well as specific rhetorical strategies* (see highlighted words). If you compare the outline with the finished essay on page 531, you will see that changes were made in the writing process. This is to be expected: it demonstrates the writer's flexibility and creativity.

I. Introduction	First, define genocide and why the lack of awareness of the Rwandan Genocide is dangerous. Introduce the idea that various types of media (which examples should I use?) fail to report the full story, adding to the lack of awareness. Explain the basic information about the Rwandan genocide and the fact that people my age don't know much about it. Include the causes for this lack of information and its effects.
II. Claim 1: College students are underinformed	College students do not fathom why it is important for them to pay attention to historical events like the Rwandan genocide, and why it should concern them personally. Describe my process for collecting student opinions. Use comments and quotations from interviews as examples: How much do college-age students know about the Rwandan genocide? What are their feelings about this event? Do they feel connected or disconnected to it? How did they get their information?

III. Background on the Genocide	Show my audience that some historical facts have been established and accepted about this event and that others are still debated (through comparison and contrast). Use this to argue that some of the perceptions from the media are shortsighted. Discuss some points of disagreement that need more attention and that are ignored in the popular media. From my interviews, it sounds like films—especially *Hotel Rwanda*—are used frequently in schools. Maybe I can connect to the analysis of the films I have watched, and start to show some cause and effect. Focus on the debate about causes of the genocide? Or on the role of particular countries?
IV. Claim 2: Genocide films don't always accomplish their educational purpose	List the many films that were made about the Rwandan genocide and classify them by discussing: (1) the filmmakers' purposes for making the films (from published interviews I have read), (2) the limitations of film as a way of showing the full story (connect with the historical accounts), (3) the limits of using film as a way of teaching students about the Rwandan genocide. Note how films tend to focus on individuals rather than on the whole of the tragedy and the fact that students didn't seem to learn much from them?
Conclusion 1: Films alone don't make an effective teaching tool	Bring together the historical information with the descriptions of the films and the views of the filmmakers to argue why film isn't the best teaching tool. Use this to lead into my recommendations for solving this problem. Films can produce an important emotional reaction, but to avoid future genocides, citizens need to understand the deeper reasons for genocide. Media doesn't accomplish that.
Conclusion 2: Recommendations for better educational techniques	Explain that going beyond just showing films about the genocide can have two effects: (1) it can help avoid future genocides because citizens will be informed enough to demand actions by the international community and (2) it can help students be better critical thinkers, rather than simply watching and accepting a historical account they get from the media. Maybe offer better ways to use the films? Or other teaching techniques, to make some recommendations?

Though not in a traditional form, this outline lays out the structure of the essay and guides Gingrich as she starts to draft. It shows the logical progression from point to point, helping Gingrich develop a richer thesis and a clear line of argument. And it helps her consider how various rhetorical and writing strategies can be used in her draft. From here, Gingrich can decide where to insert her specific evidence and how to develop her main claims.

DRAFTING

At this point, some of the most difficult work is behind you. Congratulate yourself—there are few people who know as much as you do about your subject. You are an authority: You have information, statistics, statements, ideas from other writers and researchers, and your own experiences and observations. You also have a variety of materials to keep you going: annotated articles, summaries, syntheses that show the connections between sources, and your own thesis statement. And you have a working plan for organizing all that information in ways that keep your own point central. It is now time to articulate your positions by drafting your essay.

While drafting a researched project has many similarities to the processes discussed throughout this book, the key difference is *the need to incorporate the ideas of others to forward your own ends.* The effective use of sources requires both creativity and scrupulous honesty. On the one hand, you want to use other people's information and ideas when and where they serve *your* purpose and *your* ideas. On the other hand, the sources you cite or quote must be used *fairly* and *honestly.* You must quote accurately, cite your sources properly, and document those sources with care.

This honest incorporation of sources into your draft can be done in two stages:

- Note where each piece of information originated, using your annotated articles, notes, and bibliographic records.
- Check your work: after you have written your first draft, go back and compare what you have written to the notes you took.

As you draft, consider where each claim you make and each piece of information you present came from, and add an in-text citation to the source. In some cases, that information or claim may draw on more than one source. Though this process might seem inefficient, it is the part of the drafting process that allows you to build on only the premises that have strong support and helps you follow the information to viable conclusions.

REVISING

You have been revising since the first day of the project—with notes, annotations, a working thesis, and a working outline. You thought about several subjects, but you chose one. You started with a focus but revised it as you thought, read, and wrote. You tested and synthesized ideas and continually revised your working thesis. Now you have a complete draft to revise. Follow these steps to make the process as effective and efficient as possible.

1. **Assess the adequacy of the content.** If something is missing in your data, track down the information. If a source or quotation no longer seems relevant, have the courage to delete it. If the evidence for one side of an argument appears stronger than you initially thought, change your position and your thesis. *Being willing to make such changes is not a sign of poor research and writing. Rather, it demonstrates that you have become more knowledgeable and sophisticated about your subject.*
2. **Decide whether your claims are supported by evidence.** When you find a claim that needs support, look back over your notes and annotated articles to see if you have the evidence you need to support that claim. If so, add a summary, paraphrase, or quotation, along with an in-text citation. If you can't find enough support for your claim, you have two options.
   - If you believe that the claim is credible and important to your argument, do another search for evidence to support it.
   - If the claim seems tangential to your argument or is not supported by the evidence you have, you may need to revise or discard it.
3. **Consider the overall organization of the paper.** Skim the beginnings of sections and paragraphs to see that they are in a coherent order. If an example on page 4 would work better as a lead-in for the whole paper, reorder your material accordingly. One technique that works well is to annotate your own paper—that is, make notes in the margin that trace the argument as it develops ("This paragraph does this, the next one does that . . ."). This will allow you to find gaps in the logic or places where the transition from one idea to another isn't clear, and you can then revise accordingly. This step might take several sessions.
4. **Revise for style.** After the structure and evidence of the paper are in place, move on to matters of style. Using techniques you've learned here and in class, check to see that each paragraph is a coherent unit, that sentences are precise and clear, and that your word choice is appropriate to the audience and purpose.
5. **Gather input from others.** Ask your teacher, friends, or classmates for their responses. Accept their criticism gracefully, but ask them to explain *why* they think a change would help. Will the change make your purposes clearer? Will it be more appropriate for your audience? Don't feel that you must make every change that readers suggest. You must make the final decision.

PeerResponse

These instructions will help you give and receive constructive advice about the rough draft of your proposal and annotated bibliography. You may use these guidelines for an in-class workshop, a take-home review, or a computer e-mail response.

Writer: Before you exchange drafts with another reader, write out the following information about your own rough draft.

1. On the draft, clearly label your thesis and note the specific audience to whom your essay is written and the purpose the essay is meant to serve.
2. Underline and label the parts of your paper that represent your own original claims and those that are the work of other writers.
3. Label places where you have paraphrased or summarized sources.
4. Write a brief note to your reviewers that describes three major concerns about your ability to complete this project, and ask for suggestions on how they might be overcome.

Reader: Without making any comment, read the entire draft from start to finish. As you *reread* the draft, answer the following questions.

1. Review the thesis that the writer has identified, then look for parts of the paper that seem to drift from that thesis.
2. For each claim, assess whether you believe the evidence presented is sufficient to support that claim. Ask questions in the margin that challenge the writer to better defend those claims where appropriate.
3. Consider the audience and purpose of the essay and identify any places (1) that are unlikely to interest that audience, (2) where that audience is likely to question the evidence presented, and (3) where the essay seems to drift from its intended purpose.
4. Look over the places where the author seems to use material from other sources. Is the source of each piece of information clearly documented? Is it clear what information is from a source and what are the writer's own thoughts? Does each citation have a proper entry in the Works Cited or References page?
5. Address the writer's concerns from number 4, above.

Guidelines for Revision

- **Revise in stages:** Don't try to multitask; it is more efficient and effective to complete one revision task at a time, beginning with large issues such as organization and working your way down to careful editing.
- **Check that each claim you have made is supported:** Read the draft, pausing each time you make a claim, and be sure that there is adequate evidence to make that claim credible. If possible, ask a classmate to look for unsupported claims.
- **Check that the types of supporting evidence you include are appropriate to your audience, purpose, and genre:** Remember that the amount and type of information required of an academic paper might be very different than that of a Web site or pamphlet, and that some audiences value specific kinds of information (statistics, quotations, etc.) more than others.
- **Check to be sure that each piece of information is properly cited in the text:** Using the guidelines in this chapter, be sure that all information gathered from sources has an in-text citation that corresponds with the Works Cited or References list.
- **Consider the tone, style, and grammar of your paper:** Revise any sentence or word choice that is not consistent with your purpose, audience, and genre of your document as a whole.

Postscript on the Writing Process

One of the key differences between a documented essay and other forms of writing is the need for extra care in both the quality of your evidence and the way you cite sources. Before you hand in your paper, check the following:

1. Does each part of your essay contribute to your overall thesis? Print out your thesis statement and read over the paper to be sure that each part really fits that main purpose.
2. Is the evidence you presented in keeping with the academic standards for reliability of the field or discipline? Double-check each source that you have included to be sure that it is credible and reliable—and be especially wary of Web sources.

3. Check each citation within the paper to be sure that it conforms to MLA or APA style. Have a handbook with you as you check, or use the guidelines in this chapter for each type of source.
4. Carefully proofread your Works Cited or References page, referring to citation guidelines. Check also for proper indentations, line spacing, capitalization, and use of italics or quotation marks.
5. Check with your teacher to be sure that the heading of your paper conforms to the standards of the class.

DOCUMENTING SOURCES

13.7
Use proper MLA or APA documentation

Academic essays are prepared in a strict format established by discipline-based organizations such as the Modern Language Association (MLA) and the American Psychological Association (APA). The prescribed manuscript format is used for a number of reasons:

- it provides a standardized system that experts have agreed upon
- it allows for proper documentation and citation of sources
- it provides a method for formatting pages that allows readers (as well as editors and teachers) to validate the credibility of the essay's claims and support.

When writing an academic essay, it is important to follow the rules for page layout and citation. For an example of a correctly formatted MLA paper, see the student essay by Carrie Gingrich at the end of this chapter.

One of the most important facets of academic format is the citation system. Both MLA and APA documentation styles require the citation of sources in the text of your paper, followed by an entry in the Works Cited (MLA style) or References (APA style) list at the end of your paper. Use footnotes only for content or supplementary notes that explain a point covered in the text or offer additional information.

MLA in-text documentation and Works Cited format are explained first, APA in-text documentation and References format in the following section.

In-Text Documentation: MLA Style

Watch the Animation on MLA Style

Give the author's name and the page number in parentheses following your use of a fact, paraphrase, or direct quotation from a source. These in-text citations refer your readers to the complete documentation of the source in a Works Cited or Works Consulted list at the end of the paper. As you cite your sources in the text, use the following guidelines.

If you cite the author in the text, indicate only the page number in parentheses.

> According to Alan J. Kuperman, "There are four potential explanations for the RPF pursuing a violent challenge that provoked such tragic consequences" (63).

If the author is unknown, use a short version of the title in the parentheses.

> Whether in an attempt to reconcile the injustices done to the Hutus or in a moment of blind stupidity, the Belgians put the Hutu majority in charge when they left ("Genocide in Rwanda" 55).

If the source is unpublished, cite the name or title used in your Works Cited.

> In an informal interview, one teacher noted that the effectiveness of using films in the classroom has not been carefully studied (Robbins).

If the source is from the Internet or the Web, use the author, or if there is no author, use the title. Include page or paragraph numbers if provided (as, for example, in a PDF document).

> Many Web sites now provide the stories of those who lived through the genocide of 1994 (*Rwandan Survivors*).

If your bibliography contains more than one work by an author, cite the author, a short title, and page number. The following examples show various ways of citing a reference to Donald Clarke's article "A Tale of Two Movies."

> In "A Tale of Two Movies," Clarke discusses the effectiveness of films by comparing the differing approaches of two directors (2).

> Clarke compares *Shooting Dogs* with *Hotel Rwanda*, exalting *Shooting Dogs* because it was shot in the same locations that the original story took place ("A Tale" 14).

> *Hotel Rwanda* has been criticized because of its stereotypical Hollywood methods (Clarke, "A Tale" 14).

Note: Use a comma between author and title, but not between title and page number.

MLA

If a source has two or three authors, cite all authors' names in the text or in parentheses.

> It has been suggested that the RPF under Kagame's influence and leadership conducted "an unmistakable pattern of killings and persecutions aimed at the Hutu populations" (Herman and Peterson 6).

Note: If there are three authors, use commas to separate them: (Herman, Peterson, and Jones 9).

If a source has more than three authors, you may either list all authors' names, separated by commas, or give the name of the author listed first followed by the abbreviation *et al.*, meaning "and others."

> Teachers should integrate the study of history, culture, politics, literature, and film in order to give the most accurate picture (Jamieson et al. 96).

If you cite several volumes from the same source, precede the page number with the volume number and a colon.

> The definition of genocide is increasingly complex (Johnson 2:931).

Note: If you cite only one volume of a multivolume work, you need not list the volume number in an in-text citation, but you must list it in Works Cited.

If you cite a quotation or information that is itself cited in another source, use the abbreviation *qtd. in* for "quoted in" to indicate that you have used an indirect source for your information or quotation. (If possible, however, check the original source.)

> As Frantz Fanon asserts, "The colonized man finds his freedom in and through violence" (qtd. in Moore 54).

If you cite two or more authors or works as sources for a fact, idea, or plan, separate the citations with a semicolon.

> The Belgians made ethnic conflicts more concrete by using identity cards, which many scholars believed caused the later conflicts (Longman 925; "Genocide in Rwanda" 54–57; "Case Study: Genocide in Rwanda, 1994").

Content or Supplementary Notes You may include footnotes or endnotes in your paper when you have an important idea, a comment on your text, or additional information or sources *that would interrupt the flow of your ideas in the text.* During her research, Gingrich read about the debate over the role of reputed hero Paul Rusesabagina in the aftermath of the genocide, and she described the controversy in a supplementary endnote. Here is a first draft of that note.

> 1. While Paul Rusesabagina is depicted as a hero in *Hotel Rwanda* and in many stories about the Rwandan genocide, the historical record is not clear.

MLA

Some have suggested that Rusesabagina was an opportunist rather than a hero; others suggest that Rusesabagina's role has been criticized for political purposes and to keep the blame from President Kagame.

Works Cited List: MLA Style

After you have revised your essay and are certain that you will not change any in-text documentation, you are ready to write your list of sources. Depending on what you include and your teacher's guidelines, it will be one of the following:

- Works Cited list (only those works actually cited in your essay)
- Works Consulted list (works cited *and* other works that have influenced your thinking)
- Selected Bibliography (works cited and the most important other works)
- Annotated List of Works Cited (works cited, followed by a short description and evaluation of each source)

A Works Cited list alphabetically orders, by author's last name, all sources cited in your research paper. Each citation indicates the medium of publication of the source, such as print, Web, DVD, television, and so on. If the author is unknown, alphabetize by the first word (excluding *A, An,* or *The*) of the title. Use the following abbreviations for missing information other than an unknown author:

n.p. (no place of publication)
n.p. (no publisher given)
n.d. (no date of publication given)
n. pag. (no pagination in source)

The first line of each citation begins at the left margin, and succeeding lines are indented one-half inch. (You can use the hanging indent function of Microsoft Word to accomplish this effectively.) Double-space the entire Works Cited list with no extra space between entries.

Following are examples of MLA-style entries in a Works Cited list, organized by kind of source. Use the citations as models for your own Works Cited list. For additional information and examples, see the *MLA Handbook for Writers of Research Papers* (seventh edition, 2009).

Note: In your essay or manuscript, citations of titles of articles, poems, and short stories should be surrounded by quotation marks ("The Story of an Hour"). Titles of books, plays, novels, magazines, journals, and collections should be italicized (*Caramelo, National Geographic*).

Print Periodicals: MLA Style

For all articles published in print periodicals, give the author's name, the title of the article, and the name, number, and date of the publication. For newspapers and magazines, add complete dates and inclusive page numbers. Use the first page number and a plus sign if an article is not printed on consecutive pages. For all professional journals, add volume numbers, issue numbers, years of publication, and inclusive page numbers. Add *Print* as the medium of access for articles in printed periodicals.

For an article from a scholarly journal, order the information as follows, omitting information that does not apply. For an illustration of an article and its citation, see page 514.

Author's Last Name, First Name. "Title of Article." *Title of Periodical* Volume number. Issue number (date): Page numbers. Print.

For an article from a commercial periodical such as a newspaper, order the information as follows:

Author's Last Name, First Name. "Title of Article." *Title of Periodical* Day Month Abbreviated Year, edition: Page numbers. Print.

See page 518 for articles you access on the Web or in online databases.

Article in a Weekly or Biweekly Magazine

Packer, George. "All the Angry People: A Man out of Work Finds Community at Occupy Wall Street." *New Yorker* 5 Dec. 2011: 32-40. Print.

Article in a Monthly or Bimonthly Magazine

Dobbs, David. "Beautiful Brains: Why Do Teenagers Act the Way They Do?" *National Geographic* Oct. 2011: 36-37. Print.

Marano, Hara Estroff. "The Bs Get an A: New Studies Link Vitamins to Preserving Memory, Mood, and Cognitive Mastery at All Ages." *Psychology Today* Jan.-Feb. 2011: 42+. Print.

Article in a Scholarly Journal

All entries for scholarly publications such as professional journals should include the volume, issue, year of publication, page numbers (when available), and the medium of access. For an illustration of a scholarly journal article and its citation, see page 514.

Poole, Adrian. "The Disciplines of War, Memory, and Writing: Shakespeare's *Henry V* and David Jones's *In Parenthesis*." *Critical Survey* 22.2 (2010): 91-104. Print.

(Note that the titles of books cited with in a title are italicized: *Henry V* and *In Parenthesis*)

Article in a Newspaper

Omit the introductory article (*New York Times* instead of *The New York Times*). If the masthead indicates an edition (late ed.), include it in your entry. Newspaper articles do not usually appear on consecutive pages, so indicate the page number on which the article begins and then put a plus sign + to indicate that the article continues on later pages. Indicate section numbers (A, B, C) when appropriate.

Buckley, Cara. "Deal Restores Public Housing Subsidies." *New York Times* 1 July 2010: A26+. Print.

Citing an Article in a Print Periodical

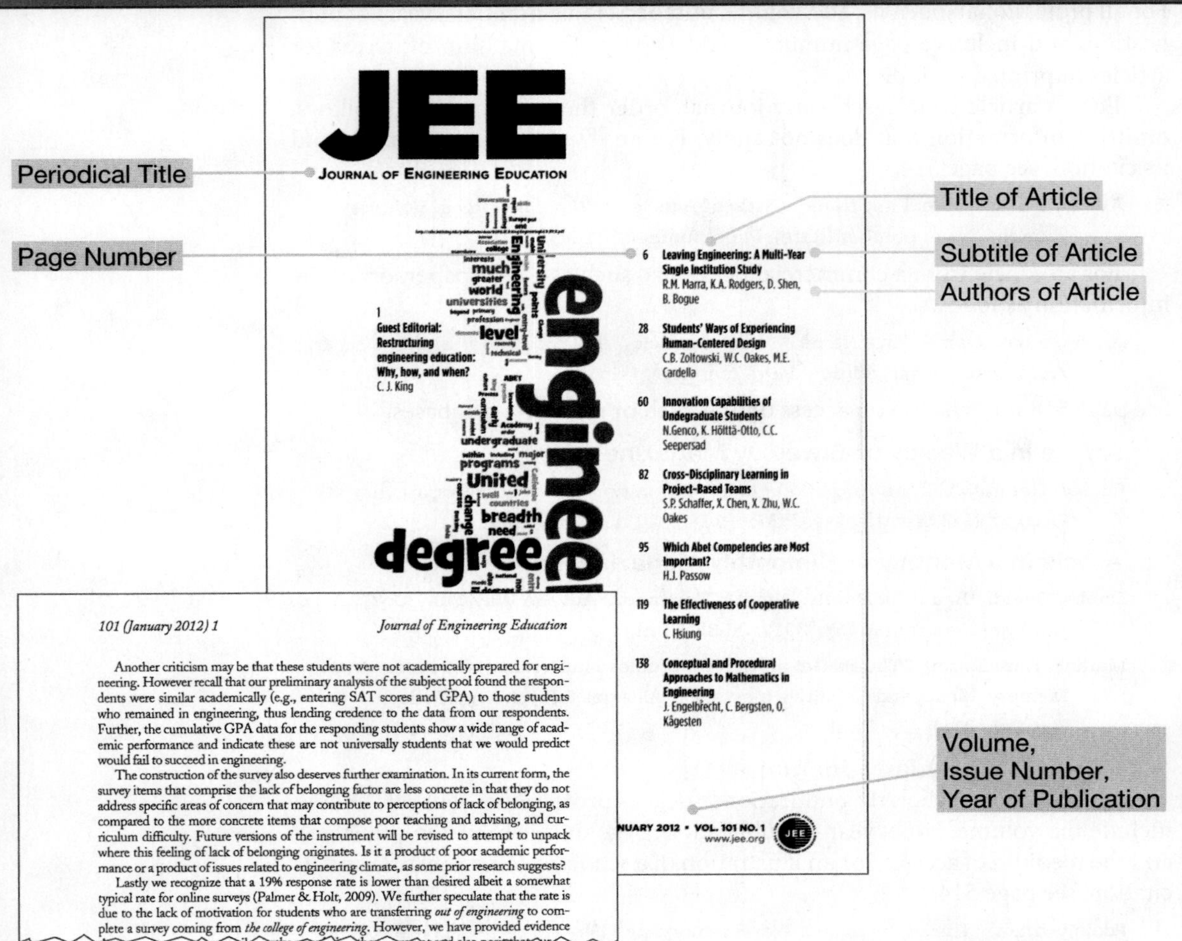

101 (January 2012) 1 *Journal of Engineering Education*

Another criticism may be that these students were not academically prepared for engineering. However recall that our preliminary analysis of the subject pool found the respondents were similar academically (e.g., entering SAT scores and GPA) to those students who remained in engineering, thus lending credence to the data from our respondents. Further, the cumulative GPA data for the responding students show a wide range of academic performance and indicate these are not universally students that we would predict would fail to succeed in engineering.

The construction of the survey also deserves further examination. In its current form, the survey items that comprise the lack of belonging factor are less concrete in that they do not address specific areas of concern that may contribute to perceptions of lack of belonging, as compared to the more concrete items that compose poor teaching and advising, and curriculum difficulty. Future versions of the instrument will be revised to attempt to unpack where this feeling of lack of belonging originates. Is it a product of poor academic performance or a product of issues related to engineering climate, as some prior research suggests?

Lastly we recognize that a 19% response rate is lower than desired albeit a somewhat typical rate for online surveys (Palmer & Holt, 2009). We further speculate that the rate is due to the lack of motivation for students who are transferring *out of engineering* to complete a survey coming from *the college of engineering*. However, we have provided evidence

MLA

Works Cited Format

Marra, R. M., et al. "Leaving Engineering: A Multi-Year Single Institution Study." *Journal of Engineering Education* 101.1 (2012): 6-27. Print.

In-Text Citation

Marra et al. conclude that "lack of belonging may be the strongest factor for all students" (23).

APA

References Format

Marra, R. M., Rodgers, K. A., Shen, D., & Bogue, B. (2012). Leaving engineering: A multi-year single institution study. *Journal of Engineering Education, 101*(1), 6–27.

In-Text Citation

Marra, Rodgers, Shen, and Bogue (2012) conclude that "lack of belonging may be the strongest factor for all students" (p. 23).

MLA

Unsigned Article in a Newspaper

"Subprime Commission." *Investor's Business Daily* 14 Sept. 2009: A1. Print.

Op Ed (Commentary) Article or Column

Saunders, Debra J. "Occupy Fannie and Freddie." *San Francisco Chronicle* 10 Nov. 2011: A18. Print.

Published Interview

Obama, Barack. Interview by Peter Baker. *New York Times* 12 Oct. 2010: B1+. Print.

Unsigned Editorial in a Newspaper

"Bring Home $1 Trillion: Territorial Tax System Would Make America More Competitive." Editorial. *Washington Times* 24 Oct. 2010: B2. Print.

Review

Garner, Dwight. "Fiction Writer Plays Tourist in Real World." Rev. of *Distrust That Particular Flavor* by William Gibson. *New York Review of Books* 1 Jan. 2012: C1+. Print.

Print Books: MLA Style

Order the information as follows, omitting information that does not apply. For an illustration of a book and its citation, see page 516.

Author's Last Name, First Name. "Title of Article or Part of Book." *Title of Book*. Ed. or Trans. Name. Edition. Number of volumes. City of Publication: Name of Publisher, year of publication. Print.

Book by One Author

Isaacson, Walter. *Steve Jobs*. New York: Simon, 2011. Print.

Two or More Works by Same Author

Morrison, Toni. *Jazz*. New York: Knopf, 1992. Print.

—. *Song of Solomon*. New York: Knopf, 1977. Print.

(The names of well-known publishers are usually shortened to the first key word. Thus, Alfred A. Knopf Publishing becomes "Knopf," "Houghton Mifflin Co." becomes "Houghton," and "Harcourt Brace Jovanovich, Inc." becomes "Harcourt.")

Book with Two or Three Authors

Aiken, Michael, Lewis A. Ferman, and Harold L. Sheppard. *Economic Failure, Alienation, and Extremism*. Ann Arbor: U of Michigan P, 1968. Print.

Delli Carpini, Michael X., and Bruce A Williams. *After Broadcast News: Media Regimes, Democracy, and the New Information Environment*. Cambridge: Cambridge UP, 2011. Print.

Citing A Book

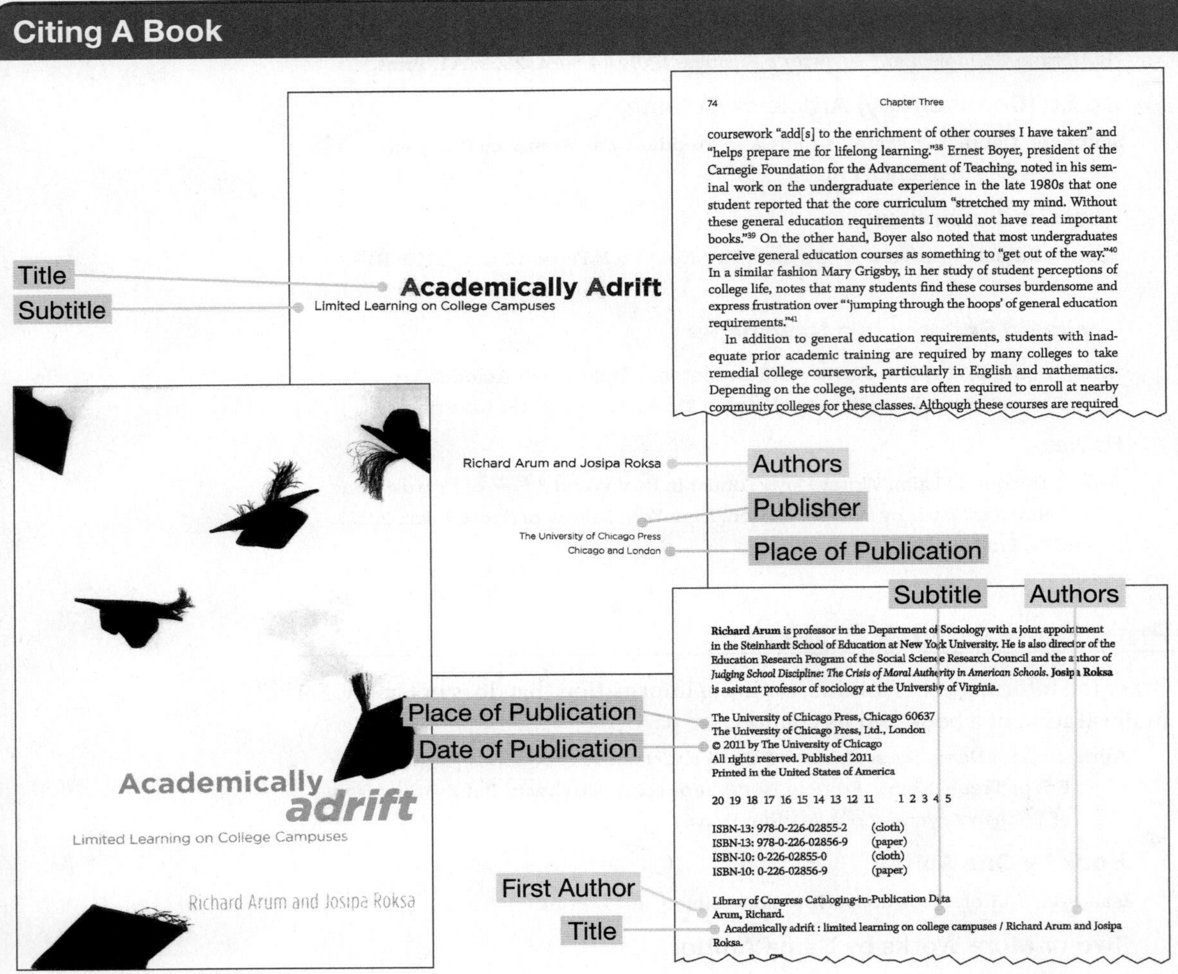

Title
Subtitle
Academically Adrift
Limited Learning on College Campuses
Richard Arum and Josipa Roksa
Authors
Publisher
The University of Chicago Press
Chicago and London
Place of Publication
74 Chapter Three
coursework "add[s] to the enrichment of other courses I have taken" and "helps prepare me for lifelong learning."[38] Ernest Boyer, president of the Carnegie Foundation for the Advancement of Teaching, noted in his seminal work on the undergraduate experience in the late 1980s that one student reported that the core curriculum "stretched my mind. Without these general education requirements I would not have read important books."[39] On the other hand, Boyer also noted that most undergraduates perceive general education courses as something to "get out of the way."[40] In a similar fashion Mary Grigsby, in her study of student perceptions of college life, notes that many students find these courses burdensome and express frustration over "'jumping through the hoops' of general education requirements."[41]
In addition to general education requirements, students with inadequate prior academic training are required by many colleges to take remedial college coursework, particularly in English and mathematics. Depending on the college, students are often required to enroll at nearby community colleges for these classes. Although these courses are required
Academically adrift
Limited Learning on College Campuses
Richard Arum and Josipa Roksa
Subtitle
Authors
Richard Arum is professor in the Department of Sociology with a joint appointment in the Steinhardt School of Education at New York University. He is also director of the Education Research Program of the Social Science Research Council and the author of Judging School Discipline: The Crisis of Moral Authority in American Schools. Josipa Roksa is assistant professor of sociology at the University of Virginia.
Place of Publication
Date of Publication
The University of Chicago Press, Chicago 60637
The University of Chicago Press, Ltd., London
© 2011 by The University of Chicago
All rights reserved. Published 2011
Printed in the United States of America
20 19 18 17 16 15 14 13 12 11 1 2 3 4 5
ISBN-13: 978-0-226-02855-2 (cloth)
ISBN-13: 978-0-226-02856-9 (paper)
ISBN-10: 0-226-02855-0 (cloth)
ISBN-10: 0-226-02856-9 (paper)
First Author
Title
Library of Congress Cataloging-in-Publication Data
Arum, Richard.
Academically adrift : limited learning on college campuses / Richard Arum and Josipa Roksa.

MLA

Works Cited Format

Arum, Richard, and Josipa Roksa. *Academically Adrift: Limited Learning on College Campuses.* Chicago: U of Chicago P, 2011. Print.

In-Text Citation

The influential book *Academically Adrift* references the work of Ernest Boyer, who had also found that general education was perceived by students as "something to get out of the way" (qtd. in Arum and Roksa 74).

APA

References Format

Arum, R., & Roksa, J. (2011). *Academically adrift: Limited learning on college campuses.* Chicago, IL: University of Chicago Press.

In-Text Citation

The influential book *Academically Adrift* references the work of Ernest Boyer, who had also found that general education was perceived by students as "something to get out of the way" (as cited in Arum & Roksa, 2011, p. 74).

MLA

(The words University and Press are commonly shortened to U and P wherever they appear in citations.)

Book with More Than Three Authors

Andolina, Molly, et al. *A New Engagement: Political Participation, Civic Life, and the Changing American Citizen*. Oxford: Oxford UP, 2006. Print.

Unknown or Anonymous Author

Encyclopedia of White-Collar Crime. Westport: Greenwood, 2007. Print.

Book with an Author and an Editor

Shakespeare, William. *Othello*. Ed. Kim F. Hall. Boston: Bedford, 2007. Print.

Edited Book

Giberson, Greg A., and Thomas Moriarity, eds. *What We Are Becoming*. Logan: Utah State UP, 2010. Print.

Translation

Morejon, Nancy. *Looking within Mirar Adentro*. Trans. Gabriel Abudu. Detroit: Wayne State UP, 2002. Print.

Article or Chapter in an Edited Book

Wiederhold, Eve. "Rhetoric, Literature, and the Ruined University." *Composition and/or Literature: The End(s) of Education*. Ed. Linda S. Bergmann and Edith M. Baker. Urbana: NCTE, 2006. Print.

Work in More Than One Volume

Morrison, Samuel Eliot, and Henry Steele Commager. *The Growth of the American Republic*. 2 vols. New York: Oxford UP, 1941. Print.

Work in an Anthology

Chopin, Kate. "The Awakening." *Harper Single-Volume American Literature*. Ed. Donald McQuade et al. 3rd ed. New York: Longman, 1999. Print.

Encyclopedia or Dictionary Entry

"Don Giovanni." *The Encyclopaedia Britannica*. 2010 ed. Print.

Government Document by Known Author

Chilton, Bart. *Ponzimonium*. Commodity Futures Trading Commission. Washington: GPO, 2011. Print.

Government Document by Unknown Author

United States. Dept. of Agriculture. Dietary Guidelines Advisory Committee. *Dietary Guidelines for Americans, 2010*. Washington: GPO, 2010. Print.

(*GPO* stands for "Government Printing Office.")

Unpublished Dissertation

Shusko, Christa M. "The Body of Love: Conceiving Perfection in the Oneida Community." Diss. Syracuse U, 2010. Print.

Pamphlet

West Nile Virus: Protect Yourself and Fight the Bite. Windsor, Ontario: Health Canada, 2010. Print.

Web Sources: MLA Style

MLA asks that you identify sources you access on the open Web and in online databases by giving Web as the medium of publication. It no longer requires that URLs be given, though writers are encouraged to include a URL when the citation information is not adequate to allow readers to find a source easily. The basic features of an Internet citation, abbreviated below, appear in complete form on the MLA home page at www.mla.org; the Purdue Online Writing Lab also provides useful information on MLA guidelines at http://owl.english.purdue.edu/. Use the sample citations that follow as models for your own citations. For additional examples, consult the MLA Web site or the *MLA Handbook*.

1. Name of author, editor, translator, director, performer, if known
2. Title of article, short story, poem, or other short work in quotation marks; or title of a longer work, such as a book, in italics
3. Publication information for a print version of the source, if known
4. Title of periodical, database, scholarly project, or Web site (italicized), or for a site with no title, a description such as *home page*
5. Name of the editor of the project or database (if available)
6. The name of any organization sponsoring the Web site
7. Date of electronic publication, update, or posting
8. Medium of access (Web) and date when researcher accessed the source or site
9. Electronic address or URL only if readers are not likely to find the site without it

Web Site

American Medical Association. AMA, Mar. 2011. Web. 12 Nov. 2011.

Document from a Web Site

Trapp, Douglas. "Faces of the Uninsured." *American Medical Association*. AMA, 28 Sept. 2009. Web. 25 Oct. 2011.

Scholarly Project Web Site

Human Genome Project: Resources. American Institute of Biological Sciences, 2010. Web. 20 June 2011.

(If the online source includes paragraph numbers instead of page numbers, use *par.* with the number.)

Magazine Article Online

Sykes, Tom. "The Real Downton Abbey: The Juiciest Bits from 'The Lost Legacy of Highclere Castle.'" *The Daily Beast*. The Daily Beast, 1 Jan. 2012. Web. 7 Jan. 2012.

Anonymous Magazine Article Online

"Russian Nuclear Submarine Burns with Sailors Still Onboard." *USNews.com*. US News & World Report, 30 Dec. 2011. Web. 6 Jan. 2012.

Article from an Online Subscription Database

To cite online material from a database to which a library subscribes, first give the print publication information. Then complete the citation by giving the name of the database (italicized), the medium of access (in this case, Web) and the date of access. See page 520 for an illustration of an online database source and its citation.

DeGaynor, Elizabeth. "Annotated Bibliography of Materials for Spirituality in the Classroom." *Delta Kappa Gamma Bulletin* 77.2 (2010): 21-26. *Academic Search Premier*. Web. 14 Feb. 2011.

Newspaper Article Online

Crompton, Janice. "Shale Puts Area in Spotlight." *Pittsburgh Post-Gazette*. Pittsburgh Post-Gazette, 29 Dec. 2011. Web. 25 Jan. 2012.

Newspaper Opinion Article Online

Mathews, Jay. "5 Reasons Why For-Profits Will Survive." *Washington Post*. Washington Post, 28 Nov. 2011. Web. 15 Jan. 2012.

Unsigned Newspaper Editorial Online

"Romney Will Say Anything." Editorial. *Union Leader*. Union Leader, 30 Dec. 2011. Web. 4 Jan. 2012.

Letter to the Editor Online

Rhoades, Sam J. "Shameful Cartoon." Letter. *Tulsa World*. Tulsa World, 27 Aug. 2011. Web. 6 Sept. 2011.

Review

French, Philip. "The Girl with the Dragon Tattoo." Rev. of *The Girl with the Dragon Tattoo*, dir. David Flincher. *The Observer*. The Guardian, 31 Dec. 2011. Web. 1 Feb. 2012.

E-book

Fitzgerald, F. Scott. *The Great Gatsby*. 1925. South Australia: U of Adelaide, 2010. Ebooks@adelaide, 2010. Web. 3 Nov. 2011.

Citing an Article from an Online Subscription Database

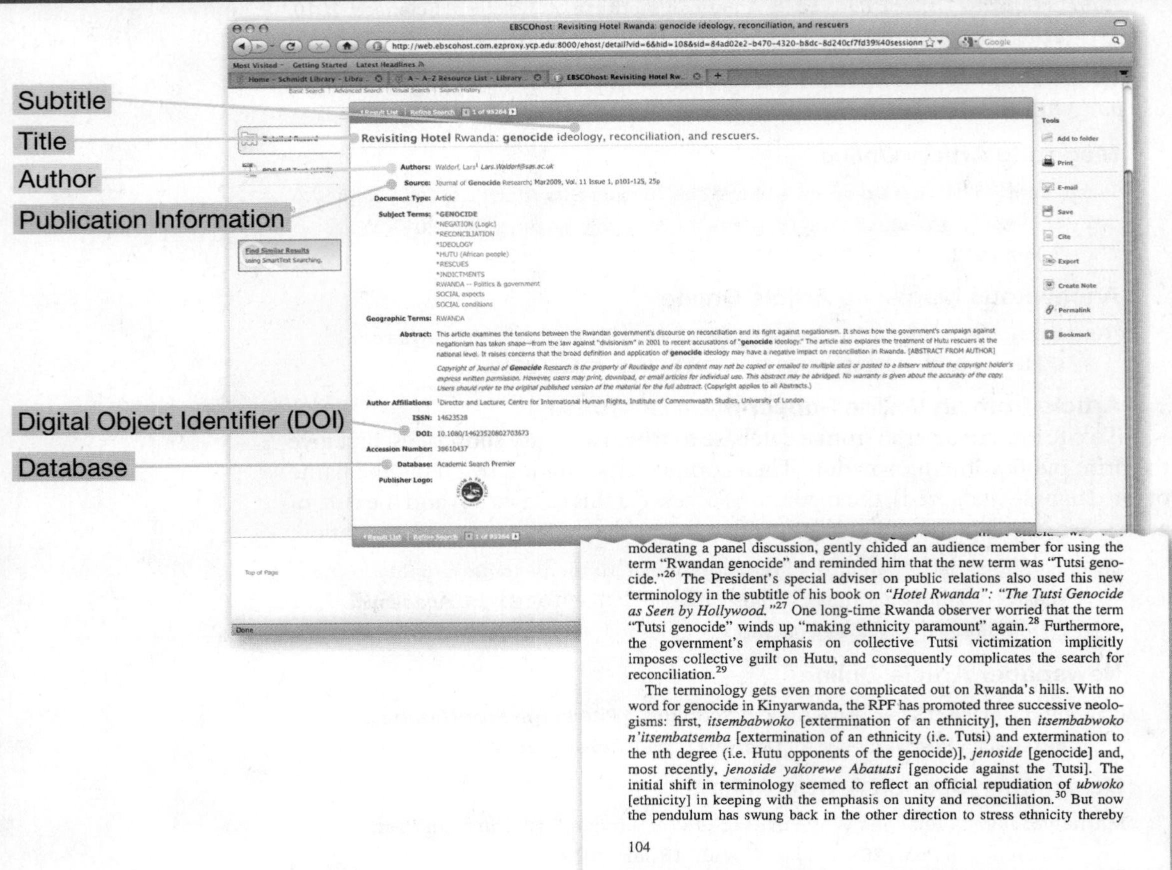

moderating a panel discussion, gently chided an audience member for using the term "Rwandan genocide" and reminded him that the new term was "Tutsi genocide."[26] The President's special adviser on public relations also used this new terminology in the subtitle of his book on *"Hotel Rwanda": "The Tutsi Genocide as Seen by Hollywood."*[27] One long-time Rwanda observer worried that the term "Tutsi genocide" winds up "making ethnicity paramount" again.[28] Furthermore, the government's emphasis on collective Tutsi victimization implicitly imposes collective guilt on Hutu, and consequently complicates the search for reconciliation.[29]

The terminology gets even more complicated out on Rwanda's hills. With no word for genocide in Kinyarwanda, the RPF has promoted three successive neologisms: first, *itsembabwoko* [extermination of an ethnicity], then *itsembabwoko n'itsembatsemba* [extermination of an ethnicity (i.e. Tutsi) and extermination to the nth degree (i.e. Hutu opponents of the genocide)], *jenoside* [genocide] and, most recently, *jenoside yakorewe Abatutsi* [genocide against the Tutsi]. The initial shift in terminology seemed to reflect an official repudiation of *ubwoko* [ethnicity] in keeping with the emphasis on unity and reconciliation.[30] But now the pendulum has swung back in the other direction to stress ethnicity thereby

104

MLA

Works Cited Format

Waldorf, Lars. "Revisiting Hotel Rwanda: Genocide Ideology, Reconciliation, and Rescuers." *Journal of Genocide Research* 11.1 (2009): 101-25. *Academic Search Premier.* Web. 7 Feb. 2012.

In-Text Citation

In his study of genocide ideology, Lars Waldorf traces attitudes toward ethnicity in varied areas of Rwanda, noting an "emphasis on unity and reconciliation" in Rwanda's hill regions (104).

APA

References Format

Waldorf, L. (2009). Revisiting Hotel Rwanda: Genocide, ideology, reconciliation, and rescuers. *Journal of Genocide Research, 11*(1), 101–25. doi: 10.1080/14623520802703673

In-Text Citation

In his study of genocide ideology, Waldorf (2009) traces attitudes toward ethnicity in varied areas of Rwanda, noting an "emphasis on unity and reconciliation" in Rwanda's hill regions (p. 104).

Poem

Wheatley, Phillis. "On Being Brought from Africa to America." *Poems on Various Subjects, Religious and Moral*. Philadelphia, 1786. *Electronic Text Center*. U of Virginia Lib., Nov. 2006. Web. 4 June 2008. <http://www.vcu.edu/engweb/webtexts/Wheatley/brought.html>.

Podcast

Biello, David. "Global Warming Is Undeniable." Podcast. *Scientific American*. Scientific American, 1 Aug. 2010. Web. 30 Sept. 2011.

Blog

Merriman, James. "Clearing Up Confusion on Charter School Accountability." Blog posting. *New York Charter Schools Blog*. New York City Charter Schools Center, 1 Aug. 2011. Web. 6 Sept. 2011. < http://www.nyccharterschools.org/meet/blog>.

Posting to a Discussion List

Baron, Dennis. "The Laws of English Punctuation." *WPA-L Discussion List*. Arizona State U, 23 Oct. 2011. Web. 17 Dec. 2011.

Synchronous Communications (MOOs, MUDs)

Grigar, Dene. Online defense of dissertation "Penelopeia: The Making of Penelope in Homer's Story and Beyond." *LinguaMOO*. U of Texas, 25 July 1995. Web. 25 July 2011. <telnet:/_/lingua._utdallas._edu:8888>.

E-Mail Communication

Rhames, Timothy. "RE: Building Online Communities." Message to the author. 30 May 2011. E-mail.

Map

Map of the Battlefield of Gettysburg. Map. New York: H. H. Lloyd, 1864. *Map Collections 1500–2004*. *American Memory*. Lib. of Congress, 2 May 2007. Web. 15 May 2011. <http://memory.loc.gov/cgi-bin/query/h?ammem/gmd:@field(NUMBER+@band(g3824g+cw0333000)>.

Other Sources: MLA Style

Film

Win Win. Dir. Thomas McCarthy. Perf. Paul Giamatti, Amy Ryan, Jeffrey Tambor. Fox Searchlight, 2011. DVD.

Recording

Bocelli, Andrea. *Concerto: One Night in Central Park*. Sugar/Decca, 2011. CD.

Author. Title. Publication Information. Other key elements.

MLA

Television or Radio Broadcast

"Man Seeks God." Narr. Ray Suarez. *PBS News Hour*. Public Broadcasting Corporation, 26 Dec. 2011. Television.

Performance

Bocelli, Andrea. Central Park, New York City. 15 Sept. 2011. Performance.

Letter

McCarthy, Cormac. Letter to the author. 22 Feb. 2008. TS.

(*TS* stands for "typescript.")

Lecture or Speech

Snyder, Rachel Louise. "The Post Sweatshop World." York College of Pennsylvania. 12 Oct. 2011. Lecture.

(In this case, it is best to avoid using an in-text citation by mentioning the speaker's name in the text. If the title is unknown, omit it.)

Personal Interview

Miller, J. Philip. Personal interview. 19 Mar. 2011.

Personal Survey

Information Literacy Questionnaire. Personal survey. 15 Mar. 2011.

Cartoon

Cagle, Daryl. "Kim Jong Il Dead." Cartoon. *Cagle Post.com.* 19 Dec. 2011. Web. 23 Dec. 2011.

Advertisement

Give the name of the product or company, then the label *Advertisement.* Follow with the usual publication information.

Prius by Toyota. Advertisement. *Newsweek* May 2011: 2. Print.

Painting, Sculpture, or Photograph

Indicate the artist's name first, followed by the title, the date of composition, and the medium. List the museum or collection, the owner if indicated, and the city.

Marc, Franz. *Deer in the Forest II.* 1914. Oil on canvas. Staatliche Kunsthalle, Karlsruhe.

Vermeer van Delft, Jan. *The Astronomer*. 1668. Musée du Louvre, Paris. *Louvre*. Web. 3 Jan. 2009.

Publication on CD-ROM, Diskette, or Magnetic Tape

"World War II." *Encarta*. Seattle: Microsoft, 2010. CD-ROM.

Bocking, Stephen. "Biodiversity: The Interplay of Science, Valuation, and Policy." DVD-ROM. *American Institute of Biological Sciences*, 2010.

MLA

In-Text Documentation: APA Style

Give the author's name and date of publication when you use a summary or paraphrase. If you quote material directly, give the author's name, the date, and the page number. (Use *p.* for one page and *pp.* for more than one page.) These citations will direct your reader to your References list, where you give complete bibliographical information. As you cite your sources, use the following guidelines.

Watch the Animation on APA Style

If you do not name the author in the text, give the author and date in parentheses at the end of the citation.

> According to one historian, "by the time the [UN] force was ready to deploy, the genocide was over" (Longman, 2009, p. 930).

Note: The use of this quotation succinctly captures the fact that the UN did not act quickly enough—a key point that Longman is trying to make.

If you cite the author in the text, indicate the date in parentheses immediately following the author's name, and cite the page number in parentheses following the quotation.

> According to Timothy Longman (2009), their advances caused bloodshed and turmoil on the border and throughout the northern portion of Rwanda, displacing many Hutus (pp. 926–29).

Note: The citation shows the source of the summary throughout the paragraph.

If you include a long direct quotation (40 or more words), indent the passage one-half inch from the left margin. Omit the enclosing quotation marks. Place the period at the end of the passage, not after the parentheses that include the page reference.

> Alan J. Kuperman develops four potential explanations for the RPF pursuing a violent challenge that provoked such tragic consequences. One possibility is that the Tutsi rebels did so irrationally, without thinking of expected consequences. A second is that they did contemplate consequences, but their expectations did not include retaliation against civilians. (63)

If you are paraphrasing or summarizing material (no direct quotations), you may omit the page number.

> Montgomery (2007) asserts that the world was told that that an unknown source fired a missile at Habyrimana's plane and even today the matter is still uncertain.

Note: Although the APA style manual says that writers may omit page citations for summaries and paraphrases, check with your instructor before you do so.

If you have previously cited the author and date of a study, you may omit the date.

> Montgomery further points out that it was the very night after signing the peace treaty that President Habyrimana's plane was shot down.

If the work has two to five authors, cite all authors in your text or in parentheses in the first reference.

Note: In your text, write "Herman and Peterson"; in a parenthetical citation, use an ampersand: "(Herman & Peterson)."

> Herman and Peterson (2010) believe the RPF (Rwandan Patriotic Front) under Kagame's influence and leadership conducted "an unmistakable pattern of killings and persecutions aimed at the Hutu populations"(p. 6).

> An article in a socialist journal asserts that the RPF (Rwandan Patriotic Front) under Kagame's influence and leadership conducted "an unmistakable pattern of killings and persecutions aimed at the Hutu populations" (Herman & Peterson, 2010, p. 6).

For subsequent citations, cite both names each time if a work has two authors. If a work has three to five authors, give the last name of the first author followed by *et al.* Include the year for the first citation within a paragraph.

> Herman et al. (2011) made similar claims.

If a work has six or more authors, use only the last name of the first author and the abbreviation *et al.* followed by the date.

> Some historians have compared the Rwandan genocide to other genocides in India and Germany (Schuster et al., 2009).

If a work has no author, give the first few words of the title (italicized, if a book or report, or in quotes, if an article or chapter) and the year.

> Whether in an attempt to reconcile the injustices done to the Hutus or in a moment of blind stupidity, the Belgians put the Hutu majority in charge when they left ("Genocide in Rwanda," 2008).

If the source is from the Internet or the Web, use the author, or if there is no author, use the title.

> Some Web sites provide a space for Rwanda survivors like Tharcisse Mukama to tell their story (*Rwanda Survivors*, 2006).

APA

If the author is a corporation, cite the full name of the company in the first reference.

> The Rwandan genocide continues to be a subject of intense interest for scholars (Yale University, 2011).

If the source is an unpublished personal communication (e-mail, letter, memo, interview, phone conversation), provide an in-text citation, but do not include the source in your References list.

> As Professor Lilley explained, "The genocide is more than an isolated historical event; it is one instance of ethnic violence that has been repeated all too frequently" (personal interview, October 21, 2010).

If you are citing a government document, give the originating agency, its abbreviation (if any), the year of publication, and (if you include a direct quotation) the page number.

> The geography of Rwanda is described as "covered by grasslands and small farms extending over rolling hills, with areas of rugged mountains that extend southeast from a chain of volcanoes in the northwest" (Department of State [DOS], 2010, p. 3).

If your citation refers to several sources, list the authors and dates in alphabetical order.

> Belgians made ethnic conflicts more concrete by using identity cards, which many scholars believed caused the later conflicts ("Case Study: Genocide in Rwanda, 1994," 2010; "Genocide in Rwanda," 2008; Longman, 2009).

Note: This entry synthesizes a number of sources to summarize the historical events. Where page numbers are available, the writer includes them. In some cases, Web sources do not have page numbers.

References List: APA Style

Make a separate list, titled References (no underlining or quotation marks), to appear after your text but before any appendixes. Include only those sources used in preparing your essay. List the sources cited in your text *alphabetically* by author's last name. Use only *initials* for authors' first and middle names. If the author is unknown, alphabetize by the first word in the title (but not *A, An,* or *The*). In titles, capitalize only the first word, proper names, and the first word following a colon. Begin the first line of each reference flush left and indent subsequent lines one-half inch. Double-space the entire References list. The APA recommends using italics for titles of books, journals, and other documents.

APA

Following are samples of APA-style reference list entries. For additional information and examples, consult the *Publication Manual of the American Psychological Association* (sixth edition, 2010).

Periodicals: APA Style

The following examples illustrate how to list articles in magazines and periodicals.

Note: Do *not* underline, italicize, or put quotation marks around titles of articles. *Do* italicize titles of magazines or periodicals. Italicize the volume number for magazines, if there is one, and omit the *p.* or *pp.* before any page numbers. If an article is not printed on continuous pages, give all page numbers, separated by commas.

Article in a Weekly or Biweekly Magazine

Gawande, A. (2011, January 24). The hot spotters: Can we lower medical costs by giving the neediest patients better care? *The New Yorker,* 41–50.

Article in a Monthly or Bimonthly Magazine

Gaffney, D. (2008, January). Fly the eco-friendly skies. *Popular Science, 46,* 48–49.

Unsigned Article in a Magazine

On the agenda: NHS reforms pose fresh challenges. (2011, 29 July). *PR Week,* 6.

Article in a Journal with Continuous Pagination

Italicize the volume number and do not include "pp." APA style requires repeating all number digits: Write 2552–2555. If the article has a DOI, include it (see page 529).

Dusinberre, M., and Aldrich, D. (2011). Hatoko comes home: Civil society and nuclear power in Japan. *Journal of Asian Studies, 70,* 683–705.

Article in a Journal That Paginates Each Issue Separately

Italicize the volume number followed by the issue number (not italicized) in parentheses. If the article has a DOI, include it (see page 529).

Moniz, E. (2011). Why we still need nuclear power. *Foreign Affairs, 90*(6), 83–94.

Article in a Newspaper

Use p. or pp. before newspaper section and page numbers.

Giordano, R. (2011, January 19). New Jersey approves a record number of charter schools. *Philadelphia Inquirer,* p. A1.

Unsigned Article in a Newspaper

U.S. grant will expand charter schools in state. (2010, August 18). *Providence Journal,* p. 3.

Op Ed Piece

Weller, S. (2009, November 22). Charters aren't labs for public education. *Denver Post,* p. D4.

APA

Unsigned Editorial

Charter feud must end [Editorial]. (2011, January 21). *Philadelphia Inquirer*, p. A14.

Books: APA Style

A Book by One Author

Cisneros, S. (2002). *Caramelo.* New York, NY: Random House.

Book by Several Authors

For books with up to six authors, use last names followed by initials and an ampersand (&) before the name of the last author. For books with more than six authors, use last name and initial of the first author followed by "et al."

Delli Carpini, M. X., & Williams, Bruce A. (2011). *After broadcast news: Media regimes, democracy, and the new information environment.* Cambridge, England: Cambridge University Press.

Andolina, M., et al. (2006). *A new engagement: Political participation, civic life, and the changing American citizen.* Oxford, England: Oxford University Press.

Additional Books by Same Author

List the author's name for all entries. Note that in-text citations are distinguished by copyright year. In the case of two works by the same author with the same copyright date, assign the dates letters *a, b* according to their alphabetical arrangement.

Morrison, T. (1977). *Song of Solomon.* New York, NY: Knopf.

Morrison, T. (1992). *Jazz.* New York, NY: Knopf

Unknown or Anonymous Author

Encyclopedia of white-collar crime. (2007). Westport, CT: Greenwood.

Book with an Author and an Editor

Shakespeare, W. (2006). *Othello* (K. Hall, Ed.). Boston, MA: Bedford St. Martin's Press.

Note: APA suggests that you include the name of the publisher in as brief a form as possible.

Work in an Anthology

Chopin, K. (1989). The story of an hour. In E. V. Roberts & H. E. Jacobs (Eds.), *Literature: An introduction to reading and writing* (pp. 304–306). Englewood Cliffs, NJ: Prentice Hall.

Note: Titles of poems, short stories, essays, and articles in a book are not italicized or put in quotation marks. Only the title of the anthology is italicized.

APA

Translation

Lefranc, J. R. (1976). *A treatise on probability* (R. W. Mateau & D. Trilling, Trans.). New York, NY: Macmillan. (Original work published 1952)

Article or Chapter in an Edited Book

Wiederhold, E. (2006). Rhetoric, literature, and the ruined university. In L. Bergmann & E. Baker (Eds.). *Composition and/or literature: The end(s) of education* (pp. 73–92). Urbana, IL: National Council of Teachers of English Press.

Government Document: Known Author

Machenthun, K. M. (1973). *Toward a cleaner aquatic environment.* Environmental Protection Agency. Office of Air and Water Programs. Washington, DC: U.S. Government Printing Office.

Government Document: Unknown Author

Dietary Guidelines Advisory Committee. (2010). *Dietary Guidelines for Americans, 2010.* Washington, DC: U.S. Government Printing Office.

Dissertation (Published)

Wagner, E. (1988). On-board automatic aid and advisory for pilots of control-impaired aircraft. *Dissertation Abstracts International, 49*(8), 3310. (UMI No. AAd88-21885)

Electronic and Internet Sources: APA Style

See section 7 of the *APA Manual* for the latest information on citing electronic sources. The basic features of an electronic or Internet citation, given in abbreviated form below, are available for downloading from the APA home page. Use the sample citations that follow as models for your own citations.

1. Name of author (if given)
2. Title of article (with APA capitalization rules)
3. Title of periodical or electronic text (italicized)
4. Volume number and/or pages (if any)
5. If information is retrieved from an electronic database (e.g., ABI/FORM, PsycInfo, Electric Library, Academic Universe), give the print information only or the publication's home page URL, if known.
6. When a digital object identifier (DOI) is available, include it instead of the URL.
7. Use the words "Retrieved" (include date here only if the publication is undated) "from" (give the URL). Use the words "Available from" to indicate that the URL leads to information on how to obtain the cited material rather than the complete address of the material itself.

8. Do not use angle brackets around a URL.
9. If the citation ends with the URL, do not follow the URL with a period.

APA style does not cite personal communications such as e-mail in a References list. Cite such references in the text only. Also, you may vary the in-text citation by mentioning the name of the author(s) or the work in your text, in which case you need only cite the date parenthetically.

Article in a Journal with DOI Assigned

Jackson, B., et al. (2007, May). Does harboring hostility hurt? *Health Psychology, 26*(3), 333–340. doi: 10.1037/0278-6133.26.3.333

Article in a Journal with No DOI Assigned

Arakji, R. Y., & Lang, K. R. (2008). Avatar business value analysis: A method for the evaluation of business value creation in virtual commerce. *Journal of Electronic Commerce Research, 9*, 207–218. Retrieved from http://www.csulb.edu/journals/jecr/

Article in an Internet-Only Journal

Twyman, M., Harries, C., & Harvey, N. (2006, January). Learning to use and assess advice about risk. *Forum: Qualitative Social Research,* 7(1), Article 22. Retrieved from http://www.qualitative-research.net

Article in a Newspaper

Greenhouse, L. (2004, June 25). Justices, in 5–4 vote, raise doubts on sentencing rules. *New York Times.* Retrieved from http:www.nytimes.com

Work from an Online Subscription Database

DeGaynor, E. (2011, Winter). Annotated bibliography of materials for spirituality in the classroom. *Delta Kappa Gamma Bulletin* 77(2): 21–26. Retrieved from www.dkg.org

(Even if you accessed the article from a database like Academic Search Premier, APA prefers a "retrieved from" line that includes the URL of the periodical's home page on the Web.)

Message Posted to an Online Forum

Baron, D. (2011, October 23). The laws of English punctuation. Message posted to WPA-l, archived at https://lists.asu.edu/cgi-bin/wa?A1=ind1110&L=WPA-L#185

Blog

Cambridge, B. (2007, April 24). ACT survey conclusion: More grammar instruction. *NCTE Literacy Education Updates.* Retrieved May 6, 2007, from http://ncteblog.blogspot.com

Author. Title. Publication Information. Other key elements.

Other Sources: APA Style

Review

Watch the Video on Formatting an APA Paper

Garner, D. (2012, January 1). Fiction writer plays tourist in real world. [Review of the book *Distrust that particular flavor*, by William Gibson]. *New York Review of Books*: C1.

Published Interview

Baker, Peter. (2010, October 12). The education of President Obama [Interview with Obama, B.]. p. B1.

Film

McCarthy, T. (Director). (2011). *Win win* [Motion Picture]. United States: Fox Searchlight.

Recording

Bocelli, A. (2011). O Sole Mio. On *Concerto: One Night in Central Park* [CD]. New York: Sugar/Decca.

Television or Radio Program

Suarez, R. (Producer). (2011, December 26). *PBS News Hour*. Washington, DC: Public Broadcasting Corporation.

(Proportions shown in the following MLA-format paper are adjusted to fit space limitations of this book. Follow actual dimensions discussed and your instructor's directions.)

½"

1"

Gingrich 1

[Watch the Animation on MLA Format Papers

Carrie Gingrich

/double space

Professor Lilley

WRT 202

26 April 2011

Learning about the Rwandan Genocide:

/double space

Misconceptions and Film

Genocides. They have occurred throughout history. Some are still painfully familiar, some are overlooked, some have been forgotten. The Rwandan genocide has not been overlooked or forgotten, but it continues to be widely misunderstood. This essay demonstrates how the media, especially film depictions, created an ongoing misunderstanding, and how the exclusive use of films to teach this event in the classroom can continue the silence and misunderstanding, leaving open the possibility of genocides to come.

The thesis statement lays out the specific topic and shows the purpose of the study.

There are both generally accepted cultural and historical facts about the Rwandan genocide and points of debate about its causes. This paper demonstrates through interviews that college-age Americans, including those who have seen films about the Rwandan genocide, lack awareness of what actually happened. And it analyzes the shortcomings of films about the genocide and discusses the responsibility of both the media and the educational system for failing to correct those misunderstandings—and in some cases for creating them. Films about the genocide were meant to portray and preserve what happened; the stated goal of many filmmakers was to help viewers learn from the genocide. However, the films oversimplify the genocide and, in doing so, they perpetuate and confirm as "fact" many misconceptions. They present the genocide as a simple morality tale rather than as something students should study and question.

1" 1"

This paragraph gives an overview of the paper, preparing readers for what follows.

Writer explains the importance of the study—why it should matter to the audience.

Recalling the Events of the Rwandan Tragedy

To fully understand the Rwandan tragedy, students must have a deeper cultural understanding and historical knowledge than the films provide. While the films present frightening images of the genocide itself, they do not educate students about the cultural

1"

This section introduction keeps the reader focused on the overall topic while introducing the background section.

MLA

Gingrich 2

causes of genocide or about the role of the international community in what transpired.

This paragraph provides historical background and shows what students should know about these events in order to be more fully informed.

For example, to better understand the reasons for the Rwandan genocide, students should know more about three ethnic groups: the Twa, the Hutu, and the Tutsi. The Twa were the first and the smallest group to migrate into Rwanda; the second group was the Hutu; and the third group was the Tutsi. A caste system developed in which the majority of Tutsi tended to be in the higher class. While some might see the conflicts between these tribes as the cause of the genocide, most experts agree that genocide would not have occurred without the influence of Belgian colonial rule. The Belgians made ethnic conflicts more concrete by using identity cards, which said one of three things: Twa, Hutu, or Tutsi, and as noted in *the Encyclopedia of Race and Racism*, "For the first time in the history of Rwanda, the terms 'Hutu' and 'Tutsi' came to identify two groups, one branded indigenous, the other exalted as alien" (Longman 925; "Genocide in Rwanda" 54-57; "Case Study"). And, in an effort to gain favor in the eyes of the Belgians, often the Tutsis followed suit. After years of Belgian colonization, the Belgians attempted to set up a Rwandan form of government and then left. Whether in an attempt to reconcile the injustices done to the Hutus or in a moment of blind stupidity, the Belgians put the Hutu majority in charge ("Genocide in Rwanda" 55).

Gingrich synthesizes a few sources to summarize events. Where page numbers are available, she includes them. Web sources often do not have page numbers.

MLA

This sentence paraphrases the conclusions of this article.

Thousands of Hutus wanted revenge or justice for the years of oppression in which they had lived under the Belgian rule through the Tutsis. As a result, thousands of Tutsis and moderate Hutus fled Rwanda into the surrounding countries: Democratic Republic of Congo, Burundi, Tanzania, and Uganda. Those who had fled Rwanda, after living as refugees, wanted to return to their home-land after the Belgian colonization. A group of Tutsi and moderate Hutu rebels formed in Uganda and made advances into Rwanda. They called themselves the Rwandan Patriot Front (RPF). According to Timothy Longman, their advances caused bloodshed and turmoil on the border and throughout the northern portion of

The citation shows the source of the summary throughout the paragraph.

Rwanda, displacing many Hutus (926-29). Alan J. Kuperman develops

> four potential explanations for the RPF pursuing a violent challenge that provoked such tragic consequences. One possibility is that the Tutsi rebels did so irrationally, without thinking of expected consequences. A second is that they did contemplate consequences, but their expectations did not include retaliation against civilians. A third is that the RPF expected violence against Tutsi civilians regardless of whether it challenged the Hutu regime, and so perceived little extra risk from doing so. The final possibility is that the rebels expected their challenge to provoke genocidal retaliation but viewed this as an acceptable cost of achieving their goal of attaining power in Rwanda. (63)

This extended quotation is presented in block style. The page number is included after the period at the end.

Other countries contributed to the coming genocide as well. The French, allies of the new Hutu government, assisted (through weapon supplies) in driving the RPF back across the Rwandan-Uganda border. The RPF, though they had been making significant gains and were well organized, could not stand against the French-supported Hutu militia. Later the RPF resumed attacks on the northern border of Rwanda, and this time the conflict drew international attention. The UN put pressure on the Hutu government to accept a cease-fire; eventually, the Hutu government relented. The UN sent in a force of peace monitors to help the two parties come to an agreement. UN troops helped organize the signing of the peace treaty between Hutu President Habyrimana and the RPF. Although peace seemed to be on the horizon, the opposite was true. The very night after signing the treaty, President Habyrimana's plane was shot down on its return to Kigali. The world was told that an unknown source fired a missile at Habyrimana's plane, and even today the truth of the matter is still uncertain (Montgomery 2007).

This introductory sentence forms a transition to the new paragraph, while continuing the discussion of the role of other countries in this genocide.

After the plane was shot down, the genocide began and the world did little to stop it. Beginning in April 1994 and continuing

The details of the genocide are corroborated from two different sources.

MLA

Gingrich 4

for 100 days, more than 800,000 Rwandans were slaughtered, an average of 10,000 people per day (Caplan; Montgomery). As the chaos began, the primary concern of other nations was that their own citizens were evacuated safely out of the country. Rather than stopping the killings, the UN troops in Rwanda were initially ordered not to use their weapons except in self-defense, and even then they could not fire until fired upon. According to Timothy Longman, "by the time the [UN] force was ready to deploy, the genocide was over" (930). Journalist Andrew Wallis accused the world, primarily the UN, for not coming to Rwanda's aid and for refusing to be responsible for that neglect. Wallis criticized the UN's pointless attempt to bring evil-doers to justice, questioning the process through which the justice is administered. He compared the world's response to the Nazi genocide to the world's response to the Rwandan genocide, questioning why the Nazis received fairer and more expedient trials than did the Rwandans. Wallis emphasized that justice that is delayed is the same thing as justice that is denied. Those concerns continue to be the topic of analyses of the events, but are often overlooked in the film versions of the history.

The introductory phrase identifies the source of the information that follows and shows the credibility of the author. It also reinforces the main point of this paragraph.

Gingrich forms a transition back to the main focus of the paper—the way the films fail to show the full story.

Hotel Rwanda: Educating Students about the Rwandan Genocide?

This brief review of some of the factors leading to the Rwandan genocide indicates the many important cultural and historical factors that one must understand in order to grasp the causes of genocide. So how much knowledge do current college students have of this relatively recent event? To examine that question, I began by interviewing ten college freshmen.

This section relies on the primary field research Gingrich did, which is blended with the secondary source information.

It may seem that studying the perspectives of contemporary American college freshmen about the Rwandan genocide is not worthwhile. After all, these students were toddlers when the Rwandan genocide took place. However, the fact that they were too young to remember those fateful days makes them perfect to demonstrate the misconceptions conveyed through the classroom and the media used there. We can thus learn a good deal by gauging

This paragraph addresses possible objections of readers and demonstrates the exigency of this research method.

Gingrich 5

their historical knowledge of this event and how their lack of knowledge leaves the possibility of future tragedies like this one.

All ten of the students reported learning of the genocide not from their parents or other sources, but from school. Unfortunately, the "truth" that they learned is a combination of ignorance and misconception. One particular film remains the most pervasive way that current college students have learned about the Rwandan genocide. Indeed, it has become a somewhat common practice in American high schools to show the film *Hotel Rwanda* in history class. Of the ten college students interviewed from various high schools, eight had seen *Hotel Rwanda*, one thought maybe she had seen parts of a movie about Rwanda, and the remaining one did not know there were movies on the subject. None were aware of the other films. It is for this reason that *Hotel Rwanda* is better known than other films made about the Rwandan genocide. Sadly, however, the showing of this film in classrooms across America has done little to increase awareness of the Rwandan genocide. In ten interviews with college freshmen, not a single one could identify the main point of the film beyond the fact that it was about two groups of people and one group was trying to kill the other. Only two of them followed up on the topic outside school to learn more. Their understanding of what caused the genocide was shaky at best. Their understanding of the UN's involvement or lack thereof was nonexistent.

Gingrich summarizes the findings of her research.

In the second half of this paragraph, Gingrich connects her field research to her main thesis—that the films don't do a good enough job of informing.

Asked if the genocide personally affected them, all agreed that it affected the people of Rwanda the most. Three of the students claimed that they would have been affected more if they had either known a Rwandan or if they had been in Rwanda during the genocide. Only one said he was personally affected on an emotional level. But he also noted that it was so terrible he did not want to think about what it would have been like to have been there. That is, he preferred not to cope with the facts of what actually happened.

The media's influence on who knows what and what they know is clearly seen in the interviews of these ten college freshmen.

This introductory sentence summarizes the importance of Gingrich's findings in the field research.

Gingrich continues to reference her findings from the field research to keep her own contributions to the topic primary.

Gingrich addresses possible audience questions here: Is the problem the use of film, or of this particular film? She goes on to address this by analyzing other films.

Gingrich draws on the work of film experts. She cites their ideas without quoting them directly. Readers can refer to the Works Cited list to find the original source.

Their first exposure to the genocide was through film. For most of them it was their only exposure. None of these freshmen had read any research articles about the genocide or studied it seriously. So their knowledge is bounded by what that one film told them. The problem is that media such as film tends to narrow rather than broaden our perspectives; yet audiences walk away thinking they know the truth.

Other Genocide Films

Of the four films, *Hotel Rwanda* is most often criticized for resembling stereotypical Hollywood films (Clarke)—but it is also the one which is most often viewed in classrooms. Perhaps this is true because it was made in a Hollywood fashion, receiving greater publicity than the films that came out before it, and continues to be more widely known than the films that came after it. The fact that *Hotel Rwanda* is the film about this event most commonly used in schools might raise another question: Is it possible that choosing a different film for use in the classroom would be a more effective educational method? After all, *Hotel Rwanda*, though clearly the most popular of the films, was only one of four films released between 2004 and 2007 with the express purpose of raising awareness about the Rwandan genocide (Brooks). And there is evidence that showing films has had some success in raising awareness. However, using only film to prevent the genocide from being forgotten has consequences. Below is a chart of four of these films, comparing and contrasting the films' perspectives.

Shooting Dogs is the second most publicized of the four films, largely because it was the first full-length film about the genocide that was filmed in its original location. Clarke compares *Shooting Dogs* favorably with *Hotel Rwanda* because it was shot in the same locations that the original story took place, and because it included survivors of the genocide in the making of the movie, both on and off the set. Contrary to Clarke's opinion, Johns finds fault with the

Gingrich 7

Table 1

Rwanda Filmography

	Hotel Rwanda	Sometimes in April	Shooting Dogs	Shake Hands with the Devil
Release Date	2004	2005	2005	2007
Rating (alternative rating)	PG-13	Not Rated TV-MA	R	R
Producer	Metro Golden Mayer-American	Independent	Independent-British-German	Independent-Canadian
Filming Location	South Africa	Original Locations	Original Locations	Original Locations
Perspective the Film is told from	Rwandan, Hutu man married to a Tutsi woman	Rwandan, Hutu man married to a Tutsi woman	Catholic Priest and British Teacher	UN Lieutenant
Main Character-Fiction vs. Nonfiction	Protagonist -Nonfiction	Protagonist -fiction	Protagonist Priest -Nonfiction Protagonist Teacher -Fiction	Protagonist -Nonfiction
Focus	Hotel manager who shelters people in the Des Milles Hotel	A soldier who finds some reconciliation with what happened ten years prior in the genocide	Catholic priest who sacrifices all he has to save the people he loves	UN general who refuses to leave Rwanda, staying behind to protect the innocent

(Caton-Jones; Dwyer; George; Nicol; Peck; Siegel; Spottiswoode.)

The chart allows readers to grasp some basic but important information in a quick, organized way.

director, Caton-Jones, accusing Caton-Jones of traumatizing his cast by making them relive the nightmares they had survived.

Gingrich draws attention to the differences among her sources' approach to the topic.

The information in parentheses gives background without interrupting the main point of the sentence.

Shake Hands with the Devil did not receive as much recognition for being filmed in its original locations because it was not the first film to have done so; the same is true for *Sometimes in April*. In his 2009 article, Keenan (unlike both Clarke and John) focused on the current life of one of the people represented in the films, not the actors in the film. Keenan writes about Paul Rusesabagina (the protagonist of *Hotel Rwanda*) and the influence he gained by the fact that his story was told in the film. This influence also came to Romeo Dallaire, the only other historical character depicted in the films who is still living. Both men play active roles in their own countries as well as internationally, and the fact that their stories were dramatized through film only increased their influence.

In the end, since all the films tend to focus on specific characters, the full historical record is often lost.

The previous paragraph, consisting of just one sentence, emphasizes Gingrich's main point and helps transition to her conclusion.

Conclusions and Recommendations

On an emotional level, the films can help to combat the silence about what happened. Each film has a distinctively gut wrenching scene: in *Hotel Rwanda*, the hotel manager is riding down a road in a van and stops the car fearing it has gone off the road, only to find that the road is covered in bodies for as far as the eye can see, causing the car to lurch back and forth as it runs over them. *Shooting Dogs* features a crowd of machete-waving men waiting for the UN troops to leave so they can begin hacking to death the people left behind; in the next scene, in eerie silence the camera scans the grounds where the bodies lie as fallen, twisted in their own pools of blood. *Shake Hands with the Devil* includes a scene in which the general finally acknowledges what has been going on around him for the last hundred days, as he stops his jeep and stares into the face of a girl lying alongside the road who had been raped before being murdered. *Sometimes in April* shows us the protagonist gazing in silent agony at the rain falling, the rain that comes every April, reminding him of all that happened, all that he did and did not do.

Gingrich uses descriptive language to describe these visual scenes from the films.

Each scene makes the audience understand what happened on an emotional level; yet the scenes do not put all the pieces together, they do not tell the whole story, and they do not challenge students to examine the key historical questions discussed in the brief outline of the events discussed above. In this way, film is an insufficient medium for teaching students about these events.

Gingrich makes a claim and then immediately provides an example to support it.

For example, while each of the films glances at the key question of who shot down President Habyrimana's plane—the catalyst of the genocide—none makes this question central. Though historians still have not concluded with certainty who shot the plane down, there are possible scenarios, each of which can help us better consider the larger picture ignored in the films:

A. Tutsi civilians shot down the plane because the President was Hutu. This is not seen as likely because the President had just signed the peace treaty with the RPF, the rebel forces primarily composed of Tutsis.

B. RPF rebels (not under Kagame's direction) shot down the plane because the President was Hutu. This seems more likely than A, since the President had signed the treaty with the RFP, yet the RPF was not sure the President would hold up his end of the bargain.

C. Kagame had the plane shot down. Though much of the case is circumstantial, political reasons makes this scenario very plausible.

D. The President's men (Hutu militia) shot down the plane. This is plausible because the historical evidence suggests that men serving under the President thought he was giving in to international pressure and being too lenient.

E. Hutu extremists, the Interhamwe, shot the plane down. While this is not as plausible as C or D, it would become more credible if the Interhamwe had received instructions from the Hutu militia (Caton-Jones; George; Peck; Spottiswoode).

This statement reinforces one of Gingrich's key points: the films show only a limited perspective. This point is reinforced throughout the paragraph.

Further, none of the films shows that the genocide took place all across the country of Rwanda, in countless different ways. Instead, films tend to portray one story. They are based on facts, but they focus on a fictionalized storyline surrounding specific individuals. Since, as my interviews showed, it is only through films that people of my generation seem to be getting their information, their historical knowledge is minimal. Through one film, students learn limited information, and after that, they do not receive or seek additional information. And though the films are only one person's interpretation, their effect is large—that version becomes the only knowledge that many people have. In the end, to educate students, teachers must go beyond the media.

Following a transition from one of her key points, Gingrich makes her next point and provides an example.

Gingrich blends the source information into her own main points, never letting the other authors control her paper.

Though the emotional impact of the films is important, they ignore other important questions. For example, they do not help students to consider the roles of the United States of America and President Kagame in this genocide. Edward Herman, for example, suggests that the United States was guilty not only for acting as a bystander but also for being an accomplice and perpetrator in the genocide. Herman states that the United States assisted in weakening Rwanda's economy before the genocide and played an influential part in the decision to pull the UN troops out of Rwanda. The films also do not address issues like those raised by Johnson, who focuses upon what is taking place in Rwanda now. He states that the U.S. government should realize that what its politicians (especially Hillary Clinton) are saying may be causing Rwandans to return the same kind of people to power who influenced the genocide.

Neither do the films seriously address the role of President Kagame, as raised by both Herman and the author of "President Paul Kagame Under Scrutiny" (2010), who agree that Kagame made unethical decisions once in power. According to some journalists and historians, Kagame seems to have been involved in both the attempted and successful assassinations of security personnel and generals, as well as the harassment of politicians and journalists

MLA

who opposed him. Nor do the films address Herman's theory that Kagame had the President's plane shot down, which causes him to question Caplan's belief that the Tutsis were the main victims of the genocide or that the Hutus are the sole perpetrators of the genocide and solely responsible for the death of so many Rwandans.

These examples make the key point: the films are not adequate to truly understanding the history.

The controversy surrounding Kagame's current decisions is clearly not the only issue that is not addressed sufficiently in the films—and which could make for worthwhile classroom discussion. Herman and Peterson believe the RPF (Rwandan Patriotic Front) under Kagame's influence and leadership conducted "an unmistakable pattern of killings and persecutions aimed at the Hutu populations" (Herman and Peterson 6). Herman also brings into question the speed and efficiency with which a Hutu-run government was overthrown and replaced by a Tutsi-run government. So, though the films may raise awareness on an emotional level, they fail to raise questions that might spur students to investigate the facts and historical theories at a more intellectual level. If such questions are raised, students could not only learn more about the facts of the genocide, but could be taught to question the authority of any one media source.

What happened in Rwanda during those one hundred days can only be understood by moving beyond the limited perspective of a film. To understand the genocide, students must be asked to do more than watch one movie or even to read one book; they must be willing to read multiple perspectives and to wade through conflicting media reports. They must be asked to question what is presented in a single film in order to achieve the necessary historical perspectives that can help to create more educated citizens and to avoid future atrocities.

Gingrich returns to and reinforces her main point in the final sentence.

Each item included in a Works Cited list is directly referenced in the text of the paper.

The name of the publication is italicized. The name of the sponsoring organization is not.

For academic journals, the volume, number, and year are listed.

For each item, the medium (Web, Print, DVD, etc..) is listed.

Films are listed alphabetically by the name of the director.

With Web sources, the date of access is given because electronic sources can be updated or revised frequently.

The major performers in a film are often listed.

In a multivolume work, the volume cited is listed.

The title of the specific entry in a reference work is listed.

Works Cited

Brooks, Richard. "Atrocities against the Tutsis in Rwanda." *Sunday Times*, Sunday Times, 20 Feb. 2005. Web. 1 Mar. 2011.

Caplan, G. "Remembering Rwanda or Denying it?" *Peace Review* 21.3 (2009): 280-85. Print.

"Case Study: Genocide in Rwanda." *Gendercide Watch*. Gendercide Watch, n.d. Web. 20 Feb. 2011.

Caton-Jones, Michael, dir. *Shooting Dogs*. Perf. John Hurt, Claire-Hope Ashitey, and Hugh Dancy. Metrodome, 2005. DVD.

Clarke, Donald. "A Tale of Two Movies." *Irish Times*. Irish Times, 17 Mar. 2006. Web. 2 Mar. 2011.

Dwyer, Michael. "Darkness Falls." *Irish Times*. Irish Times, 31 Mar. 2006. Web. 20 Feb. 2011.

George, Terry, dir. *Hotel Rwanda*. Perf. Don Cheadle. Lion's Gate/ United Artists, 2004. DVD.

"Genocide in Rwanda." *Encyclopedia of Race and Racism*. Ed. John Hartwell Moore. Vol. 2. 52-59. Print.

1" Herman, Edward S., and David Peterson. "Rwanda and the Democratic Republic of Congo in the Propaganda System." *Monthly Review* 62.1 (2010): 20-36. Print. 1"

Johns, Ian. "Shooting Dogs." *The Times*. United Kingdom Times, 29 July 2006. Web. 1 Mar. 2011.

Johnson, R. "Rwanda Takes a Strict Line on Genocide Denial: The U.S. Should Support That." *Christian Science Monitor*. 28 June 2010. Web.

Keenan, Dan. "Hero of 'Hotel Rwanda' to Visit Dublin." *Irish Times*. Irish Times, 1 Sept. 2009. Web. 25 Feb. 2011.

Kuperman, Alan J. "Provoking Genocide: A Revised History of the Rwandan Patriotic Front." *Journal of Genocide Research* 6.1 (2004): 61-84. Web. 2 Feb 2011.

Longman, Timothy. "Rwanda." *Encyclopedia of Genocide and Crimes against Humanity* Ed. Dinah L. Shelton. Vol. 2. 925-33. Web. 20 Feb. 2011.

Montgomery, Sue. "Genocide Survivor's Story of Hope and Courage." *Vancouver Sun*. Vancouver Sun, 7 Apr. 2007. Web. 2 Feb. 2011.

Nicol, Patrica. "Fresh from the Dark Heart of Africa." *The Sunday Times*. 26 March 2006. Web. 17 Feb 2011.

1"

Gingrich 13

Peck, Raoul, dir. *Sometimes in April*. Perf. Idris Elba, Oris Erhuero, Carole Karemara, and Debra Winger. HBO Films, 2005. DVD.

"President Paul Kagame under Scrutiny." *Economist* 7 Aug. 2010. 43-44. Print.

Siegel, Robert. "Interview: Don Cheadle Discusses Playing the Role of Paul Rusesabagina in the Movie 'Hotel Rwanda.'" *All Things Considered*. National Public Radio. 22 Dec 2004. Web. 22 Feb 2011.

Spottiswoode, Roger, dir. *Shake Hands with the Devil*. Perf. Roy Dupuis. Regent Films, 2007. DVD.

Wallis, Andrew. "Even Now, World Fails Rwanda." *USA Today*. Gannett, 28 Apr. 2010. Web. 13 Feb. 2011.

The medium in which a film or video was watched is listed (Film, DVD, or Web).

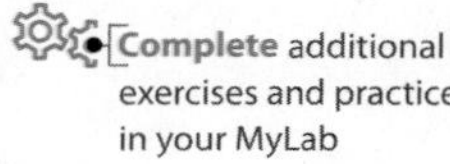

Complete additional exercises and practice in your MyLab

Appendix: Writing under Pressure

What You Will Learn

In this appendix you will learn to:

A.1 Write essay exams and other timed writing.

THE main chapters of this text assume that you have several days or even weeks to write your paper. They work on the premise that you have time to read model essays, time to think about ideas for your topic, and time to prewrite, write several drafts, and receive feedback from other members of your class. Much college writing, however, occurs on midterm or final examinations, when you may have only fifteen to twenty minutes to complete the whole process of writing. When you must produce a "final" draft in a few minutes, your writing process may need drastic modification.

A typical examination has some objective questions (true/false, multiple-choice, definition, short-answer) followed by an essay question or two. For example, with just twenty-five minutes left in your Western civilization midterm, you might finish the last multiple-choice question, turn the page, and read this essay question:

> Erich Maria Remarque's *All Quiet on the Western Front* has been hailed by critics the world over as the "twentieth century's definitive novel on war." What does Remarque's novel tell us about the historical, ideological, national, social, and human significance of twentieth-century warfare? Draw on specific illustrations from the novel, but base your observations on your wider perspective on Western civilization.

Overwhelmed by panic, you find the blood drains from your face and your fingers feel icy. You now have twenty-two minutes to write on the "historical, ideological, national, social, and human significance of twentieth-century warfare." Do you have to explain everything about modern warfare? Must you use specific examples from the novel? Everything you remembered about the novel has now vanished. Bravely, you pick up your pen and start recounting the main events of the novel, hoping to show the instructor at least that you read it.

You can survive such an essay question, but you need to prepare yourself emotionally and intellectually. The following advice comes from senior English majors who have taken dozens of essay examinations in their four years of college.

These seniors answer the question, What advice would you give to students who are preparing to take an essay examination?

- Even though I'm an English major, I'm perfectly petrified of writing impromptu essays. My advice is to calm yourself. Read the question. Study key words and concepts. Before beginning, write a brief, informal outline. This will organize your ideas and help you remember them as well. Take a deep breath and write. I would also recommend *rereading* the question while you are writing, to keep you on track.
- Before you begin, read the instructions. Know what the teacher expects. Then try to organize your thoughts into a list—preferably a list that will become your main paragraphs. Don't babble to fill space. Teachers hate reading nonsense. Reread what you've written often. This will ensure that you won't repeat yourself. Proofread at the end.
- My advice would be first to learn how to consciously relax and practice writing frequently. *Practice!!!* It's important to practice writing as much as possible in any place possible, because the more writing you do, the better and easier it becomes. Also, your belief that it *can* be done is critical!
- Know the information that you will be tested on well enough so that you can ask yourself tough and well-formed questions in preparation. You should be able to predict what essay questions your professor will ask, at least generally. I always go to the test file or ask friends for sample essay questions that I can practice on. Then I practice writing on different areas of the material.

The common threads in these excerpts of advice are to know your audience, analyze key terms in the question, make a sketch outline, know the material, practice writing before the test, and proofread when you finish writing. Knowing how to read the question and practicing your writing before the test will help you relax and do your best.

Know Your Audience

A.1
Write essay exams and other timed writing.

Teachers expect you to answer the question they have asked, not just to give information that you know. Because teachers must read dozens of essays, they are impressed by clear organization and detail. Although they demand specific examples and facts from the text, they want you to explain how these examples *relate* to the overall question. In a pile of two hundred history exams graded by one professor, margins featured comments like "Reread the question. This doesn't answer the question." "What is your main point? State your main point clearly." "Give more specific illustrations and examples." Keep this teacher in mind as you write your next essay response.

Analyze Key Terms

Understanding the key terms in the question is crucial to writing an essay under pressure. Teachers want you to respond to *their* specific question, not to write down information. The following key terms indicate teachers' expectations and suggest how you should organize your answer.

Watch the **Animation** on Essay Exams

Discuss: A general instruction that means "write about." If the question says *discuss,* look for other key words to focus your response.

Describe: Give sensory details or particulars about a topic. Often, however, this general instruction simply means "discuss."

Analyze: Divide a topic into its parts, and show how the parts are related to each other and to the topic as a whole.

Synthesize: Show how the parts relate to the whole or how the parts make sense together.

Explain: Show relationships between specific examples and general principles. Explain what (define), explain why (causes/effects), and/or explain how (analyze process).

Define: Explain what something is. As appropriate, give a formal definition, describe it, analyze its parts or function, describe what it is not, and/or compare and contrast it with similar events or ideas.

Compare: Explain similarities and (often) differences. Draw conclusions from the observed similarities and differences.

Contrast: Explain key differences. Draw conclusions from the observed differences.

Illustrate: Provide specific examples of an idea or process.

Trace: Give the sequence or chronological order of key events or ideas.

Evaluate: Determine the value or worth of an idea, thing, process, person, or event. Set up criteria and provide evidence to support your judgments.

Solve: Explain your solution; show how it fixes the problem, why it is better than other alternatives, and why it is feasible.

Argue: Present both sides of a controversial issue, showing why the opposing position should not be believed or accepted and why your position should be accepted. Give evidence to support your position.

Interpret: Offer your understanding of the meaning and significance of an idea, event, person, process, or work of art. Support your understanding with specific examples or details.

Make a Sketch Outline

The key terms in a question should not only focus your thinking but also suggest how to organize your response. Use the key terms to make a sketch outline of your response. You may not regularly use an outline when you have more time to write an essay, but the time pressure requires that you revise your normal writing process.

Assume that you have twenty-five minutes to read and respond to the following question from a history examination. Read the instructions carefully, note the key terms, and make a brief outline to guide your writing.

Answer *one* of the following. Draw on the reading for your answer. (25 pts)

1. Define *globalization,* then explain both the advantages and disadvantages of globalization for both modern and third-world countries. Based on your explanation, argue for or against globalization as a means of improving the standard of living in both modern and third-world countries.
2. Explain the arguments that the United Nations does and does not play a positive role in international relations (discuss and illustrate both sides of the argument). Then take a stand—citing the evidence for your position.

Let's assume that because you know more about the United Nations, you choose the second question. First, you should identify and underline key words in the question. The subject for your essay is the *United Nations* and its role in *international relations*. You need to *explain* the reasons why the UN does or does not have a positive effect on international relations. You will need to *discuss* and *illustrate* (give specific examples of) both sides of the controversy. Finally, you need to *take a stand* (argue) for your belief, citing *evidence* (specific examples from recent history) of how the UN has or has not helped to resolve international tensions.

Based on your rereading and annotation of the key words of the question, make a brief outline or list, perhaps as follows.

I. Reasons (with examples) why some believe the UN is effective

- **A.** Reason 1 + example
- **B.** Reason 2 + example

II. Reasons (with examples) why some believe the UN is not effective

- **A.** Reason 1 + example
- **B.** Reason 2 + example

III. Reasons why you believe the UN is effective

Refer to reasons and examples cited in I, above, but explain why these reasons and examples outweigh the reasons cited in II, above.

With this sketch outline as your guide, jot down reasons and examples that you intend to use, and then start writing. Your outline will make sure that you cover all the main points of the question, and it will keep your essay organized as you concentrate on remembering specific reasons and examples.

Warming Up: Journal Exercise

For practice, analyze at least one question from two of the following subject areas. First, underline key terms. Then, in your journal explain what these terms ask you to do. Finally, sketch an outline to help organize your response. If you are not familiar with the topics, check a dictionary or Google the key terms. (Do not write the essay.)

Biology

- Describe the process by which artificial insulin was first produced.
- What is reverse transcriptase and how was it used in genetic engineering?
- Humans—at least most of us—walk on two legs as opposed to four. How might you account for this using a Darwinian, Lamarckian, and Theistic model?

History

- Discuss the significant political developments in the English colonies in the first half of the eighteenth century.
- Account for the end of the Salem witchcraft delusion, and discuss the consequences of the outbreak for Salem Village.

Human Development

- Discuss evidence for nature versus nurture effects in human development.
- Contrast Piaget's, Vygotsky's, and Whorf's ideas on connections between language and thought.

Humanities

- How and why did early Christian culture dominate the Roman Empire? In terms of art and architecture, discuss specific ways in which the early Christians transformed or abolished the Greco-Roman legacy.

Literature

- Aristotle wrote that a tragedy must contain certain elements, such as a protagonist of high estate, recognition, and reversal, and should also evoke pity and fear in the audience. Which of the following best fits Aristotle's definition: *Hamlet, Death of a Salesman*, or *The Old Man and the Sea?* Explain your choice.

Psychology

- Contrast Freud's and Erikson's stage theories of personality.
- What is meant by triangulation of measurement (multiple methodology)?

Know the Material

It goes without saying that you must know the material in order to explain concepts and give specific examples or facts. But what is the best way to review the material before an exam so that you can recall examples under pressure? The following three study tactics will improve your recall.

First, read your text actively. Do not just mark key passages with a highlighter. Write marginal notes to yourself. Note key concepts in the margin. Ask questions. Make connections between an idea in one paragraph and something you read earlier. Make connections between what you read in the text and what you heard in class.

Second, do not depend only on your reading and class discussion. Join or form a study group that meets regularly to review course material. Each person in the group should prepare a question for review. Explaining key ideas to a friend is an excellent way to learn the material.

Finally, use your writing to help you remember. Do not just read the book and your notes and head off for the test. Instead, review your notes, *close* your notebook, and write down as much as you can remember. Review the assigned chapters in the text, close the book, and write out what you remember. If you can write answers to questions with the book closed, you know you're ready for an essay examination.

Warming Up: Journal Exercise

Get out the class notes and textbook for a course that you are currently taking. Annotate your notes with summary comments and questions. In the margins, write out the key ideas that the lecture covered. Then write out questions that you still have about the material. Annotate the margins of the textbook chapter that you are currently reading. Write summary comments about important material. Write questions in the margins about material that you do not understand. Note places in the text that the instructor also covered in class.

Practice Writing

As several senior English majors have suggested, practicing writing short essays *before* an examination will make you feel comfortable with the material and reduce your panic. A coach once noted that while every athlete wants to win, only the true winners are willing to *prepare* to win. The same is true of writing an examination. Successful writers have already completed 80 percent of the writing process *before* they walk into an examination. They have written notes in the margins of their notebooks and textbooks. They have discussed the subject with other students. They have closed the book and written out key definitions. They have prepared questions and practiced answering them. Once they read a question, they are prepared to write out their "final" drafts.

Warming Up: Journal Exercise

For an upcoming examination in one of your other courses, write out three possible essay questions that your instructor might ask. For each question, underline the key words, and make a sketch outline of your response. Set a timer for fifteen minutes, and write out your response to *one* of your questions.

Proofread and Edit

In your normal writing process, you can put aside your draft for several days and proofread and edit it later. When you are writing under pressure, however, you need to save three or four minutes at the end to review what you have written. At this point, one effective strategy is to draw a line at the end of what you have written, write "Out of Time," and then write one or two quick sentences explaining what you planned to say: "If I had more time, I would explain how the UN's image has become more positive following the crises in Israel and Iraq." Then use your remaining two or three minutes to reread what you have written, making sure that your ideas are clear and that you have written in complete sentences and used correct spelling and punctuation. If you don't know how to spell a word, at least write "sp?" next to a word to show that you think it is spelled incorrectly.

Sample Essay Questions and Responses

The following are sample essay questions, students' responses, and instructors' comments and grades.

HISTORY 100: WESTERN CIVILIZATION

Examination II over Chapter 12, class lectures, and Victor Hugo's *The Hunchback of Notre Dame*

Essay I (25 Points)

What was the fifteenth-century view of "science" as described in *The Hunchback?* How did this view tend to inhibit Claud Frollo in his experiments in his closet in the cathedral?

Answer 1

An excellent response. Your focus an superstition and heresy along with the specific examples of the roasted mouse, the "Philosopher's Stone," and La Esmeralda's goat illustrate the fifteenth-century view of science and its inhibiting effect. Grade: A

The fifteenth-century view of "science" was characterized by superstition and heresy. In *The Hunchback of Notre Dame,* for example, we see superstition operating when the king's physician states that a gunshot wound can be cured by the application of a roasted mouse. Claud Frollo, a high-ranking church official, has a thirst for knowledge, but unfortunately it pushes beyond the limits of knowledge permitted by the church. When he works in his closet on the art of alchemy and searches for the "Philosopher's Stone" (gold), he is guilty of heresy. Frollo has read and mastered the arts and sciences of the university and of the church, and he wants to know more. He knows that if he presses into the "Black Arts," the Devil will take his soul. And indeed, the "Devil" of passion does. Frollo feels inhibited because many of the experiments he has performed have made him guilty of heresy and witchcraft in the eyes of the church. And this seems to be the case in almost anything "new" or out of the ordinary. La Esmeralda, for instance, is declared "guilty" of witchcraft for the training of her goat. Her goat appears to have been possessed by the Devil himself, when, in fact, all the girl is guilty of is training the goat to do a few simple tricks. All in all, the fifteenth-century view of "science" was one not of favor, but of oppression and fear. Thankfully, the Renaissance came along!

Answer 2

Give more examples from the novel and show how the fifteenth-century view actually inhibited Frollo. Otherwise, generally good response. (Why was creating the Earth such a religious "ordeal"?) Grade: B

The fifteenth-century view of science was that according to the Bible, God was the creator of all, and as to scientific theory, the subject was moot. No one was a believer in the scientific method—however, we do find some science going on in Claud Frollo's closet, alchemy. At that time he was trying to create gold by mixing different elements together. Though alchemy seems to be the only science of that time period, people who practiced it kept it to themselves. We even find King Louis IX coming to Frollo, disguised, to dabble in a little of the science himself. At this time people were rejecting the theory of the Earth revolving around the sun because, as a religious ordeal, God created the Earth and man, and they are the center of all things, so there were no questions to be answered by science, because the answer was God.

Answer 3

Needs more specific illustrations from the novel. Frollo is inhibited by his lack of scientific method and the censure of the church. Underline title of novel: The Hunchback of Notre Dame. Grade: C

According to The Hunchback of Notre Dame, the view of "science" in the fifteenth century was basically alchemy, that is, being able to turn base metals into gold. Everything else that we would regard as scientific today was regarded as sorcery or magic in the fifteenth century. What inhibited Claud Frollo in his experiments of turning base metals into gold was that, according to the laws of alchemy, one needed "The Philosopher's Stone" to complete the experiment, and Claud Frollo was unable to find this particular stone.

Answer 4

During the period that the *Hunchback* took place, the attitude toward science was one of fear. Because the setting was in the medieval world, the people were afraid to admit to doing some things that were not being done by a majority of people. The overall view during that period was to keep one's own self out of trouble. The fright may be the result of the public executions which were perhaps Claud Frollo's deterrent in admitting to performing acts of science which others are uneducated in. Claud Frollo was outnumbered in the area of wanting to be "educated" and he kept to himself because he feared the people. He was in a position that didn't give him the power to try and overcome people's attitude of fear toward science. If he tried, he risked his life.

State your ideas more clearly. Your response doesn't answer the question. Very limited in your examples of science. Grade: D

BIOLOGY 220: ECOLOGY
FINAL EXAMINATION

Essay II (20 Points)

Water running down a mountainside erodes its channel and carries with it considerable material. What is the basic source of the energy used by the water to do this work? How is the energy used by water to do this work related to the energy used by life in the stream ecosystem?

Answer 1

The process begins with the hydrologic cycle. The sun radiates down and forces evaporation. This H_2O gas condenses and forms rain or snow, which precipitates back to earth. If the precipitation falls on a mountain, it will eventually run down the hillside and erode its channel. (Some water will evaporate without running down the hill.) The energy used by water to do its work relates directly to the energy used by life in the stream system. The sun is an energy input. It is the source of energy for stream life just as it is the source of energy for the water. Through photosynthesis, the energy absorbed by the stream is used by higher and higher trophic levels. So the sun is the energy source for both running water and the life in the stream. It all starts with solar energy.

Good response. Clear focus on the hydrologic cycle, photosynthesis, and solar energy and the source of energy for both the stream and its ecosystems. Grade: A

Answer 2

Ultimately, the sun is the basic source of energy that allows water to do the work it does. Solar power runs the hydrologic cycle, which is where water gets its energy. Heat evaporates water and allows molecules to rise in the atmosphere, where it condenses in clouds. Above the ground, but still under the effects of gravity, water has potential energy at this point. When enough condensation occurs, water drops back to the ground, changing potential energy to kinetic energy, which is how water works on mountainsides to move materials. As water moves materials, it brings into streams a great deal of organic matter, which is utilized by a number of heterotrophic organisms. That is the original

Very clear explanation of the hydrologic cycle, but response doesn't explain how source of energy for the stream ecosystem is related, through photosynthesis, to solar energy. Grade: B

source of energy for the ecosystems and also how energy used by water is related to the energy that is used by life in streams.

Answer 3

Reread the question. The basic source of energy is solar power. You almost discover the answer when you discuss photosynthesis, but after that, you get off track again. Grade: C–

The actual energy to move the water down the mountains is gravitational pull from the center of the earth. The stream's "growth" from the beginning of the mountain-top to the base starts out with being a heterotrophic system. This is because usually there is not enough light to bring about photosynthesis for the plants and in turn help other organisms' survival, so the streams use outside resources for energy. Once the stream gets bigger (by meeting up with another stream), it is autotrophic. It can produce its own energy sources. When the water reaches the base and becomes very large, it falls back to a heterotrophic system because the water has become too deep for light to penetrate and help with photosynthesis.

Text Credits

11–13 Roy Hoffman, "On Keeping a Journal." *Newsweek on Campus,* October 1983. Copyright © 1983 by Roy Hoffman. Reprinted by permission of the author.

24–26 Elizabeth Wong, "The Struggle to be an All-American Girl," *Los Angeles Times.* Reprinted by permission of the author.

26–27 Robert Zoellner, "I'm Ok But You're Not," *The Coloradoan.* Reprinted with permission of the author.

31–34 Neil H. Petrie, "Athletes and Education" (originally titled "Colleges Give Their Student Athletes an Especially Reprehensible Form of Hypocrisy"). *Chronicle of Higher Education,* February 24, 1988. Copyright © 1988. Reprinted with the permission of the publisher.

34–36 Neil H. Petrie, "On Writing 'Athletes and Education.'" *Chronicle of Higher Education,* February 24, 1988. Copyright © 1988. Reprinted with the permission of the publisher.

45 From "Sierra" by John Muir.

49–50 Richard Rodriguez, "This Boy's Desire." Copyright © 1983 by Richard Rodriguez. Originally appeared in *California* magazine (December 1983). Reprinted by permission of Georges Borchardt, Inc., on behalf of the author.

51–52 Junot Díaz, "In Mrs. Crowell's Library." First published in Joel Lovell, "The Educational Experiences that Changed a Life." *New York Times Magazine,* September 18, 2011. Reprinted by permission of Junot Díaz and Aragi Inc.

52 Michelle A. Rhee, "Calvin in Motion." Excerpt from Joel Lovell, "The Educational Experiences that Changed a Life." *New York Times Magazine,* September 18, 2011. Reprinted by permission of the author.

53 Lisa Randall, "Just Ask. Then Keep Asking." Excerpt from Joel Lovell, "The Educational Experiences that Changed a Life." *New York Times Magazine,* September 18, 2011. Reprinted by permission of the author, Lisa Randall, Professor of Physics, Harvard University, and author of *Knocking on Heaven's Door* and *Warped Passages.*

53–56 Daniel "Nene" Alejandrez, "Cesar Chavez Saved My Life." Reprinted with permission from *Sojourners,* (800) 714-7474, www.sojo.net.

69–71 Todd Petry, "Wind Catcher. " Student essay reprinted with permission.

72–74 Juli Bovard, "Red Chevy." Student essay reprinted with permission.

82–84 Barbara Ehrenreich, "Teach Diversity with a Smile." Copyright © 1991 by Barbara Ehrenreich. Reprinted by permission of International Creative Management, Inc.

92–95; 340–341 King, Martin Luther, Jr. "Letter from a Birmingham Jail" by Martin Luther King, Jr. Copyright © 1963 by Dr. Martin Luther King, Jr., copyright renewed 1991 by Coretta Scott King. Reprinted by arrangement with The Heirs to the Estate of Martin Luther King, Jr., c/o Writers House, Inc. as agent for the proprietor, New York, NY.

119–122 Allyson McGrath, "Rhetorical Analysis of Gregory Petsko's Open Letter top George M. Philip." Student essay reprinted with permission.

123–127 Jennifer Koester and Sonja H. Browe, "Two Responses to Deborah Tannen." Student essay reprinted with permission.

136–138 Nathan Brown, "Open Letter to Chancellor Linda P. B. Katehi." Reprinted by permission of the author, Nathan Brown, Assistant Professor of English and Critical Theory at the University of California, Davis.

139 Matthew Barakat, "Ex-Mortgage CEO Sentenced to Prison for $3B Fraud." Associated Press, June 21, 2011. Used with permission of The Associated Press. Copyright © 2012.

139 Chris V. Thangham, "Homeless man gets 15 years for stealing $100." *Digital Journal,* January 17, 2009. Reprinted by permission of Digital Journal, Inc.

141 © Brad Roberts. Reprinted by permission.

142 Ch. 5, figure: Storing the Power of the Wind. Sources: Xcel Energy National Renewable Energy Laboratory, graphic by Thomas McKay and Jonathan Moreno, *The Denver Post,* December 15, 2006.

148 © 1999–2009 Rosetta Stone Ltd. All Rights Reserved.

151–152 Charles Rosen and Henri Zerner, excerpt from "Scenes from the American Dream." *New York Review of Books,* August 1, 2000. Copyright © 2000 NYREV, Inc. Used with permission.

153–155 Carolyn Kleiner Butler, "Coming Home," appeared in *Smithsonian,* January, 2005, pp. 22–23. Reprinted by permission.

158–160 Karyn M. Lewis, "Some Don't Like Their Blues at All." Student essay reprinted with permission.

165–167 "Drivers on Cell Phones are as Bad as Drunks." University of Utah Study. Link at http://unews.utah.edu/p/?r=062206-1

167–168 Abigail Sullivan Moore, "Gimme an A (I Insist)." *The New York Times,* April 24, 2004. Copyright © 2004 New York Times. All rights reserved. Used with permission.

169–170 Charles McGrath, "How Many Stephen Colberts Are There?" *The New York Times Magazine,* January 4, 2012. Copyright © 2012 New York Times. All rights reserved. Used with permission.

170–172 Deborah Solomon, "Doctor's Orders: An Interview of Regina Benjamin." *The New York Times,* January 7, 2011. Copyright © 2011 The New York Times. All rights reserved. Used with permission.

173–175 Elizabeth Larsen, "Surfin' the Louvre," first appeared in *The Utne Reader* May/June 1998. Used by permission of the author.

189–194 Jennifer Macke, "Permanent Tracings." Student essay reprinted with permission.

201–202 Caterina Fake, "FOMO and Social Media." March 15, 2011. Caterina.net.

205–206 David Sirota, "How Baseball Explains Modern Racism." By permission of David Sirota and Creators Syndicate, Inc.

208–209 La Mer Steptoe, "Multiracialness," from *All Things Considered,* June 13, 2001. Reprinted with permission.

209–213 Suze Orman,"How to Take Control of Your Credit Cards," Money Matters Column, *Yahoo Finance,* posted Thursday, September 22, 2005.

213–218 Deborah Tannen, "How Male and Female Students Use Language Differently." Reprinted by permission of the author.

244–246 Nancie Brosseau, "Anorexia Nervosa." Student essay reprinted with permission.

236–243 Chris Blakely, "White Lies: White-Collar Crime in America." Student essay reprinted with permission.

253–255 "Android v. iPhone." Copyright © 2012 Consumers Union of U.S., Inc., Yonkers, New York 10703-1057, a nonprofit organization. Reprinted with permission from the January 2012 issue of Consumer Reports® for educational purposes only. www .ConsumerReports.org.

255–256 Eric Asimov, "Bud Lite, Coors Lite, Miller Lite: Is There Any Difference?" *The New York Times Magazine,* October 2, 2011. Copyright © 2011 The New York Times. All rights reserved. Used with permission.

256–258 Paul Richard, "'American Gothic,' Pitchfork Perfect." *The Washington Post,* March 10, 2006. Used with permission.

259–261 Manohia Dargis, "The Maids Now Have Their Say." *The New York Times Magazine,* October 2, 2011. Copyright © 2011 The New York Times. All rights reserved. Used with permission.

262–265 David Sedaris, "Today's Special" from *Me Talk Pretty One Day.* Copyright © 2000 by David Sedaris. By permission of Little Brown and Company, and Don Congdon Associates, Inc. All rights reserved.

277–281 Courtney Klockeman, "Vulgar Propriety." Student essay reprinted with permission.

285–286 Frank Trippett, "A Red Light for Scofflaws." *Time* magazine, January 24, 1983.

286–288 Janet Bodnar, "7 Strategies to Avoid the College Debt Trap." *Kiplinger's Personal Finance,* August 25, 2010. Copyright © 2010 The Kiplinger Washington Editors. All rights reserved. Used by permission.

291–293 Richard Arum and Josipa Roksa, "Your So-Called Education." *The New York Times,* May 14, 2011. Reprinted by permission of the authors.

293 Lynn O'Shaughnessy, "But Can They Write?" *The New York Times,* April 17, 2011. Copyright © 2011 The New York Times. All rights reserved. Used with permission.

294–296 James Surowiecki, "Debt by Degrees." Copyright © 2011 Conde Nast. All rights reserved. Originally published in *The New Yorker,* November 21, 2011. Reprinted by permission.

296–299 David Leonhardt, "Even for Cashiers, College Pays Off." *The New York Times,* June 25, 2011. Copyright © 2011 The New York Times. All rights reserved. Used with permission.

298 Ch. 9 bar graph: Net present value of lifetime earnings, by education from Michael Greenstone and Adam Looney, "Where is the Best Place to Invest $102,000 — In Stocks, Bonds, or a College Degree?" The Hamilton Project, June 25, 2001. Reprinted with permission.

299–304 Gregory Petsko, "An Open Letter to George M. Philip, President of the State University of New York at Albany."

305–308 Deborah Tannen, "The Argument Culture," from *The Argument Culture.* Copyright © 1997 by Deborah Tannen. Reprinted by permission of ICM Partners.

322–328 Adam Richman, "Can Citizen Journalism Pick Up the Pieces?"

346–351 Cathleen Cleaver, "The Internet: A Clear and Present Danger?" Copyright © Cathleen Cleaver. Reprinted with permission. Student essay reprinted with permission.

353–356 Farhad Manjoo, "You Have No Friends." *The Washington Post,* January 14, 2009. From Slate, Copyright © 2009 The Slate Group. All rights reserved. Used by permission.

356 Ch. 10, circle graph: Social networking gets the most online time adapted from "What Americans Do Online: Social Media and Games Dominate Activity," Nielsen, August 2012.

357–358 Sarah Kliff, ". . . And Why I Hate It." *Newsweek,* August 20, 2007. Copyright © 2007 The Newsweek/Daily Beast Company LLC. All rights reserved. Used by permission.

358–361 Jennifer Holladay, "Cyberbullying." *Teaching Tolerance,* 38 (Fall 2010), pp. 42–45. Reprinted with permission from Teaching Tolerance, A Project of the Southern Poverty Law Center. www.tolerance.org.

361–363 danah boyd and Alice Marwick, "Bullying as True Drama." *The New York Times,* September 22, 2011. Reprinted by permission of the authors. danah boyd is a Senior Researcher at Microsoft Research and a Research Assistant Professor at New York University. Alice Marwick is a Postdoctoral Researcher at Microsoft Research and a Visiting Researcher at Harvard Law School.

363–366 Miguel Helft, "Facebook Wrestles With Free Speech and Civility." *The New York Times,* December 12, 2010. Copyright © 2010 The New York Times. All rights reserved. Used with permission.

367–370 Neil L. Waters, "Why You Can't Cite Wikipedia in My Class." *Communications of the ACM,* September 2007. Reprinted by permission of the author.

370–372 Mark Wilson, "Professors Should Embrace Wikipedia." *Inside Higher Ed.* April 1, 2008. Reprinted by permission of the author.

372–375 Nicholas Carr, "Does the Internet Make You Dumber?" *The Wall Street Journal,* June 5, 2010. Copyright © 2010 by Nicholas Carr. Used by permission of the author.

391–398 Crystal Sabatke, "Welfare Is Still Necessary for Women and Children in the U.S." Student essay reprinted with permission.

402 Excerpt from "Because I could not stop for death" is reprinted by permission of the publishers and the Trustees of Amherst College from *The Poems of Emily Dickinson,* Thomas H. Johnson, ed., Cambridge, Mass.: The Belknap Press of Harvard University Press. Copyright © 1951, 1955, 1979 by the President and Fellows of Harvard College.

402 e.e. cummings, lines from "anyone lived in a pretty how town" copyright 1940, © 1968, 1991 by the Trustees for the E.E. Cummings Trust, from *Complete Poems: 1904–1962* by E.E. Cummings, edited by George J,. Firmage. Used by permission of Liveright Publishing Corporation.

402 Excerpt from "The Road Not Taken" from *The Poetry of Robert Frost,* edited by Edward Connery Lathem. Copyright © 1923, 1969 by Henry Holt and Company. Copyright 1951 by Robert Frost. Reprinted by permission of Henry Holt and Company, LLC.

406–407 W.H. Auden, "Musee des Beaux Arts." Copyright © 1940 and renewed 1968 by W.H. Auden from *Collected Poems of W.H. Auden* by W.H. Auden. Used by permission of Random House, Inc., and Curtis Brown Ltd.

413–419 Toni Cade Bambara, "The Lesson" from *Gorilla, My Love* by Toni Cade Bambara. Copyright © 1972 by Toni Cade Bambara. Used by permission of Random House, Inc.

422 Aurora Levins Morales, "Child of the Americas," from *Getting Home Alive* by Aurora Levins Morales and Rosario Morales. © 1986 Firebrand Books. Ann Arbor, MI. Used with permission.

423–425 Taylor Mali, "Miracle Workers." Reprinted by permission of the author. For more information, visit TAYLOR MALI.com.

425–426 Joy Harjo, "Perhaps the World Ends Here," from *The Woman Who Fell from the Sky* by Joy Harjo. Copyright © 1994 by Joy Harjo. Used by permission of W. W. Norton & Company, Inc.

426–427 Wislawa Szymborska, "The End and The Beginning," from *View with a Grain of Sand: Selected Poems by Wislawa Szymborska,* translated from the Polish by Stanislaw Baranczak and Clare Cabanagh. Copyright © 1995 Houghton Mifflin Harcourt Publishing Company. Copyright © Czytelnik, Warszawa. Reprinted by permission of Houghton Mifflin Harcourt Publishing Company. All rights reserved.

427–428 Yusef Komunyakaa, "Facing It," from *Pleasure Dome: New and Collected Poems.* Copyright © 2001 by Yusef Komunyakaa. Reprinted by permission of Wesleyan University Press.

437–439 Grace Rexroth, "Facing it." Student essay reprinted with permission.

440–441 Pat Russell, "Death — The Final Freedom." Student essay reprinted with permission.

468 Ch. 12 figure: excerpt from scholarly article with notes from Joya Uraizee, "Gazing at the Beast: Describing Mass Murder in Deepa Mehta's Earth and Terry George's Hotel Rwanda," in *Shofar: An Interdisciplinary Journal of Jewish Studies,* Volume 28, Number 4. Copyright © 2010 Purdue University. Reprinted with permission.

477–482 Carrie Gingrich, "Learning about the Rwandan Genocide: Misconceptions and Film," and Sample Research Proposal and Annotated Bibliography with Notes. Student essay reprinted with permission.

514 Ch. 13 figures: JEE Cover and excerpt from scholarly article with notes are reprinted by permission of American Society for Engineering Education.

516 Ch. 13 figures: title page, copyright page, and p. 74 from *Academically Adrift: Limited Learning on College Campuses* by Richard Arum and Josipa Roksa. Copyright © 2011 by The University of Chicago. Reprinted by permission of The University of Chicago Press.

520 Ch. 13 figure: excerpt from "Revisiting Hotel Rwanda," by Lars Waldorf from *Journal of Genocide Research*, 11.1 (2009). Reprinted by permission of the author.

Photo Credits

6 Frank & Ernst reprinted by permission of Newspaper Enterprise Association, Inc.

51 Rolf Vennenbernd/dpa/Corbis

52 Susan Walsh/AP/Corbis

53 Imago Stock & People/Newscom

53 imago stock&people/Newscom

67 Mike Flippo/Shutterstock

100 "Day and Night" by M. C. Escher. © 1997 Cordon Art- Baarn - Holland. All rights reserved"

133 Courtesy of the Library of Congress

133 Courtesy of the Library of Congress

134 Swim Ink 2, LLC/Corbis

135 Jim Goldberg/Magnum Photos

137 Wayne Tilcock/AP Images

139 Shreveport Louisiana Police Dept.

140 Corbis

140 AP Images

141 Brad Roberts

143 Courtesy of adbusters.org

146 The New Yorker Collection 2005 Robert Mankoff from cartoonbank.com. All Rights Reserved.

147 Alfred Eisenstaedt/Time Life Pictures/Getty Images

147 Gordon Parks/Corbis

152 Printed by permission of the Norman Rockwell Family Agency Copyright © 1960 The Norman Rockwell Family Entities

154 Sal Veder/AP Images

169 Cliff Owen/AP Images

170 Allstar Picture Library/Alamy

201 Ramin Talaie/Getty Images

207 Bill Watterson/Universal UClick

224 Poulsons Photography/Shutterstock

228 Erich Lessing/Art Resource, NY

259 Everett Collection

289 © UNICEF/HQ89-0052/Gilles Vauclair

346 DOONESBURY © G.B. Trudeau. Reprinted with permission of UNIVERSAL PRESS SYNDICATE. All rights reserved.

364 Jim Wilson/The New York Times/Redux Pictures

373 Mick Coulas/Revel-Ink

376 Mike Keefe, InToon.com

406 Scala/Art Resource, NY

601 © Michael Maslin/The New Yorker Collection/ www.cartoonbank.com

Index

T